Promoting the Educational Success of Children and Youth Learning English

Promising Futures

Committee on Fostering School Success for English Learners:
Toward New Directions in Policy, Practice, and Research

Ruby Takanishi and Suzanne Le Menestrel, *Editors*

Board on Children, Youth, and Families
and
Board on Science Education

Division of Behavioral and Social Sciences and Education

Health and Medicine Division

A Consensus Study Report of

The National Academies of
SCIENCES · ENGINEERING · MEDICINE

THE NATIONAL ACADEMIES PRESS
Washington, DC
www.nap.edu

THE NATIONAL ACADEMIES PRESS   500 Fifth Street, NW   Washington, DC 20001

This study was supported by contracts between the National Academy of Sciences and the Administration for Children and Families of the U.S. Department of Health and Human Services (HHSP233201400020B, Order No. HHSP23337020); the Foundation for Child Development (NAS-20-13D); the Health Resources and Services Administration of the U.S. Department of Health and Human Services (HHSH250200976014I, Order No. HHSH25034022T); the Heising-Simons Foundation (2014-158); the McKnight Foundation (14-596); and the U.S. Department of Education (HHSP233201400020B, Order No. HHSP23337018). Any opinions, findings, conclusions, or recommendations expressed in this publication do not necessarily reflect the views of any organization or agency that provided support for the project.

International Standard Book Number-13:   978-0-309-45537-4
International Standard Book Number-10:   0-309-45537-5
Library of Congress Control Number: 2017947
Digital Object Identifier: https://doi.org/10.17226/24677

Additional copies of this publication are available for sale from the National Academies Press, 500 Fifth Street, NW, Keck 360, Washington, DC 20001; (800) 624-6242 or (202) 334-3313; http://www.nap.edu.

Suggested citation: National Academies of Sciences, Engineering, and Medicine. (2017). *Promoting the Educational Success of Children and Youth Learning English: Promising Futures*. Washington, DC: The National Academies Press. https://doi.org/10.17226/24677.

The National Academies of
SCIENCES · ENGINEERING · MEDICINE

The **National Academy of Sciences** was established in 1863 by an Act of Congress, signed by President Lincoln, as a private, nongovernmental institution to advise the nation on issues related to science and technology. Members are elected by their peers for outstanding contributions to research. Dr. Marcia McNutt is president.

The **National Academy of Engineering** was established in 1964 under the charter of the National Academy of Sciences to bring the practices of engineering to advising the nation. Members are elected by their peers for extraordinary contributions to engineering. Dr. C. D. Mote, Jr., is president.

The **National Academy of Medicine** (formerly the Institute of Medicine) was established in 1970 under the charter of the National Academy of Sciences to advise the nation on medical and health issues. Members are elected by their peers for distinguished contributions to medicine and health. Dr. Victor J. Dzau is president.

The three Academies work together as the **National Academies of Sciences, Engineering, and Medicine** to provide independent, objective analysis and advice to the nation and conduct other activities to solve complex problems and inform public policy decisions. The National Academies also encourage education and research, recognize outstanding contributions to knowledge, and increase public understanding in matters of science, engineering, and medicine.

Learn more about the **National Academies of Sciences, Engineering, and Medicine** at www.nationalacademies.org.

The National Academies of
SCIENCES · ENGINEERING · MEDICINE

Consensus Study Reports published by the National Academies of Sciences, Engineering, and Medicine document the evidence-based consensus on the study's statement of task by an authoring committee of experts. Reports typically include findings, conclusions, and recommendations based on information gathered by the committee and the committee's deliberations. Each report has been subjected to a rigorous and independent peer-review process and it represents the position of the National Academies on the statement of task.

Proceedings published by the National Academies of Sciences, Engineering, and Medicine chronicle the presentations and discussions at a workshop, symposium, or other event convened by the National Academies. The statements and opinions contained in proceedings are those of the participants and are not endorsed by other participants, the planning committee, or the National Academies.

For information about other products and activities of the National Academies, please visit www.nationalacademies.org/about/whatwedo.

v

Acknowledgments

The committee and project staff express our deep gratitude to all who generously contributed their time and expertise to inform the development of this report.

To begin, we thank the sponsors of this study for their support. The committee's work was funded by the Administration for Children and Families of the U.S. Department of Health and Human Services, the Foundation for Child Development, the Health Resources and Services Administration (HRSA) of the U.S. Department of Health and Human Services, the Heising-Simons Foundation, the McKnight Foundation, and the U.S. Department of Education. Many individuals volunteered significant time and effort to address and educate committee members during our public information meetings. Their willingness to share their perspectives and experiences was essential to the committee's work. We also thank the many other stakeholders who shared information with the committee over the course of the study.

The committee also expresses our sincere appreciation for the opportunity to work with the dedicated members of the staff of the National Academies of Sciences, Engineering, and Medicine on this important project. We are thankful to the project staff: Francis Amankwah, Sarah Blankenship, Marthe Folivi, Annalee Gonzales, Rebekah Hutton, Suzanne Le Menestrel, Sheila Moats, Rebecca Nebel, Heidi Schweingruber, Amy Stephens, and Tina Tran. The committee is also grateful to Lisa Alston, Pamella Atayi, Faye Hillman, and Stacey Smit for their administrative and financial assistance on this project. We are also thankful for the administrative support of Alisa Decatur. The committee gratefully acknowledges

Natacha Blain, Kimber Bogard, and Bridget Kelly of the Board on Children, Youth, and Families; Robert Hauser, former executive director of the Division of Behavioral and Social Sciences and Education; Mary Ellen O'Connell, executive director of the Division of Behavioral and Social Sciences and Education; Dr. Victor Dzau, president of the National Academy of Medicine; and Clyde Behney, executive director of the Health and Medicine Division, for their guidance throughout this important study. The committee thanks the staff of the Office of Reports and Communication of the Division of Behavioral and Social Sciences and Education: Eugenia Grohman, Viola Horek, Patricia L. Morison, Kirsten Sampson Snyder, Douglas Sprunger, and Yvonne Wise. We also wish to thank Daniel Bearss and Rebecca Morgan for their outstanding research and fact-checking assistance.

We are grateful to Lauren Tobias of Maven Messaging & Communications for her thoughtful work as the communications consultant for this study. We thank Beatriz Arias, Julie Esparza-Brown, Kathy Lindholm-Leary, Amy Markos, Soyoung Park, and Marlene Zepeda for their valuable commissioned papers, which informed our report. We are appreciative of Rona Briere for the diligent and thorough editorial assistance she provided in preparing this report.

Reviewers

This Consensus Study Report has been reviewed in draft form by individuals chosen for their diverse perspectives and technical expertise. The purpose of this independent review is to provide candid and critical comments that will assist the National Academies of Sciences, Engineering, and Medicine in making each published report as sound as possible and to ensure that the report meets the institutional standards for objectivity, evidence, and responsiveness to the study charge. The review comments and draft manuscript remain confidential to protect the integrity of the deliberative process.

We wish to thank the following individuals for their thoughtful reviews of this report: Maria S. Carlo, Department of Teaching and Learning, University of Miami; Donna Christian, Center for Applied Linguistics; James Cummins, Institute for Studies in Education, University of Toronto, Ontario; Claude N. Goldenberg, Graduate School of Education, Stanford University; Magdalena Ruz Gonzalez, Multilingual Academic Support, Curriculum and Instructional Services, Los Angeles County Office of Education; Carol Scheffner Hammer, Communication Sciences and Disorders, Teachers College, Columbia University; Patricia K. Kuhl, Institute for Learning and Brain Sciences and Speech and Hearing Sciences, University of Washington; Laurie Olsen, Sobrato Early Academic Language, Sobrato Family Foundation; Mariela M. Páez, The Carolyn A. and Peter S. Lynch School of Education, Boston College; Laida Restrepo, School of Speech and Hearing Science, Arizona State University; Gillian Stevens, Department of Sociology and Population Research Laboratory, University of Alberta; and

Gabriela Uro, English Language Learner Policy and Research, Council of the Great City Schools.

Although the reviewers listed above provided many constructive comments and suggestions, they were not asked to endorse the conclusions or recommendations of this report nor did they see the final draft before its release. The review of this report was overseen by P. David Pearson, Language and Literacy and Cognition and Development, Graduate School of Education, University of California, Berkeley, and Douglas S. Massey, Department of Sociology and Public Affairs, Princeton University. They were responsible for making certain that an independent examination of this report was carried out in accordance with the standards of the National Academies and that all review comments were carefully considered. Responsibility for the final content rests entirely with the authoring committee and the National Academies.

Contents

Boxes, Figures, and Tables

FIGURES

TABLES

Summary

E ducating dual language learners (DLLs) and English learners (ELs) effectively is a national challenge with consequences both for individuals and for American society.[1] Despite their linguistic, cognitive, and social potential, many ELs—who account for more than 9 percent of enrollment in grades K-12 in U.S. schools—are struggling to meet the requirements for academic success, and their prospects for success in postsecondary education and in the workforce are jeopardized as a result.

A defining characteristic of DLLs/ELs is their demographic diversity. They are members of every major racial/ethnic group and include both U.S.- and foreign-born youth. Most come from Latin America and Asia, with Mexico being their leading country of origin. They speak a wide range of languages, including Chinese, French Creole, Fulani, Korean, and Spanish, as well as other languages spoken in Europe, Asia, and other parts of the world. Relative to other U.S. children, DLLs/ELs are far more likely to live in poverty and in two-parent families with low levels of education.

At the same time, DLLs/ELs have assets that may serve them well in their education and future careers. Those who become proficient in both a home or primary language ("L1") and English ("L2") are likely to reap benefits in cognitive, social, and emotional development and may also be

---

[1] When referring to young children ages birth to 5 in their homes, communities, or early care and education programs, this report uses the term "dual language learners" or "DLLs." When referring to children ages 5 and older in the pre-K to 12 education system, the term "English learners" or "ELs" is used. When referring to the broader group of children and adolescents ages birth to 21, the term "DLLs/ELs" is used.

protected from brain decline at older ages. In addition, the cultures, languages, and experiences of English learners are highly diverse and constitute assets for their development, as well as for the nation (Conclusion 3-1).[2] This report addresses both the assets that DLLs/ELs bring to their education and the factors that support or may impede their educational success.

THE PROBLEM

The Committee on Fostering School Success for English Learners: Toward New Directions in Policy, Practice, and Research was convened by the National Academies of Sciences, Engineering, and Medicine through its Board on Children, Youth, and Families and the Board on Science Education. The committee's task was to examine how evidence based on research relevant to the development of DLLs/ELs from birth to age 21 can inform education and health policies and related practices that can result in better educational outcomes.[3]

Educational Achievement and Attainment

The committee identified key challenges that may impact the language development and educational attainment of DLLs/ELs. The available evidence clearly indicates that these children and youth lag behind their English-monolingual peers in educational achievement and attainment. Limited proficiency in English poses a high barrier to academic learning and performance in schools where English is the primary language of instruction and assessment. Moreover, DLLs/ELs face a number of additional barriers to educational success and the availability of learning opportunities that go beyond their English proficiency, such as poverty and attending under-resourced schools.

Competing Views Held by Society

Both society at large and many educational and health professionals hold competing views about whether dual language learning should be supported early in a child's development and later in school. Some believe that learning two languages early in a child's life is burdensome, while others

---

[2] The conclusions and recommendations in this report are numbered according to the chapter of the main text in which they appear.

[3] This study was sponsored by the Administration for Children and Families of the U.S. Department of Health and Human Services, the Foundation for Child Development, the Health Resources and Services Administration of the U.S. Department of Health and Human Services, the Heising-Simons Foundation, the McKnight Foundation, and the U.S. Department of Education.

believe that young children are "hardwired" to learn one or more languages easily and that nothing needs to be done to promote their language development. In their extremes, both of these views can be detrimental to the development of effective policies and practices concerning the education of DLLs/ELs.

Language of Classroom Instruction

One of the most intensely debated aspects of educational policy and practice for ELs focuses on the language of classroom instruction. Educators and researchers agree that to succeed in school and participate in civic life in the United States, all children must develop strong English proficiency and literacy skills. The debate centers on the questions of the best ways to support the acquisition of English and the ongoing role of children's L1 as their English skills deepen, the social and cultural costs of losing proficiency in L1, the role of education programs in systematically supporting L1, and community and parental values that may promote English-only approaches.

Diverse Social, Cultural, and Linguistic Backgrounds

Given the steady increase in diversity among DLLs/ELs in the United States, a key challenge for educators is understanding the social, cultural, and linguistic backgrounds of the children they serve and creating the conditions of trust and respect necessary for effective instruction. Educators draw on their own experiences with cross-ethnic relations, language learning, and racialized understandings of U.S. society and may feel unprepared to support the school success of ELs.

WHAT SCIENCE REVEALS ABOUT BILINGUALISM

Scientific evidence clearly points to a universal, underlying human capacity to learn two languages as easily as one. DLLs have an impressive capacity to manage their two languages when communicating with others. For instance, they are able to differentiate the use of each language according to the language known or preferred by the people to whom they are speaking. Recent research evidence also points to cognitive advantages, such as the ability to plan, regulate their behavior, and think flexibly, for children and adults who are competent in two languages. At the same time, however, there are striking individual differences among bilingual children in their pathways to proficiency and ultimate levels of achievement in their two languages. **Language competence varies considerably among dual language learners. Multiple social and cultural factors—including parents' immigrant generational status and years in the United States, socioeconomic** status, exposures to the risks of poverty, the perceived status of the home language in the community, and neighborhood resources—may help explain this variation (Conclusion 4-7).

The Relationship Between First and Second Languages

The available evidence is mixed as to whether there is a critical period for learning a second language, although researchers agree that there is no strict cut-off point after which it is no longer possible to acquire an L2. A key question is the extent to which ability in the first language supports or hinders the acquisition of a second. Some immigrant parents may fear that talking with their child in the L1 will compromise the child's ability to learn English and succeed in U.S. schools because development of the L1 will slow and perhaps even interfere with English acquisition. Teachers also express this concern. Yet there is no evidence to indicate that the use of two languages in the home or the use of one in the home and another in an early care and education (ECE) setting confuses DLLs or puts the development of one or both of their languages at risk. Given adequate exposure to two languages, young children have the capacity to develop competence in vocabulary, morphology, syntax, and pragmatics in both (Conclusion 4-2).

School Readiness

L1 language skills have been shown to promote a variety of L2-related school readiness skills. While DLLs typically show greater competence or dominance in one language, transfer between languages is likely to occur once they build a sufficiently strong base in their L1. More advanced language learners are able to transfer or apply strong skills in their first language to learning or using an L2. However, transfer is less likely to occur when DLLs' overall language skills are underdeveloped. In contrast, children given the opportunity to develop competence in two or more languages early in life benefit from their capacity to communicate in more than one language and may show enhancement of certain cognitive skills, as well as improved academic outcomes in school (Conclusion 4-3).

Moreover, research indicates that children's language development benefits from the input of adults who talk to them in the language in which the adults are most competent and with which they are most comfortable. DLLs' language development, like that of monolingual children, benefits from the amount and quality of child-directed language—that is, language that is used frequently in daily interactions, is contingent on the child's language and focus of attention, and is rich and diverse in words and sentence types. For most DLL families, this quantity and quality of child-directed language are more likely to occur in the home language, not English (Conclusion 4-5).

Achievement of English Proficiency

One of the major and most puzzling questions for researchers, policy makers, the media, and the public since the 1974 Supreme Court issued its decision in the case of *Lau v. Nichols*[4] has been how long it does or should take ELs to achieve proficiency in English so they can benefit from participation in classrooms in which English is the language of instruction. Decisions about ELs' readiness to benefit from English-only instruction have been based largely on "reclassification" tests devised by individual states. Once ELs achieve defined cut-off scores on these tests and meet other criteria in some cases, they are reclassified as non-EL or fully English proficient. Research shows that it can take from 5 to 7 years for students to learn the English necessary for participation in a school's curriculum without further linguistic support. This is due in part to the increasing language demands of participation in school learning over time, especially with respect to the language used in written texts beyond the early primary years. Thus, students may require help with English through the upper elementary and middle school grades, particularly in acquiring proficiency in the academic uses of English. While of critical importance, "academic language" has been difficult to define, and is variously characterized in functional, grammatical, lexical, rhetorical, and pragmatic terms. As a result, efforts to support its development in classrooms have been inconsistent, just as efforts to assess its development have been problematic (Conclusion 6-1).

Long-Term English Learners

Over the past decade, increasing attention has been paid to students labeled as "long-term English learners." Typically these are students who have not been reclassified as English-proficient after 7 years, although no common definition of the term exists across schools, school districts, and states. Evidence suggests that many schools are not providing adequate instruction to ELs in acquiring English proficiency, as well as access to academic subjects at their grade level, from the time they first enter school until they reach the secondary grades. Many secondary schools are not able to meet the diverse needs of long-term ELs, including their linguistic, academic, and socioemotional needs (Conclusion 6-6).

---

[4]A landmark court case granting linguistic accommodations to students with limited proficiency in English.

WHAT IS HAPPENING IN PRACTICE

Early Care and Education

Most, if not all, ECE teachers and staff will work with DLLs during their careers and will need to understand effective practices that promote these young children's healthy development, learning, and achievement. Although no empirical studies have examined the impacts of ECE programs on DLLs' development in particular, findings from the developmental literature can guide the design of services for the youngest DLLs and their families, with special attention to their dual language status. In particular, the quality of language interactions in ECE for infants and toddlers in general has been shown to be related to later verbal and cognitive development. **All ECE teachers of DLLs can learn and implement strategies that systematically introduce English during the infant, toddler, and preschool years while simultaneously promoting maintenance of the home language— an important principle. Not all teachers can teach in all languages, but all teachers can learn specific strategies that support the maintenance of all languages (Conclusion 5-6).**

Oral language skills, such as vocabulary and listening comprehension, grammatical knowledge, and narrative production, have received particular attention from both researchers and educators seeking to identify and meet the learning needs of DLLs, who often do not receive support for advanced levels of oral language development. Early proficiency in both L1 and English at kindergarten entry is critical to becoming academically proficient in a second language. When DLLs are exposed to English during the preschool years, they often show a preference for speaking English and a reluctance to continue speaking their L1. DLLs who fail to maintain proficiency in their home language may lose their ability to communicate with parents and family members and may risk becoming estranged from their cultural and linguistic heritage. **DLLs benefit from consistent exposure to both their L1 and English in ECE settings. Research is limited on how much and what type of support for each language is most effective in supporting bilingual development (Conclusion 5-5).**

Home Visiting

The federal Maternal, Infant, and Early Childhood Home Visiting Program targets a population that includes a high proportion of families who are non-English speakers with DLLs. It is critical that, as they serve these families, home visiting practitioners and policy makers understand the strategies and elements of effective practices for promoting the healthy development, learning, and achievement of these children, with the goal of promoting optimal developmental and educational outcomes.

Pre-K to 12 Practices

Attention to how ELs are faring in grades pre-K to 12 comes at a pivotal time in American schools, when schools throughout the nation are teaching to higher curricular standards in core subject areas, including math, English language arts, and science. All students, including ELs, are expected to engage with academic content that is considerably more demanding than it used to be, and they must now demonstrate deeper levels of understanding and analysis of that content. ELs face the tasks of simultaneously achieving English proficiency and mastering grade-level academic subjects.

Two broad approaches are used to teach English to ELs in grades K-12: (1) English as a second language (ESL) approaches, in which English is the predominant language of instruction, and (2) bilingual approaches, in which both English and students' home languages are used for instruction. **Syntheses of evaluation studies that compare outcomes for ELs instructed in English-only programs with outcomes for ELs instructed bilingually find either that there is no difference in outcomes measured in English or that ELs in bilingual programs outperform ELs instructed only in English. Two recent studies that followed students for sufficient time to gauge longer-term effects of language of instruction on EL outcomes find benefits for bilingual compared with English-only approaches (Conclusion 7-1).**

Oral language proficiency[5] plays an important role in content area learning for ELs. Instructional approaches developed for students who are proficient in English offer a learning advantage for ELs as well. However, these approaches are likely to be insufficient for improving the literacy achievement of ELs absent attention to oral language development. **The following characteristics of instructional programs support ELs' oral language development: specialized instruction focused on components of oral language proficiency, opportunities for interaction with speakers proficient in the second language, feedback to students during conversational interactions, and dedicated time for instruction focused on oral English proficiency (Conclusion 7-2).**

Research has identified seven practices or guidelines for educating ELs in grades K-5:

1. Provide explicit instruction in literacy components.
2. Develop academic language during content area instruction.
3. Provide visual and verbal supports to make core content comprehensible.
4. Encourage peer-assisted learning opportunities.

---

[5] The committee defines oral language proficiency as both receptive and expressive oral language, as well as specific aspects of oral language, including phonology, oral vocabulary, morphology, grammar, discourse features, and pragmatic skills (August and Shanahan, 2006).

5.   Capitalize on students' home language, knowledge, and cultural assets.
6.   Screen for language and literacy challenges and monitor progress.
7.   Provide small-group academic support in literacy and English language development for students.

Young adolescent ELs enter middle school (typically ages 10-14) at what can be a turning point in their educational trajectory. Whether they are classified during their middle school years as long-term English learners or are newcomers to American classrooms, ELs face new challenges in middle school that influence their opportunities to learn both English and the rigorous academic subject matter required by today's higher state standards. Their degree of success in meeting these requirements will have consequences for their career and postsecondary education prospects. Research points to three promising practices for middle school EL instruction: (1) teachers should use the L1 to develop academic English in specific content areas in middle schools; (2) teachers should use collaborative, peer-group learning communities to support and extend teacher-led instruction; and (3) texts and other instructional materials should be at the same grade level as those used by English-proficient peers.

Research on ELs' language and academic subject learning in middle school is consistent with findings from studies conducted with children in the previous grades and supports the identification of promising practices during the primary grades (pre-K to 5). However, the developmental needs of young adolescent ELs—specifically their cognitive and social development—and their adaptation to a different organizational structure and expectations for student independence in middle school are important factors to consider in designing and implementing instructional strategies in middle school. The processes of identity formation and social awareness, which increase during adolescence, point to the importance of teacher beliefs about ELs and their attitudes toward learning English when working with middle school ELs (Conclusion 8-3).

Research on instructional practices for ELs in high school is less available than that on practices for elementary school. Nonetheless, recommendations for instructional practices associated with positive language and literacy outcomes for adolescents in general are applicable to ELs as well, and practices for ELs in elementary and middle school continue to be relevant in high school instruction. Research has identified nine promising practices with clear relevance to the education of ELs in high school:

1.   Develop academic English and its varied grammatical structures and vocabulary intensively as part of subject-matter learning.

2. Integrate oral and written language instruction into content area teaching.
3. Provide regular structured opportunities to develop written language skills.
4. Develop the reading and writing abilities of ELs through text-based, analytical instruction using a cognitive strategies approach.
5. Provide direct and explicit comprehension strategy instruction.
6. Provide opportunities for extended discussion of text meaning and interpretation.
7. Foster student motivation and engagement in literacy learning.
8. Provide regular peer-assisted learning opportunities.
9. Provide small group instructional opportunities to students struggling in areas of literacy and English language development.

Assessment of DLLs/ELs

Assessment of the educational progress of DLLs/ELs can yield concrete and actionable evidence of their learning. Sound assessment provides students with feedback on their learning, teachers with information with which to shape instruction and communicate with parents on the progress of their children, school leaders with information on areas of strength and weakness in instruction, and system leaders with an understanding of the overall performance of their programs. Well-established standards for assessing students and educational systems exist to guide practice. However, there is a gap between these professional standards, developed by consensus among relevant disciplines in the scientific community, and how assessments of DLLs/ELs at the individual student and system levels are actually conducted.

Current assessment practices vary across states, which will have primary responsibility for these assessments as the Every Student Succeeds Act (ESSA) of 2015 is implemented in school year 2017-2018, with its directive that school districts within a state share common assessment practices for identification of students as ELs and their exit from EL status. To conduct an accurate assessment of the developmental status and instructional needs of DLLs/ELs, it is necessary to examine their skills in both English and their home language. During the first 5 years of life, infants, toddlers, and preschoolers require developmental screening, observation, and ongoing assessment in both languages to support planning for individualized interactions and activities that will support their optimal development (Conclusion 11-1). Moreover, the appropriate use of assessment tools and practices, as well as the communication of assessment results to families and decision makers, requires that all stakeholders be capable of understanding and interpreting the results of academic assessments administered to ELs in English or their home language, as well as English language proficiency assessments. Collaboration among states, professional organizations, researchers, and other stakeholders to develop common assessment frameworks and assessments is advancing progress toward this end (Conclusion 11-4).

SPECIFIC POPULATIONS OF ENGLISH LEARNERS

In accordance with the statement of task for this study, the committee sought evidence on promising practices for ELs who are homeless and those who are unaccompanied or undocumented minors. However, such evidence is generally not specific to these populations or is lacking altogether. Systematic evaluations of practices with these specific populations are therefore needed. Evidence on promising and effective practices for migrant ELs is very limited as well. Services for migrant students vary considerably, with some states and districts having well-planned and coordinated services and others having less adequate programs and services.

Gifted and Talented ELs

Three factors have the strongest influence on the identification of ELs for gifted and talented programs: (1) the assessment tools used, including measures of real-life problem solving; (2) professional development for teachers, which leads to a reduction in their bias toward ELs; and (3) district-level support. Evidence on the effects of programs for gifted and talented ELs is limited.

Children and Youth Living on Tribal Lands

Language revitalization is an urgent matter for members of communities whose languages are in danger of extinction. Speakers remain for only 216 of the perhaps 1,000 indigenous heritage languages once spoken among American Indians and Alaska Natives in North America. For most American Indian groups, language is a key to cultural identity, and efforts to revitalize their language by teaching it to young tribal members is an important step toward maintaining and strengthening tribal culture. The reclamation of indigenous heritage languages is an important goal for many American Indian and Alaska Native communities. Some school systems see this goal as being in conflict with the school's efforts to promote English language and literacy. However, the evidence indicates that participation in strong language revitalization programs can have a positive impact on student achievement in school (Conclusion 9-2).

DLLs/ELs with Disabilities

DLLs/ELs with disabilities constitute a relatively small and under-studied portion of the K-12 population. They make up about 9 percent of the DLL/EL population and 8 percent of all students with disabilities, yet these small percentages represent more than 350,000 children. DLLs/ELs are less likely than their non-DLL/EL peers to be referred to early intervention and early special education programs, with potentially serious consequences. Evidence indicates that early childhood education, home visiting, health, and other professionals are not identifying all DLLs/ELs with special needs—such as those with autism spectrum disorder and language impairment—who could benefit from such programs (Conclusion 10-1).

The Care and Education Workforce for DLLs/ELs

Adults who interact with DLLs/ELs bear a great responsibility for their health, development, and learning. For ECE professionals, each state sets its own policies regarding employment qualifications for both the public and private sectors. Exceptions are Head Start and Military Child Care, for which requirements are set by the federal agencies. In public and private preschools, about 25 percent of teachers meet state licensing requirements. Within state-funded pre-K programs, certification, licensure, or endorsement is required.

Similarly, each state has its own requirements for K-12 teacher certification. Some states have established criteria at the preservice level, whereas others have specialist requirements beyond initial certification. Although all 50 states plus the District of Columbia offer a certificate in teaching ESL, the range of knowledge and skills required by each state varies. The professional preparation and quality of teachers and administrators, including principals and superintendents, differentiates between more and less effective schools.

Among the many factors that affect student performance, research conducted on all populations of students has produced strong evidence that the quality of the teacher has a significant impact on students' educational success. The issue of preparing teachers to educate ELs effectively is especially salient for states with large EL populations and those with increasing numbers of these students. Across the nation, more than 340,000 teachers are certified/licensed EL teachers working in Title III programs. Three of the nine states[6] with the highest percentages of ELs plus the District of Colum-

---

[6] Alaska, California, Colorado, Florida, Illinois, Nevada, New Mexico, Texas, and Washington.

bia estimate a need for more than 15,000 certified EL teachers in the next 5 years, and Nevada alone will require more than 16,000, an increase of 590 percent. The educator workforce, including ECE providers, educational administrators, and teachers, is inadequately prepared during preservice training to promote desired educational outcomes for DLLs/ELs. The great variability across state certification requirements influences the content offered to candidates by higher education and other preparation programs to provide them with the knowledge and competencies required by effective educators of these children and youth. The emergence of alternative teacher preparation programs is promising, but traditional institutions of higher education remain the major source of new teachers, and changes in these institutions may therefore be required to increase the pipeline of well-prepared teachers of DLLs/ELs (Conclusion 12-1).

RECOMMENDATIONS FOR MEETING THE CHALLENGES

The committee formulated 14 recommendations for policy, practice, and research and data collection focused on addressing the challenges described above in caring for and educating DLLs/ELs from birth to grade 12. The 10 recommendations related to practice and policy are listed below.

Recommendation 1: Federal agencies with oversight of early childhood programs serving children from birth to age 5 (such as the Child Care and Development Fund and Maternal, Infant, and Early Childhood Home Visiting Program) and state agencies with oversight of such programs should follow the lead of Head Start/Early Head Start by providing specific evidence-based program guidance, practices, and strategies for engaging and serving dual language learners and their families and monitor program effectiveness.

Recommendation 2: Federal, state, and local agencies and intermediary organizations with responsibilities for serving children birth to age 5 should conduct social marketing campaigns to provide information about the capacity of infants, toddlers, and preschoolers—including those with disabilities—to learn more than one language.

Recommendation 3: Federal and state agencies and organizations that fund and regulate programs and services for dual language learners (e.g., Office of Head Start, U.S. Department of Health and Human Services, state departments of education and early learning, state child care licensing agencies) and local education agencies that serve English learners in grades pre-K to 12 should examine the adequacy and appropriateness of district- and school-wide practices for these children and adolescents. Evidence of effective practices should be defined according to the Every Student Succeeds Act.

Recommendation 4: Federal and state agencies and organizations that fund and regulate programs and services for dual language learners (DLLs) (e.g., Office of Head Start, U.S. Department of Health and Human Services, state departments of education and early learning, state child care licensing agencies) and English learners (ELs) in grades pre-K to 12 should give all providers of services to these children and adolescents (e.g., local Head Start and Early Head Start programs, community-based child care centers, state preschool and child development programs) and local education agencies information about the range of valid assessment methods and tools for DLLs/ELs and guidelines for their appropriate use, especially for DLLs/ELs with disabilities. The Institute of Education Sciences and the National Institutes of Health should lead the creation of a national clearinghouse for these validated assessment methods and tools, including those used for DLLs/ELs with disabilities.

Recommendation 5: The U.S. Department of Education should provide more detailed guidelines to state education agencies (SEAs) and local education agencies (LEAs) on the implementation of requirements regarding family participation and language accommodations in the development of individualized education plans and Section 504 accommodation plans for dual language learners/English learners who qualify for special education. The SEAs and LEAs, in turn, should fully implement these requirements.

Recommendation 6: The U.S. Department of Health and Human Services and the U.S. Department of Education should direct programs to strengthen their referral and linkage roles in order to address the low rates of identification of developmental disorders and disabilities in dual language learners/English learners (DLLs/ELs) and related low rates of referral to early intervention and early childhood special education services. In addition, the U.S. Department of Education should address underidentification of DLLs/ELs in its analyses, reports, and regulations in order to examine the multidimensional patterns of underrepresentation and overrepresentation at the national, state, and district levels in early childhood (birth to 5) and by grade (pre-K to 12) and for all disability categories.

Recommendation 7: Local education agencies serving American Indian and Alaska Native communities that are working to revitalize their indigenous heritage languages should take steps to ensure that schools' promotion of English literacy supports and does not compete or interfere with those efforts.

Recommendation 8: Research, professional, and policy associations whose members have responsibilities for improving and ensuring the high quality of educational outcomes among dual language learners/English learners (DLLs/ELs) should implement strategies designed to foster assessment literacy—the ability to understand and interpret results of academic assessments administered to these children and adolescents in English or their primary language—among personnel in federal, state, and local school agencies and DLLs/ELs families.

Recommendation 9: State and professional credentialing bodies should require that all educators with instructional and support roles (e.g., teachers, care and education practitioners, administrators, guidance counselors, psychologists and therapists) in serving dual language learners/English learners (DLLs/ELs) be prepared through credentialing and licensing as well as pre- and in-service training to work effectively with DLLs/ELs.

Recommendation 10: All education agencies in states, districts, regional clusters of districts, and intermediary units and agencies responsible for early learning services and pre-K to 12 should support efforts to recruit, select, prepare, and retain teachers, care and education practitioners, and education leaders qualified to serve dual language learners/English learners. Consistent with requirements for pre-K to 12, program directors and lead teachers in early learning programs should attain a B.A. degree with certification to teach dual language learners.

1

Introduction

Educating children and youth who are dual language learners (DLLs) or English learners (ELs) effectively is a national challenge with consequences for both individuals and society at large. (The essential distinction between DLLs and ELs is that the latter term refers to children and youth in the pre-K to 12 education system; see Box 1-1 for detailed definitions.) ELs account for more than 9 percent of the 2013-2014 K-12 enrollment in American schools (National Center for Education Statistics, 2016). Despite their linguistic, cognitive, and social potential, many of them are struggling to meet the requirements for academic success, a challenge that jeopardizes their prospects in postsecondary education and the workforce (National Center for Education Statistics, 2015; Office of English Language Acquisition, 2016).

A defining characteristic of DLLs/ELs is their demographic diversity. They are members of every major racial/ethnic group and include both U.S.- and foreign-born youth. Most come from Latin America and Asia, with Mexico being their leading country of origin. They speak a wide range of languages, including Chinese, French Creole, Fulani, Korean, and Spanish, as well as other languages spoken in Europe, Asia, and other parts of the world, including variations of these languages—regional dialects and Cuban-Spanish, for example. DLL/ELs are highly concentrated in traditional immigrant destinations such as California and Texas. However, they increasingly live in new destination states, such as North Carolina, Georgia, and Pennsylvania, which are not prepared to meet the needs of the growing number of ELs in their schools. Relative to other populations

---

BOX 1-1
Key Terminology in This Report

The focus of this report is on children from birth to age 5 and students in grades pre-K to 12 (ages 3-21 years)[a] who learn English as their second language. The use of different terms to characterize the population that is the focus of this report reflects the lack of consensus among policy makers, practitioners, and researchers on the terminology to be used in relevant policies and practices. The terms also have evolved over time in response to social changes (see Chapter 2 for discussion of changes in terminology based on applicable laws). In the face of this complexity, the committee elected to use the federal definitions below to describe the children and youth addressed in this report. At the same time, it should be noted that the terminology used in studies and legislation discussed in the text has been preserved.

Children Birth to Age 5 Not in the Pre-K to 12 Education System

The U.S. Office of Head Start uses the term "dual language learner" (DLL), which is defined as follows:

> Dual language learners are children learning two (or more) languages at the same time, as well as those learning a second language while continuing to develop their first (or home) language (Administration for Children and Families and U.S. Department of Health and Human Services, 2013, p. 3).

Children and Youth Ages 3-21 in the Pre-K to 12 Education System

The federal definition of an English learner (EL), as articulated in Elementary and Secondary Education Act of 1965 (ESEA), has been revised over successive ESEA reauthorizations in 1978, 1994, 2001, and 2015. Currently, Sec. 8101 of ESEA defines an EL as follows:

---

of children and youth, DLLs/ELs are far more likely to live in poverty and in two-parent families with low levels of education.

The purpose of this report is to examine how scientific evidence relevant to the development of DLLs/ELs from birth to age 21 can inform education and health policy and related practices that can result in better educational outcomes. The Statement of Task for the study is presented in Box 1-2.

The term English Learner, when used with respect to an individual, means an individual—(A) who is aged 3 through 21; (B) who is enrolled or preparing to enroll in an elementary school or secondary school; (C)(i) who was not born in the United States or whose native language is a language other than English; (ii)(I) who is a Native American or Alaska Native, or a native resident of the outlying areas; and (II) who comes from an environment where a language other than English has had a significant impact on the individual's level of English language proficiency; or (iii) who is migratory, whose native language is a language other than English, and who comes from an environment where a language other than English is dominant; and (D) whose difficulties in speaking, reading, writing, or understanding the English language may be sufficient to deny the individual—(i) the ability to meet the challenging State academic standards; (ii) the ability to successfully achieve in classrooms where the language of instruction is English; or (iii) the opportunity to participate fully in society.[b]

Implications for This Report

When referring to children birth to age 5 in their homes, communities, or early care and education (ECE) programs, this report uses the term "dual language learners" or "DLLs." When referring to children and youth ages 5-21 in the pre-K to 12 education system, the report uses the term "English learners" or "ELs." When referring to the broader population of children and youth from birth to age 21, the term "DLL/EL" is used. Note that both DLL and EL include children ages 3-5 who are in pre-K or elementary school. Accordingly, both terms as used herein encompass children in this age group.

---

[a]The federal definition of English learner extends to age 21 because this is the age at which students are required to exit public schools or high school regardless of whether they have received a high school diploma. The term does not refer to those students who have graduated high school or have dropped out, only those who remain in high school. Extending the age to 21 is important for students who have entered school in the later grades or have not attained English proficiency. Thus, this report focuses on students who are currently enrolled in school.
[b]Section 8101 of the Elementary and Secondary Education Act of 1965 (as amended through P.L. 114-95, enacted December 10, 2015).

STUDY APPROACH

The study committee comprised 19 members with expertise in assessment; demography; early, elementary, and secondary education; linguistics; neurosciences; preparation of educators; psychology; public health; public policy; sociology; and special education (see Appendix A for biosketches of the committee members). The committee met six times in person, held two public information-gathering sessions, and conducted two site visits to school districts in urban and suburban areas in the western and mid-Atlantic regions of the United States.

The first public session included panel presentations focused on demog-

BOX 1-2
Statement of Task

An ad hoc committee under the auspices of the National Academies of Sciences, Engineering, and Medicine will establish one committee to address the continuum of young English language learners (ELLs) and dual language learners (DLLs) with two focus areas addressing the development of language and cultural influences from the home to the community, birth to age 8; and systems and policies affecting EL/DLL children and youth in grades K-12, including standards and practices across diverse contexts to foster educational achievement among young ELLs/DLLs. The committee will come to consensus on findings and recommendations that aim to inform a research agenda to address gaps in the knowledge base, policies that impact young ELLs, and practices in the range of settings where young DLLs/ELLs learn, grow, and develop, including homes, classrooms, and health care settings. The committee will explore the implementation implications of its recommendations within the frame of cost and scalability. The committee will review the evidence from international and U.S. studies including, but not limited to, the following disciplines: neuroscience, developmental psychology, linguistics, demography, general education, special education, sociology, public health, maternal and child health, home visiting, public policy, and cultural anthropology. Evidence will be drawn from high-quality research, including peer-reviewed literature and government reports and reflecting various study designs (e.g., descriptive, longitudinal, qualitative, mixed methods, experimental and quasi-experimental).

In this document,* the term "ELL" is used to refer to a child from a home where a language other than English is spoken and who may be learning two (or more) languages at the same time. "ELLs" encompasses "dual language learners" (DLLs), "limited English proficient" (LEP), "language minority," "bilingual," and other common terms used in the field for children who speak a language other than English.

Birth to Age 8 Focus

This focus area will be on the foundational elements of language development, developmental progress, school entry, and practices for early school success for young ELLs who are dual language learners (whether that is a heritage, native, or a second language). The birth to age 8 focus area will include the following questions:

1. How do young ELLs/DLLs develop? What are the normative learning trajectories across domains, including socio-emotional as well as language and knowledge development in any/all languages spoken by a child?
2. What are the roles of languages, culture, and cultural identity in the development of young ELLs/DLLs?
3. What practices and principles show evidence of positively affecting socio-emotional well-being, health, language and literacy development in home languages and English, and content learning for young ELLs/DLLs 0-8

years old across various settings (e.g., home, child care, health care, school, inclusive settings)?

4. What strategies and practices show evidence of supporting young ELLs/DLLs who are also children with disabilities, homeless, from migrant families, or living on tribal lands?

5. What strategies and practices show evidence of supporting optimal transitions establishing a learning progression in a continuum of education for young ELLs/DLLs from birth through third grade (i.e., between home, early childhood education and care settings, pre-K, kindergarten, and through third grade)? What are the barriers to implementing a continuum of education for young ELLs/DLLs?

6. How does the literature inform promising practices in the identification, screening, and assessment of ELLs/DLLs, from birth through third grade, to reliably document the progress of young children's learning, health, and development?

7. How does the literature inform improvements needed in data collection and measurement of young ELLs/DLLs to enhance the next generation of research and evaluation studies in this area?

8. How does the literature identify promising practices including dual language approaches of early learning (birth to grade 3) programs and systems, that are linguistically and culturally responsive to young ELLs/DLLs and their parents/families and promote long-term learning, health, and academic achievement among ELLs/DLLs?

K-12 Focus Area

This focus area will be grounded in elucidating instructional practices and systems including dual language approaches that can help EL/DLLs attain both new content as well as the newly emerging English language proficiency standards. Among several questions, the committee will address:

1. What should an effective language program look like when applying appropriate dual language approaches?

2. What are the key features of English as a second language (ESL)/English language development (ELD) instruction that foster acquisition of the complex social and academic uses of language delineated in the new content standards?

3. How should ESL/ELD instruction be coordinated and integrated with the "regular" core content instructional program particularly in dual language programs?

4. What principles should govern how educational or health care programs provide language development and rigorous academic content for ELLs and DLLs particularly in dual language programs?

5. How should the diversity of the ELLs/DLLs student population be addressed? For example, what should language instruction look like for ELLs at different levels of English language proficiency and heritage language proficiency?

continued

BOX 1-2 Continued

6. What are appropriate time expectations for progress in various components of content and language development, as measured by summary assessments that can be applied to accountability systems?
7. What are the competencies of teachers and staff working with ELLs and DLLs in educational and health care or medical home settings?

---

*This document refers to the text of the Statement of Task and uses different terminology than what the committee decided to adopt.

---

raphy and data collection, policies, effective classroom practices, and growing up as a DLL/EL. The second public session included panel presentations of educators and parents of DLLs/ELs and addressed the preparation of educators and out-of-school-time programs for DLLs/ELs. The site visits encompassed classroom observations; focus groups; and interviews with students, teachers, school administrators, parents, and support personnel.

The committee conducted an extensive critical review of the literature pertaining to the development and education of DLLs/ELs published after release of the report *Improving Schooling for Language Minority Children: A Research Agenda* (National Research Council and Institute of Medicine, 1997). This review began with an English language search of online databases, including ERIC, Scopus, PsycInfo, and Web of Science. Committee members and project staff used online searches to identify additional literature and other resources. Attention was given to consensus and position statements issued by relevant experts and professional organizations. Research reports in peer-reviewed journals of the disciplines relevant to this study received priority. In the process of reviewing the literature, the committee members engaged in interdisciplinary and interprofessional discussions to achieve consensus where possible.

This report also builds on several recent publications of the National Academies of Sciences, Engineering, and Medicine, most notably *The Integration of Immigrants into American Society* (National Academies of Sciences, Engineering, and Medicine, 2015). Box 1-3 lists those reports.

GUIDING PRINCIPLES

The committee's research and deliberations led to the formulation of five guiding principles that provide a framework for this report (see

Box 1-4). These principles relate to policy contexts, capacity, culture and social organizations, the importance of early experience, and complexity and cascades. Empirical support for these principles is incorporated throughout the report.

Policy Contexts

Federal and state policies, from their inception, have influenced the educational opportunities and experiences of DLLs/ELs (see Chapter 2).

BOX 1-3
Related Publications of the National Academies
of Sciences, Engineering, and Medicine

Advancing the Power of Economic Evidence to Inform Investments in Children, Youth, and Families (National Academies of Sciences, Engineering, and Medicine, 2016a)

Allocating Federal Funds for State Programs for English Language Learners (National Research Council, 2011)

Eager to Learn: Educating Our Preschoolers (National Research Council, 2000a)

Early Childhood Assessment: Why, What, and How (National Research Council, 2008)

Educating Language-Minority Children (National Research Council and Institute of Medicine, 1998)

From Neurons to Neighborhoods: The Science of Early Childhood Development (National Research Council and Institute of Medicine, 2000)

Improving Schooling for Language Minority Children: A Research Agenda (National Research Council and Institute of Medicine, 1997)

The Integration of Immigrants into American Society (National Academies of Sciences, Engineering, and Medicine, 2015)

Keeping Score for All: The Effects of Inclusion and Accommodation Policies on Large-Scale Educational Assessment (National Research Council, 2004)

Language Diversity, School Learning, and Closing Achievement Gaps: A Workshop Summary (National Research Council, 2010)

Minority Students in Special and Gifted Education (National Research Council, 2002)

Parenting Matters: Supporting Parents of Children Ages 0-8 (National Academies of Sciences, Engineering, and Medicine, 2016b)

Testing English Language Learners in U.S. Schools (National Research Council, 2000b)

Transforming the Workforce for Children Birth Through Age 8: A Unifying Foundation (Institute of Medicine and National Research Council, 2015)

NOTE: All of these publications are available for free download at http://www.nap.edu.

BOX 1-4
Guiding Principles

Policy Contexts. National, state, and local policies, including those governing standards, instructional practices, educator preparation, and assessment methods, determine educational opportunities for ELs.

Capacity. Children have the capacity to learn more than one language if given appropriate opportunities. Fulfillment of this capacity can be accomplished with no harm and has benefits.

Culture and Social Organizations. Language learning is a cultural and socially embedded process. Families and communities, other institutions, and schools are influential in the language development and educational attainment of DLLs/ELs.

Importance of Early Experience. For DLLs/ELs, early, rich development of the child's first language is a beneficial foundation for learning English in school.

Complexity and Cascades. Language is a complex system, takes time to develop, and has cascading effects across a range of domains of the well-being of children and youth.

The U.S. Supreme Court ruled on statutory protections regarding ELs regardless of their national origins on the basis of Title VI of the Civil Rights Act, which led to the Court's unanimous decision affirming appropriate actions to remedy educational inequalities in the K-12 grades. While explicitly stated for K-12 students,[1] these protections apply to all federally funded programs, including Head Start and home visiting programs, and therefore apply to all DLLs and ELs in those programs.

As these programs have been reformed over successive reauthorizations, issues regarding how effectively they meet the needs of DLLs and ELs have arisen. The needs of these children and youth are addressed by multiple federal policies (e.g., the Every Student Succeeds Act [ESSA], the Individuals with Disabilities Education Act [IDEA]) and programs (e.g., general education, special education, bilingual education). States, and especially local school districts, implement federal policies aimed at improving professional development for educators and leaders to impart the skills and strategies required to address the needs of DLLs/ELs, make sense of contradictory or conflicting guidelines and policies across policy realms, and

---

[1] *Lau v. Nichols*, 414 U.S. 563 (1974).

resolve tensions in programmatic decisions and plans that cut across both general and special education.

Capacity

Language lies at the center of all human development. DLLs face the promises and challenges associated with learning both a home or primary language (L1) and English (L2).[2] Those who become proficient in the two languages are likely to reap benefits in cognitive, social, and emotional development (Halle et al., 2014) and also may be protected from brain decline at older ages (Bak et al., 2014; Bialystok, 2011; Bialystok et al., 2012). Conversely, those who do not acquire the English skills needed to succeed in school may lag behind their peers educationally and may face barriers to full civic participation and professional advancement in a global economy.

The achievement of proficiency in English need not occur at the expense of DLLs'/ELs' continued development of L1. Children who lose their L1 in the course of acquiring English may risk their connections to their families and cultures, in addition to forfeiting the benefits of fluent bilingualism. Consequently, with the understanding that strong English skills are essential for educational success in the United States, a goal of this report is to identify factors that support the development of children's skills in *both* L1 and L2.

A growing body of evidence indicates that young children can attain proficiency in more than one language provided they have sufficient language input. Children enter the world with powerful learning mechanisms that enable them to acquire two languages from birth without difficulty (see Chapter 4) and with potential benefits. The expression of this capacity for dual language learning, however, is critically dependent on early language experiences (e.g., Saffran, 2014) within families and communities and on the programs available to children before they enter school. Acknowledgment of children's early capacity to learn two or more languages recognizes that bi/multilingualism is a natural human attribute, exemplified in many countries throughout the world (e.g., European Commission, 2006). Indeed, the majority of the world's population is bi- or multilingual (Marian and Shook, 2012).

Culture and Social Organizations

As noted above, language learning is a socially embedded process that takes place within families, cultural communities, and other social

---

[2] The terms "L1" and "L2" are used throughout this report to refer to a child's first and second language, respectively.

institutions. Like learning in other domains, it is a cultural phenomenon constituted by the interacting influences of individual, interpersonal, and institutional dimensions (García and Markos, 2015). Understanding this intersection between the individual and the environment is important to fostering development and learning, not only with respect to the language learning of DLLs/ELs, but also more broadly. Individuals use their language skills and capacities in the contexts of social relationships and cultural norms that are always embedded in institutional environments—families, communities, schools, youth organizations, and peer groups. Thus, understanding and addressing the social learning contexts of DLLs/ELs transcends an exclusive focus on language.

Importance of Early Experience

Research points to the importance of early experience in language learning and in particular, the ways in which early L1 development can promote learning English (L2) in DLLs/ELs. Three lines of research support this notion. First, research on brain development indicates that relatively more neural brain plasticity exists in infancy and early childhood than at later stages of development and that early language experiences shape brain development in significant ways. At the same time, early stages of brain development shape children's capacity for language learning (see Chapter 4). Second, studies on the age of acquisition in learning a second language indicate greater proficiency in children who are exposed to L2 before 3 years of age (or at least by the end of kindergarten) than in those exposed at later ages (De Houwer, 2011; Dupoux et al., 2010; Meisel, 2011; Ortiz-Mantilla et al., 2010). Third, studies in early education and economics show that investments in early childhood education can enhance overall well-being and academic outcomes for DLLs who speak Spanish (Barnett et al., 2007; Burchinal et al., 2015; Durán et al., 2010; García and García, 2012; García and Jensen, 2009; Gormley, 2008; Gormley et al., 2008; Han, 2008).

Complexity and Cascades

Language is a complex and dynamic system (e.g., De Bot et al., 2007), and language acquisition involves the integration of perceptual, lexical, grammatical, semantic, and sociocultural knowledge. Development in these components of language acquisition is affected by interrelated factors—ranging from biology; to social interactions with family members, teachers, and peers; to policies in schools. Variation in these factors may explain the striking individual differences in language and other skills seen among DLLs/ELs, while also offering a wide range of opportunities for promoting language learning.

KEY CHALLENGES FOR POLICY AND PRACTICE

This section identifies the key challenges that can impact the language development and educational attainment of DLLs/ELs, as well as factors that may constrain potential solutions to these challenges.

A Wide Achievement Gap

A large educational achievement and attainment gap exists between ELs and their monolingual English peers (e.g., National Center for Education Statistics, 2015). In 2015, for example, the reading achievement gap between non-EL and EL students was 36 points at the 4th-grade level and 44 points at the 8th-grade level (Office of English Language Acquisition, 2016). In 2013-2014, the 4-year adjusted cohort high school graduation rate for ELs was 63 percent—far lower than the rate for students living in low-income families (75%); in that same period, the overall high school graduation rate was 82 percent (National Center for Education Statistics, 2015).

Many of these disparities are driven not only by limited knowledge of English but also by the same factors that lead to lower rates of achievement in other groups of students, such as poverty and underresourced schools. Relative to their non-EL peers, ELs live in families with higher rates of poverty and lower rates of parental education. They also are disproportionately concentrated in schools with limited resources and relatively high concentrations of ELs and low-income students (Adair, 2015; Carhill et al., 2008; Gándara and Rumberger, 2008). As a result, ELs face a number of barriers to educational success and a lack of learning opportunities that go beyond their English proficiency.

Limited proficiency in English also poses a high barrier to academic learning and performance in schools where English is the primary language of instruction and assessment. As discussed in greater depth in Chapter 9, a disparity exists between professional standards for assessing EL students and the way in which assessment of ELs at the individual student and system levels is actually conducted. Chapter 8 reviews this disparity for DLLs/ELs with disabilities and the potential consequences for misclassification.

The Federal Role in the ESSA Era

Although provisions of the 2015 ESSA are aimed at returning decision-making authority around accountability to states, the federal government continues to play an important role in the education of ELs. One important federal role is to protect the civil rights of ELs, as required by court decisions such as *Lau v. Nichols*[3] and federal statutes such as the Title VI of the Civil Rights Act[4] and the Equal Educational Opportunities Act of 1974.[5] Legal actions, however, must be initiated by local actors, and are both costly and lengthy.

Under ESSA, although states have flexibility in how elements of accountability index systems are weighted, states are now required to report on English language proficiency as part of ESSA Title I accountability[6] in addition to standardizing procedures for assessing proficiency within states. Because English language proficiency is assessed only for students who have EL status, and the numbers of those students vary significantly across schools, the ways in which those assessments are accomplished are likely to vary significantly. Theoretically, there could be as many different accountability plans as there are states—a concern for the civil rights community, which has traditionally relied on federal mechanisms to ensure the equity guaranteed by federal laws.

Considerations of Cost and Scalability

Although it is difficult to draw causal conclusions about policy impacts, the academic failure rates of the nation's ELs indicate that many current policies prevent these children and youth from reaching their full potential. These poor outcomes impose large costs on ELs, their families, and society as a whole. Several economic impact studies have quantified the societal economic burdens associated with failing to invest in and successfully educate American children and youth who face substantial barriers to success (e.g., Belfield et al., 2012; Heckman, 2006). According to these studies, the greatest cost associated with society's failure to help young people reach their full potential tends to come in the form of lost lifetime earnings and the associated tax revenues (e.g., Belfield et al., 2012; Heckman, 2006). This cost may be particularly high in the case of the inadequate education of ELs, given that the nation is missing an opportunity to cultivate fully biliterate, productive members of the workforce. ELs begin school with a linguistic asset that, if further developed, could lead to higher labor market returns and social outcomes than are now realized (e.g., Gándara and Hopkins, 2010).

Many policies and practices could be revised to improve the education of ELs, thereby increasing their economic value to society, as well as the

---

[3] *Lau v. Nichols*, 414 U.S. 563 (1974).
[4] Title VI of the Civil Rights Act of 1964, 42 U.S.C. 2000d, et seq.
[5] Equal Educational Opportunities Act of 1974 (EEOA), Section 1703(f).
[6] A summary of EL assessment final regulations as of early 2017 under ESSA can be found at https://www2.ed.gov/policy/elsec/leg/essa/essaassessmentfactsheet1207.pdf [February 23, 2017].

quality of their lives. In formulating its recommendations for improving current policies and practices relative to DLLs/ELs, the committee considered the resource implications of the proposed reforms. The Great Recession during the late 2000s substantially threatened the fiscal stability of the United States and the rest of the world, and while the U.S. economy is on the mend, resources remain constrained. And although many state budgets have modestly improved since the Great Recession, they, too, are constrained, consumed in particular by the rising costs of health care (National Association of State Budget Officers, 2015). As resources are allocated, therefore, policy makers and program administrators will increasingly be required to document the costs of various interventions and, where possible, weigh those costs against the anticipated benefits.

The issue of determining the appropriate level of resources and funding for pre-K to 12 education has received a great deal of attention in the research, policy, and legal communities (for reviews, see Downes and Stiefel, 2008; Koski and Hahnel, 2007). Very little of this research and policy discussion has focused on the incremental costs associated with the education of ELs in particular (Jimenez-Castellanos and Topper, 2012). Indeed, documenting those costs is difficult, and many schools and districts fail to keep careful records on the portion of expenditures designated for EL-specific education (e.g., Report on Arizona by the National Conference of State Legislatures, 2005). Even when careful cost records are available, determining the appropriate or adequate level of funding is challenging.

In addition to cost considerations, reformers will face challenges when programs and policies are brought to scale with large and varied populations in different settings. Evaluating the implementation and scalability of policy reforms is now considered good practice (Schneider and McDonald, 2007).

Competing Beliefs About Dual Language Learning

One of the greatest challenges in the education of DLLs/ELs is the opposing views held by society at large and by many educational and health professionals about whether dual language learning should be supported early in a child's development and later in classrooms (see Chapters 4, 5, and 7).

One view holds that dual language learning early in a child's life is burdensome because it exceeds the normal limits of young learners' capacity (e.g., Baker, 2011; Volterra and Taeschner, 1978). This view leads to either (1) exposing children early in development only to their L1 because exposure to English as an additional language will confuse them, or conversely, (2) exposing children only to English because exposure to their L1 will confuse them and create barriers to their learning English. Both of these alternatives suppress opportunities to develop fluency in two languages early in children's lives.

The other view is just the opposite—that young children are "hard-wired" to learn one or more languages easily and that as a result, nothing needs to be done to promote their language development. The evidence indicating that young children are particularly efficient and effective second language learners has focused primarily on language learning in nonschool settings and has not always considered the complexities of language learning in school contexts. While young children may be within the sensitive period for language learning and have sophisticated learning capacities, the role of exposure and experience is critical (see Chapter 4).

Both of these views, in their extremes, can be detrimental to policies and practices regarding the education of DLLs/ELs.

Competing Assumptions About the Role of Families

Families and home environments are the most salient and enduring contexts in which DLLs learn and develop. Understanding the demographic profiles of DLLs' families is important for understanding the families as learning contexts, but does not capture the rich processes that both characterize and distinguish how the families foster DLLs' language development.

Debate is ongoing about the ways in which family poverty may affect children's language experiences and, in turn, their language development. This debate is relevant to the present discussion given that, as noted above, many DLLs live in low-income households. One school of thought highlights differences in language environments between wealthier families and those who live in poverty (see Chapter 4 for more in-depth discussion). Certainly the early language experiences of children are vital to language learning. However, a focus on group averages (comparing groups of children from low-income families with those from middle- or high-income families) obscures the striking variability in language inputs experienced by children in families from the same income strata, including DLLs living in poverty who are from the same ethnic and language background (Song et al., 2012).

Many researchers have adopted a language socialization lens that considers the cultural forces that affect children's experiences and development in examining and understanding educational disparities across socioeconomic groups (Miller and Sperry, 2012). According to this perspective, processes related to culture-specific parenting goals, practices, and beliefs and home language and literacy practices related to bilingualism are key aspects of the family that are unique to DLLs (e.g., García and García, 2012; Li et al., 2014).

Determining What Constitutes Effective
Instructional Policies and Practices

Instructional policies and practices designed to meet the needs of DLLs/ELs can have a positive impact on the overall well-being of these children and youth, as well as their learning outcomes in school (August and Shanahan, 2006; Baker et al., 2014; García and Frede, 2010; Genesee et al., 2006). Children can acquire advanced levels of proficiency in a second language in school when they are presented with appropriate and continuous instruction to that end.

Acquiring proficiency in a second language for academic purposes takes time (see Chapter 6). ELs come to school with the resources of their home language: they have an underlying neural architecture for language, with existing connections between various components, such as how sounds perceived are related to sounds produced; they have a system of concepts on which the language is built; they know that elements of a language (e.g., words) can be combined to make sentences; they know about the referential functions of language, what people might say in various sociocultural situations (e.g., greetings, expressions of appreciation, politeness rituals); and (most important) they have an inclination to read or infer the intentions of others in events and interactions in which they are engaged (Tomasello, 2003). These skills and knowledge constitute a foundation for the acquisition of a second language in school.

One of the most intensely debated aspects of education policy and practice for ELs has centered on the language of classroom instruction (Gándara and Hopkins, 2010). Educators and researchers agree that to succeed in school and participate in civic life in the United States, all children must develop strong English proficiency and literacy skills. The debate centers on the question of how best to support the acquisition of English and the ongoing role of L1 as English skills deepen, the social and cultural costs of losing proficiency in L1, the role of education programs in systematically supporting L1, and community values that may promote English-only approaches. Many practical questions remain around the best methods for promoting English language development while continuing to support multiple home languages in English-only classroom settings. Furthermore, as discussed below, the educator workforce has not been prepared to teach ELs, and addressing educator capacity is a long-term effort (Putman et al., 2016).

Inadequate Preparation of Educators

Given the steady increase in diversity among DLLs/ELs in the U.S. population, a key challenge for educators is understanding the social, cultural, and linguistic backgrounds of the children they serve and creating the conditions of trust and respect necessary for effective instruction (e.g., Loeb et al., 2014). The educational backgrounds of a child's parents and the social and financial resources available to the family and in the community influence the child's home learning environment. Children are exposed to and competent in different cultures, languages, and social norms and as a result, may evidence a variety of culturally specific behaviors, languages, and social norms. They may be newcomers to the United States, have had traumatic journeys, have special needs or disabilities, speak more than one language in their home, or have lived in the United States for several generations and have family members who speak little English. Panethnic categories in actuality encompass a wide range of cultural groups with unique identities, migration histories, sociodemographic profiles, language experiences, and prior schooling experiences (see Chapter 3). Educators draw on their own experiences with cross-ethnic relations, language learning, and racialized understandings of U.S. society and may feel unprepared to support the school success of ELs. Chapter 10 reviews what is known about building the workforce to care for and educate DLLs/ELs.

ORGANIZATION OF THE REPORT

The committee was tasked with applying what is known about language development from birth to age 21, reviewing effective educational practices for DLLs/ELs during this age span, and recommending policies and practices that can change the troubling educational trajectories of these children and youth. Chapter 2 addresses the policy changes since the 1960s that have shaped the educational experiences and achievement of DLLs/ELs and suggests what changes are likely under the 2015 ESSA reauthorization. The diverse demographic landscape of the EL population discussed in Chapter 3 magnifies the challenges to educators of providing a good education to all. Chapter 4 focuses on the foundations of and influences on early language development from birth to age 5. A review of promising and effective early care and education practices for DLLs from birth to age 5 follows in Chapter 5.

Chapter 6 focuses on the development of English proficiency for ELs during the K-12 grades. Chapter 7 addresses education for ELs during the pre-K to 12 grades, while Chapter 8 focuses on promising and effective practices in education for ELs in these grades. Chapter 9 reviews promising and effective practices in education for ELs from specific populations, and Chapter 10 addresses DLLs and ELs with disabilities. Chapter 11 examines promising and effective practices in assessment and measurement of the educational progress of DLLs/ELs. The issue of building the workforce to care for and educate DLLs/ELs is considered in Chapter 12. Finally, Chapter 13 presents the committee's recommendations for policy and practice and outlines a research agenda focused on improving policies and practices to support the educational success of DLLs/ELs.

The report concludes with three appendixes. Appendix A provides the biosketches of committee members and staff; Appendix B lists the state requirements for teacher certification; and Appendix C profiles the population of ELs by state and the number of certified/licensed Title III teachers available to teach those ELs.

BIBLIOGRAPHY

Adair, J.K. (2015). *The Impact of Discrimination on the Early Schooling Experiences of Children from Immigrant Families.* Washington, DC: Migration Policy Institute.

Administration for Children and Families and U.S. Department of Health and Human Services. (2013). *Report to Congress on Dual Language Learners in Head Start and Early Head Start Programs.* Available: https://www.acf.hhs.gov/sites/default/files/opre/report_to_congress.pdf.

August, D., and Shanahan, T. (2006). *Developing Literacy in Second-Language Learners: Report of the National Literacy Panel on Language Minority Children and Youth, Executive Summary.* Mahwah, NJ: Lawrence Erlbaum Associates.

Bak, T.H., Nissan, J.J., Allerhand, M.M., and Deary, I.J. (2014). Does bilingualism influence cognitive aging? *Annals of Neurology, 75*(6), 959-963.

Baker, C. (2011). *Foundations of Bilingual Education and Bilingualism* (5th ed.). Bristol, UK: Multilingual Matters.

Baker, S., Lesaux, N., Jayanthi, M., Dimino, J., Proctor, C.P., Morris, J., Gersten, R., Haymond, K., Kieffer, M.J., Linan-Thompson, S., and Newman-Gonchar, R. (2014). *Teaching Academic Content and Literacy to English Learners in Elementary and Middle School. IES Practice Guide.* NCEE 2014-4012. Available: https://ies.ed.gov/ncee/wwc/Docs/PracticeGuide/english_learners_pg_040114.pdf [June 7, 2016].

Barnett, W.S., Yaroz, D.J., Thomas, J., Jung, K., and Blanco, D. (2007). Two-way immersion in preschool education: An experimental comparison. *Early Childhood Research Quarterly, 22*(3), 277-293.

Belfield, C.R., Levin, H.M., and Rosen, R. (2012). *The Economic Value of Opportunity Youth.* Washington, DC: Corporation for National and Community Service.

Bialystok, E. (2011). Reshaping the mind: The benefits of bilingualism. *Canadian Journal of Experimental Psychology = Revue Canadienne de Psychologie Experimentale, 65*(4), 229-235.

Bialystok, E., Craik, F.I., and Luk, G. (2012). Bilingualism: Consequences for mind and brain. *Trends in Cognitive Sciences, 16*(4), 240-250.

Burchinal, M., Magnuson, K., Powell, D., and Soliday Hong, S. (2015). Early childcare and education. In R. Lerner (Ed.), *Handbook of Child Psychology and Developmental Science* (7th ed., vol. 4, pp. 223-267). Hoboken, NJ: Wiley.

Carhill, A., Suárez-Orozco, C., and Páez, M. (2008). Explaining English language proficiency among adolescent immigrant students. *American Educational Research Journal, 45*(4), 1155-1179.

De Bot, K., Lowie, W., and Verspoor, M. (2007). A dynamic systems theory approach to second language acquisition. *Bilingualism: Language and Cognition, 10*(1), 7-21.

De Houwer, A. (2011). The speech of fluent child bilinguals. In P. Howell and J.V. Borsel (Eds.), *Multilingual Aspects of Fluency Disorders* (pp. 3-23). Bristol, UK: Multilingual Matters.

Downes, T.A., and Stiefel, L. (2008). Measuring equity and adequacy in school finance. In H.F. Ladd and E.B. Fiske (Eds.), *Handbook of Research in Education Finance and Policy* (pp. 222-237). New York: Routledge.

Dupoux, E., Peperkamp, S., and Sebastián-Gallés, N. (2010). Limits on bilingualism revisited: Stress "deafness" in simultaneous French–Spanish bilinguals. *Cognition, 114*(2), 266-275.

Durán, L.K., Roseth, C.J., and Hoffman, P. (2010). An experimental study comparing English-only and transitional bilingual education on Spanish-speaking preschoolers' early literacy development. *Early Childhood Research Quarterly, 25*(2), 207-217.

European Commission. (2006). *Europeans and Their Languages*. Available: http://ec.europa.eu/public_opinion/archives/ebs/ebs_243_en.pdf [October 3, 2016].

Gándara, P.C., and Hopkins, M. (2010). *Forbidden Language: English Learners and Restrictive Language Policies*. New York: Teachers College Press.

Gándara, P., and Rumberger, R.W. (2008). Defining an adequate education for English learners. *Education, 3*(1), 130-148.

García, E.E., and Frede, E.C. (2010). *Young English Language Learners: Current Research and Emerging Directions for Practice and Policy*. New York: Teachers College Press.

García, E.E., and García, E.H. (2012). *Understanding the Language Development and Early Education of Hispanic Children*. New York: Teachers College Press.

García, E.E., and Jensen, B. (2009). Early educational opportunities for children of Hispanic origins. *Social Policy Report, XXIII*(II).

García, E.E., and Markos, A. (2015). Early childhood education and dual language learners. In W.E. Wright, S. Boun, and O. García (Eds.), *Handbook of Bilingual and Multilingual Education* (pp. 301-318). Sussex, UK: Wiley Blackwell.

Genesee, F., Lindholm-Leary, K.J., Saunders, W.M., and Christian, D. (2006). *Educating English Language Learners: A Synthesis of Research Evidence*. New York: Cambridge University Press.

Gormley, W. (2008). The effects of Oklahoma's pre-K program on Hispanic children. *Social Science Quarterly, 89*(4), 916-936.

Gormley, W.T., Phillips, D, and Gayer, T. (2008). Preschool programs can boost school readiness. *Science, 320*(5884), 1723-1724.

Halle, T.G., Whittaker, J.V., Zepeda, M., Rothenberg, L., Anderson, R., Daneri, P., Wessel, J., and Buysse, V. (2014). The social-emotional development of dual language learners: Looking back at existing research and moving forward with purpose. *Early Childhood Research Quarterly, 29*(4), 734-749.

Han, W.J. (2008). The academic trajectories of children of immigrants and their school environments. *Developmental Psychology, 44*(6), 1572-1590.

Heckman, J.J. (2006). Skill formation and the economics of investing in disadvantaged children. *Science, 312*(5782), 1900-1902.

Institute of Medicine and National Research Council. (2015). *Transforming the Workforce for Children Birth Through Age 8: A Unifying Foundation*. L. Allen and B.B. Kelly (Eds.). Committee on the Science of Children Birth to Age 8: Deepening and Broadening the Foundation for Success; Board on Children, Youth, and Families. Washington, DC: The National Academies Press.

Jimenez-Castellanos, O., and Topper, A.M. (2012). The cost of providing an adequate education to English language learners: A review of the literature. *Review of Educational Research, 82*(2), 179-232.

Koski, W.S., and Hahnel, J. (2007). The past, present, and possible futures of educational finance reform litigation. In H.F. Ladd and E.B. Fiske (Eds.), *Handbook of Research in Education Finance and Policy* (pp. 42-60). New York: Routledge.

Li, J., Fung, H., Bakeman, R., Rae, K., and Wei, W. (2014). How European American and Taiwanese mothers talk to their children about learning. *Child Development, 85*(3), 1206-1221.

Loeb, S., Soland, J., and Fox, L. (2014). Is a good teacher a good teacher for all? Comparing value-added of teachers with their English learners and non-English learners. *Educational Evaluation and Policy Analysis, 36*(4), 457-475.

Marian, V., and Shook, A. (2012). The cognitive benefits of being bilingual. *Cerebrum: The Dana Forum on Brain Science*, 13.

Meisel, J.M. (2011). *First and Second Language Acquisition: Parallels and Differences*. Cambridge, UK: Cambridge University Press.

Miller, P.J., and Sperry, D.E. (2012). Déjà vu: The continuing misrecognition of low-income children's verbal abilities. In S.T. Fiske and H.R. Markus (Eds.), *Facing Social Class: How Societal Rank Influences Interaction* (pp. 109-130). New York: Russell Sage.

National Academies of Sciences, Engineering, and Medicine. (2015). *The Integration of Immigrants into American Society*. Washington, DC: The National Academies Press.

National Academies of Sciences, Engineering, and Medicine. (2016a). *Advancing the Power of Economic Evidence to Inform Investments in Children, Youth, and Families*. Washington, DC: The National Academies Press.

National Academies of Sciences, Engineering, and Medicine. (2016b). *Parenting Matters: Supporting Parents of Children Ages 0-8*. Washington, DC: The National Academies Press.

National Association of State Budget Officers. (2015). *State Expenditure Report: Examining 2013-2015 State Spending*. Washington, DC: National Association of State Budget Officers.

National Center for Education Statistics. (2015). *EDFacts Data Groups 695 and 696, School Year 2013-14*. Available: http://nces.ed.gov/ccd/tables/ACGR_RE_and_characteristics_2013-14.asp [October 5, 2016].

National Center for Education Statistics. (2016). *English Language Learners in Public Schools*. Available: https://nces.ed.gov/programs/coe/indicator_cgf.asp [October 12, 2016].

National Conference of State Legislatures. (2005). *Arizona English Language Learner Cost Study*. Washington, DC: National Conference of State Legislatures.

National Research Council. (2000a). *Eager to Learn: Educating Our Preschoolers*. B.T. Bowman, M.S. Donovan, and M.S. Burns (Eds.). Committee on Early Childhood Pedagogy, Commission on Behavioral and Social Sciences and Education. Washington, DC: National Academy Press.

National Research Council. (2000b). *Testing English-Language Learners in U.S. Schools: Report and Workshop Summary*. K. Hakuta and A. Beatty (Eds.). Committee on Educational Excellence and Testing Equity, Board on Testing and Assessment, Division of Behavioral and Social Sciences and Education. Washington, DC: National Academy Press.

National Research Council. (2002). *Minority Students in Special and Gifted Education*. M.S. Donovan and C.T. Cross (Eds.). Committee on Minority Representation in Special Education; Board on Behavioral, Cognitive, and Sensory Sciences; Division of Behavioral and Social Sciences and Education. Washington, DC: National Academy Press.

National Research Council. (2004). *Keeping Score for All: The Effects of Inclusion and Accommodation Policies on Large-Scale Educational Assessment*. J.A. Koenig and L.F. Bachman (Eds.). Committee on Participation of English Language Learners and Students with Disabilities in NAEP and Other Large-Scale Assessments, Board on Testing and Assessment, Division of Behavioral and Social Sciences and Education. Washington, DC: The National Academies Press.

National Research Council. (2008). *Early Childhood Assessment: Why, What, and How*. C.E. Snow and S.B. Van Hemel (Eds.). Committee on Developmental Outcomes and Assessments for Young Children; Board on Children, Youth, and Families; Board on Testing and Assessment; Division of Behavioral and Social Sciences and Education. Washington, DC: The National Academies Press.

National Research Council. (2010). *Language Diversity, School Learning, and Closing Achievement Gaps: A Workshop Summary*. M. Welch-Ross (Rapporteur). Committee on the Role of Language in School Learning: Implications for Closing the Achievement Gap, Center for Education, Division of Behavioral and Social Sciences and Education Washington, DC: The National Academies Press.

National Research Council. (2011). *Allocating Federal Funds for State Programs for English Language Learners*. Panel to Review Alternative Data Sources for the Limited-English Proficiency Allocation Formula under Title III, Part A, Elementary and Secondary Education Act; Committee on National Statistics and Board on Testing and Assessment; Division of Behavioral and Social Sciences and Education. Washington, DC: The National Academies Press.

National Research Council and Institute of Medicine. (1997). *Improving Schooling for Language-Minority Children: A Research Agenda*. D. August and K. Hakuta (Eds.). Committee on Developing a Research Agenda on the Education of Limited English Proficient and Bilingual Students, Commission on Behavioral and Social Sciences and Education, Division of Behavioral and Social Sciences and Education. Washington, DC: National Academy Press.

National Research Council and Institute of Medicine. (1998). *Educating Language-Minority Children*. D. August and K. Hakuta (Eds.). Committee on Developing a Research Agenda on the Education of Limited-English-Proficient and Bilingual Students, Commission on Behavioral and Social Sciences and Education, Division of Behavioral and Social Sciences and Education. Washington, DC: National Academy Press.

National Research Council and Institute of Medicine. (2000). *From Neurons to Neighborhoods: The Science of Early Childhood Development*. J.P. Shonkoff and D.A. Phillips (Eds.). Committee on Integrating the Science of Early Childhood Development; Board on Children, Youth, and Families; Division of Behavioral and Social Sciences and Education. Washington, DC: National Academy Press.

Office of English Language Acquisition. (2016). *English Learners' (ELs') Results from the 2015 Nation's Report Card*. Washington, DC: U.S. Department of Education. Available: http://www.ncela.us/files/fast_facts/OELA_FF_NAEP_2015_For_Grades48.pdf [October 4, 2016].

Ortiz-Mantilla, S., Choudhury, N., Alvarez, B., and Benasich, A.A. (2010). Involuntary switching of attention mediates differences in event-related responses to complex tones between early and late Spanish-English bilinguals. *Brain Research, 1362*, 78-92.

Putman, H., Hansen, M., Walsh, K., and Quintero, D. (2016). *High Hopes and Harsh Realities: The Real Challenges to Building a Diverse Workforce*. Available: https://www.brookings.edu/wp-content/uploads/2016/08/browncenter_20160818_teacherdiversity reportpr_hansen.pdf [September 2016].

Saffran, J. (2014). Sounds and meanings working together: Word learning as a collaborative effort. *Language learning, 64*(Suppl. 2), 106-120.

Schneider, B.L., and McDonald, S.-K. (2007). *Scale-up in Education: Ideas in Principal* (Vol. 1). Lanham, MD: Rowman & Littlefield Publishers.

Song, L., Tamis-LeMonda, C.S., Yoshikawa, H., Kahana-Kalman, R., and Wu, I. (2012). Language experiences and vocabulary development in Dominican and Mexican infants across the first 2 years. *Developmental Psychology, 48*(4), 1106.

Tomasello, M. (2003). *Constructing a Language: A Usage-Based Theory of Language Acquisition*. Cambridge, MA: Harvard University Press.

Volterra, V., and Taeschner, T. (1978). The acquisition and development of language by bilingual children. *Journal of Child Language, 5*(2), 311-326.

2

Policy Context

S peaking, reading, and writing in different languages are complex phenomena that have been viewed from many disciplinary and social perspectives. The committee's task was to recommend policies and practices that will enhance successful educational outcomes for dual language learners (DLLs) and English learners (ELs) in the United States from birth through grade 12.[1] ELs are a large and highly diverse population of children and youth exposed to multiple languages at various points during the first two decades of their lives. This chapter examines the evolution of federal policies that have shaped practice in the education of ELs over the past 50 years, federal and state policies that govern early care and education (ECE) for DLLs and whether they are consistent with promising and effective practices,[2] and current federal and state policies related to K-12 education for ELs that have followed the advent of the Every Student Succeeds Act (ESSA) of 2015.

OVERVIEW OF POLICIES GOVERNING THE EDUCATION OF ENGLISH LEARNERS, 1965-2015

Policies matter. In the context of this report, they set assumptions and expectations for what and how ELs should learn in schools and regulate their learning environments. In reviewing the evolution of policies relevant

---

[1] The terms "DLL" and "EL" as used in this report are defined in Box 1-1 in Chapter 1.

[2] See Chapter 5 for a more comprehensive review of promising and effective practices for DLLs in ECE.

to the education of ELs, it is important to distinguish between targeted, EL-specific policies and general education and special education policies that relate to broader populations that include ELs, and to consider their relationships.

EL-Specific Policies

Federal policies affecting ELs have their origins in the Civil Rights initiatives and the War on Poverty that were priorities of the L. B. Johnson administration in the 1960s.[3] Using the framework of Ruiz (1984),[4] these early policies addressed language learning for ELs as either a means of solving a "problem" to provide equal opportunity or a "right" to access English learning while being educated through the student's first or primary language (i.e., bilingual education). Framing education in terms of problems and rights carries clear assumptions about deficits in students and inaction or violations by systems that need to be addressed through enforcement. Only rarely does one see statements referring to bilingualism as an asset, even in the nonbinding "Whereas . . ." portions of the relevant legislation or in court rulings that might reflect Ruiz's third perspective of language as a resource. It is important to recognize these historical origins of EL policies when considering policies related to children's access to learning English and to grade-level content instruction.

In 1968, Congress passed the Bilingual Education Act as Title VII of the Elementary and Secondary Education Act (ESEA), representing the first federal action specifically addressing the educational needs of ELs. The law authorized modest, targeted grants to local education agencies (LEAs) for the implementation of bilingual education programs that used the primary language of ELs to help ensure that they could continue learning subject matter content while acquiring English proficiency. There was an almost immediate reaction to the requirement that the programs be bilingual—an issue that became the contentious focus of subsequent reauthorizations of ESEA. Pressure came from antibilingual, English-only groups such as U.S.

---

[3] Early funding for federal bilingual programs was influenced by Cuban refugees in the Coral Gables bilingual programs. An earlier influence was the 1930 Lemon Grove case involving segregation of ELs in which school officials argued that the segregation of Mexican children would facilitate the learning of English and allow special attention to the "language difficulties" of Mexican American children who entered school speaking only Spanish (García, 1989; McLemore and Romo, 2005). These early developments and the *Mendez v. Westminister School District* case of 1946 in which it was argued that Spanish-speaking children learn English more readily in mixed classrooms laid the foundation for the Supreme Court *Brown v. Board of Education* desegregation case.

[4] Ruiz's framework analyzes language policy according to how it treats language diversity— as a problem, a right, or a resource.

English,[5] as well as lobbying by school districts in which large numbers of different languages in the EL population made bilingual programs impractical. Special alternative instructional programs (SAIPs) using only English were allowed with a funding cap, and congressional debates on ESEA reauthorization centered on the specific cap (4-10% in 1984, increased to 25% for programs not requiring instruction in the native language in 1988 [Stewner-Manzanares, 1988] after intense lobbying by the Reagan administration). Two pieces of legislation pertinent specifically to the Native American population are described in Box 2-1.

During this same period, the courts became active in their interpretation of the Civil Rights Act of 1964[6]—most notably Title VI, which declared, "No person in the United States shall, on the grounds of race, color, or national origin, be excluded from participation in, be denied the benefits of, or be subjected to discrimination under any program or activity receiving Federal financial assistance." In 1974, the U.S. Supreme Court unanimously ruled that the San Francisco Unified School District was in violation of this act for failing to provide 2,856 Chinese schoolchildren access to learning English or to the basic content of schooling because they had not developed the level of English proficiency necessary to benefit from subject matter instruction in English.[7] The Court stated, "There is no equality of treatment merely by providing students with the same facilities, textbooks, teachers, and curriculum; for students who do not understand English are effectively foreclosed from any meaningful education." The Court declared, "Imposition of a requirement that, before a child can effectively participate in the educational program, he must already have acquired those basic skills is to make a mockery of public education."

Congress followed the *Lau* decision by incorporating and extending its principles into the Equal Educational Opportunities Act of 1974.[8] According to that act, no state could deny students the right to equal education as a result of "failure by an educational agency to take *appropriate action* to overcome language barriers that impede equal participation by its students in its instructional programs [emphasis added]," regardless of whether federal funds were involved.

The controversy surrounding the bilingual emphasis of ESEA entered into the interpretation of the *Lau* decision. Shortly after the ruling, the Carter administration created a task force to enforce *Lau* that was decidedly in favor of bilingual remedies in the elementary grades. The task force

---

[5]U.S. English is a lobbying organization founded in 1983 that promotes the idea that English should be the official language of the United States.

[6]Civil Rights Act of 1964, P.L. 88-352, 78 Stat. 241 (1964).

[7]*Lau v. Nichols*, 414 U.S. 563 (1974).

[8]Equal Educational Opportunities Act of 1974, P. L. 93-380, 88 Stat. 515 (1974).

BOX 2-1
The Indian Self-Determination and Educational
Assistance Act of 1975 and the Native American
Languages Preservation Act of 1990

The processes of loss of language and cultural heritage that were set in motion in the 19th century when children were taken from indigenous families and communities and placed in boarding schools continue to erode what remains of the indigenous languages and cultures of North America. The policy of language and cultural replacement at the time called for forbidding instruction in schools in any Indian language for all schools on Indian reservations, based on the claim that "the education of Indians in the vernacular is not only of no use to them, but is detrimental to their education and civilization."[a]

In passing the Indian Self-Determination and Educational Assistance Act in 1975, Congress enabled indigenous communities to decide how to educate their children. The Native American Languages Act of 1990[b] recognized the rights of communities to "preserve, protect, and promote the rights and freedom to use, practice, and develop Native American languages," and to do so in educational programs that used those languages as means of instruction in school. This act was amended in 2006 as the Esther Martinez Native American Languages Preservation Act,[c] which provided funds through grants to support language revitalization efforts in many communities through the Administration for Native Americans. Communities can apply for grants to support in-school, after-school, and summer programs in indigenous communities across America; develop suitable curriculum; deliver instruction in indigenous languages; train American Indian language teachers; and develop intergenerational programs that promote the learning and use of indigenous languages in homes and communities.

---

[a]*Use of English in Indian Schools* (extract from the Annual Report of the Commissioner of Indian Affairs, September 21, 1887) (Prucha, 1975, 1990).
[b]Public Law 101-477, *Title I–Native American Languages Act,* October 30, 1990.
[c]Public Law 109-394, *Esther Martinez Native American Languages Preservation Act of 2006* (amends the Native American Programs Act of 1974 to provide for the revitalization of Native American languages through Native American language immersion programs).

---

identified three types of acceptable programs: (1) transitional bilingual education programs (TBEs), (2) bilingual/bicultural programs, and (3) multilingual/multicultural programs. The task force stated that English-only programs were inferior: "Because an ESL [English as a second language] program does not consider the affective nor cognitive development of students in this category and time and maturation variables are different here than for students at the secondary level, an ESL program *is not* appropriate [emphasis in original]" (Ramsey, 2012, p. 159). These rules, which the administration did not turn into regulations—widely interpreted as a political decision (Crawford, 2004)—were nevertheless used in U.S. Office of Civil Rights negotiations with local districts in support of bilingual programming (Crawford, 2004).

The period from the mid-1970s through the 1980s saw an interest in studies comparing students in bilingual and alternative English-only programs (attempting to control for confounding factors through experimental or quasi-experimental designs). The question of "bilingual or not" became the primary policy question under consideration. The American Institutes for Research (Danoff et al., 1978) produced a congressionally mandated evaluation of Title VII-funded bilingual programs and found few positive effects for bilingual education. The report was heavily criticized for its methodological flaws and exposed divisions among supporters on each side. Senior administration staff in the Office of Policy, Budget and Evaluation of the [then] U.S. Department of Health, Education, and Welfare entered into the controversy, reviewing studies they deemed methodologically acceptable and conducting a frequency count of studies that supported either side or were equivocal (Baker and de Kanter, 1983). These results were mixed as well, leading to the department's conclusion that federal policy should not favor bilingual education.

Subsequently, the same office commissioned two evaluation studies to shed further light on the bilingual versus English-only question, using statistical methodologies considered cutting-edge at the time. The National Research Council (1992) reviewed these studies, concluding that both "suffered from excessive attention to the use of elaborate statistical methods intended to overcome the shortcomings in the research designs" and that "the absence of clear findings in [the studies] that distinguish among the effects of treatments and programs relating to bilingual education does not warrant conclusions regarding differences in program effects, in any direction" (p. 104). Better designs and more sophisticated meta-analyses would be required to answer the question.[9]

In the absence of convincing evaluation research on the effectiveness of bilingual education and vigorous political resistance to the approach on the part of English-only advocates, a policy middle ground took root in the ruling by the Fifth Circuit Court of *Castaneda v. Pickard*.[10] In that ruling, Judge Carolyn Randall defined standards that a district must follow to take "appropriate action" under the Equal Educational Opportunities Act: that

---

[9] Studies examining this question continued beyond the 1980s, and interest in this topic has not abated. Several studies (Francis et al., 2006; Greene, 1997; Rolstad et al., 2005) used meta-analytic techniques in examining the effectiveness of bilingual versus English-only approaches, and therefore took into account the program effects found in each study even if they were not statistically significant. Three studies funded by the U.S. Department of Education (Francis et al., 2006; Slavin and Cheung, 2003; Tong et al., 2008) used quasi-experimental designs.

[10] *Castaneda v. Pickard*, 648 F.2d 989 (5th Cir. 1981).

(1) the educational approach must be based on "sound educational theory"; (2) the program must be implemented adequately; and (3) after a period of time, the program must be evaluated for its effectiveness. This ruling can be seen as a position that does not endorse any particular program, but requires thoughtfulness in whatever method or theory underlies a program

This general approach was an acceptable compromise during the Reagan and George H. W. Bush administrations, during which the U.S. Office of Civil Rights issued guidance delineating these standards for reviewing programs for ELs. These so-called "Castaneda standards" remain to this day as the foundation for Title VI enforcement activities by the U.S. Office of Civil Rights and the U.S. Department of Justice. This framing of the issues in district and state implementation of EL programs in a recent "Dear Colleagues" letter (U.S. Department of Justice and U.S. Department of Education, 2015) is discussed in more detail later in this chapter.

Shift to Standards-Based Reform

Equally important are the shifts in federal education policy toward systemic changes and standards (Cohen, 1995; Smith and O'Day, 1991). The release of *A Nation at Risk: The Imperative for Educational Reform* (Gardner et al., 1983), the report of Ronald Reagan's National Commission on Excellence in Education, triggered a series of events that led to the "standards-based reform" movement (Cross, 2015; Jennings, 2015). Following on the Charlottesville Education Summit convened by President George H. W. Bush and the National Governors Association (whose education chair was Governor Bill Clinton of Arkansas), a strong push toward deregulation at the federal level in exchange for demonstration of state educational outcomes ensued (Takona and Wilburn, 2004).

Early in the Clinton administration, Congress passed the Goals 2000: Educate America Act of 1994,[11] which established state standards. The reauthorization of ESEA, called the Improving America's Schools Act of 1994, followed suit by authorizing programs based on the standards. Because the federal government lacks the authority to prescribe the content of instruction for states and districts, each state was free to develop its own standards. The rhetoric shifted from accountability for spending of federal funds to accountability for demonstrated results.

This shift changed the way in which the Bilingual Education Act was envisioned. It had consisted mainly of targeted local grants and capacity building for the field (such as fellowship programs to produce the next generation of university faculty). The new policy shift created school- and system-wide grants to whole schools and LEAs, taking the first steps away

---

[11] Goals 2000: Educate America Act, P. L. 103-227 (1994).

BOX 2-2
States' Goals Regarding Bilingual Education Programs

A recent review of state dual language policies and programs (Boyle et al., 2015) uncovered seven states (Delaware, Georgia, New Mexico, North Carolina, Rhode Island, Utah, and Washington) with explicit goals or value statements promoting the use of dual language or bilingual education programs. Five states (Connecticut, Illinois, New Jersey, New York, and Texas) mandate that districts with 20 or more English learners (ELs) at the same grade level from the same language background provide bilingual education programs. Three states (Delaware, Georgia, and Utah) have established special dual language initiatives. As of fall 2016, 23 states and the District of Columbia had adopted policies to recognize students who acquire proficiency in two languages with a specialized seal or endorsement on their high school diploma (see Box 2-3). On the other end of the spectrum, two states (Arizona and Massachusetts) have explicit laws that limit the conditions under which students can be placed in bilingual education programs. California's Proposition 227 of 1998 previously restricted bilingual education, but in November 2016 the state passed Proposition 58 and lifted these restrictions. Massachusetts may be moving away from these restrictions on bilingual education as well. Massachusetts currently permits dual language programming and has a bill (Language Opportunities for Our Kids) that, if passed, would allow for the use of languages other than English for instructing ELs.

In their 2012-2013 consolidated state performance reports (CSPRs), 39 states and the District of Columbia indicated that districts receiving federal Title III funding had implemented at least one dual language program during that year. In total, these programs featured more than 30 different partner languages. States most frequently reported dual language programs with Spanish (35 states and the District of Columbia), Chinese (14 states), American Indian languages (12 states), and French (7 states and the District of Columbia) as the partner languages (Boyle et al., 2015).

---

from "nonsystemic" approaches targeting specific projects or grade levels to support specific students (see Box 2-2).

In 2001, Congress passed the No Child Left Behind Act of 2001 (NCLB)[12] with strong bipartisan support, which became a signature education bill of the George W. Bush presidency. NCLB added strong accountability provisions for students' attainment of standards and for reduction of gaps among subgroups of students, including ELs. Title I of the bill accomplished its goal of making schools, local districts, and states accountable for the performance of ELs, with corrective actions required of systems failing to meet the bill's requirements.

---

[12]No Child Left Behind Act of 2001, P. L. 107-110 (2001).

BOX 2-3
Seal of Biliteracy

The Seal of Biliteracy is a notable initiative by multiple states to recognize and support biliteracy among all students, not just English learners (ELs) (Giambo and Szecsi, 2015). Since 2011, when the first state (California) adopted the Seal of Biliteracy, 23 states and the District of Columbia have adopted a statewide seal. Schools and districts have begun to institute Bilingual Pathway Awards that recognize significant progress in the development of biliteracy throughout various stages of a student's academic progression (i.e., preschool and elementary awards in addition to the high school Seal of Biliteracy award on the diploma). The purposes of the seal are

- to encourage students to study languages,
- to certify attainment of biliteracy skills,
- to recognize the value of language diversity,
- to provide employers with a method of identifying individuals with language and biliteracy skills,
- to provide universities with a method that recognizes and gives credit to applicants for attainment of high-level skills in multiple languages,
- to prepare students with 21st-century skills that will benefit them in the labor market and the global society, and
- to strengthen intergroup relationships and honor the multiple cultures and languages in a community.

All students who meet criteria for the award have the seal on their high school diploma. Criteria vary depending on the type of language learner (i.e., students whose first language is English who are learning a second language versus ELs who are developing proficiency in their primary language while also mastering English), as well as on the assessment process outlined by states, districts, and schools. Typically, the criteria include attainment of a stated level of proficiency in English language arts plus demonstration of proficiency in the other language (e.g., criteria available through advanced placement, international baccalaureate testing, or American Council on the Teaching of Foreign Languages (2015) testing and a variety of locally selected criteria, especially for languages for which established formal tests are not available). The assessment process may include tests developed at the district level that are aligned with the World Language Standards; a Linguafolio approach as developed by the National Council of State Supervisors for Languages (2016); or some combination of assessments along with coursework, requirements, and performance (e.g., oral interview or presentation).

While the Seal of Biliteracy recognizes the value of bilingualism and biliteracy, its implementation raises significant challenges that need to be recognized. These challenges include the availability of qualified teachers; aligned instructional materials; an appropriate assessment system to support instruction, monitor student progress, and evaluate program effectiveness; and a research base.

SOURCE: Californians Together and Velasquez Press (2016).

The notion of standards also found its way into accountability for English language proficiency as the driver for EL programs in Title III. NCLB required states to adopt English language proficiency standards that they would develop as part of Title III, and to administer annual assessments aligned with these standards. Separate accountability requirements (annual measurable achievement objectives [AMAOs]) for a combination of student performance on the state English language proficiency and content tests were instituted. Title III funding for schools became based entirely on the numbers of ELs rather than competitive grants (National Research Council, 2011).

Emergence of the Common Core

NCLB/ESEA was up for reauthorization in 2007, but when President Obama took office in 2009, the nation was in a deep recession, and political prospects for an immediate reauthorization of the law appeared dim. Given that the steep requirement for adequate yearly progress caused most districts and states to fail under the law's accountability provisions, the Obama administration invited states to request waivers allowing for flexibility.

As part of efforts to deal with the Great Recession of 2008, the American Recovery and Reinvestment Act of 2009 (ARRA) directed $10 billion in additional funds to education. Through the Race to the Top Program (U.S. Department of Education, 2009, p. 2), states were required to address the Obama administration's priorities:

- Adopting standards and assessments that prepare students to succeed in college and the workplace to compete in the global economy.
- Building data systems that measure student growth and success, and inform teachers and principals about how they can improve instruction.
- Recruiting, developing, rewarding, and retaining effective teachers and principals, especially where they are needed most.
- Turning around the lowest-achieving schools.

In addition, ARRA provided support for consortia of states to develop common assessments for specified content areas. The resulting Partnership for Assessment of Readiness for College and Careers and Smarter Balanced Assessment Consortium developed assessments aligned with the Common Core State Standards in English language arts, literacy, and mathematics, creating synergies between the Common Core and state needs for relief from the NCLB accountability provisions.

The Common Core and its variants gave educators a new appreciation of the role of language in the learning of academic content and how it is measured in assessments. With encouragement from the U.S. Department of Education through various initiatives—most notably the ARRA-funded Race to the Top competition and the waivers enabling NCLB flexibility—states were required to adopt college- and career-ready content standards as part of their applications. Significantly, the NCLB waiver application required each state to adopt state English language proficiency (ELP) standards corresponding to the college- and career-ready standards. This requirement led to a shift in the nature of the ELP standards as a result of changes in how language would be used to address the new content standards (for example, the Common Core State Standard for mathematical practice expects students to "construct viable arguments and critique the reasoning of others").

A valuable document that guided this process was a report of the Council of Chief State Schools Officers (2012) known as the "ELP/D Framework," which describes the English language proficiency required for students to engage in learning the grade-level course content specified by the Common Core State Standards and Next Generation Science Standards. In so doing, the report builds an explicit bridge between academic content and students' use of language. This integration of standards for academic content and English language proficiency communicates to mainstream content teachers who otherwise would gravitate toward teaching the vocabulary of their content that they are expected to focus on how students engage in using language to learn through discourse, argumentation, and text-based evidence. It also can help build bridges between designated English language development teachers and content teachers who in some cases may work in isolation from each other (Valdés et al., 2014).

Another notable trend was the move away from federally driven, top-down accountability models under NCLB. Most educators now agree that the punitive approach to accountability, with required actions for schools and districts failing to meet annual measurable objectives and adequate yearly progress, did not build system capacity for improvement. Additionally, it served to narrow the curriculum to reading and math, especially in the grade levels where assessment was required.

Despite their controversial nature and local tailoring by states, the Common Core State Standards also served as an impetus for educators to consider deeper learning and social/cultural skills. The committee that developed the National Research Council (2012, p. 65) report *Education for Life and for Work* was asked to create research-based definitions of various competencies that would go beyond the analytical focus of the Common Core. The committee reached three conclusions:

1. Cognitive competencies have been more extensively studied than have intrapersonal and interpersonal competencies, showing consistent, positive correlations (of modest size) with desirable educational, career, and health outcomes. Early academic competencies are also positively correlated with these outcomes.

2. Among intrapersonal and interpersonal competencies, conscientiousness (staying organized, responsible, and hardworking) is most highly correlated with desirable educational, career, and health outcomes. Antisocial behavior, which has both intrapersonal and interpersonal dimensions, is negatively correlated with these outcomes.

3. Educational attainment—the number of years a person spends in school—strongly predicts adult earnings and also predicts health and civic engagement. Moreover, individuals with higher levels of education appear to gain more knowledge and skills on the job than do those with lower levels of education, and to be able, to some extent, to transfer what they learn across occupations. Since it is not known what mixture of cognitive, intrapersonal, and interpersonal competencies accounts for the labor market benefits of additional schooling, promoting educational attainment itself may constitute a useful complementary strategy for developing 21st century competencies.

The federal definition of ELs also recognizes competencies that go beyond core academic skills when it refers to recognizing ELs' need to access "the opportunity to participate fully in society" (ESSA Section 8101).

CURRENT POLICIES FOR DUAL LANGUAGE LEARNERS

As children's enrollment in early learning programs has increased during the past two decades (National Institute for Early Education Research, 2015), efforts to forge stronger connections between these programs and the K-12 grades have emerged at the school, district, and state levels (Bornfreund et al., 2015; Ritchie and Gutmann, 2013). These efforts, known as P-3 or pre-K to grade 3 initiatives, seek to align standards, curriculum, and instruction starting with pre-K and extending at least to grade 3. States have aligned their early learning and K-12 standards. Their aim is to create a seamless, continuous educational experience for children from birth to age 8, to sustain learning gains made in effective early education programs, and to continue to build on these gains in the K-3 grades and beyond.

During the Obama administration, the U.S. Department of Education acted to expand its oversight to include early education. Early education for young children with disabilities was in place as part of the Individuals with Disabilities Education Act (IDEA). Then Secretary of Education Arne Duncan established a new position of deputy assistant secretary for early learning in the elementary and secondary education division. The federal definition of early learning spans birth to age 8, thus overlapping with the K-3 grades or ages 5-8 of the existing K-12 division. These two entities coexist, and their concerns regarding DLLs are reflected in the overlapping age span specifications in the statement of task for this study (see Box 1-2 in Chapter 1).

Early learning is now among the provisions of ESSA,[13] the 2015 reau-thorization of ESEA. ESSA reinforces original provisions of ESEA allowing Title I funds to be used for early learning programs from birth. Districts seeking to expand their pre-K programs are using Title I funds for that pur-pose, but the funds thus invested are estimated at only about 3 percent of Title I funds (states are not required to report on the use of Title I funds for early learning). ESSA also directs states to develop policies designed to forge closer connections between early learning programs and K-12 education, specifically K-3, including alignment of educational experiences. Preschool Development Grants will continue to support that work. Some states, such as Minnesota and Oregon, are beginning to issue relevant policy guidance.

The policy context in the ESSA era will provide more opportunities for schools, districts, and states to create programs for DLLs that start early with pre-K at ages 3 and 4 and are well aligned with grades K-3 and beyond. As discussed in Chapter 5, research findings indicate that starting early to build second language competence while supporting the home or primary language is a promising program strategy and policy direc-tion. These findings point to the need to provide more DLLs with pre-K programs that support their first language while developing their English proficiency, especially for academic learning and rich literacy development.

P-3 or pre-K to grade 3 initiatives are likely to increase at the district level as a result of both ESSA guidelines and the expansion of state-funded pre-K programs that provide more DLLs with educational experiences prior to kindergarten. At present, however, research on and evaluations of these efforts are limited. Except for Lindholm-Leary's (2015b) evaluation of the Sobrato Early Academic Language (SEAL) model (see Chapter 5), none of the longitudinal studies of pre-K programs that have tracked students from pre-K into the K-12 grades have included analyses of DLLs (e.g., Zellmann and Kilburn, 2015). The remainder of this section begins by reviewing the landscape of state-funded pre-K programs, in which nearly one-third of the nation's 4-year-olds are currently being educated (National Institute

---

[13] Every Student Succeeds Act of 2015, P. L. 114-95, 114 Stat. 1177 (2015).

for Early Education Research, 2015). It then turns to policies related to the Head Start and Early Head Start programs, which serve more than 1 million children and their families (Administration for Children and Families, 2015), reaching approximately 42 percent of eligible preschool-age children and 4 percent of infants and toddlers living at or below the federal poverty level (Schmit and Matthews, 2013). The committee was unable to find policies governing DLL early learning and family engagement practices for programs funded by the Child Care and Development Fund, which provides subsidies to low-income workers to pay for child care services.

State Pre-K Policies Related to Literacy, Language, and Content Learning

In contrast with the K-12 system, the goals of pre-K programs are focused primarily on preparing children for academic success in kindergarten. To that end, all states have issued early learning and development standards (ELDS) for increasing children's kindergarten readiness, and many states have developed standards for younger ages as well.

Espinosa and Calderon (2015) reviewed the ELDS of 21 states and the District of Columbia with respect to their attention to the education of DLLs.[14] The authors first classified states according to their approach to DLLs' home language development. Specifically, states were classified into those that promote the following approaches: dual language (DL), English language development (ELD), and English immersion (EI). Roughly consistent with the approaches taken in K-12 education, the DL approach encourages a bilingual workforce, as well as the development of bilingual and biliterate children, typically through assessments of children in English and their home language. In a DL educational setting, at least 50 percent of instructional time is in the child's home language, and 50 percent is focused on English language development. On the other end of the spectrum, states with an EI approach emphasize rapid acquisition of English in an English-only instructional environment and do not explicitly support home language maintenance. States with an ELD approach fall in between the DL and EI states; these states prioritize English instructional environments but also recognize the value of the home language in supporting the child's long-term learning and overall well-being. The ELD approach uses the home language to transition to an English-only environment as quickly

---

[14] States with high shares of DLLs and states that are members of the North Carolina–led K-3 Assessment Consortium were selected for the review. These states include Alaska, Arizona, California, Delaware, Georgia, Hawaii, Illinois, Iowa, Maine, Maryland, Massachusetts, New Jersey, New York, North Carolina, North Dakota, Oregon, Rhode Island, South Carolina, Texas, Washington, and Wisconsin, along with the District of Columbia.

as possible and can be compared to the transitional bilingual education or English as a second language approach taken in K-12 education.

In addition to classifying the states according to their home language approaches, Espinosa and Calderon (2015) reviewed each state's standards on a number of other indicators, such as whether the standards include clear statements about the major goals for DLL education, how the stated goals meet the needs of DLLs, and whether the standards include a separate domain for DLL language acquisition. They found that most (16) of the states they reviewed have set an ELD approach to their early learning standards. They highlight the standards of California, Illinois, and New Jersey as providing model language for other states. California is one of the few states that provides a clear statement of philosophy about the goals for DLL learning; establishes a separate set of domains for DLLs on English language and home language development; and addresses DLLs' needs in communication, language, literacy, and social-emotional development (California Department of Education, 2009).

State Pre-K Policies Concerning Access to Services and Family Engagement

Eligibility for public pre-K programs varies substantially across states. Ten states currently do not fund such programs, while several fund small programs that are accessible to a modest number of children—typically those from low-income families. In 1995, Georgia became the first state to provide pre-K publicly for all 4-year-olds in the state. Several states, such as Florida, Georgia, Oklahoma, and West Virginia, as well as the District of Columbia, provide high levels of access to free, voluntary pre-K for all 4-year-olds (National Institute for Early Education Research, 2015).

Of the 53 state-funded programs in 40 states, 22 report DLL enrollment levels, and DLLs represent an estimated 19 percent of the enrollment in those 22 states (National Institute for Early Education Research and Center on Enhancing Early Learning Outcomes, 2014). Surprisingly, many of the states that do not report DLL enrollment, including Arizona, California, Florida, and New York, are those that likely have high shares of DLLs given their history as immigrant destinations. Immigrants and Hispanics are less likely than nonimmigrants and non-Hispanics to enroll in quality child care and education programs. A number of explanations have been offered for this differential, including financial barriers and a shortage of high-quality programs in immigrant and Hispanic neighborhoods (e.g., Crosnoe, 2007; Fortuny et al., 2010; Magnuson et al., 2006; National Task Force on Early Childhood Education for Hispanics, 2007; Takanishi, 2004).

Programs can encourage the involvement of DLLs through a number of strategies, such as approaching families from a strength-based perspective, implementing culturally and linguistic responsive services, and using community resources to support family engagement. The extent to which state policy encourages these practices varies greatly. In their review of a subset of state ELDS, Espinosa and Calderon (2015) identify seven states with specific recommendations on how to engage DLL families in the education of their children. Serving as a potential model to follow, California's curriculum framework acknowledges the importance of family engagement and provides educators with a set of practices designed to form meaningful relationships with families (California Department of Education, 2009). Examples of these practices include the following: "highlight the many ways in which families are already involved in their children's education"; "provide opportunities for parents and family members to share their skills with staff, the children in the program, and other families"; and "hold an open house or potluck dinner for families in the program" (California Department of Education, 2009, p. 16).

Head Start and Early Head Start Policies Related to Literacy, Language, and Content Learning

As the primary agency responsible for overseeing and regulating Head Start grantees, the Office of Head Start (OHS) issues requirements to programs on learning standards, assessment, and curriculum. OHS also provides general program planning and technical assistance around implementation of the program requirements. *The Head Start Child Development and Early Learning Framework* is a document that describes program requirements for development and learning, monitoring of progress, alignment of curricula, and general program planning (Office of Head Start, 2010b). The framework was updated in 2015 to include infants through preschoolers, and includes requirements in the domain of English language development focused specifically on the education of DLLs (Office of Head Start, 2015). The framework provides guidance on learning expectations for DLLs and stresses the importance of giving children the opportunity to express their knowledge in their home language: "Children who are dual language learners need intentional support for the development of their home language as well as for English acquisition" (Office of Head Start, 2015, p. 35). The framework also emphasizes the importance of choosing "assessment instruments, methods, and procedures that use the languages or languages that most accurately reveal each child's knowledge, skills, and abilities" (Office of Head Start, 2010b, p. 5). Thus, the current Head Start approach can be classified as one that promotes biliteracy and bilingualism in DLLs. A 2013 report to Congress[15] from the Office of Planning, Research, and Evaluation (OPRE) states that the majority of children in Head Start programs were exposed to an adult speaking their home language in the classroom or during home visits (Office of Planning, Research, and Evaluation, 2013). There has, however, been no comprehensive evaluation of Head Start grantees on the degree of support for home language development, the quality of language inputs, or the amount of time spent using children's native language in the classroom.

Head Start Policies Concerning Access to Services and Family Engagement

Approximately one-third of children in Head Start come from homes in which a language other than English is spoken—Spanish in the overwhelming majority of cases (Administration for Children and Families, 2014). The OPRE (2013) report notes that within Head Start, DLLs were less likely than children from monolingual English homes to be enrolled in programs that offered full-day, center-based ECE, but there were no measurable quality differences in the type of care received by DLLs and non-DLLs (Office of Planning, Research, and Evaluation, 2013).

Head Start and Early Head Start provide detailed guidance to programs on how to engage families, referred to as the Parent, Family, and Community Engagement (PFCE) framework (Office of Head Start, 2011). The framework encourages practices that are culturally responsive and offer a set of outcomes that can be used to evaluate family engagement practices, such as the extent to which families "participate in the leadership development, decision-making, program policy development, or in community and state organizing activities to improve children's development and learning experiences" (Office of Head Start, 2011, p. 5). OHS also encourages programs to develop data-driven family engagement practices and evaluate themselves regularly, including by using a program preparedness checklist to help them assess their services to families of DLLs.

Through OHS's Cultural and Linguistic Responsiveness National Center, grantees in both Head Start and Early Head Start programs also receive guidance on how to improve outreach, services, and outcomes for DLLs. A recently developed toolkit is designed to help programs evaluate and strengthen their methods for communicating with parents whose primary language is not English and be more culturally and linguistically responsive to children and families.[16]

---

[15]The Head Start Act requires OPRE to prepare a report to Congress on the characteristics of and services provided to DLLs in Head Start.

[16]Head Start also is governed by a set of "multicultural principles," released and recently updated by OHS. These principles include the following: (1) Every individual is rooted in

According to OPRE's (2013) report to Congress, almost 80 percent of parents of DLLs in Early Head Start reported that they had attended group activities for parents and their children during the past year, nearly two-thirds of parents of DLLs reported that they had attended an Early Head Start social event, and 57 percent had attended parent education meetings or workshops (Office of Planning, Research, and Evaluation, 2013). To date, there have been no formal evaluations of the extent to which Head Start grantees use the toolkits and checklists provided by the program to increase access to and engagement of DLL families in their services.

The Migrant and Seasonal Head Start (MSHS) Program is designed specifically for Spanish-speaking migrant DLL families. MSHS differs from traditional programs in being structured to address the residential mobility of these families. It provides open and continuous enrollment so that families can follow crop-harvesting schedules, and often provides transportation for the children (Diversity Data Kids, 2014).

CURRENT POLICIES FOR ENGLISH LEARNERS K-12

Federal K-12 Policies Related to Literacy, Language, and Content Learning

ESSA, enacted on December 10, 2015, has broad implications for ELs through several notable changes related to their inclusion in state plans, school accountability, and entry/exit procedures for status as an EL. Among the most notable changes in the law are the following:

- ESSA shifts the locus of decision-making authority for accountability to states and localities and limits federal authority in allowing exceptions. States are expected to administer and report academic assessments annually in grades 3-8 and once in high school, along

---

culture. (2) The cultural groups represented in the communities and families of each Head Start program are the primary sources for culturally relevant programming. (3) Culturally relevant and diverse programming requires learning accurate information about the culture of different groups and discarding stereotypes. (4) Addressing cultural relevance in making curriculum choices is a necessary, developmentally appropriate practice. (5) Every individual has the right to maintain his or her own identity while acquiring the skills required to function in our diverse society. (6) Effective programs for children with limited English speaking ability require continued development of the first language while the acquisition of English is facilitated. (7) Culturally relevant programming requires staff who reflect the community and families served. (8) Multicultural programming for children enables children to develop an awareness of, respect for, and appreciation of individual cultural differences. (9) Culturally relevant and diverse programming examines and challenges institutional and personal biases. (10) Culturally relevant and diverse programming and practices are incorporated in all systems and services and are beneficial to all adults and children (Office of Head Start, 2010a, pp. 11-69).

with science assessments in three grade spans. These assessments are intended to identify schools (not districts) that are in need of comprehensive or targeted assistance, and to support a system of technical assistance that is evidence based as determined by the state.

- States may include students formerly classified as ELs in the EL subgroup for academic assessment purposes for a period of up to 4 years after they have been reclassified (previously this period was unspecified in law, but up to 2 years was allowed in regulation).

- Student progress toward English language proficiency, formerly part of a separate Title III accountability system, is now part of Title I accountability, and in their accountability plans, states must describe their rules for how this student progress is to be accomplished. The law addresses the complex issue of how to include recently arrived ELs in academic assessments by allowing states to choose between two alternatives for Title I accountability during their first 2 years in the system.

- Overall, states are encouraged to be more innovative in their assessment and accountability systems, including being allowed to use a variety of readiness and engagement indicators (Section (c)(4)(B)(v)), and up to seven states will be allowed to develop Innovative Assessment Pilots that may use locally developed assessments and performance assessments. States are required to develop standardized entry and exit procedures for determining whether a student is an EL that are consistent across districts within the state.

- Title III directs attention in the state report to long-term ELs—students who have been enrolled in U.S. schools for more than 6 years without being reclassified as English-proficient—and to recently reclassified students.

- Of symbolic importance, the law replaces the term "limited English proficient" with "English learner."

- The law explicitly directs individual states to address early education, which will likely contribute to considerable variation across states in the provision of a sound primary education for children. For ELs, Title III includes preschool teachers under its purposes (Section 3102) for professional development, and it also specifically refers to early childhood education programs as part of the stated purposes of the EL formula subgrants (Section 3115). Further, the nonregulatory guidance document issued by the U.S. Department of Education for Title III notes that the law specifies requirements that local plans include assurance of coordination of activities and data sharing with early learning programs (U.S. Department of Education, 2016).

- The law shifts responsibility for early education and pre-K programs to the U.S. Department of Health and Human Services (HHS), with the intent of encouraging coordination with other early childhood programs currently administered by the department, such as Early Head Start, Head Start, and child care programs.

ESSA also includes requirements for family engagement in Titles I, III, and IV. Title I calls for schools to inform parents about placement of their child in a language instruction educational program, the reason for such placement, their child's level of English proficiency, programs available to their child, assessment results, teacher qualifications, improvement plans, and school report cards. All communications must be provided in a form understandable to the parent and, to the extent practical, in the parents' home language. Title III requires schools "to promote parental, family, and community participation in language instruction educational programs for the parents, families, and communities of English learners."[17] Within Title IV is a provision for assistance and support to state and local education agencies, schools, and educators for strengthening partnerships with parents and families of ELs. To that end, grants will be awarded to state-wide organizations for the establishment of family engagement centers to implement parent and family engagement programs and provide training and technical assistance to state and local education agencies and organizations that support family-school partnerships. The rulemaking process to implement ESSA still needs to be established before the law takes effect beginning in the 2017-2018 school year.

State K-12 Policies Related to Literacy, Language, and Content Learning

Federal assistance to support ELs in grades K-12 is provided through ESSA, Title I, Parts A and B (Migrant Education); Title III English Acquisition state grants, Native American and Alaska Native Children in School (NAM) discretionary grants, and National Professional Development Project grants; and Title VII Indian, Part A Native Hawaiian, and Alaska Native Education grants.

States play an important role in implementing the federal policies related to these programs and in ensuring that districts are in compliance with these policies. As previously mentioned, the U.S. Department of Justice and the Office of Civil Rights in the U.S. Department of Education issued a "Dear Colleague" letter outlining the legal obligations of states, districts, and schools to ELs under civil rights laws (U.S. Department of Justice and

---

[17] See https://www.gpo.gov/fdsys/pkg/BILLS-114s1177enr/pdf/BILLS-114s1177enr.pdf [February 21, 2017].

U.S. Department of Education, 2015). The letter states that even if state education agencies do not provide educational services directly to ELs, they have a responsibility under civil rights laws to "provide appropriate guidance, monitoring and oversight to school districts to ensure EL students receive appropriate services" (U.S. Department of Justice and U.S. Department of Education, 2015, p. 6). The letter offers guidance on areas that frequently result in noncompliance by school districts. They include identification and assessment of ELs in a timely, valid, and reliable manner; provision of educationally sound language assistance programs; sufficient staffing and support for language assistance programs; equal opportunities for ELs to participate in all curricular and extracurricular activities; avoidance of unnecessary segregation; evaluation of ELs in a timely and appropriate manner for special education and disability-related services, with language needs considered in evaluations for these services; meeting the needs of ELs who opt out of language assistance programs; monitoring and evaluation of ELs' progress in language assistance programs; evaluation of the effectiveness of the district's language assistance programs to ensure that such programs enable ELs to achieve parity of participation in standard instructional programs in a reasonable amount of time; and meaningful communication with parents (U.S. Department of Justice and U.S. Department of Education, 2015, pp. 8-9). To a large extent, state policy related to K-12 education revolves around finance, identification, reclassification, performance monitoring, standards setting, parent and family involvement, and educator quality. Some states also set policies related to use of the home language for instructional purposes.

States also support ELs by monitoring LEA compliance with state statutes related to ELs, specifying teacher certification and licensing requirements for teachers who serve ELs (see Chapter 10), establishing language proficiency standards aligned with the state's academic content standards, and annually assessing the English language proficiency and content area knowledge of all ELs. Furthermore, states support ELs by providing additional funds to districts beyond the average per-student dollar amounts. Funding amounts vary significantly among states, but states generally use the same types of funding models (Wixom, 2015):

- Formula funding—Financial support for EL programs is distributed through the state's primary funding formula; this is the most common funding method. Funding formulas typically use weights, dollar amounts, or teacher allocations to distribute the funds.
- Categorical funding—Districts receive EL funds outside of the state's primary funding formula through budget line items. Funding methods vary from state to state; for example, some states may

provide a dollar amount per child, while others may provide grants for specific programs.

- Reimbursement—The state reimburses districts for the cost of EL programs after the costs have been accrued and upon approval of the state superintendent. This model allows states to limit funding to certain specific expenses.

According to a recent report from the Education Commission of the States (Wixom, 2015, p. 4), "State funding systems have the potential to incentivize districts to shuffle ELs around different programs depending on funding availability, exit ELs from language programs too quickly or let students remain in EL programs longer than they should."

CONCLUSIONS

Conclusion 2-1: Under the Every Student Succeeds Act (ESSA) , states now play a more critical role in providing guidance to and monitoring districts and schools to ensure that English learners (ELs) are not denied services under the law or discriminated against because of their race, ethnicity, or national origin. ESSA provides increased decision-making authority to states regarding the inclusion of ELs in state accountability plans, in how the accountability index for Title I is constructed, in how ELs' academic achievement and progress toward English language proficiency are assessed, and in how districts respond to schools identified for state assistance.

Conclusion 2-2: As a result of changes in the Every Student Succeeds Act, schools rather than districts are now accountable for English learners' (ELs') progress toward English language proficiency. This change may have unintended consequences for many schools with small numbers of ELs that fall below the minimum state-determined sample size for accountability reporting as they are not required to disaggregate outcome data by EL status, making it difficult to track the progress of this subgroup.

Conclusion 2-3: Districts are expected to provide supports to schools in need of assistance and are the policy unit in which much of the improvement work will be carried out. Uncertainty exists as to the capacity of districts to play support roles, whether the state accountability system will provide the required information on English learners' educational progress, and how states and intermediary agencies will help build and ensure district capacity.

Conclusion 2-4: Early education programs have diverse funding sources and hence different applicable regulations for program delivery. While Head Start has issued clear guidance concerning what constitutes quality programs for young children and the engagement of families of dual language learners (DLLs), comparable guidance regarding DLLs does not exist for child care and home visiting programs. State-level guidance to state-funded pre-K programs varies by state; few states have addressed standards and practices regarding DLLs.

Conclusion 2-5: Greater state flexibility in accountability under the Every Student Succeeds Act has led to concerns among civil rights and other organizations focused on underserved populations, such as English learners (ELs), about protecting the legal rights of ELs to an appropriate education as guaranteed under the Supreme Court decision in *Lau v. Nichols,* the Equal Educational Opportunities Act of 1974, and other relevant laws. The Dear Colleague Letter provides an important framework for states in ensuring that ELs are receiving the services to which they are entitled.

BIBLIOGRAPHY

Administration for Children and Families. (2014). *Child Care and Development Block Grant Act.* Available: http://www.acf.hhs.gov/sites/default/files/occ/ccdbgact.pdf [January 4, 2017].

Administration for Children and Families. (2015). *Head Start Services.* Available: http://www.acf.hhs.gov/programs/ohs/about/head-start [January 4, 2017].

American Council on the Teaching of Foreign Languages, National Association of Bilingual Education, National Council of State Supervisors for Languages, and TESOL International Association. (2015). *Guidelines for Implementing the Seal of Biliteracy.* Available: http://www.actfl.org/sites/default/files/pdfs/SealofBiliteracyGuidelines_0.pdf [June 14, 2016].

Baker, K., and De Kanter, A.A. (1983). *Bilingual Education: A Reappraisal of Federal Policy.* Lanham, MD: Lexington Books.

Bornfreund, L., Cook, S., Lieberman, A., and Loewenburg, A. (2015). *From Crawling to Walking. Ranking States on Birth-3rd Grade Policies That Support Strong Readers.* Washington, DC: New America.

Boyle, A., August, D., Tabaku, L., Cole, S., and Simpson-Baird, A. (2015). *Dual Language Education Programs: Current State Policies and Practices.* Available: http://www.air.org/sites/default/files/downloads/report/Dual-Language-Education-Programs-Current-State-Policies-April-2015-rev.pdf [December 5, 2016]

California Department of Education. (2009). *Preschool English Learners: Principles and Practices to Promote Language, Literacy, and Learning—A Resource Guide* (2nd ed.). Available: http://www.cde.ca.gov/sp/cd/re/documents/psenglearnersed2.pdf [November 18, 2016].

Californians Together and Velasquez Press. (2016). *State Laws Regarding the Seal of Biliteracy.* Available: http://sealofbiliteracy.org [June 14, 2016].

Cohen, D.K. (1995). What is the system in systemic reform? *Educational Researcher, 24*(9), 11-31.

Council of Chief State School Officers. (2012). *Framework for English Language Proficiency Development Standards Corresponding to the Common Core State Standards and the Next Generation Science Standards.* Available: http://www.ccsso.org/Documents/2012/ELPD%20Framework%20Booklet-Final%20for%20web.pdf [November 18, 2016].

Crawford, J. (1992). *Language Loyalties: A Source Book on the Official English Controversy*: Chicago, IL: University of Chicago Press.

Crawford, J. (2004). *Educating English learners: Language Diversity in the Classroom.* Los Angeles, CA: Bilingual Educational Services.

Crosnoe, R. (2007). Early childcare and the school readiness of children from Mexican immigrant families. *International Migration Review, 41*(1), 152-181.

Cross, C.T. (2015). *The Shaping of Federal Education Policy over Time.* Available: http://www.ecs.org/clearinghouse/01/19/16/11916.pdf [June 14, 2016].

Danoff, M.N., Coles, G., McLaughlin, D., and Reynolds, D. (1978). *Evaluation of the Impact of ESEA Title VII Spanish/English Bilingual Education Program: Overview of Study and Findings.* Palo Alto, CA: American Institutes for Research.

Darling-Hammond, L., Wilhoit, G., and Pittenger, L. (2014). Accountability for college and career readiness: Developing a new paradigm. *Education Policy Analysis Archives, 22*(86), 1.

Diversity Data Kids. (2014). *Targeting Vulnerable Populations: Responding to the Needs of Migrant and Seasonal Worker Families.* Available: http://www.diversitydatakids.org/files/Policy/Head%20Start/Logic/Targeting%20Vulnerable%20Populations_Migrant%20and%20Seasonal%20Head%20Start.pdf [September 8, 2016].

Espinosa, L.M., and Calderon, M. (2015). *State Early Learning and Development Standards/Guidelines, Policies & Related Practices.* Boston, MA: Build Initiative.

Fortuny, K., Hernandez, D.J., and Chaudry, A. (2010). *Young Children of Immigrants: The Leading Edge of America's Future.* Brief No.3. Washington, DC: The Urban Institute.

Francis, D., Lesaux, N., and August, D. (2006). Language of instruction. In D.L. August and T. Shanahan (Eds.), *Developing Literacy in Second-Language Learners* (pp. 365-413). New York: Routledge.

García, M. (1989). *Mexican Americans.* New Haven, CT: Yale University Press.

Gardner, D.P., Larsen, Y.W., Baker, W., Campbell, A., and Crosby, E.A. (1983). *A Nation At Risk: The Imperative for Educational Reform.* Washington, DC: National Commission on Excellence in Education, U.S. Department of Education.

Giambo, D.A., and Szecsi, T. (2015). Promoting and maintaining bilingualism and biliteracy: Cognitive and biliteracy benefits & strategies for monolingual teachers. *The Open Communication Journal, 9*(Suppl. 1), 56-60.

Greene, J.P. (1997). A meta-analysis of the Rossell and Baker review of bilingual education research. *Bilingual Research Journal, 21*(2-3), 103-122.

Jennings, J.F. (2015). *Presidents, Congress, and the Public Schools: The Politics of Education Reform.* Cambridge, MA: Harvard Education Press.

Lindholm-Leary, K.J. (2015a). *Fostering School Success for English Learners K-12: Language and Academic Development of Dual Language Learners during the School Years.* Unpublished manuscript commissioned by the Committee on Fostering School Success for English Learners: Toward New Directions in Policy, Practice, and Research. Child and Adolescent Development, San Jose State University, CA.

Lindholm-Leary, K.J. (2015b, March 9). *Sobrato Family Foundation, Early Academic and Literacy Project after Five Full Years of Implementation. Final Research Report.* Cupertino, CA: Sobrato Family Foundation.

Magnuson, K., Lahaie, C., and Waldfogel, J. (2006). Preschool and school readiness of children of immigrants. *Social Science Quarterly, 87*(5), 1241-1262.

McLemore, D., and Romo, H.D. (2005). *Racial and Ethnic Relations in America* (7th ed.). New York: Pearson.

National Council of State Supervisors for Languages. (2016). *Linguafolia National Fact Sheet.* Available: http://ncssfl.org//wp-content/uploads/2016/03/LinguaFolio.National FactSheet.2015-2016.Updated.February2016.pdf [June 14, 2016].

National Institute for Early Education Research. (2015). *The State of Preschool 2014: State Preschool Yearbook.* Available: http://nieer.org/wp-content/uploads/2016/08/Yearbook2014_full3.pdf [December 5, 2016].

National Institute for Early Education Research and Center on Enhancing Early Learning Outcomes. (2014). *Young Immigrants and Dual Language Learners: Participation in Pre-K and Gaps at Kindergarten.* Available: http://ceelo.org/wp-content/uploads/2014/11/ceelo_nieer_webinar_equity_immigrant_dll_pre_k_slides_final.pdf [July 30, 2015].

National Research Council. (1992). *Assessing Evaluation Studies: The Case of Bilingual Education Strategie*s. M.M. Meyer and S.E. Fienberg (Eds.). Panel to Review Evaluation Studies of Bilingual Education, Committee on National Statistics, Commission on Behavioral and Social Sciences and Education, Division of Behavioral and Social Sciences and Education. Washington, DC: National Academy Press.

National Research Council. (2011). *Allocating Federal Funds for State Programs for English Language Learners.* Panel to Review Alternative Data Sources for the Limited-English Proficiency Allocation Formula under Title III, Part A, Elementary and Secondary Education Act; Committee on National Statistics and Board on Testing and Assessment; Division of Behavioral and Social Sciences and Education. Washington, DC: The National Academies Press.

National Research Council. (2012). *Education for Life and Work: Developing Transferable Knowledge and Skills in the 21st Century.* J.W. Pellegrino and M.L. Hilton (Eds.). Committee on Defining Deeper Learning and 21st Century Skills, Board on Testing and Assessment, Board on Science Education, Division of Behavioral and Social Sciences and Education. Washington, DC: The National Academies Press.

National Task Force on Early Childhood Education for Hispanics. (2007). *Para Nuestros Ninos: Expanding and Improving Early Education for Hispanics.* Available: http://fcd-us.org/sites/default/files/PNNExecReport.pdf [December 20, 2015].

Office of Head Start. (2010a). *Revisiting and Updating the Multicultural Principles for Head Start Programs Serving Children Ages Birth to Five.* Available: https://eclkc.ohs.acf.hhs.gov/hslc/hs/resources/ECLKC_Bookstore/PDFs/Revisiting%20Multicultural%20 Principles%20for%20Head%20Start_English.pdf [November 18, 2016]

Office of Head Start. (2010b). *The Head Start Child Development and Early Learning Framework.* Available: http://eclkc.ohs.acf.hhs.gov/hslc/tta-system/teaching/eecd/Assessment/Child%20Outcomes/HS_Revised_Child_Outcomes_Framework(rev-Sept2011).pdf [November 17, 2016].

Office of Head Start. (2011). *The Head Start Parent, Family, and Community Engagement Framework.* Available: http://eclkc.ohs.acf.hhs.gov/policy/im/acf-im-hs-11-06 [January 4, 2017].

Office of Head Start. (2015). *Head Start Early Learning Outcomes Framework: Birth to Five.* Washington, DC: U.S. Department of Health and Human Services, Administration for Children and Families. Available: http://eclkc.ohs.acf.hhs.gov/hslc/hs/sr/approach/pdf/ohs-framework.pdf [December 7, 2015].

Office of Planning, Research, and Evaluation. (2013). *Report to Congress on Dual Language Learners in Head Start and Early Head Start Programs*. Available: http://www.acf.hhs.gov/programs/opre/resource/report-to-congress-on-dual-language-learners-in-head-start-and-early-head [July 30, 2015].

Prucha, F.P. (Ed.). (1975). *Documents of United States Indian Policy* (1st ed.). Lincoln: University of Nebraska Press.

Prucha, F.P. (Ed.). (1990). *Documents of United States Indian Policy* (2nd ed.). Lincoln: University of Nebraska Press.

Ramsey, P.J. (2012). *The Bilingual School in the United States: A Documentary History*. Charlotte, NC: Information Age.

Ritchie, S., and Gutmann, A. (Eds.). (2013). *FirstSchool: Transforming PreK-3rd Grade for African American, Latino, and Low-Income Children*. New York: Teachers College Press.

Rolstad, K., Mahoney, K., and Glass, G.V. (2005). The big picture: A meta-analysis of program effectiveness research on English language learners. *Educational Policy, 19*(4), 572-594.

Ruiz, R. (1984). Orientations in language planning. *NABE Journal, 8*(2), 15-34.

Schmit, S., and Matthews, H. (2013). *Investing in Young Children: A Fact Sheet on Early Care and Education Participation, Access, and Quality*. Available: http://www.clasp.org/issues/child-care-and-early-education/in-focus/investing-in-young-children-a-fact-sheet-on-early-care-and-education-participation-access-and-quality [September 4, 2015].

Slavin, R.E., and Cheung, A. (2003). *Effective Reading Programs for English Language Learners: A Best-Evidence Synthesis*. Baltimore, MD: Johns Hopkins University Center for Research on the Education of Students Placed At Risk.

Smith, M.S., and O'Day, J. (1991). Educational equality: 1966 and now. In D.A. Verstegen and J.G. Ward (Eds.), *Spheres of Justice in Education*. New York: Harper Collins.

Stewner-Manzanares, G. (1988). *The Bilingual Education Act: Twenty Years Later*. New Focus, Occasional Papers in Bilingual Education, Number 6. New Focus. Office of Bilingual Education and Minority Affairs, Washington, DC.

Takanishi, R. (2004). Leveling the playing field: Supporting immigrant children from birth to eight. *Future of Children, 14*(2), 61-79.

Takona, J.P., and Wilburn, R.J. (2004). *Primer to Developing a Successful Pre-service Teacher Portfolio*. Lanham, MD: University Press of America.

Tong, F., Irby, B., Lara-Alecio, R., and Mathes, P. (2008). English and Spanish acquisition by Hispanic second graders in developmental bilingual programs: A 3-year longitudinal randomized study. *Hispanic Journal of Behavioral Sciences, 30*(4), 500-529.

U.S. Department of Education. (2009). *Race to the Top: Executive Summary*. Available: https://www2.ed.gov/programs/racetothetop/executive-summary.pdf [June 10, 2016].

U.S. Department of Education. (2016). *Non-Regulatory Guidance: English Learners and Title III of the Elementary and Secondary Education Act (ESEA), as Amended by the Every Student Succeeds Act*. Available: http://www2.ed.gov/policy/elsec/leg/essa/essatitleiiiguidenglishlearners92016.pdf [November 18, 2016].

U.S. Department of Justice and U.S. Department of Education. (2015). *English Learners Dear Colleague Letter*. Available: http://www2.ed.gov/about/offices/list/ocr/letters/colleague-el-201501.pdf [June 14, 2016].

Valdés, G., Kibler, A., and Walqui, A. (2014). *Changes in the Expertise of ESL Professionals: Knowledge and Action in an Era of New Standards*. Alexandria, VA: TESOL International Association.

Wixom, M.A. (2015). *State-Level English Language Learner Policies*. Denver, CO: Education Commission of the States.

Zellmann, G.L., and Kilburn, M.R. (2015). *The Hawaii Preschool-Third Grade Education Reform Initiative: How Well Did P-3 Work?* Santa Monica, CA: RAND Corporation.

3

The Demography of the English
Learner Population

A prerequisite for understanding English learners (ELs) is a systematic analysis of their demographic characteristics and of whether and how these characteristics differ from those of their non-EL peers. These are not simple matters. Nonetheless, existing descriptions of ELs yield some generalizations about their overall demographic characteristics and can help in better understanding the supports that may be needed by ELs and their families for these children and youth to succeed in school.

Before proceeding, a note on the terminology used in this chapter is in order. As explained in Chapter 1 (see Box 1-1), the term "dual language learner (DLL)" is used in this report to refer to children from birth to age 5 in their homes, communities, or early care and education programs; the term "English learner (EL)" is used to refer to children and youth ages 3-21 in the pre-K to 12 education system; and the term "DLL/EL" is used to refer to the broader population of children and youth from birth to age 21. The major data sources cited in this chapter generally provide demographic information only for ELs. Therefore, as reflected in the chapter's title, the text focuses on this group. Nonetheless, the discussion, as well as the conclusions at the end of the chapter, often may be relevant to DLLs, and in some cases these children are explicitly included in the cited research. Finally, the term "indigenous heritage language learners" is used to refer to American Indian, Alaska Native, and Native Hawaiian students whose first language is English and who are learning their heritage language.

The population of ELs is demographically diverse (Espinosa, 2013; García et al., 2009; Hammer et al., 2011). ELs vary in their home language, language abilities, age, race/ethnicity, immigration circumstances, generational status in the United States, geographic distribution, academic achievement, parental characteristics and socioeconomic resources, disability status, nativity status, and other demographic attributes (Capps, 2015; Fry, 2007). Thus, while on average, ELs have a number of unique characteristics that distinguish them from the general population of non-ELs (Capps, 2015; Fry, 2007), broad comparisons of ELs with non-ELs mask significant heterogeneity within both groups.

Describing the characteristics of ELs is complicated for several reasons beyond this demographic diversity. First, definitions of ELs differ across datasets. Many studies identify ELs simply by using parental reports on home language use and the English proficiency of their children (e.g., Cleave et al., 2010; Winsler et al., 2014). Other studies rely on information on program participation to distinguish ELs from non-ELs. A major limitation of this latter approach is that it can understate actual variations in language proficiency among children. To overcome this limitation, some scholars use such methods as specialized language proficiency tests and statistical models to distinguish the two groups (Farrington et al., 2015; Niehaus and Adelson, 2013). In the U.S. Census and the American Community Survey (ACS), ELs can be identified only using proxy indicators that capture whether children speak English less than "very well" (Ruiz Soto et al., 2015). The Census and the ACS ask language proficiency questions about all respondents ages 5 and older who speak only English at home. For respondents who speak a language other than English at home, the Census and ACS further distinguish among those who speak English very well, well, not well, and not at all.[1] The data collection process also is complicated by the difficulty of translating survey instruments, disproportionate nonresponse rates driven by suspicion of government or fear of deportation among some subgroups, missing data for some age groups, and difficulties in obtaining representative samples through phone surveys. A recent report (O'Hare et al., 2016) suggests that young children, particularly those under age 5, have a higher net census undercount than any other age group when they live in difficult-to-count places, such as areas with multiunit buildings and a high proportion of renters, or in difficult-to-count households, such as multigenerational and highly mobile families or households with complex relationships. Evidence also suggests that some adults believe young children need not be reported on the census form. In addition, data analyses typically group ELs into broad racial or ethnic categories such as Asian or

---

[1]Both the Census and the ACS ask the following question: "Does this person speak a language other than English at home?" If the response to this question is yes, the following question is then asked: "How well does this person speak English?" While these questions can provide useful insight into the characteristics of ELs, they have several limitations, including the fact that they do not capture children's proficiency in writing and reading English.

Hispanic, disregarding the socioeconomic and language diversity of such groups.

Variations in the identification of ELs across datasets have several implications for the description of their demographic profiles. Among the most important of these implications is that the variations limit the ability to estimate the size of the population of ELs accurately. As Capps (2015) reports, estimates of the number of ELs in the United States range from 2.6 million, based on U.S. Census definitions, to approximately 4.9 million, based on data from the U.S. Department of Education. One possible reason for this disparity is that, whereas the census definitions are based on responses to questions on language use at home, the U.S. Department of Education identifies ELs using various criteria (e.g., nativity status; reading, writing, and spoken English proficiency) that usually are captured in school administrative data (U.S. Department of Education, 2016). Differences in the definition of ELs across datasets also may result in selectivity in the types of ELs identified across studies. In other words, the ability to draw reliable conclusions about ELs from multiple datasets is limited by the challenge of comparing the outcomes of children who may differ in their familiarity with two or more languages or language varieties, as well as their language skills.

Despite the above challenges, existing data are used in this chapter to serve a simple instrumental purpose—to develop a broad portrait of ELs from which inferences can be drawn regarding who they are and how they differ from or are similar to the broader population of non-ELs.

THE ORIGINS OF ENGLISH LEARNERS

The annual number of immigrants admitted to the United States increased from about 320,000 in the 1960s to approximately 1 million in the following decade (Martin and Midgely, 2006). By 2013, the foreign-born population numbered 46 million, up from approximately 10 million in the mid-1960s (Connor et al., 2013; Fix and Passel, 2003).

Children of immigrants are the fastest-growing and one of the most diverse segments of the child population in the United States (Capps et al., 2005). In 2004, Latinos made up 21.4 percent of the total U.S. population under 5 years of age, and 23 percent of all babies born in the United States in that year were born to Latina mothers (both foreign- and U.S.-born) (Castro et al., 2010).

Between 1995 and 2010, first- and second-generation youth and young adults of immigrant origin accounted for half of the population growth among those ages 16-26 (Batalova and Fix, 2011). In 2010, first-generation youth accounted for 10.3 percent and second-generation youth for 14.1 percent of all people in the United States ages 16-26—together making

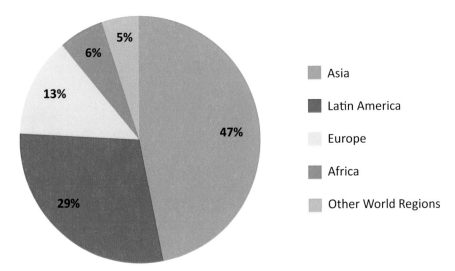

FIGURE 3-1 Region of origin of new immigrants to the United States, 2013.
SOURCE: Data from Jensen et al. (2015).

up roughly one-fourth of the total population of this age group (Batalova and Fix, 2011). These young people represent the future workforce in the United States and will play an important role in the vibrancy of the U.S. economy and local communities. As noted above, they are a highly heterogeneous group, with different home languages, different ages at arrival, varying proficiency in English, differing legal status, diverse racial and ethnic identities, and varying educational outcomes (Crosnoe and López Turley, 2011; Rumbaut, 2004; Suárez-Orozco et al., 2010).

As the size of the foreign-born population in the United States has increased, so, too, has the number of countries and regions of origin of immigrants. Whereas 88 percent of all immigrants who arrived between 1820 and 1920 came from Europe (Massey, 1999), recent immigrants arriving since 1965 are distinguished by their non-European origins (Jensen et al., 2015; Martin and Midgely, 2006), coming largely from Latin America and Asia. As of 2013, Mexico was the birthplace of 28 percent of all immigrants currently living in the United States (Krogstad and Keegan, 2015). As shown in Figure 3-1, approximately half of all new immigrants arriving in the United States in 2013 arrived from Asia (47.1%), followed by Latin America (29.5%),[2] Europe (12.5%), Africa (6.2%), and other world

---

[2] In this instance, the term *Latin America* follows the definition of the U.S. Census Bureau and the United Nations, which includes Mexico, the countries of Central and South America, and the Caribbean.

regions (4.7%) (Jensen et al., 2015). According to the Pew Research Center (2012), Asian Americans are now the fastest-growing, highest-income, and best-educated racial/ethnic group in the United States.

Immigration trends contribute to the changing profile of the U.S. population of children and youth. Overall, about 1 in 5 children between 5-17 years old now live in immigrant families (García et al., 2009; Landale et al., 2011). Combined, the foreign-born population and U.S.-born individuals with immigrant parents account for 25 percent of the overall U.S. population (National Research Council, 2015). Recent immigration trends also are associated with changes in the distribution of languages spoken in the United States. In the past three decades, the percentage of the U.S. population speaking only English has declined, while the percentage speaking a language other than English has increased. Spanish is the most commonly spoken non-English language in U.S. homes, even among non-Hispanics (Gonzalez-Barrera and Lopez, 2013). According to Rumbaut and Massey (2013), 89 percent of the U.S. population spoke only English in 1980, compared with 79.7 percent in 2010 (see Figure 3-2). The use of non-English languages is an essential part of immigrants' identities, and this cultural

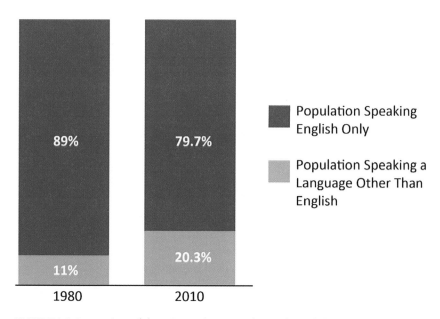

FIGURE 3-2 Proportions of the U.S. population speaking only English versus a language other than English, 1980 and 2010.
SOURCE: Data from Rumbaut and Massey (2013).

role of language is reflected in the diverse set of mother-tongue languages currently being used within immigrant families and their communities (Ruiz Soto et al., 2015).

ELs of Hispanic Origin

Hispanic populations, which can be white, black, or of mixed race/ethnicity, are growing and dispersing across the United States. Hispanics make up 20 percent or more of the kindergarten population in 17 states, concentrated especially in the West and Southwest. In 2012, 25 percent of all newborns in the United States were Hispanic. Mexico may no longer be the main source of new U.S. immigrants, although Mexico currently remains the major country of origin of immigrants in the United States (González-Barrera et al., 2015). While many of the Mexican families in the United States have been in the country for many years, Mexican Americans have a long history of circular migration to the United States, and their children may have experienced schooling in both the United States and Mexico (Migration Policy Institute, 2014; Zúñiga, 2013). Hispanic populations also include immigrants who speak an indigenous language—sometimes in addition to Spanish—from Mexico and Central America and who also know or are learning English.

In a qualitative study of Central American immigrant families residing in Los Angeles, Lavadenz (2008) found that linguistic diversity among Central Americans who migrated to the United States served to identify each group with its homeland and linked compatriots to one another. She demonstrated that Central America is not uniformly Spanish-speaking, and indigenous languages—such as the Mayan languages spoken in Guatemala—are often overlooked. Even in countries that speak Spanish, each country has different pronunciations and vocabulary, and regions such as Belize and parts of Nicaragua have strong influences of English because of colonization.

The Hispanic or Latino population also is culturally diverse, although most come from countries where Spanish is spoken (see Table 3-1). Additionally, as of 2015 Hispanics/Latinos represented the largest ethnic group in the United States at 54 million, or 17 percent of the nation's population (U.S. Census Bureau, 2015). When population figures for 2012 are presented by nativity, Mexicans are the largest group of Hispanic origin, representing 64.2 percent of the U.S. Hispanic population, Puerto Ricans are the second-largest at 9.3 percent, with Cubans at 3.7 percent and Salvadorans at 3.7 percent. The remaining 19 percent of the U.S. Hispanic population comes from countries, such as Guatemala, Dominica, Columbia, and Honduras. Table 3-1 shows that Mexico is also the country of origin of the largest number of ELs.

The largest percentages of the U.S. Hispanic population are those younger than 5 (4.9%) and 5-9 (4.9%)—preschool- and school-age children (Brown and Patten, 2014). Overall, Hispanics are a young population, with a median age of 27; U.S.-born Hispanics have an even younger median age of 18 (Brown and Patten, 2014).

ELs of Asian Origin

The countries from which ELs of Asian origin come are also considerably diverse (see Table 3-1). According to the 2010 Census, the largest populations of Asian origin in the United States are Chinese, Asian Indian, Filipino, Vietnamese, Korean, and Japanese, in that order (Frey, 2015), which together make up at least 84 percent of the total U.S. Asian population. Various Asian subgroups, such as Bangladeshis, Burmese, Cambodians, Hmong, Laotians, Pakistanis, and Thais, also exist in significant numbers (Pew Research Center, 2012). The Chinese, whose history dates back to the 1840s in the United States, are the oldest and largest population of Asian origin in the United States (Lee and Zhou, 2015), numbering about 4 million in the 2010 Census. The Vietnamese, whose numbers in the U.S. population rose after the Vietnam War ended in 1975, are one of the newest Asian groups in the United States.

According to Lee and Zhou (2015), contemporary Asian immigrants exemplify "hyper-selectivity," meaning that on average, they have higher levels of education and higher skills than others in their home countries; they also are more highly educated than the average American. There are exceptions to this generalization, such as some Southeast Asian immigrants, but it nonetheless remains largely true.

The different origins and immigration histories of Asian groups result in differing social and demographic attributes. Recently arrived Vietnamese, Koreans, and Asian Indians are a relatively young population. For example, 40 percent of the U.S. Asian Indian population in 2010 had arrived since 2000, and one-quarter of the total U.S. Asian Indian population is under age 18 (Frey, 2015). Whereas early Chinese immigrants were low-skilled and originated from areas in the southern region of Guangdong Province, contemporary Chinese immigrants are of diverse origins and socioeconomic backgrounds. According to Lee and Zhou (2015), Chinese immigrants now come primarily from mainland China, Hong Kong, and Taiwan, but some come from Southeast Asia and the Americas. Although all ethnic Chinese share an ancestral written language that may vary in versions of the written characters, they also speak a variety of regional dialects, including Cantonese, Mandarin, Hakka, Taiwanese, and others (Lee and Zhou, 2015).

TABLE 3-1 Origin Countries of Foreign-Born Children Who Are English Learners (ELs)

Country	Percentage
Mexico	41.28
China	4.54
Dominican Republic	3.60
Vietnam	3.49
Philippines	3.48
Korea	3.03
El Salvador	2.78
Guatemala	2.19
Cuba	2.16
Haiti	2.00
India	1.94
Thailand	1.90
Japan	1.40
Honduras	1.38
Colombia	1.17
Other Central and South American countries	7.01
European Countries	5.97
African countries	4.36
Other countries	6.32
All Foreign-Born	100.00

NOTE: ELs are defined based on responses to the American Community Survey (ACS) question of how well individuals who speak a language other than English at home speak English. ELs thus are defined as children who speak English less than "very well." As noted in footnote 2, language information from the ACS has its limitations. However, because ACS data are extensive and nationally representative, they are still useful in providing a broad picture of the characteristics of children who can be classified as ELs.
SOURCE: Data from the American Community Survey, 2008-2012.

ELs of Native Hawaiian or Pacific Islander Origin

More than 1.2 million Native Hawaiians and Pacific Islanders were living in the United States as of 2010 (U.S. Census Bureau, 2012). While Native Hawaiians and many Pacific Islanders are U.S. citizens, some Pacific Islanders are foreign-born and vary in their immigration status. Among the

Native Hawaiians and Pacific Islanders, Native Hawaiians are the largest ethnic group, numbering more than 527,000, followed by Samoans and Guamanian or Chamorros. Ethnic groups in this population also include Tongan, Fijian, Marshallese, Palauan, Tahitian, and many others (Empowering Pacific Islander Communities and Asian Americans Advancing Justice, 2014).

Pacific Islander immigrants to the United States often face a lack of culturally competent indigenous heritage language programs to help them navigate the U.S. immigration system and other services, such as education. Nearly 29 percent of Native Hawaiians and Pacific Islanders speak a language other than English at home, primary among these being Samoan, Tongan, Hawaiian, and Chamorro. Marshallese (78%) and Fijian Americans (77%) are most likely to speak a language other than English at home. Nearly 9 percent of Native Hawaiians and Pacific Islanders report limited proficiency in English on average. Marshallese Americans have a higher-than-average rate of limited English proficiency (41%) among Native Hawaiian and Pacific Islander groups, and in more than one in four Marshallese American households (26%), everyone in the household over age 14 has limited English proficiency or speaks English less than "very well" (Empowering Pacific Islander Communities and Asian Americans Advancing Justice, 2014). This rate is similar to that of Latinos and higher than that of Asian Americans (Empowering Pacific Islander Communities and Asian Americans Advancing Justice, 2014).

ELs of European Origin

Research is limited on immigrants to the United States from Eastern Europe and their children. After the collapse of the communist regime in Eastern Europe in the early 1990s, the number of these immigrants increased significantly, from 1.3 million in 1995 to 4.3 million in 2006 (Migration Information Source, 2009). Many highly educated researchers, professors, and scientists left their countries of origin seeking better economic and professional opportunities when the economies of previously communist states disintegrated, and wars erupted in Bosnia and Herzegovina (Ispa-Landa, 2007). As a result, Eastern European immigrants generally have higher educational attainment relative to immigrants from such regions as Mexico and Latin America. According to Gold (2007), the percentage of immigrants born in the former Soviet Union with a bachelor's degree or higher (60%) is greater than that of all foreign-born people in the United States (26%), and these highly educated immigrants are likely to have a good command of the English language when they arrive. Given their high human capital, occupational success, and favorable reception in the United States, families and children of highly educated immigrants relative to those of less well educated immigrants generally have an easier time adapting to their new environment, report higher levels of satisfaction and psychological well-being, are more geographically dispersed within the United States, are less likely to reside in ethnic communities, have high levels of interaction with the U.S.-born population, and regard their children's education and school progress in the United States as important goals (Nesteruk and Marks, 2011).

At the same time, communication difficulties and uncertainty about how to handle schooling situations often result in cultural gaps between these parents and their children despite the parents' relatively high education levels (Nesteruk, 2010). Nesteruk and Marks (2011) report that although each Eastern European country has its unique culture, language, and traditions, as these parents became more acculturated, they practiced an "American" style of parenting that involved more child-centered approaches and permissiveness—giving children choices and negotiating with them. The challenge for these immigrants, as for those from other cultures, was to find an acceptable balance between the two cultures. Eastern European immigrant parents often reported difficulties with their children's diminishing obedience and respect for the authority of parents, elders, and teachers. This finding is consistent with those of previous research on Latin American, Asian, Middle Eastern, and African immigrant parents in the United States who lack extended family to reinforce important language and cultural norms (Nesteruk and Marks, 2011). Relative to the overall immigrant population, however, common immigrant issues such as language brokering and parent-child role reversal are less relevant to immigrants in professional occupations, who, as noted, generally have greater success in being incorporated (Nesteruk, 2010).

ELs of African or Caribbean Origin

The growth in the number of black immigrants in the United States is another dimension of recent immigration trends that has implications for the nation's language diversity. Research indicates that the voluntary black immigrant population in the United States increased by more than 2,000 percent between 1965 and 2013 (Anderson, 2015). Black immigrants, especially those from Africa, are now one of the fastest-growing immigrant groups in the nation (Capps et al., 2011; Rumbaut, 1994; Thomas, 2011c), and their young children are one of the fastest-growing segments of the U.S. child population (Hernandez, 2012).

Research reveals significant variation in the English proficiency of black immigrant groups (Thomas, 2010, 2011a, 2011b). These variations are associated in part with the language characteristics of countries within the two main world regions from which these immigrants originate—the

Caribbean and Africa. Relative to those from Africa, Caribbean immigrants have a longer history of migration to the United States, accounting for approximately 49 percent of the black immigrant population (Thomas, 2012). Although the majority come from English-speaking countries such as Jamaica and Trinidad and Tobago, many others, including those from Haiti and the Dominican Republic, have French and Spanish language backgrounds (Thomas, 2012).

African immigrants, accounting for about 33 percent of the black immigrant population, immigrate to the United States mainly through the Diversity Visa Program, although a growing number of African immigrants from countries such as Somalia and Ethiopia arrive as refugees (Thomas, 2011a). As with their Caribbean counterparts, black immigrants from Africa largely originate from English-speaking countries; many, however, come from non-English-speaking backgrounds, including countries in which French, Portuguese, and Arabic are the primary languages (Thomas, 2010). South American countries such as Brazil, Colombia, and Venezuela account for a smaller proportion of the black immigrant population, and their main languages are Spanish and Portuguese.

Mitchell (2015) provides the most recent information on the languages spoken at home by black immigrant children. According to his estimates, 40 percent of black immigrant children speak Spanish at home, reflecting the increasing number of black immigrants from Central America, Latin America, and the Caribbean. Another 18.1 percent speak French Creole; 7.5 percent speak French; and the remaining 34 percent speak an assortment of languages, including Yoruba, Fulani, Swahili, Portuguese, and Arabic.

ELs Born in the United States

While the countries of origin of immigrant ELs are considerably diverse, it is important to note that the majority of children in the U.S. EL population are born in the United States and are birthright citizens. As shown in Figure 3-3, the percentage of ELs born in the United States is greater than the percentage of their foreign-born peers at every age between 5 and 17. Figure 3-3 also shows that the majority of U.S.-born ELs have at least one immigrant parent.

At the same time, the distributions presented in Figure 3-3 have important implications for understanding other issues. For example, the high concentration of foreign-born ELs in the older age group implies that they are the most likely of the three major groups shown in the figure to complete high school with low levels of English proficiency. This pattern does not appear to be driven by older ages at arrival among foreign-born ELs: foreign-born ELs arrive in the United States at a younger average age (4.97

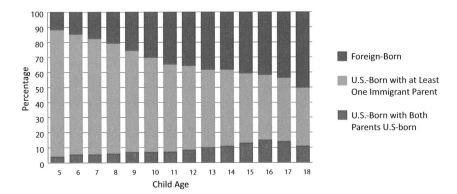

FIGURE 3-3 Immigrant generation of English learners (ages 5-18 and enrolled in school), 2008-2012.
SOURCE: Migration Policy Institute analysis of the American Community Survey, 2008-2012, presented by Capps (2015).

years) relative to foreign-born non-ELs (7.6 years). Instead, foreign-born ELs appear to find themselves in disadvantaged structural contexts that limit their access to services needed to improve their English proficiency. Figure 3-3 also shows that children exposed to English earlier in life (i.e., U.S.-born children with one or both immigrant parents) account for considerably lower percentages of those graduating from high school as ELs. Finally, the fact that U.S.-born children account for almost 50 percent of ELs at age 18 indicates that the existing education system neglects a significant number of these children.

Group differences among immigrant children often reflect disparities in the types of parents who choose to emigrate from another country to the United States. East Asian immigrant children, for example, are likely to have college-educated parents, while Mexican immigrant children are likely to have no parent with a high school degree (Crosnoe and López-Turley, 2011).

American Indian and Alaska Native Indigenous Heritage Language Learners

The ACS codes 381 distinct non-English languages, 169 of which are Native North American languages, although the speakers of these latter languages number less than half a million (Siebens and Julian, 2011). The most common Native North American languages spoken by American Indian and Alaska Native individuals ages 5 and older include Navajo, spoken by more people—an estimated 169,471—than any other Native

North American language; Yupik, with 18,950 speakers; Dakota, with 18,616 speakers; Apache, with 13,063 speakers; Keres, with 12,945 speakers; and Cherokee, with 11,610 speakers (Siebens and Julian, 2011). Fully 87 percent of the population ages 5 years and older living in an American Indian or Alaska Native area speak only English at home. The percentage of those who live in an American Indian or Alaska Native area who report speaking a Native North American language at home does not vary greatly across age groups, although the highest percentage doing so is among those ages 18-64, at 5.6 percent, followed those ages 5-17 and 65 and older, each at 5.1 percent (Siebens and Julian, 2011). Among those who identified as American Indian or Alaska Native, the most likely to maintain the home language are members of the older generation, among whom more than 1 in 5 ages 65 and older speak a Native North American language at home, while about 1 in 10 of those ages 5-17 do so. Spanish speakers (5% of the population residing in American Indian or Alaska Native areas) are almost as common as speakers of Native North American languages.

THE GEOGRAPHIC DISTRIBUTION OF ENGLISH LEARNERS

ELs are located in every state of the United States, as well as the U.S. territories and commonwealths (e.g., Guam, Puerto Rico); in American Indian and Alaska Native communities; and on American Indian tribal lands. On the U.S. mainland, California and Texas have the highest share of ELs, who represent 9 percent of children ages 5-18 enrolled in school; Arizona, Illinois, Nevada, New York, and Washington also have large concentrations of ELs (Capps, 2015). Collectively, California, Florida, New York, and Texas house 58 percent of second-generation immigrant youth (Enchautegui, 2014). The lowest percentages of ELs (approximately 3% of school-enrolled children in this age group) are found in states such as Idaho, Maine, Montana, North Dakota, South Dakota, Utah, and Vermont (Capps, 2015). U.S. Department of Education data show that the states of Alaska, California, Colorado, Florida, Kansas, Nevada, New Mexico, Oregon, Texas, Hawaii, and Washington enrolled 10-25 percent ELs among K-12 students in the school year 2012-2013 (Capps, 2015).

Within states, an emerging feature of the geographic distribution of ELs is their notable levels of residential and schooling segregation. The best example of this phenomenon is seen in the segregation experiences of Hispanic ELs. Estimates indicate that an increasing number of these children attend schools where they account for 90 to 100 percent of the student population (Carnock and Ege, 2015). Other dimensions of the segregation experiences of Hispanic children include their high concentrations in poor and disadvantaged neighborhoods, as well as their linguistic segregation. Carnock and Ege (2015), for example, argue that the linguistic segregation of Hispanics can be observed across several levels, including their segregation into schools with other poor children who are also ELs, and within schools, where they are likely to be in bilingual programs or classes in which most of the children are classified as ELs. Compared with the evidence on segregation among Hispanic ELs, less is known about the experiences of their non-Hispanic peers. Nevertheless the high prevalence of racial/ethnic segregation in housing and schooling in the United States suggests that the segregation experiences of Hispanic ELs are likely to be shared by ELs from other minority groups.

Historically, ELs have tended to cluster in large urban areas in immigrant enclaves, such as Chicago, Houston, Los Angeles, Miami, and New York City (Uro and Barrio, 2013). Gateway cities such as these continue to have high concentrations of ELs. Recent years, however, have seen a shift to destination sites across the United States, in small towns as well as in cities, in the nation's interior and along its coasts (Massey, 2008; Singer, 2004, 2015) (see Figure 3-4).

Using U.S. census data, Singer (2004) notes that newly emerging immigrant gateways experienced rapid growth of both the foreign-born and U.S.-born since the 1970s. Immigrants and their families in metropolitan areas were more likely to live in suburbs than in inner cities. The author also reports that the recent arrivals to the newest immigrant gateways, who originated mainly from Asian countries or Mexico, were likely to have low English proficiency, which also continued to be the case among immigrants residing longer in the traditional post–World War II gateways. Singer (2015) also adds a new category of major emerging gateways—those with

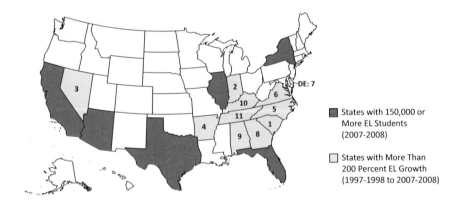

FIGURE 3-4 States with large and rapidly growing populations of English learners (ELs).
NOTE: Numbers on the map show the ranking of states in EL growth.
SOURCE: National Clearinghouse for English Language Acquisition, State Title III Information System © 2010 Migration Policy Institute.

THE DEMOGRAPHY OF THE ENGLISH LEARNER POPULATION

the fastest contemporary growth rates. This category includes Atlanta, Austin, Charlotte, Las Vegas, Orlando, and Phoenix, which together accounted for 8 percent of the total foreign-born population in the United States in 2014. The author notes that immigrants continued to find opportunities in both more established and emerging and reemerging gateways. New York City, for example, saw an increase of nearly 900,000 immigrants between 2000 and 2014, while Houston and Miami each gained more than 500,000.

Previous research shows notable variations in settlement within and among immigrant groups. Studies show, for example, that for Asian populations, the major settlement areas differ by national group. According to 2010 census data reported by Frey (2015), Boston, Los Angeles, New York, San Francisco, and San Jose had the largest Chinese populations, accounting for 54 percent of the total U.S. Chinese population. Chicago, Los Angeles, New York, San Francisco, and Washington (DC) had the largest populations of Asian Indians. Filipinos lived predominantly in Honolulu, Los Angeles, New York, San Diego, and San Francisco, which housed 43 percent of that group. Vietnamese lived predominantly in Dallas, Houston, Los Angeles, San Jose, and Washington (DC); Koreans in Chicago, Los Angeles, New York, Seattle, and Washington (DC); and Japanese in Honolulu, Los Angeles, New York, San Francisco, and Seattle, which accounted for 52 percent of the total U.S. Japanese population. Saint Paul Public Schools in Minnesota reported 31.5 percent Asian students in 2014, with the highest percentage in grade 11 (40.7%). Almost three of four Asian students in that district were identified as ELs (69%), and one in five were Hmong (Saint Paul Public Schools Office of Accountability, 2015).

According to Siebens and Julian (2011), speakers of Native North American languages were concentrated most heavily in the states of Alaska, Arizona, and New Mexico, which accounted for 65 percent of this population. Their highest concentration—37,000—was in Apache County, Arizona. The urban areas with the largest number of American Indians and Alaska Natives in 2010 were Albuquerque, Anchorage, Los Angeles, New York City, Oklahoma City, and Phoenix (Norris et al., 2012).

The states with the largest Hispanic population were California at 14,539,578 (38.2% of the state population) and Texas at 9,959,855 (38.2%) (Brown and Patten, 2014). New destination states, such as North Carolina (8.7% Hispanic), Nevada (27.3%), Pennsylvania (6.1%), Virginia (8.4%), and Washington (11.7%), have experienced substantial increases in their Hispanic populations in recent years as Hispanics have dispersed throughout the United States (see Table 3-2). The rapid increases in the Hispanic populations in these new destination states have resulted in many towns and cities and school districts experiencing significant changes in the ethnolinguistic composition of their populations for which they were not prepared.

TABLE 3-2 States Where the Percentage Change in the Hispanic Population Was Greater Than 100 Percent from 2000 to 2012

State	2000	2012	Increase, 2000-2012	Percentage Change, 2000-2012
Georgia	434,375	903,300	468,925	108.0
North Carolina	377,084	845,420	468,336	124.2
Virginia	333,482	687,008	353,526	106.0
Maryland	230,992	510,448	279,456	121.0
Oklahoma	173,746	356,077	182,331	104.9
Tennessee	116,692	306,710	190,018	162.8
Arkansas	85,303	197,146	111,843	131.1
Alabama	72,152	185,188	113,036	156.7
Iowa	80,204	160,566	80,362	100.2
Kentucky	56,922	133,726	76,804	134.9
Delaware	37,811	78,597	40,786	107.9
Mississippi	37,301	76,139	38,838	104.1
South Dakota	10,101	23,402	13,301	131.7
North Dakota	7,429	16,459	9,030	121.6
Vermont	5,260	10,662	5,402	102.7

NOTE: States are listed in descending order of number of Hispanic residents in 2012.
SOURCE: Adapted from Brown and Patten (2014). Data from Pew Research Center's Hispanic Trends Project tabulations of 2000 Census (5% IPUMS) and 2012 American Community Survey (1% IPUMS). IPUMS = Integrated Public Use Microdata Series.

Collectively, new destination gateways increased their share of the U.S. immigrant population from 18.2 percent in 2000 to 20.8 percent in 2010. Medium-sized metropolitan areas and small metro and nonmetro areas gained as the numbers of immigrants declined in traditional urban gateways, although the allure of these new destinations weakened in the late 2000s as a result of the U.S. economic recession (Ellis et al., 2014). Ellis and colleagues (2014) speculate that increasingly hostile environments for immigrants and their children and locally based anti-immigration initiatives may have affected the propensity of immigrants to locate in some of these new destinations (Ayón, 2015).

Schools remain at the forefront of the integration of immigrant children and youth into U.S. society, and some schools are clearly more prepared to support the educational success of ELs than others. The majority of immigrants studied by Griffith (2008) reported that communities in the Midwest were doing a good job at the elementary level, while those in communities in the South had less favorable perceptions of their children's elementary schools.

Griffith (2008, p. 194) found that Southern schools were "less sanguine in their reception of new immigrants" than Midwestern schools but were nevertheless making efforts to accommodate the new students by offering instruction in English as a second language (ESL) (Griffith, 2008). Although this was a small regional study, the schools Griffith studied in two Northern sites went well beyond merely teaching English to newcomers. In addition to offering ESL classes, those schools made efforts to learn about the cultural backgrounds of immigrant children; helped teachers understand the conditions that refugee children might have experienced; made efforts to deal with ethnic tensions that arose among Anglo, Somali, Latino, and Asian youth; and brought in volunteer bilingual adult members of each immigrant group to facilitate communication among students, families, and staff. They also made continuing attempts to involve parents in the schools and hired immigrants as teachers' aides in an attempt to make the students and their families feel welcome. Griffith found that new immigrant children sometimes proved beneficial to rural school districts losing enrollment. One school in a rural area of Minnesota, for example, experienced an influx of new Hmong students between 2000 and 2003 that revitalized the local elementary school, saving it from closing.

The inadequate language competency of teachers remains a major challenge to the provision of services for the growing number of ELs. School districts may attempt to bring in parents or members of an underrepresented language group to translate for students and assist them in the classroom, but these assistants often lack the formal teaching credentials required of English-speaking teachers and may lack the academic skills needed to guide students in the school curricula. The availability of teachers with the training required to meet the educational needs of ELs also varies widely. In a paper commissioned for this report, for example, Arias and Markos (2016) indicate that the ratio of ELs to teachers certified in ESL/ bilingual education (BLE) is 1:10 in traditional immigrant destinations such as California and Florida, but 1:391 in new immigrant destinations such as Kansas.[3] (For a more detailed discussion of workforce issues related to ELs, see Chapter 10.)

Other suburban school districts with predominantly white populations have found it challenging to respond to the increasing racial/ethnic diversity driven largely by immigration (Jones-Correa, 2008). In Maryland in 2000,

---

[3] The full commissioned paper is titled *Characteristics of the Workforce Who Are Educating and Supporting Children Who Are English Language Learners* (Arias and Markos, 2016).

for example, the population of Montgomery County's public schools represented 163 countries and spoke 123 different languages, and 31 percent of their households did not speak English at home. There were 12,000 ELs who took special courses in English for speakers of other languages. In 2003, the county's public schools for the first time had a majority minority student population—45 percent white, 22 percent African American, 19 percent Latino, and 14 percent Asian American (Jones-Correa, 2008). In Virginia, Fairfax County's schools saw similar increases in racial/ethnic diversity, and in 2003 had a student population representing more than 120 different languages spoken at home (Jones-Correa, 2008). Politics, federal and state mandates, court cases, budget constraints, professional interests, and bureaucratic considerations all influenced policy making and the changes the districts had to implement to meet the needs of their changing student population.

SOCIOECONOMIC CHARACTERISTICS AND STATUS OF ENGLISH LEARNERS

Family Income and Poverty

As noted earlier, children in immigrant families are more likely than their counterparts with U.S.-born parents to grow up in economically disadvantaged circumstances (Borjas, 2011; Capps, 2015; Fry, 2007). Research on exposure to poverty during early childhood suggests that it can have negative consequences for the development of children and their educational outcomes. Table 3-3 shows the distribution of ELs and non-ELs by quintiles of family income. Several striking patterns are obvious in these distributions. On average, ELs are more likely to live in families in the lowest-income quintiles, while non-ELs are concentrated in the highest-income families. These patterns indicate that ELs are more likely than non-ELs to grow up in socioeconomic contexts that have negative consequences for child development.

Despite their collective disadvantage, the economic circumstances of ELs vary considerably by race/ethnicity. Hispanic ELs, for example, are most likely to live in the poorest families, followed closely by American Indian and black ELs/indigenous heritage language learners. White and Asian ELs live in relatively more favorable economic circumstances. The exception to the general statement that ELs are more likely than their non-EL counterparts to live in families with the lowest incomes is blacks, among whom the percentages of ELs and non-ELs in the poorest families are roughly the same.

A related perspective on the economic circumstances of ELs and non-ELs comes from analysis of the distribution of children in families that are

TABLE 3-3 Percentage Distribution of English Learners (ELs) and Non-ELs by Race/Ethnicity and Family Income Quintile

| | Family Income Quintile | | | | |
	Quintile 1	Quintile 2	Quintile 3	Quintile 4	Quintile 5
ELs					
All	34.6	27.4	16.8	11.6	9.7
Hispanic	40.2	30.5	16.0	8.3	5.0
Black	36.3	26.7	16.0	11.8	9.2
White	21.3	20.3	19.1	19.4	20.0
Asian and Pacific Islander	25.7	20.2	15.6	14.7	23.8
American Indian	37.7	31.4	14.1	9.8	7.0
Non-ELs					
All	19.3	19.6	20.2	20.4	20.5
Hispanic	28.3	26.7	19.8	14.5	10.8
Black	37.8	23.8	15.9	11.4	11.1
White	13.3	17.1	21.3	23.9	24.4
Asian and Pacific Islander	10.4	12.7	15.0	21.2	40.8
American Indian	33.9	26.0	18.1	12.4	9.6

NOTES: The range of family incomes found in each quintile is as follows: Quintile 1: $0 to $26,919; Quintile 2: $26,200 to $52,000; Quintile 3: $52,201 to $81,659; Quintile 4 $81,660 to $128,425; and Quintile 5: $128,426 and above. Sample = children ages 5-18. ELs are defined based on responses to the American Community Survey question of how well individuals who speak a language other than English at home speak English. ELs thus are defined as children who speak English less than "very well."
SOURCE: Data are from the American Community Survey, 2008-2012.

at or under 185 percent of the federal poverty line (see Figure 3-5). Fully 65 percent of all ELs meet the threshold for free or reduced-price school lunches, compared with 36 percent of non-ELs. Hispanic and American Indian ELs/indigenous heritage language learners are most likely to qualify for free or reduced-price lunches and white ELs the least likely. Once again, the general economic disadvantage of ELs remains robust across race except for blacks, among whom equal proportions of ELs and non-ELs live in families at or below 185 percent of the federal poverty line.

Most explanations for the economic risks experienced in childhood focus on the effects of parental characteristics on children's welfare. Parental educational attainment, for example, is considered to be a leading determi-

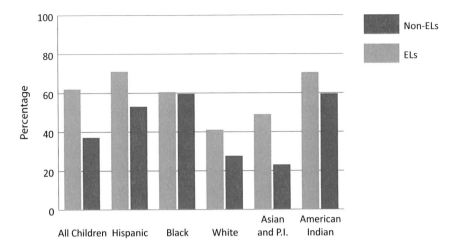

FIGURE 3-5 Percentage of children in families at or below 185 percent of the federal poverty line.
NOTE: Sample = children ages 5-18. ELs = English learners; P.I. = Pacific Islander.
SOURCE: Data are from the American Community Survey, 2008-2012.

nant of child poverty (Wood, 2003). Yet among immigrants, the range of parental influences is more diverse. Research indicates that the economic welfare of immigrant children also is positively associated with parental levels of English proficiency (Thomas, 2011a); in part, this relationship stems from the positive implications of English proficiency for wages (Chiswick and Miller, 2010; Dávila and Mora, 2004).

The distributions of the highest parental levels of education presented in Table 3-4 reveal some of the critical inequalities in parental human capital found among ELs and non-ELs. ELs are more likely to have parents with low levels of schooling. About 38 percent live in families where the highest level of parental schooling is less than a complete high school education, compared with 8.1 percent among non-ELs. Inequalities in parental educational attainment are observed within race and are most profound among Hispanic children. Almost half of all Hispanic ELs (49.8%) have parents who did not graduate from high school, compared with 26 percent among Hispanic non-ELs.

Figure 3-6 presents comparisons of English language proficiency among the parents of ELs and non-ELs. It focuses on children without a parent who speaks English at least "very well," who account for more than half of all ELs. In contrast, the percentage of non-ELs with parents who do not speak English very well is relatively low (7.9%). The parents of Hispanic

TABLE 3-4 Parental Educational Distributions of English Learners (ELs) and Non-ELs, by Race/Ethnicity

	Below Complete High School	High School Graduate	Some College	Bachelor's or More
ELs				
All	38.4	21.8	19.1	20.8
Hispanic	49.8	24.2	16.5	9.6
Black	21.7	21.1	32.6	24.7
White	18.2	18.5	25.8	37.5
Asian and Pacific Islander	23.6	17.7	12.7	46.1
American Indian	11.9	35.0	43.4	9.7
Non-ELs				
All	8.1	18.2	33.2	40.5
Hispanic	26.5	23.8	30.4	19.4
Black	11.1	25.2	41.3	22.4
White	2.9	16.0	33.2	47.9
Asian and Pacific Islander	8.9	11.4	12.3	67.5
American Indian	10.1	27.0	45.1	17.8

NOTE: Sample = children ages 5-18. ELs are defined as children who speak English less than "very well."
SOURCE: Data are from the American Community Survey, 2008-2012.

and Asian non-ELs are exceptions to this pattern: approximately one-third of non-ELs in both groups have parents with low levels of English proficiency. Hispanic and Asian non-ELs thus experience a notable mismatch between their own English-speaking skills and those of their parents. In such cases, non-EL children typically act as language brokers who help their parents interact with community and educational institutions.

Families, Household Contexts, and Language Use

Families are the first setting within which the socialization of children occurs. Among immigrants, they further perform cultural functions and exert social and economic influences that can either facilitate or constrain children's integration (Alba and Holdaway, 2013; Glick, 2010). Table 3-5

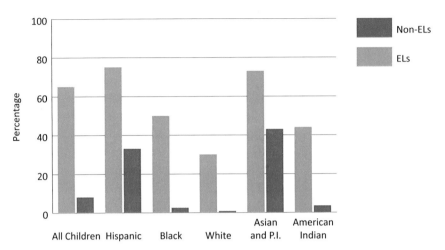

FIGURE 3-6 Percentage of children with parents who speak English less than "very well."
NOTE: Sample = children ages 5-18. ELs = English learners; P.I. = Pacific Islander.
SOURCE: Data are from the American Community Survey, 2008-2012.

compares the family structures of ELs and non-ELs. The table shows that, regardless of EL status, all children are on average less likely to live in single-parent than in two-parent households. For the most part, these patterns hold across race, except for blacks. Among blacks, ELs are less likely than non-ELs to live in single-parent households. This difference appears to reflect the lower prevalence of single-parent households among black immigrants relative to U.S.-born blacks (Brandon, 2002). Table 3-5 also shows that ELs are slightly more likely than non-ELs to live in households with no resident parent—probably a reflection of unaccompanied minors originating from Central America and Asia. As the table indicates, moreover, the percentage of Hispanic and Asian ELs living in households with no resident parent is much higher than the respective percentages among their non-EL peers.

Demographic research on the ways in which families shape the language development of their children focuses on two perspectives. The first examines the association between having immigrant parents in ethnically endogamous marriages, or marriages among couples of the same ethnicity, and level of English proficiency. Studies indicate that children in such immigrant families have lower levels of English proficiency relative to other children of immigrants (Alba et al., 2002; Ishizawa, 2004). The second perspective examines variations in the languages used at home by immigrant children (Capps, 2015; Capps et al., 2005). As expected, recent data

TABLE 3-5 Family Structures of ELs and Non-ELs, by Race/Ethnicity

	Single-Parent Household	Two-Parent Household	No Resident Parent
ELs			
All	25.57	65.92	8.51
Hispanic	30.01	61.14	8.85
Black	37.91	49.63	12.46
White	14.34	81.39	4.27
Asian and Pacific Islander	14.31	71.94	13.75
American Indian	37.00	48.44	14.56
Non-ELs			
All	27.15	66.52	6.33
Hispanic	32.52	60.59	6.89
Black	53.27	32.52	14.21
White	21.04	73.36	5.60
Asian and Pacific Islander	12.49	81.34	6.17
American Indian	40.67	45.13	14.20

NOTE: Sample = children ages 5-18. ELs are defined as children who speak English less than "very well."
SOURCE: Data are from the American Community Survey, 2008-2012.

from the 2008-2012 ACS indicate that this variation is higher among ELs than among non-ELs. While all ELs speak a language other than English at home, only 16 percent of non-ELs do so. The diversity of languages spoken at home by ELs is captured in Figure 3-7. Spanish is by far the most common of these languages (73%), followed by Chinese[4] (4%) and Vietnamese (3%).

Homeless ELs

A final perspective on children's living arrangements comes from examination of ELs who are homeless. According to the National Center for Homeless Education (2015), approximately 190,785 ELs were homeless in the United States in 2013-2014—a 9.1 percent increase over the number

---

[4]The term "Chinese" encompasses a number of languages, such as Mandarin, Cantonese, and others.

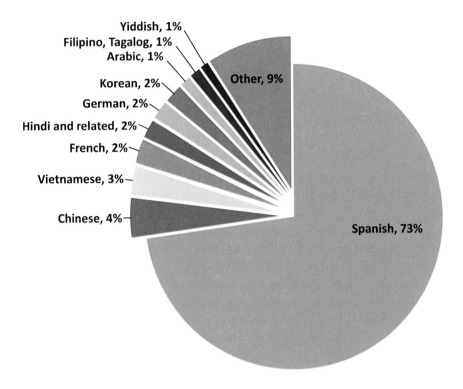

FIGURE 3-7 Top 10 languages spoken by English learners (ages 5-18 and enrolled in school), 2008-2012.
SOURCE: Migration Policy Institute analysis of the American Community Survey, 2008-2012, presented by Capps (2015).

in 2012-2013. In both periods, ELs represented the largest subgroup of homeless children who were enrolled in U.S. schools. Homeless children have lower levels of academic achievement than their nonhomeless peers (Cutuli et al., 2013; Rafferty, 1998) and are exposed to a number of risk factors that can negatively affect their development. Homeless ELs also may face other challenges, such as living as unaccompanied minors or living with various types of disabilities (National Center for Homeless Education, 2015), that can compound these risk factors.

In terms of geographic distribution, homeless ELs are most likely to be found in Western and Southwestern states such as Arizona, California, New Mexico, and Texas that have high concentrations of ELs. In these states, 10 percent or more of all homeless students enrolled in pre-K to grade 12 are ELs (National Center for Homeless Education, 2015). Comparatively lower percentages of ELs are found among homeless children in Midwestern states such as Ohio and in the Southeast (Georgia, South Carolina, Mississippi, and Tennessee). In these states, ELs account for less than 4 percent of the total number of homeless students in pre-K to grade 12.

Transnational Youth

Scholars use the concept of transnationalism to describe immigrants' long-term maintenance of cross-border ties to their communities of origin. Although critics have argued that the overall proportion of such immigrants is low and that as a result, transnationalism has little sustained effect on the process of immigrant adaptation, social networks often connect immigrants to their communities of origin and remain important in cross-border communication with friends and family members left behind (Mouw et al., 2014).

Children of parents who are members of tight-knit transnational communities or who participate in transnational organizations that keep them firmly connected to their ancestral homelands are more likely than children of nontransnational parents to sustain ties with relatives, peers, and community events and remain active in their communities of origin, as well as to maintain proficiency in their home language. Children may attend part of their school years in their country of origin and part in the United States, or spend time in U.S. schools and return to their country of origin to continue their education. Children in their country of origin with family members in the United States also may see migration, rather than education, as a route to a better socioeconomic future. As a result, they may not view schooling in their home country as worthwhile and may underachieve educationally while in their home country and separated from their family members (Gindling and Poggio, 2012). These children may later migrate to the United States to join their family members and be behind their classmates in academic skills.

Adjustment to migration is a complex process that differs for immigrant children with different characteristics. Because language acquisition becomes more challenging as children grow older, learning English is more difficult for children who migrate when they are older (Chiswick and Miller, 2008). Similarly, children who are younger when they reunite with families from which they have been separated are generally more respectful of authority and may adapt to a new school, new culture, and new educational system more readily relative to teenagers, who may have a more difficult time with integration into the academic and social life at U.S. schools (Gindling and Poggio, 2012).

Using data from the New Immigrant Survey, Gindling and Poggio (2012) found that children separated from their parents as a result of migration, compared with children who migrated with their parents or were born in the United States, were much more likely to be significantly older than other children in their grade who entered school at the appropriate age and moved on to the next grade each year. The impact of separation was also greater for children who migrated at older ages or were separated from their parents during their teenage years. The impact of separation from the mother was greater than that of separation from the father. The authors also found that dropout rates were higher for youth who were separated from their families during migration than for those who migrated with their parents, and their results suggested that the higher dropout rates of Latino immigrant children as compared with non-Latino immigrant children were due largely to the impact of family separation during migration.

Gindling and Poggio (2012) conducted a teacher survey whose results indicated that children separated from their parents during migration may have less success relative to those who do not experience such separation because they are assigned to a grade below their age level when they arrive in the United States, possibly as a result of their lack of English skills. Capps (2015 [analysis of 2008-2012 ACS]) reports that ELs ages 15-18 were less likely to be enrolled in school relative to other U.S. children of that age.

Parents' and children's social status as transnational migrants creates unique dynamics in families and may be reflected in difficult adjustments to U.S. schools. While some of these children may have exposure to English language instruction prior to coming to the United States, many arrive in U.S. classrooms as ELs. For many of the parents of these children, the hardships of family separation often are compounded by other challenges associated with their migration, making it difficult for them to participate in school activities with their children.

Undocumented ELs

Another dimension of recent immigration trends is the increasing salience of undocumented immigrant status. The size of the undocumented immigrant population increased from 8.6 million in 2000 to 11.5 million in 2011, leveling off at an estimated 11.2 million in 2014 (Passel and Cohn, 2016; Pew Hispanic Center, 2014; Zong and Batalova, 2016). Undocumented status affects not only immigrants' access to better-paying jobs and social services, but also the educational outcomes of their children (Bean et al., 2011, 2015; Suarez-Orozco and Yoshikawa, 2013; Yoshikawa and Kalil, 2011). Recent estimates suggest that more than half of all ELs have an undocumented immigrant parent (Capps, 2015).

Growing up in the United States without authorized immigration status or with parents who are unauthorized immigrants can be stressful for children and adolescents. According to a report from the Pew Hispanic Center (Passel, 2006), in 2005, children accounted for 1.8 million (16%) of the approximately 11.1 million undocumented immigrants living in the United States. Capps and Fortuny (2006) estimate that more than three-quarters of children of immigrants living in the United States are U.S. citizens, and over half live in mixed-status families, with some children being U.S.-born and others being unauthorized. These authors do not break out the percentage of these children whose home language is other than English, but it is safe to say that many of them are ELs. In mixed-status families, one or more siblings who are not U.S. citizens may face deportation, while those who were born in the United States may remain. Resources available to children who are U.S. citizens, such as financial aid for college, are unavailable to undocumented siblings (Pérez, 2014).

In addition, through social relations, deportability can be transferred to "legal" residents and citizens. For example, there are many children of undocumented immigrants who are U.S. citizens but because of their parents' unauthorized status may be viewed as "illegal" (Boehm, 2009). Even if they are recognized as citizens, the fate they face if their undocumented parents or guardians are deported has known negative outcomes. Moreover, the children of undocumented immigrants often are forced to grow up without their parents being involved in their school lives because of fears of deportation, a circumstance that has been tied to poor academic outcomes (Abrego, 2014; Dreby, 2015a).

These issues are important for future immigration policies as schools seek ways to incorporate the large population of undocumented immigrant children and children of undocumented parents. Although undocumented immigrants tend to be concentrated in those states with the highest numbers of immigrants, they can be found in most U.S. states, and they represent many different countries of origin (Passel and Cohn, 2011). Spanish-speaking countries, such as El Salvador, Guatemala, Honduras, and Mexico, are the countries of origin of the largest percentages of unauthorized immigrants. The Urban Institute (2011) estimated that in 2008-2009, 3.5 million U.S. citizen children had noncitizen Mexican parents. Passel and Cohn (2014) found that although Mexicans represent a majority of unauthorized immigrants in the United States (52% in 2012), both their numbers and their share have declined in recent years. But as the number of unauthorized Mexicans declined, the numbers of unauthorized immigrants from South America, European countries, and Canada held steady (Passel and Cohn, 2014), and unauthorized immigrants from Asia, the Caribbean, Central America, and other countries grew slightly. The Philippines also is the top country of origin for unauthorized immigrants in Alaska and Hawaii. Also among the largest contributors of unauthorized immigrants in the United States are India, China, and Korea (Passel and Cohn, 2014).

One of the major challenges for U.S. schools relative to ELs is determining the strengths of these youth in their home languages and English.

Undocumented ELs or ELs with undocumented family members may be reluctant to identify as immigrant children because of their status or the status of their family members. In a report for the Immigration Policy Institute, Gonzales (2007) documents the plight of these students, who are seldom able to go to college, cannot work legally in the United States without DACA[5] status, in some states cannot obtain a driver's license or attend public universities, and cannot put their education to good use. Many get discouraged and drop out before completing high school, while others are honor roll students, class officers, and valedictorians and aspire to give back to their communities by becoming teachers, doctors, lawyers, and social activists.

These youth express fears about family separation and have various legal misunderstandings (Dreby, 2013). Many have experienced significant tensions at the local level in communities that have seen an increase in the number of unauthorized students in their schools and non-English-speaking undocumented residents in their midst (Zúñiga and Hamann, 2009; Zúñiga and Hernández-Leon, 2005). Abrego (2014) reports that the persistently negative representation of undocumented immigrants as "criminals" affects how immigrant children understand and experience "illegality" in their day-to-day lives. She found that the undocumented immigrants she interviewed feared deportation; had a general sense of insecurity; and often felt that they could not depend on police, emergency services, or authority figures to protect them.

Many undocumented students have joined other undocumented youth and made claims as students in school settings and beyond through such organizations as the DREAM Act Movement (Nicholls, 2013). A number of these students have formed a national organization, United We Dream, that has developed a "toolkit" for students, parents, teachers, and other school personnel to help them enable undocumented youth to be successful in their educational pursuits (United We Dream, 2015).

Immigration policy plays an important role for these youth in shaping their incorporation patterns and trajectories into adulthood. Undocumented youth share a confusing and contradictory status in terms of their legal rights and the opportunities available to them. Families and children may adopt subordinate statuses and deferential behaviors, such as acting quietly, drawing little attention to themselves, or feeling isolated, and they are often fearful of seeking help from teachers or others because of their

---

[5]Deferred Action for Childhood Arrivals (DACA) was enacted in 2010 to prevent the deportation of those who meet certain criteria, such as age at arrival, possession of a high school diploma, and time in the United States. Meeting these criteria allows undocumented residents to obtain a 2-year work permit, Social Security number, and driver's license.

undocumented status and their fear of deportation (Abrego, 2006, 2008, 2014; Gonzales, 2007).

Undocumented status also affects children of other national origin groups, such as Pacific Islanders who are not from countries with a compact of free association with the United States.[6] Immigrants from Kiribati, Papua New Guinea, Samoa, Tokelau, Tonga, and others must apply for legal permanent resident status to work and live in the United States legally. Between 2002 and 2012, U.S. courts deported more than 2,700 persons to the Pacific Islands, mainly to Fiji, Micronesia, Tonga, and Western Samoa (Empowering Pacific Islander Communities and Asian Americans Advancing Justice, 2014).

Unaccompanied Minors

In recent years, most unaccompanied minors (defined as children under age 18 who do not have a parent or legal guardian and are detained because of their lack of lawful immigration status in the United States) have originated from three Central American countries—El Salvador, Guatemala, and Honduras—with others coming from Mexico (Kandel and Seghetti, 2015) (see Box 3-1).

The U.S. Department of Homeland Security (2016) reports an overall increase in the apprehension of unaccompanied children from Central America at the Southwest border, specifically in the Rio Grande Valley of Texas. The U.S. Office of Refugee Resettlement arranges for these children to be cared for initially through a network of state-licensed care providers that are required to provide classroom education, medical services, and case management while they attempt to reunite the child with a family member. Family unit apprehensions also are high, totaling 68,445 in 2014 and 39,838 in 2015 along the U.S. Southwest border.

The term "immigrant bargain" (Smith, 2005) has been used to describe immigrant families' hopes that their children's academic success will be a form of repayment for parental sacrifice. Oral histories of migration experiences and decisions are passed down to children as a way of instilling educational values and responsibility toward the family (Stanton-Salazar, 2001). Parental sacrifice is at times paid back in the form of succeeding educationally and making parents proud, or contributing to the household financially by seeking employment (Katz, 2014). Some parents choose to

---

[6] Countries with a compact of free association have an agreement with the United States to allow a military presence in their country in exchange for allowing residents to live and work in the United States as "nonimmigrants" but without citizenship, although they may serve in the U.S. military. They include the Federated States of Micronesia, the Marshall Islands, and Palau.

BOX 3-1
Hadwin's Story

Hadwin* is almost 19. He arrived in the United States from Guatemala at age 16 as an unaccompanied minor and was placed in the 9th grade because of his age. His native language is Mam, a Mayan language, and he is now learning both Spanish and English. He works at a restaurant from 4 to 11 PM and attends a high school for immigrant students in a large urban school district during the day. Hadwin appreciates the kindness of his teachers, and because he does not have family in the United States, his teachers are the persons he trusts and turns to as family:

> They started to teach me slowly things and started to teach me the most easy words. And I started to learn. Before in my country I didn't know that I'm going to speak English one day. I didn't imagine that, and now I'm here, I'm speaking English. Not very well, but I'm trying to and I'm actually proud of myself because most of my friends said to me, 'How can you do it if you just went to school for three years in your country?' That was hard for me but when I came here, I was 16 and I take school seriously, not playing around, take every class seriously. And now I'm speaking English and I want to go to college now. I really care about school, about education now. . . . In my country, my family was very poor so they didn't have money to pay all the materials that were needed in school, so here I got opportunity. . . . I know what I'm going to do in my life now. But I need that education in my life and I'm going to fight for it.

Hadwin also has a strong relationship with the chef in the restaurant where he works, who always asks him what he is learning at school and encourages him to practice his English at the restaurant. Many of the immigrant students arriving in U.S. schools may speak more than one language. Hadwin, like many others, is proud of his native language. Most of the people in the area of his country where

---

send their children to the United States even if unable to accompany them because they believe their children will have better educational opportunities or opportunities to learn English in the United States. Upper-middle-class families from such countries as Hong Kong, and Taiwan sometimes send middle and high school-age students to study abroad living with their mothers while fathers remain in the home country. Other families may send children to the United States to live with extended family or family contacts while both parents remain in the home country (Waters, 2002, 2003).

Divided families and parenting across borders have been well documented (Arias, 2013; Dreby, 2010, 2012, 2015a; Orellana et al., 2001). Unless parents can maintain regular contact with their children, younger children may become emotionally withdrawn, and adolescents may become quite independent or act out aggressively (Dreby, 2015b), which can negatively impact their ability to thrive in an academic setting.

he lived speak Mam, but the country is also trying to teach them Spanish. He worries that as people in his community begin to speak Spanish, they will lose their native language, and maintaining his native language is important to him. He explained: "Spanish is not my first language, my native language is Mam, so I start to speak Mam and then I start to learn Spanish. So I don't even know like very well the Spanish. I just speak a little bit. But I'm trying to learn both languages [English and Spanish] so now I'm always asking questions of them [teachers] in Spanish and English. What does this mean? What's that mean? And always asking questions. . . . I'm always trying to speak Mam with my family because I don't want to forget it. I just want to keep it."

Hadwin's main problems at school are bullying by other students who cut in front of the immigrant students in cafeteria lines and push them around: "They don't care about us. We are short and we cannot do nothing, even fight. So I would like more security to take care of us, because we sometimes have fights in the cafeteria and we cannot do nothing about it. They are taller people than us or we cannot do nothing."

Hadwin feels it is important for school staff to understand the different immigration experiences of the students: "He has to know, or she, about every single student because, like here in [this school] we came from different countries. I come from Guatemala. They come from Ethiopia, different countries, different continents, actually. And I would like to say that he or she has to know about every individual student, his story or their story and start to give them the right education they need."

———————

*The student's name has been changed.

SOURCE: As told to the committee during an interview conducted January 19, 2016.

Once families unite, and during the reunification process, children and youth may miss caretakers and friends left behind and may feel like strangers when they join their biological family after long separation (Foner, 2014). While both parents and children have reported difficulties resulting from separation and in the years following reunification, most families demonstrate strength, determination, resourcefulness, and resilience in dealing with the challenges presented by migration (Suárez-Orozco et al., 2011).

Refugees

Newcomers with refugee or asylum status are unable or unwilling to return to their country of origin because of persecution, and they may have left close or extended family members behind. In 2013, 34 percent of refugees admitted to the United States were under age 18 (Martin and Yankay,

2014). The leading states receiving these refugees were Texas (10.7%), California (9.1%, and Michigan (6.7%) (Martin and Yankay, 2014). As a result of these relocations, as well as migrations, children in these families often experience separations and reunifications of different members of the family over time.

Family contexts have critical implications for the functioning of children and youth. Disruptions in family systems are likely to have implications for their well-being, including psychological repercussions for those who have been separated from parents who have emigrated to the United States and those who arrive in the United States without their parents (Suárez-Orozco and Suárez-Orozco, 2001; Suárez-Orozco et al., 2011). These experiences may contribute to the difficulties faced by some of these children and youth in school (Gindling and Poggio, 2012.

The U.S. Department of Homeland Security reported that 69,909 refugees were admitted to the United States during 2013, the majority coming from Iraq (28%), Burma (23%), Bhutan (13%), and Somalia (11%) (Martin and Yankay, 2014). In that year, China, Egypt, and Ethiopia were the leading countries of origin of those granted either affirmative or defensive asylum in the United States. The leading countries of nationality of "follow-to-join" refugees, consisting of spouses and children under 21, were China, Haiti, and Ethiopia (Martin and Yankay, 2014).

U.S. military involvement in Southeast Asia and the end of the Vietnam War in the early 1970s led to waves of Vietnamese, Laotian, and Cambodian refugees. The U.S. government set up centers, such as that in the military base at Camp Pendleton in Southern California, to help these refugees learn English and adjust to the United States. The refugees were initially dispersed to several parts of the country as part of the refugee resettlement process. These families were often sponsored by churches or civic organizations. Many later resettled in major Asian settlement areas, such as the Los Angeles, California, metropolitan area, and Houston and Dallas in Texas (Frey, 2015).

The Vietnamese are a bifurcated group: a significant portion are poorly educated and have not graduated from high school, and another significant portion are highly educated and have attained at least a college degree. The positive educational selectivity of the elite and middle-class emigrants who fled Vietnam before the fall of Saigon enabled them to transfer skills and mindsets to the new U.S. contexts of resettlement (Lee and Zhou, 2015). Immigration among these groups has increased in recent decades, associated with family reunification in the United States, and many of these newcomer children are ELs. Lee and Zhou (2015) note that between 1990 and 2010, the Vietnamese population in the United States nearly tripled, to 1.74 million, and this figure likely underestimates the numbers of Vietnamese immigrants because others came as part of the larger refugee exodus from Southeast Asia.

Another group of refugees, Cubans, arrived initially in the post-Castro period, fleeing a political regime that was ideologically at war with the United States. They were warmly received as political refugees, assisted in relocation, and given monthly allowances and other government assistance (Rodriguez, 2008). The early Cuban refugees were predominantly skilled, upper-class, white, and entrepreneurial and were more likely to speak English than the later waves of Cuban refugees, referred to as the Marielitos' migration, who were less privileged (Borjas, 2015). Some families who remained in Cuba sent their children to the United States on what were known as "Peter Pan flights," hoping to join them later.

Although the U.S. government attempted to relocate Cuban refugees to various parts of the United States, many reestablished their ethnic communities in Miami and Los Angeles. Some of the first federally funded bilingual education programs, such as the transitional bilingual program at Coral Way Elementary School, were established in Miami as the U.S. government tried to facilitate the refugees' integration. There were sufficient numbers of elite, well-educated Cubans among the refugees to staff the bilingual programs as teachers and administrators. Approximately half a million Cubans have become legal permanent residents in the United States since 1981, and Cuba consistently ranks among the top 10 source countries for legal permanent residents. Since the beginning of the normalization process between Cuba and the United States in 2014, Cuban migration has increased. A "wet foot/dry foot" practice toward Cuban migrants has evolved, according to which those who do not reach dry land in the United States are returned to Cuba unless they cite fears of persecution. Those who reach the U.S. shore successfully are generally permitted to remain and become legal permanent residents within 1 year. They also are eligible to receive government benefits (Wasem, 2009).

ENGLISH PROFICIENCY ACROSS IMMIGRANT GENERATIONS

A significant percentage of ELs are born in the United States or are U.S.-born children of immigrants. Studies on language assimilation among immigrants have found that with succeeding generations, their use of mother-tongue languages decreases as their levels of English proficiency increase (Ishizawa, 2004; Thomas, 2010). The proportion of children who are ELs can be expected to decrease accordingly.

Table 3-6 presents the distribution of children who speak English less than very well by race/ethnicity and generation, based on ACS data. In general, the distributions conform to this expectation. In each immigrant generation, however, the highest prevalence of ELs is found among non-

TABLE 3-6 Distribution of Children Who Speak English Less Than Very Well, by Race/Ethnicity and Generation

	Hispanic	Black	White	Asian and Pacific Islander
First Generation	32.67	19.19	15.25	35.21
Second Generation	19.33	3.83	4.50	15.57
Third Generation	5.18	0.50	0.85	3.54

NOTES: Sample = children ages 5-18. English learners (ELs) are defined based on responses to the American Community Survey question of how well individuals who speak a language other than English at home speak English. ELs thus are defined as children who speak English less than "very well."
SOURCE: Data are from the American Community Survey, 2008-2012.

white children, highlighting the dual challenge of navigating both low levels of English proficiency and racial/ethnic minority status. First-generation children, especially those who are Hispanic or Asian, are the most likely to have poor English-speaking skills. By the second generation, the percentage of children who speak English less than very well declines, reflecting the expected gains in English proficiency among the U.S.-born or second-generation children of immigrants. Yet this decline is inconsistent across ethnic categories. Approximately 20 percent of second-generation Hispanic children and 16 percent of second-generation Asian children speak English less than very well, compared with less than 5 percent of U.S.-born blacks and non-Hispanic whites. By the third and higher generations, many of the group differences in English proficiency disappear; even within the third generation, however, at least 5 percent of Hispanic children still speak English less than very well—the highest percentage across ethnic categories.

In general, these estimates reflect the patterns of English proficiency found among immigrant groups in previous studies. According to Brown and Patten (2014), for example, approximately 11.5 percent of the Hispanic U.S.-born population reported that English was spoken less than very well in the home, compared with 29.8 percent of the foreign-born Hispanic population. The majority of both U.S.-born and foreign-born Hispanics reported that English was spoken very well or only English was spoken at home. Among the more recent foreign-born Hispanic immigrants, those who arrived in 2006 or later, 48 percent reported that English was spoken less than very well at home. Asians reported a slightly higher percentage of those who spoke English less than very well.

However, data from the 2010 U.S. census show that Asian children generally are proficient in English, with 37 percent of those ages 5-17 speaking English at home and only 16 percent speaking English less than very well

(Frey, 2015). Data from the 2010 census and the 2006-2010 ACS reveal that among Asians ages 5 and older, 46 percent of Chinese, 46 percent of Koreans, and 53 percent of Vietnamese did not speak English very well. Fewer Asian Indians (22%), Filipinos (22%), and Japanese (24%) did not speak English very well (Frey, 2015).

A study of Mexican-born immigrants in Los Angeles yields a membership-exclusion perspective on the integration of immigrants (Bean et al., 2015). The authors emphasize the importance of societal membership for integration and the impact of the extent to which unauthorized status leads to conditions that limit schooling gains for children of immigrants, including those born in the United States. These researchers identify three major components of integration—economic, spatial, and linguistic. They argue that linguistic integration is important because learning English in the United States is a prerequisite for other kinds of incorporation. They argue, however, that in looking at linguistic integration, it is important to consider both language acquisition and preservation of the heritage language. Their study revealed that among later generations of the Mexican immigrant population in Los Angeles, a preference for the English language only was almost universal (99% of the 3.5 generation). In their sample, among the second generation whose parents were both Mexican-born, members of the extended family on both sides were likely to speak Spanish, but the percentage speaking Spanish well declined dramatically in the third generation. This finding is similar to the experiences of white European immigrants, among whom there is scarcely any survival of mother tongue preference by the third generation. First- and second-generation immigrants from Mexico are on average more likely than immigrants from other countries to have low levels of English proficiency upon arrival in the United States because they are less likely to have been exposed to English in school or at work.

According to Bean and colleagues (2015), a major factor in membership exclusion for immigrants of Mexican origin and succeeding generations is legal status. They argue that "unauthorized status, reinforced by immigration and immigrant policies of the United States over the past forty years, hinders the integration of Mexican Americans" (p. 6). They found that youth whose parents had legal status were able to take greater advantage of new opportunities. For third-generation males, they found that, despite long-term residence in the United States, there was an education lag, with few Mexican Americans in their sample reaching beyond high school and with minimal educational gains from the second to the third generation, although incomes increased slightly. The authors propose that the unauthorized status of parents created conditions that affected educational attainment among their children, even those children who had U.S. citizenship. Parents' lack of legal status, low levels of education, long working hours, and limited English proficiency limited their own ability to deal with their children's schooling issues. The authors also argue that the poverty associated with unauthorized migration contributes to social isolation, strong family norms about working versus the high costs of pursuing postsecondary education, living in poor neighborhoods, female-headed households, unemployment, and low-quality schools, all factors that influence the educational attainment of second and third generations.

CONCLUSIONS

Conclusion 3-1: The cultures, languages, and experiences of English learners are highly diverse and constitute assets for their development, as well as for the nation.

Conclusion 3-2: Many English learners grow up in contexts that expose them to a number of risk factors (e.g., low levels of parental education, low family income, refugee status, homelessness) that can have a negative impact on their school success, especially when these disadvantages are concentrated.

Conclusion 3-3: As the population of English learners continues to diversify, limitations of current data sources compromise the capacity to provide a more comprehensive description of the population's characteristics for policy makers, administrators, and teachers who have responsibilities for their education.

BIBLIOGRAPHY

Abrego, L.J. (2006). "I can't go to college because I don't have papers": Incorporation patterns of Latino undocumented youth. *Latino Studies, 4*(3), 212-231.

Abrego, L.J. (2008). Legitimacy, social identity, and the mobilization of law: The effects of Assembly Bill 540 on undocumented students in California. *Law & Social Inquiry, 33*(3), 709-734.

Abrego, L.J. (2014). Latino immigrants' diverse experiences of "illegality." In C. Menjívar and D. Kanstroom (Eds.), *Constructing Immigrant "Illegality": Critiques, Experiences, and Responses* (pp. 139-161). New York: Cambridge University Press.

Alba, R., and Holdaway, J. (2013). *The Children of Immigrants at School: A Comparative Look at Integration in the United States and Western Europe.* New York: NYU Press.

Alba, R., Logan, J., Lutz, A., and Stults, B. (2002). Only English by the third generation? Loss and preservation of the mother tongue among the grandchildren of contemporary immigrants. *Demography, 39*(3), 467-484.

Anderson, M. (2015). *A Rising Share of the U.S. Black Population Is Foreign Born; 9 Percent Are Immigrants; and While Most Are from the Caribbean, Africans Drive Recent Growth.* Washington, DC: Pew Research Center. Available: http://www. pewsocialtrends. org/2015/04/09/a-rising-share-of-the-us-black-populationis-foreign-born [January 5, 2017].

Arias, P. (2013). International migration and familial change in communities of origin: Transformation and resistance. *Annual Review of Sociology, 39*, 429-450.

Arias, M.B., and Markos, A.M. (2016). *Characteristics of the Workforce Who Are Educating and Supporting Children Who Are English Language Learners.* Unpublished manuscript commissioned by the Committee on Fostering School Success for English Learners: Toward New Directions in Policy, Practice, and Research, Washington, DC.

Ayón, C. (2015). *Economic, Social, and Health Effects of Discrimination on Latino Immigrant Families.* Washington, DC: Migration Policy Institute.

Batalova, J., and Fix, M. (2011). *Up for Grabs: The Gains and Prospects of First- and Second-Generation Young Adults.* Washington, DC: Migration Policy Institute.

Bean, F.D., Leach, M.A., Brown, S.K., Bachmeier, J.D., and Hipp, J.R. (2011). The educational legacy of unauthorized migration: Comparisons across U.S.-immigrant groups in how parents' status affects their offspring. *International Migration Review, 45*(2), 348-385.

Bean, F.D., Brown, S.K., and Bachmeier, J.D. (2015). *Parents without Papers: The Progress and Pitfalls of Mexican American Integration.* New York: Russell Sage Foundation.

Boehm, D.A. (2009). "¿Quien Sabe?": Deportation and temporality among transnational Mexicans. *Urban Anthropology and Studies of Cultural Systems and World Economic Development, 38*(2/3/4), 345-374.

Borjas, G.J. (2011). Poverty and program participation among immigrant children. *The Future of Children, 21*(1), 247-266.

Borjas, G.J. (2015). *The Wage Impact of the Marielitos: A Reappraisal.* (NBER Working Paper No. 21588). Cambridge, MA: National Bureau of Economic Research

Brandon, P.D. (2002). The living arrangements of children in immigrant families in the United States. *International Migration Review, 36*(2), 416-436.

Brown, A., and Patten, E. (2014). *Statistical Portrait of Hispanics in the United States, 2012.* Washington, DC: Pew Research Center's Hispanic Trends Project. Available: http://www.pewhispanic.org/2014/04/29/statistical-portrait-of-hispanics-in-the-unitedstates-2012 [November 6, 2016].

Capps, R. (2015). *Trends in Immigration and Migration of English and Dual Language Learners.* Presentation to the National Research Council Committee on Fostering School Success for English Learners, Washington, DC, May 28. Available: http://www.nationalacademies.org/hmd/~/media/Files/Activity%20Files/Children/DualLanguageLearners/2015-MAY-28/1Capps%20Randy.pdf [November 18, 2016].

Capps, R., and Fortuny, K. (2006). *Immigration and Child and Family Policy.* Washington, DC: Urban Institute.

Capps, R., Fix, M.E., Ost, J., Reardon-Anderson, J., and Passel, J.S. (2005). *The Health and Well-Being of Young Children of Immigrants.* Washington, DC: Urban Institute.

Capps, R., McCabe, K., and Fix, M. (2011). *New Streams: Black African Migration to the United States.* Washington, DC: Migration Policy Institute.

Carnock, J.T., and Ege, E. (2015). *The Triple Segregation of Latinos, ELLs: What Can We Do?* Available: https://www.newamerica.org/education-policy/edcentral/latinos-segregation [January 5, 2017].

Castro, D.C., Peisner-Feinberg, E., Buysse, V., and Gillanders, C. (2010). Language and literacy development of Latino dual language learners: Promising instructional practices. In O. Saracho and B. Spodek (Eds.), *Contemporary Perspectives on Language and Cultural Diversity in Early Childhood Education* (pp. 65-93). Scottsdale, AZ: Information Age.

Chiswick, B.R., and Miller, P.W. (2008). A test of the critical period hypothesis for language learning. *Journal of Multilingual and Multicultural Development, 29*(1), 16-29.

Chiswick, B.R., and Miller, P.W. (2010). Occupational language requirements and the value of English in the U.S. labor market. *Journal of Population Economics, 23*(1), 353-372.

Cleave, P.L., Girolametto, L.E., Chen, X., and Johnson, C.J. (2010). Narrative abilities in monolingual and dual language learning children with specific language impairment. *Journal of Communication Disorders, 43*(6), 511-522.

Connor, P., Cohn, D., and Gonzalez-Barrera, A. (2013). *Changing Patterns of Global Migration and Remittances.* Washington, DC: Pew Research Center.

Crosnoe, R., and López-Turley, R.N. (2011). K-12 educational outcomes of immigrant youth. *The Future of Children, 21*(1), 129-152.

Cutuli, J.J., Desjardins, C.D., Herbers, J.E., Long, J.D., Heistad, D., Chan, C.-K., Hinz, E., and Masten, A.S. (2013). Academic achievement trajectories of homeless and highly mobile students: Resilience in the context of chronic and acute risk. *Child Development, 84*(3), 841-857. https://doi.org/10.1111/cdev.12013.

Dávila, A., and Mora, M.T. (2004). English-language skills and the earnings of self-employed immigrants in the United States: A note. *Industrial Relations: A Journal of Economy and Society, 43*(2), 386-391.

De Bot, K., and Kroll, J.F. (2002). Psycholinguistics. In N. Schmitt (Ed.), *Introduction to Applied Linguistics.* London, UK: Arnold.

Dreby, J. (2010). *Divided by Borders: Mexican Migrants and Their Children.* Berkeley: University of California Press.

Dreby, J. (2012). The burden of deportation on children in Mexican immigrant families. *Journal of Marriage and Family, 74*(4), 829-845.

Dreby, J. (2015a). *Everyday Illegal: When Policies Undermine Immigrant Families.* Berkeley: University of California Press.

Dreby, J. (2015b). U.S. immigration policy and family separation: The consequences for children's well-being. *Social Science & Medicine, 132,* 245-251.

Ellis, M., Wright, R., and Townley, M. (2014). The Great Recession and the allure of new immigrant destinations in the United States. *International Migration Review, 48*(1), 3-33.

Empowering Pacific Islander Communities and Asian Americans Advancing Justice. (2014). *A Community of Contrasts: Native Hawaiians and Pacific Islanders in the United States, 2014.* Available: http://empoweredpi.org/wp-content/uploads/2014/06/A_Community_of_Contrasts_NHPI_US_2014-1.pdf [May 2017].

Enchautegui, M.E. (2014). *Immigrant Youth Outcomes: Patterns by Generation and Race and Ethnicity.* Washington, DC: Urban Institute.

Espinosa, L.M. (2013). *Early Education for Dual Language Learners: Promoting School Readiness and Early School Success.* Washington, DC: National Center on Immigrant Integration Policy, Migration Policy Institute.

Farrington, A.L., Lonigan, C.J., Phillips, B.M., Farver, J.M., and McDowell, K.D. (2015). Evaluation of the utility of the revised Get Ready to Read! for Spanish-Speaking English-language learners through differential item functioning analysis. *Assessment for Effective Intervention, 40*(4), 216-227.

Fix, M., and Passel, J.S. (2003). *U.S. Immigration: Trends and Implications for Schools.* Washington, DC: Urban Institute.

Foner, N. (2014). Intergenerational relations in immigrant families. In M. Halter, M. Johnson, K. Viens, C. Wright, Z.D. Barany, and P.D. Stachura (Eds.), *What's New About the "New" Immigration?: Traditions and Transformations in the United States since 1965* (pp. 113-130). New York: Palgrave Macmillan.

Frey, W.H. (2015). *Diversity Explosion: How New Racial Demographics Are Remaking America.* Washington, DC: Brookings Institution Press.

Fry, R. (2007). *How Far Behind in Math and Reading Are English Language Learners?* Washington, DC: Pew Hispanic Center.

García, E.E., Jensen, B.T., and Scribner, K.P. (2009). The demographic imperative. *Educational Leadership, 66*(7), 8-13.

Gindling, T.H., and Poggio, S.Z. (2012). Family separation and reunification as a factor in the educational success of immigrant children. *Journal of Ethnic and Migration Studies, 38*(7), 1155-1173.

Glick, J.E. (2010). Connecting complex processes: A decade of research on immigrant families. *Journal of Marriage and Family, 72*(3), 498-515.

Gold, S.J. (2007). Russia. In M.C. Waters, R. Ueda, and H.B. Marrow (Eds.), *The New Americans: A Guide to Immigration since 1965.* Cambridge, MA: Harvard University Press.

Gonzales, R.G. (2007). Wasted talent and broken dreams: The lost potential of undocumented students. *Immigration Policy in Focus, 5*(13), 1-11.

González-Barrera, A., and Lopez, M.H. (2013). *Spanish Is the Most Spoken Non-English Language in U.S. Homes, Even among Non-Hispanics.* Washington, DC: Pew Research Center.

González-Barrera, A., Lopez, H.L. and Rohal, M. (2015). *More Mexicans Leaving Than Coming to the U.S.* Washington, DC: Pew Research Center.

Griffith, D. (2008). New Midwesterners, New Southerners: Immigration Experiences in Four Rural American Settings. In D.S. Massey (Ed.), *New Faces in New Places: The Changing Geography of American Immigration* (pp. 179-210). New York: Russell Sage Foundation.

Guendelman, S., Schauffler, H.H., and Pearl, M. (2001). Unfriendly shores: How immigrant children fare in the U.S. health system. *Health Affairs, 20*(1), 257-266.

Hammer, C.S., Jia, G., and Uchikoshi, Y. (2011). Language and literacy development of dual language learners growing up in the United States: A call for research. *Child Development Perspectives, 5*(1), 4-9.

Hernandez, D.J. (2012). Young children in black immigrant families from Africa and the Caribbean. In R. Capps and M. Fix (Eds.), *Young Children of Black Immigrants in America: Changing Flows, Changing Faces* (pp. 75-117). Washington, DC: Migration Policy Institute.

Hixson, L., Hepler, B.B., and Kim, M.O. (2012). *The Native Hawaiian and Other Pacific Islander Population: 2010.* Washington, DC: U.S. Census Bureau.

Immigration Policy Center. (2007). *Dreams Deferred: The Costs of Ignoring Undocumented Students.* Washington, DC: Immigration Policy Center.

Ishizawa, H. (2004). Minority language use among grandchildren in multigenerational households. *Sociological Perspectives, 47*(4), 465-483.

Ispa-Landa, S. (2007). Europe: Central and Southeastern. In M.C. Waters, R. Ueda, and H.B. Marrow (Eds.), *The New Americans: A Guide to Immigration since 1965* (pp. 433-444). Cambridge, MA: Harvard University Press.

Jensen, E.B., Knapp, A., Borsella, C., and Nestor, K. (2015). *The Place of Birth Composition of Immigrants to the United States: 2000 to 2013.* Washington, DC: U.S. Census Bureau.

Jones-Correa, M. (2008). Race to the top? The politics of immigrant education in suburbia. In R. Massey (Ed.), *New Faces in New Places: The Changing Geography of American Immigration* (pp. 308-340). New York: Russell Sage Foundation.

Kandel, W. A. and Seghetti, L. (2015) *Unaccompanied Alien Children: An Overview.* U.S. Congressional Research Service Report R43599. Available: http://www.refworld.org/docid/55eebcfd4.html [November 7, 2016].

Katz, V.S. (2014). *Kids in the Middle: How Children of Immigrants Negotiate Community Interactions for Their Families.* New Brunswick, NJ: Rutgers University Press.

Krogstad, J.M., and Keegan, M. (2015). *From Germany to Mexico: How America's Source of Immigrants Has Changed over a Century.* Washington, DC: Pew Research Center.

Landale, N.S., Thomas, K.J., and Van Hook, J. (2011). The living arrangements of children of immigrants. *The Future of Children, 21*(1), 43-70.

Lavadenz, M. (2008). Visibly hidden: Language, culture, and identity of Central Americans in Los Angeles. *Association of Mexican American Educators Journal, 2*(1), 16-26.

Lee, J., and Zhou, M. (2015). *The Asian American Achievement Paradox*. New York: Russell Sage Foundation.

Levitt, P., and Waters, M.C. (2002). *The Changing Face of Home: The Transnational Lives of the Second Generation*. New York: Russell Sage Foundation.

Martin, D.C., and Yankay, J.E. (2014). *Refugees and Asylees: 2013*. Washington, DC: Office of Immigration Statistics.

Martin, P.L., and Midgley, E. (2006). Immigration: Shaping and reshaping America. *Population Bulletin, 61*(4).

Massey, D.S. (1999). Why does immigration occur?: A theoretical synthesis. In C. Hirschman, P. Kasinitz, and J. DeWind (Eds.), *The Handbook of Immigration Migration* (pp. 34-52). New York: Russell Sage Foundation.

Massey, D.S. (2008). *New Faces in New Places: The Changing Geography of American Immigration*. New York: Russell Sage Foundation.

Migration Information Source. (2009). *Country Data on Immigration*. Available: http://www.migrationpolicy.org [May 2017].

Migration Policy Institute. (2014). *Select Diaspora Populations in the United States: The Mexican Diaspora*. Washington, DC: Migration Policy Institute.

Mitchell, C. (2015). *White House, Ed. Dept. Partner to Address Needs of Black English-Language Learners*. Available: http://blogs.edweek.org/edweek/learning-the-language/2015/10/number_of_black_english-langua.html [June 21, 2016].

Mouw, T., Chavez, S., Edelblute, H., and Verdery, A. (2014). Binational social networks and assimilation: A test of the importance of transnationalism. *Social Problems, 61*(3), 329-359.

National Center for Homeless Education (2015). *Federal Data Summary School Years 2011-12 to 2013-14: Educating Homeless Children*. Available: http://center.serve.org/nche/downloads/data-comp-1112-1314.pdf [January 5, 2017].

National Academies of Sciences, Engineering, and Medicine. (2015). *The Integration of Immigrants into American Society*. Washington, DC: The National Academies Press. doi:https://doi.org/10.17226/21746.

Nesteruk, O. (2010). Heritage language maintenance and loss among the children of Eastern European immigrants in the United States. *Journal of Multilingual and Multicultural Development, 31*(3), 271-286.

Nesteruk, O., and Marks, L.D. (2011). Parenting in immigration: Experiences of mothers and fathers from Eastern Europe raising children in the United States. *Journal of Comparative Family Studies, 42*(6), 809-825.

Nicholls, W. (2013). *The Dreamers: How the Undocumented Youth Movement Transformed the Immigrant Rights Debate*. Palo Alto, CA: Stanford University Press.

Niehaus, K., and Adelson, J.L. (2013). Self-concept and native language background: A study of measurement invariance and cross-group comparisons in third grade. *Journal of Educational Psychology, 105*(1), 226.

Norris, T., Vines, P.L., and Hoeffel, E.M. (2012). *The American Indian and Alaska Native Population: 2010*. Washington, DC: U.S. Department of Commerce, Economics and Statistics Administration, U.S. Census Bureau.

O'Hare, W.P., Mayol-Garcia, Y., Wildsmith E., and Torres, A. 2016. *The Invisible Ones: How Latino Children Are Left Out of Our Nation's Census Count*. Bethesda, MD: Child Trends Hispanic Institute and the National Association of Latino Elected and Appointed Officials Education Fund.

Orellana, M.F., Thorne, B., Chee, A., and Lam, W.S.E. (2001). Transnational childhoods: The participation of children in processes of family migration. *Social Problems, 48*(4), 572-591.

Passel, J.S. (2006). *Size and Characteristics of the Unauthorized Migrant Population in the U.S.* Washington, DC: Pew Hispanic Center.

Passel, J.S., and Cohn, D. (2011). *Unauthorized Immigrant Population: National and State Trends, 2010.* Washington, DC: Pew Hispanic Center.

Passel, J.S., and Cohn, D. (2014). *Unauthorized Immigrant Totals Rise in 7 States, Fall in 14: Decline in Those from Mexico Fuels Most State Decreases.* Washington, DC: Pew Research Center Hispanic Trends.

Passel, J.S., and Cohn, D. (2016). *Unauthorized Immigrant Population Stable for a Half a Decade.* Washington, DC: Pew Research Center.

Pérez, Z.J. (2014). *Removing Barriers to Higher Education for Undocumented Students.* Washington, DC: Center for American Progress. Available: https://cdn.americanprogress.org/wp-content/uploads/2014/12/UndocHigherEd-report2.pdf [March 21, 2017].

Pew Hispanic Center. (2014). *Unauthorized Immigrant Population Trends for States, Birth Countries and Regions.* Available: http://www.pewhispanic.org/2014/12/11/unauthorized-trends [June 21, 2016].

Pew Research Center. (2012). *The Rise of Asian Americans.* Washington, DC: Pew Research Center Social & Demographic Trends. Available: http://www.pewsocialtrends.org/files/2012/06/SDT-Rise-of-Asian-Americans.pdf [June 20, 2016].

Rafferty, Y. (1998). Meeting the educational needs of homeless children. *Educational Leadership, 55*(4), 48-53.

Rodriguez, C.E. (2008). *Latinas/os in the United States: Changing the Face of America.* Berlin, Germany: Springer Science & Business Media.

Ruiz Soto, A.G., Hooker, S., and Batalova, J. (2015). *Top Languages Spoken by English Language Learners Nationally and by State.* Washington, DC: Migration Policy Institute.

Rumbaut, R.G. (1994). Origins and destinies: Immigration to the United States since World War II. *Sociological Forum, 9*(4), 583-621.

Rumbaut, R. (2004). Ages, life stages, and generations cohorts: Decomposing the immigrant first and second generations in the United States. *International Migration Review, 38*(3), 1160-1205.

Rumbaut, R.G., and Massey, D.S. (2013). Immigration & language diversity in the United States. *Daedalus, 142*(3), 141-154.

Saint Paul Public Schools Office of Accountability. (2015). *Asian Students in Saint Paul Public Schools.* Presentation for Committee of the Board. Saint Paul: Saint Paul Public Schools.

Siebens, J., and Julian, T. (2011). Native North American Languages spoken at home in the United States and Puerto Rico: 2006–2010. *American Community Services Briefs, 10*(10).

Singer, A. (2004). *The Rise of New Immigrant Gateways.* Washington, DC: Brookings Institution Press.

Singer, A. (2015). *Metropolitan Immigrant Gateways Revisited, 2014.* Washington, DC: Brookings Institution Press.

Smith, R. (2005). *Mexican New York: Transnational Lives of New Immigrants.* Oakland: University of California Press.

Stanton-Salazar, R.D. (2001). *Manufacturing Hope and Despair: The School and Kin Support Networks of U.S.-Mexican Youth.* New York: Teachers College Press.

Suárez-Orozco, C., and Suárez-Orozco, M.M. (2001). *Children of Immigration.* Cambridge, MA: Harvard University Press.

Suárez-Orozco, C., Gaytán, F.X., Bang, H.J., Pakes, J., O'Connor, E., and Rhodes, J. (2010). Academic trajectories of newcomer immigrant youth. *Developmental Psychology, 46*(3), 602.

Suárez-Orozco, C., Bang, H.J., and Kim, H.Y. (2011). I felt like my heart was staying behind: Psychological implications of family separations and reunifications for immigrant youth. *Journal of Adolescent Research, 26*(2), 222-257.

Suárez-Orozco, C., and Yoshikawa, H. (2013). Undocumented status: Implications for child development, policy, and ethical research. In M.G. Hernandez, J. Nguyen, C.L. Saetermoe, and C. Suárez-Orozco (Eds.), *Frameworks and Ethics for Research with Immigrants: New Directions in Child and Adolescent Development* (pp. 61-78). San Francisco, CA: Jossey-Bass.

Thomas, K.J. (2010). Household context, generational status, and English proficiency among the children of African immigrants in the United States. *International Migration Review, 44*(1), 142-172.

Thomas, K.J. (2011a). Familial influences on poverty among young children in black immigrant, U.S.-born black, and nonblack immigrant families. *Demography, 48*(2), 437-460.

Thomas, K.J. (2011b). Socio-demographic determinants of language transition among the children of French- and Spanish-Caribbean immigrants in the U.S. *Journal of Ethnic and Migration Studies, 37*(4), 543-559.

Thomas, K.J. (2011c). What explains the increasing trend in African emigration to the U.S.? *International Migration Review, 45*(1), 3-28.

Thomas, K.J. (2012). *A Demographic Profile of Black Caribbean Immigrants in the United States*. Washington, DC: Migration Policy Institute.

United We Dream. (2015). *Toolbox*. Available: http://unitedwedream.org/toolbox [November 6, 2016].

Urban Institute. (2011). *The Urban Institute Children of Immigrants Data Tool*. Available: http://datatool.urban.org/charts/datatool/pages.cfm [November 18, 2016].

Uro, G., and Barrio, A. (2013). *English Language Learners in America's Great City Schools: Demographics, Achievement, and Staffing*. Washington, DC: Council of the Great City Schools.

U.S. Census Bureau. (2015). *2011-2015 American Community Survey 5-Year Estimates*. Available: https://factfinder.census.gov/faces/tableservices/jsf/pages/productview.xhtml?src=CF [March 15, 2017].

U.S. Department of Education. (2016). *Tools and Resources for Identifying All English Learners*. Available: https://www2.ed.gov/about/offices/list/oela/english-learner-toolkit/chap1.pdf [January 5, 2017].

U.S. Department of Homeland Security. (2016). *Southwest Border Unaccompanied Alien Children Statistics FY 2015*. Available: https://www.cbp.gov/newsroom/stats/southwest-border-unaccompanied-children/fy-2015 [June 21, 2016].

Wasem, R.E. (2009). *Cuban Migration to the United States: Policy and Trends*. U.S. Congressional Research Service Report 7-5700. Available: www.crs.gov R40566 [February 2017].

Waters, J.L. (2002). Flexible families: "Astronaut" households and the experiences of lone mothers in Vancouver, British Columbia. *Social and Cultural Geography, 3*(2), 117-134.

Waters, J.L. (2003). Satellite kids in Vancouver. In M. Charney, B. HYeoh, and T.C. Kiong (Eds.), *Asian Migrants and Education* (pp. 165-184). Dordrecht, the Netherlands: Kluwer.

Winsler, A., Burchinal, M.R., Tien, H.-C., Peisner-Feinberg, E., Espinosa, L., Castro, D.C., LaForett, D.R., Kim, Y.K., and De Feyter, J. (2014). Early development among dual language learners: The roles of language use at home, maternal immigration, country of origin, and socio-demographic variables. *Early Childhood Research Quarterly, 29*(4), 750-764.

Wood, D. (2003). Effect of child and family poverty on child health in the United States. *Pediatrics, 112*(Suppl. 3), 707-711.

Yoshikawa, H., and Kalil, A. (2011). The effects of parental undocumented status on the developmental contexts of young children in immigrant families. *Child Development Perspectives, 5*(4), 291-297.

Zong, J., and Batalova, J. (2016). *Frequently Requested Statistics on Immigrants and Immigration in the United States.* Washington, DC: Migration Policy Institute. Available: http://www.migrationpolicy.org/article/frequently-requested-statistics-immigrants-and-immigration-united-states [November 6, 2016].

Zúñiga, V. (2013). Migrantes internacionales en las escuelas Mexicanas: Desafíos actuales y futuros de política educativa. *Sinéctica, 40,* 1-12.

Zúñiga, V., and Hamann, E.T. (2009). Sojourners in Mexico with U.S. school experience: A new taxonomy for transnational students. *Comparative Education Review, 53*(3), 329-353.

Zúñiga, V., and Hernández-Leon, R. (2005). *New Destinations: Mexican Immigration in the United States.* New York: Russell Sage Foundation.

4

Dual Language Learners: Capacities and Influences on Language Development

The goals of this chapter are twofold. The first is to review the evidence on young children's underlying capacity for dual language development. Understanding young children's capacity for dual language learning is critical for having evidence-based expectations that shape parents' and other caregivers' decisions about whether and how to raise children bilingually. These findings can also inform families, educators, education administrators, health professionals, and policy makers about the most advantageous learning environments for dual language learners (DLLs)[1] that will enhance their opportunities to learn the language (English) that is essential for their educational success in the United States. Multiple sources of evidence are relevant to this issue. This evidence includes studies with international samples outside of the United States and samples that varied widely in socioeconomic status, and studies with experimental, quasi-experimental, and correlational designs. In most of these studies, the children began learning their two languages from birth or before the age of 3. Although the samples from these studies may not be representative of the U.S. population of DLLs, they make a strong case for the human potential to learn more than one language and offer a picture of what is possible for DLLs in the United States.

The second goal of this chapter is to examine the factors that may influence the full expression of this capacity among DLLs in the United States.

---

[1] As indicated in Chapter 1 (see Box 1-1), the term "dual language learner (DLL)" is used in this report to refer to children birth to age 5 in their homes, communities, or early care and education (ECE) programs.

Not all DLLs in the United States realize the potential of becoming fully proficient in English and their home language, as indicated by the striking variation among children in their trajectories and ultimate levels of achievement in their first (L1) and second (L2) languages. Thus, the second part of the chapter identifies the factors that help explain individual differences in the development of children's language competencies. Three general sources of evidence were brought to bear on this issue. First were studies focused on the factors that benefit the learning of both L1 and L2. Second were correlational studies of children who began to learn a second language at different ages (specifically, before age 3 or after age 5). Most of these studies involved children who spoke a language other than English at home and began to learn English when they entered preschool or child care centers. A third source of evidence was experimental studies of monolingual children (mainly English speakers) learning a foreign language. Five broad categories of explanatory factors emerged from this literature: (1) timing of second language learning; (2) development of the home language; (3) the quantity and quality of language input; (4) cross-linguistic influences of L1 on L2 learning; and (5) broader sociocultural influences (beyond the quantity and quality of language experienced by children), including family socioeconomic status, school, and community contexts, that affect children's opportunities to learn English and maintain their L1 and cultural heritage.

THE UNIVERSAL CAPACITY FOR DUAL LANGUAGE LEARNING

This section reviews research on children's underlying capacity for dual language development from birth to 5 years of age. It begins with a review of research that has examined early stages in the development of critical components of dual language development: (1) language discrimination and speech perception; (2) early word learning, encompassing phonotactics (sounds), word segmentation and recognition, and associative word learning; (3) early vocabulary development; and (4) morphosyntactic[2] development. Examining infants' and toddlers' language development during their early formative years gives insights into their capacity for learning language at the very outset. The section then illustrates DLLs' capacity for adaptation and flexibility in response to the challenges of dual language learning

---

[2]Morphosyntax, also referred to as grammar, describes how words are combined to make larger units such as phrases and sentences (e.g., the order in which subjects, verbs, and objects should appear in order to be correct in a language). It also describes how words are formed in a language (e.g., how nouns are pluralized, how verbs indicate past or present tense). Taken together, rules of morphology and syntax describe what is a well-formed sentence. Morphosyntactic rules are different for different languages. Morphosyntactic development refers to children's and adults' acquisition of the morphosyntactic rules or constraints that operate on the languages they are learning.

by reviewing research on communicative and cognitive aspects of their development.

Language Discrimination and Speech Perception

DLLs' ability to discriminate among languages early in development is an important foundation for building two, or more, linguistic systems (Bosch and Sebastián-Gallés, 1997; see also Sebastián-Gallés, 2010, for a review of these studies). Language discrimination abilities allow the learner to separate different languages and connect the structural and functional properties of each (such as its sounds, words, and grammatical constraints). In addition, the ability to process speech sounds at 7 months of age correlates with the size of children's vocabulary during the second year of life in both monolinguals (Kuhl, 2009; Tsao et al., 2004) and DLLs (Silvén et al., 2014). Thus, it is important to understand these early building blocks of dual language learning as precursors of subsequent and more complex aspects of language development.

Studies have shown that DLL infants have the language discrimination abilities they need to differentiate between the two languages they hear in their environments. When given the choice to listen to English or Tagalog, for example, neonates (ages 0 to 5 days) who had been exposed only to English listened to English more than Tagalog (Byers-Heinlein et al., 2010) because English was familiar to them and therefore preferred. In contrast, infants who had been exposed to both English and Tagalog during pregnancy and since birth could discriminate between the two languages and listened to both equally, indicating that both were familiar to them. Early discrimination abilities have likewise been documented in infants learning a different language combination—Spanish and Catalan—two languages that are much more similar to one another than English and Tagalog (Bosch and Sebastián-Gallés, 2001).

Other studies have shown that DLL infants may have enhanced language discrimination abilities. Monolinguals are unable to discriminate between languages that are rhythmically similar (e.g., Dutch and British English or Spanish and Italian) before 5 months of age (Bosch and Sebastián-Gallés, 2000; Nazzi et al., 2000), whereas bilingual infants have been found to distinguish between rhythmically similar languages (such as Spanish or Catalan) at 4.5 months of age (Bosch and Sebastián-Gallés, 1997). Rhythmic differences are a useful starting point for identifying other properties of the languages being heard. DLLs, for instance, use the rhythmic properties of their two languages to begin building the vocabularies and grammars of those languages (Gervain and Werker, 2013a). To take an example, languages differ in basic word order. The two most common word orders are subject-verb-object, in which the verb precedes the object (*the cat chased the dog*) and subject-object-verb, in which the object precedes the verb (*the cat the dog chased*). Word order and prosody or rhythm are correlated, and infants can use the cues of prosodic prominence to figure out word order in their developing languages. One study found that infants 7 months of age who were learning two languages with different word orders could exploit the prosodic differences in the two languages to segment noun phrases from continuous speech (Gervain and Werker, 2013a). These findings attest to the capacity of DLLs to use cues in language input to abstract higher-order features of language.

Infants also are adept at learning the specific sounds and sound sequences of language. Languages differ in the sounds used to construct words and convey meaning. Sounds that carry meaning in individual words, such as /l/ and /r/ in English, are called phonemes; using /l/ instead of /r/ changes the meaning of the word (e.g., *lot* and *rot*). These sounds are not phonemic in Japanese, so that interchanging /l/ and/r/ when speaking Japanese does not change the meaning of individual words. Extensive research has shown that infants begin life with the ability to discriminate many consonant and vowel sounds found in the world's languages, regardless of their experience with specific languages (e.g., Trehub, 1976; Werker and Tees, 1984). These findings point to an important capacity for DLLs to discriminate many of the sound segments they need to construct two languages.

Experience does matter, however. Researchers have found that infants' ability to discriminate speech sounds becomes language-specific during the second half of the first year of life (at about 6-9 months of age) (Gervain and Werker, 2013b; Kuhl et al., 2006). They continue to discriminate acoustic contrasts that are phonemic in their native language after this age, but gradually begin to lose the ability to discriminate contrasts that are not phonemic in that language. Monolingual infants perceive language-specific vowel contrasts by 6-8 months of age (Bosch and Sebastián-Gallés, 2003; Kuhl et al., 1992) and consonant contrasts somewhat later, by 10-12 months of age (Werker and Tees, 1984). DLLs go through a similar reorganization in speech perception at roughly the same ages (Albareda-Castellot et al., 2011; Burns et al., 2007; Sundara et al., 2008; Vihman et al., 2007).

Not all phonemic contrasts are equally easy to learn, and as a result, DLL infants whose languages contain contrasts that are difficult to discriminate may take longer than monolinguals to discriminate some of the contrasts in the languages they are learning. Sebastián-Gallés and Bosch (2002) explored the ability of monolingual and bilingual infant learners of Spanish and Catalan with respect to the Catalan-specific contrast /e-ɛ/, as in English "late" and "let" (Sebastián-Gallés and Bosch, 2002). This phonetic contrast is not phonemic in Spanish, and adult Spanish speakers thus have difficulty perceiving it (Sebastián-Gallés and Bosch, 2002). The authors found that infants in all three language groups (monolingual in each language and bilingual) could distinguish the Catalan contrast at 4 months, whereas only the monolingual Catalan learners could discriminate the contrast at 8 months. The bilingual infants could discriminate this contrast a bit later, at 12 months of age. The researchers suggest as an explanation for their results that the Spanish-Catalan bilingual infants may have treated the /e- / contrast in Catalan as a single category because it is a single phonemic category in Spanish. As a result, they required more time and possibly more input to disentangle the subtle distributional properties of these sounds in Catalan and Spanish. The important point here is that the perceptual performance of DLL infants may differ from that of monolinguals because of competing phonetic properties of their two languages, which can be quite subtle at times and may thus require more exposure to learn.

At the same time, neuroimaging evidence indicates that the strategies used by DLLs may differ in kind or degree from those used by their monolingual counterparts insofar as bilingual and monolingual toddlers show different patterns of brain activity during performance of the same task (Conboy and Mills, 2006; Ferjan Ramirez et al., 2016; Shafer et al., 2011). Conboy and Mills (2006) used event-related potential (ERP) techniques to study the neural responses of bilingual Spanish-English toddlers ages 19-22 months during a task in which they listened to known and unknown words (Conboy and Mills, 2006). The DLL and monolingual toddlers exhibited different patterns of activation, with the DLLs showing relatively greater activation in the right hemisphere, as well as ERP effects that were distributed more broadly across the brain. These findings illustrate that experience with language shapes "the organization of brain activity for language processing" (Conboy, 2013, p. 19), which in turn may alter the way in which the brain processes and acquires language in future stages of development.

The developments reviewed to this point provide infants with fundamental building blocks for continued language development. The next sections review what research reveals about how they use those building blocks to construct larger and more complex units of language—the sound combinations, words, and grammars of their languages.

Early Word Learning

Three different but interrelated lines of research are relevant to early word learning in DLL infants: phonotactics, word segmentation and recognition, and associative word learning. Research in these domains is relatively limited, and thus the evidence is still emerging. Nevertheless, a coherent understanding of this stage of dual language learning is already beginning to emerge, one that emphasizes processes common to all language learners and those reflecting variability linked to unique features of dual language learning.

Phonotactics

Languages differ not only in their phonemic inventories, as noted earlier, but also in the sequences of phonemes they use to construct words. This property is referred to as phonotactics—the permissible sequences of sounds in a given language. Infants learn the sound sequences of their languages from exposure to those languages over time. Learning the phonotactic regularities of two languages early in development does not appear to be more challenging than learning those of only one. Sebastián-Gallés and Bosch (2002), for example, found that 10-month-old monolingual Catalan infants preferred listening to Catalan-sounding pseudowords that used Catalan phonotactics over Spanish words that did not use Catalan phonotactics. The Catalan-dominant bilinguals also preferred listening to the Catalan pseudowords, as expected. The Spanish-dominant bilinguals exhibited a mild preference for words that conformed to Catalan phonotactics over words that violated Spanish phonotactic constraints. And the Spanish monolinguals exhibited no preference, as would be expected since the contrast was specific to Catalan. These findings indicate that dual language learning does not compromise infants' ability to learn the phonotactic constraints of a language or to recognize words (Vihman et al., 2007), and that the amount of language exposure or relative language proficiency can influence DLLs' development of phonotactic knowledge (see also Garcia-Sierra et al., 2011).

Word Segmentation and Recognition

A number of researchers have examined DLL infants' ability to extract words from continuous speech. Doing so is difficult for all infants since there are no clear acoustic cues that signal the beginnings and endings of words when they occur in continuous speech, so infants must know the phonotactic regularities of their language(s). In a study of DLL infants learning Spanish and Catalan and monolingual infants learning Spanish or Catalan, infants preferred familiar to new words, indicating that they perceived differences between the two (Bosch et al., 2013). Both dual and monolingual language groups exhibited more advanced segmentation abilities at 8 months (namely, a novelty effect) than at 6 months (a familiarity effect). French-English dual language 8-month-old infants also were able to segment familiar words from both languages in continuous speech (Polka and Sundara, 2003).

At the same time, evidence suggests that it takes time for children to acquire stable detailed representations of the sounds that make up words and, in some instances, DLLs may take longer to do so than monolingual learners. Ramon-Casas and colleagues (2009) examined whether 18-month-old bilingual Catalan-Spanish, monolingual Spanish, and monolingual Catalan children could recognize mispronounced words. Critically, the mispronounced words were created by exchanging the Catalan-specific /I-ɛ/ contrast in some words, a contrast that does not exist in Spanish, thereby producing target words such as *fish* and *fesh* that should sound like two different words in Catalan but like the same word in Spanish. They found that the Catalan monolinguals more often recognized the correctly pronounced target word (*fish*), suggesting that they perceived the mispronunciation. In contrast, neither the monolingual Spanish children nor the Spanish-Catalan bilinguals displayed differential recognition of the correctly and incorrectly pronounced word. These results suggest that bilinguals may take longer than monolinguals to learn certain phonological properties of one of their two languages because the task is more complex than that faced by monolingual children. It may be that DLLs take longer than monolinguals to establish stable phonological representations of word forms because they are exposed to less input in each language or to non-native input in one or both of their languages.

Associative Word Learning

Further insights into infants' early word-learning capacities come from studies that have examined their ability to associate novel words with referents or objects. To examine young learners' associative word learning ability, Byers-Heinlein and colleagues (2013) examined 12- and 14-month old DLLs and monolingual infants on a word-learning task involving new words that differed phonetically in several ways (e.g., *lif* and *neem* differ in all three of their phonemes). The monolingual participants were from English-speaking families, while the DLL participants had been exposed to English and another language from birth. The children were first exposed to novel word-object pairings several times—for example, the word *lif* was presented with a novel object shaped like a molecule, and the word *neem* was presented with a novel object shaped like a crown. During the test phase, following the familiarization phase, the children were presented with either the same word-object pairing or a switched pair in which a familiar word was shown with another object. Infants' differential looking times during the switched and nonswitched trials is considered evidence that they have learned the new word-object pair, and presumably the meaning of the new word. The findings of this study suggest that neither the monolingual nor DLL infants detected a violation of the previous word-object pairings at 12 months of age, but both groups succeeded, with no difference in performance between them, at 14 months of age.

Learning to associate objects with novel words comprised of minimal pairs—words that differ by only one phoneme, such as the pair /bih/ and

/dih/, is more difficult. Fennel and colleagues (2007) found that infants who were learning one language could learn associations between new words comprised of minimal pairs and their referents at 17 months of age, whereas DLLs were able to learn these associations only at 20 months of age, suggesting that they needed more time to succeed at this difficult task. Further research by Fennell and Byers-Heinlein (2014), as well as Mattock and colleagues (2010), revealed that DLLs could succeed at this demanding task at the earlier age (17 months) when the sounds were produced by bilingual speakers. In contrast, 17-month-old monolingual children were unable to learn novel minimal pairs of words produced by bilingual speakers. These findings illustrate that the experimental conditions for studying DLLs may not always match the conditions in which the children have actually learned and used language, and that the language environment experienced by DLLs is not simply the sum of two monolingual environments. There may be qualitative differences between the input to which bilinguals are exposed in each language and the input from monolingual speakers of the corresponding languages.

There is evidence that DLL infants demonstrate adaptability when learning two languages; for example, they are more likely than their monolingual counterparts to accept mispronounced words since they may be spoken by non-native speakers, and they are able to use visual information about mouth shape to discriminate languages for an extended period in development (Werker, 2012). Additional evidence on the adaptable strategies used by DLLs to learn language comes from research examining the use of the "mutual exclusivity" constraint. Mutual exclusivity is thought to help monolingual children in word learning such that when they hear a new word, they tend to associate it with a novel object rather than an object for which they already have a label. This has been shown experimentally in 17-month-old monolingual infants and young children (e.g., Halberda, 2003; Markman, 1989). Yet while mutual exclusivity may be a useful heuristic for learning one language, where objects are often associated with only one common label, this is not the case for children learning more than one language, where objects usually have more than one label. A number of studies of DLLs have shown that they are less likely than their monolingual counterparts to apply the mutual exclusivity constraint in experimental situations (e.g., Bosch and Ramon-Casas, 2014; Byers-Heinlein and Werker, 2009; Houston-Price et al., 2010). Analyses of DLLs' natural language use also indicate that they often have labels in both languages for the same objects (Pearson et al., 1993), in violation of the mutual exclusivity constraint. That children learning more than one language do not honor the mutual exclusivity constraint also shows how their pattern of development is different from that of monolingual learners.

Early Vocabulary Development

When simultaneous DLLs' scores on standardized vocabulary measures and/or parent report measures are examined separately, they often are lower than those of monolingual children learning only one of the languages, even after controlling for socioeconomic factors (Hoff et al., 2012, discussed in greater detail later). However, they are at the same level as or higher than the scores of monolinguals when both languages are considered together. On their own, these results give the impression that DLLs have reduced capacity for vocabulary learning. However, assessing one language of DLLs does not provide a complete picture of their vocabulary knowledge. In a landmark study of Spanish-English bilingual children in the United States (8-30 months of age; average socioeconomic status 2.2 on a 5-point scale, with 1 being highest), Pearson and colleagues (1993) found no differences between DLL and monolingual children when the DLLs were given credit for knowing words in both languages, or what is referred to as conceptual vocabulary.[3] Hoff and colleagues (2012) also examined the vocabulary and grammatical development of Spanish-English bilingual infants and toddlers in the United States. Their study included 47 Spanish-English bilingual children and 56 monolingual English-speaking children from high socio-economic environments. Overall, they found that the monolingual children scored higher than the bilingual children on both English vocabulary and grammar indices from the MacArthur Communication Development Index when each language was considered separately. In contrast to the single-language results, however, there were no significant differences between the two groups of children when total vocabulary in English and Spanish was calculated and when combinatorial speech in both languages was assessed. These results have been replicated by researchers around the world working with different language combinations and children at different socioeconomic levels (see De Houwer, 2009, for a review).

Morphosyntactic Development

Evidence that DLLs exhibit the same language-specific and appropriate grammatical knowledge as monolinguals at similar ages would provide additional evidence that DLLs have the capacity to acquire two languages without jeopardizing the development of either. This section reviews studies on the grammatical development of DLLs from approximately 2 to 5 years of age. The reviewed research addresses the following three interrelated questions: (1) Do DLLs acquire separate grammatical systems? (2) Do the

---

[3]Scoring for conceptual vocabulary gives credit for each word that refers to a different concept regardless of the language of that word; words that refer to the same concept are counted only once.

grammars of DLLs exhibit the same developmental patterns as those of children learning only one language? and (3) Is the rate of grammatical development affected by the acquisition of two languages?

Do DLLs Acquire Separate Grammatical Systems?

An early and predominant issue in research on the grammatical development of DLLs is whether they acquire differentiated grammatical systems and if so, how early in development this is evident (Genesee, 1989). There is, in fact, consensus among researchers that DLLs acquire separate grammatical systems for the most part and under most circumstances (see De Houwer [2009, App. G, p. 350], for a synopsis of studies that support this view) and that this is evident from the earliest stages of grammatical development.

One source of evidence that led researchers to think initially that DLLs were "mixing up" their languages is the phenomenon known as *code switching* (sometimes called *code mixing*).[4] When DLLs code switch (that is, use elements from their two languages in the same utterances), they usually do so in ways that respect the grammatical constraints of each language (see Genesee, 2002, for a review). For example, if a developing Spanish-English DLL child uses words from English when speaking with a Spanish-speaking person, the English words will be inserted into a Spanish grammatical phrase so that the word order of Spanish is respected. DLLs also usually avoid affixing grammatical morphemes (the smallest unit of meaning in a language) from one language to words in the other language. Such grammatically constrained code switching is observed as soon as DLLs begin combining words into simple two-word utterances. That DLL children code switch in this way attests to their having acquired the underlying grammatical constraints of the two languages.

Further evidence that DLLs have separate grammars is that during the two-word and multiword stage of their language development, they produce many more single-language than mixed-language utterances (De Houwer, 2009; Genesee et al., 1995; Schelletter et al., 2001). If DLLs were, in fact, acquiring undifferentiated grammatical systems, the majority of their utterances would be expected to violate the constraints of one or both languages, as predicted by Volterra and Taeschner (1978), because they would not have reached the stage in development when differentiation of the two grammars had occurred. The neurolinguistic evidence is also consistent with these conclusions (Kovelman et al., 2008b).

---

[4]Researchers who study language development and use in bilingual children tend to use the term code mixing.

Do the Grammars of DLLs Exhibit the Same Developmental Patterns as Those of Children Learning Only One Language?

Studies of the grammatical development of DLLs indicate that for the most part, they acquire language-specific and appropriate patterns in each language and that these are the same patterns exhibited by monolinguals, other things being equal (see De Houwer [2011] for a review). With respect to general patterns of morphosyntactic development, DLLs, like young monolingual learners, go through one-word, two-word, and then multiword stages of development, and they do so at approximately the same ages. It has been well established that monolingual children begin to produce two-word combinations after they have acquired about 200 words (e.g., see Bloom, 1993; Hoff et al., 2012; Marchman and Bates, 1994); the same link between vocabulary size and early word combinations is seen in DLLs (David and Li, 2004; Junker and Stockman, 2002; Patterson, 1998). There is also a correlation between vocabulary size and overall complexity of utterances produced by both DLL and monolingual children (Marchman et al., 2004).

With respect to specific aspects of grammar, it has been found that, at a given age or mean length of utterance (MLU),[5] DLL and monolingual children learning the same languages usually demonstrate knowledge of the same grammatical structures and constraints (see De Houwer [2011] for a review of relevant studies). Spanish-English DLLs, for example, exhibit language-specific and appropriate use of predicates and closed-class words[6] in both languages (Conboy and Thal, 2006). Spanish-English DLLs and same-age typically developing monolingual English learners in the United States do not differ on finite verb accuracy and use of obligatory overt subjects in English (mean age 5 years, 7 months; range 4 years, 5 months to 6 years, 5 months) (Gutiérrez-Clellen et al., 2008). In short, DLLs and young monolinguals show the same general developmental patterns and relationships.

Is the Rate of Grammatical Development Affected by the Acquisition of Two Languages?

When milestones in grammatical development are examined and when adequate amounts of exposure to each language are available to the learner,

---

[5] MLU is the average number of words or morphemes in a stretch of language use, often 100 words. It is generally interpreted as an indicator of level of grammatical development in young learners.

[6] Function or closed-class words are words such as prepositions, conjunctions, articles, and auxiliaries; these words play an important role in establishing relationships between words in a sentence, but they lack referential meaning.

there is no evidence that DLLs are likely to fall behind norms established for monolingual learners. This finding holds for indices such as MLU (Paradis and Genesee, 1996); emergence of two-word combinations (around 2 years of age), noted previously; production of short sentences with some inflectional morphemes (around 30-36 months of age); and production of complex utterances/sentences (around 48 months of age) (see De Houwer [2009, p. 37] for a summary of language development milestones from birth to age 5). The robust similarity in the emergence of these milestones in monolingual children and DLLs learning different language combinations implies a universal, underlying human capacity to learn two languages as easily as one.

Communicative and Cognitive Capacity of Dual Language Learners

Additional evidence for DLLs' capacity for learning more than one language early in development comes from studies that have examined their communicative competence using two languages and their cognitive flexibility.

Communicative Competence

DLLs demonstrate impressive capacity to manage their two languages when communicating with others. Systematic examination of this issue has demonstrated that even very young DLLs use their two languages in communicatively appropriate and competent ways—they differentiate use of each language according to the language known or preferred by the people to whom they are speaking. Research on this question has examined DLLs in early stages of verbal development when they are producing mainly one- and two-word utterances, because it is during this stage of development that communication might be expected to be most challenging. Genesee and colleagues (1995) studied 2-year-old children from varied socioeconomic backgrounds who were acquiring French and English simultaneously from their parents, who used the one parent/one language pattern with their children. They found that the children were able to use the appropriate language with each parent. In a follow-up study, English-French DLLs (average age of 2 years, 2 months) were able to use their languages appropriately with strangers, indicating that DLLs' ability to use their two languages differentially and appropriately did not depend on prior experiences with particular speakers and, moreover, was within their capacity from the earliest stages of development (Genesee et al., 1996).

DLLs also demonstrate impressive control over the use of their languages, even though both are still developing (Comeau et al., 2003, 2010; see Petitto et al., 2001, for similar evidence from children learning oral and sign languages simultaneously). In a quasi-experimental study, for example, 2- and 3-year-old French-English bilingual children who used the "wrong language" with a monolingual interlocutor/stranger whom they had never met before switched languages when the interlocutors indicated that they did not understand what the child had said (Comeau et al., 2007). Of particular importance, the children switched languages even when their interlocutors used a very general prompt, such as "What?," that did not indicate the source of the breakdown, indicating that managing their two languages was not a challenge. Taken together, this evidence is difficult to reconcile with concerns that early dual language learning can engender confusion.

Cognitive Flexibility

Recent evidence points to certain cognitive advantages among children (and adults) who are competent in two languages (see Baum and Titone [2014] for an overview, including opposing views, on this issue). This section briefly reviews these advantages.

Executive functioning refers to a set of cognitive abilities that allows individuals to plan, control their attention, regulate their behavior, and think flexibly (Miyake et al., 2000). It has been argued that learning and using two languages enhances executive functioning because bilinguals engage the areas of the brain (the prefrontal cortex, the inferior parietal lobule, and the basal ganglia) that are involved in reducing potential interference between their languages and ensuring the activation of the appropriate language depending upon the situation. Thus, bilinguals often exhibit a broad set of advantages that are related to the ability to control their focus of attention. These advantages include the ability to switch their focus of attention, reason about others' mental states, and reflect on the structure of language itself (Bialystok, 1999; Bialystok and Senman, 2004; Bialystok and Shapero, 2005; Bialystok et al., 2003, 2008; Carlson and Meltzoff, 2008; Costa et al., 2008; Friesen and Bialystok, 2012; Kapa and Colombo, 2013; Martin-Rhee and Bialystok, 2008; see Gordon, 2016, for a recent review) a process known as metalinguistic awareness.

A bilingual advantage in switching attention has been observed in DLL infants as young as 7 months of age who are better able than monolinguals to reorient their attention to a new location to obtain a reward (Kovács and Mehler, 2009) and 8-month-olds who, unlike their monolingual counterparts, can visually discriminate when a speaker switches from French to English (Sebastián-Gallés et al., 2012). Such advantages also have been observed in DLLs (English-Welsh) who begin to learn a second language as late as 4-6 years of age (Kalashnikova and Mattock, 2014). Bilinguals may have advantages as well in spatial and verbal working memory—other components of executive functioning—even after controlling statistically for socioeconomic status and vocabulary (e.g., Blom et al., 2014), and these effects may emerge as early as 18 months of age (Brito and Barr, 2012).

Although evidence suggests that bilinguals may exhibit an advantage in short-term memory (Morales et al., 2013), this advantage appears to be unstable and has been attributed to vocabulary size rather than bilingualism per se (e.g., Engel de Abreu et al., 2011). Moreover, advantages in visual attention and visual perception have not always been observed (Schonberg et al., 2014). In addition, a number of researchers have openly questioned whether monolinguals and bilinguals differ in their behavioral performance on cognitive control tasks (Abutalebi et al., 2012; de Bruin et al., 2015; Duñabeitia and Carreiras, 2015; Dunabeitia et al., 2014; Hernandez and Kohnert, 2015; Hilchey and Klein, 2011; Paap and Greenberg, 2013; Paap et al., 2014). In a recent meta-analysis of the cognitive advantages of bilingualism, de Bruin and colleagues (2015) suggest a bias toward publishing studies with results that support the bilingual advantage. Some evidence also suggests that cognitive control may be heritable (Friedman et al., 2008; Lee et al., 2012) and that it is related to socioeconomic status (Noble et al., 2005) and parenting style (Bernier et al., 2010), evidence that argues against the importance of bilingualism per se.

In response to suggestions of bias, researchers have sought to identify the circumstances under which bilingual advantages are observed (Baum and Titone, 2014). These advantages are observed most commonly among bilinguals who became highly proficient in both of their languages at early ages (Gordon, 2016). That a cognitive advantage may not be reported in all studies under all conditions is not surprising since the kinds of performance and reasoning examined—problem solving, planning, and divergent thinking—are likely to be influenced by multiple factors, of which bilingualism is only one. Thus, different results may be found under subtly different testing conditions and for children of different backgrounds. Moreover, it appears likely that the relationship between bilingual competence and cognitive ability is one not simply of positive or negative but of varied and complex effects. In addition to advantages, for example, there are what might be considered disadvantages associated with bilingualism. Specifically, relative to their monolingual counterparts, adult bilinguals often show slower access for words presented in isolation (Pelham and Abrams, 2014) and in phrases (Sadat et al., 2012) and lower levels of oral fluency (Portocarrero et al., 2007).

In summary, there is no evidence to indicate that use of two languages in the home during the birth to 5 period poses a risk to children's development of one or both languages. Given adequate exposure to two languages, young children can acquire full competence in both. Nonetheless, DLLs and monolinguals do not exhibit exactly the same developmental trajectories or exactly the same skills in each language. In addition to the factors discussed in the next section on influences, differences can arise because DLLs face complexities that monolingual learners do not; specifically, they are learning two or more languages with different phonological, lexical, and morphosyntactic properties that may be ambiguous or incompatible with one another. These differences are perfectly normal and typical for DLLs, even though they result in these children's looking and sounding different from monolingual children of the same age. Finally, current evidence suggests that dual language learning does not appear to pose communicative or cognitive challenges, and to the contrary, it may under some conditions enhance the child's cognitive resources.

INFLUENCES ON DUAL LANGUAGE LEARNING

Children's impressive capacity to acquire at least two languages is seen across multiple components of language, with certain sensitivities arising before birth. However, capacity does not imply competence, and there are striking individual differences among children in their trajectories and ultimate levels of achievement in their two languages. What factors explain individual differences in the development of DLLs' language competencies? This section reviews evidence that points to the following categories of influence: (1) timing of second language learning; (2) development of the home language (L1); (3) the quantity and quality of language input; (4) cross-linguistic influences of L1 on L2 learning; and (5) broad sociocultural influences, including family, socioeconomic status, school, and community contexts, that affect children's opportunities to learn English and maintain their L1 and cultural heritage. Understanding the influence of these factors on development is important for understanding DLLs and for optimizing their language learning.

Timing of Second Language Learning

Both developmentalists and the public strongly believe that there is a "critical" period for language learning, and indeed the evidence is strong that such a period exists in the case of first language learning (Lenneberg, 1967; Werker and Hensch, 2015). However, the evidence for a critical period in the case of second language learning is mixed and controversial. The literature on dual language learning uses the phrase *age of acquisition* (AoA) to refer to the learner's age when beginning to acquire an L2 (Hernandez and Li, 2007). An AoA effect is seen for L2 learning, with early exposure being consistently associated with relatively higher levels of L2 attainment relative to later exposure (Flege et al., 1995, 1999; Mackay and Flege, 2004; Munro et al., 1996). It should be noted, however, that there are individual cases in which later exposure can result in native-like proficiency on tests of English grammar (Birdsong, 1992). The facilitative effects of early exposure might be explained by the trajectory of early brain development and align with findings discussed earlier that young children have the neural capacity to learn two or more languages from birth (see Box 4-1 for further discussion). There is also evidence that age of exposure to L2 affects processing of certain components of language (phonology, morphology, and syntax) more than others (such as semantics and vocabulary) (Johnson and Newport, 1989; Mitchell et al., 2013; Weber-Fox and Neville, 1996). There continues to be debate about whether and when the capacity to fully learn an L2 begins to decline, with researchers acknowledging that there is no strict cut-off point after which it is no longer possible to acquire an L2. And, as will be reviewed in a subsequent section, DLLs' L2 proficiency (like proficiency in L1) depends to a large degree on the quantity and quality of language to which they are exposed.

BOX 4-1
Effects of Early Exposure on the Brain
of Dual Language Learners

One of the key questions concerning brain development is how exposure to two languages at an early age affects the brain signals observed. In a seminal study, Conboy and Mills (2006) presented bilingual toddlers ages 19-22 months with a set of words; the word lists were child-specific to ensure that they would contain words that were known and unknown to each child. The electrical activity associated with vocabulary was assessed using an electroencephalogram (EEG). Each child was assessed in each language to determine his or her ability and language dominance. The dominance pattern observed in each group ("high" and "low" vocabulary) led to differences in the lateral asymmetry of an early positive EEG component (P100) that is known to relate to level of vocabulary. Moreover, known and unknown words varied on brain components that occurred later as well as for the "high" and "low" vocabulary groups based on total conceptual vocabulary scores. These results show the importance of experience for brain development.

EEG evidence also supports a prolonged period of recognition of speech sounds in both languages (Garcia-Sierra et al., 2011). In this experiment, DLL infants from Texas were presented with speech sounds in both their languages. Information about the exposure to each language also was gathered within the home. Neural signatures indicating recognition of speech sounds in both languages appeared at 10-12 months, and this ability improved with age. Furthermore, infants' word production skills were related to the ability to recognize speech sounds and the amount of exposure in each language at home.

Early Versus Late Exposure

Early exposure to L2 input is consistently associated with better language skills in L2 (e.g., Dupoux et al., 2010; Meisel, 2011; Ortiz-Mantilla et al., 2010). For example, children exposed to proficient speakers in L1 and L2 before 3 years of age (simultaneous bilinguals) outperformed children with an onset of L2 exposure later than age 3 (often referred to as sequential or successive bilinguals) in morphology and phonology in both languages (Weber-Fox and Neville, 1996, 2001). Similar studies have shown better performance in reading, phonological awareness, and overall competence in both languages (Kovelman et al., 2008a). These AoA effects are especially strong in areas of phonology, morphology, and syntax—domains of language that Hernandez and Li (2007) argue rely on sensorimotor processing. In phonology, for example, late L2 learners show clear accents, even after years of speaking the L2.

Additionally, and as noted earlier, children exposed to two languages simultaneously demonstrate the same developmental trajectory in each language as that seen in monolingual children, for the most part (De Houwer, 2009), provided they have adequate exposure to each (a topic covered later in this chapter). Similarities in language development between simultaneous DLLs and monolingual children have been found in the acquisition of vocabulary and grammar and in the relations between children's vocabulary and grammatical development in each language, among other measures (Conboy and Thal, 2006; Marchman et al., 2004; Parra et al., 2011).

Neural Development and Age-of-Acquisition Effects

The benefits of early exposure to L2 for the language development of DLLs may be explained by developmental changes in the brain (see Box 4-2). When dual language learning occurs from birth to 3 years of age, the neurocognitive changes in the brain are the same or nearly so for both (or all) languages being learned. When children begin to acquire an L2 after approximately 3 years of age, however, some neural commitment to the language already learned has occurred, so the brain is not in the same state it was in earlier. In fact, magnetic resonance imaging (MRI) studies of cortical thickness show no differences in brain structure between simultaneous bilinguals (exposed to L2 before age 3) and monolinguals, whereas "late bilinguals" (those who acquired L2 after gaining proficiency in L1) had modified brain structures relative to the other two groups (Klein et al., 2014). Even a delay of 1 year may change the way the brain acquires language (Pierce et al., 2015). As a result, the processes, rates, and outcomes of learning are likely to be the same or highly similar for both languages when dual language learning occurs during infancy and toddlerhood—provided

---

BOX 4-2
Neural Foundations for Dual Language Learning

Many parts of the brain in both the left and right hemispheres are involved in language processing. These regions include the frontal lobe, which has been implicated in cognitive control and in which Broca's area is located; the temporal lobe, which contains the auditory cortex and Wernicke's area; the motor cortex; and regions within the parietal and occipital cortices. Thus, the ability to learn and understand language relies on neural mechanisms that reside in different areas of the brain and are connected via axons and dendrites (white matter[a]). Exposure (to language) plays a critical role in the development of these networks by determining which connections are created and retained (Werker and Hensch, 2015). Thus, infants are not born already "wired for" language; rather, experience establishes the wiring. The relevance of brain development to DLLs, who may not all be exposed to both of their eventual languages from birth, is that these areas develop at different ages.

The visual areas of the brain develop first and are important for joint attention and early word learning. For example, infants with larger increases in white matter within the splenium (the posterior end of the corpus callosum[b]) between 6 and 24 months of age produce more words at 24 months relative to those with smaller increases in white matter during this period (Swanson et al., 2015). The auditory sensory cortex involved in learning language sounds also develops earlier than other areas, and this may be why people who learn a second language later in life often have difficulty perceiving the sounds of a second language and speak with an accent. The frontal cortex, which is critical for planning the order in which words of a sentence are spoken, develops last. Studies have shown that less proficient bilinguals have increased activity in the prefrontal cortex related to language processing (Abutalebi, 2008; Abutalebi et al., 2008; Luk et al., 2012), suggesting that older bilingual children may recruit different brain areas than those used by younger bilinguals to perceive second language sounds. Research also shows (Hernandez and Li, 2007; Hernandez et al., 2005) that three separate factors—age of acquisition, language proficiency, and cognitive control—contribute to the brain architecture of bilingualism, and the interaction between the existing brain architecture and the environment at different ages is highly relevant to understanding dual language learning (Institute of Medicine and National Research Council, 2015).

---

[a]The white matter of the brain is composed of nerve fibers and myelin, a fatty sheath that surrounds the nerve fiber.
[b]A broad band of nerve fibers joining the two hemispheres of the brain.

---

learners experience adequate exposure to each language—in contrast to L2 exposure that occurs after 3 years of age (Pierce et al., 2015).

In particular, neural systems crucial for sensorimotor learning and coordination undergo rapid organization and reorganization early in life (Hernandez and Li, 2007) and may be responsible for declines in plasticity that result in difficulty forming complex mappings later in life (Bates, 1999; Bates et al., 1997; Hensch, 2004; Pickett et al., 1998). Rates of synaptogenesis[7] and pruning[8] occur earlier in the sensory cortices that process speech sounds than in the "higher" brain networks involved in combining words into sentences. Early and rapid changes to sensorimotor systems may be important to language since the articulation of speech sounds is a sensorimotor process. A child's developing skills in L1 and L2 pronunciation require precise control and temporal coordination of articulatory actions in the speech apparatus (tongue, lips, jaw, larynx, etc.) (Hernandez and Li, 2007).

Finally, simultaneous and successive bilinguals differ in neural circuitry between the left and right regions of the brain and among brain areas involved in language control (Berken et al., 2016). Specifically, earlier AoA for an L2 leads to stronger functional connectivity, which may allow simultaneous bilinguals to regulate the two competing language systems efficiently (Abutalebi and Green, 2007; Green, 1998; Stocco et al., 2014), thereby leading to more efficient language control networks. In contrast, late L2 onset means learning of language occurs after networks have been established, and the individual must rely on modifications of existing circuitry (Berken et al., 2016).

Children exposed to an L2 early in development also have more exposure to and practice using the language, which supports proficiency with the language. Testing of AoA and proficiency together for their associations with neural responses yields conflicting results as to which is the stronger predictor of brain activation patterns (Hernandez and Li, 2007; Rossi et al., 2006; Steinhauer et al., 2009). Proficient bilinguals, whether early or late learners, show strikingly similar neural responses for both L1 and L2 that differ from the neural responses of less proficient bilingual individuals (e.g., Abutalebi et al., 2001; Chee, 2006; Perani et al., 1998). Still, greater AoA effects are seen for syntactic than for semantic processing tasks (Hernandez et al., 2007a; Waldron and Hernandez, 2013; Wartenburger et al., 2003; Weber-Fox and Neville, 1996).

Development of the Home Language (L1)

To what extent does ability in L1 support or hinder the acquisition of L2? Some immigrant parents may fear that talking with their child in L1 will compromise the child's ability to learn English and subsequently succeed in U.S. schools because the development of L1 will slow and perhaps even interfere with English acquisition. Teachers also express this concern.

---

[7] Synapses are the connections between neurons (nerve cells). Synaptogenesis is the formation of these connections.
[8] Pruning is the elimination of extra neurons or synapses.

To the contrary, however, growing evidence indicates that strong L1 literacy and vocabulary facilitate the development of skills in a second and even third language (Brisk and Harrington, 2007).

The importance of L1 skills for learning a new language is evident during the emergence of language, as indicated by experimental studies aimed at teaching a new language to toddlers. Koening and Woodward (2012), for example, examined monolingual English-speaking toddlers' ability to learn words for objects in Dutch versus English. Toddlers with large English vocabularies successfully learned the words in Dutch, whereas those with low English vocabulary scores responded at chance levels. These findings suggest that having a large vocabulary in their native language supports toddlers' ability to learn words in another language.

Cross-language associations have been documented for phonology (Kohnert et al., 2010) as well as semantic priming, in which hearing a word such as "table" leads to faster recognition of a related item such as "chair" (Singh, 2014). Priming effects for DLL toddlers also have been shown to exist for words that are phonologically similar across the two languages (Von Holzen and Mani, 2012).

Studies of deaf children learning American Sign Language (ASL) and English offer strongly compelling evidence that L1 development facilitates L2 development, illustrating the effect even across different modalities. Boudreault and Mayberry (2006) compared the L2 (English) proficiency of two groups of deaf children: (1) those who had begun to acquire ASL early and (2) those who had begun to acquire ASL later and had acquired no language earlier in development. Across all syntactic structures (e.g., simple sentences, passive sentences, relative classes), the grammatical judgments of the deaf children who had learned ASL at an early age were more accurate than those of the deaf children who had not done so. In a subsequent study, children who were more proficient in ASL also scored higher on tests of English reading (Mayberry, 2007). Thus, it appears that learning a language early establishes a general foundation that can be engaged for later language learning and literacy.

L1 language skills also have been shown to promote a variety of school readiness skills in L2. Spanish language literacy and growth in Spanish vocabulary, for example, have been shown to contribute to the development of reading skills in English as an L2 (Rinaldi and Páez, 2008; see August and Shanahan [2006] for a review). In a study of toddlers of low-income Mexican and Dominican immigrant mothers, rates of growth in the diversity of the children's expressive vocabulary (words a child can produce) during book sharing (from ages 1 to 5 years) in either L1 or L2 predicted a variety of school readiness skills (narrative coherence, vocabulary, math skills, print knowledge) tested predominantly in English when children were 5 years of age (Tamis-LeMonda et al., 2014a). Cross-language facilitation also was seen in a study of Latino/a English DLLs from low-income migrant families who were followed longitudinally from kindergarten to second grade to identify predictors of rate of growth in vocabulary (Leacox and Jackson, 2014). Although the low-income DLLs lagged behind their monolingual peers in vocabulary growth in English, high initial Spanish receptive vocabulary (words a child understands) at kindergarten was associated with greater growth in English receptive vocabulary over time.

In contrast to these studies of cross-language associations, correlations between measures of L1 and L2 and the ability to process information efficiently are sometimes seen only within languages (Marchman et al., 2010). In a test of speech processing efficiency and vocabulary development in 30-month-old Spanish-English DLL toddlers, children with larger Spanish vocabularies and faster processing speeds in Spanish did not process words faster in English. Similarly, Marchman and colleagues (2004) found in a study of 23.5-month-olds who were learning English and Spanish simultaneously that within-language were stronger than cross-language vocabulary-grammar associations.

In summary, several studies indicate that L1 development can facilitate L2 learning. Evidence in support of this finding comes from studies that report significant positive cross-language associations and transfer from L1 to L2 over time. DLLs typically show greater competence or dominance in one language; equivalent competence in both languages is rare. Differential dominance often can be explained by different amounts of exposure to each language (reviewed in the next section). The young language learner is still building the foundations of each language, and there is as yet little to transfer from the dominant to the nondominant language. Even so, once the young child builds a sufficiently strong base in L1, transfer between languages is likely to occur. The more advanced language learner is able to transfer or apply strong skills in one language to learning or using the weaker language. However, transfer is less likely to occur when language skills are underdeveloped.

Quantity and Quality of Language Input

Children's development in both L1 and L2 depends on the language that is directed to them. Notably, infants and toddlers learn best under conditions of one-on-one interactions, in which talk is directed to them. Language simply overheard by toddlers has not been found to be related to growth in vocabulary or other aspects of language development (Ramírez-Esparza et al., 2014; Rowe, 2012; Weisleder and Fernald, 2013). Two features of language input and children's language experiences that may affect DLLs' early language development are examined in the following sections: (1) the quantity of exposure to each language; and (2) the quality of language input, including the diversity of the input, contingent responsiveness, the speaker's proficiency in the language, and engagement in literacy and learning activities (which offer children opportunities to hear diverse language and quantity of language).

Quantity of Exposure

As might be expected, children's development in their L1 and L2 depends on the amount of exposure to each (e.g., De Houwer, 2009; Hoff et al., 2012; Place and Hoff, 2011; Song et al., 2012). A review of 182 empirical studies on DLLs indicated that differences among children in their language and literacy development depended on the quantity of their exposure to each language (Hammer et al., 2014), as well as when they were first exposed to their L2 (as discussed above in the section on timing of second language learning).

Most researchers who have examined the early vocabulary development of DLLs have found a significant association between exposure to each language and vocabulary size (e.g., Barnes and Garcia, 2013; Bialystok et al., 2010; De Houwer et al., 2014; Hoff et al., 2012; Oller et al., 2007; Thordardottir, 2011). In a set of studies with DLL toddlers exposed to Spanish and English, for example, estimates of input in each language were related to the percentage of words toddlers were reported to produce in Spanish and English (Hoff et al., 2012; Place and Hoff, 2011). These results are discussed in terms of associations between amount of exposure and proficiency. These researchers found that Spanish-English bilingual children with more exposure to Spanish than English generally achieved higher scores in Spanish than in English; those with more exposure to English than Spanish tended to achieve higher scores in English than in Spanish; and those with similar exposure to both achieved similar scores in each.

Hoff and colleagues (2012) demonstrated the role of relative exposure in the vocabulary and grammatical development of Spanish-English bilingual infants and toddlers in the United States. The parents of the bilingual and monolingual participants in this study had equally high levels of education and, importantly, most had college-level education. The children were assessed three times between 1 and 3 years of age. The monolinguals scored higher than the DLLs on measures of single-language vocabulary in English, the onset of combinatorial speech (two-word utterances), grammatical complexity, and mean length of utterance; this differential was evident at all three testing times and was estimated to correspond to about a 3-month lag for the DLLs. Notwithstanding group differences, there was considerable overlap in the English scores of the monolingual and DLL children. In fact, DLL participants who had had more than 70 percent exposure to English did not differ from the monolingual children who had had 100 percent exposure. In contrast to the single-language results, no differences were found when the DLLs' performance in both languages was considered together. In particular, there were no significant differences when total vocabulary in English and Spanish and combined speech in both English and Spanish were calculated.

Language exposure in each language also was found to be correlated with the vocabulary development of bilingual French-English 5-year-olds living in Montreal (Thordardottir, 2011) compared with monolingual French- and monolingual English-speaking children of the same age whose mothers did not differ from those of the bilingual children on education and nonverbal cognitive ability. The study findings revealed a strong and consistent association between exposure to a language and scores on vocabulary measures in that language, with more exposure producing higher scores, as expected. Similar findings have been replicated in longitudinal studies of children of other language backgrounds, including Basque and Spanish-French (Barnes and Garcia, 2013) and Finnish and Dutch (Silvén and Rubinov, 2010).

Beyond vocabulary, relative exposure to L1 and L2 also is related to measures of phonology and grammar. A study of Spanish-English DLLs ages 22 to 25 months (Parra et al., 2011) found that children's relative amount of exposure to their two languages was related not only to their productive vocabulary size but also to their phonological memory and grammar in each language. The percentage of children's home exposure to English was related to their nonword repetition accuracy for English-like but not for Spanish-like words. These findings show that relative exposure to L1 and L2 has language-specific relationships to phonological memory and that exposure effects are usually language-specific rather than cross-linguistic.

Although the above studies indicate that the proportion of exposure to each language predicts skills in vocabulary and/or grammar, they differ on estimates of just how much exposure is required to fully support children's language development. In one study, no difference between DLL and monolingual 5-year-old children was found if the former had had at least 40-60 percent exposure to each language (Thordardottir, 2011). In contrast, even a difference of 10-20 percent in exposure to English was associated with reduced vocabulary scores in Spanish among a group of Spanish-dominant Spanish-English DLLs living in the United States who ranged in age from 16 to 20 months (Deanda et al., 2016). Similar results were found in English for English-dominant Spanish-English DLLs. These differences across studies may be attributable to the age of the children. The effects of exposure may be more pronounced among younger learners when the lexical system is relatively immature (Deanda et al., 2016). By implication, and as suggested by the results of Thordardottir (2011), differences may diminish and even disappear with age as DLLs have more cumulative exposure to each language (see also Paradis et al., 2014).

As children's exposure to a language increases, so does their speed at processing new information in the language. As is seen for vocabulary, associations between exposure and processing speed are language-specific. In one longitudinal study, Spanish-English bilingual children from families of a broad range of socioeconomic status were followed between ages 30 and 36 months, and their relative exposure to each language predicted their efficiency in real-time language processing and expressive and receptive vocabularies in that language (Hurtado et al., 2014). Thus, opportunities to practice real-time comprehension in a language sharpen processing skills as well.

Relative exposure to L1 and L2 also was found to affect the phonemic inventories of preschool-age children attending Head Start (Gildersleeve-Neumann et al., 2008). Monolingual English-speaking children ages 3-4 years were compared with English-Spanish bilingual children who either were exposed predominantly to English or received relatively equal exposure to both languages. Outcomes, including phoneme accuracy and error pattern frequencies, were measured over time. Children with the greatest cumulative exposure to English made the fewest errors, on average; conversely, children who were exposed to relatively more Spanish showed the highest maintenance of Spanish phonemic patterns and frequent vocalization errors in English, particularly syllable-level error patterns. Over time, however, rates of growth in phonetic skills were equivalent across the three groups.

When interpreting findings on relative language exposure, it is important to note that some of the previously discussed studies focused on the proportion of exposure to each language, whereas others focused on the absolute amount of exposure to each. Often, the proportion-based approach (for instance, that a DLL is hearing 40% English) leads to erroneous assumptions about the actual amount of language input. Moreover, people often assume that DLLs are, on average, exposed to less input in each language relative to monolinguals because they are exposed to two languages during the same time as monolinguals are exposed to one. However, a lower percentage of exposure does not necessarily mean less input. A DLL with half as much exposure to each language as a monolingual receives to one language could actually receive more input in one or both of those languages. If, for example, the Spanish-speaking parent of a Spanish-English DLL is more attentive to and talks more with her child than the Spanish-speaking parent of a monolingual child, the DLL may in fact experience more absolute language input than the monolingual child (see De Houwer et al. [2014] for more discussion of this issue). Thus it is likely that the amount of input, rather than the proportion of input, is the better predictor of DLLs' proficiency in their L1 and L2.

Quality of Language Input

Studies of the quality of the language input DLLs receive, in contrast to their relative exposure to L1 and L2, have been limited. The features that define language quality change as children gain new skills in language and cognition over the course of their development. During the emergence of language (from about 10 to 18 months of age), word learning is slow. At this time, children benefit from hearing a large amount of language; a variety of words with which to label and describe objects, people, and events; language that is temporally contingent on their attention and communications; and relatively simple grammatical constructions. As children's vocabularies and grammatical skills expand, between 18 months and 3 years of age, they continue to benefit from rich language input, particularly diversity in words and increasingly complex grammatical forms (Institute of Medicine and National Research Council, 2015). By around 3 years of age, children use and understand relatively decontextualized language that goes beyond the here and now, and they benefit from inferential questions that challenge them to reason about everyday situations and storylines in books (Kuchirko et al., 2015). By the pre-K years, children actively participate in give-and-take narrative exchanges and can co-construct personal narratives about the past and future, story narratives during booksharing, and fantasy narratives during pretend play (Uccelli et al., 2005).

The sections that follow examine some of these quality features of language, particularly those that support the language development of DLLs: the diversity of vocabulary to which children are exposed (that is, the number of different words in the input), the contingent responsiveness of language input, and caregiver engagement of children in literacy activities (with a focus on the use of questions during booksharing activities). Additionally, parents' proficiency in the input languages can affect the quality of language addressed to children, which in turn can predict children's language development. These factors are critical to consider in light of growing evidence that it is the quality of language directed to children that most strongly influences language development (Golinkoff et al., 2015), even after controlling for the sheer amount or quantity of language input (Rowe, 2012).

Diversity of the input The diversity of parental language (across and within different levels of socioeconomic status), reflected in the use of different word types and the different ideas conveyed by those words, is positively associated with children's vocabulary size, rate of vocabulary growth (e.g.,

Hart and Risley, 1995; Hoff, 2003, 2006; Tamis-LeMonda et al., 2012a), phonological awareness, listening comprehension (Sénéchal et al., 2006), cognitive skills, preacademic skills, and school performance (Marchman and Fernald, 2008). Although most studies on the benefits of parents' lexical diversity for children's language development focus on monolingual children, their findings extend to DLLs as well. In a longitudinal study of DLLs of Mexican and Dominican descent, low-income immigrant mothers' increased use of different word types during booksharing with their 2- to 5-year-old children was associated with children's vocabulary growth in the respective language. In turn, children's language skills predicted their narrative skills, emergent literacy, and emergent math at 5 years of age (Tamis-Lemonda et al., 2014a). In another study, Latino mothers of Spanish-learning infants varied substantially in the quantity and diversity of their language input to their children. Infants of relatively talkative mothers heard three times as many different words and more complex sentences as did infants of less talkative mothers, and these differences related to the children's vocabulary size at age 2 (Hurtado et al., 2008). These results also corroborate arguments made previously that the percentage of exposure to L1 and L2 may not be the most useful measure of the amount of exposure to each.

Exposure to rich language early in language development is especially important because it facilitates children's skills at real-time language processing and consequently vocabulary building. In one study of Spanish-speaking Mexican families of low socioeconomic status, the amount of speech directed to infants predicted how efficiently they processed familiar words in real time, based on a measure of how quickly they became oriented to pictures of familiar words. It also was associated with the children's expressive vocabularies at 24 months (Weisleder and Fernald, 2013).

Additionally, the ways in which parents use language—referred to as the pragmatic functions of language—can influence children's language development by affecting the complexity of sentence structures, as well as children's opportunities to participate in conversations. Parents who frequently use commands and directives (also referred to as regulatory language) may cut short the rich vocabulary and conversational turn taking that occurs when they ask questions. Asking a child, "What do you want to do next?" is more likely to elicit a conversational response than is "Do that." This point is illustrated by a study in which supportive language input to 2- and 3-year-olds (in families of middle to high socioeconomic status) took the form of conversations in which mothers asked their children questions and engaged them in conversational exchanges (Hoff, 2006).

An analysis of the use of child-directed language by low-income immigrant U.S. Latino mothers of 2-year-old DLLs showed that directive/regulatory language contained a preponderance of pronouns, whereas referential language—in which mothers used language to talk about objects and events in everyday life—contained many nouns, adjectives, verbs, and adverbs. In turn, referential but not regulatory language was related to the size of DLL toddlers' expressive vocabularies in English and Spanish (Tamis-LeMonda et al., 2012b). The grammatical complexity of parental language, including the variety of different syntactic structures in which verbs appear, likewise predicts monolingual children's vocabulary (Hoff, 2003; Hoff and Naigles, 2002) and grammatical development (Huttenlocher et al., 2010), although comparable research on DLLs is scarce.

Contingent responsiveness Responsive language experiences, defined as input that is prompt, contingent, and positively connected to a child's interests and actions, predict gains in monolingual children's language, especially during the first 2 years of life (e.g., Bornstein et al., 2008; Landry et al., 2006). Contingent responses to infant behaviors promote word learning by increasing the likelihood that infants will hear words that are the focus of their attention, thereby reducing referential ambiguity and easing the mapping of words to objects and events in the environment (Tamis-LeMonda et al., 2014b). One study with DLL toddlers of Spanish-speaking Dominican and Mexican immigrant mothers found that the mothers were contingently responsive to the toddlers; when the toddlers touched or acted on objects, the mothers followed with labels and descriptions for those objects within 2 seconds (Tamis-LeMonda et al., 2013).

The importance of contingent responsive language input for children's language development is likely due to children's ability to learn words for things and events that interest them and are already the focus of their attention (Hirsh-Pasek et al., 2015; Konishi et al., 2014). Consequently, it has been found that children whose parents talk to them about what interests them have more advanced vocabularies than children whose parents frequently redirect their attention and label objects that are not of interest to them (e.g., Konishi et al., 2014). Although research in this area is based primarily on the experiences of monolingual children, there is mounting evidence for the supportive role of contingently responsive language in the language development of DLLs (e.g., David and Wei, 2008).

Speaker's proficiency For DLLs, as for monolinguals, the proficiency of a caregiver's language skills in L1 and L2—including the use of correct grammatical forms and diverse vocabulary—powerfully affects their language trajectories in each language. Caregivers who engage with their children in a language in which they are proficient and with which they are comfortable may also benefit their children socially.

Many immigrant parents use English with their children with the aim of supporting their children's English language development. However, parents' proficiency in English has been found to determine whether this strategy is effective. Parental English language proficiency is often measured through parent report—by asking parents to rate how well they understand, speak, write, and read English (as separate questions), or asking them to rate their proficiency level on a scale ranging from having few words or phrases (low proficiency) to native-like proficiency with good vocabulary and few grammatical errors (high proficiency) (e.g., Baker, 2014; Goldstein et al., 2010). However, many DLLs are not exposed to proficient English. More than 40 percent of Latino children, for example, have at least one parent with limited English proficiency (Hernandez et al., 2007b); children of Mexican, Dominican, and Central American descent in particular are less likely to have parents who are proficient in English relative to other Latino children whose parents have different educational backgrounds, are bilingual, and are of different generational status in the United States (Hernandez, 2006).

When the source of input for one or both of a DLL's languages is a non-native speaker, the child may hear grammatical forms that deviate from monolingual norms and in turn may reproduce these forms. In a case study, for example, a Spanish-English bilingual child who used many more overt subjects in Spanish than is typical of Spanish monolingual children actually heard more overt subjects in the Spanish used by her English-speaking mother, who was a non-native speaker of Spanish (Paradis and Navarro, 2003) (see De Houwer [2009, pp. 285-286] for synopses of other studies that have found a relationship between adult usage and DLLs' productions).

A DLL can benefit from hearing English early in development from a parent who is comfortable with and competent in English (Kovelman et al., 2008a). Use of L2 by immigrant parents promotes children's language development only if the parents have achieved a threshold level of proficiency in that language (Paradis et al., 2011a). For simultaneous Spanish-English DLLs, the proportion of input that is provided by native speakers of English predicts their English skills after controlling for the total amount of language exposure (Place and Hoff, 2011). Conversely, when parents are limited in English proficiency, talking to their children in English can also compromise the children's native (L1) language development without yielding significant gains in English (Hammer et al., 2009; McCabe et al., 2013; Paradis et al., 2011a).

Parental English language proficiency also was found to relate to children's segmental accuracy on phonological production tasks (i.e., the percentage of consonants and vowels children produce correctly) in a sample of 5.9-year-old Spanish-English DLLs (Goldstein et al., 2010). In another study, associations between Mexican mothers' English proficiency and their preschoolers' reading and math scores were examined in a nationally representative sample (Baker, 2014). Mothers' English proficiency predicted their children's reading (but not math) achievement as a result of its influence on the mediating variable of home literacy involvement in English. Thus, DLLs' education and development may be enhanced by programs aimed at enhancing mothers' English proficiency and home literacy activities.

In a related vein, and as noted earlier, speaker proficiency also relates to DLLs' ability to learn associations between new words that comprise minimal phonemic pairs and their referents during early language emergence. Infants who are learning one language succeed at such tasks around 17 to 20 months of age, whereas infants learning two languages from birth do not succeed until 20 months of age (Fennell et al., 2007; Werker et al., 2002). However, follow-up research (Fennell and Byers-Heinlein, 2014; Mattock et al., 2010) indicates that success on this demanding task may depend on whether pronunciation of the novel words to be learned in the study matches the language environment in which the children were actually learning language. Early abilities to discriminate among specific phonemes are affected by the phonetic properties of caregiver speech (Fennell and Byers-Heinlein, 2014).

Over time, DLLs who speak their L1 and are exposed increasingly to their L2, typically English, often as a result of schooling in L2 and/or contact with native speakers of that language, often show an increasing preference for using L2 (see also Chapter 6 for a discussion of reclassification issues in grades K-12). Consequently, the L1 may begin to weaken, resulting in deviations in the speakers' underlying knowledge and their differential use of specific grammatical structures and constraints compared with typical monolingual patterns (Montrul, 2008). The importance of parents' language proficiency for DLLs' language development extends into adulthood. Jia and colleagues (2002) found that the L2 skills of adults who were immigrants as children depended on their immigrant parents' fluency in English.

Parents' language proficiency also is important for the quality of parent-child interactions more broadly, which in turn can influence children's language learning. Parents may inadvertently limit their ability to convey certain information to children when they communicate in a language they do not know well (McCabe et al., 2013). Children enjoy better relationships with their caregivers (Oh and Fuligni, 2010) and are less likely to be alienated from them (Tabors, 1997) when they are able to communicate in their parents' heritage language (McCabe et al., 2013).

The social and cognitive benefits that have been documented in children fluent in two or more languages, discussed earlier, speak to the importance of maintaining skills in L1 to promote bilingual proficiency. Often, however, the integration of immigrant families into a predominantly English-speaking society can lead to a shift from a non-English primary language to English over generations (National Task Force on Early Childhood

Education for Hispanics, 2007). Therefore, as English becomes part of the child's experiences, the issue of L1 preservation becomes more relevant to understanding development and learning. Use of the first language in various settings, for example, is associated with the development of a healthy ethnic identity in early childhood (Bialystok, 2001) and mitigates the potential negative psychological effects of losing L1 and weakening relationships with parents and family members (Tseng and Fuligni, 2000; Wong-Filmore, 2000). The formation of cultural identity also is related to language use (Espinosa, 2010a). Loss of L1 may compromise children's sociocultural understanding of and appropriate interactions in the families and communities in which they reside. In some cases, moreover, loss of the L1 has been associated with a sense of shame or disregard for the family's culture, furthering minimizing developmental opportunities (Hakuta and D'Andrea, 1992; Wong-Fillmore, 1991).

Engagement in literacy and learning activities Children's participation in literacy activities such as shared book reading, storytelling, reciting nursery rhymes, and singing songs supports their language growth and emergent literacy in several ways. There is ample evidence for the benefits of shared book reading and exposure to print with respect to children's vocabulary size, phonemic awareness, print concept knowledge, and positive attitudes toward literacy (Bus et al., 1995; Dickinson and Tabors, 1991; Lyytinen et al., 1998; Raikes et al., 2006; Sénéchal et al., 1996; Snow and Dickinson, 1990; Wagner et al., 1994; Watson, 2001). In particular, research indicates strong associations between dialogic reading—adults' use of "wh" questions and informative feedback during booksharing—and children's language skills within and across developmental time (Reese and Newcombe, 2007; Sénéchal, 1997; Whitehurst et al., 1988, 1994). Additionally, dialogic reading relates to children's independent storytelling skills, emergent literacy, vocabulary growth, print awareness, and memory (Fiorentino and Howe, 2004; Kang et al., 2009; Schick and Melzi, 2010).

The benefits of dialogic reading generalize to DLL preschoolers (Kuchirko et al., 2015; Luo and Tamis-LeMonda, 2017). For instance, Latino DLL preschoolers whose teachers encouraged them to co-construct stories from wordless books (i.e., adopting a dialogic booksharing style) demonstrated superior print-related language and storytelling skills at the end of the preschool year compared with DLL preschoolers whose teachers did not adopt this style (Schick, 2015). It appears, however, that DLLs engage in literacy and other learning activities less often than monolingual children, which may contribute to the relatively low performance of some DLLs in school. Many explanations for these disparities in literacy and learning experiences are possible, including concentrated disadvantage experienced by many families with DLLs and low access to books in languages other than English (Raikes et al., 2006). Research also has documented less frequent reading by immigrant compared with nonimmigrant parents (Quiroz et al., 2010).

Notably, findings of comparatively low literacy activities in some Spanish-immigrant families are not always replicated in studies involving other immigrant groups. One study found that Asian DLL parents endorsed reading books at bedtime more frequently than did Euro-American parents. Their children also were significantly more involved in preacademic activities such as learning letters, numbers, and math skills; playing alphabet and number games; engaging in computer activities; and visiting the library (Parmar et al., 2008). These findings, however, may be explained by differences in socioeconomic status across studies; for example, the Asian immigrant families in this study were from middle- to high-income backgrounds. It also is important to note that Asians who immigrate from some countries in Southeast Asia (e.g., Hmong, Cambodia, Mynamar) show patterns similar to Spanish-immigrant families who have lower levels of education and fewer economic resources (see, e.g., Council on Asian Pacific Minnesotans, 2012).

Television and other technologies   There is a paucity of research on the potential role of electronic tools in DLLs' learning since most such studies are conducted with monolinguals. Nonetheless, work on television viewing in relation to toddlers' language learning has shown few benefits (Linebarger and Walker, 2005) and even some impairment of learning (Hudon et al., 2013). Similarly, electronic board books have limited learning benefits for toddlers (Sosa, 2016). In contrast, electronic books, educational programs, and computer apps may provide opportunities for DLLs, particularly those who ordinarily experience little exposure to English, to hear proficient English (e.g., Leacox and Jackson, 2014). However, evidence showing that apps do not help monolingual infants and toddlers learn language (Roseberry et al., 2014) suggests that their DLL counterparts are unlikely to benefit. Nonetheless, additional research is needed on this question.

Cross-Linguistic Influences of L1 on L2 Learning

While the evidence reviewed in the first section of this chapter indicates that for the most part, DLLs keep their languages separate, at times they differ from monolinguals in their language usage in ways that can be attributed to cross-linguistic influences. There is no evidence that cross-linguistic influences are pervasive (i.e., broad in scope) or long-lasting, except possibly in the case of children who acquire an L2 after their L1 (see Meisel [2007] and Paradis et al. [2011b] for reviews). Evidence of such influences is discussed in this section.

Because languages of the world vary in the extent to which they differ in structure, a critical task for parents and teachers of multilingual English learners is to understand how development in the components of a child's native language may affect the acquisition of English. If for example, the child's native language is similar to English (e.g., Dutch), initial learning of English may be easier than if the native language is different from English (e.g., Hmong). Indeed, cross-language similarities and differences may account for some of the discrepant findings on transfer of skills from L1 to L2 reviewed above, and may influence children's rate of learning a second language and ultimate level of proficiency discussed earlier.

Influence of L1 on L2 Speech Perception

After a certain age, humans' phonological representations are fairly fixed. There is a major gap in the literature, however, on what that age is for English contrasts that do not exist in other languages (such as *ship* versus *sheep* for native Spanish speakers). Empirical evidence on how English L2 speech perception becomes more difficult as a function of age and whether certain contrasts are more difficult at certain ages and for speakers of certain native languages could provide information on the optimal instruction for DLLs of different ages with different L1 backgrounds. Older children have been shown to improve their perception and identification of non-native vowel sounds with as a little as 5 hours of training, and such training has been shown to be more effective for 7- to 8-year-olds than for adults (Giannakopoulou et al., 2013). Similarly, a study of phonological production and perception found that Korean children surpassed Korean adults in the production of certain English vowels, supporting the idea that the older L2 learners are, the less likely they are to be able to establish new vowel categories needed for accurate L2 vowel production and perception (Baker et al., 2008). This is yet another area in which the evidence strongly suggests that earlier exposure leads to better L2 learning. But more evidence is needed on effective techniques for speech perception training for children of different ages who are native speakers of different languages (e.g., Spanish vs. Mandarin).

Morphology

Morphological differences in the L1s of DLLs (e.g., Spanish versus Hmong) may result in different patterns of English (L2) learning. Hmong, for example (unlike English and Spanish), is a tone language in which morphological structures such as plurals are marked lexically instead of by suffixes. A number of studies have examined how native Hmong-speaking preschoolers who begin to learn English in preschool learn words in English and in their native Hmong (Kan, 2014; Kan and Kohnert, 2008). After these children had been exposed to English for 6 months, there was no evidence that they could learn words in English as quickly as they did in their native Hmong (Kan and Kohnert, 2008). After the children had been exposed to English for 14 months, they still recalled more words in their native Hmong than in English (Kan, 2014). Subsequent analyses showed that knowledge of L2 predicted children's ability to retain the new words they learned in L2. Thus, these findings indicate that Hmong children's ability to learn and retain words quickly in L2 depended on other aspects of their L2 knowledge. One potential explanation for why native Hmong speakers do not appear to benefit from their L1 vocabularies when learning English as their L2 may be phonological and morphological differences between Hmong and Spanish (versus English). In contrast with English and Hmong, there may be sizable overlap between Spanish and English sounds with high phonotactic probabilities and the ways in which plurals are made.

Words

The structure of the words children learn—reflected in the structure of the input they receive—also may influence their development of proficiency in English as a second language. Studies of children learning only one language strongly suggest that language learning builds on itself (e.g., Reznick and Goldfield, 1992). The language-learning environment consists of many different kinds of statistical regularities, among words themselves as well as among words and kinds of entities in the world. Children learning one language have been shown to be highly sensitive to these regularities and to use them to learn new words (Gathercole and Min, 1997; Gleitman, 1990; Golinkoff and Hirsh-Pasek, 2006, Imai and Gentner, 1997; Pinker, 2013; Waxman, 2009; Yoshida and Smith, 2003). By implication, another reason for different patterns of L2 (English) learning by DLLs who speak different L1s may involve the composition of their early vocabularies. Children learning Korean, Mandarin, and other East Asian languages as their native language often show a "verb bias," or a tendency to learn words for actions before learning words for solid objects (Choi and Gopnik, 1995; Tardif, 1996, 2017; Tardif et al., 1997)—a pattern that contrasts with that generally found in native monolingual English speakers (Nelson et al., 1993). Perhaps learning an L1 that emphasizes different word classes than English (i.e., nouns or verbs, either through frequency or word position) poses a greater challenge to certain L1 groups learning English as an L2.

Influence of DLLs' Grammars on One Another During Development

One salient type of cross-linguistic influence in DLLs is the substitution of a word order rule from one language to the other. In a study on young Cantonese-English DLLs (ages 2 to 4 years) in Hong Kong, Yip and Matthews (2007) noted the placement of relative clauses before the noun they modified. They found that their Cantonese-dominant participants used the relative clause word order of Chinese rather than that of English. For example, the children would ask, "Where's *the Santa Claus give me the gun?*" instead of the target English form, "Where's the gun *that Santa Claus give (gave) me?*" (Yip and Matthews, 2007, p. 155). Nicoladis (2002, 2003) also found cross-linguistic influence in French-English children's use of compound words. The order in which such words are created is usually the opposite in French and English—for example, *brosse à dents* (brush-teeth) in French versus toothbrush in English. Nicoladis found that French-English bilingual children were more likely than monolinguals to reverse the word order in their compound words in both languages.

Cross-linguistic influences also have been noted that alter the frequency of DLLs' usage of optional but correct grammatical patterns relative to monolinguals. Paradis and Navarro (2003), for example, examined the use of sentential subjects by a Spanish-English DLL girl from the age of 1 year, 9 months to 2 years, 6 months compared with that of Spanish monolinguals of a similar age. The Spanish-English DLL girl in this study used more overt subjects in her Spanish sentences—subjects that were sometimes redundant in the conversation—relative to two Spanish monolingual children her age. The authors suggest that the child was more likely to use subjects in her Spanish than is typical among monolingual Spanish-speaking children because English requires a subject.

How long do cross-linguistic influences persist in development? Some researchers, such as Yip and Matthews (2007), have documented the increase and then decline of certain cross-linguistic structures in the language of DLLs over time during the preschool years. Studies of simultaneous bilinguals provide evidence that some aspects of cross-linguistic influence are temporary, but research with school-age second language learners suggests that these influences can be more extended. Serratrice and colleagues (2009) asked Italian-English DLLs ages 6 to 10 years and their monolingual peers to judge whether certain plural noun phrases were grammatical. The DLLs, even those in the oldest group, showed some cross-linguistic influence in their performance on this task because they sometimes accepted noun phrases as grammatical in one language when those phrases actually had the morphosyntactic structure of the other language. Such research suggests that interactions between dual language systems may be a permanent feature of sequential DLLs' grammars.

Sociocultural Influences

The broader sociocultural context in which DLLs grow up influences their language development, especially those aspects that are valued and rewarded in school settings. An ecocultural approach to language learning highlights the intersecting multiple contexts in which children develop (Bronfenbrenner, 1979; Weisner, 2002) and the shared values and practices of cultural communities that affect their language-learning experiences (Heath, 1982; Tamis-LeMonda and Song, 2012). Parents from different cultural communities, and even those within the same cultural group, provide different language experiences to their DLL children, and these differences play out in children's language development, school readiness, and later academic success, as reviewed earlier. Moreover, DLLs may be exposed to more than one language in the home and other informal educational settings, and those settings may be characterized by aspects of the immigrant experience and other risk factors, such as poverty, low levels of parental education, and lack of access to resources that support literacy. These circumstances are important given that language practices in home, neighborhood, and school settings are highly relevant to early language and literacy outcomes (Goldenberg, 2006; Nord and Griffin, 1999; Tabors, 1997; Tabors et al., 2001).

As described in Chapter 3, DLLs in the United States are on average more likely than monolingual English-speaking children to live in poverty and to have parents with limited formal education, especially if their parents are recent immigrants. Living in poverty, however, does not necessarily lead to poor outcomes. It is critical to contextualize these vulnerability factors, recognizing that in general, developmental and educational vulnerability is attributable not only to characteristics of DLL families such as low parental education, but also to many interrelated entities and factors outside the family, including the quality and resources of the neighborhood and schools and the value society ascribes to different foreign languages, as well as national differences in the value attached to multilingualism. The following sections review research relevant to these issues (see Box 4-3).

Cultural Practices Regarding Communication

Parents from different communities and ethnicities display similarities and differences in their communicative interactions with children, with many such practices being rooted in cultural norms and beliefs (Schieffelin and Ochs, 1986; Tamis-LeMonda and Song, 2012). Parents generally are similar in relying on spoken language, as well as nonverbal forms of communication including gaze, touch, and gesture, to communicate with their

BOX 4-3
Effects of Parents' Generational and Socioeconomic Status

The majority of dual language learners (DLLs) are children of immigrant parents who vary in their length of residency in the United States, from recent immigrants to those who have lived in the United States for several generations (Hernandez et al., 2008). Being the child of an immigrant or U.S.-born parent and the extent to which the family is integrated into mainstream society both are associated with DLLs' development and learning (e.g., Center for Early Care and Education Research—Dual Language Learners, 2011).

A key way in which parents' generational status and duration of residency in the United States affect children's developing skills in language is through parents' L1 and L2 skills. Parents' skills in language influence how soon children learn and how proficient they become in the languages spoken to them. In U.S. Latino households, for example, first-generation caregivers tend to communicate in their native language (Veltman, 2000), whereas second-generation families are not as uniform in their preferred language, using L1 to varying degrees (Hurtado and Vega, 2004). By the third generation, L2 is the primary language used at home (Arriagada, 2005). In line with these generational shifts in language use, Hammer and colleagues (2012) found that Latino children of immigrant mothers had larger Spanish vocabularies relative to children of later-generation mothers. Moreover, the variation in the length of time that immigrant families have been in the United States has implications for the language directed to children. Research reveals, for example, that low-income immigrant Dominican mothers increased substantially the amount of English they directed to their children across their first 5 years of life, whereas low-income immigrant Mexican mothers used primarily Spanish throughout their children's early childhood years—a difference attributed to the greater number of years Dominican mothers had been in the United States, which aided their skills in English. In turn, Dominican and Mexican children differed in their trajectories of English and Spanish language growth, with the former showing faster gains in English vocabulary during early childhood than the latter (Escobar and Tamis-LeMonda, 2015; Tamis-LeMonda et al., 2014a).

DLLs with first-generation immigrant parents frequently begin school lagging behind their monolingual peers in language and school readiness skills (Oller and Eilers, 2002), and those delays often persist throughout the school years (Place and Hoff, 2011). These disparities typically are attributed to children's DLL status, although these children's delayed language and learning outcomes are likely also due in part to their poverty status and the low education levels of many immigrant DLL families in the United States. A study of DLL Singaporean kindergartners in the United States, for example, showed that those children from households of low socioeconomic status were most at risk for low proficiency in both languages (Chinese, Malay, or Tamil and English) (Dixon et al., 2012), whereas children from households of middle and high socioeconomic status were most likely to demonstrate high English proficiency.

Parents' socioeconomic status (typically measured by parental education and income) directly affects children's language development across the first years of life through the quality and quantity of child-directed language (Hoff, 2003, 2006). Children from low-income households, for instance, have been shown to receive on average less language input, less varied input, and more negative input (such as reprimands) relative to their peers in environments of higher socioeconomic status (Hart and Risley, 1995; Hoff, 2006). To the extent that some children in low-income households experience low quantity and quality of language, this situation can create a double risk factor for their language development. Impoverished language input is associated with children's abilities to process language information in real time, as summarized earlier. A study of English-learning (monolingual) toddlers from families of low and high socioeconomic status, for example, found that at 18 months, toddlers in the high socioeconomic status group looked more quickly at the correct object after hearing a word relative to toddlers from the low socioeconomic status group. Although both groups improved in processing speed with increasing age, children from families of low socioeconomic status had achieved the processing efficiency at 24 months that their peers from better-off families had achieved at 18 months. Thus differences in socioeconomic status can lead to a 6-month language gap by 2 years of age (Fernald et al., 2013). There is additional evidence indicating that poverty has adverse consequences for brain development (Farah, 2010; Johnson et al., 2016).

Several cautions are warranted, however, in interpreting findings pertaining to the development of DLLs living in poverty. First, there exist enormous variations in the language experiences and skills of children from low-income households, paralleling those seen in middle-income samples (Song et al., 2012). Consequently, any adverse outcomes associated with poverty, including slower processing speed, should generalize to children exposed to little language, regardless of their household socioeconomic status. Second, Hart and Risley's (1995) findings were based on comparisons of small samples at two extremes—children of welfare recipients and children of professors—yet have often been overgeneralized (Michaels, 2013). Third, although Hart and Risley found that early language disparities predicted 3rd-grade language, long-term predictions were not seen for reading, writing, spelling, and math or standardized IQ outcomes (Hart and Risley, 1995; Michaels, 2013).

In fact, there is widespread agreement that the adverse effects of poverty on children's learning and development are exacerbated in the context of other risks, beyond the sheer amount of language input to children. Marcella and colleagues (2014), for example, examined the relationship between cumulative family risk (including a single-parent household, poverty, receipt of welfare, low maternal education, and maternal depression) and family literacy activities among 3-year-old children in low-income families (primarily of Latino descent). They found that those children in families with the most cumulative risk engaged in the fewest literacy activities. Literacy activities are a valuable context for language interactions, and children who rarely participate in these types of activities are at risk for later cognitive delay (Rodriguez and Tamis-LeMonda, 2011).

children, yet differ in their relative emphases on these various modes of communication.

Parents of different cultural backgrounds also are similar in communicating about objects, events, actions, and the experiences of self and others using grammatical forms (e.g., nouns and verbs) that map onto fundamental, universal concepts. However, they vary in the content (i.e., topics) of their communications—for example, in their differential use of language as a tool to impart knowledge versus to regulate child behavior. Thus, both the forms (structure and content) and functions (purpose) of parent-infant communications are products of culture.

Use of gesture is one aspect of communication that varies across cultural communities. Gestures (such as pointing) that accompany words can help children who are first learning language to match words to referent objects by "narrowing the search space" and enabling children to perceive the word and stimulus as "belonging together" (Rader and Zukow-Goldring, 2010). Research has shown that gestures support English-speaking monolingual children's word learning (e.g., Rowe and Goldin-Meadow, 2009) and also predict cognitive skills in DLL Latino toddlers (Tamis-LeMonda et al., 2012b). Gestural communication may be especially prevalent in certain cultural communities. In particular, a high reliance on such communication has been documented in certain Latino (particularly Mayan) communities, in which much of children's learning occurs through "keen observation" of the people around them (Rogoff et al., 2003). One study found that 2-year-old U.S. children of Mexican immigrant mothers displayed more gesture use and higher skills at sequencing and imitating actions and following commands that incorporate gestures (despite lower expressive language) relative to children from other ethnic backgrounds during their first 2 years (Tamis-LeMonda et al., 2012b). When social interactions between Mexican and Dominican DLLs of low-income backgrounds were compared with those of monolingual children from low-income African American backgrounds, Mexican immigrant mothers in particular were found to be most responsive to the gestures produced by their infants relative to mothers in the other groups (Tamis-LeMonda et al., 2012b), and used gestures frequently to teach their toddlers a new task of how to string beads (Luo and Tamis-LeMonda, 2016). Reliance on gesture as a communicative tool can aid language learning if gestures are coupled with child-directed speech, but impede language learning if they substitute for language inputs. It is important to consider how children and parents from different cultural backgrounds communicate in ways beyond spoken language when interpreting differences in spoken language among DLLs from different cultural backgrounds.

Neighborhood Context

Beyond the family, features of communities and neighborhoods create or restrict opportunities to foster DLLs' learning, use of language, and sense of identity. These features encompass community elements both structural (physical spaces shared by people) and psychological (beliefs, values, history, and practices shared by people).

The extent to which the home languages of DLLs are valued in their communities is a key aspect of these children's daily lives. Researchers have distinguished between mature and immature immigrant-receiving communities (Urzúa and Gómez, 2008). Mature communities are more likely than immature ones to have a longer history of being a relocation area for immigrant groups. As a result, they may have community resources that serve the basic needs of immigrants (e.g., housing and employment opportunities) and foster a sense of community within immigrant groups, as well as positive attitudes toward bilingualism (Urzúa and Gómez, 2008). In contrast, immature immigrant-receiving communities may have a shorter history as relocation areas and thus have fewer resources for immigrant groups, which can create a sense of isolation and limit opportunities to speak the home language with other people.

The presence and value of different languages in a community can be observed within a community's shared spaces (e.g., neighborhoods, city blocks, town limits) and specific community structures (e.g., playgrounds, community resource centers, churches, grocery stores)—spaces where people who live in the community come together and interact. Such opportunities for diverse and frequent linguistic interactions increase the likelihood that DLLs will become bilingual and biliterate. Reese and Goldenberg (2006) found that in neighborhoods where most signs were written in both English and the community members' native languages and where native languages were used frequently in commercial transactions and community activities, DLLs were more likely to acquire the native language.

Community influences are illustrated by a study of family access to printed materials across 35 communities in the United States. Communities with high concentrations of Latinos were less likely to have printed materials, and available materials were more likely to be in Spanish, relative to communities with higher income and education levels, which had access to more literacy materials in English (Reese and Goldenberg, 2006). Additionally, low-income communities have fewer print resources available to children relative to middle-income communities, placing children from poor households (a disproportionate number of which are dual language households) on divergent paths to literacy and language development well before they start school (Neuman and Celano, 2001). These inequities span the quantity and quality of literacy materials, public spaces and places for reading, and even the types of literacy materials available at public institutions such as child care centers and libraries (Neuman and Celano, 2001). In turn, community (together with family) language characteristics were related to the literacy outcomes in Spanish and English of children in kindergarten and first grade. Thus in early stages of children's literacy development, communities can influence Spanish-speaking children's literacy through language-learning opportunities.

Parents of DLLs can promote a sense of community through their efforts to socialize their children in ways that maintain important features of their culture of origin (Hughes et al., 2006). Immigrant parents may seek out community organizations that offer L1 classes, schools in which the curriculum of the country of origin is taught, or religious institutions that promote children's ethnic and cultural identity. These goals for cultural maintenance may encourage parents of DLLs to select neighborhoods or communities that afford their children opportunities to interact with other children and families from their cultures of origin. In a study of Chinese language schools in Chicago, Lu (2001) found that parents sent their children to Chinese schools as a way of maintaining their Chinese identity, by learning Chinese and participating in community activities. Similarly, Inman and colleagues (2007) found that Indian Asian immigrant parents brought their children to religious activities as a way of preserving their ethnic identity. Such socialization practices of parents of DLLs may shift through successive generations as families move from ethnic enclaves to more diverse neighborhoods and as they gain an understanding of U.S. racial stratification (Hughes et al., 2006).

Summary

A number of factors have been shown to influence the development of dual language proficiency. Early relative to later exposure to English as a second language can facilitate its learning if the language being heard is spoken by speakers who are fluent and proficient. It is also critically important, however, for young children who are beginning to learn an L2 a few years after birth to continue to develop their L1, as many cases of positive transfer from L1 to L2 have been documented when L1 is strong. Literacy experiences such as book reading also are associated with diverse and rich language that promotes language skills in children. Parents' immigrant generation status and education, the status of L1 in the community, and neighborhood features all relate to parents' use of language with their children and with the children's language skills. Parents from different cultural communities have differing views and practices concerning their role as teachers of their children and how much and how they communicate with their children (including variations in gesture use and other nonverbal modes of communication). These differences influence children's language development insofar as they affect how parents and others use language, communicate, and interact with DLLs.

CONCLUSIONS

Conclusion 4-1: Children learning two languages from birth or within the first 3 years of life exhibit many similarities with monolingual children in their developmental trajectories and their skills in each language. At the same time, those trajectories or outcomes can differ between the two groups. Dual languages learners (DLLs) may take longer to learn subtle aspects of language that differ between the two languages, they may use alternative learning strategies to manage input from the two languages, and their levels of proficiency may reflect variations in language input and its quality. Even though these differences sometimes result in DLLs sounding different from monolingual children of the same age, these differences are in most cases normal and typical for children learning two languages at the same time, and not an indication of disorder, impairment, or disability.

Conclusion 4-2: There is no evidence to indicate that the use of two languages in the home or the use of one in the home and another in an early care and education setting confuses dual languages learners or puts the development of one or both of their languages at risk. Given adequate exposure to two languages, young children have the capacity to develop competence in vocabulary, morphology, syntax, and pragmatics in both.

Conclusion 4-3: Children given the opportunity to develop competence in two or more languages early in life benefit from their capacity to communicate in more than one language and may show enhancement of certain cognitive skills, as well as improved academic outcomes in school.

Conclusion 4-4: The cognitive, communicative, cultural, and economic benefits of knowing English and another language are most likely to occur when individuals have high levels of linguistic and functional competence in both languages, including speaking, listening, reading, and writing in both. This is most likely to occur if development of the home language is maintained throughout the preschool and school years as dual languages learners learn English.

Conclusion 4-5: Research indicates that children's language development benefits from the input of adults who talk to them in the language in which the adults are most competent and with which they are most comfortable. Dual languages learners' (DLLs') language development, like that of monolingual children, benefits from the amount and quality of child-directed language—that is, language that is used frequently in daily interactions, is contingent on the child's language and focus of attention, and is rich and diverse in words and sentence types. For most DLL families, this quantity and quality of child-directed language are more likely to occur in the home language, not English.

Conclusion 4-6: Dual language learners' language development can benefit from shared book reading and storytelling that are characterized by diverse and rich language that promotes interaction and engagement between another person and the child. Infants and toddlers have not been shown to learn language from television or computer applications that do not involve interactions with other people.

Conclusion 4-7: Language competence varies considerably among dual language learners. Multiple social and cultural factors—including parents' immigrant generational status and years in the United States, socioeconomic status, exposures to the risks of poverty, the perceived status of the home language in the community, and neighborhood resources—may help explain this variation.

BIBLIOGRAPHY

Abutalebi, J. (2008). Neural aspects of second language representation and language control. *Acta Psychologica, 128*(3), 466-478.

Abutalebi, J., and Green, D. (2007). Bilingual language production: The neurocognition of language representation and control. *Journal of Neurolinguistics, 20*(3), 242-275.

Abutalebi, J., Cappa, S.F., and Perani, D. (2001). The bilingual brain as revealed by functional neuroimaging. *Bilingualism: Language and Cognition, 4*(2), 179-190.

Abutalebi, J., Annoni, J.M., Zimine, I., Pegna, A.J., Seghier, M.L., Lee-Jahnke, H., Lazeyras, F., Cappa, S.F., and Khateb, A. (2008). Language control and lexical competition in bilinguals: An event-related fMRI study. *Cerebral Cortex, 18*(7), 1496-1505.

Abutalebi, J., Della Rosa, P.A., Green, D.W., Hernandez, M., Scifo, P., Keim, R., Cappa, S.F., and Costa, A. (2012). Bilingualism tunes the anterior cingulate cortex for conflict monitoring. *Cerebral Cortex, 22*(9), 2076-2086.

Albareda-Castellot, B., Pons, F., and Sebastián-Gallés, N. (2011). The acquisition of phonetic categories in bilingual infants: New data from an anticipatory eye movement paradigm. *Developmental Science, 14*(2), 395-401.

Arriagada, P.A. (2005). Family context and Spanish-language use: A study of Latino children in the United States. *Social Science Quarterly, 86*(3), 599-619.

August, D., and Shanahan, T. (2006). *Developing Literacy in Second-Language Learners: Report of the National Literacy Panel on Language Minority Children and Youth, Executive Summary*. Mahwah, NJ: Lawrence Erlbaum Associates.

Baker, C.E. (2014). Mexican mothers' English proficiency and children's school readiness: mediation through home literacy involvement. *Early Education and Development*, 25(3), 338-355.

Baker, W., Trofimovich, P., Flege, J. E., Mack, M., and Halter, R. (2008). Child—Adult Differences in second-language phonological learning: The role of cross-language similarity. *Language and Speech*, 51(4), 317-342.

Barnes, J., and Garcia, I. (2013). Vocabulary growth and composition in monolingual and bilingual Basque infants and toddlers. *International Journal of Bilingualism*, 17(3), 357-374.

Bates, E. (1999). Language and the infant brain. *Journal of Communication Disorders*, 32, 195-205.

Bates, E., Thal, D., Trauner, D., Fenson, J., Aram, D., Eisele, J., and Nass, R. (1997). From first words to grammar in children with focal brain injury. *Developmental Neuropsychology*, 13(3), 275-343.

Baum, S., and Titone, D. (2014). Moving toward a neuroplasticity view of bilingualism, executive control and aging. *Applied Psycholinguistics*, 35(5), 857-894.

Berken, J.A., Chai, X., Chen, J.K., Gracco, V.L., and Klein, D. (2016). Effects of early and late bilingualism on resting-state functional connectivity. *Journal of Neuroscience*, 36(4), 1165-1172.

Bernier, A., Carlson, S.M., and Whipple, N. (2010). From external regulation to self-regulation: Early parenting precursors of young children's executive functioning. *Child Development*, 81(1), 326-339.

Bialystok, E. (1999). Cognitive complexity and attentional control in the bilingual mind. *Child Development*, 70(3), 636-644.

Bialystok, E. (2001). *Bilingualism in Development*. Cambridge, UK: Cambridge University Press.

Bialystok, E., and Senman, L. (2004). Executive processes in appearance-reality tasks: The role of inhibition of attention and symbolic representation. *Child Development*, 75(2), 562-579.

Bialystok, E., and Shapero, D. (2005). Ambiguous benefits: The effect of bilingualism on reversing ambiguous figures. *Developmental Science*, 8(6), 595-604.

Bialystok, E., Majumder, S., and Martin, M.M. (2003). Developing phonological awareness: Is there a bilingual advantage? *Applied Psycholinguistics*, 24(1), 27-44.

Bialystok, E., Craik, F., and Luk, G. (2008). Cognitive control and lexical access in younger and older bilinguals. *Journal of Experimental Psychology. Learning, Memory, and Cognition*, 34(4), 859-873.

Bialystok, E., Luk, G., Peets, K.F., and Yang, S. (2010). Receptive vocabulary differences in monolingual and bilingual children. *Bilingualism: Language and Cognition*, 13(4), 525-531.

Birdsong, D. (1992). Ultimate attainment in second language acquisition. *Language*, 68(4), 706-755.

Blom, E., Küntay, A.C., Messer, M., Verhagen, J., and Leseman, P. (2014). The benefits of being bilingual: Working memory in bilingual Turkish–Dutch children. *Journal of Experimental Child Psychology*, 128, 105-119.

Bloom, L. (1993). *The Transition from Infancy to Language: Acquiring the Power of Expression*. Cambridge, UK: Cambridge University Press.

Bornstein, M.H., Tamis-LeMonda, C.S., Hahn, C.-S., and Haynes, O.M. (2008). Maternal responsiveness to young children at three ages: Longitudinal analysis of a multidimensional, modular, and specific parenting construct. *Developmental Psychology, 44*(3), 867.

Bosch, L., and Ramon-Casas, M. (2014). First translation equivalents in bilingual toddlers' expressive vocabulary. Does form similarity matter? *International Journal of Behavioral Development, 38*(4), 317-322.

Bosch, L., and Sebastián-Gallés, N. (1997). Native-language recognition abilities in 4-month-old infants from monolingual and bilingual environments. *Cognition, 65*(1), 33-69.

Bosch, L., and Sebastián-Gallés, N. (2000). *Exploring Four-Month-Old Infants' Abilities to Discriminate Languages from the Same Rhythmic Class.* Paper presented at the XIIth Biennial International Conference on Infant Studies, Brighton, UK.

Bosch, L., and Sebastián-Gallés, N. (2001). Evidence of early language discrimination abilities in infants from bilingual environments. *Infancy, 2*(1), 29-49.

Bosch, L., and Sebastián-Gallés, N. (2003). Simultaneous bilingualism and the perception of a language-specific vowel contrast in the first year of life. *Language and Speech, 46*(2-3), 217-243.

Bosch, L., Figueras, M., Teixidó, M., and Ramon-Casas, M. (2013). Rapid gains in segmenting fluent speech when words match the rhythmic unit: Evidence from infants acquiring syllable-timed languages. *Frontiers in Psychology, 4*(106).

Boudreault, P., and Mayberry, R.I. (2006). Grammatical processing in American Sign Language: Age of first-language acquisition effects in relation to syntactic structure. *Language and Cognitive Processes, 21*(5), 608-635.

Brisk, M.E., and Harrington, M.M. (2007). *Literacy and Bilingualism: A Handbook for All Teachers* (2nd ed.). New York: Routledge.

Brito, N., and Barr, R. (2012). Influence of bilingualism on memory generalization during infancy. *Developmental Science, 15*(6), 812-816.

Bronfenbrenner, U. (1979). *The Ecology of Human Development: Experiments by Design and Nature.* Cambridge, MA: Harvard University Press.

Burns, T.C., Yoshida, K.A., Hill, K., and Werker, J.F. (2007). The development of phonetic representation in bilingual and monolingual infants. *Applied Psycholinguistics, 28*(3), 455-474.

Bus, A.G., van IJzendoorn, M.H., and Pellegrini, A.D. (1995). Joint book reading makes for success in learning to read: A meta-analysis on intergenerational transmission of literacy. *Review of Educational Research, 65*(1), 1-21.

Byers-Heinlein, K., and Werker, J.F. (2009). Monolingual, bilingual, trilingual: Infants' language experience influences the development of a word-learning heuristic. *Developmental Science, 12*(5), 815-823.

Byers-Heinlein, K., Burns, T.C., and Werker, J.F. (2010). The roots of bilingualism in newborns. *Psychological Science, 21*(3), 343-348.

Byers-Heinlein, K., Fennell, C.T., and Werker, J.F. (2013). The development of associative word learning in monolingual and bilingual infants. *Bilingualism: Language and Cognition, 16*(1), 198-205.

Carlson, S.M., and Meltzoff, A.N. (2008). Bilingual experience and executive functioning in young children. *Developmental Science, 11*(2), 282-298.

Center for Early Care and Education Research—Dual Language Learners. (2011). *Research Brief #5: Early Care and Education Quality Measures: A Critical Review of the Research Related to Dual Language Learners.* Chapel Hill: University of North Carolina, FPG Child Development Institute, Center for Early Care and Education Research—Dual Language Learners.

Chee, M.W. (2006). Dissociating language and word meaning in the bilingual brain. *Trends in Cognitive Sciences, 10*(12), 527-529.

Choi, S., and Gopnik, A. (1995). Early acquisition of verbs in Korean: A cross-linguistic study. *Journal of Child Language, 22*(3), 497-529.

Comeau, L., Genesee, F., and Lapaquette, L. (2003). The modeling hypothesis and child bilingual codemixing. *International Journal of Bilingualism, 7*(2), 113-126.

Comeau, L., Genesee, F., and Mendelson, M. (2007). Bilingual children's repairs of breakdowns in communication. *Journal of Child Language, 34*(1), 159-174.

Comeau, L., Genesee, F., and Mendelson, M. (2010). A comparison of bilingual and monolingual children's conversational repairs. *First Language, 30*(3-4), 354-374.

Conboy, B. (2013). Neuroscience research: How experience with one or multiple languages affects the developing brain. In Governor's State Advisory Council on Early Learning and Care Sacramento (Ed.), *California's Best Practices for Young Dual Language Learners Research Overview Papers* (pp. 1-50). Sacramento: Child Development Division, California Department of Education.

Conboy, B.T., and Mills, D.L. (2006). Two languages, one developing brain: Event-related potentials to words in bilingual toddlers. *Developmental Science, 9*(1), F1-F12.

Conboy, B.T., and Thal, D.J. (2006). Ties between the lexicon and grammar: Cross-sectional and longitudinal studies of bilingual toddlers. *Child Development, 77*(3), 712-735.

Costa, A., Hernandez, M., and Sebastián-Gallés, N. (2008). Bilingualism aids conflict resolution: Evidence from the ANT task. *Cognition, 106*(1), 59-86.

Council on Asian Pacific Minnesotans. (2012). *Asian Pacific Students in Minnesota: Facts not Fiction.* Saint Paul: Council on Asian Pacific Minnesotans.

David, A., and Li, W. (2004). To what extent is codeswitching dependent on a bilingual child's lexical development? *Sociolinguistica, 18*(1), 1-12.

David, A., and Wei, L. (2008). Individual differences in the lexical development of French-English bilingual children. *International Journal of Bilingual Education and Bilingualism, 11*(5), 598-618.

de Bruin, A., Treccani, B., and Della Sala, S. (2015). Cognitive advantage in bilingualism: An example of publication bias? *Psychological Science, 26*(1), 99-107.

De Houwer, A. (2009). *Bilingual First Language Acquisition.* Bristol, UK: Multilingual Matters.

De Houwer, A. (2011). The speech of fluent child bilinguals. In P. Howell and J.V. Borsel (Eds.), *Multilingual Aspects of Fluency Disorders* (pp. 3-23). Bristol, UK: Multilingual Matters.

De Houwer, A., Bornstein, M.H., and Putnick, D.L. (2014). A bilingual–monolingual comparison of young children's vocabulary size: Evidence from comprehension and production. *Applied Psycholinguistics, 35*(6), 1189-1211.

Deanda, S., Arias-Trejo, N., Poulin-Dubois, D., Zesiger, P., and Friend, M. (2016). Minimal second language exposure, SES, and early word comprehension: New evidence from a direct assessment. *Bilingualism: Language and Cognition, 19*(1), 162-180.

Dickinson, D.K., and Tabors, P. (1991). Early literacy: Linkages between home, school, and literacy achievement at age five. *Journal of Research in Childhood Education, 6*, 30-46.

Dickinson, D.K., and Tabors, P.O. (2001). *Beginning Literacy with Language: Young Children Learning at Home and School.* Baltimore, MD: Paul H. Brookes.

Dixon, L.Q., Wu, S., and Daraghmeh, A. (2012). Profiles in bilingualism: Factors influencing kindergartners' language proficiency. *Early Childhood Education Journal, 40*(1), 25-34.

Duñabeitia, J.A., and Carreiras, M. (2015). The bilingual advantage: Acta est fabula? *Cortex, 73*, 371-372.

Duñabeitia, J.A., Hernandez, J.A., Anton, E., Macizo, P., Estevez, A., Fuentes, L.J., and Carreiras, M. (2014). The inhibitory advantage in bilingual children revisited: Myth or reality? *Experimental Psychology, 61*(3), 234-251.

Dupoux, E., Peperkamp, S., and Sebastián-Gallés, N. (2010). Limits on bilingualism revisited: Stress "deafness" in simultaneous French–Spanish bilinguals. *Cognition, 114*(2), 266-275.

Engel de Abreu, P.M.J., Gathercole, S.E., and Martin, R. (2011). Disentangling the relationship between working memory and language: The roles of short-term storage and cognitive control. *Learning and Individual Differences, 21*(5), 569-574.

Escobar, K., and Tamis-Lemonda, C. (2015). Understanding the variability in Latino children's dual-language development. In N.J. Cabrera, B. Leyendecker, and R. Bradley (Eds.), *Positive Development of Minority Children* (vol. 27). Ann Arbor, MI: Springer.

Espinosa, L.M. (2010a). *Getting it Right for Young Children from Diverse Backgrounds: Applying Research to Improve Practice.* Upper Saddle River, NJ: Pearson.

Espinosa, L.M. (2010b). Language and literacy for bilingual and monolingual children. In V. Washington and J.D. Andrews (Eds.), *Children of 2020: Creating a Better Tomorrow* (pp. 73-80). Washington, DC: National Association for the Education of Young Children.

Farah, M.J. (2010). Mind, brain, and education in socioeconomic context. In *The Developmental Relations among Mind, Brain and Education* (pp. 243-256). Rotterdam: Springer Netherlands.

Fennell, C., and Byers-Heinlein, K. (2014). You sound like Mommy: Bilingual and monolingual infants learn words best from speakers typical of their language environments. *International Journal of Behavioral Development, 38*(4), 309-316.

Fennell, C.T., Byers-Heinlein, K., and Werker, J.F. (2007). Using speech sounds to guide word learning: The case of bilingual infants. *Child Development, 78*(5), 1510-1525.

Ferjan Ramirez, N., Ramirez, R.R., Clark, M., Taulu, S., and Kuhl, P.K. (2016). Speech discrimination in 11-month-old bilingual and monolingual infants: A magnetoencephalography study. *Develomental Science*, 1-16. DOI:10.1111/desc.12427.

Fernald, A., Marchman, V.A., and Weisleder, A. (2013). SES differences in language processing skill and vocabulary are evident at 18 months. *Developmental Science, 16*(2), 234-248.

Fiorentino, L., and Howe, N. (2004). Language competence, narrative ability, and school readiness in low-income preschool children. *Canadian Journal of Behavioural Science/ Revue Canadienne des Sciences du Comportement, 36*(4), 280-294.

Flege, J.E., Munro, M.J., and Mackay, I.R.A. (1995). Effects of age of second-language learning on the production of English consonants. *Speech Communication, 16*(1), 1-26.

Flege, J.E., Yeni-Komshian, G.H., and Liu, S. (1999). Age constraints on second-language acquisition. *Journal of Memory and Language, 41*(1), 78-104.

Friedman, N.P., Miyake, A., Young, S.E., DeFries, J.C., Corley, R.P., and Hewitt, J.K. (2008). Individual differences in executive functions are almost entirely genetic in origin. *Journal of Experimental Psychology: General, 137*(2), 201-225.

Friesen, D., and Bialystok, E. (2012). Metalinguistic ability in bilingual children: The role of executive control. *Rivista Psicholinguistica Applicata, 12*(3), 47-56.

Garcia-Sierra, A., Rivera-Gaxiola, M., Percaccio, C.R., Conboy, B.T., Romo, H., Klarman, L., Ortiz, S., and Kuhl, P.K. (2011). Bilingual language learning: An ERP study relating early brain responses to speech, language input, and later word production. *Journal of Phonetics, 39*(4), 546-557.

Gathercole, V.C.M., and Min, H. (1997). Word meaning biases or language-specific effects? Evidence from English, Spanish, and Korean. *First Language, 17*(49), 31-56.

Genesee, F. (1989). Early bilingual development: One language or two? *Journal of Child Language, 16*(1), 161-179.

Genesee, F. (2002). Portrait of the bilingual child. In V. Cook (Ed.), *Portraits of the Second Language User* (pp. 219-250). Clevedon, UK: Multilingual Matters.

Genesee, F., Nicoladis, E., and Paradis, J. (1995). Language differentiation in early bilingual development. *Journal of Child Language, 22*(3), 611-632.

Genesee, F., Boivin, I., and Nicoladis, E. (1996). Talking with strangers: A study of bilingual children's communicative competence. *Applied Psycholinguistics, 17*(4), 427-442.

Gervain, J., and Werker, J.F. (2013a). Prosody cues word order in 7-month-old bilingual infants. *Nature Communications, 4,* 1490.

Gervain, J. and Werker, J.F. (2013b). Learning non-adjacent regularities at 0;7. *Journal of Child Language, 40*(4), 860-872.

Giannakopoulou, A., Uther, M., and Ylinen, S. (2013). Enhanced plasticity in spoken language acquisition for child learners: Evidence from phonetic training studies in child and adult learners of English. *Child Language Teaching and Therapy, 29*(2), 201-218.

Gildersleeve-Neumann, C.E., Kester, E.S., Davis, B.L., and Pena, E.D. (2008). English speech sound development in preschool-aged children from bilingual English-Spanish environments. *Language, Speech, and Hearing Services in Schools, 39*(3), 314-328.

Gleitman, L. (1990). The structural sources of verb meanings. *Language Acquisition, 1*(1), 355.

Goldenberg, C. (2006). Involving parents of English learners in their children's schooling . *Instructional Leader, 29*(3), 1-3.

Goldstein, B.A., Bunta, F., Lange, J., Rodriguez, J., and Burrows, L. (2010). The effects of measures of language experience and language ability on segmental accuracy in bilingual children. *American Journal of Speech-Language Pathology, 19*(3), 238-247.

Golinkoff, R.M., and Hirsh-Pasek, K. (2006). Baby wordsmith: From associationist to social sophisticate. *Current Directions in Psychological Science, 15*(1), 30-33.

Golinkoff, R.M., Deniz Can, D., Soderstrom, M., and Hirsh-Pasek, K. (2015). (Baby)talk to me: The social context of infant-directed speech and its effects on early language acquisition. *Current Directions in Psychological Science, 24,* 339-344.

Gordon, K.R. (2016). High proficiency across two languages is related to better mental state reasoning for bilingual children. *Journal of Child Language, 43*(2), 407-424.

Green, D.W. (1998). Mental control of the bilingual lexico-semantic system. *Bilingualism: Language and Cognition, 1*(02), 67-81.

Gutiérrez-Clellen, V.F., Simon-Cereijido, G., and Wagner, C. (2008). Bilingual children with language impairment: A comparison with monolinguals and second language learners. *Applied Psycholinguistics, 29*(1), 3-19.

Hakuta, K., and D'Andrea, D. (1992). Some properties of bilingual maintenance and loss in Mexican background high-school students. *Applied Linguistics, 13*(1), 72-99.

Halberda, J. (2003). The development of a word-learning strategy. *Cognition, 87*(1), B23-B34.

Hammer, C.S., Davison, M.D., Lawrence, F.R., and Miccio, A.W. (2009). The effect of maternal language on bilingual children's vocabulary and emergent literacy development during Head Start and kindergarten. *Scientific Studies of Reading, 13*(2), 99-121.

Hammer, C.S., Komaroff, E., Rodriguez, B.L., Lopez, L.M., Scarpino, S.E., and Goldstein, B. (2012). Predicting Spanish–English bilingual children's language abilities. *Journal of Speech, Language, and Hearing Research, 55*(5), 1251-1264.

Hammer, C.S., Hoff, E., Uchikoshi, Y., Gillanders, C., Castro, D.C., and Sandilos, L.E. (2014). The language and literacy development of young dual language learners: A critical review. *Early Childhood Research Quarterly, 29*(4), 715-733.

Hart, B., and Risley, T.R. (1995). *Meaningful Differences in the Everyday Experience of Young American Children.* Baltimore, MD: Paul H. Brookes.

Heath, S.B. (1982). What no bedtime story means: Narrative skills at home and school. *Language in Society, 11*(1), 49-76.

Hensch, T. K. (2004). Critical period regulation. *Annual Review of Neuroscience, 27,* 549-579.

Hernandez, D. (2006). *Young Hispanic Children in the U.S.: A Demographic Portrait Based on Census 2000. Report to the National Task Force on Early Childhood Education for Hispanics.* Tempe: Arizona State University.

Hernandez, A.E., and Kohnert, K.J. (2015). Investigations into the locus of language-switching costs in older adult bilinguals. *Bilingualism: Language and Cognition, 18*(1), 51-64.

Hernandez, A.E., and Li, P. (2007). Age of acquisition: Its neural and computational mechanisms. *Psychological Bulletin, 133*(4), 638-650.

Hernandez, A.E., Li, P., and MacWhinney, B. (2005). The emergence of competing modules in bilingualism. *Trends in Cognitive Sciences, 9*(5), 220-225.

Hernandez, A.E., Hofmann, J., and Kotz, S.A. (2007a). Age of acquisition modulates neural activity for both regular and irregular syntactic functions. *Neuroimage, 36*(3), 912-923.

Hernandez, D.J., Denton, N.A., and Macartney, S.E. (2007b). Demographic trends and the transition years. In R.C. Pianta, M.J. Cox, and K.L. Snow (Eds.), *School Readiness and the Transition to Kindergarten in the Era of Accountability* (pp. 217-281). Baltimore, MD: Paul H. Brookes.

Hernandez, D.J., Denton, N.A., and Macartney, S.E. (2008). Children in immigrant families: Looking to America's future. *Social Policy Report, 22*(3), 3-23.

Hilchey, M.D., and Klein, R.M. (2011). Are there bilingual advantages on nonlinguistic interference tasks? Implications for the plasticity of executive control processes. *Psychonomic Bulletin and Review, 18*(4), 625-658.

Hirsh-Pasek, K., Michnick Golinkoff, R., Berk, L.E., and Singer, D.G. (2009). *A Mandate for Playful Learning in Preschool: Presenting the Evidence.* Oxford, UK and New York: Oxford University Press.

Hoff, E. (2003). The specificity of environmental influence: Socioeconomic status affects early vocabulary development via maternal speech. *Child Development, 74*(5), 1368-1378.

Hoff, E. (2006). How social contexts support and shape language development. *Developmental Review, 26*(1), 55-88.

Hoff, E., and Naigles, L. (2002). How children use input to acquire a lexicon. *Child Development, 73*(2), 418-433.

Hoff, E., Core, C., Place, S., Rumiche, R., Señor, M., and Parra, M. (2012). Dual language exposure and early bilingual development. *Journal of Child Language, 39*(1), 1-27.

Houston-Price, C., Caloghiris, Z., and Raviglione, E. (2010). Language experience shapes the development of the mutual exclusivity bias. *Infancy, 15*(2), 125-150.

Hudon, T.M., Fennell, C.T., and Hoftyzer, M. (2013). Quality not quantity of television viewing is associated with bilingual toddlers' vocabulary scores. *Infant Behavior and Development, 36*(2), 245–254.

Hughes, D., Rodriguez, J., Smith, E.P., Johnson, D.J., Stevenson, H.C., and Spicer, P. (2006). Parents' ethnic-racial socialization practices: A review of research and directions for future study. *Developmental Psychology, 42*(5), 747-770.

Hurtado, A., and Vega, L.A. (2004). Shift happens: Spanish and English transmission between parents and their children. *Journal of Social Issues, 60*(1), 137-155.

Hurtado, N., Marchman, V.A., and Fernald, A. (2008). Does input influence uptake? Links between maternal talk, processing speed and vocabulary size in Spanish-learning children. *Developmental Science, 11*(6), F31-F39.

Hurtado, N., Grueter, T., Marchman, V.A., and Fernald, A. (2014). Relative language exposure, processing efficiency and vocabulary in Spanish–English bilingual toddlers. *Bilingualism: Language and Cognition, 17*(1), 189-202.

Huttenlocher, J., Waterfall, H., Vasilyeva, M., Vevea, J., and Hedges, L.V. (2010). Sources of variability in children's language growth. *Cognitive Psychology, 61*(4), 343-365.

Imai, M., and Gentner, D. (1997). A cross-linguistic study of early word meaning: Universal ontology and linguistic influence. *Cognition, 62*(2), 169-200.

Inman, A.G., Howard, E.E., Beaumont, R.L., and Walker, J.A. (2007). Cultural transmission: Influence of contextual factors in Asian Indian immigrant parents' experiences. *Journal of Counseling Psychology, 54*(1), 93-100.

Institute of Medicine and National Research Council. (2015). *Transforming the Workforce for Children Birth Through Age 8: A Unifying Foundation*. L. Allen and B.B. Kelly (Eds.). Committee on the Science of Children Birth to Age 8: Deepening and Broadening the Foundation for Success; Board on Children, Youth, and Families. Washington, DC: The National Academies Press.

Jia, G., Aaronson, D., and Wu, Y. (2002). Long-term language attainment of bilingual immigrants: Predictive variables and language group differences. *Applied Psycholinguistics, 23*(4), 599-621.

Johnson, J.S., and Newport, E.L. (1989). Critical period effects in second language learning: The influence of maturational state on the acquisition of English as a second language. *Cognitive Psychology, 21*(1), 60-99.

Johnson, S.B., Riis, J.L., and Noble, K.G. (2016). State of the art review: Poverty and the developing brain. *Pediatrics, 137*(4). DOI:10.1524/peds.2015-3075.

Junker, D.A., and Stockman, I.J. (2002). Expressive vocabulary of German-English bilingual toddlers. *American Journal of Speech-Language Pathology, 11*(4), 381-394.

Kalashnikova, M., and Mattock, K. (2014). Maturation of executive functioning skills in early sequential bilingualism. *International Journal of Bilingual Education and Bilingualism, 17*(1), 111-123.

Kan, P.F. (2014). Novel word retention in sequential bilingual children. *Journal of Child Language, 41*(2), 416-438.

Kan, P.F., and Kohnert, K. (2008). Fast mapping by bilingual preschool children. *Journal of Child Language, 35*(3), 495-514.

Kang, J.Y., Kim, Y.-S., and Pan, B.A. (2009). Five-year-olds' book talk and story retelling: Contributions of mother-child joint bookreading. *First Language, 29*(3), 243-265.

Kapa, L.L., and Colombo, J. (2013). Attentional control in early and later bilingual children. *Cognitive Development, 28*(3), 233-246.

Klein, D., Mok, K., Chen, J.K., and Watkins, K.E. (2014). Age of language learning shapes brain structure: A cortical thickness study of bilingual and monolingual individuals. *Brain and Language, 131*, 20-24.

Koenig, M.A., and Woodward, A.L. (2012). Toddlers learn words in a foreign language: The role of native vocabulary knowledge. *Journal of Child Language, 39*(2), 322-337.

Kohnert, K., Kan, P.F., and Conboy, B.T. (2010). Lexical and grammatical associations in sequential bilingual preschoolers. *Journal of Speech, Language, and Hearing Research, 53*(3), 684-698.

Konishi, H., Kanero, J., Freeman, M.R., Golinkoff, R.M., and Hirsh-Pasek, K. (2014). Six principles of language development: Implications for second language learners. *Developmental Neuropsychology, 39*(5), 404-420.

Kovács, Á.M., and Mehler, J. (2009). Cognitive gains in 7-month-old bilingual infants. *Proceedings of the National Academy of Sciences of the United States of America, 106*(16), 6556-6560.

Kovelman, I., Baker, S.A., and Petitto, L.A. (2008a). Age of first bilingual language exposure as a new window into bilingual reading development. *Bilingualism (Cambridge, England), 11*(2), 203-223.

Kovelman, I., Baker, S.A., and Petitto, L.-A. (2008b). Bilingual and monolingual brains compared: A functional magnetic resonance imaging investigation of syntactic processing and a possible "neural signature" of bilingualism. *Journal of Cognitive Neuroscience, 20*(1), 153-169.

Kovelman, I., Shalinsky, M.H., Berens, M.S., and Petitto, L.A. (2008c). Shining new light on the brain's "bilingual signature": A functional near infrared spectroscopy investigation of semantic processing. *Neuroimage, 39*(3), 1457-1471.

Kuchirko, Y., Tamis-LeMonda, C. S., Luo, R., and Liang, E. (2015). "What happened next?": Developmental changes in mothers' questions to children. *Journal of Early Childhood Literacy, 16*(4), 498-521.

Kuhl, P.K. (2009). Early language acquisition: Phonetic and word learning, neural substrates, and a theoretical model. In B. Moore, L. Tyler, and W. Marslen-Wilson (Eds.), *The Perception of Speech: From Sound to Meaning* (pp. 103-131). New York: Oxford University Press.

Kuhl, P.K., Williams, K.A., Lacerda, F., Stevens, K.N., and Lindblom, B. (1992). Linguistic experience alters phonetic perception in infants by 6 months of age. *Science, 255*(5044), 606-608.

Kuhl, P.K., Stevens, E., Hayashi, A., Deguchi, T., Kiritani, S., and Iverson, P. (2006). Infants show a facilitation effect for native language phonetic perception between 6 and 12 months. *Developmental Science, 9*(2), F13-F21.

Landry, S.H., Smith, K.E., and Swank, P.R. (2006). Responsive parenting: Establishing early foundations for social, communication, and independent problem-solving skills. *Developmental Psychology, 42*(4), 627-642.

Leacox, L.R. and Jackson, C.W. (2014). Language-bridging and technology to enhance vocabulary development for young bilinguals. *Journal of Early Childhood Literacy, 14*, 175-197.

Lee, T., Mosing, M.A., Henry, J.D., Trollor, J.N., Ames, D., Martin, N.G., Wright, M.J., and Sachdev, P.S. (2012). Genetic influences on four measures of executive functions and their covariation with general cognitive ability: The Older Australian Twins Study. *Behavior Genetics, 42*(4), 528-538.

Lenneberg, E.H. (1967). *Biological Foundations of Language.* New York: John Wiley & Sons.

Linebarger, D.L., and Walker, D. (2005). Infants' and toddlers' television viewing and language outcomes. *American Behavioral Scientist, 48*(5), 624-645.

Lu, X. (2001). Bicultural identity development and Chinese community formation: An ethnographic study of Chinese schools in Chicago. *Howard Journal of Communications, 12*(4), 203-220.

Luk, G., Green, D.W., Abutalebi, J., and Grady, C. (2012). Cognitive control for language switching in bilinguals: A quantitative meta-analysis of functional neuroimaging studies. *Language and Cognitive Processes, 27*(10), 1479-1488.

Luo, R., and Tamis-LeMonda, C.S. (2016). Mothers' verbal and nonverbal strategies in relation to infants' object-directed actions in real time and across the first three years in ethnically diverse families. *Infancy, 21*(1), 65-89.

Luo, R., and Tamis-LeMonda, C.S. (2017). Reciprocity between maternal questions and child contributions during book-sharing. *Early Childhood Research Quarterly, 38*, 71-83.

Lyytinen, P., Laakso, M.-L., and Poikkeus, A.-M. (1998). Parental contribution to child's early language and interest in books. *European Journal of Psychology of Education, 13*(3), 297-308.

Mackay, I.R.A., and Flege, J.E. (2004). Effects of the age of second language learning on the duration of first and second language sentences: The role of suppression. *Applied Psycholinguistics, 25*(3), 373-396.

Marcella, J., Howes, C., and Fuligni, A.S. (2014). Exploring cumulative risk and family literacy practices in low-income Latino families. *Early Education & Development, 25*(1), 36-55.

Marchman, V.A., and Bates, E. (1994). Continuity in lexical and morphological development: A test of the critical mass hypothesis. *Journal of Child Language, 21*(2), 339-366.

Marchman, V.A., and Fernald, A. (2008). Speed of word recognition and vocabulary knowledge in infancy predict cognitive and language outcomes in later childhood. *Developmental Science, 11*(3), F9-F16.

Marchman, V.A., Martínez-Sussmann, C., and Dale, P.S. (2004). The language specific nature of grammatical development: Evidence from bilingual language learners. *Developmental Science, 7*(2), 212-224.

Marchman, V.A., Fernald, A., and Hurtado, N. (2010). How vocabulary size in two languages relates to efficiency in spoken word recognition by young Spanish–English bilinguals. *Journal of Child Language, 37*(4), 817-840.

Markman, E.M. (1989). *Categorization and Naming in Children: Problems of Induction.* Cambridge, MA: MIT Press.

Martin-Rhee, M.M., and Bialystok, E. (2008). The development of two types of inhibitory control in monolingual and bilingual children. *Bilingualism: Language and Cognition, 11*(1), 81-93.

Mattock, K., Polka, L., Rvachew, S., and Krehm, M. (2010). The first steps in word learning are easier when the shoes fit: Comparing monolingual and bilingual infants. *Developmental Science, 13*(1), 229-243.

Mayberry, R.I. (2007). When timing is everything: Age of first-language acquisition effects on second-language learning. *Applied Psycholinguistics, 28*(3), 537-549.

McCabe, A., Tamis-LeMonda, C.S., Bornstein, M.H., Cates, C.B., Golinkoff, R., Guerra, A.W., Hirsh-Pasek, K., Hoff, E., Kuchirko, Y., and Melzi, G. (2013). Multilingual children. *Social Policy Report, 27*(4), 1-36.

Meisel, J.M. (2007). The weaker language in early child bilingualism: Acquiring a first language as a second language? *Applied Psycholinguistics, 28*(3), 495-514.

Meisel, J.M. (2011). *First and Second Language Acquisition: Parallels and Differences.* Cambridge, UK: Cambridge University Press.

Michaels, S. (2013). Commentary. Déjà vu all over again: What's wrong with Hart and Risley and a "linguistic deficit" framework in early childhood education? *Learning Landscapes, 7*(1) 23-41.

Mitchell, S., Myles, F., and Marsden, E. (2013). *Second Language Learning Theories.* New York: Routledge.

Miyake, A., Friedman, N.P., Emerson, M.J., Witzki, A.H., Howerter, A., and Wager, T.D. (2000). The unity and diversity of executive functions and their contributions to complex "frontal lobe" tasks: A latent variable analysis. *Cognitive Psychology, 41*(1), 49-100.

Montrul, S.A. (2008). *Incomplete Acquisition in Bilingualism: Re-Examining the Age Factor* (vol. 39). Philadelphia, PA: John Benjamins.

Morales, J., Calvo, A., and Bialystok, E. (2013). Working memory development in monolingual and bilingual children. *Journal of Experimental Child Psychology, 114*(2), 187-202.

Munro, M.J., Flege, J.E., and Mackay, I.R.A. (1996). The effects of age of second language learning on the production of English vowels. *Applied Psycholinguistics, 17*(3), 313-334.

National Task Force on Early Childhood Education for Hispanics. (2007). *Expanding and Improving Early Education for Hispanics Executive Report.* Available: http://fcd-us.org/sites/default/files/PNNExecReport.pdf [July 2017].

Nazzi, T., Jusczyk, P.W., and Johnson, E.K. (2000). Language discrimination by English-learning 5-month-olds: Effects of rhythm and familiarity. *Journal of Memory and Language, 43*(1), 1-19.

Nelson, K., Hampson, J., and Shaw, L.K. (1993). Nouns in early lexicons: Evidence, explanations and implications. *Journal of Child Language, 20*(1), 61-84.

Neuman, S.B., and Celano, D. (2001). Access to print in low-income and middle-income communities. An ecological study of four neighborhoods. *Reading Research Quarterly, 36*(1), 8-26.

Newmeyer, F. (1986). *The Politics of Linguistics.* Chicago, IL: University of Chicago Press.

Nicoladis, E. (2002). What's the difference between "toilet paper" and "paper toilet"? French-English bilingual children's crosslinguistic transfer in compound nouns. *Journal of Child Language, 29*(4), 843-863.

Nicoladis, E. (2003). Cross-linguistic transfer in deverbal compounds of preschool bilingual children. *Bilingualism: Language and Cognition, 6*(1), 17-31.

Noble, K.G., Norman, M.F., and Farah, M.J. (2005). Neurocognitive correlates of socioeconomic status in kindergarten children. *Developmental Science, 8*(1), 74-87.

Nord, C.W., and Griffin, J.A. (1999). Educational profile of 3- to 8-year-old children of immigrants. In D.J. Hernandez (Ed.), *Children of Immigrants: Health, Adjustment, and Public Assistance* (pp. 348-409). Washington, DC: National Academy Press.

Oh, J.S., and Fuligni, A.J. (2010). The role of heritage language development in the ethnic identity and family relationships of adolescents from immigrant backgrounds. *Social Development, 19*(1), 202-220.

Oller, D.K., and Eilers, R.E. (2002). *Language and Literacy in Bilingual Children.* Clevedon, UK: Multilingual Matters.

Oller, D.K., Pearson, B.Z., and Cobo-Lewis, A.B. (2007). Profile effects in early bilingual language and literacy. *Applied Psycholinguistics, 28*(2), 191-230.

Ortiz-Mantilla, S., Choudhury, N., Alvarez, B., and Benasich, A.A. (2010). Involuntary switching of attention mediates differences in event-related responses to complex tones between early and late Spanish–English bilinguals. *Brain Research, 1362*, 78-92.

Paap, K.R., and Greenberg, Z.I. (2013). There is no coherent evidence for a bilingual advantage in executive processing. *Cognitive Psychology, 66*(2), 232-258.

Paap, K.R., Johnson, H.A., and Sawi, O. (2014). Are bilingual advantages dependent upon specific tasks or specific bilingual experiences? *Journal of Cognitive Psychology, 26*(6), 615-639.

Paradis, J., and Genesee, F. (1996). Syntactic acquisition in bilingual children. *Studies in Second Language Acquisition, 18*(1), 1-25.

Paradis, J., and Navarro, S. (2003). Subject realization and crosslinguistic interference in the bilingual acquisition of Spanish and English: What is the role of the input? *Journal of Child Language, 30*(2), 371-393.

Paradis, J., Nicoladis, E., Crago, M., and Genesee, F. (2011a). Bilingual children's acquisition of the past tense: A usage-based approach. *Journal of Child Language, 38*(3), 554-578.

Paradis, J., Genesee, F., and Crago, M.B. (2011b). *Dual Language Development and Disorders: A Handbook on Bilingualism and Second Language Learning* (2nd ed.). Baltimore, MD: Paul H. Brookes.

Paradis, J., Tremblay, A., and Crago, M. (2014). French-English bilingual children's sensitivity to child-level and language-level input factors in morphosyntactic acquisition. *Input and Experience in Bilingual Development, 13*, 161-180.

Parmar, P., Harkness, S., and Super, C.M. (2008). Teacher or playmate? Asian immigrant and Euro-American parents' participation in their young children's daily activities. *Social Behavior and Personality: An International Journal, 36*(2), 163-176.

Parra, M., Hoff, E., and Core, C. (2011). Relations among language exposure, phonological memory, and language development in Spanish–English bilingually developing 2-year-olds. *Journal of Experimental Child Psychology, 108*(1), 113-125.

Patterson, J.L. (1998). Expressive vocabulary development and word combinations of Spanish–English bilingual toddlers. *American Journal of Speech-Language Pathology, 7*(4), 46-56.

Pearson, B.Z., Fernandez, S.C., and Oller, D.K. (1993). Lexical development in bilingual infants and toddlers: Comparison to monolingual norms. *Language Learning, 43*(1), 93-120.

Pelham, S.D., and Abrams, L. (2014). Cognitive advantages and disadvantages in early and late bilinguals. *Journal of Experimental Psychology: Learning, Memory, and Cognition,* 40(2), 313-325.

Perani, D., Paulesu, E., Galles, N.S., Dupoux, E., Dehaene, S., Bettinardi, V., Cappa, S.F., Fazio, F., and Mehler, J. (1998). The bilingual brain. Proficiency and age of acquisition of the second language. *Brain, 121*(10), 1841-1852.

Petitto, L.A., Katerelos, M., Levy, B.G., Gauna, K., Tétreault, K., and Ferraro, V. (2001). Bilingual signed and spoken language acquisition from birth: Implications for the mechanisms underlying early bilingual language acquisition. *Journal of Child Language, 28*(2), 453-496.

Pickett, E.R., Kuniholm, E., Protopapas, A., Friedman, J., and Lieberman, P. (1998). Selective speech motor, syntax and cognitive deficits associated with bilateral damage to the putamen and the head of the caudate nucleus: A case study. *Neuropsychologia, 36*(2), 173-188.

Pierce, L.J., Chen, J.-K., Delcenserie, A., Genesee, F., and Klein, D. (2015). Past experience shapes ongoing neural patterns for language. *Nature Communications, 6*(10073). Available: https://www.nature.com/articles/ncomms10073 [June 2017].

Pinker, S. (2013). *Learnability and Cognition: The Acquisition of Argument Structure.* Cambridge, MA: The MIT Press.

Place, S., and Hoff, E. (2011). Properties of dual language exposure that influence 2-year-olds' bilingual proficiency. *Child Development, 82*(6), 1834-1849.

Polka, L., and Sundara, M. (2003). *Word Segmentation in Monolingual and Bilingual Infant Learners of English and French.* Paper presented at the Proceedings of the 15th International Congress of Phonetic Sciences, Barcelona, Spain.

Portocarrero, J.S., Burright, R.G., and Donovick, P.J. (2007). Vocabulary and verbal fluency of bilingual and monolingual college students. *Archives of Clinical Neuropsychology, 22*(3), 415-422.

Quiroz, B.G., Snow, C.E., and Zhao, J. (2010). Vocabulary skills of Spanish–English bilinguals: Impact of mother–child language interactions and home language and literacy support. *International Journal of Bilingualism, 14*(4), 379-399.

Rader, N.D.V., and Zukow-Goldring, P. (2010). How the hands control attention during early word learning. *Gesture, 10*(2-3), 202-221.

Raikes, H., Alexander Pan, B., Luze, G., Tamis-LeMonda, C.S., Brooks-Gunn, J., Constantine, J., Banks Tarullo, L., Raikes, H.A., and Rodriguez, E.T. (2006). Mother–child bookreading in low-income families: Correlates and outcomes during the first three years of life. *Child Development, 77*(4), 924-953.

Ramírez-Esparza, N., García-Sierra, A., and Kuhl, P.K. (2014). Look who's talking: Speech style and social context in language input to infants are linked to concurrent and future speech development. *Developmental Science, 17*(6), 880-891.

Ramon-Casas, M., Swingley, D., Sebastián-Gallés, N., and Bosch, L. (2009). Vowel categorization during word recognition in bilingual toddlers. *Cognitive Psychology, 59*(1), 96-121.

Reese, L., and Goldenberg, C. (2006). Community contexts for literacy development of Latina/o children. *Anthropology & Education Quarterly, 37*(1), 42-61.

Reese, E., and Newcombe, R. (2007). Training mothers in elaborative reminiscing enhances children's autobiographical memory and narrative. *Child Development, 78*(4), 1153-1170.

Reznick, J.S., and Goldfield, B.A. (1992). Rapid change in lexical development in comprehension and production. *Developmental Psychology, 28*(3), 406-413.

Rinaldi, C., and Páez, M. (2008). Preschool matters: Predicting reading difficulties for Spanish-speaking bilingual students in first grade. *Learning Disabilities, 6*(1), 71-84.

Rodriguez, E.T., and Tamis-LeMonda, C.S. (2011). Trajectories of the home learning environment across the first 5 years: Associations with children's vocabulary and literacy skills at prekindergarten. *Child Development, 82*(4), 1058-1075.

Rogoff, B., Paradise, R., Arauz, R.M., Correa-Chávez, M., and Angelillo, C. (2003). Firsthand learning through intent participation. *Annual Review of Psychology, 54*(1), 175-203.

Roseberry, S., Hirsh-Pasek, K., and Golinkoff, R.M. (2014). Skype me! Socially contingent interactions help toddlers learn language. *Child Development, 85*(3), 956-970.

Rossi, S., Gugler, M.F., Friederici, A.D., and Hahne, A. (2006). The impact of proficiency on syntactic second-language processing of German and Italian: Evidence from event-related potentials. *Journal of Cognitive Neuroscience, 18*(12), 2030-2048.

Rowe, M.L. (2012). A longitudinal investigation of the role of quantity and quality of child-directed speech in vocabulary development. *Child Development, 83*(5), 1762-1774.

Rowe, M.L., and Goldin-Meadow, S. (2009). Early gesture selectively predicts later language learning. *Developmental Science, 12*(1), 182-187.

Sadat, J., Martin, C.D., Alario, F.X., and Costa, A. (2012). Characterizing the bilingual disadvantage in noun phrase production. *Journal of Psycholinguistic Research, 41*(3), 159-179.

Schelletter, C., Sinka, I., and Garman, M. (2001). Early nouns in bilingual acquisition: A test of the separate development hypothesis. In M. Georgiafentis, P. Kerswill, and S. Varlokosta (Eds.), *Working Papers in Linguistics* (vol. 5, pp. 301-317). Reading, UK: University of Reading.

Schick, A. (2015). Wordless book-sharing styles in bilingual preschool classrooms and Latino children's emergent literacy skills. *Journal of Early Childhood Literacy, 15*(3), 331-363.

Schick, A., and Melzi, G. (2010). The development of children's oral narratives across contexts. *Early Education and Development, 21*(3), 293-317.

Schieffelin, B.B., and Ochs, E. (1986). *Language Socialization Across Cultures* (no. 3). New York: Cambridge University Press.

Schonberg, C., Sandhofer, C.M., Tsang, T., and Johnson, S.P. (2014). Does bilingual experience affect early visual perceptual development? *Frontiers in Psychology, 5*, 1429.

Sebastián-Gallés, N. (2010). Bilingual language acquisition: Where does the difference lie? *Human Development, 53*(5), 245-255.

Sebastián-Gallés, N., and Bosch, L. (2002). Building phonotactic knowledge in bilinguals: Role of early exposure. *Journal of Experimental Psychology: Human Perception and Performance, 28*(4), 974-989.

Sebastián-Gallés, N., Albareda-Castellot, B., Weikum, W.M., and Werker, J.F. (2012). A bilingual advantage in visual language discrimination in infancy. *Psychological Science, 23*(9), 994-999.

Sénéchal, M. (1997). The differential effect of storybook reading on preschoolers' acquisition of expressive and receptive vocabulary. *Journal of Child language, 24*(1), 123-138.

Sénéchal, M., LeFevre, J.-A., Hudson, E., and Lawson, E.P. (1996). Knowledge of storybooks as a predictor of young children's vocabulary. *Journal of Educational Psychology, 88*(3), 520-536.

Sénéchal, M., Ouellette, G., and Rodney, D. (2006). The misunderstood giant: On the predictive role of vocabulary to reading. In S.B. Neuman and D. Dickinson (Eds.), *Handbook of Early Literacy* (vol. 2, pp. 173-182). New York: Guilford Press.

Serratrice, L., Sorace, A., Filiaci, F., and Baldo, M. (2009). Bilingual children's sensitivity to specificity and genericity: Evidence from metalinguistic awareness. *Bilingualism: Language and Cognition, 12*(2), 239-257.

Shafer, V.L., Yu, Y.H., and Datta, H. (2011). The development of English vowel perception in monolingual and bilingual infants: Neurophysiological correlates. *Journal of Phonetics, 39*(4), 527-545.

Silvén, M., and Rubinov, E. (2010). Language and preliteracy skills in bilinguals and monolinguals at preschool age: Effects of exposure to richly inflected speech from birth. *Reading and Writing, 23*(3), 385-414.

Silvén, M., Voeten, M., Kouvo, A., and Lundén, M. (2014). Speech perception and vocabulary growth: A longitudinal study of Finnish–Russian bilinguals and Finnish monolinguals from infancy to three years. *International Journal of Behavioral Development, 38*(4), 323-332.

Singh, L. (2014). One world, two languages: Cross-language semantic priming in bilingual toddlers. *Child Development, 85*(2), 755-766.

Snow, C.E., and Dickinson, D.K. (1990). Social sources of narrative skills at home and at school. *First Language, 10*(29), 87-103.

Song, L., Tamis-LeMonda, C.S., Yoshikawa, H., Kahana-Kalman, R., and Wu, I. (2012). Language experiences and vocabulary development in Dominican and Mexican infants across the first 2 years. *Developmental Psychology, 48*(4), 1106.

Sosa, A.V. (2016). Association of the type of toy used during play with the quantity and quality of parent-infant communication. *JAMA pediatrics, 170*(2), 132-137.

Steinhauer, K., White, E.J., and Drury, J.E. (2009). Temporal dynamics of late second language acquisition: Evidence from event-related brain potentials. *Second Language Research, 25*(1), 13-41.

Stocco, A., Yamasaki, B., Natalenko, R., and Prat, C.S. (2014). Bilingual brain training: A neurobiological framework of how bilingual experience improves executive function. *International Journal of Bilingualism, 18*(1), 67-92.

Sundara, M., Polka, L., and Molnar, M. (2008). Development of coronal stop perception: Bilingual infants keep pace with their monolingual peers. *Cognition, 108*(1), 232-242.

Swanson, M.R., Wolff, J.J., Elison, J.T., Gu, H., Hazlett, H.C., Botteron, K., Styner, M., Paterson, S., Gerig, G., Constantino, J., Dager, S., Estes, A., Vachet, C., and Piven, J. (2015). Splenium development and early spoken language in human infants. *Developmental Science.* Available: http://dx.doi.org/10.1111/desc.12360 [November 6, 2016].

Tabors, P. (1997). *One Child, Two Languages: A Guide for Preschool Educators of Children Learning English as a Second Language.* Baltimore, MD: Paul H. Brookes.

Tabors, P.O., Snow, C.E., and Dickinson, D.K. (2001). Homes and schools together: Supporting language and literacy development. In D.K. Dickinson and P.O. Tabors (Eds.), *Beginning Literacy with Language* (pp. 313-334). Baltimore, MD: Paul H. Brookes.

Tamis-LeMonda, C.S., and Song, L. (2012). Parent-infant communicative interactions in cultural context. In I.B. Weiner, R.M. Lerner, E. Easterbrooks, and J. Mistry (Eds.), *Handbook of Psychology* (2nd ed., vol. 6). Hoboken, NJ: John Wiley & Sons.

Tamis-LeMonda, C.S., Baumwell, L., and Cristofaro, T. (2012a). Parent–child conversations during play. *First Language, 32*(4), 413-438.

Tamis-LeMonda, C.S., Song, L., Leavell, A.S., Kahana-Kalman, R., and Yoshikawa, H. (2012b). Ethnic differences in mother–infant language and gestural communications are associated with specific skills in infants. *Developmental Science, 15*(3), 384-397.

Tamis-LeMonda, C.S., Kuchirko, Y., and Tafuro, L. (2013). From action to interaction: Infant object exploration and mothers' contingent responsiveness. *IEEE Transactions on Autonomous Mental Development, 5*(3), 202-209.

Tamis-LeMonda, C.S., Song, L., Luo, R., Kuchirko, Y., Kahana-Kalman, R., Yoshikawa, H., and Raufman, J. (2014a). Children's vocabulary growth in English and Spanish across early development and associations with school readiness skills. *Developmental Neuropsychology, 39*(2), 69-87.

Tamis-LeMonda, C.S., Kuchirko, Y., and Song, L. (2014b). Why is infant language learning facilitated by parental responsiveness? *Current Directions in Psychological Science, 23*(2), 121-126.

Tardif, T. (1996). Nouns are not always learned before verbs: Evidence from Mandarin speakers' early vocabularies. *Developmental Psychology, 32*(3), 492-504.

Tardif, T. (2017). Culture, language and emotion: Explorations in development. In M.D. Sera, M. Maratsos, and S.M. Carlson (Eds.), *Minnesota Symposia on Child Psychology* (vol. 38). Hoboken, NJ: Wiley.

Tardif, T., Shatz, M., and Naigles, L. (1997). Caregiver speech and children's use of nouns versus verbs: A comparison of English, Italian, and Mandarin. *Journal of Child Language, 24*(3), 535-565.

Thordardottir, E. (2011). The relationship between bilingual exposure and vocabulary development. *International Journal of Bilingualism, 15*(4), 426-445.

Trehub, S. E. (1976). The discrimination of foreign speech contrasts by infants and adults. *Child Development, 47*(2), 466-472.

Tsao, F.-M., Liu, H.-M., and Kuhl, P.K. (2004). Speech perception in infancy predicts language development in the second year of life: A longitudinal study. *Child Development, 75*(4), 1067-1084.

Tseng, V., and Fuligni, A.J. (2000). Parent-adolescent language use and relationships among immigrant families with East Asian, Filipino, and Latin American backgrounds. *Journal of Marriage and Family, 62*(2), 465-476.

Uccelli, P., Hemphill, L., Pan, B.A., and Snow, C. (2005). Conversing with toddlers about the nonpresent: Precursors to narrative development in two genres. In L. Balter and C.S. Tamis-LeMonda (Eds.), *Child Psychology: A Handbook of Contemporary Issues* (2nd ed., pp. 215-237). New York: Taylor & Francis.

Urzúa, A., and Gómez, E. (2008). Home style Puerto Rican: A study of language maintenance and use in New England. *Journal of Multilingual and Multicultural Development, 29*(6), 449-466.

Veltman, C. (2000). The American linguistic mosaic: Understanding language shift in the United States. In S.L. McKay and S.-l.C. Wong (Eds.), *New Immigrants in the United States: Readings for Second Language Educators* (pp. 58-93). Cambridge, UK: Cambridge University Press.

Vihman, M.M., Thierry, G., Lum, J., Keren-Portnoy, T., and Martin, P. (2007). Onset of word form recognition in English, Welsh, and English–Welsh bilingual infants. *Applied Psycholinguistics, 28*(3), 475-493.

Volterra, V., and Taeschner, T. (1978). The acquisition and development of language by bilingual children. *Journal of Child Language, 5*(2), 311-326.

Von Holzen, K., and Mani, N. (2012). Language nonselective lexical access in bilingual toddlers. *Journal of Experimental Child Psychology, 113*(4), 569-586.

Wagner, R.K., Torgesen, J.K., and Rashotte, C.A. (1994). Development of reading-related phonological processing abilities: New evidence of bidirectional causality from a latent variable longitudinal study. *Developmental Psychology, 30*(1), 73-87.

Waldron, E.J., and Hernandez, A.E. (2013). The role of age of acquisition on past tense generation in Spanish-English bilinguals: An fMRI study. *Brain and Language, 125*(1), 28-37.

Wartenburger, I., Heekeren, H.R., Abutalebi, J., Cappa, S.F., Villringer, A., and Perani, D. (2003). Early setting of grammatical processing in the bilingual brain. *Neuron, 37*(1), 159-170.

Watson, R. (2001). Literacy and oral language: Implications for early literacy acquisition. *Handbook of Early Literacy Research, 1*, 43-53.

Waxman, S. (2009). How infants discover distinct word types and map them to distinct meanings. In J. Colombo, P. McCardle, and L. Freund (Eds.), *Infant Pathways to Language: Methods, Models, and Research Disorders* (pp. 99-118). New York: Psychology Press.

Weber-Fox, C.M., and Neville, H.J. (1996). Maturational constraints on functional specializations for language processing: ERP and behavioral evidence in bilingual speakers. *Journal of Cognitive Neuroscience, 8*(3), 231-256.

Weber-Fox, C.M, and Neville, H.J. (2001). Sensitive periods differentiate processing of open- and closed-class words: An ERP study of bilinguals. *Journal of Speech, Language, and Hearing Research, 44*(6), 1338-1353.

Weisleder, A., and Fernald, A. (2013). Talking to children matters early language experience strengthens processing and builds vocabulary. *Psychological Science, 24*(11), 2143-2152.

Weisner, T.S. (2002). Ecocultural understanding of children's developmental pathways. *Human Development, 45*(4), 275-281.

Werker, J. (2012). Perceptual foundations of bilingual acquisition in infancy. *Annals of the New York Academy of Sciences, 1251*(1), 50-61.

Werker, J.F., and Hensch, T.K. (2015). Critical periods in speech perception: New directions. *Annual Review of Psychology, 66*, 173-196.

Werker, J.F., and Tees, R.C. (1984). Cross-language speech perception: Evidence for perceptual reorganization during the first year of life. *Infant Behavior and Development, 7*(1), 49-63.

Werker, J.F., Fennell, C.T., Corcoran, K.M., and Stager, C.L. (2002). Infants' ability to learn phonetically similar words: Effects of age and vocabulary size. *Infancy, 3*(1), 1-30.

Whitehurst, G.J., Falco, F.L., Lonigan, C.J., Fischel, J.E., DeBaryshe, B.D., Valdez-Menchaca, M.C., and Caulfield, M. (1988). Accelerating language development through picture book reading. *Developmental psychology, 24*(4), 552.

Whitehurst, G.J., Arnold, D.S., Epstein, J.N., Angell, A.L., Smith, M., and Fischel, J.E. (1994). A picture book reading intervention in day care and home for children from low-income families. *Developmental Psychology, 30*(5), 679.

Wong-Fillmore, L. (1991). When learning a second language means losing the first. *Early Childhood Research Quarterly, 6*(3), 323-346.

Wong-Fillmore, L. (2000). Loss of family languages: Should educators be concerned? *Theory into Practice, 39*(4), 203-210.

Yip, V., and Matthews, S. (2007). *The Bilingual Child. Early Development and Language Contact.* Cambridge, UK: Cambridge University Press.

Yoshida, H., and Smith, L.B. (2003). Shifting ontological boundaries: How Japanese- and English-speaking children generalize names for animals and artifacts. *Developmental Science, 6*(1), 1-17.

5

Promising and Effective Early Care and Education Practices and Home Visiting Programs for Dual Language Learners

A large and growing share of the children under age 5 in the United States have a first language (L1) that is not English, and many of these children are served by early care and education (ECE) programs (Espinosa et al., 2017). The proportion of U.S. children from birth to age 5 who are identified as dual language learners (DLLs)[1] and are enrolled in ECE programs is greater than the percentage of children identified as English learners (ELs) in kindergarten and is growing across the nation (National Institute for Early Education Research, 2013). Illustrating the greater representation of DLLs during the early childhood years, while approximately 30 percent of children enrolled in the federal Head Start/Early Head Start Programs have been identified as DLLs (Office of Head Start, 2015b), just 9 percent of all children in U.S. K-12 public schools were identified as ELs in the 2011-2012 school year (Child Trends, 2014). In addition, more than one-quarter of the children served in Head Start and Early Head Start Programs live in households where a language other than English is spoken (Migration Policy Institute, 2016). Consequently, most if not all ECE teachers and staff will work with DLLs during their careers and will require an understanding of the elements and strategies of effective practices that promote the healthy development, learning, and achievement of DLLs.

---

[1] When referring to young children ages birth to 5 in their homes, communities, or ECE programs, this report uses the term "dual language learners" or "DLLs." When referring to children ages 5 and older in the pre-K to 12 education system, the term "English learners" or "ELs" is used. When referring to the broader group of children and adolescents ages birth to 21, the term "DLLs/ELs" is used.

U.S. policy makers at all levels of government generally agree that investments in children's early learning and healthy development promote equity and reduce costs to society in the long run. Compared with the K-12 education system, however, the delivery of ECE to young children is far more dispersed across multiple agencies and funding streams at the federal, state, and local levels.[2] A review conducted by the U.S. Government Accountability Office in 2012 identified 45 federally funded programs that directly provide early learning programs or financially support children ages birth through 5.[3] At the federal level, about 50 percent of eligible low-income children are served by the Head Start and Early Head Start programs. More than 850,000 eligible families receive subsidies for child care through the Child Care Development Fund (Administration for Children and Families, 2014). In addition, 40 states now fund pre-K programs, which vary widely across states in their eligibility criteria, delivery mechanisms, funding sources, and learning standards. Likewise, the policies and regulations that govern ECE programs vary substantially across states, localities, and programs.

This chapter reviews relevant research on guiding principles, programs, practices, and strategies that promote positive developmental and educational outcomes for DLLs in home visiting programs and ECE settings. While a robust body of research addresses the developmental trajectories of DLLs (see Chapter 4), and a small but growing body of research deals with effective programs and practices for preschool-ages DLLs, there are no known studies of the effects of specific ECE practices for DLL infants and toddlers (Fuligni et al., 2014). Therefore, this chapter reviews relevant research on features of high-quality ECE for infants and toddlers generally, combined with the developmental literature on DLLs reviewed in earlier chapters, to arrive at findings and conclusions about effective practices for the youngest DLLs.

DEVELOPMENTAL CHARACTERISTICS OF DUAL LANGUAGE LEARNERS

The years from birth through age 5 are critical for building the foundational knowledge and language skills required for future success in school and life. It is clear that early experiences shape development in a dynamic process that is interactive and cumulative (Institute of Medicine and

---

[2] See Kagan and Reid (2008) for a thorough account of the history of early childhood education in the United States. See also Herfeldt-Kamprath and Hamm (2015) for an explanation of the funding streams and state and local efforts to improve the delivery of education and health care to infants and toddlers.

[3] Among the 45 programs, 12 have an explicit purpose of providing early learning or child care services.

National Research Council, 2015). Decades of research have shown that high-quality ECE can improve school readiness scores and promote overall development for children living in poverty (Camilli et al., 2010; Wong et al., 2008; Yoshikawa et al., 2013). Recent data suggest that ECE services provided early (by age 2) and continuously are particularly effective in giving DLLs added language advantages at kindergarten entry (Yazejian et al., 2015).

If the benefits of ECE programs in improving school readiness, school achievement, and lifelong learning are to be achieved and sustained, the specific developmental characteristics of DLLs need to be understood and integrated into the learning environments and educational practices of these programs. Many of the developmental characteristics of children ages birth to 3 and 3 to 5 are distinct from those of other age groups, and the policies, standards, licensing requirements, and practices of ECE systems vary across these two age groups.

Birth to Age 3: Infant and Toddler Development, Care, and Education

As described by Lally and White-Tennant (2004), all infants and toddlers need a safe, healthy, engaging, and secure environment where they can develop social attachments and physical and intellectual abilities, as well as build positive self-identities and trust of others. The authors argue that it is critical for humans to experience protective environments and high-quality care during the first 3 years of life because this is a period of rapid brain growth that influences all later functioning. They assert that long-term school success must begin with effective care and education in infancy. This assertion echoes the findings of the influential National Research Council and Institute of Medicine (2000) report *Neurons to Neighborhoods: The Science of Early Childhood Development*, which identifies social-emotional strengths developed during the first 3 years as critical to all future learning. During these first 3 years, when children are highly dependent on responsive and nurturing adults, the quality of their care and learning opportunities will literally shape the neurocognitive architecture of their brains (Harvard National Center on the Developing Child, 2011).

Across most theories of early development, social interactions and relationships are viewed as the foundation for language, cognitive, and socioemotional development (Bowlby, 1969; Bronfenbrenner, 1979; Erikson, 1965; Vygotsky, 1978). *Neurons to Neighborhoods* (National Research Council and Institute of Medicine, 2000, p. 341) emphasizes this aspect of early development: "Young children's relationships with their primary caregivers have a major impact on their cognitive, linguistic, emotional, social, and moral development. These relationships are most growth-promoting when they are warm, nurturing, individualized, responsive in a contingent and reciprocal manner, and characterized by a high level of 'goodness of fit.'"

The family's culture also plays a significant role in adult-child interactions. The intimate work of raising very young children is greatly influenced by a family's culture. Many aspects of infant/toddler care and adult interactions vary significantly among different cultures. Examples of practices closely tied to a family's culture include

- feeding and nutrition,
- sleep patterns and arrangements,
- positioning and physical closeness of the infant or toddler,
- who uses language and when and how, and
- the role of extended family networks in raising the child (Lynch and Hanson, 2011; National Center on Cultural and Linguistic Responsiveness, n.d.).

The ability to listen attentively, speak with clarity, and communicate personal needs depends on social interactions and relationships with attentive adults that include meaningful language exchanges beginning during infancy. It is crucial that ECE programs recognize the impact of relationships on development across all domains and create the conditions for close, positive, responsive, and individualized caregiver-child relationships (National Research Council, 2000).

Specific features of positive adult-child interactions that have been linked to cognitive and language development in infants and toddlers include adult responsiveness to infant cues, sensitivity, positive affect, empathy, warmth, joint attention,[4] verbalization, and adult-child synchrony (Halle et al., 2011). In addition, the construct of joint attention has been positively associated with language development as well as social-emotional and some aspects of cognitive development (Dodici et al., 2003; Markus et al., 2000). These terms have been operationalized in slightly different ways across measures of infant/toddler and adult interaction scales, but the basic constructs generally agree. Responsiveness and sensitivity, for example, typically include both physical and verbal responsiveness to the child's cues (Atkins-Burnett et al., 2015). Such "contingent responsiveness" (see also Chapter 4) requires that early care providers be emotionally and physically available and able to read the child's signals of interest, enjoyment, or distress. Adult warmth can be communicated through smiling, praise, facial expressions, and tone of voice.

---

[4]Joint attention is shared focus on an object or event by the child and adult, as well as the understanding of both that the focus is shared.

An important feature of infant/toddler development is children's growing ability to regulate their own behavior (Cook et al., 2004). Having consistent routines and setting positive limits have been shown to help older infants and toddlers manage their behavior (Strain and Bovey, 2011; Winton et al., 2008). ECE providers can support the cognitive development of infants and toddlers by providing them with diverse and interesting materials and helping them actively explore how the world works; rolling balls up and down a ramp, for example, helps toddlers develop a concept of gravity. During this period of development, children have an endless curiosity about how things work and abundant motivation to discover new concepts. Adults promote emerging conceptual understandings by helping young children reason, organize their knowledge, and solve problems; scaffolding their levels of play; and directing their attention to salient features of the environment (Lobo and Galloway, 2008).

The many ways in which caregivers promote language and early literacy development are discussed in Chapter 4. For all children across all settings, the quantity and quality of adult language that is directed to a child, as well as the diversity of that language, are related to cognitive and language outcomes (Dodici et al., 2003; Hart and Risley, 1995; Huttenlocher et al., 2002; National Institute of Child Health and Human Development Early Child Care Research Network, 2005) (for a contrasting view, see Dudley-Marling and Lucas [2009]). The posing of questions with adequate wait time, conversational turn taking, extended vocabulary, and diversity of talk all have been identified as important dimensions of ECE providers' behavior that promote young children's language development (Booth, 2006; Hudson, 1990; Hurtado et al., 2008; Tamis-LeMonda et al., 1996).

In addition to positive, trusting, and nurturing relationships, certain parent and caregiver behaviors have been shown to foster the development of early literacy skills, such as an interest in books and print; enjoyment of being read to; oral language abilities, including vocabulary size and narrative skills; listening comprehension; differentiating between pictures and print; and book handling (DeBruin-Parecki et al., 2000). Strong empirical evidence shows that these emergent literacy skills are developmental precursors to future reading and writing abilities (Hammer et al., 2007; Whitehurst and Lonigan, 1998). As pointed out in Chapter 4, the language skills that infants and toddlers develop before they are able to retell a story or identify letters of the alphabet predict more advanced oral language abilities during the preschool years, and are important for kindergarten readiness and later reading comprehension (Gardner-Neblett and Iruka, 2015).

Specific types of experiences during children's first 3 years will support the development of these early literacy skills. ECE providers can foster both specific literacy skills and a love of literacy by engaging infants and toddlers with age-appropriate books; using a variety of words, such as adjectives, adverbs, and verbs, in addition to nouns and pronouns and speaking in complex sentences; and creating emotionally positive experiences with books and reading activities (National Research Council, 1998; Whitehurst et al., 1994).

Another important feature of ECE programs is the relationship between the ECE professionals and parents and family members (Halgunseth et al., 2013; Raikes et al., 2006). Family engagement with ECE programs has been linked to multiple important child outcomes across all groups of families and ages of children (Fantuzzo et al., 2004; Jeynes, 2012). Positive, mutually respectful relationships between ECE professionals and parents promote open and ongoing communication about the child's experiences and progress, as well as any potential concerns (Zero to Three, 2010). By coordinating their approaches and sharing information, ECE staff and parents can create a more consistent and predictable environment that promotes healthy development.

Considerable evidence reveals that while school-family partnerships are important for improved outcomes for all children, families of DLLs often have lower levels of school engagement relative to families of their monolingual counterparts and face unique barriers to making these connections with ECE settings. Although there have been no empirical studies on the impacts of ECE programs on the development of DLL infants and toddlers in particular, it is reasonable to use findings from the developmental literature to guide the design of services for very young DLLs and their families with special attention to their dual language status (see Chapter 4 for a full discussion of language and brain development in DLLs). The research on general infant/toddler ECE also is applicable in many respects to DLLs. Multiple studies have found that infant/toddler care for both DLLs and monolinguals tends to be of lower quality than care provided during the preschool years (Burchinal et al., 2015; National Institute of Child Health and Human Development Early Child Care Research Network, 2005). Since the earliest years are so important for language and social-emotional development, and the impacts of ECE on children's cognitive, language, and social development tend to be stronger for younger children, these findings have important implications for program improvement (Burchinal et al., 2015). Box 5-1 describes a promising program for low-income Latina mothers and their infants that is designed to increase the responsive language interactions that are so important to the later verbal and cognitive development of infants and toddlers.

BOX 5-1
Promising Program for Low-Income Spanish-Speaking Families

Habla Conmigo! (Talk with Me!) teaches Latina mothers how to engage in more language interactions with their infants. Anne Fernald, a Stanford University psychology professor working in the Language Learning Lab, Center for Infant Studies, began this program in 2012 with the goal of increasing the amount and quality of Latina parent-infant talk. She found a high degree of variability in the amount of talk among parents in low-income Spanish-speaking homes. Infants who heard more child-directed speech developed greater efficiency in language processing and learned new words more quickly. Results of the initial evaluation of this program have shown robust positive effects. Relative to the mothers and children in the control group, mothers in the *Habla Conmigo!* program were communicating more and using higher-quality language with their 18-month-olds, and their 2-year-olds were showing significantly more advanced language skills (Marchman et al., 2017). According to Fernald, "What's most exciting is that by 24 months the children of more engaged moms are developing bigger vocabularies and processing spoken language more efficiently. Our goal is to help parents understand that by starting in infancy, they can play a role in changing their children's life trajectories."

Ages 3 to 5: The Prekindergarten Years

The prekindergarten years are a sensitive period for language development. If young children lack sufficient opportunities to acquire language, persistent, lifelong language deficits may result (Kuhl et al., 2005). This is also a time of rapid social-emotional and cognitive growth. During these years, children move from using simple sentences to communicate basic ideas and needs to having extended and detailed conversations with many back-and-forth exchanges about experiences, ideas, and feelings (Biemiller, 2009; Dickinson et al., 2010; Hirsh-Pasek et al., 2015).

A common theme across multiple studies (see Chapter 4 for a full review) is the role of individual factors in predicting second-language outcomes. Individual differences, including the child's L1, cognitive abilities, previous learning experiences, cultural background, and prior knowledge, can play an important role in the process of learning a second language. Thus, it may prove beneficial for preschool programs to collect information about DLLs' background, including their family, culture, early exposure to language(s), prior knowledge, and skills in each language. Knowledge about these individual factors provides important background information about each child's developmental context and how to design specific instructional activities that are responsive to their unique learning needs.

Importance of Oral Language and Early Literacy Skills for DLLs' Academic Success

Research with both monolingual and DLL populations has found that vocabulary is one of the best predictors of reading comprehension, that vocabulary is more than just learning words, and that it is learned in multiple contexts both at home and at school (Fiorentino and Howe, 2004; Weisberg et al., 2013). The differences in vocabulary learning between DLLs and their monolingual counterparts usually do not indicate language delays or potential learning problems but are a typical feature of early dual language learning (see Chapter 4). Conboy (2013, p. 19) clearly makes this point:

> Bilingual lexical learning leads to initially smaller vocabularies in each separate language than for monolingual learners of those same languages, and *total vocabulary sizes* (the sum of what children know in both their languages) in bilingual toddlers are similar to those of monolingual toddlers (Pearson et al., 1997). Thus, the differences noted in brain activity across bilingual and monolingual children should not be interpreted as evidence of a delay induced by bilingualism, but rather, as a distinct developmental pattern of specialization linked to experience with each language (emphasis in original).

Given that vocabulary size is a key goal in preschool and important to future reading comprehension, it is critical for ECE teachers to understand this difference between DLL and monolingual preschoolers. To determine a preschool DLL's vocabulary size, one must assess the words a child knows in both languages. If a DLL preschooler does not know the English word for *window*, for example, the child may understand the concept of a window but know a different word, such as *ventana*.

Oral language skills (e.g., vocabulary, listening comprehension), grammatical knowledge, and narrative production have garnered particular attention from both educators and researchers attempting to meet the learning needs of DLLs. Research with young Spanish-speaking DLLs from low socioeconomic backgrounds has found that they may be at risk for delays in their early literacy development because of their weaker oral language abilities (Espinosa and Zepeda, 2009; Mancilla-Martinez and Lesaux, 2011). Given the importance of oral language abilities for future reading skills and the fact that DLLs often do not receive adequate support for advanced levels of oral language development (Espinosa and Gutiérrrez-Clellan, 2013), ECE providers need instructional guidance on what constitutes a rich and engaging language environment for DLLs.

DLLs have varying amounts of exposure and environmental support for each of their languages, and their proficiency in both their L1 and English varies accordingly. A preschool DLL may be fluent in both languages, proficient in the L1 but know very little English, have some English conversational language abilities but little English academic language skill, or have minimal proficiency in both languages (Páez and Rinaldi, 2006; Place and Hoff, 2011). Recently, several studies have shown that lower levels of English proficiency at kindergarten entry are related to later school and specifically English reading difficulties (Galindo, 2010; Halle et al., 2012). And in a secondary analysis of the Early Childhood Longitudinal Study, Kindergarten Class of 1998-99 (ECLS-K) dataset, Halle and colleagues (2012) found that when DLLs became more proficient in English during the preschool years, they had better overall achievement in math, science, and reading that lasted through 8th grade. These studies underscore the importance of systematic exposure to English during the preschool years to the future school performance of DLLs. Recent research on the amount of time it takes for DLLs to become reclassified as fully proficient in English in school (see Chapter 6) also has found that early proficiency in both L1 and English at kindergarten entry is critical to the process of becoming academically proficient in a second language (Thompson, 2015; see also Chapter 10).

Other Learning and Developmental Domains

Additional learning and developmental domains that are important to academic success for preschool DLLs include math, executive function skills, social-emotional development, and loss of L1.

Math The ways in which different languages describe math concepts influence young children's understanding of those concepts (e.g., Mandarin and Korean) (Chang and Sandhofer, 2009; Sarnecka et al., 2011). Chang and Sandhofer (2009), for example, investigated factors that influence young children's early understanding of math concepts. They compared English- and Mandarin-speaking parents' use of counting and number vocabulary when reading picture books to their DLL children and found that the Mandarin-speaking parents used three times more number words than their English-speaking counterparts in the study. The authors attribute this finding to the different syntactic characteristics of each language. Mandarin does not denote plurals, so the parents had to use more number words, thus providing the child with more specific number language input. In addition, the way different languages express some math concepts may make those concepts easier for children to grasp. In Korean, for example, fractions are termed "of four parts, one," instead of "one-fourth." This feature of the language makes the math concept of fraction more transparent and was related to higher scores for Korean students relative to their English-speaking peers on a fraction concept test (Paik and Mix, 2003; Sandhofer and Uchikoshi, 2013). Finally, some research has found that when preschool DLLs know certain math concepts, such as the number 5, in one language, they are likely to know the concept in their other language as well or can learn it easily (Sarnecka et al., 2011). This finding indicates that conceptual knowledge about number appears to transfer across languages and in turn, that preschool teachers should learn about both the salient features of DLLs' L1 and what mathematical concepts they know in that language.

Executive function skills During the preschool years, bilingual children have shown advantages in executive function tasks that require selectively attending to competing options and suppressing interfering information, skills that are important to school readiness (Bialystok and Viswanathan, 2009; see also Chapter 4 for more detailed discussion). Although controversial, findings of a bilingual advantage in executive function skills have been noted across cultural and socioeconomic groups, as well as different language combinations (e.g., English-Spanish, English-Mandarin, English-French, and English-Tamil) (Carlson and Meltzoff, 2008; Sandhofer and Uchikoshi, 2013). However, these cognitive advantages depend on the extent to which the child is bilingual and may be related to other aspects of development, such as culture and genetic traits. DLLs who show strong skills in both of their languages show larger executive control advantages than those who are stronger in one language (Bialystok and Majumder, 1998; Sandhofer and Uchikoshi, 2013). Thus it is important for ECE programs serving DLLs to consider the amount and frequency of exposure in each language.

Social-emotional development Evidence indicates that DLLs have comparable or better social-emotional competencies relative to their monolingual English peers (Crosnoe, 2007; Halle et al., 2014). These competencies are important for school readiness and need to be recognized and built upon by ECE providers, preschool teachers, and school administrators.

Using data from the ECLS-K cohort, Crosnoe (2007) found that kindergarten teachers rated the Spanish-speaking children of recent Mexican American immigrants more positively than their English-only counterparts on such aspects of social-emotional competence as self-control and externalizing and internalizing behaviors. Others have found evidence that the use of DLLs' L1 in ECE programs has a positive effect on their peer and teacher relationships and acts for them as a protective factor for some outcomes, including social-emotional competencies, although these findings may also be related to culturally based patterns of parenting (Winsler et al., 2014).

Loss of L1 When DLLs are exposed to English during the preschool years, they often start to show a preference for speaking English and a reluctance to continue speaking their L1 (Hakuta and D'Andrea, 1992; Oller and Eilers, 2002; Wong-Filmore, 1991). ECE professionals and program administrators need to understand that there are developmental risks associated with loss of a child's L1. Children who do not develop and maintain proficiency in their home language may lose their ability to communicate with parents and family members and risk becoming estranged from their cultural and linguistic heritage (Wong-Filmore, 1991; see Chapter 6 for a more detailed discussion). DLLs who have a strong base in their L1 and acquire high levels of English proficiency will realize the cognitive, linguistic, social, and cultural benefits of becoming bilingual as well as the ability "to establish a strong cultural identity, to develop and sustain strong ties with their immediate and extended families, and thrive in a global multilingual world" (Espinosa, 2006, p. 2).

Implications for Effective Practices for Preschool DLLs

Research on the developmental characteristics of preschool children in general and the impact of dual language learning on cognitive, language, social, and cultural development during the preschool years has the following implications for preschool programs serving DLLs:

- The cognitive, social-emotional, language, and literacy development of DLLs may vary depending on their early language experiences and cultural backgrounds. Therefore, ECE teachers need to have in-depth conversations with parents to learn about DLLs' family practices, languages, and cultural values.
- Preschool DLLs need systematic exposure to English to prepare them for success in kindergarten and beyond. However, important benefits are lost if the acquisition of English comes at the expense of continuing development in the child's L1.
- Because bilingualism conveys some social, cultural, linguistic, and cognitive advantages, ECE programs can best serve DLL preschoolers by
  - providing them with high-quality language experiences and support in mastering both of their languages, recognizing that the cognitive advantages of bilingualism are greatest when DLLs have comparable levels of proficiency in both their languages; and

o understanding that DLLs may have social-emotional advantages in the classroom relative to their monolingual peers, such as greater self-control and interpersonal skills, that need to be recognized and leveraged for improved academic achievement.

RESEARCH ON EFFECTIVE PROGRAM MODELS AND INSTRUCTIONAL STRATEGIES FOR DUAL LANGUAGE LEARNERS

This section reviews research on effective models and instructional strategies for home visiting and ECE programs.

Home Visiting Programs

The federal Maternal, Infant, and Early Childhood Home Visiting (MIECHV) Program targets[5] a population with a high proportion of families who are non-English speakers with DLLs. It is critical that home visiting practitioners and policy makers understand the strategies and elements of effective practices that promote the healthy development, learning, and achievement of these children. Yet while there is a robust body of research on the developmental trajectories of DLLs, the effectiveness of evidence-based home visiting models has not been studied specifically in this population.

Families of DLLs differ on important demographic variables, such as socioeconomic status, number of children in the home, family structure, early language and literacy practices, and commitment to home language and culture maintenance, that influence development and learning (see Chapter 3) (Espinosa et al., 2017; Winsler et al., 2014). Within this population are factors that influence the risk of poor educational outcomes, such as poverty linked to toxic stress;[6] high rates of maternal depression; and high rates of trauma linked to neighborhood, school, or domestic violence. At the same time, specific protective factors that build resilience in children, such as high rates of father involvement, child-centeredness and family warmth, stronger family and ethnic community supports, strong beliefs in education, and trust in and respect for educational and health professionals

---

[5]Home visiting services funded by MIECHV are targeted at pregnant mothers and young families and their children who are living in communities with high rates of poverty, teenage births, violence, or other criteria discussed later in this chapter.

[6]Toxic stress response can occur when a child experiences strong, frequent, and/or prolonged adversity without adequate adult support. This kind of prolonged activation of the stress response systems can disrupt the development of brain architecture and other organ systems and have damaging effects on learning, behavior, and health across the life span (Harvard National Center on the Developing Child, 2016).

(Toppelberg and Collins, 2010), explain why some DLLs in families that have recently immigrated fare better in certain developmental domains than their U.S.-born peers. The federal MIECHV program represents a unique opportunity to address those aspects of DLLs' home environments that negatively affect their development.

Emergence of the Maternal, Infant, and Early Childhood Home Visiting Program

Many states funded home visiting programs prior to MIECHV (and continue to do so) with other federal funding sources, as well as through state appropriations for education, child welfare, health, and other social services (Johnson, 2009).[7,8] Extensive research has documented that home visits by a trained professional (nurse, social worker, early childhood educator, or other) during pregnancy and the early years can improve the lives of children and families. This research has documented the benefits of the most common evidence-based home visiting models on a range of long-term outcomes, such as preventing child abuse and neglect, supporting positive parenting, improving maternal and child health, and promoting child development and school readiness (Sama-Miller et al., 2016). Home visiting programs are concerned not only with the child's healthy development but also with the development and health of parents and family, particularly their mental health and well-being. Families of DLLs often are eligible to enroll voluntarily in home visiting programs as a result of their economic status and other factors (see Box 5-2). Despite the promise of these home visiting programs, however, the committee identified several problems with how they serve DLLs and their families.

MIECHV provides grants to states, territories, and tribal entities to fund home visiting programs based on home visiting service delivery models that have demonstrated effectiveness according to specific criteria of the U.S. Department of Health and Human Services (HHS). The Home Visiting Evidence of Effectiveness (HomVEE) study is a major ongoing

---

[7] The 2010 Patient Protection and Affordable Care Act amended Title V of the Social Security Act to create the MIECHV program (Health Resources and Services Administration, 2011), and Congress approved $100 million in initial funding for the program. In 2014, funding increased to $371 million, and the program served 145,561 parents and children in 825 of the 3,142 counties in the 50 states, the District of Columbia, and five territories (23% of all rural counties and 29% of all urban counties) (Health Resources Services Administration, 2015a, 2015b). In 2015, funding was further increased to $386 million. MIECHV has funded more than 1.4 million home visits since 2012. It is administered by two agencies within the U.S. Department of Health and Human Services (HHS): the Health Resources and Services Administration (HRSA) and the Administration for Children and Families (ACF).

[8] Other federal sources of funding for home visiting programs include Temporary Assistance for Needy Families, the Maternal and Child Health Services Block Grant, and Medicaid.

BOX 5-2
Populations Served by the Maternal, Infant, and Early Childhood Home Visiting (MIECHV) Program

MIECHV is expected to comply with Title IV of the Civil Rights Act, which ensures that "Limited English Proficient [sic]" persons have meaningful access to all programs and activities. States are required to conduct needs assessments to identify and reach out to families living in "at-risk" communities—defined as those with high rates of poverty, premature birth, low birth weight, infant mortality, crime, domestic violence, high school dropout, substance use, unemployment, teen birth rate, or child maltreatment* and—in some states—communities with high populations of refugees and Americans Indians (Michalopoulos et al., 2015; Schmitt et al., 2015). An estimated one-third of high-need counties receive funding from MIECHV (Health Resources and Services Administration, 2015b).

Families living in poverty are explicit targets of the MIECHV mandate. Nearly 80 percent of families participating in the MIECHV program had household incomes at or below 100 percent of the federal poverty level when they enrolled in home visiting services. While information on the demographic characteristics of participants is limited, an evaluation of evidence-based home visiting programs by Boller and colleagues (2014) found that only 14 percent of participating families spoke a language other than English as their primary language at home (most—86%—spoke English), and only 24 percent were identified as Hispanic. Of the participating Hispanic families, half reported speaking English as their primary language; other language groups were also underrepresented in the sample. These numbers are lower than their representation in the target populations: a language other than English is spoken at home by 73.3 percent of Hispanics (U.S. Census Bureau, 2013) and 21.1 percent of the general U.S. population (U.S. Census Bureau, 2014). This percentage is higher, likely close to 30 percent, among families with young children as well as those living in poverty, of which Hispanics make up 24 percent (U.S. Census Bureau, 2016). Based on these statistics, the percentages of the populations of Hispanics, non-English speakers, and DLLs being served by home visiting programs should be higher.

The difference between the actual numbers served and the composition of the population strongly suggests that families speaking a language other than English and Hispanics are underrepresented among those served by the MIECHV program. In more recent information provided by the MIECHV program, the primary language exposure of children enrolled in home visiting was English for 77 percent of children, Spanish for 15 percent of children, and an unspecified variety of other languages for the remaining 8 percent. This discrepancy raises questions about compliance with Title VI of the Civil Rights Act.

---

*See http://www.hhs.gov/about/news/2015/02/19/hhs-awards-386-million-to-support-families-through-the-home-visiting-program.html [February 22, 2017].

federal initiative tasked with documenting the effectiveness of home visiting models. HomVEE has reviewed 44 existing home visiting service delivery models, 19 of which have been found to demonstrate effectiveness (Avellar et al., 2016). Four of these models—Early Head Start-Home Based Program, Healthy Families America, Nurse-Family Partnership, and Parents as Teachers—are those most commonly adopted at the state level, although they differ in their program goals, their target populations, program intensity and duration, required qualifications of home visitors, and the flexibility localities have in designing their programs (Michalopoulos et al., 2015). To determine the effectiveness of a home visiting model, HomVEE reviews the evidence of its impact on eight major outcomes. While all of these eight outcomes are relevant to DLLs and their families, the discussion here highlights aspects of five critical outcomes of particular relevance to this report—child health, child development (including language) and school readiness, linkages and referrals to other community resources and supports, maternal health, and positive parenting practices.

Evaluations of Home Visiting Models

There have been two major evaluations of home visiting models: HomVEE and the HHS-funded Mother and Infant Home Visiting Program Evaluation (MIHOPE).

Home Visiting Evidence of Effectiveness Study (HomVEE) HomVEE, a major ongoing national study being conducted by Mathematica Policy Research (Avellar et al., 2016), is tasked with documenting the effectiveness of home visiting models and identifying those models that meet the HHS criteria for an "evidence-based early childhood home visiting service delivery model." The evaluation considers only models aimed at improving outcomes in at least one of the following eight domains: (1) child health; (2) child (including language) development and school readiness; (3) family economic self-sufficiency; (4) linkages and referrals; (5) maternal health; (6) positive parenting practices; (7) reductions in child maltreatment; and (8) reductions in juvenile delinquency, family violence, and crime. A home visiting model must meet one of the following criteria for HHS to consider it evidence-based:

- at least one high- or moderate-quality impact study must find favorable, statistically significant impacts in two or more of the eight outcome domains; or
- at least two high- or moderate-quality impact studies using non-overlapping study samples must find one or more favorable, statistically significant impacts in the same domain.

The most recent HomVEE report reviews 44 existing home visiting service delivery models (Avellar et al., 2016), 19 of which demonstrated effectiveness according to the HHS criteria. Seven of these 19 models had favorable effects on in the same domain (e.g., child health, maternal health, child development and school readiness, positive parenting practices) in two or more samples, while 8 had favorable effects on child and language development and school readiness.[9] Studies of the 4 most common models assessed child language development using such measures as the Peabody Picture Vocabulary Test, Communicative Development Inventories, and Preschool Language Scales in English. However, none of these studies assessed the development of L1 (when applicable), which would have been feasible as versions of these measures are available and commonly used for Spanish as well as other languages.

The most recent HomVEE report (Avellar et al., 2016) concludes that most of the program models analyzed had favorable effects, which varied across models, and that all 19 models deemed evidence-based according to the HHS criteria had favorable impacts for at least 1 year after enrollment. However, none of these studies disaggregated DLL subgroups, leaving some question as to whether these home visiting models are equally effective in supporting the families of monolinguals and DLLs:

> The HomVEE review identified several gaps in the existing research literature on home visiting models that limit its usefulness for matching program models to community needs . . . more evidence is needed about the effectiveness of HV models for different types of families with a range of characteristics. . . . HomVEE found little or no research on the effectiveness of home visiting program models for immigrant families that have diverse cultural backgrounds or may not speak English as a first language. (Avellar et al., 2016, p. 17)

Mother and Infant Home Visiting Program Evaluation (MIHOPE) study One of the key findings of the HHS-funded MIHOPE study was that states focused their funds on expanding the four most common evidence-based home visiting models noted earlier.[10] According to the MIHOPE report (Michalopoulos et al., 2015), home visiting programs have three functions: (1) to assess family needs, (2) to educate and support parents, and (3) to help families gain access to services, with the overall goal of improving outcomes for families throughout their children's early years and beyond.

---

[9] See http://homvee.acf.hhs.gov/Outcome/2/Child-Development-and-School-Readiness/3/1 [February 23, 2017].

[10] (1) Early Head Start-Home Based Program Option, (2) Healthy Families America, (3) Nurse-Family Partnership, and (4) Parents as Teachers. For complete descriptions of these models, see Michalopoulos et al. (2015).

Although only 8 percent of the mothers in the evaluation sample reported poor English-speaking ability, Michalopoulos and colleagues (2015) found that these families may be more of a challenge to serve if home visitors and other service providers are unable to speak in the mother's L1. In addition, the authors note that losing L1 may put individuals at risk for chronic health conditions and mental health problems.

Access to Services and Engagement of Families of DLLs

Boller and colleagues (2014) found that agencies implementing home visiting programs struggled to maintain caseloads and to deliver services of the intended intensity. Importantly, higher-risk families were most likely to leave the program earlier, between 6 and 12 months. Enrolling and retaining families who speak a language other than English may be more challenging because of the accumulation of additional risk factors, such as underutilization of health services and Head Start and the undocumented status of parents. These factors may contribute to the underrepresentation of the families of DLLs in home visiting programs (see Box 5-1).

The extent to which programs reach out to families with DLLs varies substantially across localities and program types. For instance, New York's assessment reported on four operating home visiting programs, only one of which explicitly targeted families with literacy and language barriers (Michalopolous et al., 2015). The committee reviewed each state's MIECHV information fact sheet[11] and in contrast with some early childhood programs, such as Head Start and Early Head Start, could find no explicit references to serving immigrant families or families who speak a language other than English. Thus no state-level information is available on strategies for outreach and engagement targeting these groups.

Competencies Required of Home Visitors Serving Families of DLLs

A home visiting professional who does not share the cultural and linguistic background of the families being served may find it difficult to achieve the program goals, although sharing a background does not guarantee the absence of misconceptions or biases that may compromise the ability to serve families well. Home visitors often function independently in a highly unstructured environment, which requires manageable caseloads and additional supervision and support. It is critical to have the linguistic and cultural competence to interact with families that speak a language other than English and have specific immigration, refugee, or cultural

---

[11] See http://mchb.hrsa.gov/programs/homevisiting/states [February 23, 2017].

backgrounds (Pumariega et al., 2013); also essential is to have knowledge of child development to support DLLs' L1.

MIHOPE provides information about the qualifications and educational and linguistic backgrounds of home visitors (Michalopoulos et al., 2015). The majority of both supervisors and home visitors describe themselves as non-Hispanic white, and no data are available regarding the language skills of these professionals.

The MIECHV Technical Assistance Coordinating Center (Health Resources and Services Administration, 2016) summarizes critical HV core competencies. While cultural, linguistic, and developmental competencies are critical for serving families of DLLs, the report makes no mention of them, suggesting that the program does not consider them. In this connection, it is important to note that, according to a 2009 policy statement by the American Academy of Pediatrics, nurse-based programs are more effective than those that are not nurse-based, but programs that are staffed by paraprofessionals of the same cultural backgrounds as the target populations are as if not more effective if the paraprofessionals are retained for 2 or more years.[12]

An in-depth qualitative study of 14 immigrant Latina mothers illustrates the importance of some of these cultural and linguistic core competencies. It also documents how highly the participating mothers valued home visiting services and the bilingual/bicultural paraprofessional staff—who themselves were immigrants—that delivered the services (Paris, 2008). The study details many aspects of the relationships between the home visitors and participants that merit further investigation, such as

- use of bicultural and multilingual paraprofessionals as home visitors in communities that are mistrustful of outsiders;
- use of home visitors who are trained in relationship-building skills;
- provision of support and referral to services for immigrant mothers in the context of a trusting relationship with the home visitor; and
- use of paraprofessional home visitors who have "social proximity" to the communities they serve (i.e., live in the same communities or ones similar to those they are serving) and can help mothers navigate a new country/culture.

Approach to L1 and dual language development The general public, even speakers of languages other than English, holds significant misconceptions about dual language development. Even well-intended professionals may exhibit implicit biases (Banaji and Greenwald, 2013). To the best of the committee's knowledge, neither the federal MIECHV nor state programs

---

[12] See http://pediatrics.aappublications.org/content/123/2/598.full [February 23, 2017].

have policies or guidelines with respect to supporting the development of L1. It is unclear whether home visitors receive any training in providing such support, or what guidance families receive about the benefits of supporting the development of L1 for optimal language development and early stimulation for infants and young children. Misinformation, bias and discrimination, and misconceptions about how to ensure that a child learns English may lead untrained home visitors to convey erroneous views to the families they are supporting, with negative consequences for the child's development. As discussed in Chapter 4, maximizing cognitive and language stimulation at home requires that parents use the language they know best. Doing so provides a solid cognitive-linguistic base for emerging literacy and school-based reasoning and facilitates learning English and other languages later on. Home visiting services that encourage parents to take a positive view of dual language development bolster exposure to and use of L1, which protects against the loss of L1—an unfortunate but frequent occurrence. Low-status languages (such as Spanish) are more likely to be lost to attrition than high-status languages (such as French or German), requiring a proactive stance toward their maintenance and growth on the part of the home visitor. Support for the development of L1 needs to extend to young children with delays and disabilities (Toppelberg and Collins, 2016; see Chapter 9).

As noted above, neither federal nor state home visiting programs have guidelines for a coherent, science-based approach to DLLs' language development. Nor is support for L1 development explicitly stated as an outcome or task of home visiting services. While evidence-based home visiting models have overall beneficial impacts on language outcomes, it is unclear how these outcomes are achieved in DLLs without an explicit and proactive approach to support for L1.

Screening and assessment of DLLs One of the goals of MIECHV is the early screening and identification of children with developmental delays and their appropriate linkage and referral for services (early identification is discussed in Chapter 9). Relative to their monolingual peers, however, DLLs with developmental delays and disabilities are less likely to be identified and referred for early intervention. The risk of underidentification is particularly significant for language delays, which can erroneously be attributed to normal bilingual development. (Overidentification is less likely in the early years, but may occur if low English abilities due to a lack of opportunity to learn English are misinterpreted as a language delay in a normally developing child.) Home visitors can play a crucial role in the early identification and referral of these DLLs.

Mental health considerations Home visitors serving families of DLLs need to be aware of the risks and exposures outlined previously in this chapter that can lead to mental health problems as well as recognizable signs of depression and psychological trauma, and of available resources for addressing these issues. The negative impact on children of institutional and individual discrimination, for example, has been documented (Brown, 2015). This and other traumas may lead to posttraumatic stress disorder, major depression, sleep disorders, alcohol and substance abuse, and other mental health disorders. As a result, home visitors and their supervisors need to be knowledgeable about such resources as the National Child Traumatic Stress Network, which lists resources and evidence-based practices for addressing the consequences of psychological trauma.[13]

At the same time, it is important to note that, despite the accumulation of risk in subgroups of families of DLLs, their strength and resilience in the face of adversity has been well documented (Oppedal and Toppelberg, 2016; Toppelberg and Collins, 2010). Home visiting programs that target DLLs and their families with research-based methods and guidance may provide additional supports that help mitigate the effects of these experiences.

Early Care and Education Programs

Although nonparental care during early childhood has become normative for children in the United States, and high-quality ECE services appear to be especially important for DLLs, published work on the early care arrangements of DLLs overall is relatively scarce (Burchinal et al., 2015; Hirshberg et al., 2005; Loeb et al., 2004). Some research has found that parents whose primary language is not English are less likely to use formal center-based ECE settings and more likely to use informal care, such as that provided by relatives, than families that speak only English, especially when children are ages 0-4 (Cannon et al., 2012; Halle et al., 2009; Hirshberg et al., 2005). A few studies have found that immigrant families of DLLs prefer programs in which their home language is used (Ward et al., 2011), while others have found that some Latino families express a desire for their children to learn English during the preschool years (Vesely, 2013). Some evidence indicates that when DLLs do attend formal ECE programs (described in Table 5-1), they are more likely than other groups to experience poor-quality services (Karoly and Gonzalez, 2011; Matthews and Ewen, 2006).

A recent study examined the ECE experiences of infant/toddler and preschool-age DLLs using the nationally representative Early Childhood Lon-

---

[13] See http://www.nctsn.org/resources [February 23, 2017].

TABLE 5-1 Formal Early Care and Education Programs

Program	Description
Head Start	Head Start aims to promote the school readiness and healthy development of children ages 3 and 4 living in poor households.* It is the largest federal program focused on meeting the developmental needs of children from low-income families. Launched in 1965, it was most recently reauthorized by the Head Start for School Readiness Act. Head Start services usually include a 9-month educational program, as well as nutritional, social, and some medical services. In 2014, the program served more than 1 million children and their families (Administration for Children and Families, 2015), reaching approximately 40 percent of the nation's eligible children (Schmit and Matthews, 2013). The Office of Head Start provides grants to approximately 1,700 public and nonprofit organizations for the administration of program services (Administration for Children and Families, 2015).
Early Head Start	Early Head Start extends the education and child care services of Head Start to children ages 0-3. It also provides home visits for low-income pregnant women and their families to conduct needs assessments and offer individualized information, as well as referrals to additional resources and services related to parenting and general child well-being. In 2016, there were 149,986 Head Start slots (National Head Start Association, 2016).
Migrant and Seasonal Head Start	A smaller program within Head Start, Migrant and Seasonal Head Start provides child care services to nearly 30,000 children of migrant farm workers. It was created to ensure that young children would not be cared for by their parents in the fields, where they could potentially be exposed to dangerous chemicals and extreme weather conditions (National Migrant and Seasonal Head Start Association, 2015).
Child Care and Development Fund	This block grant program provides federal funding to states, territories, and tribes to assist low-income parents with the cost of child care so they can work or receive education and/or training. Participating families receive either a voucher that can be used to pay for child care in a state-approved facility or a contracted slot in a child care facility. The program enables families to enroll in center-based facilities and preschools that are funded privately by nonprofit and for-profit entities. In 2013, approximately 1.45 million children and more than 870,000 families received child care assistance on a monthly basis from this program.

continued

TABLE 5-1 Continued

Program	Description
State-Funded Prekindergarten Programs	An estimated 4 percent of the nation's 3-year-olds and 29 percent of its 4-year-olds are served by state-funded prekindergarten programs (Barnett et al., 2015). The Every Student Succeeds Act of 2015 (ESSA) includes competitive grant funding for early childhood education, to be administered jointly by the U.S. Department of Education and the U.S. Department of Health and Human Services. The goals of this new funding are to improve access to and the quality of preschool by enhancing coordination and collaboration across the various systems that provide early childhood education. Most state programs are administered by the state education department and consist of mixed delivery systems; however, public funding for preschool also is provided to students in community-based and private child care centers and nursery schools (Bornfreund, 2015; Demma, 2015).

*In 2015, a family of four earning less than $24,250 was considered below the federal poverty level (U.S. Department of Health and Human Services, Office of the Assistant Secretary for Planning and Evaluation, 2015).

gitudinal Study-Birth Cohort (ECLS-B) dataset (Espinosa et al., 2013). This study found that the proportion of DLLs in nonparental care was lower than the proportion of English-only children at all ages assessed (9, 24, and 52 months). About one-third of the DLLs and one-half of the English-only children were in an out-of-home ECE setting at 9 and 24 months, whereas about two-thirds of DLLs and three-fourths of English-only children were in some form of ECE at 52 months. When the analysis adjusted for family demographic variables, however, no reliable differences were found between DLL and English-only families in the use of ECE programs. This finding suggests that the use of nonparental ECE services is driven by such factors as socioeconomic status rather than language status. Some differences were noted, however, in the types of ECE DLLs attended even after controlling for family demographic factors: DLLs were more likely than English-only children to be in a relative's care at 9 and 24 months and less likely than all other groups to be in child care homes. Significantly, once the analysis controlled for family demographics, the quality of services did not differ between programs that DLLs attended at 2 years and center-based ECE they attended at 52 months. Informal family-based child care programs, which preschool DLLs attended at slightly higher rates than their

English-only counterparts at 52 months, were found to be of lower quality than the center-based programs after adjusting for demographic variables.

This study found further that the youngest DLLs—infants and toddlers—were most likely to have a provider who spoke their home language when they were cared for by relatives (93%) or in a child care home. The data collected for the study do not reveal to what extent or how these ECE providers used the DLLs' home language with infants and toddlers in the ECE setting, only that they had the ability to do so. In contrast, only 23 percent of the children attending center-based programs at 52 months had a provider who spoke and reported using the children's home language in the classroom. This study also found that DLL infants and toddlers were most likely to receive bilingual services when they were 9 months old; less likely at 24 months; and unlikely at 52 months, when they were more likely to attend center-based ECE (Espinosa et al., 2013). Notably, informal care by relatives and in family child care settings was found to be lower in overall quality than center-based care. In summary, this large nationally representative study shows that in the United States, DLLs who attend center-based ECE programs have fewer opportunities than their infant and toddler counterparts to develop proficiency in both of their languages, as English is the most common language used for instruction in preschools.

Taken together, these findings represent a challenge to the ECE professional community. Evidence indicates that DLLs benefit greatly from high-quality center-based ECE services, as well as from exposure to their first language in addition to a second (e.g., English). Yet currently, most center-based ECE programs have limited capacity to offer bilingual support (Adair, 2015). In addition, most infant and toddler DLLs receive informal ECE services, which often are rated lower in overall quality than center-based programs. These informal settings are where the youngest DLLs are most likely to experience support for continued development of their home language, but least likely to experience stimulating interactions that support conceptual and academic learning that is important to kindergarten readiness. The challenge for policy and practice, then, is how to both improve overall quality in informal ECE and increase the capacity of center-based programs to provide culturally and linguistically responsive care and education and to support the development of both languages.

Effective Preschool Practices

Strong evidence across multiple studies and decades of research indicates that a year or two of high-quality center-based ECE for 3- and 4-year-olds will improve these children's early language, literacy, and mathematics skills at kindergarten entry (Barnett, 2011; Gormley et al., 2004; Karoly and Gonzalez, 2011; Peisner-Feinberg et al., 2001; Yoshikawa et al.,

2013). A meta-analysis integrating evaluations conducted between 1965 and 2007 of 84 diverse early education programs for young children found significant impacts of preschool attendance across cognitive, language, and school achievement outcomes (Duncan and Magnusen, 2013). Specifically, this meta-analysis found evidence of about a third of a year of additional learning, beyond what might have occurred without access to ECE. Other studies have yielded similar results. These studies include well-known small demonstration programs such as Perry Preschool (Schweinhart et al., 2005), which resulted in long-term positive schooling and life outcomes, as well as evaluations of large publicly funded preschool programs such as Head Start, which typically yield more modest effects (Puma et al., 2012). When analyzed across studies, the average impact of ECE on long-term academic success has been found to be larger than the average impact of many other well-known educational interventions, including class-size reductions in elementary schools and comprehensive school reform (Borman et al., 2003). A set of secondary analyses was conducted using the 2011 ECLS-K and the ECLS-B national datasets in combination with the evaluation results of the Tulsa Early Childhood Four-Year-Old Program and Boston Public School Prekindergarten Program. These analyses found that high-quality universal prekindergarten programs could dramatically reduce or even eliminate gaps in reading and math achievement at kindergarten entry between children of color—specifically African American and Hispanic children—and their white peers, as well as between low-income children and their higher-income peers (Friedman-Krauss et al., 2016, p. 15).

When their quality is relatively high, ECE programs show larger impacts on children's development and achievement immediately after the program and are most likely to result in long-term academic gains that are measurable later in schooling (Yoshikawa et al., 2013). While not everyone agrees on the essential features of high-quality preschool or why some effects appear to diminish during the elementary school years (Barnett, 2011), findings from rigorous experimental studies, several meta-analyses, and research reviews all highlight certain common elements generally considered to be part of a high-quality program for all preschool children (see Box 5-3).

These program features have been shown to be important for multiple outcomes (Barnett, 2011; Camilli et al., 2010; Pianta et al., 2009; Schweinhart et al., 2006). These outcomes include improved school readiness skills, particularly in the academic areas of language, literacy, and mathematics (Barnett et al., 2007; Magnuson and Waldfogel, 2008). Some studies also have shown that children who attend high-quality preschool programs have better academic achievement in high school, are more likely to complete high school and enroll in postsecondary education (Barnett, 2008; Campbell et al., 2012; Heckman et al., 2015), and exhibit higher lev-

---

BOX 5-3
Common Features of High-Quality Preschool Programs

- Positive and mutually respectful teacher-child relationships and home-school partnerships (National Association for the Education of Young Children, 2008)
- Intentional teaching of important foundational skills (Burchinal et al., 2015)
- Responsiveness to each family's culture and language (Office of Head Start, 2015a)
- Ratios of teacher to child of 1 to 10 or less, and a maximum class size of 20 children (Roopnarine and Johnson, 2013)
- Effective family engagement (Hammer et al., 2011)
- Age-appropriate materials available for exploration (Hirsh-Pasek et al., 2009)
- Comprehensive curricula, developmentally sequenced, and focused on specific content (Clements, 2007)
- Ongoing assessment to guide instructional decision making and monitor progress (Beltrán, 2012)
- Qualified, responsive, and skilled teachers (Castro et al., 2011)
- Opportunities for children to learn and practice new vocabulary
- Individualized adult-child conversations that promote language and positive relationships
- Responsive and enriched language interactions
- Dedicated time for teachers and staff to plan together (Roopnarine and Johnson, 2013)
- Intensive and ongoing professional development that includes classroom coaching (Zaslow et al., 2010)

SOURCES: Barnett et al. (2007); Camilli et al. (2010); Dickinson (2011); Dickinson and Neuman (2006); Espinosa and Magruder (2003); Goldenberg et al. (2013).

---

els of adult functioning with significant cost-benefit returns on investment (Heckman, 2010; Heckman et al., 2015). Further, many of these features of high-quality preschool programs have been shown to have stronger associations with long-term outcomes for low-income children than for middle-class children (Magnuson et al., 2007).

Features of High-Quality ECE Programs for DLLs

Given the specific challenges and opportunities DLLs face in school and the growing number of such students in the United States, it is important to know how high-quality ECE programs impact these children in particular, as well as the features of quality that are important to their development and achievement and any additional educational enhancements that may be needed to improve their short- and long-term outcomes.

Most studies focused on the features of ECE programs and children's outcomes, such as those listed in Box 5-3, have either not included DLLs, not disaggregated results by language status, or administered cognitive and social assessments exclusively in English (Espinosa and López, 2007; National Research Council, 2008). Consequently, an evidence base that can inform the design of effective and high-quality ECE programs for DLLs is just beginning to emerge. Nonetheless, this emergent research is converging on findings regarding some of the elements of ECE programs that are important for DLLs: (1) the global quality of the ECE environment (including its positive emotional climate), (2) the language of instruction, (3) specific instructional and assessment practices, (4) teacher/provider qualifications and language abilities, and (5) home-school collaboration practices (Castro, 2014; Espinosa, 2013).

Since features of high-quality ECE instruction have been linked to positive language, literacy, and mathematics outcomes for most children, there is probably considerable overlap between what constitutes effective practice for monolingual English speakers and DLLs (Downer et al., 2012; Espinosa, 2010, 2013). Therefore, what is known about high-quality ECE in general is likely the foundation for effective practices for DLLs. However, multiple studies have concluded that basic high-quality ECE instruction must be enhanced to meet the unique linguistic and developmental needs of DLLs (Castro et al., 2011; Espinosa, 2010; Goldenberg et al., 2013; Roberts and Neal, 2004). Certain aspects of preschool instruction, such as a focus on oral language development and early literacy and math skills, as well as the creation of social environments that foster positive peer and adult relationships, are clearly important for all children. However, most recent research identifies specific instructional accommodations or enhancements as being critical aspects of high-quality ECE for DLLs.

An emerging focus of research is how to define and measure the quality of ECE for DLLs, given that most measures of ECE classroom quality were developed for use in settings with English-only instruction and/or monolingual populations (Castro et al., 2011; Zepeda, 2015). A review of the literature from the past decade conducted by the Center for Early Care and Education Research-Dual Language Learners (CECER-DLL) found that widely used instruments for measuring the quality of ECE programs functioned similarly for DLL and English-monolingual populations in the small number of studies that have examined this question. Measures designed to examine supports for DLLs specifically appeared to capture different dimensions of the environment from those captured by the general quality measures (Center for Early Care and Education Research-Dual Language

Learners, 2011). This review of 49 commonly used measures of the quality of ECE in center-based and/or home-based settings found that "it is not possible to draw conclusions about the validity of specific measures for use with DLLs, given that there were few studies for any particular tool. Only two research studies included measures that were designed specifically for examining early care and education for DLL populations" (p. 1). Thus, specific features of quality that have been linked to important gains for DLLs typically are not part of the preschool classroom/program quality improvement process or in many cases, ECE program monitoring or evaluation systems.

Additional evidence from a nationally representative study indicates that DLLs and their English-speaking peers are impacted by ECE experiences in slightly different ways. In a secondary analysis of the ECLS-K dataset, Crosnoe (2007) found that children from Mexican immigrant families generally benefited less than their U.S. born, English-speaking counterparts and may experience some unintended consequences when they attend formal ECE programs. Crosnoe found that while children of Mexican immigrant families gained cognitively from attending ECE programs, they also jeopardized the health, social, and emotional advantages of maintaining their L1 as they became more proficient in English and assimilated into American culture (Jackson et al., 2010). DLLs benefit from high-quality ECE environments just as monolingual English speakers do, although possibly to a lesser extent, but care is necessary that the academic benefits they realize are not associated with unintended social-emotional costs.

By contrast, other research has found that when DLLs attend high-quality preschool programs, they actually experience greater gains in their emergent English abilities relative to their English-only counterparts (Gormley, 2008; Gormley et al., 2005). Some studies have shown that preschool DLLs benefit more from attending center-based ECE programs such as Head Start relative to the general Head Start population (Bloom and Weiland, 2015; Cooper and Lanza, 2014; Lee et al., 2014). As Head Start and most state prekindergarten programs target low-income families and focus explicitly on language and literacy outcomes (U.S. Department of Health and Human Services, 2010), it is indeed likely that Head Start and other center-based preschool programs provide critical exposure and opportunities to learn English prior to kindergarten for non-English-speaking preschoolers. However, DLLs most often enter these preschool programs with lower language and early literacy scores relative to their English-only peers (Gormley, 2008; Páez et al., 2011). Therefore, even though they may make equivalent or greater gains relative to those realized by their English-only peers, DLLs begin preschool with lower language scores, which persist when they enter kindergarten (e.g., 0.4 standard deviation lower) (Miller and Garcia, 2008).

Results of an evaluation of the Educare Program, a comprehensive approach to ECE for low-income children ages 0-5 (Yazejian et al., 2015), reveal that Spanish-speaking DLLs who entered the program during infancy and who were enrolled continuously had higher English language scores at age 5 than those who entered the program at age 3. Educare implements most elements of general high-quality ECE—such as lead teachers with a bachelor's degree, small child-staff ratios, ongoing professional development for teachers, continuous use of data to improve program quality, and extensive family engagement activities. Most of the DLLs enrolled in Educare (95%) speak Spanish in the home, and the majority of classrooms with DLLs (70%) have at least one adult who speaks Spanish. The Educare evaluation showed that although most instruction is conducted in English, DLLs do receive some support in their L1. Although how much or what type of L1 support is provided is unknown, the DLLs attending Educare programs did not show the decreases in their standardized Spanish language scores that have been reported in other English language immersion approaches to ECE for DLLs (Espinosa, 2013). This evaluation therefore confirmed that early and continuous English learning opportunities combined with support for continued development of the child's L1 in high-quality programs can go a long way toward reducing the achievement gap at kindergarten entry (Espinosa, 2013; Rodriguez et al., 1995; Winsler et al., 1999a).

While there are no rigorous studies or clear consensus on the types and amounts of support for each language that are most effective for DLLs, most scholars agree that high-quality early learning opportunities will positively influence the school readiness of DLLs (Barnett, 2008; Camilii et al., 2011; Espinosa, 2010). Further, while it appears that DLLs make significant English language gains when they attend high-quality preschool programs, generic high quality without attention to the unique language needs of DLLs is probably not sufficient to significantly reduce the achievement gap at kindergarten entry and ensure long-term educational success. The features of high quality measured by common preschool quality assessments most likely need to be supplemented with specific instructional practices and strategies that have been shown to promote and accelerate learning and development for DLLs (Castro et al., 2011; Espinosa, 2013; Goldenberg et al., 2013).

Language of instruction A feature of ECE programs that may be uniquely important to the learning and development of DLLs is the language of instruction. This issue has been the most intensely debated aspect of the education of DLLs in K-12 settings for decades and is often politically charged (Gándara and Hopkins, 2010). All educators and scholars agree that to succeed in school and participate in civic life in the United States, all children need to develop strong English proficiency, literacy, and academic content skills (see Chapter 7). However, questions about the ongoing role of DLLs' L1 as English skills deepen, the social and cultural costs of losing proficiency in L1, the role of ECE programs in systematically supporting and promoting L1 development, and community values that may promote English-only approaches have not been resolved. Further, many practical questions remain around the best methods for promoting English language development while continuing to support multiple L1s in English-dominant ECE settings.

As discussed above, systematic exposure to English during the preschool years will lead to rapid gains in certain aspects of English language skills by kindergarten entry. What is less clear is how to maintain these early gains when more advanced linguistic skills are needed for challenging academic content, and what role the child's L1 plays in the development of these more advanced conceptual and linguistic skills that are so necessary for later school success.

Evidence indicates, moreover, that supporting the child's L1 while adding English can promote higher levels of achievement in English (August and Shanahan, 2006; Castro et al., 2011; Méndez et al., 2015; Winsler et al., 1999a). Thus, programs that intentionally use both languages can promote emergent bilingualism, a characteristic that carries linguistic and cognitive advantages that may be valuable in later development (Saiz and Zoido, 2005), as well as advanced conceptual development. At best, then, preschool instruction that systematically uses DLLs' L1 while also introducing English contributes to growth in skills in both languages (Barnett et al., 2007; Burchinal et al., 2012; Durán et al., 2010; Winsler et al., 1999a). At worst, there is no difference in English language skills but an advantage in L1 growth when the L1 is part of the instructional model (Barnett et al., 2007; Bernhard et al., 2006; Durán et al., 2010; Farver et al., 2009; Winsler et al., 1999a).

An evaluation of the effects of state-funded preschool education in 11 states showed that DLL enrollees' average reading and math scores were higher when they received greater amounts of instruction in Spanish (Burchinal et al., 2012; Vitiello et al., 2011). Likewise, a pilot study contrasting the effects of a bilingual versus English-only targeted literacy intervention on the development of DLLs' emergent literacy skills found that the bilingual approach produced significantly higher vocabulary and print knowledge gains (Farver et al., 2009). In addition, a small, randomized trial in federally funded Head Start classrooms that differed only in teachers' language of instruction showed that enrollees in the Spanish instruction classes had higher Spanish vocabulary and phonics scores (Durán et al., 2010). This finding is important because of related research demonstrating the potential for cross-linguistic transfer of such skills to children's emergent literacy in English (Anthony et al., 2009; Atwill et al., 2010; August and Shanahan, 2006; Dickinson et al., 2004; Farver et al., 2013; Goldenberg, 2013; see Chapter 4). In summary, research clearly indicates that when DLLs are given opportunities to develop high levels of proficiency in both of their languages, they realize linguistic, cognitive, and academic advantages that are significant and lasting (Conboy, 2013; Sandhofer and Uchikoshi, 2013).

Program approaches In reality, although recent research favors a balanced approach to bilingualism, dual language instruction with the goal of biliteracy and bilingualism is not possible in many contexts. All types of ECE programs throughout the country, such as Head Start, state prekindergarten, community-based child care, and home-based child care, are today reporting not only more DLLs but also representation of a greater number of different languages among the children and families they serve. At the same time, few ECE teachers are fluent in more than one language (Adair, 2015), and few teachers certified in ECE have received focused training in cultural and linguistic diversity (Espinosa, 2009; Zepeda, 2015). In contexts in which teachers are unable to instruct in the L1s of the children in their classrooms, curriculum developers have devised strategies that teachers can implement to support these children's continued development of their L1 (Castro et al., 2006; Espinosa, 2010; Goldenberg et al., 2013; Magruder et al., 2013). For example, Goldenberg and colleagues (2013) recommend the following strategies:

- having someone (e.g., teachers, family members, volunteers who speak the child's L1) read to DLLs in their home language;
- creating books that use the child's L1 (see Box 5-4);
- teaching rhymes, letters, and numbers in DLLs' L1 (with parental or community support as needed) while providing opportunities for child-adult interaction;
- teaching all children the greetings of each other's L1s;
- highlighting cognates and connections between words in the L1 and English from storybooks and themes;
- informing parents of topics being discussed in the classroom so they can help build conceptual knowledge in the L1 at home before DLLs are exposed to them in the classroom; and
- making time and space for adults who speak the children's L1 to interact with them in that language.

While these specific strategies have not been evaluated, there is some evidence that this approach of using mainly English for instructional purposes but systematically and intentionally bringing the DLL's home language into

---

BOX 5-4
The Early Authors Program

The Early Authors Program (Bernhard et al., 2006) was an innovative effort in Miami-Dade County in Florida to provide bilingual literacy experiences for parents and young preschool-age DLLs who, because of lags in development, were deemed to be at risk for learning disabilities. This program, which operated in child development centers and programs, engaged parents and children in joint literacy activities: writing and illustrating dual language stories about themselves—identity texts—that were based on family history, events in the children's lives, and topics in which the children were interested. More than 1,000 children were randomly selected from 32 early childhood centers for participation in the intervention. They represented 800 low-income families, mostly Hispanic, African American, or Caribbean/Haitians. Over the course of the 12-month intervention, more than 3,000 dual language books were produced.

The evaluation of the intervention was based on assessments of the children's preschool language and learning skills in their dominant language, as well as observations of the children's engagement in literacy activities. The findings were encouraging. The children in the experimental group showed significant growth in language expression and comprehension, and while the intervention did not reduce their initial developmental lag, they did not fall further behind, as did the control group students. The intervention group students started and remained 2 months behind the national norms in language skills for their age group, while the control group had fallen behind by more than 5 months by the end of the study period. Most important, the children who participated in the intervention activities gained in literacy engagement and in their self-esteem.

---

the classroom can capitalize on the child's existing linguistic knowledge while applying those skills in the L1 to the task of learning English, and also build conceptual knowledge.

Specific Instructional Practices

Recent studies have documented the value of specific instructional practices for DLLs. For example, explaining the meaning of vocabulary words and using them in different contexts (Collins, 2010) can improve DLLs' reading comprehension as well as strengthen their oral language skills (Lesaux, 2009). Moreover, instructional strategies that promote narrative skills, listening comprehension, and the understanding of complex grammatical structures will improve DLL preschoolers' early English literacy skills (University of Chicago, 2010). Such strategies include the use of sensitive and responsive teachers (Burchinal et al., 2012); opportunities for individual and small-group interactions; an intentional focus on oral language development, such as listening and speaking combined with explicit vocabulary instruction (Brydon, 2010; Collins, 2010; Davison et al., 2011); skilled, interactive methods of storybook reading in both languages (Leung et al., 2011); emphasis on the development of academic English; frequent assessment of progress in both languages (Espinosa and Gutiérrez-Clellan, 2013); and strategies that promote English comprehension while leveraging knowledge of L1 as a bridge to English (Lugo-Neris et al., 2010).

As noted earlier, strategies that utilize DLLs' home language, such as reading stories in both English and the L1, have been linked to improved literacy outcomes. Using specific core words in the child's home language to activate knowledge in that language and then explicitly connecting that knowledge to English can facilitate dual language learning (Castro et al., 2010; Gillanders and Castro, 2011). Evidence also suggests that systematically incorporating elements of children's home culture can increase their engagement and interest in preschool and the primary grades (Goldenberg et al., 2008).

The underlying principle for DLLs is that they need additional supports to comprehend the meaning of lessons because they are simultaneously learning the new language and the cognitive and conceptual content. These supports may include explicit bridging between the two languages; pictorial, visual, and multimedia cues that convey meaning; interactive and physical actions linked to meanings; direct instruction on important features of English, including vocabulary and phonics; use of culturally familiar themes and materials; and working closely with families to promote the continued development of the home language. Based on a careful synthesis of these and similar research findings, Espinosa and Magruder (2015) recommend a set of instructional strategies that monolingual English-speaking teachers can use to support the goals of L1 maintenance and English language development (see Box 5-5). It is important for all ECE staff to be proficient in English and use varied vocabulary and correct grammar when implementing these specific strategies in English. Although these specific evidence-based practices need further research, the weight of the evidence points to the need for all preschool teachers to integrate and extend DLLs' knowledge in their L1 and apply it to the challenge of learning English while they are also learning new age-appropriate content.

An emerging line of research addresses the implementation of the above practices (Downer and Yazejian, 2013; Durlak, 2010; Meyers et al., 2012). Such research is needed to better understand how these evidence-based practices can be adapted to different real-world contexts and diverse populations of children, families, and teachers. Successful implementation will require clear definition of the program model and specific strategies,

---

BOX 5-5
Instructional Strategies for Monolingual Teachers That Support Dual Language Learners' (DLLs') English Language Development and L1 Maintenance

- Teachers meet with parents early in the school year to learn about the child and family, especially early language experiences.
- Recruit parents, family members, and community members to volunteer in the classroom to provide opportunities for DLLs to hear, see, speak, read, and practice their L1.
- Create visuals that represent the languages, cultures, and family practices of children in the classroom.
- Make time for frequent individual and small-group language learning experiences.
- Provide books and materials that give an authentic representation of the cultures and L1s of DLLs and their families. Have students, parents, and volunteers help read and explain them.
- Introduce key vocabulary words in the child's L1, with help from parents or community volunteers.
- Preread stories in the child's L1, with help from parents or volunteers.
- Explicitly use cognates in the L1 and English to make connections between the two languages.
- Use pictorial, real-world objects and concrete experiences to convey the meaning of words and concepts.
- Use visual cues, gestures, and signals to link content vocabulary to imprint meaning.
- Routinely assess each child's language and conceptual knowledge and skills.

SOURCE: Summarized from Espinosa and Magruder (2015).

---

sufficient professional development, coaching and/or mentoring for educators, and means of collecting data on the fidelity of implementation and indicators with which to gauge impacts on targeted outcomes. The goal of achieving educational parity and reducing the achievement gap for DLLs can help motivate the increased investments necessary to take these steps toward meeting the needs of DLLs. (For a discussion of teacher qualifications and competencies needed to utilize these instructional practices effectively, see Chapter 8.)

Family Engagement Practices

A robust research literature emphasizes the importance of school-family partnerships to improving outcomes for children of all families (Arias and Morillo-Campbell, 2008; Halgunseth et al., 2013). Although research has identified lower levels of such engagement with families of DLLs, specific practices can enable programs to reduce the "language, cultural, and social networking barriers that keep DLL families from participating in their children's schools" (Halgunseth et al., 2013, p. 135). These practices include hiring bilingual staff, demonstrating respect for the families' beliefs and customs, being flexible about the scheduling of school events, translating information into the languages of DLL families (Halgunseth et al., 2009; Ramirez, 2003), and helping families recognize that their language and culture are strengths that should be shared at home and in the program. Some members of families with DLLs may believe that the family should stop speaking their home language and shift to English. In these cases, ECE professionals can make clear that the home language is a linguistic strength and can be used in rich language interactions throughout the day and across all contexts with no fear of doing harm. Families are critical partners in the goal of maintaining and supporting home language development, and "the entire program benefits when educators incorporate diverse cultures, languages, and talents of DLL families into the program's learning environment and curriculum" (Halgunseth, 2013, p. 144). Many researchers have recommended that programs hire bilingual and bicultural family liaisons to enhance communication and help build positive relationships between DLL families and ECE programs. Specific family engagement practices proven to be effective for DLL families include the following:

- addressing the bilingual/bicultural needs of DLL families,
- developing warm and mutually respectful relationships with DLL families,
- engaging in regular two-way communication,
- using a strengths-based approach when working with DLL families,
- engaging families in supporting their children's development at home, and
- utilizing community resources to support family engagement (Aria and Morillo-Campbell, 2008; Halgunseth et al., 2013).

CONCLUSIONS

Conclusion 5-1: Similar to all young children, dual language learners (DLLs) require comprehensive care and education that includes warm, nurturing, and responsive relationships, as well as sustained,

rich, diverse, and responsive language interactions. In addition, specific instructional strategies and language scaffolds that improve English language comprehension have been shown to be important for DLLs to reduce the achievement gap with their monolingual peers at kindergarten entry.

Conclusion 5-2: Dual language learners (DLLs) need both systematic exposure to English and ongoing support for L1 maintenance and development for two major reasons: (1) DLLs exposed to both languages show as much growth in English language and literacy skills as those instructed only in English; and (2) children immersed in English at an early age often show declines in their L1 skills, and strong language skills in a child's first language have been shown to facilitate English language development.

Conclusion 5-3: The quality of language learning opportunities in both infant/toddler programs and informal early care and education (ECE) settings where many dual language learners (DLLs) are enrolled has been shown to be lower than that of preschool programs and more formal, center-based ECE programs. However, shared linguistic and cultural backgrounds between DLL families and staff in ECE programs are more likely for children ages birth to 3 and in informal ECE settings than in center-based ECE programs, allowing for more L1 support for these DLLs.

Conclusion 5-4: It is important for early care and education and home visiting providers to know specific information about individual dual language learners' backgrounds, including their early language learning opportunities, family cultural values, and prior knowledge, so they can individualize instruction and services.

Conclusion 5-5: Dual language learners benefit from consistent exposure to both their L1 and English in early care and education settings. Research is limited on how much and what type of support for each language is most effective in supporting bilingual development.

Conclusion 5-6: All early care and education teachers of dual language learners can learn and implement strategies that systematically introduce English during the infant, toddler, and preschool years while simultaneously promoting maintenance of the home language—an important principle. Not all teachers can teach in all languages, but all teachers can learn specific strategies that support the maintenance of all languages.

Conclusion 5-7: There are critical gaps in research on the federal home visiting program serving dual language learners and their families. Research is limited, specifically, regarding model effectiveness with respect to child and family outcomes such as child health and development, including language and school readiness; linkages and referrals to social and health services; maternal health; and supportive parenting practices.

Conclusion 5-8: Dual language learners (DLLs) families are currently underserved by the federal home visiting program. Although research supports the capacity of all children, including those with disabilities, to become bilingual, home visiting programs are not using the extant evidence on early language development to guide families in supporting their child's first language and understanding its importance for learning the second language and for healthy psychosocial development. Guidelines for home visitors need to include talking with parents of DLLs about the benefits of a strong L1, including as the basis for developing English language competence. In addition, DLL families are numerically underrepresented and therefore underserved by the Maternal, Infant, and Early Childhood Visiting program.

BIBLIOGRAPHY

Adair, J. K. (2015). *The Impact of Discrimination on the Early Schooling Experiences of Children from Immigrant Families*. Washington, DC: Migration Policy Institute.

Administration for Children and Families. (2014). *FY 2014 Preliminary Data Table 1— Average Monthly Adjusted Number of Families and Children Served*. Available: http://www.acf.hhs.gov/occ/resource/fy-2014-preliminary-data-table-1 [December 5, 2016].

Administration for Children and Families. (2015). *Head Start Services*. Available: http://www.acf.hhs.gov/programs/ohs/about/head-start [August 31, 2015].

Anthony, J.L., Solari, E.J., Williams, J.M., Schoger, K.D., Zhang, Z., Branum-Martin, L., and Francis, D.J. (2009). Development of bilingual phonological awareness in Spanish-speaking English language learners: The roles of vocabulary, letter knowledge, and prior phonological awareness. *Scientific Studies of Reading, 13*(6), 535-564.

Arias, M.B., and Morillo-Campbell, M. (2008). Promoting ELL Parental Involvement: Challenges in Contested Times. *Online Submission*.

Atkins-Burnett, S., Monahan, S., Tarullo, L., Xue, Y., Cavadel, E., Malone, L., and Akers, L. (2015). *Measuring the Quality of Caregiver-Child Interactions for Infants and Toddlers (Q-CCIIT)*. OPRE Report 2015-13. Washington, DC: Administration for Children and Families, U.S. Department of Health and Human Services.

Atwill, K., Blanchard, J., Christie, J., Gorin, J.S., and García, H.S. (2010). English-language learners: Implications of limited vocabulary for cross-language transfer of phonemic awareness with kindergartners. *Journal of Hispanic Higher Education, 9*(2), 104-129.

August, D., and Shanahan, T. (Eds.). (2006). *Developing Literacy in Second Language Learners: Report of the National Literacy Panel on Language-Minority Children and Youth*. Mahwah, NJ: Lawrence Erlbaum Associates.

Avellar, S., Paulsell, D., Sama-Miller, E., Del Grosso, P., Akers, L., and Kleinman, R. (2016). *Home Visiting Evidence of Effectiveness Review: Executive Summary*. Washington, DC: Office of Planning, Research and Evaluation, Administration for Children and Families, U.S. Department of Health and Human Services.

Banaji, M.R., and Greenwald, A.G. (2013). *Blindspot: Hidden Biases of Good People*. New York: Delacorte Press.

Barnett, W.S. (2006). *Research on the Benefits of Preschool Education: Securing High Returns from Preschool for All Children*. Available: https://pdfs.semanticscholar.org/d18e/3c39 7060e42fe72175378849dfbbb1a148bf.pdf [May 2017].

Barnett, W.S. (2008). *Preschool Education and its Lasting Effects: Research and Policy Implications*. Boulder, CO and Tempe, AZ: Education and the Public Interest Center and Education Policy Research Unit.

Barnett, W.S. (2011). Effectiveness of early educational intervention. *Science, 333*(6045), 975-978.

Barnett, W.S., Yarosz, D., Thomas, J., Junga, K., and Blanco, D. (2007). Two-way and monolingual English immersion in preschool education: An experimental comparison. *Early Childhood Research Quarterly, 22(3)*, 277-293.

Barnett, W.S., Carolan, M.E., Squires, J.H., Clarke Brown, K., and Horowitz, M. (2015). *The State of Preschool 2014: State Preschool Yearbook*. New Brunswick, NJ: National Institute for Early Education Research. Available: http://nieer.org/sites/nieer/files/Yearbook2014_full2_0.pdf [July 28, 2015].

Beltrán, E. (2012). *Preparing Young Latino Children for School Success: Best Practices in Assessments*. Available: http://publications.nclr.org/handle/123456789/1097 [January 31, 2015].

Bernhard, J.K., Cummins, J., Campoy, F.I., Ada, A.F., Winsler, A., and Bleiker, C. (2006). Identity texts and literacy development among preschool English language learners: Enhancing learning opportunities for children at risk for learning disabilities. *Teachers College Record, 108*(11), 2380.

Bialystok, E., and Majumder, S. (1998). The relationship between bilingualism and the development of cognitive processes in problem solving. *Applied Psycholinguistics, 19*(1), 69-85.

Bialystok, E., and Viswanathan, M. (2009). Components of executive control with advantages for bilingual children in two cultures. *Cognition, 112*(3), 494-500.

Biemiller, A. (2009). *Words Worth Teaching: Closing the Vocabulary Gap*. Columbus, OH: McGraw-Hill.

Bloom, H.S., and Weiland, C. (2015). Quantifying variation in Head Start effects on young children's cognitive and socio-emotional skills using data from the National Head Start Impact Study. *Available at SSRN 2594430*.

Boller, K., Daro, D., Del Grosso, P., Cole, R., Paulsell, D., Hart, B., Coffee-Borden, B., Strong, D., Zaveri, H., and Hargreaves, M. (2014). *Making Replication Work: Building Infrastructure to Implement, Scale-Up, and Sustain Evidence-Based Early Childhood Home Visiting Programs with Fidelity*. Princeton, NJ: Mathematica Policy Research.

Booth, A.E. (2006). Object function and categorization in infancy: Two mechanisms of facilitation. *Infancy, 10*(2), 145-169.

Borman, G.D., Hewes, G.M., Overman, L.T., and Brown, S. (2003). Comprehensive school reform and achievement: A meta-analysis. *Review of Educational Research, 73*(2), 125-230.

Bornfreund, L. (2015). *Every Student Succeeds Act and Early Learning*. Available: http://www.edcentral.org/every-student-succeeds-act-early-learning [December 14, 2015].

Bowlby, J. (1969). *Attachment and Loss*. New York: Basic Books.

Bronfenbrenner, U. (1979). Contexts of child rearing: Problems and prospects. *American Psychologist, 34*(10), 844.

Brown, C.S. (2015). *The Educational, Psychological, and Social Impact of Discrimination on the Immigrant Child.* Washington, DC: Migration Policy Institute.

Brydon, M.M. (2010). *The Effect of Rich Instruction on the Vocabulary Acquisition of Preschool Dual Language Learners.* Pittsburgh, PA: University of Pittsburgh.

Burchinal, M., Field, S., López, M.L., Howes, C., and Pianta, R. (2012). Instruction in Spanish in pre-kindergarten classrooms and child outcomes for English language learners. *Early Childhood Research Quarterly, 27*(2), 188-197.

Burchinal, M., Magnuson, K., Powell, D., and Soliday Hong, S. (2015). Early childcare and education. In R. Lerner (Ed.), *Handbook of Child Psychology and Developmental Science* (7th ed., vol. 4, pp. 1-45). Hoboken, NJ: Wiley.

Camilli, G., Vargas, S., Ryan, S., and Barnett, W.S. (2010). Meta-analysis of the effects of early education interventions on cognitive and social development. *Teachers College Record, 112*(3), 579-620.

Campbell, F.A., Pungello, E.P., Burchinal, M., Kainz, K., Pan, Y., Wasik, B.H., Barbarin, O., and Ramey, C.T. (2012). Adult outcomes as a function of an early childhood educational program: An Abecedarian Project follow-up. *Developmental Psychology, 48*(4), 1033-1043.

Cannon, J.S., Jacknowitz, A., and Karoly, L.A. (2012). *Preschool and School Readiness: Experiences of Children with Non-English-Speaking Parents.* San Francisco: Public Policy Institute of California.

Carlson, S.M., and Meltzoff, A.N. (2008). Bilingual experience and executive functioning in young children. *Developmental Science, 11*(2), 282-298.

Castro, D.C. (2014). *Research Based on Best Practices for DLLs in PreK-3rd Grade: Instructional Strategies and Language of Instruction Approaches.* Commissioned paper prepared for the National Research Summit on the Early Care and Education of Dual Language Learners, October 15, Washington, DC. Available: https://www.mcknight.org/system/asset/document/864/original/Castro_NRSECEDLL_2014.pdf [May 2017].

Castro, D.C., Gillanders, C., Machado-Casas, M., and Buysse, V. (2006). *Nuestros Niños Early Language and Literacy Program.* Chapel Hill: University of North Carolina FPG Child Development Institute.

Castro, D.C., Peisner-Feinberg, E., Buysse, V., and Gillanders, C. (2010). Language and literacy development of Latino dual language learners: Promising instructional practices. In *Contemporary Perspectives on Language and Cultural Diversity in Early Childhood Education.* (pp. 65-94). Charlotte, NC: Information Age.

Castro, D.C., Espinosa, L.M., and Paez, M.M. (2011). Defining and measuring quality in early childhood practices that promote dual language learners' development and learning. In M. Zaslow, I. Martinez-Beck, K. Tout, and T. Halle (Eds.), *Quality Measurement in Early Childhood Settings* (pp. 257-280). Baltimore, MD: Paul H. Brookes.

Center for Early Care and Education Research-Dual Language Learners. (2011). *Research Brief #5: Early Care and Education Quality Measures: A Critical Review of the Research Related to Dual Language Learners.* Chapel Hill: The University of North Carolina, FPG Child Development Institute, Center for Early Care and Education Research-Dual Language Learners.

Chang, A., and Sandhofer, C.M. (2009). Language differences in bilingual parent number speech to preschool-aged children. In *Proceedings of the Thirty-first Annual Conference of the Cognitive Science Society* (pp. 887-892).

Collins, M.F. (2010). ELL preschoolers' English vocabulary acquisition from storybook reading. *Early Childhood Research Quarterly, 25*(1), 84-97.

Conboy, B. (2013). Neuroscience research: How experience with one or multiple languages affects the developing brain. In Governor's State Advisory Council on Early Learning and Care Sacramento (Ed.), *California's Best Practices for Young Dual Language Learners Research Overview Papers* (pp. 1-50). Sacramento: Child Development Division, California Department of Education.

Cook, R.E., Klein, M.D., and Tessier, A. (2004). *Adapting Early Childhood Curricula for Children in Inclusive Settings* (Sixth Edition). Upper Saddle River, NJ: Pearson.

Cooper, B.R., and Lanza, S.T. (2014). Who benefits most from Head Start? Using latent class moderation to examine differential treatment effects. *Child Development, 85*(6), 2317-2338.

Crosnoe, R. (2007). Early childcare and the school readiness of children from Mexican immigrant families. *International Migration Review, 41*(1), 152-181.

Davison, M.D., Hammer, C., and Lawrence, F.R. (2011). Associations between preschool language and first grade reading outcomes in bilingual children. *Journal of Communication Disorders, 44*(4), 444-458.

DeBruin-Parecki, A., Perkinson, K., and Ferderer, L. (2000). *Helping Your Child Become a Reader*. Parent Booklets, International Reading Association. Available: http://files.eric.ed.gov/fulltext/ED303789.pdf [February 21, 2017].

Demma, L. (2015). *Early Care and Learning in the Every Student Succeeds Act*. Available: http://mccormickcenter.nl.edu/early-care-and-learning-in-the-every-student-succeeds-act [December 14, 2015].

Dickinson, D.K. (2011). Teachers' language practices and academic outcomes of preschool children. *Science, 333*(6045), 964-967.

Dickinson, D.K., and Neuman, S.B. (2006). *Handbook of Early Literacy Research*. New York: Guilford Press.

Dickinson, D.K., McCabe, A., Clark-Chiarelli, N., and Wolf, A. (2004). Cross-language transfer of phonological awareness in low-income Spanish and English bilingual preschool children. *Applied Psycholinguistics, 25*(3), 323-347.

Dickinson, D.K., Golinkoff, R.M., and Hirsh-Pasek, K. (2010). Speaking out for language why language is central to reading development. *Educational Researcher, 39*(4), 305-310.

Dodici, B.J., Draper, D.C., and Peterson, C.A. (2003). Early parent–child interactions and early literacy development. *Topics in Early Childhood Special Education, 23*(3), 124-136.

Downer, J., and Yazejian, N. (2013). *Measuring the Quality and Quantity of Implementation in Early Child-Hood Interventions* (OPRE Research Brief OPRE 2013-12). Washington, DC: Office of Planning, Research, and Evaluation; Administration for Children and Families; U.S. Department of Health and Human Services.

Downer, J.T., López, M.L., Grimm, K.J., Hamagami, A., Pianta, R.C., and Howes, C. (2012). Observations of teacher-child interactions in classrooms serving Latinos and dual language learners: Applicability of the Classroom Assessment Scoring System in diverse settings. *Early Childhood Research Quarterly, 27*(1), 21-32.

Dudley-Marling, C., and Lucas, K. (2009). Pathologizing the language and culture of poor children. *Language Arts, 86*(5), 362-370.

Duncan, G.J., and Magnuson, K. (2013). Investing in preschool programs. *The Journal of Economic Perspectives, 27*(2), 109-132.

Durán, L.K., Roseth, C.J., and Hoffman, P. (2010). An experimental study comparing English-only and transitional bilingual education on Spanish-speaking preschoolers' early literacy development. *Early Childhood Research Quarterly, 25*(2), 207-217.

Durlak, J. A. (2010). The importance of doing well in whatever you do: A commentary on the special section, "Implementation research in early childhood education." *Early Childhood Research Quarterly, 25*(3), 348-357.

Erikson, E. H. (1965). *Childhood and Society (Revised Edition)*. London, UK: Penguin Books.

Espinosa, L.M. (2006). Young English language learners in the U.S. *Parents as Teacher News, 2*.

Espinosa, L. (2009). *Getting it Right for Young Children from Diverse Backgrounds: Applying Research to Improve Practice*, Upper Saddle River, NJ: Pearson Education.

Espinosa, L. (2010). The importance of language and literacy development for ALL children, bilingual and monolingual. In V. Washington and J.D. Andrews (Eds.), *Children of 2020: Creating a Better Tomorrow*. Washington, DC: Children of 2020.

Espinosa, L. (2013). *Pre-K–3rd: Challenging Common Myths about Dual-Language Learners. An Update to the Seminal 2008 Report*. New York: Foundation for Child Development.

Espinosa, L., and Gutiérrez-Clellen, V. (2013). Assessment of young dual language learners in preschool. In F. Ong and J. McLean (Eds.), *California's Best Practices for Dual Language Learners: Research Overview Papers* (pp. 172-208). Sacramento, CA: Governor's State Advisory Council on Early Learning and Care.

Espinosa, L.M., and López, M.L. (2007). *Assessment Considerations for Young English Language Learners across Different Levels of Accountability*. Los Angeles, CA: National Early Childhood Accountability Task Force and First 5 LA.

Espinosa, L., and Magruder, E.S. (2015). Practical and proven strategies for teaching young dual language learners. In *Getting it RIGHT for Young Children from Diverse Backgrounds: Applying Research to Improve Practice*. Upper Saddle River, NJ: Prentice Hall. Available http://www.earlychildhoodwebinars.com/wp-content/uploads/2016/01/Chapter-4_Practical-and-Proven-Strategies-for-Teaching-Young-Dual-Language-Learners.pdf [February 2017].

Espinosa, L.M., Burchinal, M., Winsler, A., Tien, H., Castro, D.C., and Peisner-Feinberg, E. (2013). *Child Care Experiences among Dual Language Learners in the U.S.: Analyses of the Early Childhood Longitudinal Survey-Birth Cohort*. Paper presented at the Dual Language Learners in Early Care and Education, American Education Research Association Annual Meeting, San Francisco, CA.

Espinosa, L., Burchinal, M., Winsler, A., Tien, H., Castro, D., and Peisner-Feinberg, E. (2017). *Child Care Experiences among Dual Language Learners in the US: Analyses of the Early Childhood Longitudinal Survey-Birth Cohort. AERA Open, 3*(2), 1-15. doi: 10.1177/2332858417699380.

Fantuzzo, J., McWayne, C., Perry, M.A., and Childs, S. (2004). Multiple dimensions of family involvement and their relations to behavioral and learning competencies for urban, low-income children. *School Psychology Review, 33*(4), 467.

Farver, J., Lonigan, C., and Eppe, S. (2009). Effective early literacy skill development for young Spanish-speaking English language learners: An experimental study of two methods. *Child Development, 80*(3), 703-719.

Farver, J.A.M., Xu, Y., Lonigan, C.J., and Eppe, S. (2013). The home literacy environment and Latino Head Start children's emergent literacy skills. *Developmental Psychology, 49*(4), 775.

Fiorentino, L., and Howe, N. (2004). Language competence, narrative ability, and school readiness in low-income preschool children. *Canadian Journal of Behavioural Science/Revue Canadienne des Sciences du Comportement, 36*(4), 280.

Friedman-Krauss, A., Barnett, W.S., and Nores, M. (2016). *How Much Can High-Quality Universal Pre-K Reduce Achievement Gaps?* Washington, DC: Center for American Progress.

Fuligni, A.S., Hoff, E., Zepeda, M., and Mangione, P. (2014*). Development of Infants and Toddlers Who Are Dual Language Learners*. Available: http://cecerdll.fpg.unc.edu/sites/cecerdll.fpg.unc.edu/files/imce/documents/%233016_Working-Paper%232.pdf [February 1, 2017].

Galindo, C. (2010). English language learners' math and reading achievement trajectories in the elementary grades. *Young English Language Learners: Current Research and Emerging Directions for Practice and Policy*, 42-58.

Gándara, P., and Hopkins, M. (2010). *English Learners and Restrictive Language Policies*. New York: Columbia University, Teachers College.

Gardner-Neblett, N., and Iruka, I.U. (2015). Oral narrative skills: Explaining the language-emergent literacy link by race/ethnicity and SES. *Developmental Psychology, 51*(7), 889.

Gillanders, C., and Castro, D. (2011). Storybook reading for young dual language learners. *Young Children, 66*(1), 91-95.

Goldenberg, C. (2013). Unlocking the research on English learners: What we know—and don't yet know—about effective instruction. *American Educator, 37*(2), 4-11.

Goldenberg, C., Rueda, R., and August, D. (2008). Sociocultural contexts and literacy development. In D. August and T. Shanahan (Eds.), *Developing Reading and Writing in Second-Language Learners: Lessons from the Report of the National Literacy Panel on Language-Minority Children and Youth* (ch. 5, pp. 95-130). New York: Routledge.

Goldenberg, C., Nemeth, K., Hicks, J., Zepeda, M., and Cardona, L.M. (2013). Program elements and teaching practices to support young dual language learners. *California's Best Practices for Young Dual Language Learners: Research Overview Papers*, 90-118.

Gormley, Jr., W.T. (2008). The effects of Oklahoma's pre-K program on Hispanic students. *Social Science Quarterly, 89*(4), 916-936.

Gormley, Jr., W., Gayer, T., Phillips, D., and Dawson, B. (2004). *The Effects of Oklahoma's Universal Pre-K Program on School Readiness: An Executive Summary*. Washington, DC: Center for Research on Children in the United States, Georgetown University.

Gormley, Jr., W.T., Gayer, T., Phillips, D., and Dawson, B. (2005). The effects of universal pre-K on cognitive development. *Developmental Psychology, 41*(6), 872.

Hakuta, K., and D'Andrea, D. (1992). Some properties of bilingual maintenance and loss in Mexican background high-school students. *Applied Linguistics, 13*(1), 72-99.

Halgunseth, L., Peterson, A., Stark, D., and Moodie, S. (2009). *Family Engagement, Diverse Families, and Early Childhood Education Programs: An Integrated Review of the Literature*. Washington, DC: NAEYC and Pre-K Now.

Halgunseth, L., Jia, G., and Barbarin, O. (2013). Family engagement in early childhood programs: Serving families of young dual language learners. In F. Ong and J. McLean (Eds.), *California's Best Practices for Young Dual Language Learners: Research Overview Papers* (no. 4, pp. 119-171). Sacramento: California Department of Education. Available: https://www.researchgate.net/publication/266394039_Family_Engagement_in_Early_Childhood_Programs_Serving_Families_of_Dual_Language_Learners [May 2017].

Halle, T., Forry, N., Hair, E., Perper, K., Wandner, L., Wessel, J., and Vick, J. (2009). *Disparities in Early Learning and Development: Lessons from the Early Childhood Longitudinal Study–Birth Cohort (ECLS-B)*. Washington, DC: Child Trends.

Halle, T., Anderson, R., Blasberg, A., Chrisler, A., and Simkin, S. (2011). *Quality of Caregiver-Child Interactions for Infants and Toddlers (Q-CCIIT): A Review of the Literature*. OPRE 2011-25. Washington, DC: Office of Planning, Research and Evaluation, Administration for Children and Families, U.S. Department of Health and Human Services.

Halle, T., Hair, E., Wandner, L., McNamara, M., and Chien, N. (2012). Predictors and outcomes of early versus later English language proficiency among English language learners. *Early Childhood Research Quarterly, 27*(1), 1-20.

Halle, T.G., Whittaker, J.V., Zepeda, M., Rothenberg, L., Anderson, R., Daneri, P., Wessel, J., and Buysse, V. (2014). The social–emotional development of dual language learners: Looking back at existing research and moving forward with purpose. *Early Childhood Research Quarterly, 29*(4), 734-749.

Hammer, C.S., Lawrence, F.R., and Miccio, A.W. (2007). Bilingual children's language abilities and early reading outcomes in Head Start and kindergarten. *Language, Speech, and Hearing Services in Schools, 38*(3), 237-248.

Hammer, C.S., Davison, M.D., Lawrence, F.R., and Miccio, A.W. (2009). The effect of maternal language on bilingual children's vocabulary and emergent literacy development during Head Start and Kindergarten. *Scientific Studies of Reading, 13*(2), 99-121.

Hammer, C.S., Scarpino, S., and Davison, M.D. (2011). Beginning with language: Spanish-English bilingual preschoolers' early literacy development. In D. Dickinson and S. Neuman (Eds.), *Handbook on Research in Early Literacy* (vol. 3, pp. 118-135). New York: Guilford Press.

Hart, B., and Risley, T.R. (1995). *Meaningful Differences in the Everyday Experience of Young American Children.* Baltimore, MD: Paul H. Brookes.

Harvard National Center on the Developing Child. (2011). *Building the Brain's "Air Traffic Control" System: How Early Experiences Shape the Development of Executive Function. Working Paper No. 11.* Available: http://developingchild.harvard.edu/resources/building-the-brains-air-traffic-control-system-how-early-experiences-shape-the-development-of-executive-function [January 10, 2017].

Harvard National Center on the Developing Child. (2016). *Toxic Stress.* Available: http://developingchild.harvard.edu/science/key-concepts/toxic-stress [January 10, 2017].

Health Resources Services Administration. (2011). *Affordable Care Act Maternal, Infant and Early Childhood Home Visiting Program: Supplemental Information Request for the Submission of the Statewide Needs Assessment.* Available: https://www.hrsa.gov/grants/apply/assistance/homevisiting/homevisitingsupplemental.pdf [February 6, 2017].

Health Resources and Services Administration. (2015a). *Fiscal Year 2015 Justification of Estimates for Appropriations Committees.* Available: http://www.hrsa.gov/about/budget/budgetjustification2015.pdf [September 2015].

Health Resources and Services Administration (2015b). *The Maternal, Infant, and Early Childhood Home Visiting Program Partnering with Parents to Help Children Succeed.* Available: http://mchb.hrsa.gov/programs/homevisiting/programbrief.pdf [August 12, 2015].

Health Resources and Services Administration. (2016). Federal Home Visiting Program: Performance Indicators and Systems Outcome Measures – Summary. Available: https://mchb.hrsa.gov/sites/default/files/mchb/MaternalChildHealthInitiatives/HomeVisiting/Federal_Home_Visiting_Program_Performance_Indicators_and_Systems_Outcomes_Summary.pdf [February, 1, 2017].

Heckman, J. (2010). *A New Cost-Benefit and Rate of Return Analysis for the Perry Preschool Program: A Summary.* Working Paper 16180. Cambridge, MA: National Bureau of Economic Research. Available: www.nber.org/papers/w16180 [May 2017].

Heckman, J.J., Humphries, J.E., and Veramendi, G. (2015). The causal effects of education on earnings and health. Unpublished manuscript, Department of Economics, University of Chicago.

Herfeldt-Kamprath, R., and Hamm, K. (2015). *Emerging State and Community Strategies to Improve Infant and Toddler Services.* Washington, DC: Center for American Progress. Available: https://www.americanprogress.org/issues/early-childhood/report/2015/06/04/114474/emerging-state-and-community-strategies-to-improve-infant-and-toddler-services [August 12, 2015].

Hirshberg, D., Huang, D.S.-C., and Fuller, B. (2005). Which low-income parents select childcare? Family demand and neighborhood organizations. *Children and Youth Services Review, 27*(10), 1119-1148.

Hirsh-Pasek, K., Michnick Golinkoff, R., Berk, L.E., and Singer, D.G. (2009). *A Mandate for Playful Learning in Preschool: Presenting the Evidence.* Oxford, UK and New York: Oxford University Press.

Hirsh-Pasek, K., Adamson, L.B. Bakeman, R., Owen, M.T., Golinkoff, R.M., Pace, A., Yust, P.K.S., and Suma, K. (2015). The contribution of early communication quality to low-income children's language success. *Psychological Science, 26*(7), 1071-1083.

Hudson, J.A. (1990). Constructive processing in children's event memory. *Developmental Psychology, 26*(2), 180.

Hurtado, N., Marchman, V.A., and Fernald, A. (2008). Does input influence uptake? Links between maternal talk, processing speed and vocabulary size in Spanish-learning children. *Developmental Science, 11*(6), F31-F39.

Huttenlocher, J., Vasilyeva, M., Cymerman, E., and Levine, S. (2002). Language input and child syntax. *Cognitive Psychology, 45*(3), 337-374.

Institute of Medicine and National Research Council. (2015). *Transforming the Workforce for Children Birth through Age 8: A Unifying Foundation.* L. Allen and B.B. Kelly (Eds.). Board on Children, Youth, and Families; Committee on the Science of Children Birth to Age 8: Deepening and Broadening the Foundation for Success. Washington, DC: The National Academies Press.

Jackson, M., Kiernan, K., and McLanahan, S. (2010). *Nativity Differences in Child Development across Diverse Populations, Settings and Outcomes: Do Socioeconomic Resources Narrow or Widen the Gap?* Available: https://ideas.repec.org/p/pri/crcwel/wp10-11-ff.pdf.html [February 21, 2017].

Jeynes, W. (2012). A meta-analysis of the efficacy of different types of parental involvement programs for urban students. *Urban Education, 47*(4), 706-742.

Johnson, K. (2009). *State-Based Home Visiting: Strengthening Programs through State Leadership.* New York: National Center for Children in Poverty. Available: http://www.nccp.org/publications/pdf/text_862.pdf [August 18, 2015].

Kagan, S.L, and Reid, J.L. (2008). *Advancing ECE2 Policy: Early Childhood Education (ECE) and its Quest for Excellence, Coherence and Equity.* Available: http://policyforchildren.org/wp-content/uploads/2013/07/American-ECE-Policy-Final-2.10.091.pdf [February 2017].

Karoly, L.A., and Gonzalez, G.C. (2011). Early care and education for children in immigrant families. *The Future of Children, 21*(1), 71-101.

Kuhl, P. K., Conboy, B.T., Padden, D., Nelson, T., and Pruitt, J. (2005). Early speech perception and later language development: Implications for the "critical period." *Language Learning and Development, 1*(3-4), 237-264.

Lally, J.R., and White-Tennant, G. (2004). Ready for life: How Early Head Start nurtures early learning. In J. Lombardi and M. Bogle (Eds.), *Beacon of Hope: The Promise of Early Head Start for America's Youngest Children* (pp. 77-95). Washington, DC: Zero to Three Press.

Lee, R., Zhai, F., Brooks-Gunn, J., Han, W.-J., and Waldfogel, J. (2014). Head Start participation and school readiness: Evidence from the Early Childhood Longitudinal Study–Birth cohort. *Developmental Psychology, 50*(1), 202.

Lesaux, N. (2009). *Slide Presentation, Panel I: Vocabulary and Academic Language.* Presented at the Workshop on the Role of Language in School Learning: Implications for Closing the Achievement Gap, October 15-16, Hewlett Foundation, Menlo Park, CA.

Leung, C.B., Silverman, R., Nandakumar, R., Qian, X., and Hines, S. (2011). A comparison of difficulty levels of vocabulary in first grade basal readers for preschool dual language learners and monolingual English learners. *American Educational Research Journal, 48*(2), 421-461.

Lobo, M.A., and Galloway, J.C. (2008). Postural and object-oriented experiences advance early reaching, object exploration, and means-end behavior. *Child Development, 79*(6), 1869-1890.

Loeb, S., Fuller, B., Kagan, S.L., and Carrol, B. (2004). Child care in poor communities: Early learning effects of type, quality, and stability. *Child Development, 75*(1), 47-65.

Lugo-Neris, M.J., Jackson, C.W., and Goldstein, H. (2010). Facilitating vocabulary acquisition of young English language learners. *Language, Speech, and Hearing Services in Schools, 41*(3), 314-327.

Lynch, E.W., and Hanson, M.J. (2011). *Developing Cross-Cultural Competence: A Guide for Working with Young Children and Their Families* (4th ed.). Baltimore, MD: Paul H. Brookes.

Magnuson, K., and Waldfogel, J. (2008). *Steady Gains and Stalled Progress: Inequality and the Black-White Test Score Gap.* New York: Russell Sage Foundation.

Magnuson, K.A., Ruhm, C., and Waldfogel, J. (2007). The persistence of preschool effects: Do subsequent classroom experiences matter? *Early Childhood Research Quarterly, 22*(1), 18-38.

Magruder, E.S., Hayslip, W.W., Espinosa, L.M., and Matera, C. (2013). Many languages, one teacher: Supporting language and literacy development for preschool dual language learners. *Young Children, 68*(1), 8.

Mancilla-Martinez, J., and Lesaux, N.K. (2011). The gap between Spanish speakers' word reading and word knowledge: A longitudinal study. *Child Development, 82*(5), 1544-1560.

Marchman, V.A., Martínez, L.Z., Hurtado, N., Grüter, T., and Fernald, A. (2017). Caregiver talk to young Spanish–English bilinguals: Comparing direct observation and parent-report measures of dual-language exposure. *Developmental Science, 20*(1), 1-13.

Markus, J., Mundy, P., Morales, M., Delgado, C.E., and Yale, M. (2000). Individual differences in infant skills as predictors of child-caregiver joint attention and language. *Social Development, 9*(3), 302-315.

Matthews, H., and Ewen, D. (2006). *Reaching All Children? Understanding Early Care and Education Participation among Immigrant Families.* Washington, DC: Center for Law and Social Policy. Available: http://www.clasp.org/resources-and-publications/files/0267.pdf [February 3, 2017].

Mayoral, M.V. (2013). *Early Head Start Fact Sheet. Zero to Three.* Available: http://www.zerotothree.org/policy/docs/ehs-fact-sheet-ztt-04-04-2014.pdf [September 1, 2015].

Méndez, L.I., Crais, E.R., Castro, D.C., and Kainz, K. (2015). A culturally and linguistically responsive vocabulary approach for young Latino dual language learners. *Journal of Speech, Language, and Hearing Research, 58*(1), 93-106.

Meyers, D.C., Durlak, J.A., and Wandersman, A. (2012). The quality implementation framework: A synthesis of critical steps in the implementation process. *American Journal of Community Psychology, 50*(3-4), 462-480.

Michalopoulos, C., Lee, H., Duggan, A., Lundquist, E., Tso, A., Crowne, S., Burrell, L., Somers, J., Filene, J.H., and Knox, V. (2015). *The Mother and Infant Home Visiting Program Evaluation: Early Findings on the Maternal, Infant, and Early Childhood Home Visiting Program. A Report to Congress.* OPRE Report 2015-11. Washington, DC: Office of Planning, Research and Evaluation, Administration for Children and Families, U.S. Department of Health and Human Services. Available: http://www.mdrc.org/sites/default/files/MIHOPE_2015_report_to-congress.pdf [February 4, 2017].

Migration Policy Institute. (2016). *Dual Language Learners in Head Start: The Promises and Pitfalls of New Reforms.* Available: http://www.migrationpolicy.org/article/dual-language-learners-head-start-promises-and-pitfalls-new-reforms [February 6, 2017].

Miller, L.S., and Garcia, E.E. (2008). *A Reading-Focused Early Childhood Research and Strategy Development Agenda for African Americans and Hispanics at All Social Class Levels Who Are English Speakers or English Language Learners.* Phoenix: Arizona State University, Office of the Vice President for Educational Partnerships.

Morgan, P.L., Farkas, G., Hillemeier, M.M., Mattison, R., Maczuga, S., Li, H., and Cook, M. (2015). Minorities are disproportionately underrepresented in special education: Longitudinal evidence across five disability conditions. *Educational Research, 44*(5), 278-292.

National Association for the Education of Young Children. (2008). *Overview of the NAEYC Early Childhood Program Standards.* Available: https://www.naeyc.org/files/academy/file/OverviewStandards.pdf [February 4, 2017].

National Center on Cultural and Linguistic Responsiveness and National Center on Quality Teaching and Learning. (n.d.). *Screening Dual Language Learners in Early Head Start and Head Start: A Guide for Program Leaders.* Available: http://eclkc.ohs.acf.hhs.gov/hslc/tta-system/cultural-linguistic/fcp/docs/Screening-dual-language-learners.pdf [August 30, 2015].

National Head Start Association. (2016). *2016 National Head Start Profile.* Available: https://www.nhsa.org/files/resources/fact_sheet_national_0.pdf [June 2017].

National Institute for Early Education Research. (2013). *Trends in State Funded Preschool Programs: Survey Findings from 2001-2002 to 2011-2012.* Available: http://nieer.org/sites/nieer/files/Trends%20in%20State%20Funded%20Preschool%20Programs_0.pdf [October 10, 2016].

National Institute of Child Health and Human Development Early Child Care Research Network. (2005). Early child care and children's development in the primary grades: Follow-up results from the NICHD study of early child care. *American Educational Research Journal, 42*(3), 537-570.

National Migrant and Seasonal Head Start Association (2015). *Basic Facts on Migrant and Seasonal Head Start.* Available: https://www.nhsa.org/files/resources/fact_sheet_mshs.pdf [June 2017].

National Research Council. (1998). *Preventing Reading Difficulties in Young Children.* Washington, DC: National AcademyPress.

National Research Council. (2000). *Eager to Learn: Educating Our Preschoolers.* B.T. Bowman, M.S. Donovan, and M.S. Burns (Eds.), Committee on Early Childhood Pedagogy; Board on Behavioral, Cognitive, and Sensory Sciences; Division of Behavioral and Social Sciences and Education. Washington, DC: National Academy Press.

National Research Council. (2008). *Early Childhood Assessment: Why, What, and How.* C.E. Snow and S.B. Van Hemel (Eds.). Committee on Developmental Outcomes and Assessments for Young Children; Board on Children, Youth, and Families; Board on Testing and Assessment; Division of Behavioral and Social Sciences and Education. Washington, DC: The National Academies Press.

National Research Council and Institute of Medicine. (2000). *From Neurons to Neighborhoods: The Science of Early Childhood Development.* J.P. Shonkoff and D.A. Phillips (Eds.). Committee on Integrating the Science of Early Childhood Development; Board on Children, Youth, and Families; Division of Behavioral and Social Sciences and Education. Washington, DC: National Academy Press.

Office of Head Start. (2011). *The Head Start Parent, Family, and Community Engagement Framework.* Available: http://eclkc.ohs.acf.hhs.gov/hslc/standards/im/2011/pfce-framework.pdf [August 23, 2015].

Office of Head Start. (2015a). *Head Start Early Learning Outcomes Framework.* Available: http://eclkc.ohs.acf.hhs.gov/hslc/hs/sr/approach/pdf/ohs-framework.pdf [December 7, 2015].

Office of Head Start. (2015b). Head Start Program Facts. Available: https://eclkc.ohs.acf. hhs.gov/data-ongoing-monitoring/article/head-start-program-facts-fiscal-year-2015 [June 2017].

Oller, D.K., and Eilers, R.E. (2002). *Language and Literacy in Bilingual Children*. Clevedon, UK: Multilingual Matters.

Oppedal, B., and Toppelberg, C.O. (2016). Culture competence: A developmental task of acculturation. In D. Sam and J. Berry (Eds.), *The Cambridge Handbook of Acculturation Psychology* (2nd ed.). Cambridge, UK: Cambridge University Press.

Páez, M., and Rinaldi, C. (2006). Predicting English word reading skills for Spanish-speaking students in first grade. *Topics in Language Disorders, 26*(4), 338.

Páez, M., Bock, K.P., and Pizzo, L. (2011). Supporting the language and early literacy skills of English language learners: Effective practices and future directions. *Handbook of Early Literacy Research, 3*, 136-152.

Paik, J.H., and Mix, K.S. (2003). U.S. and Korean children's comprehension of fraction names: A reexamination of cross-national differences. *Child Development, 74*(1), 144-154.

Paris, R. (2008). For the dream of being here, one sacrifices...: Voices of immigrant mothers in a home visiting program. *American Journal of Orthopsychiatry, 78*(2), 141-151.

Peisner-Feinberg, E.S., Burchinal, M.R., Clifford, R.M., Culkin, M.L., Howes, C., Kagan, S.L., and Yazejian, N. (2001). The relation of preschool child-care quality to children's cognitive and social developmental trajectories through second grade. *Child Development, 72*(5), 1534-1553.

Pianta, R.C., Barnett, W.S., Burchinal, M., and Thornburg, K.R. (2009). The effects of preschool education: What we know, how public policy is or is not aligned with the evidence base, and what we need to know. *Psychological Science in the Public Interest, 10*(2), 49-88.

Place, S., and Hoff, E. (2011). Properties of dual language exposure that influence 2-year-olds' bilingual proficiency. *Child Development, 82*(6), 1834-1849.

Puma, M., Bell S., Cook R., Heid C., Broene P., Jenkins F., Mashburn A., and Downer, J. (2012). *Third Grade Follow-Up to the Head Start Impact Study: Final Report*. OPRE Report 2012-45. Washington, DC: Administration for Children and Families, U.S. Department of Health and Human Services. Available: http://www.acf.hhs.gov [February 4, 2017].

Pumariega, A.J., Rothe, E., Mian, A., Carlisle, L., Toppelberg, C., Harris, T., Gogineni, R.R., Webb, S., and Smith, J. (2013). Practice parameter for cultural competence in child and adolescent psychiatric practice. *Journal of the American Academy of Child & Adolescent Psychiatry, 52*(10), 1101-1115.

Raikes, H., Green, B.L., Atwater, J., Kisker, E., Constantine, J. ,and Chazan-Cohen, R. (2006). Involvement in Early Head Start home visiting services: Demographic predictors and relations to child and parent outcomes. *Early Childhood Research Quarterly, 21*(1), 2-24.

Ramirez, A.F. (2003). Dismay and disappointment: Parental involvement of Latino immigrant parents. *The Urban Review, 35*(2), 93-110.

Roberts, T., and Neal, H. (2004). Relationships among preschool English language learners' oral proficiency in English, instructional experience and literacy development. *Contemporary Educational Psychology, 29*(3), 283-311.

Rodriguez, J.L., Duran, D., Diaz, R.M., and Espinosa, L. (1995). The impact of bilingual preschool education on the language development of Spanish-speaking children. *Early Childhood Research Quarterly, 10*(4), 475-490.

Roopnarine, J., and Johnson, J.E. (2013). *Approaches to Early Childhood Education*. Upper Saddle River, NJ: Pearson Education.

Saiz, A., and Zoido, E. (2005). Listening to what the world says: Bilingualism and earnings in the United States. *Review of Economics and Statistics, 87*(3), 523-538.

Sama-Miller, E., Akers, L., Mraz-Esposito, A., Avellar, S., Paulsell, D., and Del Grosso, P. (2016). *Home Visiting Evidence of Effectiveness Review: Executive Summary.* Office of Planning, Research and Evaluation, Administration for Children and Families, U.S. Department of Health and Human Services. Washington, DC. Available: http://homvee. acf.hhs.gov/HomVEE_Executive_Summary_2016_B508.pdf [February 22, 2017].

Sandhofer, C., and Uchikoshi, Y. (2013). *The Relationship between Dual Language Development and Development of Cognition, Mathematics, Social-emotional Development, and Related Domains.* California's Best Practices for Young Dual Language Learners: Research Overview Papers. Sacramento: Child Development Division, California Department of Education. Available: http://www.cde.ca.gov/sp/cd/ce/documents/dllresearch papers.pdf [January 10, 2017].

Sarnecka, B.W., Wright, C.E., and Goldman, M.C. (2011). *Cross-Linguistic Associations in the Vocabularies of Bilingual Children: Number Words vs. Color Words and Common Nouns.* Paper presented at the Biennial Meeting of the Society for Research in Child Development, Pennsylvania, PA.

Schmit, S., and Matthews, H. (2013). *Investing in Young Children: A Fact Sheet on Early Care and Education Participation, Access, and Quality.* Washington, DC: Center for Law and Social Policy. Available: http://www.clasp.org/issues/child-care-and-early-education/in-focus/investing-in-young-children-a-fact-sheet-on-early-care-and-education-participation-access-and-quality [September 4, 2015].

Schmitt, S., Walker, C., and Herzfeldt-Kamprath, R. (2015). *An Investment in Our Future: How Federal Home Visiting Provides Critical Support for Parents and Children.* Washington, DC: Center for American Progress and Center for Law and Social Policy. Available: https://www.americanprogress.org/issues/early-childhood/report/2015/02/11/106406/an-investment-in-our-future [August 18, 2015].

Schweinhart, L.J., and Weikart, D.P. (2006). The High/Scope preschool curriculum comparison study. In R. Parker-Rees and J. Willan (Eds.), *Early Years Education: Major Themes in Education* (vol. 4, pp. 116-146). New York: Routledge.

Schweinhart, L.J., Montie, J., Xiang, Z., Barnett, W.S., Belfield, C.R., and Nores, M. (2005). *Lifetime Effects: The High/Scope Perry Preschool Study Through Age 40.* Monographs of the High/Scope Educational Research Foundation, #14. Ypsilanti, MI: High/Scope Press.

Slavin, R., Madden, N., Calderón, M., Chamberlain, A., and Hennessy, M. (2011). Reading and language outcomes of a multiyear randomized evaluation of transitional bilingual education. *Educational Evaluation and Policy Analysis, 33*(1), 47-58.

Strain, P.S., and Bovey, E.H. (2011). Randomized, controlled trial of the LEAP model of early intervention for young children with autism spectrum disorders. *Topics in Early Childhood Special Education, 31*(3), 133-154.

Tamis-LeMonda, C.S., Bornstein, M.H., Baumwell, L., and Melstein Damast, A. (1996). Responsive parenting in the second year: Specific influences on children's language and play. *Infant and Child Development, 5*(4), 173-183.

Thompson, K.D. (2015). English learners' time to reclassification: An analysis. *Educational Policy,* 1-34.

Toppelberg, C.O., and Collins, B.A. (2010). Language, culture, and adaptation in immigrant children. *Child and Adolescent Psychiatric Clinics of North America, 19*(4), 697-717.

Toppelberg, C.O., and Collins B.A. (2016). Dual language children: Development, mental health, and clinical implications. In R.I. Parekh (Ed.), *Cultural Sensitivity in Child and Adolescent Mental Health.* Boston: Massachusetts General Hospital Psychiatry Academy Press.

University of Chicago. (2010). *Getting on Track Early for School Success: An Assessment System to Support Effective Instruction.* Technical Report. Chicago, IL: University of Chicago.

U.S. Census Bureau. (2013). *Language Spoken at Home by Ability to Speak English for the Population 5 Years and Over (Hispanic or Latino)*. Available: https://factfinder.census.gov/faces/tableservices/jsf/pages/productview.xhtml?src=bkmk [February 2, 2017].

U.S. Census Bureau. (2014). *Age by Language Spoken at Home by Ability to Speak English for the Population 5 Years and Over*. Available: https://factfinder.census.gov/faces/tableservices/jsf/pages/productview.xhtml?pid=ACS_15_1YR_B16004&prodType=table [February 3, 2017].

U.S. Census Bureau. (2016). *2014 and 2015 Annual Social and Economic Supplements*. Available: https://www.census.gov/programs-surveys/cps/technical-documentation/complete.html [February 1, 2017].

U.S. Department of Health and Human Services. (2010). *The Head Start Child Development and Early Learning Framework: Promoting Positive Outcomes in Early Childhood Programs Serving Children 3-5*. Available: http://eclkc.ohs.acf.hhs.gov/hslc/tta-system/teaching/eecd/Assessment/Child%20Outcomes/HS_Revised_Child_Outcomes_Framework(rev-Sept2011).pdf [February 21, 2017].

U.S. Department of Health and Human Services, Office of the Assistant Secretary for Planning and Evaluation. (2015). *U.S. Federal Poverty Guidelines Used to Determine Financial Eligibility for Certain Federal Programs*. Available: https://aspe.hhs.gov/2015-poverty-guidelines [December 7, 2015].

Vesely, C.K. (2013). Low-income African and Latina immigrant mothers' selection of early childhood care and education (ECCE): Considering the complexity of cultural and structural influences. *Early Childhood Research Quarterly, 28*(3), 470-486.

Vitiello, V., Downer, J., and Williford, A. (2011). Preschool classroom experiences of dual language learners: Summary of findings from publicly funded programs in 11 states. *Dual Language Learners in the Early Childhood Classroom*, 69-91.

Vygotsky, L.S. (1978). *Mind in Society*. Cambridge, UK: Cambridge University Press.

Ward, H., Oldham LaChance, E., and Atkins, J. (2011). *New Americans: Child Care Decision-Making of Refugee and Immigrant Parents of English Language Learners*. Portland: University of Southern Maine, Muskie School of Public Service.

Weisberg, D. S., Zosh, J. M., Hirsh-Pasek, K., and Golinkoff, R. M. (2013). Talking it up: Play, language development, and the role of adult support. *American Journal of Play, 6*(1), 39.

Whitehurst, G.J., and Lonigan, C.J. (1998). Child development and emergent literacy. *Child Development, 69*(3), 848-872.

Whitehurst, G.J., Arnold, D.S., Epstein, J.N., Angell, A.L., Smith, M., and Fischel, J.E. (1994). A picture book reading intervention in day care and home for children from low-income families. *Developmental Psychology, 30*(5), 679.

Winsler, A., Diaz, R.M., Espinosa, L., and Rodriguez, J.L. (1999a). When learning a second language does not mean losing the first: Bilingual language development in low-income, Spanish-speaking children attending bilingual preschool. *Child Development, 70*(2), 349-362.

Winsler, A., Diaz, R.M., McCarthy, E.M., Atencio, D.J., and Chabay, L.A. (1999b). Mother-child interaction, private speech, and task performance in preschool children with behavior problems. *Journal of Child Psychology and Psychiatry, 40*(6), 891-904.

Winsler, A., Burchinal, M., Tien, H., Peisner-Feinberg, E., Espinosa· L., Castro, D., LaForett, D., Kim, Y.K., and De Feyter, J. (2014). Early development among dual language learners: The roles of language use at home, maternal immigration, country of origin, and sociodemographics. *Early Childhood Research Quarterly, 29*(4), 750-764.

Winton, P.J., McCollum, J.A., and Catlett, C. (2008). *Practical Approaches to Early Childhood Professional Development: Evidence, Strategies, and Resources*. Washington, DC: Zero to Three.

Wong, V.C., Cook, T.D., Barnett, W.S., and Jung, K. (2008). An effectiveness-based evaluation of five state pre-kindergarten programs. *Journal of Policy Analysis and Management,* 27(1), 122-154.

Wong-Fillmore, L. (1991). When learning a second language means losing the first. *Early Childhood Research Quarterly,* 6, 323-346.

Yazejian, N., Bryant, D., Freel, K., and Burchinal, M. (2015). High-quality early education: Age of entry and time in care differences in student outcomes for English-only and dual language learners. *Early Childhood Research Quarterly,* 32, 23-39.

Yoshikawa, H., Weiland, C., Brooks-Gunn, J., Burchinal, M.R., Espinosa, L.M., Gormley, W.T., Ludwig, J., Magnuson, K.A., Phillips, D. and Zaslow, M.J. (2013). *Investing in Our Future: The Evidence Base on Preschool Education.* Available: http://repositorio.minedu.gob.pe/bitstream/handle/123456789/4015/Investing%20in%20 Our%20Future%20The%20Evidence%20Base%20on%20Preschool%20Education. pdf?sequence=1&isAllowed=y [February 21, 2017].

Zaslow, M., Tout, K., Halle, T., Whittaker, J.V., and Lavelle, B. (2010). *Toward the Identification of Features of Effective Professional Development for Early Childhood Educators. Literature Review.* Washington, DC: Office of Planning, Evaluation and Policy Development, U.S. Department of Education.

Zepeda, M. (2015). *The Early Childhood Workforce for Dual Language Learners: What Do We Know and Where Do We Need to Go?* Unpublished commissioned paper. Los Angeles, CA: California State University, Department of Child and Family Studies.

Zero to Three. (2010). *How to Communicate with Parents.* Available: https://www.zerotothree. org/resources/92-how-to-communicate-with-parents [February 2017].

6

The Development of English Language Proficiency in Grades K-12

Policies and practices with respect to educating English learners (ELs) in the United States have historically been driven largely by beliefs and attitudes about how best to ensure that they acquire high levels of functional proficiency in English as quickly as possible (Espinosa, 2013). These beliefs and attitudes have reflected a combination of what might be regarded as common sense and scientific theories about what is best for ELs with respect to learning English. Generally speaking, educational policies and practices concerning the role of language in the education of ELs reflect four commonly held beliefs (see Cook, 1992; Cummins, 1981; and Grosjean, 1985, for earlier renditions of these ideas), all of which have been challenged by empirical research (see Genesee, 2015, for a review of that evidence):

1. Learning and using more than one language is burdensome and has associated costs and disadvantages.
2. Young children are effective and efficient (second) language learners.
3. Amount of exposure is a significant correlate of language competence.
4. The languages of bi- and multilinguals are separate neurocognitive systems.

Taken together, these beliefs have had important implications for thinking about when and how ELs should learn English and about schooling for ELs in general. For example, and of particular importance for the discussion in this chapter, how long does it or should it take ELs to achieve proficiency in English so they can benefit from participation in classrooms in which English is the language of instruction? These beliefs have shaped thinking about other educational issues as well, including the following: To what extent should ELs begin to learn English before school starts so they are prepared for formal schooling in English? What is the importance of developing the first language (L1) during the preschool years in supporting English language development and academic success in school? Should ELs receive academic instruction in the home language to ensure their ability to meet academic objectives while they learn English? and Should achievement in nonlanguage subjects (such as mathematics or science) and in English (such as reading and writing) be assessed in the same ways and, in the case of English proficiency, using the same benchmarks as are used with monolingual native English-speaking students? The influence of these beliefs and attitudes has been most evident in educational programs during the elementary and secondary school years, but has also impacted thinking about preschool education as more and more children attend preschool programs.

Although the focus in this chapter is on the development of English proficiency, it is important to point out that language proficiency is not necessarily the only or even the most important barrier to academic success among ELs. Depending on the background of specific children or groups of ELs, their academic success can be jeopardized by issues related to such factors as poverty; poor health; trauma linked to immigration and/or preimmigrant experiences; cultural differences between home and school; state, district, and school policies and practices (including assessment requirements); the quality of educational materials, instruction, and curriculum; teachers' attitudes; and inadequate teacher preparation. Individual ELs can experience a number of different challenges simultaneously (Suárez-Orozco et al., 2010), with significant and commensurate effects on their academic outcomes (Lindholm-Leary, 2010). Of these, socioeconomic status has been shown to be particularly potent (National Task Force on Early Childhood Education for Hispanics, 2007). For example, Kieffer (2008), using data from the Early Childhood Longitudinal Study (ECLS), found smaller differences between ELs and native English-speaking students who attended low-poverty versus high-poverty schools. As well, and in contrast to other research on the performance of language minority students, Lesaux and colleagues (2007) found few significant differences in reading comprehension between ELs and non-ELs where the ELs were distributed across the same schools and neighborhoods as the non-ELs. They speculate that EL status and low socioeconomic status are often confounded in other studies on ELs and that this may account for the difference in their findings.

The conclusion that EL status alone is not sufficient to explain the academic challenges of ELs in the United States also is supported by evidence that the academic performance of ELs or heritage language speakers can vary from country to country. Specifically, research has shown that immigrant ELs in Canada and Australia on average perform as well as or better than native-born students on standardized tests of academic achievement (Aydemir et al., 2008; Cobb-Clark and Trong-Ha Nguyen, 2010, respectively). Whatever the explanation for these between-country differences, suffice it to say here that the relative importance of proficiency in the language of instruction per se is an open question and probably reflects complex, national-level factors along with individual, family, and school factors. Overly simplistic notions of second language development in school and across-the-board stereotypes about the academic achievement of ELs are to be avoided, as noted in Chapter 1.

TIME TO PROFICIENCY

The question of how long it does, or should, take ELs to achieve proficiency in English so they can benefit from participation in classrooms in which English is the language of instruction[1] has engaged researchers, policy makers, the media, and the public since the 1974 Supreme Court decision in *Lau v. Nichols* granted linguistic accommodations to students with limited proficiency in English (see Chapter 2). Understanding the time it takes for ELs to develop English language proficiency is critical to the discussion of how best to educate these children and youth for several reasons, notwithstanding the importance of other factors. First, states are required to develop and implement identification/classification systems for ELs whose level of proficiency in English is deemed too low for them to be educated in mainstream classrooms without additional support.[2] States also are required to monitor ELs' progress in English proficiency once they are reclassified as fully English-proficient (Hakuta, 2011; Linquanti and Cook, 2013). (More details about these policies and their implications are provided in Chapters 2 and 9.)

Empirical evidence concerning the typical time required to achieve levels of proficiency in English that would permit ELs to benefit from all-English instruction also is necessary to establish reasonable expectations about how long ELs require additional support in learning English for academic purposes. A common view is that young learners are efficient and effective second language learners who require little systematic or long-term

---

[1] This chapter is adapted from a paper commissioned by the committee for this study (Lindholm-Leary, 2015).

[2] Children who are deemed as lacking sufficient proficiency in English to benefit fully from instruction in English-only classrooms (according to state definitions and criteria) are identified as ELs and are eligible for additional services and supports for a certain number of grades; more details are provided in Chapter 2.

intervention to enhance their acquisition of English as a second language. Proposition 227 in California (overturned by voters in November 2016), for example, allowed ELs 1 year in classes where they received specialized support in learning English before being integrated into regular classrooms with native speakers of English.

There is growing recognition that educational research on and educational policies and practices with respect to the English language development of ELs need to distinguish between language for social communication and language for academic purposes. Numerous conceptualizations of language for academic purposes have been proposed (e.g., Scarcella, 2003; Schleppelgrell, 2004; also see Goldenberg and Coleman, 2010; Snow and Ucelli, 2009, for extended discussions of this topic). For illustrative purposes, the succinct and early definition proposed by Chamot and O'Malley (1994, p. 40) is useful: "Academic language is the language that is used by teachers and students for the purposes of acquiring new knowledge and skills . . . imparting new information, describing abstract ideas, and developing students' conceptual understanding." To expand on this definition, there is also general agreement that academic language refers to the specialized vocabulary, grammar, discourse/textual, and functional skills associated with academic instruction and mastery of academic material and skill, and it can be oral or written language. Goldenberg and Coleman (2010, p. 87) characterize academic language in comparison with social-conversational language as "more formal, abstract, used in academic and explicit teaching and learning situations, more demanding cognitively, and more challenging to learn (see also Bailey, 2007)." Snow and Ucelli (2009, pp. 119-120) offer an alternative conceptualization of "more academic" compared with "more colloquial" language. Specifically, they propose that academic language can be conceptualized in terms of the communicative challenges and goals to which academic language is meant to respond. These, they argue, include representing the self and the audience, representing the message, and organizing discourse.

Box 6-1 presents an example of a teacher's use of academic language during a lesson on using graphs to represent change in the manufacturing industry in California. Specifically, this example illustrates that academic language is characterized by the use of

- technical vocabulary (such as *manufactured, line graph, trace, related rise*);
- sentence patterns that require complex grammatical constructions, such as "What might happen if there were not products to manufacture?" (e.g., Bailey, 2007; Wong-Fillmore and Fillmore, 2012);
- explicit reference to what is being talked about (e.g., ". . . the graph would then indicate a decline. *The line* would go down. . . "); and

- specific background knowledge, as illustrated by the fact that without the necessary background knowledge that was part of this lesson, the language used in this interchange would be even more challenging.

In addition, from a language teaching and learning point of view, proficiency in language for academic purposes requires that students be competent at performing sophisticated "language functions," such as the ability to

- argue persuasively for or against a point of view;
- analyze, compare, and contrast;
- evaluate alternative points of view and factual information;
- justify one's point of view or debate different points of view;
- synthesize and integrate information;
- follow or give complex directions;
- hypothesize about the causal relationship between events;
- justify a predication, as in a science experiment on osmosis;
- present a logical argument; and
- question an explanation.

BOX 6-1
Example of Academic Language

T: *Many things are manufactured in California, from airplanes to computer chips. Suppose you wanted to find out how many people worked in manufacturing jobs in California for the last 25 years. A line graph could help you. Look at the line graph on page 51 and trace the line to see changes over time. Why would the line be expected to move up over time?*

S: More jobs.

T: *That's right. Because manufacturing had increased over time, the line indicates the related rise in the number of jobs. What happened around 1990?*

S: It stays the same.

T: *Yes, the job market stabilized so there was only a slight increase—hardly discernible—in the line. What might happen if there were not products to manufacture?*

S: People lose their jobs.

S: Some would move away.

T: *That's right, and the graph would then indicate a decline. The line would go down in that case.*

NOTE: T = teacher; S = student.

It is also thought that academic language differs from one subject to another; for example, the language of mathematics is different from the language used to discuss and write about science and history. The language of different academic subjects can differ in multiple ways. To start, each subject requires knowledge of specific technical vocabulary; sometimes this means that students must learn alternative meanings of common words, such as the mathematical use of the word *table* or *times* versus the day-to-day meanings of these words. Academic language also differs from subject to subject with respect to the specific grammatical forms and discourse patterns that are typically used when talking or writing about these subjects. For example, whereas science might call for grammatical skills that allow students to formulate hypotheses using subjunctive verb forms and to express relationships in probabilistic terms (e.g., "if the boats were heavier, then they would probably sink") or to express causal relationships (e.g., "humidity is a function of both temperature and proximity to large bodies of water"), mathematics might call on these grammatical forms and discourse functions much less often. There is undoubtedly some overlap in the academic language associated with different domains, and therefore, it is usually a matter of what grammatical forms or discourse patterns are relatively common in each academic domain.

At present, however, there is no single conceptualization of academic language and the specific features it comprises. In fact, some researchers have contested the distinction between these forms of language use (e.g., MacSwan and Rolstad, 2010). In their review of work on academic language, Snow and Ucelli (2009, p. 113) note, "Despite these advances in delineating academic language, a conceptualization of academic language within a consensual analytic framework that could guide educationally relevant research is still lacking." Moreover, as noted previously, test-defined levels of proficiency do not reflect a widely held theory of language for academic purposes. As well, there is a dearth of research that has examined the development of proficiency in English as a second language for academic purposes, the factors that influence its development, and its influence on academic success.

School- and district-based policies and decisions about ELs' readiness to benefit from English-only instruction have often been based on "reclassification tests" devised by individual states using criteria that differ from state to state. Once ELs achieve defined cut-off scores on these tests and in some cases meet other criteria, they are deemed proficient and reclassified as non-EL or fully English-proficient. At that time, specialized services tailored to meet their English language learning needs are withdrawn, modified, or reduced on the assumption that they are ready to benefit from instruction in English without such supports. For the most part, the tests used to make these determinations have not been based on empirically validated theories of language proficiency for academic purposes and its development. Thus, the terms "proficiency" and "proficient" as used in the following section on time to reclassification refer to the level of performance achieved by ELs on reclassification tests, not their level of competence in English as defined by a validated theory of academic language proficiency.[3]

A large body of research is based on the results of such testing, and the committee believes it is important to review the results of this research, notwithstanding the above limitations, because the methods of classification and reclassification under investigation in these studies reflect policy and practice that until recently were prevalent. Since most studies were conducted prior to the passage of the Every Student Succeeds Act (ESSA), they do not reflect policies associated with current legislation that is slated to be implemented in school year 2017-2018. To ignore these studies is to ignore a large body of evidence on how schools have identified ELs who require additional language support and, in turn, the suitability of policies and practices that have underpinned the use of reclassification tests. Reviewing these studies helps in evaluating policies and practices that have been in place until recently and could perhaps even inform evolving policies and practices.

The following section reviews research on time to reclassification of ELs, beginning with a discussion of methodological and other measurement issues associated with the use of reclassification tests; Chapter 11 provides more in-depth discussion of psychometric issues resulting from the use of these tests. The second section examines factors that influence reclassification rates among ELs in grades K-12. This is followed by sections on retention and loss of the home language of ELs and on cross-linguistic aspects of ELs' language development. The former is intended to provide an understanding of the language development of ELs and, in particular, the extent to which they do or do not become bilingual in English and their home language. The section on cross-linguistic effects in the language development of bilinguals briefly considers research on the relationship of ELs' two languages in their development. The chapter ends with conclusions.

TIME TO RECLASSIFICATION

Methodological and Measurement Issues

Existing research on time to reclassification raises important methodological and measurement issues that complicate interpretation of its results and limit the generalizability of its findings.

First, the tests and decision criteria used to make classification and

---

[3]This is a definition of convenience that was necessitated by the lack of relevant evidence on the development of English as a second language for academic purposes among ELs in the United States.

reclassification decisions vary considerably across and within states, complicating the task of synthesizing this evidence. Moreover, the nature of the tests and procedures used to assess and classify ELs' English proficiency has changed over the years (see Chapter 11 for a more detailed discussion). Variation from state to state and across time can be linked to the fact, noted previously, that there is no widely held theory of language for academic purposes.

Second, the validity of current instruments and procedures used to predict readiness to benefit from English-only instruction has not been fully determined. Without a widely accepted and valid theory of academic language proficiency, the development of valid test instruments is difficult if not impossible. The challenge of developing valid tests is complicated further by the fact that the expression of academic language proficiency, by definition, ultimately depends on knowledge and skills in specific content domains. As a result, poor performance on a specific test of academic language proficiency may reflect a lack of relevant and specific content knowledge rather than a lack of broadly based academic language proficiency.

Third, most of the studies reviewed are cross-sectional; longitudinal studies that follow the same students over time are limited (see, however, Conger, 2009; Thompson, 2015). Cross-sectional designs provide only a snapshot of proficiency at one point in time. Moreover, most studies have focused on elementary school students; much less is known about middle and high school students, although, as discussed later in this chapter, a large number of high school students are long-term English learners (Olsen, 2010; Thompson, 2015). And many, if not most, of the students in studies on students in middle school began school in the United States in the elementary grades, so it is difficult to interpret reclassification rates for these students as evidence concerning the effects of middle school per se. In a related vein, students participating in studies differed widely in grade level at school entry and at time of classification and reclassification as fully English-proficient, as well as in length of attendance in school. As a result, it is difficult to examine time to reclassification with respect to particular grade or age ranges, although trends on this issue are evident. Furthermore, studies that compare outcomes for different program types (e.g., monolingual English versus dual language immersion) fail to distinguish between ELs who participated in all-English programs from the outset and those who had some form of dual language instruction and were subsequently transitioned to an all-English program as a result of reclassification procedures.

Fourth, most U.S. studies are based primarily or totally on Hispanic students from low-income backgrounds. Few studies have been carried out to examine variation among groups that differ with respect to cultural and language background, socioeconomic status, country of origin/birth, years of prior schooling, and other variables. Studies examining these factors are discussed separately later in this chapter.

How Long Does It Take ELs to Be Reclassified as Non-EL?

For purposes of this review, studies of elementary/middle school ELs (grades K-8) were combined and reviewed separately from studies of high school students (grades 9-12). Disaggregating findings for elementary and middle school students would have been desirable to provide a more nuanced overview. As noted above, however, many if not most students who were tested while in middle school had begun school in the United States in the elementary grades, so it is difficult to isolate middle school from prior elementary school effects.

Elementary and Middle School ELs (K-8)

This review is based on a large sample of key studies on time to reclassification. Studies were included if testing was carried out between kindergarten and grade 7 or 8. Although the criteria used to reclassify students varied among studies, a rating of "proficient" on a test or tests always indicates a higher score than a rating of "not proficient." Notwithstanding the caveats noted earlier, five general trends emerge from this review:

1. Achieving high levels of English-L2[4] proficiency during the school years is a complex process that takes considerable time.
2. Progress toward English-L2 proficiency tends to occur faster with earlier school entry and younger age at the time of entry.
3. Individual ELs vary considerably in their success at achieving proficiency in English.
4. A relatively high proportion of ELs fail to achieve proficiency in English even after many years of schooling.
5. The difficulties faced by ELs who do not achieve proficiency after more than 7 years in U.S. schools (i.e., long-term English learners, discussed later in this section) can probably be attributed to failure of the school system to provide them with coherent, appropriate, and long-term instructional support.

The studies included in this review are discussed with respect to three different but interrelated indices of reclassification: (1) the median/average number of years to reclassification as proficient in English, (2) the percent-

---

[4] "L2" attached to the name of a language indicates a second or non-native language for the student; thus, "English-L2" indicates English as a second language.

age of ELs who are reclassified as proficient at specific grade levels, and (3) the percentage of ELs who are not reclassified as proficient after a number of years of schooling. The percentage of ELs reclassified as proficient is calculated as a function of the number of students who were classified as ELs at the beginning of the study or at the beginning of the study period if the study examined data retroactively. The influence of grade level and age at entry on the attainment of a rating of proficient also is discussed.

Three studies report the average or median number of years required by ELs, on average, to attain reclassification as proficient in English, regardless of their starting grade. MacSwan and Pray (2005) estimate the average time to proficiency as 3.31 years in a group of K-5 ELs; Conger (2009) estimates the median number of years to achieve proficiency as 2 or 3 years for ELs who entered school in New York City at 5 and 6 years of age, respectively; and Umansky and Reardon (2014) estimate median time to reclassification as 8 years. Greenberg-Motamedi (2015), discussed in the subsection on high school ELs because the study also included high school students, estimate the time to reclassification as 3.8 years for all cohorts. There are likely several explanations for the variation found in these studies, including different conceptualizations of English language proficiency, technical differences among the tests themselves, and possibly student background characteristics, among other factors.

Median/average years to reclassification likely underestimates how quickly ELs achieve proficiency because these estimates are based on ELs who were (re)classified as English-proficient and do not include those who did not achieve proficient status (as in Greenberg-Motamedi, 2015, for example), or a default value is assigned based on students' entry grade if the students did not achieve proficiency by the end of the study (as in Conger, 2009). Statistics on the percentage of ELs who are classified as proficient in English at specific grade levels or after a certain number of years of schooling reveal a more sobering picture than those on mean/median years to reclassification. In a detailed analysis of eight studies published in 2006, Saunders and O'Brien (2006) conclude that kindergarten to school entry ELs, including those in all-English programs, seldom were rated "generally proficient" (less than "native-like"[5] proficiency) even by grade 3. In fact, none of the studies they review report average ratings of "native-like" proficiency-based on all ELs in a cohort until grade 5. The authors also note that rates of progress in attaining proficiency in English were "strikingly consistent" (p. 26) for students in different types of programs, including dual language and English-only programs. Students in 90:10 dual language

---

[5]The criterion "native-like" was determined by the test developers and reflects the highest level of performance on the test; it does not refer to the performance expected of or demonstrated by native speakers on the test.

programs, in which ELs received 90 percent instruction in Spanish in grades K-3 and only 10 percent instruction in English, exhibited levels of proficiency in reading, writing, and speaking English that were just as advanced, or more so, than those of ELs in 50:50 dual language programs, in which 50 percent of instruction was in English and 50 percent in Spanish, or in all-English programs. Arguably, extensive exposure to English outside school and the overall sociocultural value of English as the majority language in the United States may account, at least in part, for these findings by affording more opportunities to hear and use English outside school. In contrast, exposure in school may be relatively more important for learning a minority language, such as Spanish, because these advantages are lacking.

Saunders and O'Brien's (2006) estimated rates of time to proficiency are corroborated by the American Institutes for Research's evaluation of the implementation of Proposition 227 in California[6] (Parrish et al., 2006). These authors examined data between 1994-1995 and 2004-2005—before and after passage of Proposition 227—on how long it took ELs to be reclassified as "fully English-proficient" if they had previously been designated as "limited English-proficient." Their analysis is based on data from the state-mandated California English Language Development Test (CELDT), which includes measures of both oral (speaking, listening) and written (reading, writing) language skills. They estimate the "current probability of an EL (English learner) being redesignated to fluent English proficient status *after 10 years in California* to be less than 40 percent" (p. III-1). They go on to state: "We estimate that 75 percent of EL students are not redesignated [as fluent English proficient] *after five years of schooling* [emphasis in original]" (p. III-33).

Notwithstanding variation in the estimates of time to proficiency across studies, they all indicate that ELs require several grades or years to be rated proficient—5-7 years is frequently reported. With the exception of Lindholm-Leary (2014), who tested ELs only until grade 2, the time most commonly reported for a substantial number of ELs to achieve proficiency is 5 years. These estimates are corroborated by earlier reviews of research on this issue, which indicate that it can take ELs 5-7 years to achieve proficiency in English for academic purposes (Cummins, 1981; Lindholm-Leary and Borsato, 2006; National Research Council, 1997; Thomas and Collier, 2002).

On the one hand, some of these estimates may appear positive (e.g.,

---

[6]Proposition 227, passed in 1998, required that students who were not proficient in English be taught almost completely in English—effectively eliminating bilingual classes. In addition, it shortened the time ELs stayed in sheltered English immersion classes to 1 year (under normal circumstances) and required that ELs move from such classes to mainstream classes once they had a good working knowledge of English.

Carroll and Bailey's [2016] and MacSwan and Pray's [2005] estimates of 79 percent by grade 5 and 92 percent after 5 years, respectively). On the other hand, these studies also indicate that a substantial percentage of ELs fail to achieve proficiency in English even after 5 years of schooling in English. For example, this percentage is reported as 21 percent by MacSwan and Pray (2005), as 8 percent by Carroll and Bailey (2016), as 25 percent after 9 years by Thompson (2015), as 40 percent after 5 years by Lindholm-Leary and Hernández (2011), as 47 percent after 5 years by the California Department of Education (2014), as 28 percent by Greenberg-Motamedi (2015), and as 20 percent after 7 years among kindergarten to school entry ELs by Hakuta (2011). The full significance of these statistics becomes clear only in the context of these students' overall education: fully 10 percent to possibly 45 percent of ELs lack full proficiency in English even by the upper elementary grades, when general academic instruction has become complex, abstract, and dependent on sophisticated uses of English for academic purposes.

These studies also reveal important differences among groups of learners. Greenberg-Motamedi (2015), for example, found that speakers of Arabic, Amharic, and Korean took relatively less time to achieve proficiency in English, whereas speakers of Samoan and Spanish took relatively longer; in general, Hispanic students took more time (4.2 years), while Asian students took less (3.4 years). These differences may be due, at least in part, to differences in socioeconomic status since, as the authors note, students in schools with a relatively high percentage of students eligible for free or reduced-price lunch take longer to achieve proficiency in English relative to students in schools with lower percentages of such students (Hakuta et al., 2000). Students eligible for special education services also were found to take longer than those who were not receiving such services (5.5 versus 3.7 years). Likewise, U.S.-born ELs took less time than foreign-born ELs (3.3 versus 3.5 years) if they entered in kindergarten, but both of these groups, especially the U.S.-born students, took longer if they entered after kindergarten (4.8 versus 3.7 years). It should be noted that other factors may influence the results for foreign-born students, such as the level and nature of their prior education, the socioeconomic status and education of their parents, the medical and emotional state of the children at the time of their immigration, the qualifications of teachers, and the quality of instruction.

Researchers working outside the United States have similarly concluded that achieving proficiency in a second language takes time, even when learning starts early. In these studies, unlike most of the reclassification studies reviewed here, proficiency is defined relative to the performance of native speakers of the target language. For example, in a longitudinal study of 24 ELs (termed "ESLs" by the author) in Edmonton, Canada, Paradis (2009) found that after 21 months of exclusive exposure to English in school, only

40 percent performed within the normal range for native English speakers on a test of grammatical morpheme production (e.g., the use of "s" to pluralize nouns or "ed" to express past tense in verbs); the corresponding percentages for receptive vocabulary and story grammar were 65 and 90 percent, respectively. Research conducted in Sweden by Abrahamsson and Hyltenstam (2009) found that, compared with native Swedish speakers, only 40 percent of adults who had immigrated to Sweden during the preschool years scored in the native range on a battery of diverse language tests, even after more than 20 years of exposure. In a similar vein, research in Canada on children internationally adopted from China at ages 12-24 months showed that they scored significantly lower than nonadopted native French-speaking children matched on socioeconomic status on a variety of standardized measures of language ability, including expressive and receptive vocabulary and grammar. This was the case even after the adopted children had experienced more than 12 years of using French in their homes and been educated exclusively in that language (Delcenserie and Genesee, 2014). The adopted children did not show similar delays in general cognitive/intellectual, socioemotional, or nonverbal memory development, suggesting that their language development was uniquely affected by their delayed exposure.

These findings suggest that even when acquisition of a second language (L2) begins at an early age, several years can be required to acquire true "native-like" levels of proficiency and moreover, that L2 learners may always differ from native speakers. In a review of research on child L2 learners, Paradis (2006, p. 401) concludes that "obtaining oral language proficiency in the L2 on par with native speakers can take most of the elementary school years" and furthermore, that individual children vary considerably in their rate of L2 development. That it can take ELs so long to achieve proficiency in English for academic purposes probably reflects several factors. Of note, it probably reflects the complexity of academic language skills themselves. In addition, it could reflect a lack of systematic and explicit focus on instruction of academic English in classes with EL students. It undoubtedly also reflects the fact that native speakers of English are advancing in their level of proficiency in English for academic purposes from grade to grade. To the extent that ELs' performance on reclassification tests is compared with that of native speakers, ELs are being compared with a moving target. As result, ELs must make more yearly progress in English if they are to achieve parity with native speakers. These findings have important implications for instruction and, specifically, indicate that ELs will benefit from systemic instruction in English for academic purposes and/or additional supports throughout their education if a native-like level of proficiency in English is expected.

Effects of Age and Proficiency in English at School Entry

Evidence indicates that progress toward proficiency in English among ELs as measured by reclassification tests occurs more rapidly during the first year after school entry (and thus, presumably, during the early stages of English development in school) and declines in subsequent elementary grades. Attainment of proficiency also appears to be easier for ELs who are younger at school entry relative to those who are older (Bleakley and Chin, 2010; Conger, 2009; Greenberg-Motamedi, 2015; Johnson, 2007; Saunders and O'Brien, 2006).

To address the question of time to reclassification, Conger (2009) analyzed data from four cohorts of ELs with different ages of entry to New York City schools between 1996 and 1999. The majority of the students were eligible for free lunch, foreign-born, and from Spanish-speaking homes. A criterion of the 40th percentile on the Language Assessment Battery (LAB) was used to determine proficiency in English, which resulted in reclassification. The "probability of exit from EL status" (i.e., reclassification as non-EL) was highest for students 1 year after they entered the school system and lower in subsequent grades. The author also reports that students who were older at school entry were less likely than those who were younger to be reclassified within the first year. However, the decline in reclassification in subsequent grades was lower for ELs who were older at school entry than for those who were younger, suggesting that while older ELs make a relatively slow start in learning English, they show relatively better progress than their younger peers in subsequent grades. In a reanalysis of data reported in the eight studies included in their synthesis, Saunders and O'Brien (2006) similarly found that ELs made faster progress from low to intermediate levels of proficiency and slower progress from intermediate to high levels of proficiency. While this finding pertains to ELs regardless of the age at school entry, it most commonly applies to students who enter school in kindergarten.

The finding that younger ELs make relatively fast progress on reclassification tests initially may reflect the fact that the target for them is relatively low compared with that for ELs who are older at school entry. In other words, the language skills to be learned at older ages and in higher grades are more complex and thus more difficult to learn. In any case, the initial advantage of younger learners may have fueled the notion that they are better and faster second language learners overall relative to their older peers. Results from other studies, however, suggest that "older is better" in some cases, although this may be true only when L2 learners have had prior education, and especially literacy instruction, in their first language (L1). In these cases, the advantage of older learners may be linked to prior schooling and/or the acquisition of literacy and academic language skills in L1, both of which may transfer to L2 acquisition and facilitate the development of proficiency in that language (see also Chapter 4). Consistent with these possibilities, Lindholm-Leary and Borsato (2006) report that ELs in the United States who participated in dual language programs that provided instruction in L1 along with English in the primary grades (K-2) often attained the same or higher levels of proficiency in English, especially in domains related to academic literacy and oral language development, relative to students in all-English programs. This was true despite the fact that students in the dual language programs had had less instruction and a later start in learning English in school. Again, this finding may reflect the transfer of language, including literacy and cognitively based language skills, acquired in L1 to English.

Evidence that dual language learning can be an additive process comes from studies showing that ELs who develop high levels of proficiency in both L1 and English relative to those with low levels of bilingual proficiency are more successful at closing the achievement gap in reading with their native English-speaking peers (e.g., Lambert and Cazabon, 1994; Lindholm and Aclan, 1991; Lindholm-Leary, 2001; Lindholm-Leary and Howard, 2008). Thompson (2015) found that ELs who entered kindergarten with high levels of academic proficiency in both L1 and English were 24 percent more likely to be reclassified than students who entered kindergarten with low levels of academic proficiency in both languages. Likewise, bilingual Hispanic students have been found to have higher achievement scores, grade point averages, and educational expectations relative to their monolingual English-speaking Hispanic peers (e.g., Lindholm-Leary, 2001; Rumberger and Larson, 1998). In a related vein, Lindholm-Leary and colleagues (Lindholm-Leary, 2001; Lindholm-Leary and Hernández, 2011; Lindholm-Leary and Howard, 2008) found that former ELs (i.e., those reclassified as proficient in English) were more likely to be bilingual and to score higher on standardized tests of Spanish achievement relative to current ELs and that their English test scores were highly and significantly correlated with their scores on Spanish language tests. Thus, the highest EL achievers were those who maintained and continued to develop their Spanish, while relatively low-achieving ELs tended to have poor Spanish language skills.

In contrast, studies of ELs who enter kindergarten with relatively low levels of proficiency in English show that, while they make progress over the following grades, they usually continue to lag behind their native English-speaking peers:

- Jackson and colleagues (2014) assessed the growth trajectories of receptive vocabulary development in both Spanish and English among migrant ELs of low socioeconomic status from kindergarten through grade 2. These students began kindergarten with English receptive vocabulary scores 2 standard deviations below those of monolingual native speakers of English. They made significant progress by grade 2 and narrowed the gap, although they were still below their English-speaking peers. Their scores in Spanish vocabulary were initially at grade-level expectations, although more than half scored below grade-level expectations by grade 2. Of interest, their Spanish scores predicted their rate of English vocabulary growth; that is, students with low Spanish scores showed slower growth in English relative to students with average or higher Spanish scores.

- Mancilla-Martinez and Lesaux (2011) also found that ELs began kindergarten with much lower vocabulary levels in English compared with national norms, but made good growth and narrowed the gap by age 8, although they were still below national norms at age 11.
- Collins and colleagues (2014) studied five groups of Latino children of immigrants to examine their dual language profiles from kindergarten to grade 2: (1) dual-proficient, (2) English-proficient, (3) Spanish-proficient, (4) borderline-proficient (just below cut-off in one or both languages), and (5) limited-proficient in both languages (2 standard deviations below the norm). At entry in kindergarten, most students (63%) showed a low-performing (subgroups 4 and 5) profile in English, but most made substantial gains in both languages by grade 2; in fact, 64 percent had "proficient competent profiles" (groups 1, 2, and 3). Among the kindergartners in the "limited-proficient" subgroup, however, a third were still in this category in grade 2. Students who were "borderline-proficient" in grade 2 were "limited-proficient" in kindergarten and made only limited growth over the grades or remained "borderline."
- Lesaux and colleagues (2007) found a different pattern. They studied a linguistically diverse group of ELs, representing 33 languages, and found that although they started kindergarten with lower scores than those of native speakers, this gap had largely been closed by grade 4.

These findings are important for a number of reasons. First, they indicate that, indeed, students who begin school in kindergarten with relatively limited proficiency in English are at risk of not achieving proficiency during the early grades of schooling. Viewed differently, these findings run counter to the notion that such students are necessarily quick language learners. It would be useful to know in what other respects, if any, these two groups of ELs—those with low and those with relatively high levels of English proficiency initially—are similar and/or different from one another and from their monolingual English peers. These findings also indicate that bilingual proficiency at kindergarten entry does not jeopardize ELs' achievement in school and, to the contrary, may be advantageous, especially in the face of challenges linked to low socioeconomic status. The bilingual advantage could be linked to enhanced metalinguistic or executive functions, or both (see Chapter 4). More research on these ELs would be useful. Finally, these findings reinforce the importance of conducting early assessment to identify ELs who need additional support and the kinds of support they need, since it appears that the gap between ELs and non-ELs will otherwise widen.

High School ELs

Relative to grades K-8, much less research has focused on reclassification rates among high school ELs. Studies of newcomer high school students are particularly rare; the committee could identify only two such studies, and they are based on the same dataset (Carhill et al., 2008; Suárez-Orozco et al., 2010). Testing in the studies discussed in this section took place in grades 9 to 12; thus they are considered high school studies even though the participants may have entered their respective school systems much earlier than 9th grade. Therefore, as was observed earlier with respect to middle school ELs who entered U.S. schools in the elementary grades, the results of these studies cannot be attributed to the effects of high school alone. Nevertheless, these findings give some indication of time to reclassification among ELs who were often older when they started school in the United States and certainly older when assessed in comparison with the elementary and middle school students discussed above.

A study by Carhill and colleagues (2008) is of particular interest because the authors used a longitudinal design to examine the relationships between English proficiency and a number of contextual and individual student factors. The 274 adolescent EL participants in this study were foreign-born (from Central America, China, the Dominican Republic, Haiti, and Mexico), and all spoke a language other than English as their first language. On average, they had spent at least two-thirds of their lives in their country of birth, had been in the United States for 7 years, and were 16.7 years of age. There was a significant positive correlation between length of time in the United States and ratings of proficiency. However, even after 7 years of schooling in the United States, only 7 percent scored at norm for English speakers on the English language proficiency subtests of the Bilingual Verbal Abilities Test (Muñoz-Sandoval et al., 1998), and fully three-quarters scored more than 1 standard deviation below the average of their English-speaking peers. Also of interest, the authors examined the relationship between test performance and a number of contextual variables. They found that students from China, those who had more exposure to English in informal out-of-school contexts, and those attending schools with a low percentage of students living in poverty and a high percentage of English-proficient ELs scored relatively high on the test. Results of regression analyses that included key background and contextual variables indicated that parental factors were significant predictors of students' proficiency in English, but that opportunities to use English in informal contexts and attendance at schools with a high percentage of English-proficient ELs were stronger predictors of English proficiency. These results are important in emphasizing the number and complexity of factors beyond quality of schooling that can influence ELs' performance on reclassification tests.

A study by Umansky and Reardon (2014) is also of particular interest because it examined time to reclassification in relation to instructional program. This is one of the few studies in both the elementary/middle school and high school corpus that investigated how time to reclassification may vary as a function of ELs' educational experiences, an issue that deserves much greater attention since it provides potential insights of an educational nature about how to improve ELs' English proficiency results. The study was conducted in a large school district in California with more than 50,000 students, half of whom were classified as ELs or reclassified as proficient in English and were from diverse backgrounds. More specifically, in contrast to many studies on reclassification, Latinos made up just 25 percent of the district population and almost 50 percent of the EL school population. The students attended four program types: traditional English immersion, a transitional Spanish bilingual program,[7] a Spanish maintenance[8] bilingual program, and a Spanish dual language immersion program (see Chapter 7 for descriptions of instructional program types). Only ELs who had entered the U.S. school system in kindergarten were included in the analyses. Several important findings emerged. Overall, 60 percent of the Latino students became long-term ELs. Relative to those in the other program types, Latino ELs enrolled in dual language programs were reclassified as English-proficient at a lower rate in the elementary grades but had higher overall reclassification rates; higher English language arts academic achievement scores; and higher English reading, writing, speaking, and listening test results in the long run.

In summary, studies of high school ELs demonstrate that they do not

---

[7] A program in which ELs' home language is used for instruction along with English for the first 2-3 years of school, followed by instruction in English only. The goal of these programs is to promote full proficiency in only English and not the home language.

[8] Programs, such as 90:10 or 50:50 dual language programs, in which both English and a non-English language are used for instruction throughout the elementary and sometimes the high school grades. The goal of these programs is to promote high levels of bilingual proficiency.

achieve reclassification as English-proficient quickly, and a relatively large percentage are not reclassified even after several years in school. This finding is of particular importance as ELs enter the upper grades, when academic requirements become more demanding and more dependent on language proficiency. Studies by Umansky and Reardon (2014) and Carhill and colleagues (2008) indicate further that understanding the development of proficiency in English among ELs requires a multidimensional, longitudinal approach since development is not linear but fluctuates over grades, and is influenced by multiple factors. With regard to the latter, more attention to school-related factors, including classroom instructional practices, would be particularly useful in the future to elucidate what steps educators can take to improve the progress of ELs, especially in light of policy goals for the educational progress of ELs under ESSA.

Long-Term English Learners

The evidence reviewed to this point clearly shows the difficulty of achieving reclassification to English-proficient and, by implication, levels of English proficiency that are deemed sufficient for ELs to participate in classrooms where all instruction is in English. The most common estimates of time to reclassification range from 5 to 10 years, with 5 to 7 years being one of the more frequently reported estimates. Of course, some of these estimates are an artifact of how long the studies continued or what grade levels were examined; they also reflect the influence of a myriad of other factors, such as quality of instruction, prior schooling, literacy levels in L1 and in English, and family and community factors. Nevertheless, many ELs fail to be reclassified as English-proficient even after many years of schooling in English. Over the last 10 years, attention has begun to focus on ELs who demonstrate extraordinary difficulty in achieving proficiency in English as measured by state-mandated assessments. Also referred to as long-term English learners (LTELs) (Olsen, 2010), these most commonly are ELs who have not been reclassified after 7 years.[9] As Olsen (2010)

---

[9] California has a formal state definition for LTEL as an EL to whom all of the following apply: (1) is enrolled in grades 6 to 12, inclusive; and (2) has been enrolled in a U.S. school for 6 or more years; and (3) has remained at the same English language proficiency level for 2 or more consecutive prior years, or has regressed to a lower English language proficiency level; and (4) for students in grades 6 to 9, inclusive, has scored at the "Standard Not Met" level on the prior-year administration of the California Assessment of Student Performance and Progress-English Language Arts (CAASPP-ELA). In addition, (1) students for whom one or more of the required testing criteria are not available are categorically determined to be LTELs; and (2) the assessment component of LTEL determination for students in grades 10-12, inclusive, is based solely on the CELDT criteria outlined above. For more information, see Education Code 313.1.

234 EDUCATIONAL SUCCESS OF CHILDREN AND YOUTH LEARNING ENGLISH

notes with respect to California, schools and school districts in that state do not have a common definition of LTELs, and this is likely the case in other states as well. Olsen suggests that a simple binary distinction between LTEL and non-LTEL may not be the best or most useful way to understand and support the LTEL population:

> It is most useful, therefore, to think of a continuum from those long term English learners who are failing and whose proficiency is actually falling to those who are stagnating at a level of English proficiency managing to get by in school with very low grades, to those who are slowly progressing and doing okay in school. (p. 12)

The lack of a common definition of LTELs makes it difficult to interpret and draw general conclusions from the existing, limited research on these students.

LTELs have attracted increased attention recently because they represent a sizable segment of the EL population. Menken (2013), for example, found that LTELs made up about 33 percent of high school ELs in New York City and Chicago, about 25 percent of ELs in Colorado, and 50 percent of ELs in California. California had the largest percentage of LTELs in grades 6-12, at 12 percent; more than 75 percent of current ELs were long-term in one of every three districts in the state. Olsen (2010) similarly reports very high rates, 59 percent, of LTEL status among California ELs. Using 2000 U.S. census data, Batalova and colleagues (2007) report that 5 percent of all students in grades 6-12 nationwide were ELs and 70 percent of LTELs were Hispanic, followed by Vietnamese speakers, at 3 percent. Abedi (2008) similarly cites ethnic group differences, with Hispanic LTELs spending almost 10 years in EL status and Asians and Caucasian LTELs spending about half that time, although these differences may be confounded by other variables, such as socioeconomic status. The question arises of how to account for such group differences.

LTELs often are proficient in everyday uses of oral English but have low levels of proficiency in academic language and literacy in both English and their L1. Commonly, LTEL students reach a plateau at intermediate or lower levels of language proficiency (Olsen, 2010). Indeed, longitudinal studies that have followed LTEL students into middle or high school have found that their rates of growth in language and literacy slow over time and then plateau (Kieffer, 2008; Mancilla-Martinez et al., 2011; Nakamoto et al., 2007). Umansky and Reardon (2014), for example, report that reclassification to fully English-proficient slowed in middle school in all instructional programs they examined, including English-only and transitional, maintenance, and two-way dual language programs,[10] supporting Saunders and O'Brien's (2006) conclusion that times to proficiency appear to be comparable regardless of program type. Attainment of proficiency in English in middle school can be thwarted because increased academic tracking of ELs often occurs in these grades. As a result, ELs are often assigned to low-level academic classes (Callahan, 2005; Callahan et al., 2008, 2010; Kanno and Kangas, 2014), presumably in an effort to support their learning, but often resulting in reducing their chances of advancing beyond EL status. Because they are in classrooms that lack academic rigor, it is difficult for many of these ELs to meet the academic standards in English needed for reclassification.

LTELs are to be distinguished from other struggling high school ELs who are new arrivals, and often refugees who have experienced interrupted or limited formal education (Boyson and Short, 2003; Menken, 2013). Like LTELs, these students often exhibit low levels of English language proficiency and academic achievement compared with their peers. However, their difficulties probably are linked to the challenge of initial adjustment to a new language and culture and of developing language and literacy in English in a relatively brief period of time (Boyson and Short, 2003; Menken, 2013). In contrast, LTELs are not newcomers to the United States, and their difficulties cannot be attributed in any simple fashion to adjustment or personal issues. Menken and colleagues (2012), for example, note that by definition, LTELs have often been in the United States for 7 or more years and in fact often were born here (see also Freeman et al., 2002, in Menken, 2013). Batalova and colleagues (2007) also found that about 57 percent of LTELs were U.S.-born; 27 percent were second-generation, and 30 percent were third-generation.

In a related vein, Freeman and colleagues (2002) and Menken and colleagues (2012) report that LTELs often have had inconsistent educational programming; they are "in and out of various ESL and bilingual programs" (Freeman et al., 2002, p. 5). They also often have experienced weak, no, or inappropriate language education programs; curriculum and learning materials that are not designed to meet their linguistic needs; and limited access to the full curriculum. LTEL status may be linked as well to the characteristics of the schools they attend. Specifically, several studies have found that ELs tend to be enrolled disproportionately in schools in urban areas with a high percentage of ethnic minority and economically disadvantaged students (Callahan et al., 2010; Clewell et al., 2007; Rumberger and Gándara, 2005), characteristics of schools that put students at risk for low academic achievement (Clewell et al., 2007; Rumberger and Gándara,

---

[10] Programs in which both native speakers of English and native speakers of the non-English language participate and are taught using both languages for significant periods of time.

2005; Uriarte et al., 2011) (see Chapter 7 for more detailed discussion). A study conducted by the Urban Institute (Clewell et al., 2007) indicates that as of 2000, nearly 70 percent of ELs nationwide were enrolled in schools that fit this description.

Taken together, evidence on the family and educational histories of LTELs indicates that an explanation for the failure of LTELs to achieve English proficiency and to succeed academically is likely to be complex. In brief, explanations for the fate of LTELs can be linked to multiple dimensions of their education, including the quality and consistency of academic programming, the provision of appropriate and timely additional support services, and other characteristics of their schools (Callahan, 2005; Callahan et al., 2008, 2010; Kanno and Kangas, 2014; Menken et al., 2012). While these findings are distressing, they suggest specific areas in which changes could realistically be made to help address LTELs' long-term needs and thereby enhance their educational success. Unfortunately, however, few studies have examined alternative support strategies for LTELs and their effectiveness. In one such study, Callahan and colleagues (2010) examined the impact of English as a second language (ESL) placement on the academic achievement and course taking of ELs in high school. While acknowledging the benefits of ESL placement in meeting the students' linguistic needs, the authors also note that long-term ESL placement can marginalize students academically because of the low academic rigor in these classes. ESL placement also fails to provide ELs with opportunities to complete upper-level science and social science coursework or to take electives. Several studies have documented the potential adverse consequences of the long-term designation as EL:

- less access to classes required for high school graduation and admission to postsecondary education (e.g., Callahan, 2005; Kanno and Kangas, 2014; Parrish et al., 2006);
- potentially negative affective consequences of EL status during adolescence (Gándara et al., 2001; Maxwell-Jolly et al., 2007); and
- elevated high school dropout rates (Silver et al., 2008; Watt and Roessingh, 1994).

FACTORS THAT INFLUENCE RECLASSIFICATION RATES AMONG ENGLISH LEARNERS IN GRADES K-12

Thus far, little attention has been paid to differences among individual ELs and subgroups of ELs whose backgrounds differ. Given the considerable variation in ELs' personal, cultural, linguistic, and educational backgrounds, one would expect to see large individual variations among ELs in their reclassification rates (see, e.g., Suárez-Orozco et al., 2010). Identifying, documenting, and understanding these variations and their relationship to progress toward proficiency in English is critical for planning effective instruction that meets these students' needs. Research has examined a variety of individual, family, school, and contextual differences among ELs alluded to earlier in this chapter, including gender, socioeconomic status, place of birth (U.S.- or foreign-born), ethnic/racial/linguistic background, prior schooling, density of minority students in the school/community, parental education, and language education program (dual language or all-English). Many of these factors, but not all—such as low socioeconomic status, ethnic minority status, and no/limited/interrupted prior schooling— frequently are associated with underachievement in school among non-ELs. Unfortunately, relatively little research has examined the influence of these factors on reclassification rates among ELs, and most studies address only one or two of these factors. In this regard, it is worth noting that, according to Lindholm-Leary (2010), achievement among ELs is lower the more risk factors individual students experience.

The existing research in this area has limitations. The samples in most of the studies reviewed by the committee comprised exclusively or largely low-income Hispanic Spanish-speaking ELs. Further, most studies included students who entered at kindergarten, or possibly first grade, and did not include students who were receiving special education services. Nevertheless, the available evidence is fairly consistent in showing that student characteristics influence time to reclassification, although the quality and quantity of evidence with respect to specific factors varies. Clearly, much more research in this area is needed.

Gender

Findings from the available studies on gender are inconsistent. Four studies (Greenberg-Motamedi, 2015; Grissom, 2004; Thompson, 2015; Uriarte et al., 2011) found higher rates of classification among girls. However, four studies (Abedi, 2008; Conger, 2009; Conger et al., 2012; Johnson, 2007) failed to find this difference.

Language Background

ELs whose native language is Asian tend to be reclassified sooner and to achieve at higher levels relative to Spanish-speaking ELs (Abedi, 2008; Carhill et al., 2008; Conger, 2009; Conger et al., 2012; Greenberg-Motamedi, 2015; Grissom, 2004; Hill, 2006; Lindholm-Leary, 2011; Mulligan et al., 2012; New York Office of English Language Learners, 2009; Thompson, 2015; Uriarte et al., 2011). The reason for this difference is unclear, but it could be due to multiple factors, such as prior schooling, culture, and family circumstances and characteristics. In addition, research has shown that ELs who speak Asian languages, especially Chinese, outscore their non-EL peers on assessments (Leung and Uchikoshi, 2012; Lindholm-Leary, 2011; Mulligan et al., 2012), even after controlling for socioeconomic status, suggesting that other factors also are at play.

Socioeconomic Status

Seven of the eight studies on socioeconomic status reviewed by the committee found that ELs from relatively high socioeconomic backgrounds achieve proficiency in English more quickly than ELs from relatively low socioeconomic backgrounds. Monolingual English-speaking students from high socioeconomic backgrounds have similarly been found to score significantly higher than their peers from relatively low socioeconomic backgrounds on a variety of measures (Reardon et al., 2012). Although not specific to oral language proficiency, research findings from Kieffer (2008) and Lesaux and colleagues (2007) indicate that differences in English reading ability between ELs and non-ELs are eliminated if differences in socioeconomic status are taken into account, illustrating the important and possibly overriding influence of this factor in many of the studies whose samples comprise largely students from low socioeconomic backgrounds. Han (2014) reports that Asian ELs from relatively high socioeconomic backgrounds outperformed all other groups, while those of low socioeconomic status performed the worst. Her findings illustrate variation within a specific group, and point to the importance of factors other than race/ethnicity. They also call for caution in generalizing about ethnic groups.

U.S.- Versus Foreign-Born

All three of the studies reviewed that examined the influence of being U.S.- versus foreign-born found that this factor is important, but its effects may depend on age at entry. Conger (2009) reports that a higher percentage of U.S.-born than of foreign-born ELs achieved proficiency in English in 3 years. Greenberg-Motamedi (2015) similarly reports an advantage for U.S.-born ELs who entered school at kindergarten, but the opposite for those who entered in grades 2 to 5. Slama (2012) also found significant differences in English language proficiency favoring U.S.- over foreign-born ELs in grade 9, but these differences had disappeared by the end of grade 12. The underlying explanation for these differences is difficult to discern because of methodological issues.

English Proficiency at School Entry

While no recent studies have looked at the effect of ELs' prior schooling on the attainment of English proficiency, five studies have examined their level of proficiency in English at program entry (Greenberg-Motamedi, 2015; Johnson, 2007; Lindholm-Leary, 2013, 2014; Thompson, 2015). All five found that English proficiency scores at program entry had a positive influence on later English proficiency scores and reclassification rates. The challenge for parents and educators is how to promote ELs' proficiency in English if they live in homes and neighborhoods where another language is solely or widely used.

RETENTION AND LOSS OF THE HOME LANGUAGE

Increased cross-cultural, cross-linguistic, and cross-national communication, whether through electronic channels or face-to-face conversation suggests the importance of examining the development of ELs' proficiency in their L1s. One might argue that competence in other languages is unnecessary given the global status of English. However, evidence shows that second language speakers of English outnumber native speakers (Crystal, 2003). This fact speaks to the importance of not only learning English but also knowing other languages as well in order to interact effectively or compete for jobs with those who are bilingual in English and other world languages. Children who come to school with some competence in languages other than English are a logical place to begin an examination of this issue. Countries such as the United States with a high proportion of speakers of other languages could have an advantage in the multilingual global marketplace were ELs' skills in their L1 developed along with those in English.

The association between bilingual proficiency and higher levels of academic achievement among ELs was mentioned earlier in this chapter and is discussed in greater detail in Chapter 4. In addition, research has shown that bilingual children experience higher levels of well-being than English-dominant ELs or English-monolingual children (Han, 2014; Han and Huang, 2010). Using cohort data from the Early Childhood Longitudinal Study, Kindergarten Class of 1998-99 (ECLS-K), Han and Huang (2010) examined the behavioral trajectories of ELs up to grade 5. They found that the growth rate of problem behaviors was lower in fluent bilingual and non-English-dominant ELs than in white English-monolingual children. In contrast, monolingual ELs had the highest levels of problem behaviors by grade 5. Similarly, Collins and colleagues (2011) found that Spanish and English competencies significantly predicted dimensions of well-being and school functioning for Latino children of immigrants, and were far more important than child, home, and school variables. Taken together, the findings of these studies indicate that the optimal focus of support for the language acquisition of ELs goes beyond English because emotional, social, and behavioral benefits are associated with dual language competence. These findings corroborate the importance of cultural and personal dimensions of ELs discussed in Chapters 1 and 4 of this report.

In light of these findings, it is important to note that when the minority language of ELs is not supported at home or in school, it often undergoes attrition or may be underdeveloped relative to age-matched native speakers of the language (Block, 2012; Cohen and Wickens, 2015; Collins, 2014; Espinosa, 2007, 2010, 2013; Hammer et al., 2008, 2009, 2014; Jackson et al., 2014; Lindholm-Leary, 2014; Mancilla-Martinez and Lesaux, 2011; Oller and Eilers, 2002; Pham and Kohnert, 2014; Proctor et al., 2010). In fact, some researchers have found that ELs who began as dominant or monolingual Spanish speakers suffered so much language attrition that they were no longer considered proficient in Spanish (Lindholm-Leary, 2014; Mancilla-Martinez and Lesaux, 2011).

Loss and underdevelopment of L1 has been documented in preschool, early elementary, and high school ELs. This is the case even for Spanish, despite the fact that it is widely spoken in some communities in the United States. Loss of L1 among ELs has been documented in multiple ways, including reduced overall proficiency, reduced preference for use of the L1 (Wong-Fillmore, 1991), loss or incomplete acquisition of specific grammatical features of the language (e.g., Mueller Gathercole, 2002), reduced lexical knowledge, and slowed processing of the language relative to English (Kohnert et al., 1999, in Montrul, 2008). Language loss is not a uniform process, however. It tends to be greater

- among simultaneous than sequential bilinguals, although both experience L1 attrition, and among younger versus older immigrants (e.g., Jia and Aaronson, 2003; Yeni-Komshian et al., 2000, in Montrul, 2008);
- the earlier ELs are exposed to and begin to learn English; and
- in homes where English is used compared with those in which parents use only the minority language.

Loss tends to occur more slowly and gradually the older ELs are when exposed to the dominant language in the society, arguably because their earlier, intensive exposure to their L1 consolidates competence in that language and thus serves to protect them from the eroding influences of English. Jia and Aaronson (2003) found that the young Chinese-English ELs in their sample, who varied in age at immigration, demonstrated a shift in preference for using English as early as 12 months after their first exposure to it. Montrul (2008, p. 136) suggests that "there is a threshold for vulnerability to language loss in sequential ELs." More specifically, "minority-speaking children younger than 10 years of age show a more rapid shift to the L2 and a larger degree of L1 loss than children older than 10." Hakuta and D'Andrea (1992) likewise suggest that exposure to English before age 10 contributes to language loss in Latino children.

Processing and acquisition of the structural/grammatical properties of L1 also are susceptible to negative influences from the dominant language. Influences on processing have been demonstrated by ELs having more difficulty accessing words in their L1 and processing the L1 more slowly than the dominant language (see Montrul, 2008, for a review). Although there has been little research on the morphosyntactic development of ELs in the United States, evidence indicates that ELs often fail to acquire full mastery of the morphosyntax of their L1 once they have been exposed to English. In an early study of this phenomenon, for example, Merino (1983) examined the morphosyntactic development of Spanish-speaking ELs from low socio-economic backgrounds attending English-only schools in kindergarten to grade 4 (5-10 years of age) in the United States. She found a gradual decline in the children's general production and comprehension skills in Spanish, as well as incomplete mastery of a number of features of that language, including gender and number marking and correct use of the past tense, the subjunctive, relative clauses, and conditional verb forms. Children who used only Spanish with their parents had the strongest Spanish skills, while those who used both Spanish and English demonstrated significant loss. More recent work confirms that ELs often show poorer mastery of the morphosyntax of the L1 relative to native speakers (see Montrul and Potowski [2007] and Mueller Gathercole [2002] for Spanish-English ELs, and Song et al. [1997] for Korean-English ELs).

A shift toward English emerges as exposure to, proficiency in, and the necessity of using English increases. For young ELs, this shift often is associated with preschool and school entry. In a national large-scale survey of 1,100 Spanish, Korean, Japanese, Chinese, Khmer, and Vietnamese families in the United States, Wong-Fillmore (1991) found that 50 percent of the participating parents of ELs who were attending preschool programs in which English was used exclusively or along with the L1 reported a shift away from the L1 and toward English; in comparison, only 10 percent of parents who did not send their children to preschool programs reported such a shift. In contrast, Rodriguez and colleagues (1995) found that early exposure to English in preschool did not affect the comprehension, production, or vocabulary development of Spanish-speaking ELs in their study. Arguably, the difference in results here may be linked to differences in community language. Many of the languages spoken by the parents interviewed by Wong-Fillmore were not as well represented or used in the community at large as was Spanish, the language spoken by the parents who participated in the Rodriguez study.

Support for the primary language at home (e.g., Hakuta and D'Andrea, 1992; Wong-Fillmore, 1991) can reduce the chances and severity of loss (e.g., Collins, 2014; Collins et al., 2014; Hammer et al., 2009; Leung and Uchikoshi, 2012; Mancilla-Martinez and Lesaux, 2011). Mancilla-Martinez and Lesaux (2011), for example, found that use of Spanish in the home had a positive impact on children's vocabulary growth and did not negatively affect their English vocabulary growth, while mothers' increased use of English in the home negatively affected children's Spanish vocabulary development. Similarly, attending school programs in which the L1 is used for instruction along with English can lead to retention of the L1 (e.g., Lindholm-Leary and Borsato, 2006; Mueller Gathercole, 2002). Working with school-age ELs in Florida, Mueller Gathercole (2002) found that by grade 5, Spanish-speaking ELs in two-way immersion programs had significantly greater proficiency in Spanish grammar than their peers in all-English mainstream programs, even when the latter came from homes in which Spanish was spoken.

However, even ELs who use their L1 at home and/or attend dual language programs in the elementary grades often experience a shift to English (Wong-Fillmore, 1991). Hammer and colleagues (2009) found that L1 interactions between ELs and their mothers changed upon the children's entry to preschools in which they were instructed in English; that is, the percentage of mothers who spoke mostly English to their children increased from preschool to kindergarten. This change in mothers' language usage slowed their children's development of Spanish vocabulary. Similarly, Collins and colleagues (Collins, 2014; Collins et al., 2014) found that more use of Spanish in the home was an important predictor of academic proficiency in Spanish in the early elementary grades, but even when Spanish was the dominant language of the home, second-generation adolescents who had been schooled in English had trouble conversing fluently in Spanish with their parents or other family members (Block, 2012; Cohen and Wickens, 2015).

Participation in dual language school programs does not guarantee that ELs will continue to develop age-appropriate academic language in their L1. Proctor and colleagues (2010), for example, found that ELs who were instructed in Spanish literacy until grade 2 or 3 in transitional bilingual programs experienced decreases in Spanish reading ability relative to norms for native Spanish speakers; at the same time, ELs instructed only in English were not literate in Spanish by grade 5. Pham and Kohnert (2014) found that Vietnamese-speaking ELs who received some instruction in Vietnamese along with English showed growth in both languages from grades 2 to 5, but greater growth in English and a trend to shift to greater use of English over grade progression (see also Mueller Gathercole, 2002).

CROSS-LINGUISTIC ASPECTS OF LANGUAGE DEVELOPMENT IN ENGLISH LEARNERS

A growing body of research dating back to the 1960s reveals that the two languages of bilinguals do not exist in isolation and to the contrary, are highly interactive. This interaction has been found in multiple domains of language learning and use, including acquisition, cognitive representation and processing, and use. That this process characterizes even 2- to 3-year-old ELs indicates that it is an unconscious one that is a by-product of being bilingual (see the discussion in Chapter 4 on code switching in preschool-age dual language learners). The two languages of bilinguals share a cognitive/conceptual foundation that can facilitate the acquisition and use of more than one language for communication, thinking, and problem solving. It is the sophisticated and complex management of two linguistic systems that is thought to engender the development of superior cognitive skills in bilinguals relative to monolinguals.

Research on the acquisition, comprehension, and production of two languages during second language learning and bilingual performance has revealed that both linguistic systems are differentially accessible and activated at virtually all times (e.g., Gullifer et al., 2013; Kroll et al., 2014). Even when using only one language, bilinguals access the meaning of words in both languages, although accessibility and salience of meaning in the active language are stronger. Of particular relevance to this study, extensive evidence demonstrates cross-linguistic correlations in performance in domains of language related to literacy and academic language more generally (Genesee and Geva, 2006; Genesee et al., 2006; Riches and Genesee, 2006). Extensive reviews and detailed descriptions of this research are provided by August and Shanahan (2006) and Genesee and colleagues (2006, Ch. 4). Correlations have been reported in numerous domains of language and literacy development across a wide range of language pairs, but the magnitude of the correlations can depend on the typological similarity of the languages, the level of proficiency of the learning in one or both languages, the stage of second language learning, and the specific measures used.

Research has shown that bilinguals who code switch do so in such a way as to avoid violating the grammatical constraints of both languages, indicating a profound sensitivity to extremely subtle, subconscious knowledge governing both linguistic systems (MacSwan, 2016; Myers-Scotton, 1993; Poplack, 1980). This view of code switching is especially apt in the case of young ELs, who use all of their linguistic resources to acquire language and to communicate when they are in a stage of early development. Notwithstanding such evidence, teachers often view code switching as a cause for concern (Ramirez and Milk, 1986; Valdés-Fallis, 1978). In a study involving 278 elementary school teachers from 14 elementary schools in South Texas, for example, Nava (2009) found that a large majority of teachers, particularly those in less diverse school settings, viewed code switching negatively and discouraged their students from using it. Teachers expressed the view that code switching reflects limited proficiency in both languages, and interferes with academic and cognitive development. The way teachers, researchers, and others view children's language ability is important because it affects their views of what the children know and of their families and communities, as well as the treatment children receive in school and other service contexts.

That there are extensive and significant cross-linguistic relationships between the languages of bilinguals has significant implications for both raising and educating children bilingually since it indicates that the skills, knowledge, or strategies acquired in one language can be used to acquire or use another language. Indeed, cross-linguistic interactions are now viewed largely as facilitative or as evidence of linguistic competence or resourcefulness.

CONCLUSIONS

Conclusion 6-1: It can take from 5 to 7 years for students to learn the English necessary for participation in a school's curriculum without further linguistic support. This is due in part to the increasing language demands of participation in school learning over time, especially with respect to the language used in written texts beyond the early primary years. Thus, students may require help with English through the upper elementary and middle school grades, particularly in acquiring proficiency in the academic uses of English. While of critical importance, "academic language" has been difficult to define, and is variously characterized in functional, grammatical, lexical, rhetorical, and pragmatic terms. As a result, efforts to support its development in classrooms have been inconsistent, just as efforts to assess its development have been problematic.

Conclusion 6-2: Time to reclassification as a "fully proficient speaker of English" varies widely among English learners (ELs) with different background characteristics. Some language groups consistently take longer to attain proficiency and do so at lower rates than other groups, although variation is found within cultural and linguistic groups. This variation in time to reclassification may be due to differences in how academic language proficiency is assessed, in the adequacy of the tests used to reclassify ELs, in the quality of instruction provided to ELs, in teachers' beliefs about ELs' ability to meet high academic standards, and in teachers' attitudes about the role they should play in supporting students in school. Research does not provide clear explanations for why some ELs have more difficulty than others in attaining the English proficiency necessary for reclassification. Research is limited on pedagogical factors, such as as teacher qualifications and expectations and the quality of instruction provided, as well as on student characteristics, such as their prior educational background, the economic status of their families, their motivation, and their cultural values.

Conclusion 6-3: The languages of bilinguals do not develop in isolation from one another. Evidence indicates that certain aspects of dual language learning, processing, and usage are significantly and positively correlated and that the development of strong L1 skills supports the development of English-L2 skills. This interrelationship has been shown to be most evident in domains related to the acquisition of literacy skills and in languages that are typologically similar.

Conclusion 6-4: Evidence reveals significant positive correlations between literacy skills in English learners (ELs') L1 and the development of literacy skills in English-L2. Educational programs that provide systematic support for the development of ELs' L1 often facilitate and enhance their development of skills in English, especially literacy.

Conclusion 6-5: Evidence indicates that English learners are at risk of losing their L1 when exposure to English begins early—during the preschool or early school years; this is true even when students are in dual language programs. Loss of or reduced competence in the L1 results in reduced levels of bilingual competence and, commensurately, the advantages associated with bilingualism—cognitive enhancements, improved self-esteem, and job-related opportunities associated with competence in English and another language(s).

Conclusion 6-6: Evidence suggests that many schools are not providing adequate instruction to English learners (ELs) in acquiring English proficiency, as well as access to academic subjects at their grade level, from the time they first enter school until they reach the secondary grades. Many secondary schools are not able to meet the diverse needs of long-term ELs, including their linguistic, academic, and socioemotional needs.

BIBLIOGRAPHY

Abedi, J. (2008). Classification system for English language learners: Issues and recommendations. *Educational Measurement: Issues and Practice, 27*(3), 17-31.

Abrahamsson, N., and Hyltenstam, K. (2009). Age of onset and nativelikeness in a second language: Listener perception versus linguistic scrutiny. *Language Learning, 59*(2), 249-306.

August, D., and Shanahan, T. (2006). *Developing Literacy in Second-Language Learners: Report of the National Literacy Panel on Language Minority Children and Youth*. Mahwah, NJ: Lawrence Erlbaum Associates.

Aydemir, A., Chen, W.-H., and Corak, M. (2008). *Intergenerational Education Mobility among the Children of Canadian Immigrants*. Bonn: Institute for the Study of Labor.

Bailey, A. (2007). Introduction: Teaching and assessing students learning English in school. In A. Bailey (Ed.), *The Language Demands of School: Putting Academic English to the Test* (pp. 1-26). New Haven, CT: Yale University Press.

Batalova, J., Fix, M., and Murray, J. (2007). *The Demography and Literacy of Adolescent English Learners: A Report to the Carnegie Corporation of New York*. Washington, DC: Migration Policy Institute.

Bleakley, H., and Chin, A. (2010). Age at arrival, English proficiency, and social assimilation among U.S. immigrants. *American Economic Journal: Applied Economics, 2*(1), 165-192.

Block, N.C. (2012). Perceived impact of two-way dual immersion programs on Latino students' relationships in their families and communities. *International Journal of Bilingual Education and Bilingualism, 15*(2), 235-257.

Boyson, B.A., and Short, D. (2003). *Secondary School Newcomer Programs in the United States*. Santa Cruz: Center for Research on Education, Diversity and Excellence, University of California.

California Department of Education. (2014). *California English Language Development Test (CELDT) 2014-2015*. Available: http://dq.cde.ca.gov/dataquest/CELDT/results.aspx?year=2014-2015&level=state&assessment=2&subgroup=8&entity= [February 1, 2016].

Callahan, R.M. (2005). Tracking and high school English learners: Limiting opportunity to learn. *American Educational Research Journal, 42*(2), 305-328.

Callahan, R.M., Wilkinson, L., and Muller, C. (2008). School context and the effect of ESL placement on Mexican-origin adolescents' achievement. *Social Science Quarterly, 89*(1), 177-198.

Callahan, R.M., Wilkinson, L., and Muller, C. (2010). Academic achievement and course taking among language minority youth in U.S. schools: Effects of ESL placement. *Educational Evaluation and Policy Analysis, 32*(1), 84-117.

Carhill, A., Suárez-Orozco, C., and Páez, M. (2008). Explaining English language proficiency among adolescent immigrant students. *American Educational Research Journal, 45*(4), 1155-1179.

Carroll, P.E., and Bailey, A.L. (2016). Do decision rules matter? A descriptive study of English-language proficiency assessment classifications for English-language learners and native English speakers in fifth grade. *Language Testing, 33*(1), 23-52.

Cazabon, M.T., Nicoladis, E., and Lambert, W.E. (1998). *Becoming Bilingual in the Amigos Two-Way Immersion Program*. Santa Cruz: Center for Research on Education, Diversity and Excellence, University of California.

Chamot, A.U., and O'Malley, J.M. (1994). *The CALLA Handbook: Implementing the Cognitive Academic Language Learning Approach*. Reading, MA: Addison-Wesley.

Clewell, B.C., Murray, J., and de Cohen, C.C. (2007). *Promise or Peril?: NCLB and the Education of ELL Students*. Washington, DC: Urban Institute.

Cobb-Clark, D.A., and Nguyen, T.-H. (2010). *Immigration Background and the Intergenerational Correlation in Education* (No. 9780734042217 0734042213). Bonn: Institute for the Study of Labor.

Cohen, J., and Wickens, C.M. (2015). Speaking English and the loss of heritage language. *TESL-EJ: Teaching English as a Second Language Electronic Journal, 18*(4).

Collins, B.A. (2014). Dual language development of Latino children: Effect of instructional program type and the home and school language environment. *Early Child Research Quarterly, 29*(3), 389-397.

Collins, B.A., Toppelberg, C.O., Suárez-Orozco, C., O'Connor, E., and Nieto-Castañon, A. (2011). Cross-sectional associations of Spanish and English competence and well-being in Latino children of immigrants in kindergarten. *International Journal of the Sociology of Language, 2011*(208), 5-23.

Collins, B.A., O'Connor, E.E., Suarez-Orozco, C., Nieto-Castanon, A., and Toppelberg, C.O. (2014). Dual language profiles of Latino children of immigrants: Stability and change over the early school years. *Applied Psycholinguistics, 35*(3), 581-620.

Conger, D. (2009). Testing, time limits, and English learners: Does age of school entry affect how quickly students can learn English? *Social Science Research, 38*(2), 383-396.

Conger, D., Hatch, M., McKinney, J., Atwell, M.S., and Lamb, A. (2012). *Time to English Proficiency for English Language Learners in New York City and Miami-Dade County.* New York: The Institute for Educational and Social Policy.

Cook, V. (1992). Evidence of multicompetence. *Language Learning, 42,* 557-591.

Crystal, D. (2003). *English as a Global Language.* Cambridge, UK and New York: Cambridge University Press.

Cummins, J. (1981). Age on arrival and immigrant second language learning in Canada. A reassessment. *Applied Linguistics, 2*(2), 132-149.

de Jong, E.J., and Bearse, C. (2011). The same outcomes for all? High school students reflect on their two-way immersion program experiences. In D. Christian, D. Tedick, and T. Fortune (Eds.), *Immersion Education: Practices, Policies, Possibilities* (pp. 104-122). Bristol, UK: Multilingual Matters.

Delcenserie, A., and Genesee, F. (2014). Language and memory abilities of internationally adopted children from China: Evidence for early age effects. *Journal of Child Language, 41*(6), 1195-1223.

Espinosa, L.M. (2007). English-language learners as they enter school. In R.C. Pianta, M.J. Cox, and K.L. Snow (Eds.), *School Readiness and the Transition to Kindergarten in the Era of Accountability* (pp. 175-196). Baltimore, MD: Paul H. Brookes.

Espinosa, L.M. (2010). *Getting It Right for Young Children from Diverse Backgrounds: Applying Research to Improve Practice.* Upper Saddle River, NJ: Pearson.

Espinosa, L.M. (2013). *PreK-3rd: Challenging Common Myths about Dual Language Learners.* New York: Foundation for Child Development.

Freeman, Y.S., Freeman, D.E., and Mercuri, S. (2002). *Closing the Achievement Gap: How to Reach Limited-Formal-Schooling and Long-Term English Learners.* Portsmouth, NH: Heinemann.

Gándara, P., Gutierrez, D., and O'Hara, S. (2001). Planning for the future in rural and urban high schools. *Journal of Education for Students Placed at Risk, 6*(1-2), 73-93.

Genesee, F. (2015). Myths about early childhood bilingualism. *Canadian Psychology, 56(1),* 6-15.

Genesee, F., and Geva, E. (2006). Cross-linguistic relationships in working memory, phonological processes, and oral language. In D. August and T. Shanahan (Eds.), *Developing Literacy in Second Language Learners. Report of the National Literacy Panel on Minority-Language Children and Youth* (pp. 175-184). Mahwah, NJ: Lawrence Erlbaum Associates.

Genesee, F., Lindholm-Leary, K.J., Saunders, W.M., and Christian, D. (2006). *Educating English Language Learners: A Synthesis of Research Evidence.* New York: Cambridge University Press.

Goldenberg, C., and Coleman, R. (2010). *Promoting Academic Achievement among English Language Learners: A Guide to the Research.* Thousand Oaks, CA: Corwin.

Greenberg-Motamedi, J. (2015). *Time to Reclassification: How Long Does it Take English Learner Students in Washington Road Map Districts to Develop English Proficiency?* Available: http://ies.ed.gov/ncee/edlabs [January 20, 2016].

Grissom, J.B. (2004). Reclassification of English learners. *Education Policy Analysis Archives, 12,* 1-38.

Grosjean, F. (1985). The bilingual as a competent but specific speaker-hearer. *Journal of Multilingual and Multicultural Development, 6,* 467-477.

Gullifer, J.W., Kroll, J.F., and Dussias, P.E. (2013). When language switching has no apparent cost: Lexical access in sentence context. *Frontiers in Psychology, 4.*

Hakuta, K. (2011). Educating language minority students and affirming their equal rights research and practical perspectives. *Educational Researcher, 40*(4), 163-174.

Hakuta, K., and D'Andrea, D. (1992). Some properties of bilingual maintenance and loss in Mexican background high-school students. *Applied Linguistics, 13*(1), 72-99.

Hakuta, K., Butler, Y.G., and Witt, D. (2000). *How Long Does it Take English Learners to Attain Proficiency?* Santa Barbara: University of California, Linguistic Minority Research Institute.

Hammer, C.S., Lawrence, F.R., and Miccio, A.W. (2008). Exposure to English before and after entry into Head Start: Bilingual children's receptive language growth in Spanish and English. *International Journal of Bilingual Education and Bilingualism, 11*(1), 30-56.

Hammer, C.S., Davison, M.D., Lawrence, F.R., and Miccio, A.W. (2009). The effect of maternal language on bilingual children's vocabulary and emergent literacy development during Head Start and kindergarten. *Scientific Studies of Reading, 13*(2), 99-121.

Hammer, C.S., Hoff, E., Uchikoshi, Y., Gillanders, C., Castro, D.C., and Sandilos, L.E. (2014). The language and literacy development of young dual language learners: A critical review. *Early Childhood Research Quarterly, 29*(4), 715-733.

Han, W.J. (2014). The role of family SES and language background in shaping the well-being of children of Asian origin in the context of school mobility. *Race and Social Problems, 6*(1), 85-101.

Han, W.J., and Huang, C.C. (2010). The forgotten treasure: Bilingualism and Asian children's emotional and behavioral health. *American Journal of Public Health, 100*(5), 831-838.

Hill, E.G. (2006). *Update 2002-2004: The Progress of English Learner Students.* Sacramento: California Legislative Analysts Office.

Jackson, C.W., Schatschneider, C., and Leacox, L. (2014). Longitudinal analysis of receptive vocabulary growth in young Spanish English-speaking children from migrant families. *Language, Speech, and Hearing Services in Schools, 45*(1), 40-51.

Jia, G., and Aaronson, D. (2003). A longitudinal study of Chinese children and adolescents learning English in the United States. *Applied Psycholinguistics, 24*(1), 131-161.

Johnson, T.E. (2007). Canonical correlation of elementary Spanish speaking English language learners entry characteristics to current English language status. *Education, 127*(3), 400-409.

Kanno, Y., and Kangas, S.E.N. (2014). "I'm not going to be, like, for the AP": English language learners' limited access to advanced college-preparatory courses in high school. *American Educational Research Journal, 51*(5), 848-878.

Kieffer, M.J. (2008). Catching up or falling behind? Initial English proficiency, concentrated poverty, and the reading growth of language minority learners in the United States. *Journal of Educational Psychology, 100*(4), 851-868.

Kohnert, K.J., Bates, E., and Hernandez, A.E. (1999). Balancing bilinguals lexical-semantic production and cognitive processing in children learning Spanish and English. *Journal of Speech, Language, and Hearing Research, 42*(6), 1400-1413.

Kroll, J.F., Bobb, S.C., and Hoshino, N. (2014). Two languages in mind: Bilingualism as a tool to investigate language, cognition, and the brain. *Current Directions in Psychological Science, 23*(3), 159-163.

Lambert, W.E., and Cazabon, M. (1994). *Students' Views of the Amigos Program.* Santa Cruz, CA: National Center for Research on Cultural Diversity and Second Language Learning.

Lesaux, N.K., Rupp, A.A., and Siegel, L.S. (2007). Growth in reading skills of children from diverse linguistic backgrounds: Findings from a 5-year longitudinal study. *Journal of Educational Psychology, 99*(4), 821-834.

Leung, G., and Uchikoshi, Y. (2012). Relationships among language ideologies, family language policies, and children's language achievement: A look at Cantonese–English bilinguals in the U.S. *Bilingual Research Journal, 35*(3), 294-313.

Lindholm, K.J., and Aclan, Z. (1991). Bilingual proficiency as a bridge to academic achievement: Results from bilingual/immersion programs. *The Journal of Education, 173*(2), 99-113.

Lindholm-Leary, K.J. (2001). *Dual Language Education.* Clevedon, UK: Multilingual Matters.

Lindholm-Leary, K.J. (2010). Student and school impacts: A quantitative analysis. In L. Olsen, K. Lindholm-Leary, M. Lavadenz, E. Armas, and F. Dell'Olio (Eds.), *The PROMISE Initiative: Pursuing Regional Opportunities for Mentoring, Innovation, and Success for English Learners* (pp. 113-224). San Bernardino, CA: PROMISE Design Center, San Bernardino County Superintendent of Schools.

Lindholm-Leary, K.J. (2011). Student outcomes in Chinese two-way immersion programs: Language proficiency, academic achievement, and student attitudes. In D. Tedick, D. Christian, and T. Fortune (Eds.), *Immersion Education: Practices, Policies, Possibilities* (pp. 81-103). Avon, UK: Multilingual Matters.

Lindholm-Leary, K.J. (2013). *Understanding ELLs at Different English Proficiency Levels in Dual Language Programs.* Paper presented at the American Educational Research Association Annual Meeting, San Francisco, CA.

Lindholm-Leary, K.J. (2014). Bilingual and biliteracy skills in young Spanish-speaking low-SES children: Impact of instructional language and primary language proficiency. *International Journal of Bilingual Education and Bilingualism, 17*(2), 144-159.

Lindholm-Leary, K.J. (2015). *Fostering School Success for English Learners K-12: Language and Academic Development of Dual Language Learners during the School Years.* Unpublished manuscript commissioned by the Committee on Fostering School Success for English Learners: Toward New Directions in Policy, Practice, and Research. Child and Adolescent Development, San Jose State University.

Lindholm-Leary, K.J., and Borsato, G. (2006). Academic achievement. In F. Genesee, K. Lindholm-Leary, W. Saunders, and D. Christian (Eds.), *Educating English Language Learners* (pp. 157-179). New York: Cambridge University Press.

Lindholm-Leary, K.J., and Hernández, A. (2011). Achievement and language proficiency of Latino students in dual language programmes: Native English speakers, fluent English/previous ELLs, and current ELLs. *Journal of Multilingual and Multicultural Development, 32*(6), 531-545.

Lindholm-Leary, K.J., and Howard, E. (2008). Language and academic achievement in two-way immersion programs. In T. Fortune and D. Tedick (Eds.), *Pathways to Bilingualism: Evolving Perspectives on Immersion Education* (pp. 177-200). Oxford, UK: Blackwell.

Linquanti, R., and Cook, H.G. (2013). *Toward a "Common Definition of English Learner": A Brief Defining Policy and Technical Issues and Opportunities for State Assessment Consortia.* Washington, DC: Council of Chief State School Officers.

MacSwan, J. (2016). Codeswitching and the timing of lexical insertion. *Linguistic Approaches to Bilingualism, 6*(6), 782-787.

MacSwan, J., and Pray, L. (2005). Learning English bilingually: Age of onset of exposure and rate of acquisition among English language learners in a bilingual education program. *Bilingual Research Journal, 29*(3), 653-678.

MacSwan, J., and Rolstad, K. (2010). The role of language in theories of academic failure for linguistic minorities. In J. Petrovic (ed.) *International Perspectives on Bilingual Education: Policy, Practice, and Controversy.* (pp. 173-195). Charlotte, NC: Information Age.

Mancilla-Martinez, J., and Lesaux, N.K. (2011). The gap between Spanish speakers' word reading and word knowledge: A longitudinal study. *Child Development, 82*(5), 1544-1560.

Mancilla-Martinez, J., Kieffer, M.J., Biancarosa, G., Christodoulou, J.A., and Snow, C.E. (2011). Investigating English reading comprehension growth in adolescent language minority learners: Some insights from the simple view. *Reading and Writing, 24*(3), 339-354.

Maxwell-Jolly, J., Gándara, P., and Méndez Benavídez, L. (2007). *Promoting Academic Literacy among Secondary English Language Learners: A Synthesis of Research and Practice.* Santa Barbara: University of California, Linguistic Minority Research Institute.

Menken, K. (2013). Emergent bilingual students in secondary school: Along the academic language and literacy continuum. *Language Teaching, 46*(4), 438-476.

Menken, K., Kleyn, T., and Chae, N. (2012). Spotlight on "long-term English language learners": Characteristics and prior schooling experiences of an invisible population. *International Multilingual Research Journal, 6*(2), 121-142.

Merino, B.J. (1983). Language loss in bilingual Chicano children. *Journal of Applied Developmental Psychology, 4,* 277-294.

Montrul, S. (2008). *Incomplete Acquisition in Bilingualism Re-examining the Age Factor.* Amsterdam and Philadelphia, PA: John Benjamins.

Montrul, S., and Potowski, K. (2007). Command of gender agreement in school-age Spanish–English bilingual children. *International Journal of Bilingualism, 11*(3), 301-328.

Mueller Gathercole, V. (2002). Grammatical gender in bilingual and monolingual children: A Spanish morphosyntactic distinction. In D.K. Oller and R. Eilers (Eds.), *Language and Literacy in Bilingual Children* (pp. 207-219). Clevedon, UK: Multilingual Matters.

Mulligan, G., Halle, T., and Kinukawa, A. (2012). *Reading, Mathematics, and Science Achievement of Language-Minority Students in Grade 8.* Issue Brief, NCES 2012-028. Washington, DC: National Center for Education Statistics.

Muñoz-Sandoval, A.F., Cummins, J., Alvarado, C.G., and Ruef, M.L. (1998). *Bilingual Verbal Ability Tests: Comprehensive Manual.* Itasca, IL: Riverside.

Myers-Scotton, C. (1993). *Social Motivations for Codeswitching: Evidence from Africa.* Oxford: Clarendon Press.

Nakamoto, J., Lindsey, K.A., and Manis, F.R. (2007). A longitudinal analysis of English language learners' word decoding and reading comprehension. *Reading and Writing, 20*(7), 691-719.

National Research Council. (1997). *Improving Schooling for Language-Minority Children: A Research Agenda.* D. August and K. Hakuta (Eds.). Division of Behavioral and Social Sciences and Education, Commission on Behavioral and Social Sciences and Education, Committee on Developing a Research Agenda on the Education of Limited English Proficient and Bilingual Students. Washington, DC: National Academy Press.

National Task Force on Early Childhood Education for Hispanics. (2007). *Expanding and Improving Early Education for Hispanics Executive Report.* Tempe, AZ: Author. Available: https://www.fcd-us.org/assets/2016/04/PNNExecReport.pdf [July 2017].

Nava, G.N. (2009). Elementary teachers' attitudes and beliefs towards their students' use of code-switching in South Texas. *Lenguaje, 37(1),* 135-158.

New York Office of English Language Learners. (2009). *Diverse Learners on the Road to Success: The Performance of New York City's English Language Learners.* New York: New York Department of Education.

Oller, D.K., and Eilers, R.E. (2002). *Language and Literacy in Bilingual Children.* Avon, UK: Multilingual Matters.

Olsen, L. (2010). *Reparable Harm: Fulfilling the Unkept Promise of Educational Opportunity for California's Long Term English Learners.* Long Beach, CA: Californians Together.

Paradis, J. (2009). Second language acquisition in childhood. In E. Hoff and M. Shatz (Eds.), *Handbook of Language Development* (pp. 387-405). Oxford, UK: Blackwell.

Paradis, J., Schneider, P., and Duncan, T.S. (2013). Discriminating children with language impairment among English-language learners from diverse first-language backgrounds. *Journal of Speech, Language, and Hearing Research, 56*(3), 971-981.

Parrish, T.B., Merickel, A., Perez, M., Linquanti, R., Socias, M., Spain, A., Speroni, C., Esra, P., Brock, L., and Delancey, D. (2006). *Effects of the Implementation of Proposition 227 on the Education of English Learners, K-12: Findings from a Five-Year Evaluation. Final Report for AB 56 and AB 1116.* Palo Alto, CA: American Institutes for Research.

Pham, G., and Kohnert, K. (2014). A longitudinal study of lexical development in children learning Vietnamese and English. *Child Development, 85*(2), 767-782.

Poplack, S. (1980). Sometimes I'll start a sentence in Spanish y termino en Espanol: Toward a typology of code-switching. *Linguistics, 18*(7-8), 581-618.

Portes, A., and Schauffler, R. (1994). Language and the second generation: Bilingualism yesterday and today. *International Migration Review, 28*(4), 640-661.

Proctor, C.P., August, D., Carlo, M., and Barr, C. (2010). Language maintenance versus language of instruction: Spanish reading development among Latino and Latina bilingual learners. *Journal of Social Issues, 66*(1), 79-94.

Ramirez, A.G., and Milk, R.D. (1986). Notions of grammaticality among teachers of bilingual pupils. *TESOL Quarterly, 20*(3), 495-513.

Reardon, S.F., Valentino, R.A., and Shores, K.A. (2012). Patterns of literacy among U.S. students. *The Future of Children, 22*(2), 17-37.

Riches, C., and Genesee, F. (2006). Cross-linguistic and cross-modal aspects of literacy development. In F. Genesee, K. Lindholm-Leary, W. Saunders, and D. Christian (Eds.), *Educating English Language Learners: A Synthesis of Research Evidence* (pp. 64-108). New York: Cambridge University Press.

Rodriguez, J.L., Diaz, R.M., Duran, D., and Espinosa, L. (1995). The impact of bilingual preschool education on the language development of Spanish-speaking children. *Early Childhood Research Quarterly, 10*(4), 475-490.

Rumberger, R.W., and Gándara, P. (2005). How well are California's English learners mastering English?: Educational outcomes and opportunities for English language learners. *University of California Linguistic Minority Research Institute Newsletter, 13*(1), 1-2.

Rumberger, R.W., and Larson, K.A. (1998). Student mobility and the increased risk of high school dropout. *American Journal of Education,* 1-35.

Saunders, W., and O'Brien, G. (2006). Oral language. In F. Genesee, K.J. Lindholm-Leary, W.M. Saunders, and D. Christian (Eds.), *Educating English Language Learners: A Synthesis of Research Evidence* (pp. 14-63). New York: Cambridge University Press.

Scarcella, R. (2003). *Academic English: A Conceptual Framework.* Technical Report 2003-1. Berkeley: The University of California Linguistic Minority Research Institute.

Schleppegrell, M.J. (2004). *The Language of Schooling: A Functional Linguistics Perspective.* Mahwah, NJ: Lawrence Erlbaum Associates.

Silver, D., Saunders, M., and Zarate, E. (2008). *What Factors Predict High School Graduation in the Los Angeles Unified School District.* Santa Barbara: California Dropout Research Project.

Slama, R.B. (2012). A longitudinal analysis of academic English proficiency outcomes for adolescent English language learners in the United States. *Journal of Educational Psychology, 104*(2), 265-285.

Snow, C.E., and Uccelli, P. (2009). The challenge of academic language. In D.R. Olson, and N. Torrance (Eds.), *The Cambridge Handbook of Literacy* (pp. 112-133). New York: Cambridge University Press.

Song, M., O'Grady, W., Cho, S., and Lee, M. (1997). The learning and teaching of Korean in community schools. *The Korean Language in America, 2,* 111-127.

Suárez-Orozco, C., Gaytán, F.X., Bang, H.J., Pakes, J., O'Connor, E., and Rhodes, J. (2010). Academic trajectories of newcomer immigrant youth. *Developmental Psychology, 46*(3), 602-618.

Thomas, W., and Collier, V. (2002). *A National Study of School Effectiveness for Language Minority Students' Long-Term Academic Achievement.* Washington, DC: Center for Research on Education, Diversity and Excellence.

Thompson, K.D. (2015). English learners' time to reclassification: An analysis. *Educational Policy* [E-pub ahead of print].

Umansky, I.M., and Reardon, S.F. (2014). Reclassification patterns among Latino English learner students in bilingual, dual immersion, and English immersion classrooms. *American Educational Research Journal, 51*(5), 879-912.

Uriarte, M., Karp, F., Gagnon, L., Tung, R., Rustan, S., Chen, J., Berardino, M., and Stazesky, P. (2011). *Improving Educational Outcomes of English Language Learners in Schools and Programs in Boston Public Schools.* Boston: Center for Collaborative Education and Mauricio Gaston Institute for Latino Community Development and Public Policy, University of Massachusetts.

Valdés-Fallis, G. (1978). Code switching and the classroom teacher. *Language in Education: Theory and Practice, 4.*

Watt, D.L.E., and Roessingh, H. (1994). Some you win, most you lose: Tracking ESL student drop out in high school (1988-1993). *English Quarterly, 26*(3), 5-7.

Wong-Fillmore, L. (1991). When learning a second language means losing the first. *Early Childhood Research Quarterly, 6*(3), 323-346.

Wong-Fillmore, L., and Fillmore, C.J. (2012). *What Does Text Complexity Mean for English Learners and Language Minority Students?* Stanford University Understanding Language Project. Available: http://ell.stanford.edu/papers/language [January 24, 2017].

Yeni-Komshian, G.H., Flege, J.E., and Liu, S. (2000). Pronunciation proficiency in the first and second languages of Korean–English bilinguals. *Bilingualism: Language and Cognition, 3*(2), 131-149.

7

Programs for English Learners in Grades Pre-K to 12

This chapter begins with a discussion about connecting effective programs for dual language learners (DLLs) with effective programs and practices for English learners (ELs).[1] It then provides an overview of the English-only and bilingual programs that serve ELs in grades pre-K to 12 and the evaluation research that compares outcomes for ELs instructed in English-only programs with ELs instructed in bilingual programs. This is followed by a review of the research on instructional practices for developing ELs' oral language proficiency in grades K-12. Next, the chapter reviews district-wide practices related to the educational progress of ELs and examines the role of family engagement in ELs' educational success. The chapter ends with conclusions.

Attention to how ELs are faring in grades pre-K to 12 comes at a pivotal time in American education. Schools throughout the nation are teaching to higher curricular standards in core subject areas—English language arts, social studies, mathematics, and science (Bunch, 2013; Cantrell et al., 2009; Echevarria et al., 2011; Lara-Alecio et al., 2012). All students, including ELs, are expected to engage with academic content that is considerably more demanding than in previous years, and they must now demonstrate deeper levels of understanding and analysis of that content.

---

[1] When referring to young children ages birth to 5 in their homes, communities, or early care and education programs, this report uses the term "dual language learners" or "DLLs." When referring to children ages 5 and older in the pre-K to 12 education system, the term "English learners" or "ELs" is used. When referring to the broader group of children and adolescents ages birth to 21, the term "DLLs/ELs" is used. (See Box 1-1 in Chapter 1 for details.)

ELs face the dual tasks of achieving English proficiency while mastering grade-level academic subjects.

CONNECTING EFFECTIVE PROGRAMS FOR DUAL LANGUAGE LEARNERS BIRTH TO AGE 5 WITH ENGLISH LEARNERS IN PRE-K TO 12

Research on children's learning, programs, and policies follows a divide between early learning programs (birth to 5) and pre-K to 12 education (ages 3 to 21) in the United States (Takanishi, 2016). To address this gap, the U.S. Department of Education has issued nonregulatory guidance on how states can better connect their early education programs with pre-K to 12 education, as proposed under the Every Student Succeeds Act (ESSA) (see Chapter 2 for more detail).

The evidence is now clear that becoming proficient in English and able to perform at grade level in core academic subjects in English takes time and occurs over several grades (see Chapter 6) (Thompson, 2015; Umansky and Reardon, 2014; Valentino and Reardon, 2015). Given findings that the levels of proficiency in an EL's home language and in English at school entry are related to the time to English proficiency in the K-12 grades (Thompson, 2015), more attention is needed to how the early grades, especially K-5, build the academic language that young children need to be successful in school. The Sobrato Early Academic Literacy (SEAL) Program is an example of a pre-K to grade 3 approach that educates ELs in predominantly English settings as well as in those that are bilingual (see Box 7-1).

ENGLISH-ONLY AND BILINGUAL APPROACHES TO INSTRUCTION

This section first describes the program models used to teach ELs and then turns to findings from the evaluation research that compares outcomes for ELs taught primarily in English-only programs with ELs taught in bilingual programs. The committee notes that implementation of the programs described varies depending on attention to the professional development of educators (see Chapter 12) and to issues of fidelity of implementation (e.g., O'Donnell, 2008). Program labels may not accurately reflect what teachers do and what students experience in classrooms.

Program Models

The two broad approaches used to teach ELs English in grades pre-K to 12 are (1) English as a second language (ESL) approaches, in which English is the predominant language used for instruction, and (2) bilingual approaches, in which English and students' home languages are used for instruction. Each approach has various models (Faulkner-Bond et al., 2012) (see Table 7-1). The three models that provide instruction predominantly in English are the ESL model, the content-based ESL model, and the sheltered instruction model. "In ESL instructional programs, ESL-certified teachers provide explicit language instruction that focuses on the development of proficiency in English. In content-based ESL instructional programs, ESL-certified teachers provide language instruction that uses subject matter content as a medium for building language skills. In sheltered instructional programs, teachers provide instruction that simultaneously introduces both language and content using specialized techniques to accommodate DLL's linguistic needs" (Faulkner-Bond et al., 2012, pp. x-xiii).

The two models that provide bilingual instruction are the transitional bilingual education (TBE) model and the dual language (DL) model (Boyle et al., 2015). In TBE programs, students typically begin learning in their home language in kindergarten or grade 1 and transition to English incrementally over time. In TBE programs, while the L1 is used to leverage English, the goal is to achieve English proficiency as quickly as possible. In early-exit TBE programs, ELs generally exit prior to grade 3.

DL instructional programs vary in structure, implementation, and enrolled student populations. Unlike TBE programs, where the goal is English proficiency, DL programs aim to help students develop high levels of language proficiency and literacy in both program languages. Additionally, they aim to help students attain high levels of academic achievement and develop an appreciation for and understanding of multiple cultures (Boyle et al., 2015). There are two types of DL instructional programs. The first is a one-way dual language program that serves predominantly one group of students. The students served may be ELs who are acquiring English and developing their L1. Two other groups also can be served by this type of program: (1) predominantly English-speaking students who are developing their English and acquiring a world language, and (2) predominantly heritage language learners. The second type of DL program is a two-way DL program in which ELs and English-speaking peers receive instruction in both English and the ELs' L1 in the same classes (also called the partner language in these programs).

Findings from Evaluation Research

Syntheses of studies that compare outcomes for ELs instructed in English-only programs with outcomes for ELs instructed bilingually have found either that there are no differences in outcomes measured in English or that ELs in bilingual programs outperform those instructed only in English when outcomes are measured in English (and in the partner lan-

BOX 7-1
Sobrato Early Academic Literacy (SEAL) Program

SEAL is a promising approach that aims to connect ELs' pre-K experiences with the early primary grades, K-3, in both predominantly English and bilingual settings. As of the 2016-2017 school year, the SEAL model had expanded to 87 California schools in 16 districts, reaching more than 39,000 students (Sobrato Family Foundation, 2016). Based on Common Core State Standards and the California state preschool learning foundations, SEAL emphasizes language-rich instruction delivered through integrated thematic units that embed language development within the academic content of social studies and science, with a strong focus on oral language and vocabulary development and extensive parental engagement practices.

To promote an affirming environment and to support students' first language (L1), the SEAL model explicitly emphasizes the value of bilingualism and supports students' use of their L1 to discuss their culture, family, and identity. Building strong relationships between families and teachers is also an important component of the SEAL model. Parents are encouraged to be involved in the schools and to develop their own literacy to foster their child's development. Some of the strategies used to engage parents and families and build relationships between parents and teachers include providing classes in English as a second language for parents at the school, recruiting and training parents as classroom volunteers, communicating with parents regularly using multiple forms of communication, providing guidance for teachers on how to incorporate the culture and experiences of students from diverse backgrounds, offering book loan programs that provide students with books to read at home with their families, and conducting workshops for parents on how to support language and literacy development at home and on the importance of the L1 and the family's culture.

In 2015, an evaluation of the SEAL program examined the outcomes of Spanish-speaking students who participated in the SEAL preschool program and continued participating in the program in grades K-3. Outcome data focused on language, literacy, mathematics/cognitive, and social outcomes—components that are the focus of SEAL. After 5 full years of program implementation, the evaluation yielded the following findings (Lindholm-Leary, 2015):

- There was a high level of implementation of SEAL, with more than two-thirds of teachers being rated as high implementers. Further, there was no difference in level of implementation across school sites. While teachers were more likely to be rated as high implementers in classes with bilingual as compared with English instruction, the difference was not statistically significant.
- TSEAL students who received the full intervention from pre-K to grade 3 were compared with partial SEAL students who received the same in-

tervention in elementary school but did not participate in pre-K and may have had less elementary school experience with SEAL as well (only 1-2 years instead of 3-4). In assessments during grades 2 and 3, the English language proficiency, English reading/language arts, and math scores, as well as Spanish reading/language arts and math scores, of SEAL students who had participated in the program since kindergarten were significantly higher than the SEAL scores of students who had not.

- Developmental profiles (Desired Results Developmental Profile [DRDP], California English Language Development Test [CELDT], California Standards Test [CST], Standards-based Tests in Spanish [STS]) of SEAL students were compared with those of other groups, including district and state averages, to determine whether SEAL students were showing lower, similar, or higher performance growth on the assessments. In comparisons of the SEAL test scores with district and state averages, the SEAL scores, especially for children who had fully participated in the program from pre-K to grade 3, generally were comparable to or higher than the district and state averages. This was true at the pre-K level on the DRDP in language, literacy, and math; on the CELDT in comparisons with district and state peers (by grades 3 and 4); and on the CST and STS, on which full and sometimes partial SEAL students scored as well as or higher than district and state peers in reading/language arts and math.

- In the SEAL program, some parents choose to have their children instructed in structured English immersion (SEI) classrooms where instruction is predominantly in English, while others choose to have their children instructed bilingually. Overall, children who were instructed in SEAL SEI classrooms and those instructed in SEAL bilingual classrooms began at low levels on measures of language, literacy, and math and showed significant growth. In grades 1 and 2, students enrolled in SEI classrooms tended to score higher than students enrolled in bilingual classrooms. By grades 3 and 4, however, students receiving bilingual instruction scored similarly to or higher than students instructed in SEI classrooms.

- SEAL had a significant impact on parents and literacy activities in the home. Half of the SEAL parents reported reading to their children on a daily basis and engaging regularly in literacy-related activities. Parental engagement was significantly related to student outcomes.

These findings indicate that SEAL is a promising approach for developing English proficiency and subject matter learning based on the Common Core State Standards for low-income Hispanic/Latino students, including those living in immigrant families. A large-scale evaluation of SEAL using Common Core assessments is now under way with a representative sample of 7,000-10,000 SEAL students (Sobrato Family Foundation, 2016).

TABLE 7-1 Approaches to Teaching English Learners (ELs) in Pr-K to Grade 12

Program Names	Program Description	Teacher Description	Goals	Format
English as a Second Language Approaches				
English as a Second Language (ESL) Alternative Names: English Language Development (ELD), English for Speakers of Other Languages (ESOL)	ELs are provided with explicit language instruction to develop their language proficiency.	ESL-certified teacher[a]	English proficiency, including grammar, vocabulary, and communication skills	Students may have a dedicated ESL class in their school day or may receive pull-out ESL instruction, wherein they work with a specialist for short periods during other classes.
Content-based English as a Second Language	ELs are provided with language instruction that uses content as a medium for building language skills. Although using content as a means, instruction is still focused primarily on learning English.	ESL-certified teacher	Academic achievement, proficiency in English	Students may have a dedicated ESL class in their school day or may receive pull-out ESL instruction, wherein they work with a specialist for short periods during other classes.
Sheltered Instruction (SI) Alternative Name: Specially Designed Academic Instruction in English (SDAIE)	Instruction for ELs focuses on the teaching of academic content rather than the English language itself. Teacher uses specialized techniques to accommodate ELs' linguistic needs.	Likely to be a general education teacher but may be an ESL-certified teacher	Academic achievement, proficiency in English	Generally used in EL-only classrooms, designed specifically for ELs.

Bilingual Approaches

Program	Students	Teachers	Goals	Grade level/timing
Transitional Bilingual Education (TBE) Alternative Name: Early-Exit Bilingual Education	ELs begin in grade K or 1 by receiving instruction all or mostly in their first language (L1) and transition incrementally to English during the primary grades but may exit as late as grade 5. L1 is used to leverage second language (L2) acquisition, but L1 proficiency is not a program goal.	Teachers proficient in both English and the L1 and certified for teaching the particular grade level and bilingual education	Academic achievement, proficiency in English	Balance of L1 and L2. Some TBE programs begin with L1 exclusively, others begin with a majority of L1 and use some L2. The division of the languages across instructional time and content areas may vary from program to program.
One-Way Dual Language Program Alternative Names: Late-Exit Bilingual; Maintenance Bilingual; Developmental Bilingual Education (DBE)	Students are predominantly from one primary language group. The different kinds of language groups that can be served in these programs are ELs learning their home language and English; English-proficient students learning English and a world language; and heritage language learners[b] studying English and their heritage language (e.g., French, Navajo).	May be bilingual teachers, or teachers who teach in English who use sheltered instruction techniques to make their instruction accessible for ELs	Academic achievement, proficiency in English, bilingualism and biliteracy, cross-cultural understanding	Students typically begin in grade K or 1. Regardless of when or whether students attain proficiency in English, the program is designed to keep them enrolled through its completion (typically, the end of elementary school).

continued

260

TABLE 7-1 Continued

Program Names	Program Description	Teacher Description	Goals	Format
Two-Way Dual Language Program Alternative Names: Dual Immersion (DI), Two-Way Immersion (TWI)	Students are ELs and English-proficient students, ideally in a 50-50 mix.	May be bilingual teachers who use sheltered instructional techniques to make content comprehensible or who team teach, where one teacher communicates in English and one communicates in the second language	Academic achievement, proficiency in English, bilingualism and biliteracy, biculturalism, cross-cultural understanding	Balance of L1 and L2. Programs follow either 50:50 model or 90:10 model (which ultimately transitions to 50:50). Programs may balance languages by dividing instructional time according to content area, class period, instructor, week, or unit. The program is designed to keep them enrolled through its completion, in some cases through high school graduation.

[a]As used here, an ESL-certified teacher is a teacher with a license, credential, and/or certification to provide English language instruction to second language learners. Different states and districts may use different naming conventions to refer to this kind of instructor.

[b]A heritage language learner is a person studying a language who has some proficiency in or a cultural connection to that language through family, community, or country of origin. Heritage language learners have widely diverse levels of proficiency in the language (in terms of oral proficiency and literacy) and of connections to the language and culture. They are different in many ways from students studying the language as a foreign language.

SOURCE: Selected data from http://www2.ed.gov/rschstat/eval/title-iii/language-instruction-ed-programs-report.pdf [January 20, 2017].

guage if the control group includes speakers of partner languages and out-comes are measured in those languages). For meta-analyses of the research, see Faulkner-Bond et al. (2012), Francis et al. (2006), Greene (1997), Rolstad et al. (2005), Slavin and Cheung (2005), and Willig (1985). For reviews of the research, see Rossell and Baker (1996), Lindholm-Leary and Borsato (2006), Genesee and Lindholm-Leary (2012), and.

The committee calls attention to two studies that followed students in programs with different models for language of instruction for suf-ficient time to gauge the longer-term effects of language of instruction on EL outcomes. Umansky and Reardon (2014) examined the effects of sev-eral programs, including TBE, developmental bilingual education (DBE), English immersion (EI), and dual immersion (DI), on reclassification rates using administrative data on Latino EL kindergarten entrants to California public schools in the 2000s. Students were followed through grade 11. The study aimed to control for selection biases by holding relevant student and school characteristics constant. The study found that "two-language programs, especially those that focus on home language acquisition in the early grades, may result in longer durations of EL status prior to reclas-sification" (p. 906). However, the study also found that ELs in bilingual/DL programs have a higher long-term likelihood of becoming proficient in English, meeting an English language arts threshold, and being reclassified relative to ELs in English-only programs.

Using the same data and research design with additional controls for parental preferences, Valentino and Reardon (2015) examined the effect of these same programs on ELs' English language arts and math achievement in middle school. The study compared students with the same parental preferences and found substantial differences in the short- versus long-term effects of the different instructional models. According to the authors, "By second grade, ELs in DI classrooms have ELA [English language arts] test scores that are well below those of their peers in EI [English instruction] classrooms. At the same time, ELs in TB programs have test scores well above those of ELs in EI on both ELA and math, and those in DB have math test scores that are significantly higher than their peers in DI. However, by seventh grade, students in DI and TB programs have much higher ELA scores than those in EI classrooms" (p. 30). Explanations for short- versus long-term effects may be that ELs in DI programs spend more of their time in the early grades learning in their home languages and that assessments to measure math and English language arts may be administered in Eng-lish. A second notable result is that the test scores of ELs in DI programs far outpace those of ELs in other programs. The authors hypothesize that this may be due to the opportunity in DI programs for ELs to interact with English-speaking peers and the fact that instruction in content in their home language helps ensure that ELs do not fall behind in grade-level subjects.

BOX 7-2
Improving the Design of Studies of Language of Instruction

There is an abundance of research on the effects of language of instruction on EL outcomes; however, the design of the studies could be improved by

- providing more information about students' characteristics, such as ages, levels of language proficiency, degrees of bilingualism, family resources, and ethnicity;
- providing more details about students' school and community contexts, including the status of their languages;
- providing more details about the program models, including how much, for how long, and how each language is used;
- providing information about the experience and training of teachers involved in implementing programs and how well they are implementing key components of the programs;
- randomly assigning students to programs or conducting quasi-experiments with matched control groups; and
- following students over longer periods of time because ELs instructed bilingually tend to take additional time to acquire full proficiency in two languages, and learning languages takes time.

Moreover, continued development in the home language provides opportunities for transfer from that language to English.

Research also has begun to explore the relationship between classroom language use configurations and student outcomes. A qualitative study (Soltero-González et al., 2016) found that paired literacy instruction led to stronger literacy outcomes in both languages relative to sequential literacy instruction in which children learn mostly in their partner language first and then transition to English. However, debates about the most appropriate approaches to language instruction are ongoing. For example, drawing on the second language acquisition literature, some guidance calls for the separation of languages. This means that teachers and students are expected to use mostly one language or another in any given lesson (Howard et al., 2007). Others argue for an approach to bilingualism that allows for the mixing of languages within a classroom. Proponents of this approach, called translanguaging (García, 2009), claim that individuals with two or more languages benefit from drawing on all of their linguistic resources in classrooms (García, 2009). Studies are needed to compare the effects of the two approaches on ELs' language, literacy, and content area outcomes.

Some research related to language of instruction for ELs has been limited by selection bias because the preferences of administrators, teachers, parents, and sometimes children play a role in determining which type of instruction a student receives (Francis et al., 2006; Slavin and Cheung, 2005), as well as by the failure to take into account factors other than type of programming that might influence outcomes. Box 7-2 lists factors that need to be considered in interpreting findings from studies that compare one type of program model with another, while Box 7-3 summarizes a case study of one K-12 DL school.

BOX 7-3
Profile of a K-12 Dual Language School

The Chula Vista Learning Community Charter School (CVLCC) in Chula Vista, California, is a Spanish-English dual language school located just 7 miles north of the Mexican border near San Diego. CVLCC serves more than 1,000 students in grades K-12, 94 percent of whom are Latinos, 60.5 percent of whom are categorized as "socioeconomically disadvantaged," and 37.4 percent of whom are classified as ELs.[a] The instructional program is aligned with California's Common Core State Standards and aims to develop high-level thinking, literacy, and communication skills across the curriculum.[b] Children begin kindergarten with 50 percent instruction in English and 50 percent in Spanish (Alfaro et al., 2014).

CVLCC serves a student population that is generally at high risk for academic failure, yet a case study of the school found substantial academic gains for its students from 2005 to 2012, with the school's Academic Performance Index (API) score rising from 680 in 2005 to 880 in 2012. This accomplishment earned the school a Title I Closing the Achievement Gap Award for the 2010-2011 school year and a California Distinguished School award in 2012 (Alfaro et al., 2014). In 2012, the API score for CVLCC's ELs was 854, considerably above the score of 758 for California's ELs in grades 2-6. In 2013, the last year for which the state of California reported API scores for schools, CVLCC's scores declined somewhat, possibly reflecting the adoption and implementation of new curricular frameworks aligned with the Common Core State Standards. Averaged over 3 years, the school and all student subgroups met their growth targets for the year, with a 3-year average API of 869 for the school and 840 for ELs.[c]

At CVLCC, students learn through Spanish and English but also in Mandarin. Finding teachers who can teach science, math, literature, and history aligned with current standards in more than one language is a challenge. The success of dual language schools like CVLCC depends in large part on having teachers who not only have the professional and linguistic qualifications to teach but also are equipped with the sociocultural understanding of the life experiences of students and their families that is a prerequisite for effective teaching and learning (see Chapter 12).

Dual language instruction is considerably more complex than other forms of pedagogy. To develop its faculty, the school partnered with the San Diego State University Dual Language and English Learner Education (SDSU-DLE) Program to provide preservice and in-service professional development. This includes a

continued

BOX 7-3 Continued

1-week Paulo Freire Institute for the CVLCC teachers and administrators. The partnership began with the assumption that university and school faculty alike have much to learn from one another, and that it is important to prepare teachers to work on developing a pedagogical approach that will support students in working at grade level, irrespective of the quality of their prior schooling, their language background, or their socioeconomic status. To this end, teachers have to learn to recognize the cultural, linguistic, and social resources that students bring to the school from their homes and communities. This in turn requires that educators work with families and community members as partners in learning about their cultural and linguistic assets and in creating "inclusive learning communities, where teacher, school leadership, student, and parent each play an integral role in supporting student success" (Alfaro et al., 2014, p. 21).

CVLCC's pedagogical approach encourages teachers to engage their students in deep inquiry and dialogue about the subject matter, whether in studying history or developing writing skills across the curriculum. CVLCC teachers have designed their curriculum and instructional program to support their students' development of high-level thinking skills and to demonstrate their knowledge and skills both orally and in writing. Teachers across the languages engage in close collaboration and joint planning, and students are held to the same standards in both Spanish and English (Alfaro et al., 2014).

Instruction at CVLCC is student-centered, with students learning cooperatively and teachers facilitating learning by asking probing questions, but otherwise observing students as they grapple with ideas and probe one another's thinking. By grade 4, the students are expected to handle such academic tasks as peer editing that require high levels of proficiency in both English and Spanish. They are able to critique and offer feedback to one another on their written work. This emphasis on dialogic learning helps students develop critical thinking and oral language skills. Alfaro and colleagues (2014) report that the benefits to students are substantial, and students learn how to express themselves fluently in language that is academically appropriate.

The authors of the CVLCC case study are cautious about claiming that the experience at this one dual language school can be generalized to other schools facing the challenges of ELs' linguistically and culturally complex learning. CVLCC nevertheless shows what is possible when school leadership, teacher collaboration, and classroom instruction, all connected with a local teacher preparation institution, are aligned to support the deep learning of ELs.

---

[a]Every school in California is required by state law to publish a School Accountability Report Card (SARC). These data are from Chula Vista's 2013-2014 SARC, which was published during the 2014-2015 school year. Available: http://schools.cvesd.org/schools/cvlcc/Documents/_2014_School_Accountability_Report_Card_Chula_Vista_Learning_Community_Charter_Elementary_School.pdf [January 20, 2017].

[b]The school relies on the Freirean philosophy (1970) in its professional development program.

[c]California Department of Education: Academic Performance Index (API) Report 3 Year Average API School Report. Available: http://www.cde.ca.gov/ta/ac/ap/apireports.asp [September 28, 2016].

THE DEVELOPMENT OF ORAL LANGUAGE PROFICIENCY
IN ENGLISH LEARNERS IN GRADES K-12

This section reviews the research on instructional methods intended to develop oral English proficiency in ELs. The committee defines oral language proficiency as both receptive and expressive oral language, as well as specific aspects of oral language including phonology, oral vocabulary, morphology, grammar, discourse features, and pragmatic skills (August and Shanahan, 2006). There is some theoretical basis for this definition. Oral language differs from written language because of the differences between the physical nature of speech and writing. Speech provides auditory information, while writing provides visual information; speech is temporary, while writing is permanent; and speech has prosodic features (rhythm, stress, and intonation) that writing does not (Schallert et al., 1971). The committee also includes multiple aspects of oral language in one construct because recent empirical research indicates that all the frequently tested oral language constructs (including phonological awareness) cluster together, at least until about grade 3, when there is a split between lexical and grammatical features (Foorman et al., 2015; Language and Reading Research Consortium, 2015). Findings from this research appear to indicate that children learn words and patterns for combining words from the same social interactions. The words are analyzed, recognized, and stored as phonological patterns, but they are associated with information about co-occurrences that give grammatical information (e.g., nouns follow "a" and "the"; verbs take "ed"), so although the trajectory to mastery may be different for different elements of the system, the interconnections are there from the beginning.

The committee focused on oral language proficiency as a construct because of its important role in content area learning for ELs (August and Shanahan, 2006; Saunders et al., 2013). Evidence for its importance comes from the effect sizes for literacy outcomes for ELs compared with English-proficient students. In a review of the literature on literacy development, the effect sizes for EL outcomes were lower and more variable than those for English-proficient students exposed to the same literacy interventions, and sizable positive reading comprehension outcomes for ELs across the studies were relatively rare (August and Shanahan, 2006, p. 447). This led the authors to hypothesize that ELs' limited oral proficiency was impeding their ability to benefit from the literacy instructional routines, especially those focused on text-level skills such as reading comprehension.

The studies in this review measured phonological awareness, oral reading fluency and accuracy, receptive and expressive vocabulary, listening comprehension, grammar and syntax, and other linguistic features of English. Interventions had to focus wholly or in part on developing oral language proficiency and also had to include outcome measures of oral language proficiency. Other parameters for inclusion were that studies focused on students in grades K-12 who were learning English as a second language in the United States or other countries where English is the national language. The committee drew on studies located through systematic database searches of peer-reviewed journals using keywords for the parameters of interest; on intervention studies reported in previous syntheses that focused on instructed second language learning (e.g., Ammar and Spada, 2006; Carrier, 2003; Greenfader et al., 2015; Mackey and Oliver, 2002; O'Brien, 2007; Saunders et al., 2006; Tong et al., 2008); and on studies focused on developing oral proficiency as a component of reading or language arts instruction (e.g., Calhoon et al., 2007; Crevecoeur et al., 2014; Scientific Learning Corporation, 2004; Silverman and Hines, 2009; Solari and Gerber, 2008; Uchikoshi, 2005; Vaughn et al., 2006a, 2006b).

The committee found very few studies that met these parameters. Most studies that focused on instructed second language proficiency cited in previous syntheses (Dixon et al., 2012; Ellis, 2005; Jeon, 2007; Norris and Ortega, 2000; Saunders et al., 2013; Saunders and O'Brien, 2006; Taguchi, 2015) were conducted with adult learners or learners who were children acquiring foreign or other-than-English second languages, precluding their inclusion in this review. Some studies focused on developing these skills in ELs but did not measure these constructs as outcomes (e.g., August et al., 2009, 2014; Lesaux et al., 2010, 2014), in many cases because the studies included older children in the samples, and as children grow older, they are given assessments that require reading and writing. It is important that future intervention studies focused in part on oral language development measure it as an outcome.

From the very limited available research, the committee draws tentative inferences about the kinds of instructional practices that are beneficial for promoting oral language proficiency. Before reviewing findings related to promising practices, it is important to note that while some of the studies included in this review encouraged the kinds of classroom discourse that are aligned with new language proficiency standards (e.g., comprehending classroom discourse; speaking about grade-appropriate complex literacy and informal texts and topics; constructing grade-appropriate oral claims and supporting them with evidence; and adapting language choices to purpose, task, and audience when speaking), some did not, and virtually no studies measured ELs' discourse in these areas.

Recommended Instructional Practices to Develop Oral Language Proficiency

Practice 1: Provide Specialized Instruction Focused on Components of Oral Proficiency

Across the studies included in this review, explicit instruction in oral language components was found to be beneficial; it led to students acquiring these component skills to higher levels relative to students in the control groups who were not exposed to the interventions. ELs in the primary grades who were struggling readers benefited from instruction that developed their phonological awareness skills (e.g., Ransford-Kaldon et al., 2010; Scientific Learning Corporation, 2004; Solari and Gerber, 2008; Vaughn et al., 2006a). In one study (Vaughn et al., 2006a), this was the case for instruction in English as well as Spanish. The promising practices in these studies provided practice in phoneme discrimination, phoneme segmentation, and blending.

Explicit in-depth vocabulary teaching was beneficial for developing vocabulary knowledge and skills. For example, two studies that focused on kindergarten children (Crevecoeur et al., 2014; Silverman and Hines, 2009) provided direct instruction of vocabulary in the context of story reading. The Crevecoeur et al. (2014) study explored the effects of multimedia enhanced instruction in the form of videos aligned with the book themes (habitats). It found that the multimedia support had a positive effect on vocabulary acquisition for ELs but had no such effect for students who were English-proficient.

Several studies focused on text-level skills such as listening comprehension. One study (Uchikoshi, 2005) was successful in building kindergarten ELs' auditory comprehension and narrative skills through exposure to a high-quality children's television program that presented stories with a plot, conflict, and resolution. Narrative skills were measured by the number of words and mean clause length in stories children told based on slides that represented the story plot. Children's stories also were coded for story structure, number of main events, evaluation, temporality, reference, and storybook language. A second study conducted with kindergarteners (Solari and Gerber, 2008) found that instruction in summarizing text, identifying the main ideas in text, recalling textual facts, and making predictions and inferences resulted in improvements in listening comprehension (Solari and Gerber, 2008).

A third study (Greenfader et al., 2015) that improved the speaking skills of ELs in grades K-2 implemented a year-long drama and creative movement intervention that used movement, gesture, and expression to stimulate engaging in English verbal interactions. Language skills targeted were vocabulary, dialoging, story construction, and story recall. The students in the treatment group outperformed those in the control group who did not receive the intervention on the California English Language Development Test, a standardized language proficiency test used throughout California. Findings from this study also indicate that ELs with the most limited abilities at baseline benefited the most. A fourth study (Tong et al., 2008) made enhancements to two types of language instruction educational programs—transitional bilingual programs and structured immersion programs. A multifaceted approach was used that included daily tutorials in intensive English, storytelling and retelling that emphasized higher-order thinking skills, and a teacher-directed academic oral language activity. ELs in the intervention developed oral language proficiency (indexed by measure of expressive vocabulary as well as listening comprehension) at faster rates than students in the control groups.

A fifth study (Scientific Learning Corporation, 2004) was successful in building the auditory comprehension of elementary school ELs who were identified as at risk through Fast ForWord, an adaptive computer training program that uses games to train acoustic reception abilities and improve semantic and syntactic skills. In a sixth exploratory study, high school ELs who participated in listening strategy instruction (Carrier, 2003) showed significant improvements between pre-and posttests in discrete and video listening ability on assessments that measured discrete and video listening skills.

Several themes emerge from the above studies that are consistent with previous reviews of instructed second language acquisition (Ellis, 2005; Saunders and Goldenberg, 2010). First, as noted above, specialized instruction in components of oral language proficiency led to better outcomes for students in intervention groups compared with controls. Second, in most of the studies, oral language components were taught explicitly. Third, while this was the case, in these studies the language components were taught in language-rich environments such as read-alouds of narrative and informational texts (e.g., Crevecoeur et al., 2014). Finally, efforts were made to address the specialized needs of ELs learning content in a second language. Instruction in English was made comprehensible through such methods as multimedia use (Silverman and Hines, 2009); children's television (e.g., Uckikoshi, 2005); on-screen animation (e.g., Scientific Learning Corporation, 2004); movements and gestures (e.g., Greenfader et al., 2015); dramatization and movement (e.g., Tong et al., 2008); ongoing clarification of word meanings in multiple contexts before, during, and after reading (e.g., Crevecoeur et al., 2014); and ongoing questioning and discussion about the content presented (e.g., Solari and Gerber, 2008; Tong et al., 2008).

Practice 2: Provide Opportunities for Interaction with Speakers Proficient in the Learner's Second Language

Reviews of instructed second language learning (Dixon et al., 2012; Ellis, 2005; Saunders and Goldenberg, 2010) highlight the importance of interaction between second language learners and learners proficient in their second language. Several of the studies cited in the previous section provided structured opportunities for ELs to engage with English-proficient speakers (e.g., Calhoon et al., 2007; Silverman and Hines, 2009; Solari and Gerber, 2008). In one study (Greenfader et al., 2015), part of the lesson was dedicated to peer-to-peer interactions involving discussion and dramatization related to stories that had been read. Speaking is important because it generates feedback, forces syntactic processing, and challenges students to engage at higher proficiency levels (Johnson and Swain, 1997; Saunders and Goldenberg, 2010). It also generates more input, and substantial differences in the rate of second language acquisition are related to the amount and quality of the input students receive (Ellis, 2012).

A qualitative study by O'Day (2009) found that while coefficients for opportunities to engage in discussion with peers in the classroom are positive for both ELs and English-proficient students with regard to reading comprehension, the magnitude is small and insignificant for English-proficient students but large and significant for ELs. Some evidence suggests that for peer interactive activities to be effective, they must be carefully planned and carried out (Saunders and Goldenberg, 2010).

Practice 3: Engage in Interactional Feedback

The relationship between interactional feedback and second language learning has been an important focus of research. While many of the studies reviewed created opportunities for interaction between ELs and native English speakers, two studies explicitly examined the types of interactional feedback during conversational interactions that support ELs' language development. One study (Ammar and Spada, 2006) provides evidence that corrective feedback is beneficial. This quasi-experimental study investigated the benefits of two corrective feedback techniques—recasts and prompts—for 6th-grade ELs in Montreal acquiring English (Ammar and Spada, 2006). The intervention targeted third-person possessive determiners, "his" and "her," a difficult aspect of English grammar for French ELs. One group was a control group, one group received corrective feedback from the teacher in the form of recasts, and the third group received corrective feedback from the teacher in the form of prompts. All three groups benefited, but the experimental groups benefited the most. An interesting finding is that high-proficiency learners benefited equally from recasts and prompts, but low-proficiency learners benefited significantly more from prompts than recasts.

A second study (Mackey and Oliver, 2002) explored the effects of interactional feedback on the language development of 22 ELs in an intensive ESL center in Perth, Australia. The children ranged from ages 8 to 12 and were from a variety of L1 backgrounds. The children carried out communicative tasks in dyads with adult native English speakers. The experimental group received interactional feedback in response to their non-target-like production of question forms. That is, in the interaction and feedback group, children were engaged in tasks that provided context for the targeted structure to occur (e.g., story completion, picture sequencing). The child learners asked whatever questions were necessary to carry out the task, and the native speakers answered their questions and asked their own when necessary. Interactional feedback, including negotiation and recasts, was provided to the child learners. The control group carried out the same tasks as the interaction group but did not receive feedback. Results showed that the experimental group improved more than the control group in terms of question formation.

Practice 4: Dedicate Time for Instruction Focused on Oral English Proficiency

While research cited at the beginning of this section (August and Shanahan, 2006) suggests that oral language development is important in helping ELs succeed in text-level literacy skills (e.g., comprehension), several studies suggest that a daily block of time focused on the development of oral English language proficiency can be beneficial. One study (Saunders et al., 2006) found small positive effects on oral language proficiency for kindergarten children who received oral English language proficiency instruction during a separate block of time compared with similar children who received oral language proficiency instruction that was integrated with language arts instruction. A second study (O'Brien, 2007) found that 1st-grade Spanish-speaking ELs who received English language instruction in a separate English language development block using an explicit English language proficiency program outperformed ELs who were learning English language proficiency only as part of their language arts program. In a third study (Tong et al., 2008), a separate block of time in kindergarten and 1st grade was focused on direct teaching of English. ELs in this study outperformed control group students who did not have a separate block of time. It should be noted that this additional time block was only one component of a multifaceted approach to developing oral English language proficiency in ELs. While the research reviewed here indicates that additional time dedicated to developing oral language English language proficiency is beneficial, additional research would help clarify whether differential outcomes are attributable to a separate time block or such associated factors as fewer students, more homogeneity in classroom composition, method of instruction, or increased time or dosage itself.

Interpreting the Research

In interpreting findings from the studies reviewed above, it is important to keep in mind that factors other than the instructional method itself influence the acquisition of oral language proficiency in school-age ELs (see Chapter 6). These factors include individual, family, and teacher characteristics (e.g., proficiency in the language of instruction, teaching experience and training); school and community contexts; the attributes of the assessments used to measure student outcomes; and whether the language acquired is a national or foreign language. The committee controlled for some of these factors by focusing on children who are learning English as a second language in countries where English is the national language. Other factors not controlled for completely in the studies cited also influence acquisition, including, for instance, children's initial levels of proficiency in their L1 and English, home language literacy practices (e.g., Roberts, 2008), district and school support for instructed second language acquisition (August and Shanahan, 2006); and the specific types and characteristics of the linguistic features being taught (Boers and Lindstromberg, 2012) and measured as outcomes (Norris and Ortega, 2000).

DISTRICT-WIDE PRACTICES RELATED TO THE EDUCATIONAL PROGRESS OF ENGLISH LEARNERS

American education is characterized by its localism—there are nearly 13,500 school districts in the United States.[2] Whereas states have authority over education, with a limited federal role (see Chapter 2), local school districts are where both federal and state policies are implemented, and district implementation becomes the prevailing education policy experienced by students. Available studies typically do not identify district factors that will help educators serve their ELs more effectively (Coleman and Goldenberg, 2010). However, having a coherent academic program in which administrators and teachers are focused on doing whatever it takes to ensure ELs' academic success is the key overarching factor across studies (Coleman and Goldenberg, 2010). This section describes two district-wide efforts that

---

[2] According to the National Center for Education Statistics' data for the 2013-2014 school year, see http://nces.ed.gov/programs/digest/d15/tables/dt15_214.30.asp?current=yes [September 28, 2016].

improved outcomes for ELs. In one district, a mainly English approach was used; in the other, ELs were instructed bilingually.

Sanger Unified School District, California (K-12)

The first district example is the Sanger Unified School District. In 2004, Sanger was one of California's 98 lowest-performing districts. In addition, the child poverty rate in California's Central Valley was two to three times the national average. Fully 84 percent of the school district's students were children of color, and 73 percent were living in poverty in 2010-2011; 22 percent of students were ELs. By 2011-2012, Sanger was one of the most improved districts in California (David and Talbert, 2012). Its ELs outperformed the state on gains in percentage of proficient or advanced on the California Standards Test (CST) in English language acquisition and math. This increase was almost double the state gain. In English language arts, Sanger ELs' scores increased by 38 percentage points (from 11% to 49%) versus 20 points for the state (19% to 3%). In math, Sanger ELs' scores increased by 43 percentage points (from 19% to 62%) versus 22 points for the state (27% to 49%). Gains for Sanger's Hispanic students, students with disabilities, and socioeconomically disadvantaged students also were roughly double the state's gains from 2003 to 2011 (David and Talbert, 2012).

In 2004, seven of Sanger's schools and the district were deemed in need of improvement under provisions of the No Child Left Behind Act. David and Talbert (2012) point out that prior to the improvement efforts, the district's schools varied widely in their instructional approaches, with teachers functioning as "independent contractors," guided by individual understandings of what constituted good practice. Further, the authors report that "adults (in the district) tend[ed] to blame the students and their families for poor academic performance" (p. 19).

Confronting Sanger's own culture of low expectations for ELs was the first step in the district's reform effort. The leadership team, beginning with the superintendent, decided that the focus had to change from the adults to the students, involving a major shift in the district's culture. Superintendent Marc Johnson's belief became the district's mantra: "The only reason an adult is in this district is because it is a position that is necessary to support school learning" (p. 19). With that as a guiding premise, the blame for low student performance was placed on adults' failure to provide adequate supports for learning.

Sanger's transformation did not happen overnight. Its leadership recognized that any real improvement in students' academic learning would require attention first to the adults who had to change their own attitudes, understandings, and practices. That meant shared responsibility—

"reciprocal accountability"—for necessary and continuous effort in delving more deeply into the work, being informed by analyses of student learning data, basing decisions about adjustments in instruction on these analyses, and ensuring that teachers were supported within professional learning communities where they could develop their capacity together. To sustain the effort, the district had to rely on growing its own leadership capacity within the ranks of the current educators who had been immersed in the work of the district and who understood local conditions.

A major shift involved how adults thought about what students needed to succeed and their expectations for students' capacities to learn. Thus, diagnosing student needs and addressing them instructionally led to a mind shift that involved seeing instruction as supporting students' academic development rather than as remediation for their lack of English language proficiency. Educators also were engaged in a developmental process and sought support from colleagues and administrators for improving their practices.

The district ultimately chose instructional strategies that were hardly revolutionary or innovative, a direct instruction approach "grounded in Madeleine Hunter's elements of effective lessons," which it adopted and adapted with training and support from Data Works. The success of this approach, which involves presenting information, modeling, checking for understanding, guided practice, closure, and independent practice, convinced the district that this was a suitable strategy for ELs requiring language support.

The most important aspect of this instructional strategy was its insistence on students working with grade-level appropriate materials rather than materials geared to their current level of English proficiency. The argument was that ELs would never reach grade-level proficiency levels, let alone exceed them, if they were taught using lower-level materials. To implement this approach required teacher-directed instruction with guided and independent practice.

An important element of this approach was that English language development support was provided according to proficiency levels during a specially designated English language development period each day; the main differentiation in these leveled classes was the degree of instructional support and scaffolding rather than the use of leveled materials. Additionally, the response to intervention approach the district had in place for its special education students was expanded to provide additional support for students, including ELs, who required more assistance than could be provided through regular instructional activities. Intensive instructional support was provided to students in small groups defined by need rather than by such categories as EL or special education. Students who needed help to strengthen decoding skills, for example, were grouped together for targeted intervention for as long as needed, and were then moved out of that group when the ongoing assessments indicated they no longer needed such help.

Union City School District, New Jersey (pre-K to 12)

The rebirth of the Union City School District began with a 1-year reprieve from the state to set things right (Kirp, 2013). By school year 2013-2014, 95 percent of all students in the district had achieved proficiency (proficient plus advanced) both in English language arts and in math, and the high school had achieved a 100 percent graduation rate. At the time, the district's 13 schools served 11,457 students, 95.7 percent of whom were Hispanic, mainly immigrants from Cuba, the Dominican Republic, and Central America. Twenty-four percent were designated ELs, and 95 percent were from low-income families, as indicated by participation in the free and reduced-price lunch program.

In education, everything connects, from the crucible of the classroom, to the interplay among teachers, to the principal's skills as a leader, to the superintendent's success in creating a coherent system from a host of separate schools, to politicians' role in setting the limits of a school district's autonomy. The first step in Union City's rebirth was the selection of an administrator who was wise in the ways of the district, having served as its bilingual education supervisor in the past, to redesign the district's educational plan instead of bringing in outside consultants for the job. He, in turn, engaged several teachers from the district with expertise in math, science, and English language arts to create a curriculum guided by the state's standards. The curriculum redesign team reviewed the research on teaching and learning and insisted on one curriculum for everyone.

With state funding, the district offered free full-day pre-K programs with rich language and learning experiences both in students' L1 and in English. Students at varying levels of skill and language proficiency worked on projects in groups at learning centers. Differentiated support was provided in these small groups according to need.

For the district to succeed, collaboration was necessary. A culture of caring and mutual respect was established among administrators and teachers at all levels, among teachers within schools, between teachers and students, and between educators and parents. Teachers recognized that in addition to instructional support, the children needed understanding, patience, and emotional support. They provided support that helped initially disruptive and uncooperative students gradually advance academically and take responsibility for helping fellow students in need of academic and emotional support.

The district's turnaround was all the more impressive in that it relied not on replacing district personnel but on changing the beliefs and attitudes of teachers and administrators who were already working in the district. The adoption of a new district-wide common curriculum and a pedagogical approach that allowed students to learn at their own pace was not an easy or quick process.

Kirp (2013, p. 208) concludes his study of Union City's turnaround of its schools by identifying the following core principles:

- putting students first and at the center of decision making;
- investing in quality pre-K programs;
- relying on a rigorous, consistent, and integrated curriculum implemented by all teachers;
- diagnosing problems and finding solutions based on data on learning;
- building a culture that emphasizes high expectations of students and mutual respect between educators and students and their families;
- valuing stability and avoiding political drama; and
- engaging in continuous improvement of classroom instruction.

Summary

The following promising practices emerge from the school and district profiles described above:

- Administrative leadership at the district and school levels takes responsibility for initiating and sustaining instructional programs and practices that support the full academic development of all students, including ELs.
- ELs are recognized as capable of learning whatever society expects all children to learn in school rather than as incapable of handling the school's curriculum until they master English. This is a fundamental epistemological difference between schools that educate ELs successfully and those that do not.
- Socioemotional support is provided for both teachers and students through the creation of learning communities. In the successful districts and schools described above, administrators recognized that educating students with complex and diverse needs could be very challenging for teachers, emotionally and physically. They, like their students, required collegial support from fellow teachers and administrators to accomplish all they were expected to do.
- Teachers are encouraged to work collaboratively and support one another to improve instruction. In the cases described above, cross-disciplinary endeavors in planning and integrating instruction were

critical in supporting language and literacy development across the curriculum.

- Language-rich classroom and school environments are promoted in which communication and self-expression are encouraged.
- Teachers are linguistically, culturally, and pedagogically prepared to meet the academic and sociocultural needs of ELs.
- Instruction is adapted based on frequent analysis of student performance in formative and summative assessments.
- School and community partnerships are encouraged to augment and enrich classroom-based learning.

FAMILY ENGAGEMENT IN ENGLISH LEARNERS' EDUCATION

This section describes the ways in which families engage with schools, the opportunities associated with involving families in the education of their EL children, and state and district practices for meeting these challenges. Family engagement in children's education and in their schools can include attending parent-teacher conferences; engaging in communications among families, students, educators, and schools about the students or school programs; participating in the classroom or in school activities; becoming involved in school decisions; and providing familial support for academic achievement by emphasizing high aspirations and providing a home environment that supports learning outside of school (Epstein et al., 2002; Fan and Chen, 2001; National Research Council and Institute of Medicine, 1997; Noel et al., 2016; Wilder, 2014).

The ways in which families engage with their children's education change as children grow older—from talking, reading, and playing with the children when they are very young; to supporting them throughout their primary, middle, and high school years; to engaging in various activities both in school and at home, as well as in community and youth organizations (Harvard Family Research Project, 2014; Sibley and Dearing, 2014). In the middle and high school years, parent-teacher conferences and communications to families continue, but family roles evolve from providing direct support to encouraging their children to value education, having high aspirations for postsecondary education, and being engaged in classrooms and school activities (see the vignette in Box 7-4).

Additionally, the level of family engagement tends to decline as students move from the elementary grades to the succeeding levels of their education (Epstein and Sheldon, 2006). Part of this decline is explained by long-standing school policies and beliefs that as students grow older and more independent of their families, family activities to support classroom learning are less important than they are in elementary school. However, families of middle and high school students can be advocates for their

---

BOX 7-4
The Role of the Family in Supporting Learning
English in Middle and High Schools

Daylin Cu Ramirez, a high school junior from Alexandria, Virginia, emigrated from Guatemala to the United States with her family when she was in middle school. Sometimes she lived with her aunt in the United States, who spoke both English and Spanish and encouraged Ramirez to use English. "She said, 'You have to speak the little bit that you know, because how are you going to learn if you don't try?' And she still, when I'm with her and in the house and I'm speaking Spanish, she says, 'You have to speak English.' She was pushing me to speak, and she's still doing that."

Rameriz's cousin had been born in the United States, so he spoke both English and Spanish. "Sometimes he forgot that we don't speak English and he'd speak English to us. It was like, I don't know how to answer to him, because he doesn't practice very well the Spanish. So sometimes my uncle would say, 'You have to speak English to your cousin.'" Ramirez's younger sister also talked with her in English, which Ramirez welcomed. "When you're out with somebody that you have confidence to speak with them, you feel better than speaking to someone you don't know." Ramirez's older brother had dropped out of school to go to work, and he, too, has been learning English from their younger sister.

SOURCE: The vignette presented here is from a young adult who served on a panel on growing up multilingual at a public information-gathering session convened by the committee on May 28, 2015. She provided written permission to include her story, quotes, and name.

---

children and be assisted in accessing resources and information to help their children stay on track and meet the requirements for postsecondary institutions, whether they be 4-year colleges, apprenticeships, or workforce development programs.

Research indicates that engagement of families, including both English-speaking families and families of ELs, is associated with positive student outcomes, such as higher grades and test scores, higher language proficiency, better social skills, increased high school graduation rates, and enrollment in postsecondary education (Ferguson, 2008; Henderson and Mapp, 2002; Lindholm-Leary, 2015). Notably, immigrant parents in particular place a high value on the education of their children (Cooper et al., 1994) and on learning English themselves to provide better economic resources for their families (Public Agenda, 1998). More research is needed to examine the specific attributes of family engagement that support ELs at different grade levels and the influence of family engagement at each of these levels on ELs' educational progress, particularly at the middle and high school levels.

Barriers to Family Engagement

Despite the potential benefits of family engagement, results from a national survey among families of K-12 students indicate lower rates of family engagement in school among EL than among English-speaking families (Noel et al., 2016). Among students with English-speaking parents, 77 percent had parents who reported attending a regularly scheduled parent-teacher conference, compared with 69 percent of students who had parents either one or both of whom spoke another language (Noel et al., 2015). Similarly, 78 percent of students with English-speaking parents had parents who reported attending a school or class event, and 45 percent had parents who volunteered, compared with only 62 percent and 29 percent, respectively, among EL families.

Barriers to family engagement for EL families include the misguided perception by school personnel that the families of ELs are disinterested in the education of their children (Ramirez, 2003; Shim, 2013; Souto-Manning and Swick, 2006; Xiong and Obiakor, 2013). For example, in interviews conducted with 37 teachers and assistant teachers in an elementary school, Souto-Manning and Swick (2006) found that most of the teachers attributed students' lower performance to the parents' lack of caring about their children's education. To the contrary, studies indicate that the parents of ELs are just as likely as the parents of non-ELs to report that they want their children to succeed in school, understand the importance of school, and support their children's school experience (Cooper et al., 1994; Glick and White, 2004; Goldenberg et al., 2001; Ji and Koblinsky, 2009; Noel et al., 2015; Sibley and Dearing, 2014; Tobin et al., 2013).

There are also practical barriers to parent involvement in school activities, including time constraints due to work schedules, transportation, child care, and the scheduling of meetings or events during times when families are unable to participate (Best and Dunlap, 2012; Rah et al., 2009; Tinkler, 2002; Tucker, 2014). In addition, schools may not be able to provide translation for the variety of languages spoken by families of ELs, especially those spoken by a small number of families (Tucker, 2014).

Some parents perceive that their education or proficiency in English is insufficient for them to assist in the classroom and may also find it difficult to communicate with teachers and school staff (Lindholm-Leary, 2001; Shim, 2013; Westrich and Strobel, 2013; Xiong and Obiakor, 2013) (see Box 7-5). Further, immigrant families may not understand a school system that is different from their own experiences in their countries of origin and may fear involvement because of their undocumented status (Panferov, 2010; Souto-Manning and Swick, 2006; Tarasawa and Waggoner, 2015; Waterman and Harry, 2008). EL families also report receiving less communication from their schools relative to non-EL families. In the same national

---

BOX 7-5
Parent Perspectives*

Before I wanted to help in the classrooms but I felt ashamed or embarrassed and felt like I would not be of value or that I did not have anything to offer. I thought to myself, how can I help? But then [after training to be a volunteer] what I learned is that I am valuable and I have a lot to offer and even though I did not go to school very much, . . . four months of first grade and I did not go beyond that, I learned that there is a lot I can do to help and I am glad to be a volunteer here. Even when my kids no longer go here I still plan to help [the school].

I think what we should really change is our roots of where we come from. As Latino families we often think of well, you leave the child at school and let the teacher do all the work. But what we are learning here is this school is about collaboration and what we want is for our children to be more successful than we were. We can do that by talking to them and telling them the importance of education, and that is important, but also as ourselves, we need to make the effort and we need to be an example for them that you can do something if you try hard.

---

*Presented by parents during focus groups conducted by committee members as part of the site visits for this study.

---

survey mentioned above (Noel et al., 2016), 88 percent of English-speaking households had parents who reported receiving written communications from the school, compared with 81 percent of households without English-speaking adults. Similarly, 59 percent of the total number of students, both in English- and non-English-speaking households, had parents who reported receiving written communications specifically about their child, compared with 46 percent of households without English-speaking adults.

Knowledge and Skills to Build Positive Relationships

For all families, regardless of language background, both the school and the family require knowledge and skills to build positive relationships (Mapp, 2012; Mapp and Kuttner, 2013). A recent review of 31 studies on family engagement[3] found that a welcoming environment encourages family-school partnerships (Ferguson, 2008). Providing information on how to navigate the school system, hiring a parent-community liaison capable of communicating with the families of ELs, providing adult education

---

[3]Reviewed studies included those that focused on families with ELs and on a broad range of factors, including varied cultural and ethnic populations.

programs including English language classes for families, and establishing effective two-way communications were found to help build partnerships (Office of the Education Ombudsman, 2012; Rah et al., 2009; Tucker, 2014; Westrich and Strobel, 2013). The use of technology in the form of texting educational messages to parents has also been shown to be an effective way to provide families with regular tips to support the language development of young children in their own languages (Loeb and York, 2016).

At the state and district levels, findings from a 50-state survey (Education Commission of the States, 2015) indicate that states use a variety of levers to promote the engagement of families that include ELs. Ten of the 13 states that reported engagement policies for families with ELs had parent advisory committees at the district and/or school level. Examples of other state and district levers included district and school orientation sessions on state standards, assessments, school expectations, and general program requirements for EL programs for parents of students newly identified as ELs (New York); school support teams that included parents of ELs, in which ELs could discuss their educational and language needs (North Dakota); and the use of district-level language proficiency committees (in districts with special programming for ELs), which included a professional bilingual educator, a professional transitional language coordinator, a parent of an EL, and a campus administrator to review all pertinent information on ELs, make recommendations regarding program placement and advancement, review each EL's progress at the end of the school year, monitor the progress of former ELs, and determine the appropriateness of programs that extend beyond the school year (Texas).

CONCLUSIONS

Conclusion 7-1: Syntheses of evaluation studies that compare outcomes for English learners (ELs) instructed in English-only programs with outcomes for ELs instructed bilingually find either that there is no difference in outcomes measured in English or that ELs in bilingual programs outperform ELs instructed only in English. Two recent studies that followed students for sufficient time to gauge longer-term effects of language of instruction on EL outcomes find benefits for bilingual compared with English-only approaches.

Conclusion 7-2: The following characteristics of instructional programs support English learners' oral language development: specialized instruction focused on components of oral language proficiency, opportunities for interaction with speakers proficient in the second language, feedback to students during conversational interactions, and dedicated time for instruction focused on oral English proficiency.

Conclusion 7-3: Despite the potential benefits of family engagement in schools, results from a national survey indicate lower rates of family engagement in K-12 schools for English learner (EL) families relative to English-speaking families. Promising methods for engaging families include creating a welcoming environment, providing orientation programs, using technology to enhance two-way communication, instituting district- and school-level parent advisory committees and school support teams that include parents of ELs to support ELs' academic success and emotional well-being, and instituting adult education programs for parents of ELs.

Conclusion 7-4: Case studies of districts and schools that demonstrate their effectiveness in educating English learners (ELs) find that such districts and schools are led by superintendents and principals who foster a common commitment to high expectations for all students; invest in teacher collaboration and ongoing, focused professional development; implement a coherent instructional program for students; attend to the needs of ELs who are struggling to meet grade-level expectations; and engage families and communities.

BIBLIOGRAPHY

Alfaro, C., Durán, R., Hunt, A., and Aragón, M.J. (2014). Steps toward unifying dual language programs, common core state standards, and critical pedagogy: Oportunidades, estrategias y retos. *Association of Mexican-American Educators, 8*(2), 17-30.

Ammar, A., and Spada, N. (2006). One size fits all?: Recasts, prompts, and L2 learning. *Studies in Second Language Acquisition, 28*(4), 543-574.

August, D., and Erickson, F. (2006). Qualitative studies of classroom and school practices. In D. August and T. Shanahan (Ed.), *Developing Literacy in Second-Language Learners: Report of the National Literacy Panel on Language-Minority Children and Youth* (pp. 489-522). Mahwah, NJ: Lawrence Erlbaum Associates.

August, D., and Shanahan, T. (2006). *Developing Literacy in Second Language Learners: Report of the National Literacy Panel on Language Minority Children and Youth.* Mahwah, NJ: Lawrence Erlbaum Associates.

August, D., Branum-Martin, L., Cardenas-Hagan, E., and Francis, D.J. (2009). The impact of an instructional intervention on the science and language learning of middle grade English language learners. *Journal of Research on Educational Effectiveness, 2*(4), 345-376.

August, D., Branum-Martin, L., Cárdenas-Hagan, E., Francis, D.J., Powell, J., Moore, S., and Haynes, E.F. (2014). Helping ELLs meet the common core state standards for literacy in science: The impact of an instructional intervention focused on academic language. *Journal of Research on Educational Effectiveness, 7*(1), 54-82.

Bailey, A.L. (2007). *The Language Demands of School: Putting Academic English to the Test.* New Haven, CT: Yale University Press.

Baker, S., Lesaux, N., Jayanthi, M., Dimino, J., Proctor, C.P., Morris, J., Gersten, R. Haymond, K., Kieffer, M.J., Linan-Thompson, S., and Newman-Gonchar, R. (2014). *Teaching Academic Content and Literacy to English Learners in Elementary and Middle School.* NCEE 2014-4012. Washington, DC: National Center for Education Evaluation and Regional Assistance, Institute of Education Sciences, U.S. Department of Education.

Barnhardt, R., and Kawagley, A.O. (2005). Indigenous knowledge systems and Alaska Native ways of knowing. *Anthropology and Education Quarterly, 36*(1), 8-23.

Best, J., and Dunlap, A. (2012). *Student Achievement Beyond the Classroom: Engaging Families and Communities.* Denver, CO: Mid-Continent Research for Education and Learning.

Black, P., and Wiliam, D. (1998). Assessment and classroom learning. *Assessment in Education: Principles, Policy and Practice, 5*(1), 7-74.

Boers, F., and Lindstromberg, S. (2012). Experimental and intervention studies on formulaic sequences in a second language. *Annual Review of Applied Linguistics, 32*, 83-110.

Boyle, A., August, D., Tabaku, L., Cole, S., and Simpson-Baird, A. (2015). *Dual Language Education Programs: Current State Policies and Practices.* Washington, DC: U.S. Department of Education, Office of English Language Acquisition.

Bunch, G.C. (2013). Pedagogical language knowledge: Preparing mainstream teachers for English learners in the new standards era. *Review of Research in Education, 37*(1), 298-341.

Burns, D.A. (2011). *Examining the Effect of an Overt Transition Intervention on the Reading Development of At-Risk English-Language Learners in First Grade.* Ph.D. Dissertation. Eugene: University of Oregon.

Calderón, M., Hertz-Lazarowitz, R., and Slavin, R. (1998). Effects of bilingual cooperative integrated reading and composition on students transitioning from Spanish to English reading. *Elementary School Journal, 99*(2), 153-165.

Calhoon, M.B., Al Otaiba, S., Cihak, D., King, A., and Avalos, A. (2007). Effects of a peer-mediated program on reading skill acquisition for two-way bilingual first-grade classrooms. *Learning Disability Quarterly, 30*(3), 169-184.

Cantrell, S.C., Burns, L.D., and Callaway, P. (2009). Middle- and high-school content area teachers' perceptions about literacy teaching and learning. *Literacy Research and Instruction, 48*(1), 76-94.

Carlo, M.S., August, D., Mclaughlin, B., Snow, C.E., Dressler, C., Lippman, D.N., Lively, T.J., and White, C.E. (2004). Closing the gap: Addressing the vocabulary needs of English-language learners in bilingual and mainstream classrooms. *RRQ Reading Research Quarterly, 39*(2), 188-215.

Carrier, K.A. (2003). Improving high school English language learners' second language listening through strategy instruction. *Bilingual Research Journal, 27*(3), 383-408.

Coleman, R., and Goldenberg, C. (2010). What does research say about effective practices for English learners? Part IV: Models for schools and districts. *Kappa Delta Pi Record, 46*(4), 156.

Cooper, C.R., Azmitia, M., Garcia, E.E., Ittel, A., Lopez, E., Rivera, L., and Martinez-Chavez, R. (1994). Aspirations of low-income Mexican American and European American parents for their children and adolescents. *New Directions for Child Development, 63*, 65-81.

Council of Chief State School Officers. (2014). *English Language Proficiency (ELP) Standards with Correspondences to K-12 English Language Arts (ELA), Mathematics, and Science Practices, K-12 ELA Standards, and 6-12 Literacy Standards.* Available: http://www.ccsso.org/Documents/Final%204_30%20ELPA21%20Standards(1).pdf [December 12, 2016].

Crevecoeur, Y.C., Coyne, M.D., and McCoach, D.B. (2014). English language learners and English-only learners' response to direct vocabulary instruction. *Reading and Writing Quarterly, 30*(1), 51-78.

Crosnoe, R. (2006). *Mexican Roots, American Schools. Helping Mexican Immigrant Children Succeed.* Stanford, CA: Stanford University Press.

Cummins, J. (2003). Challenging the construction of difference as deficit: Where are identity, intellect, imagination and power in the new regime of truth? In P.P. Trifonas (Ed.), *Pedagogies of Difference: Rethinking Education for Social Change* (pp. 39-58). New York: Routledge Falmer.

Daily, S., Burkhauser, M., and Halle, T. (2010). A review of school readiness practices in the United States: Early learning guidelines and assessments. *Child Trends: Early Childhood Highlights*, *1*(3). Available: http://www.childtrends.org/wp-content/uploads/2013/05/2010-14-SchoolReadinessStates.pdf [May 2017].

David, J.L., and Talbert, J.E. (2012). *Turning around a High-Poverty School District: Learning from Sanger Unified's Success.* Available: https://crceducation.stanford.edu/sites/default/files/sanger_turnaround_10-14-12.pdf [February 15, 2017].

Denton, C.A., Anthony, J.L., Parker, R., and Hasbrouck, J.E. (2004). Effects of two tutoring programs on the English reading development of Spanish-English bilingual students. *The Elementary School Journal*, *104*(4), 289-305.

Dixon, L.Q., Zhao, J., Shin, J.-Y., Wu, S., Su, J.-H., Burgess-Brigham, R., Gezer, M.U., and Snow, C. (2012). What we know about second language acquisition: A synthesis from four perspectives. *Review of Educational Research*, *82*(1), 5-60.

Dressler, C., and Kamil, M.L. (2006). First-and second-language literacy. In D. August and T. Shanahan (Eds.), *Developing Literacy in Second-Language Learners: Report of the National Literacy Panel on Language-Minority Children and Youth* (pp. 197-238). Mahwah, NJ: Lawrence Erlbaum Associates.

Dweck, C.S. (1999). *Self-Theories: Their Role in Motivation, Personality, and Development.* Philadelphia, PA: Psychology Press.

Dweck, C.S. (2007). *Mindset: The New Psychology of Success.* New York: Ballantine Books.

Echevarria, J., Richards-Tutor, C., Chinn, V.P., and Ratleff, P.A. (2011). Did they get it? The role of fidelity in teaching English learners. *Journal of Adolescent and Adult Literacy*, *54*(6), 425-434.

Education Commission of the States. (2015). *State-Level English Language Learner Policies.* Available: http://www.ecs.org/clearinghouse/01/17/92/11792.pdf [December 12, 2016].

Eisner, E. (2005). Back to whole. *Educational Leadership: The Whole Child*, *63*(1), 14-18.

Ellis, R. (2005). Principles of instructed language learning. *System*, *33*(2), 209-224.

Ellis, R. (2012). *Language Teaching Research and Language Pedagogy.* Hoboken, NJ: John Wiley and Sons.

Epstein, J.L., and Sheldon, S.B. (2006). Moving forward: Ideas for research on school, family, and community partnerships. In C.F. Conrad and R. Serlin (Eds.), *SAGE Handbook for Research in Education: Engaging Ideas and Enriching Inquiry* (pp. 117-138). Thousand Oaks, CA: SAGE Publications.

Epstein, J.L., Simon, M.G., Salinas, K.C., Jansom, N.R., and Van Voorhis, F.L. (2002). *School, Family, and Community Partnerships: Your Handbook for Action* (2nd ed.). Thousand Oaks, CA: Corwin Press.

Fan, X., and Chen, M. (2001). Parental involvement and students' academic achievement: A meta-analysis. *Educational Psychology Review*, *13*(1), 1-22.

Faulkner-Bond, M., Waring, S., Forte, E., Crenshaw, R.L., Tindle, K., and Belknap, B. (2012). *Language Instruction Educational Programs (LIEPs): A Review of the Foundational Literature.* Washington, DC: U.S. Department of Education, Office of Planning, Evaluation and Policy Development.

Ferguson, C. (2008). *The School-Family Connection: Looking at the Larger Picture: A Review of Current Literature.* Austin, TX: National Center for Family and Community Connections with Schools.

Fitzgerald, J., and Noblit, G. (2000). Balance in the making: Learning to read in an ethnically diverse first-grade classroom. *Journal of Educational Psychology, 92*(1), 3-22.

Foorman, B.R., Koon, S., Petscher, Y., Mitchell, A., and Truckenmiller, A. (2015). Examining general and specific factors in the dimensionality of oral language and reading in 4th-10th grades. *Journal of Educational Psychology, 107*(3), 884.

Francis, D., Lesaux, N., and August, D. (2006). Language of instruction. In D. August and T. Shanahan (Eds.), *Developing Literacy in Second-Language Learners* (pp. 365-413). Mahwah, NJ: Lawrence Erlbaum Associates.

García, O. (2009). Education, multilingualism and translanguaging in the 21st century. In A. Mohanty, M. Panda, R. Phillipson, and T. Skutnabb-Kangas (Eds.), *Multilingual Education for Social Justice: Globalising the Local* (pp. 140-158). New Delhi: Orient Blackswan.

Genesee, F., and Lindholm-Leary, K. (2012). The education of English language learners. *APA Educational Psychology Handbook, 3*, 499-526.

Gersten, R., Baker, S.K., Shanahan, T., Linan-Thompson, S., Collins, P., and Scarcella, R. (2007). *Effective Literacy and English Language Instruction for English Learners in the Elementary Grades. IES Practice Guide.* NCEE 2007-4011. Washington, DC: National Center for Education Evaluation and Regional Assistance, Institute of Education Sciences, U.S. Department of Education. Available: http://ies.ed.gov/ncee/pdf/20074011.pdf [November 16, 2016].

Gewertz, C. (2014). "Platooning" on the rise in early grades. *Education Week*, February 19.

Glick, J.E., and White, M.J. (2004). Post-secondary school participation of immigrant and native youth: The role of familial resources and educational expectations. *Social Science Research, 33*(2), 272-299.

Goldenberg, C., Gallimore, R., Reese, L., and Garnier, H. (2001). Cause or effect? A longitudinal study of immigrant Latino parents' aspirations and expectations, and their children's school performance. *American Educational Research Journal, 38*(3), 547-582.

Greene, J.P. (1997). A meta-analysis of the Rossell and Baker review of bilingual education research. *Bilingual Research Journal, 21*(2-3), 103-122.

Greenfader, C.M., Brouillette, L., and Farkas, G. (2015). Effect of a performing arts program on the oral language skills of young English learners. *Reading Research Quarterly, 50*(2), 185-203.

Gunn, B., Smolkowski, K., Biglan, A., and Black, C. (2002). Supplemental instruction in decoding skills for Hispanic and non-Hispanic students in early elementary school: A follow-up. *Journal of Special Education, 39*(2), 66-85.

Guthrie, J.T. (2004). Teaching for literacy engagement. *Journal of Literacy Research, 36*(1), 1-30.

Hansen-Thomas, H. (2008). Sheltered instruction: Best practices for ELLs in the mainstream. *Kapa Delta Pi Record, 44*(4), 165-169.

Harry, B., and Klingner, J. (2007). Discarding the deficit model. *Educational Leadership, 64*(5), 16-21.

Harvard Family Research Project. (2014). *Redefining Family Engagement for Student Success.* Cambridge, MA: Harvard Graduate School of Education.

Henderson, A.T., and Mapp, K.L. (2002). *A New Wave of Evidence: The Impact of School, Family, and Community Connections on Student Achievement.* Austin, TX: National Center for Family and Community Connections with Schools.

Hood, L. (2009). "Platooning" instruction: Districts weigh pros and cons of departmentalizing elementary schools. *Harvard Education Letter, 25*(6), 1-3.

Howard, E.R., Lindholm-Leary, K.J., Sugarman, J., Christian, D., and Rogers, D. (2007). *Guiding Principles for Dual Language Education.* Washington, DC: Center for Applied Linguistics.

Institute of Medicine and National Research Council. (2015). *Transforming the Workforce for Children Birth through Age 8: A Unifying Foundation.* L. Allen and B.B. Kelly (Eds.). Board on Children, Youth, and Families; Committee on the Science of Children Birth to Age 8: Deepening and Broadening the Foundation for Success. Washington, DC: The National Academies Press.

Jeon, K.S. (2007). Interaction-driven L2 learning: Characterizing linguistic development. In A. Mackey (Ed.), *Conversational Interaction in Second Language Acquisition: A Collection of Empirical Studies* (pp. 379-403). Oxford, UK: Oxford University Press.

Ji, C.S., and Koblinsky, S.A. (2009). Parent involvement in children's education: An exploratory study of urban, Chinese immigrant families. *Urban Education, 44*(6), 687-709.

Johnson, R.K., and Swain, M. (1997). *Immersion Education: International Perspectives.* Cambridge, NY: Cambridge University Press.

John-Steiner, V., and Mahn, H. (2012). Sociocultural approaches to learning and development: A Vygotskian Framework. *Educational Psychologist, 31*(3/4), 191-206.

Kim, J.S., Olson, C.B., Scarcella, R., Kramer, J., Pearson, M., Van Dyk, D., Collins, P., and Land, R.E. (2011). A randomized experiment of a cognitive strategies approach to text-based analytical writing for mainstreamed Latino English language learners in grades 6 to 12. *Journal of Research on Educational Effectiveness, 4*(3), 231-263.

Kirp, D.L. (2013). *Improbable Scholars: The Rebirth of a Great American School System and a Strategy for America's Schools.* New York: Oxford University Press

Language and Reading Research Consortium. (2015). The dimensionality of language in young children. *Child Development, 86*(6), 1948-1965.

Lara-Alecio, R., Tong, F., Irby, B.J., Guerrero, C., Huerta, M., and Fan, Y. (2012). The effect of an instructional intervention on middle school English learners' science and English. *Journal of Research in Science Teaching, 49*(8), 997-1011.

Lesaux, N.K., Kieffer, M.J., Faller, S.E., and Kelley, J.G. (2010). The effectiveness and ease of implementation of an academic vocabulary intervention for linguistically diverse students in urban middle schools. *Reading Research Quarterly, 45*(2), 196-228.

Lesaux, N.K., Kieffer, M.J., Kelley, J.G., and Harris, J.R. (2014). Effects of academic vocabulary instruction for linguistically diverse adolescents evidence from a randomized field trial. *American Educational Research Journal, 51*(6), 1159-1194.

Lesaux, N.K., Galloway, E.P., and Marietta, S.H. (2016). *Teaching Advanced Literacy Skills: A Guide for Leaders in Linguistically Diverse Schools.* New York: Guilford.

Liang, L.A., Peterson, C.A., and Graves, M.F. (2005). Investigating two approaches to fostering children's comprehension of literature. *Reading Psychology: An International Quarterly, 26*(4-5), 387-400.

Lindholm-Leary, K.J. (2001). *Dual Language Education.* Bristol, UK: Multilingual Matters.

Lindholm-Leary, K.J. (2015). *Sobrato Family Foundation Early Academic and Literacy Project After Five Full Years of Implementation: Final Research Report.* Cupertino, CA: Sobrato Family Foundation.

Lindholm-Leary, K.J., and Borsato, G. (2006). Academic achievement. In F. Genesee, K. Lindholm-Leary, W. Saunders, and D. Christian (Eds.), *Educating English Language Learners: A Synthesis of Research Evidence* (pp. 176-222). New York: Cambridge University Press.

Llosa, L., Lee, O., Jiang, F., Haas, A., O'Connor, C., Van Booven, C.D., and Kieffer, M.J. (2016). Impact of a large-scale science intervention focused on English language learners. *American Educational Research Journal American Educational Research Journal, 53*(2), 395-424.

Loeb, S., and York, B. (2016). *Helping Parents Help their Children.* Available: https://www.brookings.edu/research/helping-parents-help-their-children [September 30, 2016].

Mackey, A., and Oliver, R. (2002). Interactional feedback and children's L2 development. *System, 30*(4), 459-477.

Mapp, K.L. (2012). *Title I and Parent Involvement: Lessons from the Past, Recommendations for the Future.* Washington, DC: Center for American Progress and the American Enterprise Institute.

Mapp, K.L., and Kuttner, P. (2013). *Partners in Education: A Dual Capacity-Building Framework for Family-School Partnerships.* Available: https://www2.ed.gov/documents/family-community/partners-education.pdf [January 18, 2017].

McMaster, K.L., Kung, S.H., Han, I., and Cao, M. (2008). Peer-assisted learning strategies: A "Tier 1" approach to promoting English learners' response to intervention. *Exceptional Children*, 74(2), 194-214.

National Center for Learning Disabilities. (2006). *Transitioning to Kindergarten: School Readiness.* Available: http://www.aft.org/sites/default/files/t2k_schoolreadiness.pdf [February 2017].

National Research Council. (1984). *Development during Middle Childhood: The Years from Six to Twelve.* W.A. Collins (Ed.). Division of Behavioral and Social Sciences and Education, Commission on Behavioral and Social Sciences and Education, Panel to Review the Status of Basic Research on School-Age Children, Committee on Child Development Research and Public Policy. Washington, DC: National Academy Press.

National Research Council and Institute of Medicine. (1997). *Improving Schooling for Language-Minority Children: A Research Agenda.* Washington, DC: National Academy Press.

Nelson, J.R., Vadasy, P.F., and Sanders, E.A. (2011). Efficacy of a tier 2 supplemental root word vocabulary and decoding intervention with kindergarten Spanish-speaking English learners. *Journal of Literacy Research*, 43(2), 184-211.

Neufeld, P., and Fitzgerald, J. (2001). Early English reading development: Latino English learners in the "low" reading group. *Research in the Teaching of English*, 64-109.

Noel, A., Stark, P., and Redford, J. (2016). *Parent and Family Involvement in Education, from the National Household Education Surveys Program of 2012: First Look.* NCES 2013-029-REV. Available: http://nces.ed.gov/pubs2013/2013028rev.pdf [February 2017].

Norris, J.M., and Ortega, L. (2000). Effectiveness of L2 instruction: A research synthesis and quantitative meta-analysis. *Language Learning*, 50(3), 417-528.

O'Brien, G.I. (2007). *The Instructional Features across Three Different Approaches to Oral English Language Development Instruction.* Ph.D. Dissertation. Los Angeles: University of Southern California.

O'Day, J. (2009). Good instruction is good for everyone—or is it? English language learners in a balanced literacy approach. *Journal of Education for Students Placed at Risk*, 14(1), 97-119.

O'Donnell, C.L. (2008). Defining, conceptualizing, and measuring fidelity of implementation and its relationship to outcomes in K-12 curriculum intervention research. *Review of Educational Research*, 78(1), 33-84.

Office of the Education Ombudsman. (2012). *Engaged Parents Successful Students: An Overview of Local and National Parent Engagement Efforts.* Available: http://www.roadmapproject.org/wp-content/uploads/2012/11/Final-Report_Engaged-Parents-Successful-Students-Report-9-12-12.pdf [January 18, 2017].

Panferov, S. (2010). Increasing ELL parental involvement in our schools: Learning from the parents. *Theory Into Practice*, 49(2), 106-112.

Pettit, S.K. (2011). Teachers' beliefs about English language learners in the mainstream classroom: A review of the literature. *International Multilingual Research Journal*, 5(2), 123-147.

Public Agenda. (1998). *Being an American Is a Privilege, Say White, African American, Hispanic and Foreign-Born Parents.* Available: http://www.publicagenda.org/press-releases/being-american-privilege-say-white-african-american-hispanic-and-foreign-born-parents [December 5, 2016].

Rah, Y., Choi, S., and Nguyen, T.S.T. (2009). Building bridges between refugee parents and schools. *International Journal of Leadership in Education, 12*(4), 347-365.

Ramirez, A.F. (2003). Dismay and disappointment: Parental involvement of Latino immigrant parents. *The Urban Review, 35*(2), 93-110.

Ransford-Kaldon, C.R., Flynt, E.S., Ross, C.L., Franceschini, L., Zoblotsky, T., Huang, Y., and Gallagher, B. (2010). *Implementation of effective intervention: An empirical study to evaluate the efficacy of Fountas and Pinnell's Leveled Literacy Intervention System (LLI). 2009-2010.* Memphis, TN: Center for Research in Educational Policy.

Roberts, T.A. (2008). Home storybook reading in primary or secondary language with preschool children: Evidence of equal effectiveness for second-language vocabulary acquisition. *Reading Research Quarterly, 43*(2), 103-130.

Rogoff, B. (2003). *The Cultural Nature of Human Development.* New York: Oxford University Press.

Rolstad, K., Mahoney, K., and Glass, G.V. (2005). The big picture: A meta-analysis of program effectiveness research on English language learners. *Educational Policy, 19*(4), 572-594.

Rossell, C., and Baker, K. (1996). The educational effectiveness of bilingual education. *Research in the Teaching of English, 30*(1), 7-74.

Ryoo, K. (2009). *Learning Science, Talking Science: The Impact of a Technology-Enhanced Curriculum on Students' Science Learning in Linguistically Diverse Mainstream Classrooms.* Ph.D. Dissertation. Stanford, CA: Stanford University.

Sáenz, L.M., Fuchs, L.S., and Fuchs, D. (2005). Peer-assisted learning strategies for English language learners with learning disabilities. *Exceptional Children, 71*(3), 231-247.

Saunders, W.M., and Goldenberg, C. (1999). Effects of instructional conversations and literature logs on limited-and fluent-English-proficient students' story comprehension and thematic understanding. *The Elementary School Journal, 99*(4), 277-301.

Saunders, W.M., and Goldenberg, C. (2010). Research to guide English Language Development instruction. In D. Dolson and L. Burnham-Massey (Eds.), *Improving Education for English Learners: Research-Based Approaches.* Sacramento, CA: CDE Press.

Saunders, W.M., and O'Brien, G. (2006). Oral language. In F. Genesee, K. Lindholm-Leary, W. Saunders, and D. Christian (Eds.), *Educating English Language Learners: A Synthesis of Research Evidence* (pp. 14-63). New York: Cambridge University Press.

Saunders, W.M., Foorman, B.R., and Carlson, C.D. (2006). Is a separate block of time for oral English language development in programs for English learners needed? *The Elementary School Journal, 107*(2), 181-198.

Saunders, W.M., Goldenberg, C., and Marcelletti, D. (2013). English language development: Guidelines for instruction. *American Educator*, 13-39.

Schallert, D.L., Kleiman, G.M., and Rubin, A.D. (1977). *Analyses of Differences Between Written and Oral Language.* Center for the Study of Reading Technical Report, 29. Champaign: University of Illinois.

Scientific Learning Corporation. (2004). Improved language skills by children with low reading performance who used FastForWord language. *MAPS for Learning, 3*(1), 1-13.

Shanahan, T., and Beck, I.L. (2006). Effective literacy teaching for English-language learners. In D. August and T. Shanahan (Eds.), *Developing Literacy in Second-Language Learners: Report of the National Literacy Panel on Language-Minority Children and Youth* (pp. 415-488). Mahwah, NJ: Lawrence Erlbaum Associates.

Shim, J.M. (2013). Involving the parents of English language learners in a rural area: Focus on the dynamics of teacher-parent interactions. *Rural Educator, 34*(3), 18-26.

288

Sibley, E., and Dearing, E. (2014). Family educational involvement and child achievement in early elementary school for American-born and immigrant families. *Psychology in the Schools, 51*(8), 814-831.

Silva, K.G., Correa-Chavez, M., and Rogoff, B. (2010). Mexican-heritage children's attention and learning from interactions directed to others. *Child Development, 81*(3), 898-912.

Silverman, R., and Hines, S. (2009). The effects of multimedia-enhanced instruction on the vocabulary of English-language learners and non-English-language learners in pre-kindergarten through second grade. *Journal of Educational Psychology, 101*(2), 305.

Slavin, R.E., and Cheung, A. (2005). A synthesis of research on language of reading instruction for English language learners. *Review of Educational Research, 75*(2), 247-284.

Sobrato Family Foundation. (2016). *Community Impact*. Available: http://www.sobrato.com/sobrato-philanthropies/sobrato-family-foundation/seal/current-sites-community-impact [November 8, 2016].

Solari, E.J., and Gerber, M.M. (2008). Early comprehension instruction for Spanish-speaking English language learners: Teaching text-level reading skills while maintaining effects on word-level skills. *Learning Disabilities Research and Practice, 23*(4), 155-168.

Soltero-González, L., Sparrow, W., Butvilofsky, S., Escamilla, K., and Hopewell, S. (2016). Effects of a paired literacy program on emerging bilingual children's biliteracy outcomes in third grade. *Journal of Literacy Research, 48*(1).

Souto-Manning, M., and Swick, K.J. (2006). Teachers' beliefs about parent and family involvement: Rethinking our family involvement paradigm. *Early Childhood Education Journal, 34*(2), 187-193.

Sullivan, A., and Brown, M. (2013). Social inequalities in cognitive scores at age 16: The role of reading. *CLS Working Papers, 2013*(13/10).

Taguchi, N. (2015). "Contextually" speaking: A survey of pragmatic learning abroad, in class, and online. *System, 48*, 3-20.

Takanishi, R. (2016). *First Things First!: Creating the New American Primary School*. New York: Teachers College Press.

Tarasawa, B., and Waggoner, J. (2015). Increasing parental involvement of English language learner families: What the research says. *Journal of Children and Poverty, 21*(2), 129-134.

Thompson, K.D. (2015). English learners' time to reclassification: An analysis. *Educational Policy, 31*(3), 330-363.

Tinkler, B. (2002). *A Review of Literature on Hispanic/Latino Parent Involvement in K-12 Education*. Denver, CO: University of Denver. Available: http://files.eric.ed.gov/fulltext/ED469134.pdf [September 30, 2016].

Tobin, J., Adair, J.K., and Arzubiaga, A. (2013). *Children Crossing Borders: Immigrant Parent and Teacher Perspectives on Preschool for Children of Immigrants*. New York: Russell Sage Foundation.

Tong, F., Lara-Alecio, R., Irby, B., Mathes, P., and Kwok, O. (2008). Accelerating early academic oral English development in transitional bilingual and structured English immersion programs. *American Educational Research Journal, 45*(4), 1011-1044.

Tong, F., Irby, B.J., Lara-Alecio, R., and Koch, J. (2014). Integrating literacy and science for English language learners: From learning-to-read to reading-to-learn. *The Journal of Educational Research, 107*(5), 410-426.

Tucker, M.S. (2014). *Fixing Our National Accountability System*. Washington, DC: National Center on Education and the Economy. Available: http://www.ncee.org/wp-content/uploads/2014/08/FixingOurNationalAccountabilitySystemWebV4.pdf [February 15, 2017].

Uchikoshi, Y. (2005). Narrative development in bilingual kindergarteners: Can Arthur help? *Developmental Psychology, 41*(3), 464-478.

Umansky, I.M., and Reardon, S.F. (2014). Reclassification patterns among Latino English learner students in bilingual, dual immersion, and English immersion classrooms. *American Educational Research Journal, 51*(5), 879-912.

Valencia, R.R. (2010). *Dismantling Contemporary Deficit Thinking: Educational Thought and Practice.* New York: Routledge.

Valentino, R.A., and Reardon, S.F. (2015). Effectiveness of four instructional programs designed to serve English learners variation by ethnicity and initial English proficiency. *Educational Evaluation and Policy Analysis, 37*(4), 612-637.

Vaughn, S., Mathes, P., Linan-Thompson, S., Cirino, P., Carlson, C. Pollard-Durodola, S., Cardenas-Hagan, E., and Francis, D. (2006a). Effectiveness of an English intervention for first-grade English language learners at risk for reading problems. *Elementary School Journal, 107*(2), 153-180.

Vaughn, S., Cirino, P.T., Linan-Thompson, S., Mathes, P.G., Carlson, C.D., Hagan, E.C., Pollard-Durodola, S.D., Fletcher, J.M., and Francis, D.J. (2006b). Effectiveness of a Spanish intervention and an English intervention for English-language learners at risk for reading problems. *American Educational Research Journal, 43*(3), 449-487.

Walker, A., Shafer, J., and Liams, M. (2004). "Not in my classroom": Teacher attitudes towards English language learners in the mainstream classroom. *NABE Journal of Research and Practice, 2*(1), 130-159.

Waterman, R., and Harry, B. (2008). *Building Collaboration between Schools and Parents of English Language Learners: Transcending Barriers, Creating Opportunities.* Practitioner Brief. Washington, DC: National Center for Culturally Responsive Educational Systems.

Westrich, L., and Strobel, K. (2013). *A Study of Family Engagement in Redwood City Community Schools.* Palo Alto, CA: John W. Gardner Center for Youth and Their Communities.

Wilder, S. (2014). Effects of parental involvement on academic achievement: A meta-synthesis. *Educational Review, 66*(3), 377-397.

Willig, A.C. (1985). A meta-analysis of selected studies on the effectiveness of bilingual education. *Review of Educational Research, 55*(3), 269-317.

Xiong, T.T., and Obiakor, F.E. (2013). Cultural connections and disconnections between non-Hmong principals and Hmong parents. *Multicultural Perspectives, 15*(1), 39-45.

8

Promising and Effective Practices for English Learners in Grades Pre-K to 12

This chapter focuses on promising and effective practices for English learners (ELs)[1] during their pre-K to grade 5 years (primary or elementary grades), middle school years (grades 6-8, typically middle or junior high school), and grades 9-12 (typically high school).[2] The elementary school years are a critical time for beginning to acquire content area knowledge and skills that provide the foundation for more advanced learning in academic disciplines required in middle and high schools. It is an equally critical time to sustain the natural curiosity and eagerness to learn that young children bring to the early grades (Institute of Medicine and National Research Council, 2015). For ELs, these grades also represent a time of adapting, many for the first time, to new cultural demands of their schools. ELs will be learning the skills and content knowledge expected of all students, but in many cases, at least for some of the time, they will be doing so in a new language and also in ways that may differ from those in their homes and cultures. The following sections review promising practices for meeting these challenges in grades pre-K to 5, 6-8, and 9-12. The chapter ends with conclusions.

---

[1] When referring to children aged 5 or older in the pre-K to 12 education system, this report uses the term "English learners" or "ELs" (see Box 1-1 in Chapter 1 for details).

[2] Grade spans are administrative decisions made by school districts that vary throughout the United States.

PROMISING AND EFFECTIVE PRACTICES FOR EDUCATING ENGLISH LEARNERS IN GRADES PRE-K TO 5

Educators expect that children's caregivers at home have prepared them for elementary school. While some widely used norms consider children's diverse cultural background, language, and beliefs (e.g., Head Start Early Learning Outcomes Framework), others may not, basing norms for language proficiency and competencies on the development of children raised in monolingual English households.

This presents a special challenge for elementary schools: How are cultural and linguistic differences in children's preparation for school to be treated? How, as Rogoff (2003, p. 17) asks, does one look at differences without making value judgments? Does the absence of certain expected skills or behaviors indicate that children are not ready to learn what others their age are learning, or does it indicate the need for additional instructional experiences designed to fill the assumed gaps in their preparation? Are skills and strengths that are promoted in families that are not mainstream recognized and appreciated, or are differences seen as deficits to be remediated? Deficit theories used to explain school outcomes for ELs have been discredited and rejected (Cummins, 2003; Harry and Klingner, 2007; Valencia, 2010), but remain influential both in instructional practice and in the design of research and interventions.

Gándara (2016) proposes an assets-based framework for viewing ELs based on current research. Upon entering elementary school, for example, children of Mexican immigrants in a nationally representative sample (Early Childhood Longitudinal Study-Kindergarten) were rated as highly socially competent and mentally healthy (Crosnoe, 2006). According to Gándara (2016), ELs are resilient and adaptive to change based on family migration, and come from families with strong beliefs in the value of educational success. They are collaborative and oriented to learning in peer group settings. Gándara argues that considering these assets rather than focusing on the deficits of ELs can lead to improved learning outcomes.

This section draws on research conducted between 1998 and 2016 that focuses on seven effective and promising practices for educating ELs in grades K-5. In many of these studies, multiple methods were used to achieve the study goals. Thus, in most cases, it is not possible to know which study components were responsible for the results. The committee describes the attributes of the studies that may have contributed to students' outcomes, but without further research, it is impossible to know with certainty their role in supporting ELs' learning of English language and content knowledge.[3]

Practice 1: Provide Explicit Instruction in Literacy Components

Research focused on developing literacy in ELs builds on literacy research conducted with English-proficient students. This research indicates that it is helpful to teach young children explicitly to hear the individual English sounds or phonemes within words (phonemic awareness); to use the letters and spelling patterns within words to decode the words' pronunciations (phonics); to read text aloud with appropriate speed, accuracy, and expression (oral reading fluency); to know the meanings of words and affixes (vocabulary); to think about what they are reading (reading comprehension); and to write with the organization, development, substance, and style appropriate to the task and audience.

A review of effective literacy instruction[4] for ELs found 12 studies published between 1997 and 2002 (see Shanahan and Beck, 2006, pp. 421-423, for a table of these studies) indicating that the general pattern found with English-proficient students appears to hold for ELs. Explicit classroom instruction focused on developing key aspects of literacy—phonemic awareness, phonics, oral reading fluency, and reading vocabulary—provides clear learning benefits for elementary school-aged ELs. More recent studies report similar findings (e.g., Llosa et al., 2016; Tong et al., 2014). However, because ELs are developing language proficiency while they are acquiring content area knowledge in a second language, research indicates that there are important considerations to keep in mind regarding instruction, as described below.

Practice 2: Develop Academic Language During Content Area Instruction

Academic language is the language used in school, in written communications, in public presentations, and in formal settings (Snow and

---

[3]The sources for this section are experimental research studies referenced in two practice guides published by the U.S. Department of Education (Baker et al., 2014; Gersten et al., 2007). The discussion also draws on experimental studies cited in a synthesis of the research on effective instruction for ELs (Shanahan and Beck, 2006) and studies published between 2014 and 2016 that met What Works Clearinghouse standards (Crevecour et al., 2014; Llosa et al., 2016; Tong et al., 2014). In all these studies, ELs performed better than control students on study outcome measures as a result of the instructional approaches that were implemented. The discussion also references qualitative studies of classroom and school practices published during the same years.

[4]The studies included those that used experimental, quasi-experimental, or single-subject research designs and resulted in significant differences in outcomes for treated groups.

Uccelli, 2009). Bailey (2007, pp. 10-11) defines being academically proficient as "knowing and being able to use general and academic vocabulary, specialized or complex grammatical structures, and multifarious language functions and discourse structures—all for the purpose of acquiring new knowledge and skills, interacting about a topic, imparting information to others." A series of experimental studies developed academic language[5] in the context of teaching content (e.g., Brown et al., 2010; Carlo et al., 2004; Llosa et al., 2016; Ryoo, 2009; Silverman and Hines, 2009; Tong et al., 2014). The majority of these studies developed language during science instruction; one did so during language arts instruction. All the studies used multifaceted instructional approaches that combined professional development for teachers with enhanced instructional routines that focused concurrently on teaching content and the associated academic language.

In one study (Tong et al., 2014), implemented with 5th-grade Hispanic ELs, the instructional approach consisted of ongoing professional development for teachers and paraprofessionals, an academic science approach that used the 5-E model of science instruction (Engage, Explore, Explain, Elaborate, and Evaluate), and the infusion of reading and writing activities into instruction (e.g., leveled questions using such verbs as "identify," "describe," "explain," and "analyze" to help ELs understand text). A second study (Llosa et al., 2016), implemented with 5th-grade ELs from a variety of first language (L1) backgrounds, also included teacher and student components. Teacher components comprised a teacher guide and professional development workshops, while student components consisted of a stand-alone, year-long, 5th-grade curriculum aligned with state science standards and using an inquiry-based approach. Language development included providing opportunities for students to discuss science in small and whole groups and engage in language development activities posted on a project website.

Practice 3: Provide Visual and Verbal Supports to Make Core Content Comprehensible

A third practice linked to positive outcomes in the development of content area knowledge in ELs is using methods that help make core content in English comprehensible. One set of methods includes the strategic use of such instructional tools as short videos, visuals, and graphic organizers. In a study conducted with 5th graders (Llosa et al., 2016), for example, scaffolding consisted of providing ELs with science terms in their L1 and using multiple modes of representation in textual and graphic formats. In another study (Silverman and Hines, 2009), kindergarten ELs who watched

---

[5]Academic language includes oral as well as written language.

short videos on the habitats they had learned about during storybook reading outperformed children who had heard the same books read aloud but did not see the videos. In this study, the multimedia addition did not have a positive effect on English-proficient students, highlighting the value of additional supports for ELs. A second way to make core content comprehensible is though verbal interactions that clarify content, such as defining words in context; asking right-there questions; coaching; and conducting whole-class, small-group, and partner discussions (e.g., Carlo et al., 2004; Tong et al., 2014).

Qualitative research (August and Erickson, 2006; O'Day, 2009) also suggests the need for supports. For instance, O'Day (2009) found that the use of literacy practices that included higher-level questioning/discussion about the meaning of text, writing instruction, and accountable talk[6] had a strong relationship to improved reading comprehension for English-proficient students, but had little discernable benefit for ELs. The author hypothesizes that these activities may have been at too high a linguistic level for ELs to benefit from them without appropriate supports. Differences also emerged with respect to teacher-student interactions. "Telling," defined as the teacher providing students with information rather than engaging them in the creation of information through coaching, recitation, or other forms of interaction, had a statistically significant positive effect on ELs' reading comprehension but a negative effect on the comprehension of English-proficient students. The difference in coefficients for this variable was larger than that for any of the many other variables in the study. The author posits that literacy practices (e.g., higher-level questioning) may have been at too high a level for ELs to benefit from them without the appropriate supports, while in the case of "telling," ELs benefited because they were provided with more support for engaging with core content in English, but this was not necessary for English-proficient students.

Practice 4: Encourage Peer-Assisted Learning Opportunities

Studies conducted with elementary school-aged ELs (e.g. Calderón et al., 1998; Calhoun et al., 2007; McMaster et al., 2008; Ryoo, 2009; Sáenz et al., 2005[7]) that were effective in developing their literacy implemented peer-assisted learning in pairs or cooperative groups of four to six students. For example, Peer Assisted Learning Strategies (PALS) was implemented in

---

[6]Accountable talk was defined as talk focused on ideas accurate and appropriate to the topic and flow of discussion, included a press for evidence from the text, involved students responding to and elaborating on each other's contributions, and reflected a more facilitative rather than directive role on the part of the teacher.

[7]Students in this study were in grades 3-6, so there is some overlap with the middle grades.

1st-grade classrooms in a dual language program (Calhoun et al., 2007). PALs consisted of a structured routine in which a teacher modeled the code-focused activities of the day; students practiced the code-focused activities in pairs for 15 minutes while the teacher supervised; and students then turned to story sharing, a partner reading activity that lasted for another 15 minutes. Teachers paired students so that one was a high-performing reader and the other was low-performing, and then taught the students to use PALS procedures. During each segment of the session, the high-performing student performed the role of coach first, and the low-performing student followed. On average, PALS students demonstrated significantly greater growth than control students on phoneme segmentation, nonsense word fluency, and oral reading fluency. Both ELs and English-proficient students responded positively to PALS, but the ELs responded with differential effects depending on the outcome measure.

A feature of all these studies is that they enabled students to talk about course content in pairs or small groups. An important principle related to second language learning is that students benefit from opportunities to interact (via speaking, listening, reading, and writing) in the second language (L2). Speaking is important to generate feedback, force syntactic processing, and challenge students to engage at higher proficiency levels (Johnson and Swain, 1997).

Practice 5: Capitalize on Students' Home Language, Knowledge, and Cultural Assets

In studies of schooling, such socioeconomic variables as race/ethnic group, immigration status, parental education level, parental employment status and income, family composition, and marital status of parents are considered if not examined (e.g., National Research Council, 1984). Cultural factors, while mentioned, are seldom examined. Yet in schools that serve as diverse a student population as those in the United States do, a sociocultural perspective on teaching and learning is arguably a necessity (John-Steiner and Mahn, 2012) if the goal is to interpret the relationship between instructional practices and learning outcomes. Analyses of the effectiveness of instructional practices requires, in addition to evidence of learning outcomes, examination of how children respond to those practices.

Children's learning behaviors and responses to instruction, especially in the early years of schooling, are culturally influenced by the socialization practices of the home and family. Ethnographic studies of socialization for learning, for example, have found that learning through observation is promoted in diverse indigenous communities around the world (Barnhardt and Kawagley, 2005; Rogoff, 2003). An experimental study by Silva and colleagues (2010), building on that ethnographic work, found that Mexican-heritage children paid close attention to and were able to learn complex tasks just by attending to instructions directed at their siblings, and the practice of learning by keen observation and intent participation documented among indigenous peoples in Mexico is one that appears to carry over in immigrant groups, even after they leave their places of origin. In considering sociocultural influences, it is important to keep in mind that a view of home-school relationships as either match or mismatch is a nuanced one, and that there are practices that are similar in some ways and different in others. Relationships shift over time as the practices in the two domains interact (Rueda et al., 2006: Volk and Acosta, 2001).

Some school districts across the nation have been experimenting with departmentalization, or "platooning," of instruction (see, e.g., Gewertz, 2014; Hood, 2009). This practice appears to be driven by policy changes, increased testing pressures, and spending cuts in education that have placed teachers at risk for burnout and emotional distress, leading ultimately to high teacher turnover rates in many districts. The argument for departmentalization in elementary schools is that teachers can be specialists in such subjects as math or science instead of having to meet the full gamut of student needs. In addition, departmentalization could help alleviate the shortage of teachers who are able to speak the home languages of ELs. One teacher could provide subject matter instruction in a language such as Spanish or Haitian Creole for five or six groups of students each day.

Elementary school teachers of self-contained classes are, by definition, generalists—they cover all or most academic subjects for their students for a school year. The most compelling argument for this traditional arrangement derives from the "whole child" movement, in which the child is the focus of education rather than curricular subjects, and the school itself is viewed as an ecological system in which students learn more than is taught (Eisner, 2005). Students also are influenced by their close and stable relationships with teachers and classmates, and teachers are able to know their students' needs and issues. For ELs, some departmentalization is inevitable. Instruction in English as a second language (ESL)/English language development (ELD) is usually provided by specialists, and whether they push in to classes or students are pulled out of their regular classes for instruction, ELs are taught these subjects by a teacher different from their principal teacher. At present, little research is available on the effects of these different instructional arrangements on ELs.

With this complexity in mind, the experimental studies reviewed (e.g., Carlo et al., 2004; Liang et al., 2005; Llosa et al., 2016, Saunders and Goldenberg, 1999) suggest that instructional routines that draw on students' home language, knowledge, and cultural assets support literacy development in English. Examples of the instructional routines in these studies include previewing and reviewing material in children's L1, storybook reading in students' L1 (Liang et al., 2005), providing opportunities for students to engage in conversational exchanges during instruction that permit some interpretation to take place in the L1 (Saunders and Goldenberg, 1999), providing L1 definitions for the targeted vocabulary (Carlo et al., 2004; Llosa et al., 2016), providing instruction in word-learning strategies that help ELs uncover the meanings of cognates when encountered in English texts (Carlo et al., 2004), and introducing key concepts by connecting them with children's prior knowledge or experiences in the home and community contexts (Llosa et al., 2016).

Findings from correlational and evaluation studies also provide support for these methods. Studies on cross-language transfer (Dressler and Kamil, 2006) indicate significant relationships between performance in ELs' L1 and L2 in word reading, spelling, vocabulary, comprehension, and reading strategies. Findings from evaluation studies comparing bilingual programs with mostly English-only programs (see Chapter 7) indicate that ELs instructed bilingually either perform on par with or outperform ELs instructed only in English over time.

Practice 6: Screen for Language and Literacy Challenges and Monitor Progress

Findings from numerous studies[8] cited in previous reviews of promising and effective instructional practices for ELs (Baker et al., 2014; Gersten et al., 2007) suggest that "districts establish procedures for and provide training for schools to screen ELs for reading problems; consider collecting progress monitoring data more than three times a year for ELs at risk of reading problems; and use data from screening and progress monitoring assessments to make decisions about the instructional support ELs need to learn to read" (Gersten et al., 2007, p. 5). Further, these studies suggest "using currently available measures, such as standardized tests, district benchmark tests, or English language assessments to screen and identify students in need of additional instructional support" (Baker et al., 2014, p. 60).

The studies specify the types of assessments that are useful at different grade spans for determining whether ELs are in need of additional instructional support. For kindergarten and 1st grade, measures include those that assess phonological awareness, familiarity with the alphabet and alphabetic principle, ability to read single words, and knowledge of basic phonics rules. For children at the end of 1st grade and in the next few grades, assessments include those that measure reading connected texts accurately

---

[8] A list of these studies appears in Gersten et al. (2007, p. 31, fn. 22). Only studies conducted between 1997 and 2016 are included.

and fluently. For students in grades 2-5, oral reading fluency measures are valid screening measures.

Two other recommendations are that districts with performance benchmarks use the same standards for ELs and English-proficient students in the early grades, but make adjustments in instruction when EL progress is not sufficient, and that teachers be trained to use formative data to guide instruction (Gersten et al., 2007, pp. 6-7). With regard to formative data, Black and Wiliam (1998) suggest that students' writing samples be used on an ongoing basis to determine areas for improvement. Students' writing samples are excellent sources for formative assessment because they shed light on language challenges that are common to all children, as well as on challenges and opportunities related to primary language influence on English (Kim et al., 2011).

Practice 7: Provide Small-Group Support in Literacy and English Language Development for English Learners Who Need Additional Support

Many of the studies of ELs in grades 1-5 support the use of small-group academic support for ELs who require more time to develop prereading and reading skills, as well as in other areas of literacy and language development (e.g. Burns, 2011; Denton et al., 2004; Gunn et al., 2002; Nelson et al., 2011; Ransford-Kaldon et al., 2010; Solari and Gerber, 2008; Vaughn et al., 2006a, 2006b). Recommendations related to these studies (Gersten et al., 2007, pp. 10-11) call for ensuring the programs are implemented for at least 30 minutes in small homogeneous groups and providing training and ongoing support for teachers, interventionists, and other school personnel on how to deliver small group instruction effectively, as well how to use effective teaching techniques that can be used outside of small group instruction. An additional important recommendation related to the studies (Baker et al., 2014) is that additional supports address language and literacy skills, such as vocabulary, listening, and reading comprehension.[9]

Instructional Approaches That Merit Additional Attention

Research related to ELs and content area outcomes in grades K-5 has focused predominantly on instructional supports to help ELs learn English and content delivered in English. Other instructional practices that have not

---

[9]Readers are referred to the two practice guides (Baker et al., 2014; Gersten et al., 2007), the August and Shanahan (2006) review, and the studies themselves for more information about the particular approaches used.

been extensively researched for elementary ELs in the United States merit further attention.

The first such practice relates to dual language programing. There is almost no research related to promising and effective methods for developing both ELs' L1 knowledge and skills and the partner language knowledge and skills of English-proficient students (e.g., Spanish or Chinese) in these programs, or to methods for equalizing status among the students from different ethnic/language backgrounds in these schools. There also is virtually no research related to the features of school-wide programs that lead to better student outcomes. Such features that influence the successful acquisition of language and content include student ratios of English speakers to partner language speakers in two-way programs, the number of instructional hours allotted to each language, the proportion of school staff and leadership that is bilingual, and the use of target languages within and across content areas (Boyle et al., 2015).

The second practice is focused on creating more engaged readers and learners. This is a matter of critical importance with respect to both language and literacy development. Children who have difficulty learning to read by the end of 3rd grade have difficulty learning academic content and the forms and structures of language that figure in academic discourse. The school's curriculum up through the 3rd grade is typically aimed at teaching students the basics of reading and writing. The emphasis in reading instruction, as reflected in the research, has privileged skill development: phonological awareness, decoding skills at the level of phonics and morphemics, and reading fluency, all of which are built on prior oral language skills.

Beginning in the 4th grade, students are expected to know how to read well enough to learn academic content by reading informational and literary texts written in more complex language than they have encountered earlier in school. This is the point at which many ELs falter. If they have managed to learn to read despite the hardships of doing so in a language they do not fully understand, and if they have become engaged readers by then, they have access to the forms and structures of language required for mastery of English. Linguists and literacy specialists have shown that there are substantial differences between spoken and written language (Biber, 2009; Gee, 2001; Halliday, 1987; Massaro, 2015; Ong, 2002; Scarcella, 2003; Schleppegrell, 2001; Snow and Uccelli, 2009), especially in the written texts that are used in school.

The importance of literacy experiences to language development was highlighted in a recent study conducted by Massaro (2015), who compared the vocabulary used in children's picture books with the vocabulary used in spoken language, whether addressed to adults or children. This study, an update and replication of an earlier study by Donald Hayes (1988), examined whether spoken language alone can prepare children for the written language of books. By comparing the language used in a large sample of picture books with adult-directed speech in a database of speech samples collected from adults speaking to other adults and with child-directed speech (the speech used by adults in speaking to children) drawn from a subset of the Child Language Data Exchange System Corpora, Massaro found a more extensive vocabulary in the picture books than in adult-to-adult speech and approximately three times as many rare word types in the picture books as in child-directed speech. Massaro found not only vocabulary differences but also important differences in grammar. Such differences highlight the value of reading picture books to children in the early years of life, and Massaro points out that the standard model that assumes reading and learning to read are "parasitic on speech" is incomplete. Learning to read also requires early exposure and access to written language forms, structures, and functions that can come only from books. Thus, students require support from teachers, both linguistically and strategically, to make sense of these materials. Families can augment these experiences by reading regularly to their children, especially during the early childhood and primary school years (Bernhard et al., 2006).

Little recognition or attention has been given to the role of literacy engagement in language development, especially for ELs. Cummins (2011) argues that literacy plays a pivotal role in the development of English proficiency because the only place ELs are likely to encounter the words, grammatical structures, and rhetorical features of academic language is in written texts. Thus, it is only through meaningful engagement with such language in written texts that students can learn academic language at all. The difficulty for ELs is that reading a language that is new to them is effortful. Students who learn to read in their native language first have knowledge and skills they can draw on when reading in a second language (Dressler and Kamil, 2006). The question for ELs who lack the opportunity to learn to read in their primary language and must do so in English is whether engagement in literacy can enable them to overcome the difficulty inherent in learning to read in a language they do not fully understand, and whether enthusiasm for literacy can overcome the language barriers that prevent easy understanding of texts and participation in the world of literacy.

The research on literacy engagement reveals that it can be the means of overcoming considerable odds against literacy attainment in English-monolingual students. The relationship between low socioeconomic status and reading attainment is a complex one, as Snow and colleagues (1998) have shown. While aspects of the home environment are assumed to constitute major risk factors for reading achievement for children from low socioeconomic status backgrounds, the school environments in which such children find themselves also are implicated. A study by Duke (2000) revealed that there are marked differences between schools serving students from families of low socioeconomic status and high socioeconomic status in the amount of print materials and the quality of print experiences available to students in their 1st-grade classrooms. Such differences affect both opportunities for reading and writing and motivation for students to become readers and writers. Duke found that "the mean proportion of time in which high-SES [socioeconomic status] students had a choice in reading materials was three times greater than for low-SES students" (p. 466). In classroom writing activities, students of low socioeconomic status spent much of their time taking dictation and working with worksheets, whereas students of high socioeconomic status were provided opportunities "to exert their agency as writers."

The case for literacy engagement as a critical factor in reading achievement is supported by research conducted over several decades. Little of this research has been done on ELs, but that hardly minimizes its relevance to them. A thorough review of that body of research is beyond the scope of this discussion, but meta-analyses by Lindsay (2010) and Mol and Bus (2011) are useful as starting points. Literacy engagement and time spent on literacy-related activities can make a difference for students who otherwise might not be expected to succeed in reading. Guthrie (2004, p. 5) cites a study using National Assessment of Educational Progress (NAEP) data in which "9 year old students whose family backgrounds were characterized by low income and low education, but who were highly engaged readers, substantially outscored students who came from backgrounds with higher education and higher income, but who themselves were less engaged readers." Large-scale longitudinal data from a nationally representative U.K. sample similarly demonstrated a causal relationship between reading engagement and reading achievement that was not dependent either on the socioeconomic status of the parents or on the cognitive or academic ability of the student (Sullivan and Brown, 2013).

Research on the development of literacy engagement conducted over the past two decades by John Guthrie and colleagues (Guthrie and Wigfield, 2004; Wigfield et al., 2016) has emphasized students' motivation for reading, the cognitive strategies involved in reading, and students' conceptual goals for learning—all of which takes place within a classroom context. Guthrie and Wigfield (2000, p. 404) argue that "although cognitive and social dimensions of engaged reading are distinguishable from the motivational dimension, engagement cannot occur without all three." The research group designed and implemented a Concept-Oriented Reading Instruction (CORI) program for teaching language arts and science in 3rd- and 5th-grade classes (Guthrie et al., 1996). The emphasis in CORI was on enhancing reading engagement by promoting motivation for reading, motivation for the use of cognitive strategies in reading, and motivation for conceptual learning. Performance assessments used in this study along with assessments of students' portfolios documented statistically significant improvements in learning outcomes as a result of enhanced student literacy engagement over the course of the study year.

Guthrie and Davis (2003) explored two pathways for reengaging students in school reading. The first involved connecting an intrinsically motivating activity to reading, in the hope that that motivation could be generalized to reading other texts. The second involved the building of stronger motivation for reading. The challenge for the researchers was to design instructional experiences—units of study on materials that were inherently interesting to students—and to make reading a part of those learning activities. They identified six classroom practices for middle school teachers to follow to reengage students in literacy: (1) build reading around rich knowledge goals, (2) connect reading to student experiences through real-world interactions, (3) provide an abundance of interesting books and materials, (4) give students a choice in what they read, (5) provide direct instruction on important and necessary reading strategies, and (6) encourage student collaboration in learning.

A second related area that merits additional attention is approaches that enhance socioemotional well-being, especially motivation to engage in school learning. One such attribute is students' growth mindset (Dweck, 1999, 2007). Growth mindset research suggests that students will be more engaged in learning when they understand that their abilities can be strengthened through effort (Dweck, 2007). Teacher beliefs about student capacity also influence learning (Pettit, 2011; Walker et al., 2004), but no studies to date have examined methods that might change teacher beliefs. It would be important to include factors related to and indicators of students' engagement, measures of mindsets regarding their learning, and teacher beliefs, as these factors relate to such outcomes as language proficiency and academic achievement. While reviews have uncovered several interventions aimed at improving ELs' engagement (e.g., Llosa et al., 2016; Tong et al., 2014), none of these studies measured student engagement during or after the interventions.

A study by Zhang and colleagues (2013) suggests that motivation and engagement are not necessarily predictive of enhanced outcomes, at least when essay writing is used as a measure of literacy achievement. This study, involving 75 Spanish-speaking 5th graders from a school in the Chicago area, investigated whether a peer-led, open-format discussion approach known as collaborative reasoning would accelerate the students' English language development. Results showed that after participating in eight discussions over a 4-week period, the collaborative reasoning group performed significantly better than the control group on measures of listening and reading comprehension. The collaborative reasoning group produced more coherent narratives in a storytelling task. The reflective essays they wrote were longer; contained more diverse vocabulary; and contained a significantly greater number of satisfactory reasons, counterarguments, and uses of text evidence. Collaborative reasoning discussions also enhanced students' interest and engagement in discussions, perceived benefits from discussions, and attitudes toward learning English. On the other hand, the study did not support the hypothesized relationship between motivation and engagement, defined by the choice of stories and texts used in the study, and language development for the ELs, as measured by their writing. Although the reflective essays produced by the collaborative reasoning group were longer, included the use of more diverse vocabulary, and contained significantly more relevant reasons, counterarguments, and uses of text evidence relative to those written by the control group, the results could not be attributed to motivation and engagement—perhaps, as the researchers comment, because the small sample size, involving just four classrooms, made it impossible to rule out sources of variation in teacher skills and enthusiasm and variations in the students as well.

Interpreting the Research

Both quantitative research and qualitative studies focused on explicit content area instruction of ELs (August and Erickson, 2006) reveal, as is the case with English-proficient students, that progress among ELs is not uniform. Some students make good progress, whereas others do not, an observation that argues for the importance of attending to the individual needs of students as part of whatever instructional approach is implemented. In some cases, while students' progress at different rates, their growth follows similar paths (Fitzgerald and Noblit, 2000; Neufeld and Fitzgerald, 2001). Other students, however, may need more intensive and qualitatively different approaches to achieve in English at levels commensurate with those of their English-proficient peers (National Institute for Child Health and Human Development, 2000).

PROMISING AND EFFECTIVE PRACTICES FOR EDUCATING ENGLISH LEARNERS IN GRADES 6-8 (MIDDLE SCHOOL)

Young adolescents (typically aged 10-14) who are ELs enter middle school at what can be a turning point in their educational trajectory. Whether they are first classified during their middle school years as long-term ELs (LTELs) (see Chapter 6) or are newcomers to American classrooms (Valdés, 2001), these youth face new challenges in middle school that influence their opportunities to learn both the English language and the rigorous academic subject matter required by today's higher state standards and the middle school curriculum itself relative to their previous school experience. For adolescents, literacy involves more abstract language and concepts than the more concrete ideas encountered during the primary grades (Duke and Carlisle, 2011; Snow and Uccelli, 2009). Whether ELs are successful in meeting these new requirements will have consequences for their high school experiences and their career and postsecondary education prospects.

Lesaux and colleagues (2014, p. 1161) capture the complex challenges facing both students and their teachers in middle schools as they pursue the dual goals of English language development and content area learning:

> Because literacy development is a multifaceted process that demands a number of separate, but related competencies (Duke and Carlisle, 2011; McCutchen, 2006; RAND Reading Study Group, 2002), there are myriad potential sources of difficulty for the learner who struggles to understand, discuss, and produce academic texts. For middle-schoolers, these competencies are largely composed of higher level processing and linguistic skills. In part, these skills are made up of knowledge that relates to literacy itself; knowledge of process, text structure, genre, and author (or reader) expectations (Beers and Nagy, 2011; RAND Reading Study Group, 2002; Saddler and Graham, 2007). They also include the ability to draw on prior knowledge, make appropriate inferences, and resolve structural and semantic ambiguities (Alexander and Jetton, 2000; Kintsch and Rawson, 2005). For the learner to undertake this complex process of comprehending and producing academic text, deep and flexible knowledge of the often abstract and complex words and phrases used in this particular register is needed.

Middle schools typically are larger organizations for students to navigate relative to primary schools. Many ELs move from having one teacher in primary school to having several teachers, each of whom is responsible for specific academic disciplines. Thus, ELs must adapt to different teachers with different approaches to subject matter instruction while mastering academic English terms tied to specific disciplines (Suárez-Orozco et al., 2008). Alternatively, some middle school ELs may be placed in "sheltered" classes for long periods of time where they are segregated from other students, with restricted access to grade-level academic courses and English-proficient peers, a practice that can have stigmatizing effects (Rumberger et al., 2006; Valdés, 2001; Walqui et al., 2010) and inhibit the development of their language proficiency, their grade-level knowledge and skills, and their motivation to learn in school.

These shifts in school organization and classroom demands occur at a time when ELs are entering early adolescence and experiencing its normative neurobiological, social, and cognitive changes (Lerner and Steinberg,

2009). While families continue to be important, peer groups and youth and community organizations can become significant influences on young adolescents, particularly on their identities as competent learners and their motivation to invest in their education. These convergences are daunting for all middle school students (Eccles, 2008) but are likely to be compounded for ELs (see Box 8-1).

BOX 8-1
How Middle School Contexts Matter for English Learners

In an ethnographic study of middle school English learners (ELs), Valdés (2001) documents the challenges confronting many of these youth who find themselves in programs that fail to provide the instructional supports they need for learning both English and the school's curriculum for their age and grade level. At the original school where Valdés was conducting her case study of four Latino newcomers, the teachers, although experienced in working with ELs, were operating under the assumption that their working-class immigrant students were unlikely to be prepared for the rigors of the regular middle school curriculum, and therefore needed an intensive program in the English language first. Students had three periods of English as a second language (ESL) and three periods of sheltered English content instruction in which they worked on materials in various subjects in basic-level English. Most activities involved seatwork during which students were admonished to be quiet and not to speak to one another, especially in Spanish.

Writing instruction involved the writing of sentences with emphasis on spelling and punctuation—lists rather than connected prose. Reading instruction was provided in a similar manner: students were given elementary school texts or the *Scholastic News*, an elementary-level weekly newspaper. Students who knew enough English to decipher the text were left to do so on their own, while the teacher worked on the vocabulary used in the text with those who did not know English at all. Nor did the sheltered classes provide the support these students needed to learn either English or the subjects that were taught in English: science, math, and "home arts."

At the beginning of the second year, the family of one of the four students in the study moved to a neighboring community, which provided Valdés an opportunity to observe how teacher beliefs about students' potential can influence the quality of the programs they are offered in middle school (Valdés, 2001). The schools in this affluent community had far fewer ELs relative to the community that was the main site of Valdés's study. Here, the ELs were primarily the children of professionals in the technology industry—Europeans, East Asians, Israelis, and Indians from India—whereas the ELs at the original study site were the children of working-class Latino immigrants. At the new site, the ELs were perceived as the willing, able, and enthusiastic learners they were, rather than as problematic and difficult to teach. They were seen as having to learn English quickly enough so

BOX 8-1 Continued

they would not be held back from taking the courses that would prepare them for college, and thus the materials provided to them were grade-appropriate. Except for two periods of English language development (ELD), the student who had transferred was enrolled in mainstream 8th-grade classes: computers, science, math, creative writing, and physical education. In the ELD classes, the aim was English proficiency, but the materials were drawn from the 8th-grade language arts and social studies curricula.

The teacher's operating assumption was that the English her students needed to learn was the English they would encounter in the courses they had to take to be prepared for the more demanding work of high school and beyond. This teacher saw herself not so much as an ESL teacher, but as a teacher of literature and history. She focused on teaching her students vocabulary and English grammar in the context of the materials they were working on, and each day, she asked her students to write to her about their evolving understanding of the language and materials. She responded to her students' comments in writing—and she attended to the thoughts they communicated rather than their grammar, spelling, or punctuation in these submissions. At the same time, she taught them the intricacies of English written communication: text structure and the use of grammatical constructions and cohesive devices in producing written essays such as those any 8th-grade student should be learning to write. Far from just learning to write sentences based on grammatical rules, the teacher had students spend 4 weeks on constructing a speculative essay on how they saw their lives unfolding over the next several decades. Valdés describes this as a "master" class—a model for how to educate ELs in middle school.

Was the working-class EL who found himself in this radically different program able to keep up with the rigors of its demanding curriculum? Valdés reports that he made excellent progress in English, although his progress was not uniformly successful, especially in his math class, as the prior year of remedial math in his previous school had not prepared him for the algebra class in his new school.

Valdés's (2001) study shows that the social context of middle schools—shaped by the sociodemographic characteristics of the ELs and how teachers perceive their capacities for learning both English and academic subjects—can result in different classroom learning experiences and outcomes (see also Kim and Viesca, 2016). Providing the conditions necessary for the kind of excellent instruction offered in the more affluent school in her study is not easy. The majority of ELs are segregated in low-performing schools. Such schools require skilled teachers who understand the needs of students who may vary considerably in prior educational experiences and preparation in middle school subjects. Effective schools for ELs begin with a school culture and educators who believe that ELs are capable of and ready for learning, irrespective of their origins, parental resources, or language backgrounds. Such schools are staffed by teachers with the pedagogical competence to teach ELs in ways that recognize the complexity and social exchanges that characterize both English learning and mastery of middle school curricula.

While practices implemented during the middle school grades are similar to those for the primary and elementary grades, their implementation and impacts are likely to be mediated by three interacting factors relevant to instruction and learning in schools. First, classroom practices examined here must take into account and adapt to students' characteristics during adolescence—cognitive, linguistic, social, and emotional—as well as levels of literacy skills gained in previous grades. Second, the organization of these schools (their size, how classrooms are organized by academic discipline) as experienced by the learner creates different opportunities to benefit from sound instruction relative to those in earlier grades. Specifically, middle and high schools vary in their missions and in how they view ELs and their potential to be educated (Kanno and Kangas, 2014; Valdés, 2001). Third, the requirements for learning and the stakes for students' prospects change as they move from primary to middle to high school based on current state education requirements. Thus, practices must be recommended with the recognition that these three sets of factors influence the educational trajectories of ELs, their opportunities to develop to their full potential, and their educational performance during these school grades.

Middle school teachers also face considerable challenges in motivating and instructing students with varying English proficiency levels, differences in their educational experiences in both the United States and their countries of origin, and varying experiences in the earlier grades of primary school, and in integrating into their instruction the sociocultural influences on how learning occurs in their students (Rumberger et al., 2006; Valdés, 2001; Walqui et al., 2010). However, there is a paucity of guidance for teachers on evidence-based instructional approaches for middle school ELs (Cisco and Padrón, 2012).

Cisco and Padrón (2012) reviewed 11 studies published from 1989 to 2010 in education journals that meet standards set by the National Research Council (2002). More recent experimental studies published up to 2016 focus on academic language and content area knowledge and skills in middle school students. Studies have focused on social studies (Vaughn et al., 2009), science (August et al., 2009, 2014), and English language arts (Kim et al., 2011; Lesaux et al., 2010, 2014). All studies were successful in developing ELs' academic language and core content knowledge associated with the interventions that were implemented. Characteristics shared by the studies were a focus on grade-level knowledge and skills; the use of rich core content to develop ELs' language and writing skills; and the provision of additional visual supports (e.g., graphic organizers, illustrations, multimedia) and language supports (e.g., bilingual glossaries) to help ELs comprehend complex content. A noteworthy aspect of all these studies is that the interventions were implemented in classrooms that contained both ELs and English-proficient students and provided regular opportunities for students to talk and work together. The heterogeneous classroom contexts and structured opportunities for collaboration promoted interactions in English between the ELs and English-proficient students, a principle of instructed second language acquisition. Pairing also was done based on students' reading scores. Once students had been paired by language background, they were matched on reading ability. Students worked in pairs for reading, writing, and vocabulary discussions. These promising intervention studies need to be replicated in additional sites.

One study at this grade level (Denton et al., 2008) investigated the effectiveness of a multicomponent reading intervention for students in grades 6-8 with severe learning difficulties. Most of the students in the sample were Spanish-speaking ELs. Students in the treatment group "received daily explicit and systematic small group intervention for 40 minutes a day over 13 weeks, consisting of a modified version of a phonics-based remedial reading program augmented with ESL practices and instruction in vocabulary, fluency, and comprehension strategies" (p. 79). There were no differences in outcomes between treatment and control students. The authors hypothesize that students with the most severe reading disabilities, particularly those that are ELs with limited oral vocabularies, require more intensive interventions (p. 79).

A small number of case studies of individual ELs and their teachers in middle schools (Kim and Viesca, 2016; Protacio, 2013; Valdés, 2001) illuminate situational factors that shape both teaching and learning in these classrooms, including criteria for small groups, whether such groups are based on skills or on a mix of English proficiency and literacy, and teacher beliefs about how students learn language. Studies of the roles of out-of-school settings and youth organizations in supporting ELs' educational success in middle schools remain rare (Zhou, 2000).

The paucity of research on effective and promising practices related to middle school ELs reveals a major gap in knowledge regarding what can be a pivotal time in the education trajectories of ELs. The use of mixed methods that combine quantitative and qualitative approaches to understanding these interventions and whether and how they are sustained in their school and district contexts would be a next step in determining whether these interventions continue to influence how ELs are taught during the regular course of a school year. Despite the limited research, however, the available evidence suggests four promising practices for middle school EL instruction, which are described below.

Promising Practice 1: Provide ELs Access to Grade-Level Core Course Content

For ELs, exposure to grade-level core course content and literacy development provides necessary and crucial access to the forms of language required for academic achievement, and indeed for attaining full proficiency in English (Fillmore, 2014). Moreover, such exposure develops in ELs the concepts and skills needed to continue to master grade-level coursework. Providing middle school ELs with materials at the same grade level as that of materials provided to their peers is important to enable them to meet the requirements for deep understanding, interpretation, and reflection on academic texts in English, as long as such instruction is coupled with evidence-based methods that support ELs in comprehending the core content. Grade-level coursework also helps ensure that students perceive such materials as worth working on, as engaging and meaningful to them (Skinner and Pitzer, 2012). Not surprisingly, engagement in reading (Guthrie, 2004), as Cummins (2011) argues, is an important factor in both language and literacy development. The texts ELs are provided within school, however, may be several years below the level appropriate for their grade (Walqui et al., 2010, pp. 52-53).

In all the studies cited above, ELs were given access to core course content. The interventions were aligned with state grade-level standards, and the support materials, such as textbooks, were grade-level texts. The science experiments conducted in two of the studies (August et al., 2009, 2014) were the same as those required of students across the grade level, including students who were gifted and talented.

Promising Practice 2: Support Comprehension and Writing Related to Core Content

When students are not entirely familiar with the academic language teachers use for instruction or the language of the texts they are using, learning grade-level core content is at best effortful. Thus, students require support from teachers, both linguistically and strategically, to make sense of classroom discourse and course materials. As noted above, characteristics shared by intervention studies were the use of visual supports (e.g., graphic organizers, illustrations, multimedia) and language supports (e.g., bilingual glossaries) to help ELs comprehend complex course content and write about the core content. In several studies, students were taught strategies to support learning. In one study (Kim et al., 2011), students were taught strategies to help them write. These strategies were focused at the word, sentence, and connected text levels. At the text level, for example, students distinguished among plot summaries, evidence or supporting details, and commentary through color coding. In a second study (August et al., 2014), students were taught strategies that enabled them to draw on cognate knowledge to comprehend challenging text and summarize text.

Practice 3: Capitalize on Students' Home Language, Knowledge, and Cultural Assets

Chapter 7 describes the positive English outcomes for ELs instructed bilingually, especially those who have had a sufficient amount of instruction in English. As was the case for studies conducted with children in grades K-5 reviewed earlier, middle school studies that showed positive effects capitalized on ELs' assets even when the instruction was delivered in English. While none of the studies were implemented in bilingual settings, the interventions included bilingual glossaries and teacher explanations in students' home languages and partner work in students' home languages for ELs who were at beginning levels of proficiency in English (August et al., 2009, 2014).

Promising Practice 4: Use Collaborative, Peer Group Learning Communities to Support and Extend Teacher-Led Instruction

Adolescents' growing awareness of their social status in peer groups in school and their community (Smetana et al., 2006), especially how they are perceived as ELs, needs to be considered in planning classroom practices (Cisco and Padrón, 2012; Kim and Viesca, 2016). It is important as well to foster the capacity to engage in dialogue with peers and teachers, especially in science (González-Howard and McNeill, 2016). Such capacities can be developed first during the primary grades and then built upon in middle school to facilitate continued, deeper learning. As discussed earlier, opportunities for middle school ELs to work collaboratively are practices used in studies that show promising learning outcomes for ELs (August et al., 2009, 2014; Lesaux et al., 2010, 2014; Vaughn et al., 2009).

Interpreting the Research

Teaching middle school ELs is a highly complex enterprise for which most teachers are not adequately prepared (DiCerbo et al., 2014). During the middle school years, teachers must not only be skilled in their academic content areas but also be knowledgeable about the subject-specific literacy development of their students and able to address both areas effectively (Lesaux et al., 2012). Research described above points to promising practices in the classroom instruction of middle school ELs. These studies constitute well-controlled interventions of different durations, sometimes part of the school year, and in specific academic subject areas (e.g., science), reflecting the departmentalized nature of middle schools. In addition to the need for replication of these studies under different implementation conditions (e.g., intensity of the professional development of teachers participating in interventions as required to develop their knowledge and skills), research also needs to focus on the full range of academic subject areas. Goldman (2012) notes that literacy needed to acquire knowledge in one subject area (history) is different from that needed to acquire knowledge in another subject area (biology). Examination of the longer-term effects of these interventions on both teacher behaviors and student progress is also needed.

Research on middle school ELs generally has not focused on social and emotional factors that influence the academic performance of ELs, including student motivation and engagement, school and classroom attendance patterns, and behavioral issues that may interfere with the high demands for learning faced by ELs. The relationship among motivation, engagement, and literacy is not easily disentangled, as Frankel and colleagues (2016) have argued. In a recent retrospective on the 1985 report of the Commission on Reading, *Becoming a Nation of Readers*, the authors expand on the report's five principles related to skilled reading. Of particular interest is their expansion on the principle of motivation for reading. At the time that report was produced, it was understood that "reading requires motivation," and motivation is a key to learning to read. Frankel and colleagues argue that reading also requires engagement, "that motivation and engagement in reading are best understood in context" (p. 12), and that the relationship between these aspects of reading changes over time as students move through school. They point out that such motivational factors as self-efficacy, intrinsic motivation for reading, and seeing the value in reading decline as students move from elementary through middle school, leading to a decline not just in reading but in school learning as students grow older. Such changes over time may pose a special challenge for ELs in middle school.

While there have been no direct studies addressing student engagement for ELs, the research on literacy engagement in middle school students appears relevant to ELs. Many ELs become classified as LTELs during middle school, and as discussed in Chapter 6, have begun to slow down in their development of English proficiency. School becomes a struggle for many such students and can have stigmatizing effects (Valdés, 2001).

A study by Guthrie and Davis (2003) aimed at motivating struggling readers in middle school is relevant here. The researchers examined the factors that contributed to the low achievement of these students and to their disengagement from reading. Struggling readers tend to be students with low reading skills—their difficulties with reading have had a dampening effect on their motivation to read, and their sense of self-efficacy suffers, as does their sense of belonging at school. Guthrie and Davis found a distinct decline in reading engagement and motivation from elementary to middle school. From 3rd to 8th grade, students come to view reading as less enjoyable, teachers as less encouraging, and reading as being more boring. Some of these differences relate to the change in school environment from self-contained classes in elementary school to the subject-specific classes in middle school. The biggest difference is in the function and use of written texts. Middle school texts are more complex and demanding than the texts used in elementary school, and students are expected to learn content from them. These texts pose a challenge for any student, but for a student who does not read well, such texts can become further evidence that they do not belong in school. Studies just described need to be conducted on middle school ELs to test whether similar findings apply to them.

Despite the limited research on ELs' learning experiences in middle school classrooms, those experiences can be a significant turning point in their educational trajectories. On the negative side, disengagement may be associated with chronic absence from classes, identification for special education services (see the case study in Annex 10-1 in Chapter 10), suspensions related to behavioral problems, or eventual dropping out of school (Burke, 2015). Alternatively, more effective instruction and engaging school climates can foster ELs' strong motivation to learn and commitment to their educational success in their middle school through high school years. Case studies of middle and high schools described in this chapter demonstrate that it is possible to improve the educational prospects of ELs not only at the classroom but also at the school level. In addition to research on improving classroom instruction and learning conditions, research on how schools sustain positive outcomes found in intervention studies of ELs is needed as part of the scaling up of effective classroom practices.

PROMISING AND EFFECTIVE PRACTICES FOR EDUCATING ENGLISH LEARNERS IN GRADES 9-12

The structure and larger size of some high schools can make the transition from middle school especially difficult for ELs (e.g., Egalite and Kasida, 2016; Leithwood and Jantzi, 2009; Nield, 2009). Some high school ELs may be newcomers to American schools with varying experiences of formal education in their countries of origin and may have experienced disruption in school or trauma as a result of their migration (see Chapter 3), while others may have been in American schools for years. In California, the state with the largest number of ELs (roughly 1.4 million), 59 percent of ELs in high schools are classified as LTELs who have attended primary and middle schools in the United States but not attained the English proficiency required for high school (Olsen, 2010). In secondary schools in California during the 2015-2016 school year, more than 77 percent of students in each grade were LTELs.[10] California is not alone in this regard. Reliable statistics, however, are not available for other states, partly because until recently, there was no clear definition for just when an EL becomes an LTEL, and in many states, LTELs have only recently been recognized as a phenomenon (Menken and Kleyn, 2010).

The new Every Student Succeeds Act (ESSA) reporting provision requires districts receiving Title III funds "to biannually report the number and percentage of students who do not achieve full proficiency in English within five years of initial classification as an EL and first enrollment in the LEA [local education agency]," the point at which ELs can be considered LTELs.[11] By that reckoning, some 57 percent of ELs in middle and high schools can be considered LTELs, as this, according to the U.S. Department of Education's Office of English Language Acquisition, is the proportion of adolescent ELs who are U.S.-born and remain classified as ELs since they entered school at age 5.[12] The actual percentage may well turn out to be much higher when districts begin to report the numbers of ELs in middle and high schools who have been classified as such for 5 years or longer.

In a recent survey of programs and services for ELs in public school districts (Lewis and Gray, 2016), 62 percent of districts with high school grades reported that they are currently enrolling ELs at the high school level (Lewis and Gray, 2016). Sixty-eight percent of districts with high school ELs provided ESL instruction during classes. Sixty-one percent provided either instruction in which the ESL teacher worked with ELs in a content class (push-in) or had ELs move out of a class for ESL services (pull-out). Forty-seven percent of the districts provided sheltered English/content instruction (Lewis and Gray, 2016).

Newcomer programs are specially designed for immigrant high school students new to the United States, but they vary widely in their services from (1) short-term (a month or a summer) to longer-term (one to several years), (2) school site-based to separate site, (3) focus on academic skills to inclusion of supplemental services (e.g., health, counseling, mental health), (4) elementary to secondary, and (5) after-school to half- to full-day. The focus of most programs is to better serve ELs with no to low English lan-

---

[10] See http://dq.cde.ca.gov/dataquest/longtermel/LongTerm.aspx?cds=00&agglevel=State &year=2015-16 [February 23, 2017].

[11] U.S. Department of Education, *Non-Regulatory Guidance: English Learners and Title III of the Elementary and Secondary Education Act (ESEA)*, as amended by the Every Student Succeeds Act (ESSA), September 23, 2016, p. 38 (http://www2.ed.gov/policy/elsec/leg/essa/ essatitleiiiguidenglishlearners92016.pdf [February 23, 2017]).

[12] Office of English Language Acquisition, *Fast Facts: Profiles of English Learners*, January 2015 (http://www2.ed.gov/about/offices/list/oela/fast-facts/pel.pdf [February 23, 2017]).

guage proficiency and to work with ELs with low literacy in their L1. While some programs focus only on English, however, others provide some primary language support and ESL. Sixteen percent of public school districts with high school grades and high school ELs reported having a newcomer program (Lewis and Gray, 2016).

High school ELs must meet graduation requirements as well as state standards for "career and college readiness" and enroll in nonremedial classes that prepare them for postsecondary education. In some schools, ELs are blocked from access to a large proportion of the core curriculum, electives, and advanced placement classes because they are locked into ELD and/or intervention classes, sometimes for much of the school day (Callahan, 2005). Kanno and Kangas (2014) document the mechanism in one high school that resulted in ELs being locked into academic tracks that precluded them from even applying to a 4-year college. They found that once students had been identified as ELs, they were invariably streamed into low-level sheltered or remedial-level nonsheltered classes, apparently with little reference to their English proficiency. The authors note that "the . . . usual pattern was that once placed in remedial-level classes, [ELs] adjusted their expectations and lost the high motivation they might have had originally" (p. 863).

Other studies have found that many students never progress out of these ELD and intervention classes (Callahan, 2005). The classes from which they are blocked are lost opportunities to be exposed to higher levels of English, critical thinking, and complex content concepts relative to those encountered in their ELD and intervention classes. They are effectively isolated from the rest of the English-speaking population at school, often in their own "ghetto" or corner of the school (Gándara and Orfield, 2012; Olsen, 2008; Orfield et al., 2014).

ELs in high school face a number of development challenges as well. The social and cultural contexts in which they are educated—during a time of life when, as adolescents, they must reconcile their school experiences with their evolving sense of self based on their personal history, sociocultural understandings, immigration status, and expectations of adulthood—can be daunting (Suárez-Orozco et al., 2008). The research on adolescent sociopsychological development suggests that the educational environment in which adolescents find themselves can profoundly influence their sense of identity, self-efficacy, and control over their future (Massey et al., 2008). In a study of academic well-being among Latino youth, for example, DeGarmo and Martinez (2006) found that perceived discrimination in school settings was "a significant contributor to academic problems." While there are group and individual differences in how students cope with perceptions of academic bias, even the most resilient can become discouraged. Viewed against that backdrop, the low 4-year adjusted cohort high school graduation rate for ELs of 63 percent (National Center for Education Statistics, 2015) is understandable. For many ELs whose families are struggling economically, the temptation to leave the unsatisfying experience of school behind and take a job to help their family survive economically or to get their own life started can be irresistible, particularly for those from cultural groups that regard the onset of adolescence as the beginning of adulthood rather than as a separate stage of life (Arnett, 2003; Esparza and Sánchez, 2008).

Overall, research examining instructional practices with ELs in secondary school is less reliable than that for ELs in elementary school. However, the Institute for Education Sciences (IES) Practice Guide offers recommendations for instructional practices associated with positive language and literacy outcomes for adolescents in general (Kamil et al., 2008) that arguably also are applicable to ELs, as well as practices for ELs in elementary and middle schools (Baker et al., 2014; Gersten et al., 2007) that continue to be relevant in high school instruction. In addition, a review of a study of the Pathways Project (U.S. Department of Education et al., 2012) is available. From these sources, the committee derived nine promising practices that can inform the education of ELs in high school (Baker et al., 2014; Gersten et al., 2007; Kamil et al., 2008; U.S. Department of Education et al., 2012):

- development of academic English (Gersten et al., 2007) and its varied grammatical structures and vocabulary (Baker et al., 2014) as part of subject matter learning;
- integration of oral and written language instruction into content area teaching (Baker et al., 2014);
- provision of regular structured opportunities to develop written language skills (Gersten et al., 2007);
- development of reading and writing abilities of ELs through text-based, analytical instruction using a cognitive strategies approach (U.S. Department of Education et al., 2012);
- provision of direct and explicit comprehension strategy instruction (Kamil et al., 2008; U.S. Department of Education et al., 2012);
- provision of opportunities for extended discussion of text meaning and interpretation (Kamil et al., 2008; U.S. Department of Education et al., 2012);
- fostering of student motivation for and engagement in literacy learning (Kamil et al., 2008);
- provision of regular peer-assisted learning opportunities; and
- provision of small-group instructional support for students struggling with literacy and English language development (Gersten et al., 2007).

The promise of these practices is apparent in a recent study of six high schools in the northeastern region of the United States (Castellón et al., 2015). The report of the Schools to Learn From study, funded by the Carnegie Corporation of New York, provides detailed descriptions of instructional practices, lessons, materials, and student work, along with results of interviews with administrators and teachers who offered their views on the educational needs of their students that guided their work. Each school was unique, but they all shared a common vision concerning the central role of schools in preparing ELs for college and careers. Schools selected for the study included those with higher-than-average EL high school graduation and postsecondary entry rates[13] (see Box 8-2).

Promising Practice 1: Develop Academic English as Part of Subject-Matter Learning

For ELs at the secondary level in particular, acquiring the forms and structures of academic English is vital to reading, writing, and engagement in the curricular content (Bailey, 2007; Scarcella, 2003; Schleppegrell, 2001). The language used in texts and other instructional materials across the curriculum is sufficiently different from the spoken language of social discourse to constitute a barrier to understanding and learning for students who have not yet developed academic English as used in content areas (Anstrom et al., 2010; Cummins, 1979; Fillmore and Snow, 2000; Schleppegrell, 2004). Overcoming this barrier requires that teachers intentionally develop ELs' language skills in the context of the curricular subjects they teach (Derewianka and Jones, 2013).

Comparisons of the use of academic language in science or social studies with the use of language in literary narratives reveal how language can vary among disciplines. No one arrives at school already proficient in specialized language, which is learned through meaningful literacy activities. The way one learns such language, whether as a native speaker of English or an EL, is by reading and engaging with materials written in that language, discussing their meaning with others, and attempting to express one's thoughts using the forms and structures one has encountered in those materials. Students who lack the requisite language or literacy skills require structured, coordinated instructional support—scaffolding (Walqui and van Lier, 2010), discussion (Zwiers et al., 2014; Zwiers, 2017, and attention

---

[13] The high schools in this study were Boston International High School and Newcomers Academy (Boston, Massachusetts), High School for Dual Language and Asian Studies (Manhattan, New York), It Takes a Village Academy (Brooklyn, New York), Manhattan Bridges High School (Manhattan, New York), Marble Hill School for International Studies (Bronx, New York), and New World High School (Bronx, New York).

BOX 8-2
Characteristics and Design Elements of High
Schools in the Schools to Learn from Study

The six schools in this study varied in the size of their EL population, from 20 percent to 83.7 percent, with slight differences in the proportion of students (80 to 100%) who qualified for free or reduced-price lunch. They were all relatively small schools (from 381 to 566 students) and varied in ethnic diversity.

The instructional practices and programs at the six schools varied as well. Instruction in English as a second language (ESL) was necessary but even more so were the many courses of the high school curriculum. Students in New York, where five of the six schools were located, had to pass a demanding set of tests to graduate from high school, while students in Massachusetts, site of the sixth school, had to complete a capstone research project and pass both the Massachusetts Comprehensive Assessment System (MCAS) and end-of-year state assessments in several subjects. Thus teachers at these schools created opportunities for students to work together for extended practice on rigorous course materials. Teachers did not just assign materials, but provided the ongoing support students needed to deal with the materials' language demands. The six schools shared the following characteristics:

- Their missions guided hiring of staff, scheduling, course programming, professional learning, and partnerships with community organizations.
- They maintained a goal of continuous improvement. Administrators and educators constantly looked for ways to improve student success and were guided by student data in adjusting instructional practices.
- Everyone shared responsibility for students' success. Teachers, administrators, staff, parents, and fellow students were ready to help when anyone required additional support.
- They were attuned to student needs and capacities. ELs, especially newcomers and those needing help in developing basic skills, received support in acquiring language and literacy skills across the content areas of the curriculum.
- They valued cultural and linguistic diversity among their students. Time and resources were devoted to ensuring that students were proud of their identities and abilities and those of their peers.

The study report notes that no particular program model or curriculum was responsible for the unusual success of the six schools, but specific design elements with related instructional practices made a difference:

- School leadership was passionate and mission-driven and worked collectively with staff toward the school's mission.
- Leadership teams of teachers and administrators engaged in staff development, leading or participating in professional development activities.
- Staff members felt respected, inspired, and valued by the leadership team.
- Improvement was provided through ongoing reflection and continual assessment of progress.
- The priority in staffing was on hiring teachers and staff who could speak the students' first languages or were themselves immigrants and on recruiting former ELs.
- Ongoing assessment and follow-through were an important design feature. In addition to the performance data routinely collected by schools and districts, educators in these schools collected data on students, their families, and their needs through diagnostic interviews and home visits.
- Social-emotional support was an integral design feature. Such support is a necessity for ELs, for whom the transition to secondary school may have involved a move to the United States, separation from family and friends, trauma, and the challenges of entering a world where little was familiar.
- A unified language development framework integrated content, the development of analytical skills and practices, alternative interpretations of content, and argumentation for those interpretations based on text analyses.
- Carefully orchestrated structures allowed for flexibility through block schedules, after-school and weekend tutoring, and "looping"—the practice of a teacher remaining with the same group of students for more than a single school year.
- Strategic partnerships with community organizations provided extracurricular options and opportunities for students, families, and faculty to augment classroom learning.

Castellón and colleagues (2015) provide numerous examples of the above practices, as do several other methodologically sound studies of the ongoing Pathways Project (Kim et al., 2011; Matuchiniak et al., 2014).

SOURCE: Summarized from Castellón et al. (2015).

to the way language is used to convey information (Bailey, 2007; Fillmore and Fillmore, 2012; Schleppegrell, 2001).

Studies of high schools provide many examples of academic language and vocabulary instruction, but rarely in isolation from content. The language development framework at Boston's International High School and Newcomer Academy (BINcA), one of the schools studied by Castellón and colleagues (2015), serves as an example of an instructional endeavor in which ELs received contextualized support for learning academic language (see Box 8-2). The school provides ESL/ELD classes, but language and literacy goals are aspects of all content courses. Teachers also work together to ensure that such goals are core practices (see Box 8-3).

Promising Practice 2: Integrate Oral and Written Language Instruction into Content Area Teaching

The integration of both oral and written language into content instruction was widely practiced in all of the high schools included in the Schools to Learn From Study, as illustrated by the BINcA example in Box 8-3. Indeed, this practice was evident in all of the instructional vignettes included in the Castellón et al. (2015) report, whether the lesson was on science, global history, or literature (see also Box 8-4).

Promising Practices 3, 4, and 5: Provide Regular Structured Opportunities to Develop Written Language Skills; Develop Reading and Writing Abilities of ELs Through Text-Based, Analytical Instruction Using a Cognitive Strategies Approach; and Provide Direct and Explicit Comprehension Strategy Instruction

The Pathways Project provides excellent examples of instructional efforts to develop reading and writing abilities and skills through text-based instruction. Descriptions of such lessons are reported in papers by researchers who have studied the project's effects on student learning in the Santa Ana School District in California (Kim et al., 2011; Matuchniak et al., 2014). The Pathways Project has tackled the problems many ELs experience in reading and writing in a language in which they are not yet fully proficient.

The approach taken by the Pathways Project to improve literacy skills for ELs was characterized as a "cognitive strategies approach," in which teachers received sustained professional development and coaching in working with ELs in mainstream (integrated) classrooms. Teachers learned techniques for teaching students the thinking tools and cognitive strategies that experienced readers and writers use to understand and interpret the texts they read or to compose and express their thoughts and ideas in writing.

BOX 8-3
Example of the Incorporation of Language and
Literacy Goals into Content Instruction

Castellón and colleagues (2015) provide an example of how organically content, language, and literacy can come together. In a 10th-grade English class at Boston's International High School and Newcomer Academy (BINcA), students had read Geoffrey Canada's plan for revitalizing the Harlem Children's Zone program. They were guided to consider whether the proposed plan was likely to be effective and for what reasons, and what they would add or change to make it more so. The teacher provided "sentence starters" as frames for students to use in discussion and writing: "I concur with the idea that. . . ; I take issue with the fact that . . .; To make this program more effective, I would . . ." The teacher then led the students in a discussion of the pros and cons of Canada's proposal to pay students to attend school. The students received an "academic discourse hand-out" to support their practice of "academic talk moves" (Michaels and O'Connor, 2015) in discussions and in writing.

The discourse starters were organized under skills students were encouraged to develop for asking questions to move a conversation forward (e.g., "What would happen if . . ."); for addressing questions that had been raised (e.g., "In response to X's question . . ."); for incorporating others into the discussion (e.g., "Can you say more about . . ."); for explaining a change of opinion or ideas based on new information or evidence ("After considering what X said about . . . I have reconsidered my opinion . . ."). During these teacher-facilitated discussions, students considered a provocative question related to educational policy and practice, but they also learned to use the language of academic discourse for writing and expressing their thoughts on the issue. Vocabulary development was part of these instructional activities, but it was not just about words that required explication or were to be committed to memory. Language was learned not through memorization of separate words, but by students' coming to understand the meanings, nuances, and functions of words, phrases, and expressions in the contexts of oral and written communications.

SOURCE: Summarized from Castellón et al. (2015).

Teachers helped students learn strategies for reading with greater understanding and engaging in higher-level thinking as they did so through direct instruction and modeling by their teachers (Kim et al., 2011; Matuchniak et al., 2014, p. 980). Students learned to apply these strategies during reading and writing activities and to practice their use in collaborative groups and independently over time. The project forcefully demonstrated that after 2 years of such instructional support, the ELs in this study had internalized these strategies and could apply them in the reading and writing they had to do in school (Matuchniak et al., 2014). The project has now entered

---

BOX 8-4
An Example of the Integration of Language
Instruction into Content Area Teaching

A class in one of the Schools to Learn From high schools—It takes a Village Academy—was studying the Vietnam War. Students were asked to jot down notes on the sequence of events leading to the war and then compare their notes with those of a classmate. The lesson built on what students had learned on previous days, and now they had to recollect the order in which events happened and details about those events. They recalled, they wrote, and they discussed their understanding of the events with one another. The students then participated in a whole-class, teacher-led discussion, and as they offered their accounts of the events and the relationships among them, the teacher pointed out connections, drew attention to vocabulary items that were used, and taught academic vocabulary in the context of the lesson. Using such strategies as think-pair-share, students were given time to practice speaking with peers before being called on to express their ideas to the whole class. The use of graphic organizers helped students see connections and relationships among ideas and to organize their thoughts before being asked to write about them. Such visual scaffolding enabled the students to gain access to the meaning of the materials they were studying, even at early stages of learning English.

SOURCE: Summarized from Castellón et al. (2015).

---

an expansion phase that involves training middle and high school teachers from four Southern California school districts.[14]

Promising Practice 6: Provide Opportunities for Extended Discussion of Text Meaning and Interpretation

Opportunities for extended discussion of text are important for all students but are crucial to the development of text understanding for ELs. The report on the Schools to Learn From study documents various instructional methods, such as Socratic Seminar[15] and the Danielson Framework,[16] for engaging students in such discussion. At the High School for Dual Language and Asian Studies, for example, 11th-grade students in a U.S. history class performed a close reading and analysis of *Korematsu v. U.S.* (1944), the landmark Supreme Court case on the constitutionality of Executive Order

---

[14] See http://education.uci.edu/research/olson_grant_911.php [February 22, 2017].
[15] See https://www.paideia.org/about-paideia/socratic-seminar [February 22, 2017].
[16] See https://www.danielsongroup.org/framework [February 22, 2017].

9066, which ordered the placement of Japanese Americans in internment camps irrespective of their citizenship (Castellón et al., 2015, pp. 46-50). ELs and non-ELs worked together, guided by probing questions about the complex and difficult language of the court ruling. Students took turns as "discussion director" or "discussion facilitator" and prepared questions that guided group discussion of the arguments contained in this historical text.

Promising Practice 7: Foster Student Motivation for and Engagement in Literacy Learning

At a high-performing science, technology, engineering, and mathematics (STEM) school in the Hell's Kitchen neighborhood of Manhattan—the Manhattan Bridges High School—Hispanic students can chose an engineering or information technology focus while also developing their bilingual academic language skills. At the time of the Schools to Learn From study, 53 percent of the students at this school were ELs, many of them having experienced an interruption in their education. These latter students were able to build on what they already knew as they made the transition to a school in a predominantly English-speaking community. The school describes its dual language focus as one that embraces a concept mentioned earlier— "translanguaging"—a mode of communication in which bilingual speakers move fluidly between languages. At Manhattan Bridges, students' home language—Spanish—is viewed as an asset to their lives to be developed, rather than as an obstacle to academic progress. Students study English and Spanish literature and engage in probing discussions of poetry and literary works in both languages. In an Advanced Placement Spanish class, students observed for the Schools to Learn From study discussed the Spanish literary movement known as the "Generation of '98." They read three types of poetry—El Romance, El Soneto, and La Silva—and were prepared to discuss their critical analyses with the class. In small groups, the students took turns presenting their analyses in Spanish. Classmates listened, asked questions, and evaluated the presentations based on a rubric the teacher had provided (Castellón et al., 2015, pp. 98-138). Students were motivated to read and to learn not only about the subjects that would lead to careers in STEM, but also about literature and the arts to gain insight into the human condition and their own lives.

Promising Practice 8: Provide Regular Peer-Assisted Learning Opportunities

While thoroughly prepared professional teachers provide the essential support required by ELs for linguistic and academic development, peers can play important roles as well. At one of the high schools in the Schools to Learn From study—Marble Hill School for International Studies—project-based learning is practiced, whereby teams of students work together on inquiry-based projects across the curriculum. Project work for newcomers or beginning ELs takes place primarily in their ESL or sheltered content classes, where teachers provide the support needed by the students to conduct research and to ensure that they receive the language and literacy instruction they require. ELs are not placed in groups with English-dominant students until they have learned enough English in ESL and sheltered classes to feel confident about working with their English-dominant peers as equals. At that point, ELs benefit from working closely with these peers, not as tutees and tutors, but as co-participants in the work of the project. Scaffolding of learning is not viewed as the exclusive responsibility of teachers, but one that students are encouraged to assume for one another as well. In a 9th-grade algebra class observed for the Schools to Learn From study, ELs worked in groups on quadratic equations that had been set up at four stations. The problem at the first station was the most difficult, so the teacher provided the support needed by students until they understood the concept well enough to move on. The problem at the next station called for the students to recall what they had already learned and to apply it to solve another problem, and so on. Finally, when students arrived at the fourth station, they found word problems, which they had to solve without teacher support. Here, they were encouraged to work together and to provide mutual support in dealing with the problems at hand (Castellón et al., 2015, pp. 139-180).

Promising Practice 9: Provide Small-Group Instructional Support for Students Struggling with Literacy and English Language Development

Among high school students classified as ELs are those whose struggles with language and literacy require instructional support beyond what teachers can ordinarily provide in the regular classroom. These students include newcomers with little prior formal education or disrupted educational experiences and LTELs who have been instructed inappropriately in previous grades. The educational needs of these two types of ELs are quite different, however.

For newcomers, the greatest need for instructional support, especially in high schools where support for students' L1 is not available, is intensive ESL. At Newcomer Academy at the Boston International High School, newcomers receive high-intensity courses in English for 2 years or a sheltered English immersion program, which is designed to give them access to academic content along with the development of English skills. Newcomers who have had interrupted formal education or limited prior schooling receive skill-building courses in their native language to prepare them for the intensive language training program.

On the other hand, LTELs who are struggling in school because of literacy problems tend to be quite proficient in spoken English but much less so in the academic English in which texts are written. Some of these students may even have fairly good decoding skills in reading but be unable to make much sense of the materials they read. As a result, their academic progress is hampered, and they may believe that they lack the ability to perform well in school. These students have varied needs, but what they do not need is more ESL or remedial reading courses, where they are provided more of what they have often been receiving for years (Olsen, 2014). Instead, what LTELs need is rigorous, intensive, and relevant support in small groups, supported by teachers who can offer the kind of attention they need to discover how language works in texts. They need to learn to use strategies such as those used in the Pathway Project.

CONCLUSIONS

Conclusion 8-1: The following instructional practices are effective in developing elementary school-aged English learners' knowledge of academic subject matter: providing explicit instruction focused on developing key aspects of literacy; developing academic language during content area instruction; providing support to make core content comprehensible; encouraging peer-assisted learning opportunities; capitalizing on students' home language, knowledge, and cultural assets; screening for language and literacy challenges and monitoring progress; and providing small-group academic support for students to learn grade-level core content.

Conclusion 8-2: Research on classroom practices does not account for the potential influence of developmental factors such as age or grade of the students and associated cognitive and social changes that may influence their learning. Thus, conclusions about effective practices are based on syntheses of research involving students in particular grades or grade spans, from kindergarten through middle school (K-8) or K-12, on the assumption that evidence-based practices apply to students in all grades and that the changing cognitive, social, and emotional development of students during those grades does not condition or interact with outcomes.

Conclusion 8-3: Research on English learners' (ELs') language and academic subject learning in middle school is consistent with findings from studies conducted with children in the previous grades and supports the identification of promising practices during the primary grades (pre-K to 5). However, the developmental needs of young adolescent ELs—specifically their cognitive and social development—and their adaptation to a different organizational structure and expectations for student independence in middle school are important factors to consider in designing and implementing instructional strategies in middle school. The processes of identity formation and social awareness, which increase during adolescence, point to the importance of teacher beliefs about ELs and their attitudes toward learning English when working with middle school ELs.

Conclusion 8-4: Literacy engagement is critical during the middle school grades. During these grades, students are required to read and learn from advanced and complex grade-level texts. For English learners (ELs), this problem is acute because instructional support for long-term ELs tends to emphasize skills instead of dealing with the barriers to their motivation to learn, engagement in the classroom, and literacy engagement.

Conclusion 8-5: Instruction that fails to address appropriately the linguistic, cultural, socioemotional, and academic needs of English learners (ELs) when they first enter elementary school leads to their lack of progress and to the growing number of long-term ELs in secondary schools, which in turn can lead to disengagement in these students. Practices for long-term ELs that focus on identifying their assets and addressing their diverse linguistic and academic needs, as well as their socioemotional reengagement and full integration into grade-level classrooms, can lead to improved academic outcomes.

Conclusion 8-6: Research on instruction in academic language has focused on the acquisition of specific skills in isolation, rather than on the integration of these skills into higher level processing and linguistic competence. Some promising practices at the middle school level for developing academic language and domain knowledge include use of the student's first language to support learning across content areas; use of collaborative and peer groups to support and extend instruction; and use of grade-level texts with appropriate supports to provide access to complex language and content.

Conclusion 8-7: The stakes for high school English learners (ELs) are particularly critical with respect to their postsecondary education and career opportunities. For newcomer students and long-term ELs, there is little research on effective approaches. ELs (including long-term

ELs) are frequently placed in intervention/remedial-level classes that have neither been designed for ELs nor shown to be effective, which precludes them from access to classes that would prepare them for college or careers.

Conclusion 8-8: There is less research on effective instructional practices for high school English learners (ELs) than for the other grade spans. However, some promising practices include a focus on academic language development that embraces all facets of academic language and includes both oral and written language across content areas; structured reading and writing instruction using a cognitive strategies approach and explicit instruction in reading comprehension strategies; opportunities for extended discussion of text and its meaning between teachers and students and in peer groups that may foster motivation and engagement in literacy learning; provision of peer-assisted learning opportunities; and rigorous, focused, and relevant support for long-term ELs.

Conclusion 8-9: Research on the literacy engagement of English learners (ELs) and its relationship to educational outcomes is limited despite its potential importance. Current research indicates that literacy engagement may be an important factor for ELs in their learning to read, in their academic language learning from school texts, and in their literacy and academic achievement. Literacy engagement may be even more important for ELs than for students whose first language is English because (1) learning to read in a language one is still learning is difficult, and literacy engagement can support ELs' efforts to learn despite those difficulties; and (2) literacy is necessary to learning academic language. If ELs do not read well and are not motivated to read, they will find it difficult to learn the academic language required for reclassification.

BIBLIOGRAPHY

Alexander, P.A., and Jetton, T.L. (2000). Learning from text: A multidimensional and developmental perspective. *Handbook of Reading Research, 3*, 285-310.

Anstrom, K., DiCerbo, P., Butler, F., Katz, A., Millet, J., and Rivera, C. (2010). *A Review of the Literature on Academic English: Implications for K-12 English Language Learners.* Arlington, VA: The George Washington University Center for Equity and Excellence in Education.

Arnett, J.J. (2003). Conceptions of the transition to adulthood among emerging adults in American ethnic groups. *New Directions for Child and Adolescent Development, 100*, 63-75.

August, D., and Erickson, F. (2006). Qualitative studies of classroom and school practices. In D. August and T. Shanahan (Ed.), *Developing Literacy in Second-Language Learners: Report of the National Literacy Panel on Language-Minority Children and Youth* (pp. 489-522). Mahwah, NJ: Lawrence Erlbaum Associates.

August, D., Branum-Martin, L., Cardenas-Hagan, E., and Francis, D.J. (2009). The impact of an instructional intervention on the science and language learning of middle grade English language learners. *Journal of Research on Educational Effectiveness, 2*(4), 345-376.

August, D., Branum-Martin, L., Cárdenas-Hagan, E., Francis, D.J., Powell, J., Moore, S., and Haynes, E.F. (2014). Helping ELLs meet the common core state standards for literacy in science: The impact of an instructional intervention focused on academic language. *Journal of Research on Educational Effectiveness, 7*(1), 54-82.

Bailey, A.L. (2007). *The Language Demands of School: Putting Academic English to the Test.* New Haven, CT: Yale University Press.

Baker, S., Lesaux, N., Jayanthi, M., Dimino, J., Proctor, C.P., Morris, J., Gersten, R., Haymond, K., Kieffer, M.J., and Linan-Thompson, S. (2014). *Teaching Academic Content and Literacy to English Learners in Elementary and Middle School.* NCES2014-4012. Washington, DC: National Center for Education Evaluation and Regional Assistance, Institute of Education Sciences, U.S. Department of Education. Available: http://ies.ed.gov/ncee/wwc/Docs/practiceguide/english_learners_pg_040114.pdf [November 6, 2016].

Barnhardt, R., and Kawagley, A.O. (2005). Indigenous knowledge systems and Alaska Native ways of knowing. *Anthropology and Education Quarterly, 36*(1), 8-23.

Beers, S.F., and Nagy, W.E. (2011). Writing development in four genres from grades three to seven: Syntactic complexity and genre differentiation. *Reading and Writing, 24*(2), 183-202.

Bernhard, J.K., Cummins, J., Campoy, F.I., Ada, F.A., Winsler, A., and Bleiker, C. (2006). Identity texts and literacy development among preschool English language learners: Enhancing learning opportunities for children at risk of learning disabilities. *Teachers College Record, 108*(11), 2380-2405.

Biber, D. (2009). Are there linguistic consequences of literacy? Comparing the potentials of language use in speech and writing. In D.R. Olson and N. Torrance (Eds.), *Cambridge Handbook of Literacy* (pp. 75-91). New York: Cambridge University Press.

Black, P., and Wiliam, D. (1998). Assessment and classroom learning. *Assessment in Education: Principles, Policy and Practice, 5*(1), 7-74.

Boyle, A., August, D., Tabaku, L., Cole, S., and Simpson-Baird, A. (2015). *Dual Language Education Programs: Current State Policies and Practices.* Washington, DC: U.S. Department of Education, Office of English Language Acquisition.

Brown, B., Ryoo, K., and Rodriguez, J. 2010. Pathway towards fluency: Using disaggregate instruction to promote science literacy. *International Journal of Science Education, 32*(11), 1465-1493.

Burke, A. (2015). *Suspension, Expulsion, and Achievement of English Learner Students in Six Oregon Districts.* REL 2015-094. Washington, DC: U.S. Department of Education, Institute of Education Sciences, National Center for Education Evaluation and Regional Assistance, Regional Educational Laboratory Northwest. Available: http://ies.ed.gov/ncee/edlabs/regions/northwest/pdf/REL_2015094.pdf [November 6, 2016].

Burns, D.A. (2011). *Examining the Effect of an Overt Transition Intervention on the Reading Development of At-Risk English-Language Learners in First Grade.* Ph.D. Dissertation Eugene: University of Oregon.

Calderón, M., Hertz-Lazarowitz, R., and Slavin, R. (1998). Effects of bilingual cooperative integrated reading and composition on students transitioning from Spanish to English reading. *Elementary School Journal, 99*(2), 153-165.

Calhoun, M.B., Al Otaiba, S., Cihak, D., King, A., and Avalos, A. (2007). Effects of a peer-mediated program on reading skill acquisition for two-way bilingual first-grade classrooms. *Learning Disability Quarterly, 30*(3), 169-184.

Callahan, R.M. (2005). Tracking and high school English learners: Limiting opportunity to learn. *American Educational Research Journal, 42*(2), 305-328.

Carlo, M.S., August, D., McLaughlin, B., Snow, C.E., Dressler, C., Lippman, D.N., Lively, T.J., and White, C.E. (2004). Closing the gap: Addressing the vocabulary needs of English-language learners in bilingual and mainstream classrooms. *RRQ Reading Research Quarterly, 39*(2), 188-215.

Castellón, M., Cheuk, T., Greene, R., Mercado-Garcia, D., Santos, M., Skarin, R., and Zerkel, L. (2015). *Schools to Learn From: How Six High Schools Graduate English Language Learners College and Career Ready.* Stanford, CA: Stanford University Graduate School of Education. Available: http://ell.stanford.edu/sites/default/files/Schools%20to%20Learn%20From%20.pdf [November 6, 2016].

Cisco, B.K., and Padrón, Y. (2012). Investigating vocabulary and reading strategies with middle grades English language learners: A research synthesis. *RMLE Online, 36*(4), 1-23.

Crevecoeur, Y.C., Coyne, M.D., and McCoach, D.B. (2014). English language learners and English-only learners' response to direct vocabulary instruction. *Reading and Writing Quarterly, 30*(1), 51-78.

Crosnoe, R. (2006). *Mexican Roots, American Schools: Helping Mexican Immigrant Children Succeed.* Stanford, CA: Stanford University Press.

Cummins, J. (1979). Linguistic interdependence and the educational development of bilingual children. *Review of Educational Research, 49*(2), 222-251.

Cummins, J. (2003). Challenging the construction of difference as deficit: Where are identity, intellect, imagination and power in the new regime of truth? In P.P. Trifonas (Ed.), *Pedagogies of Difference: Rethinking Education for Social Change* (pp. 39-58). New York: Routledge Falmer.

Cummins, J. (2011). Literacy engagement: Fueling academic growth for English learners. *The Reading Teacher, 65*(2), 142-146.

DeGarmo, D.S., and Martinez, Jr., C.R. (2006). A culturally informed model of academic well-being for Latino youth: The importance of discriminatory experiences and social support. *Family Relations, 55*(3), 267-278.

Denton, C.A., Anthony, J.L., Parker, R., and Hasbrouck, J.E. (2004). Effects of two tutoring programs on the English reading development of Spanish-English bilingual students. *The Elementary School Journal, 104*(4), 289-305.

Denton, C.A., Wexler, J., Vaughn, S., and Bryan, D. (2008). Intervention provided to linguistically diverse middle school students with severe reading difficulties. *Learning Disabilities Research and Practice, 23*, 79-89.

Derewianka, B., and Jones, P. (2013). *Teaching Language in Context.* Oxford, UK: Oxford University Press.

DiCerbo, P.A., Anstrom, K.A., Baker, L L., and Rivera, C. (2014). A review of the literature on teaching academic English to English language learners. *Review of Educational Research, 84*(3), 446-482.

Dressler, C., and Kamil, M.L. (2006). First-and second-language literacy. In D. August and T. Shanahan (Eds.), *Developing Literacy in Second-Language Learners: Report of the National Literacy Panel on Language-Minority Children and Youth* (pp. 197-238). Mahwah, NJ: Lawrence Erlbaum Associates.

Duke, N. (2000). For the rich, it's richer: Print experiences and environments offered to children in very low- and very high-socioeconomic status first-grade classrooms. *American Educational Research Journal, 37*(2), 441-478.

Duke, N., and Carlisle, J.F. (2011). Comprehension development. *Handbook of Reading Research, 4*, 199-228.

Dweck, C.S. (1999). *Self-Theories: Their Role in Motivation, Personality, and Development.* Philadelphia, PA: Psychology Press.

Dweck, C.S. (2007). *Mindset: The New Psychology of Success.* New York: Ballantine Books.

Eccles, J.S. (2008). Agency and structure in human development. *Research in Human Development, 5*(4), 231-243.

Egalite, A.J., and Kisida, B. (2016). School size and student achievement: A longitudinal analysis. *School Effectiveness and School Improvement, 27*(3), 1-12.

Esparza, P., and Sánchez, B. (2008). The role of attitudinal familism in academic outcomes: A study of urban, Latino high school seniors. *Cultural Diversity and Ethnic Minority Psychology, 14*(3), 193-200.

Fitzgerald, J., and Noblit, G. (2000). Balance in the making: Learning to read in an ethnically diverse first-grade classroom. *Journal of Educational Psychology, 92*(1), 3-22.

Frankel, K.K., Becker, B.L., Rowe, M.W., and Pearson, P.D. (2016). From "What is reading?" to What is literacy? *Journal of Education, 196*(3), 7-17.

Gándara, P. (2016, November 30). *Educating Immigrant Students and Emergent Bilinguals in an Anti-Immigrant Era.* American Educational Research Association Centennial Lecture Series. Brooklyn, NY: Brooklyn Museum.

Gándara, P., and Orfield, G. (2012). Segregating Arizona's English learners: A return to the "Mexico Room"? *Teachers College Record, 114*(090302), 1-27.

Gee, J.P. (2001). Reading as situated language: A sociocognitive perspective. *Journal of Adolescent and Adult Literacy, 44*(8), 714-725.

Gersten, R., Baker, S.K., Shanahan, T., Linan-Thompson, S., Collins, P., and Scarcella, R. (2007). *Effective Literacy and English Language Instruction for English Learners in the Elementary Grades.* IES Practice Guide. NCEE 2007-4011. Washington, DC: National Center for Education Evaluation and Regional Assistance, Institute of Education Sciences, U.S. Department of Education. Available: http://ies.ed.gov/ncee/pdf/20074011.pdf [November 6, 2016].

Gewertz, C. (2014). "Platooning" on the rise in early grades. *Education Week,* February 19.

Goldman, S.R. (2012). Adolescent literacy: Learning and understanding content. *The Future of Children, 22*(2), 89-116.

González-Howard, M., and McNeill, K.L. (2016). Learning in a community of practice: Factors impacting English-learning students' engagement in scientific argumentation. *Journal of Research in Science Teaching, 53*(4), 527-553.

Gunn, B., Smolkowski, K., Biglan, A., and Black, C. (2002). Supplemental instruction in decoding skills for Hispanic and non-Hispanic students in early elementary school: A follow-up. *Journal of Special Education, 39*(2), 66-85.

Guthrie, J.T. (2004). Teaching for literacy engagement. *Journal of Literacy Research, 36*(1), 1-30.

Guthrie, J.T., and Davis, M.H. (2003). Motivating struggling readers in middle school through an engagement model of classroom practice. *Reading and Writing Quarterly, 19*(1), 59-85.

Guthrie, J.T., and Wigfield, A. (2000). Engagement and motivation in reading. In M.L. Kamil, P.B. Mosenthal, P.D. Pearson, and R. Barr (Eds.), *Handbook of Reading Research* (Vol. 3) (pp. 403-422). New York and London: Routledge.

Guthrie, J.T., and Wigfield, A. (2004). Roles of motivation and engagement in reading comprehension assessment. In S. Paris and S. Stahl (Eds.), *Assessing Children's Reading Comprehension.* Mahwah, NJ: Lawrence Erlbaum Associates.

Guthrie, J.T., Van Meter, P., McCann, A.D., Wigfield, A., Bennett, L. Poundstone, C.C., Rice, M.E., Faibisch, F.M., Hunt, B., and Mitchell, A.M. (1996). *Growth of Literacy Engagement: Changes in Motivation and Strategies during Concept-Oriented Reading Instruction. Reading Research Quarterly, 31*(3), 306-332. Available: https://msu.edu/~dwong/CEP991/CEP991Resources/Guthrie-MotRdng.pdf [February 16, 2017].

Halliday, M.A.K. (1987). Spoken and written modes of meaning. In R. Horowitz and S.J. Samuels (Eds.), *Comprehending Oral and Written Language* (pp. 55–82). San Diego, CA: Academic Press.

Harry, B., and Klingner, J. (2007). Discarding the deficit model. *Educational Leadership, 64*(5), 16-21.

Hayes, D.P. (1988). Speaking and writing: Distinct patterns of word choice. *Journal of Memory and Language, 27*, 572-585.

Hood, L. (2009). "Platooning" instruction: Districts weigh pros and cons of departmentalizing elementary schools. *Harvard Education Letter, 25*(6), 1-3.

Institute of Medicine and National Research Council. (2015). *Transforming the Workforce for Children Birth through Age 8: A Unifying Foundation.* L. Allen and B.B. Kelly (Eds.). Board on Children, Youth, and Families; Committee on the Science of Children Birth to Age 8: Deepening and Broadening the Foundation for Success. Washington, DC: The National Academies Press.

Johnson, R.K., and Swain, M. (1997). *Immersion Education: International Perspectives.* Cambridge, NY: Cambridge University Press.

John-Steiner, V., and Mahn, H. (2012). Sociocultural approaches to learning and development: A Vygotskian Framework. *Educational Psychologist, 31*(3/4), 191-206.

Kamil, M.L., Borman, G.D., Dole, J., Kral, C.C., Salinger, T., and Torgesen, J. (2008). *Improving Adolescent Literacy: Effective Classroom and Intervention Practices: A Practice Guide.* NCEE 2008-4027. Washington, DC: National Center for Education Evaluation and Regional Assistance, Institute of Education Sciences, U.S. Department of Education. Available: http://ies.ed.gov/ncee/wwc [November 16, 2016].

Kanno, Y., and Kangas, S.E.N. (2014). "I'm not going to be, like for the AP": English language learners' limited access to advanced college-preparatory courses in high school. *American Educational Research Journal, 51*(5), 848-878.

Kim, J.I., and Viesca, K.M. (2016). Three reading-intervention teachers' identity positioning and practices to motivate and engage emergent bilinguals in an urban middle school. *Teaching and Teacher Education, 55*, 122-132.

Kim, J.S., Olson, C.B., Scarcella, R., Kramer, J., Pearson, M., Van Dyk, D., Collins, P., and Land, R.E. (2011). A randomized experiment of a cognitive strategies approach to text-based analytical writing for mainstreamed Latino English language learners in grades 6 to 12. *Journal of Research on Educational Effectiveness, 4*(3), 231-263.

Kintsch, W., and Rawson, K.A. (2005). Comprehension. In S.G. Paris and S.A. Stahl (Eds.), *Children's Reading Comprehension and Assessment* (pp. 71-92). New York: Routledge.

Leithwood, K., and Jantzi, D. (2009). A review of empirical evidence about school size effects: A policy perspective. *Review of Educational Research, 79*(1), 464-490.

Lerner, R.M., and Steinberg, L. (2009). *Handbook of Adolescent Psychology* (2nd Edition). Hoboken, NJ: John Wiley and Sons.

Lesaux, N.K., Kieffer, M.J., Faller, S.E., and Kelley, J.G. (2010). The effectiveness and ease of implementation of an academic vocabulary intervention for linguistically diverse students in urban middle schools. *Reading Research Quarterly, 45*(2), 196-228.

Lesaux, N.K., Russ Harris, J., and Sloane, P. (2012). Adolescents' motivation in the context of an academic vocabulary intervention in urban middle school classrooms. *Journal of Adolescent and Adult Literacy, 56*(3), 231-240.

Lesaux, N.K., Kieffer, M.J., Kelley, J.G., and Harris, J.R. (2014). Effects of academic vocabulary instruction for linguistically diverse adolescents: Evidence from a randomized field trial. *American Educational Research Journal, 51*(6), 1159-1194.

Lewis, L., and Gray, L. (2016). *Programs and Services for High School English Learners in Public School Districts: 2015-16.* NCES 2016-150. Washington, DC: National Center for Education Statistics, U.S. Department of Education. Available: http://nces.ed.gov/pubsearch [October 19, 2016].

Liang, L.A., Peterson, C.A., and Graves, M.F. (2005). Investigating two approaches to fostering children's comprehension of literature. *Reading Psychology: An International Quarterly, 26*(4-5), 387-400.

Lindsay, J. (2010). *Children's Access to Print Material and Education-Related Outcomes: Findings from a Meta-Analytic Review.* Naperville, IL: Learning Point Associates.

Llosa, L., Lee, O., Jiang, F., Haas, A., O'Connor, C., Van Booven, C.D., and Kieffer, M.J. (2016). Impact of a large-scale science intervention focused on English language learners. *American Educational Research Journal, 53*(2), 395-424.

Massaro, D. (2015). Two different communication genres and implications for vocabulary development and learning to read. *Journal of Literacy Research, 47*(4), 505-527.

Massey, E.K., Gebhardt, W.A., and Garnefski, N. (2008). Adolescent goal content and pursuit: A review of the literature from the past 16 years. *Developmental Review, 28*(4), 421-460.

Matuchniak, T., Olson, C.B., and Scarcella, R. (2014). Examining the text-based, on-demand, analytical writing of mainstreamed Latino English learners in a randomized field trial of the Pathway Project Intervention. *Reading and Writing, 27*(6), 973-994.

McCutchen, D. (2006). Cognitive factors in the development of children's writing. In C. MacArthur, S. Graham, and J. Fitzgerald (Eds.), *Handbook of Writing Research* (pp. 115-130). New York: Guilford Press.

McMaster, K.L., Kung, S.H., Han, I., and Cao, M. (2008). Peer-assisted learning strategies: A "Tier 1" approach to promoting English learners' response to intervention. *Exceptional Children, 74*(2), 194-214.

Menken, K., and Kleyn, T. (2010). The long-term impact of subtractive schooling in the educational experiences of secondary English language learners. *International Journal of Bilingual Education and Bilingualism, 13*(4), 399-417.

Michaels, S., and O'Connor, C. (2015). Conceptualizing talk moves as tools: Professional development approaches for academically productive discussions. In L.B. Resnick, C. Asterhan, and S. Clarke (Eds.), *Socializing Intelligence through Academic Talk and Dialogue* (pp. 347-362). Washington, DC: American Educational Research Association.

Mol, S. E. and Bus, A. (2011). To read or not to read: A meta-analysis of print exposure from infancy to early adulthood, *Psychological Bulletin, 137*(2), 267-296.

National Center for Education Statistics. (2015). *EDFacts Data Groups 695 and 696, School Year 2013-14.* Available: http://nces.ed.gov/ccd/tables/ACGR_RE_and_characteristics_2013-14.asp [October 5, 2016].

National Institute of Child Health and Human Development. (2000). *Report of the National Reading Panel. Teaching Children to Read: An Evidence-Based Assessment of the Scientific Research Literature on Reading and its Implications for Reading Instruction* (NIH Publication No. 004769). Washington, DC: U.S. Government Printing Office.

National Research Council. (1984). *Development during Middle Childhood: The Years from Six to Twelve.* W.A. Collins (Ed.). Panel to Review the Status of Basic Research on School-Age Children, Committee on Child Development Research and Public Policy, Commission on Behavioral and Social Sciences and Education. Washington, DC: National Academy Press.

National Research Council. (2002). *Scientific Research in Education*. R.J. Shavelson and L. Towne (Eds.), Division of Behavioral and Social Sciences and Education, Center for Education, Committee on Scientific Principles for Education Research. Washington, DC: The National Academies Press.

Nelson, J.R., Vadasy, P.F., and Sanders, E.A. (2011). Efficacy of a tier 2 supplemental root word vocabulary and decoding intervention with kindergarten Spanish-speaking English learners. *Journal of Literacy Research*, 43(2), 184-211.

Neufeld, P., and Fitzgerald, J. (2001). Early English reading development: Latino English learners in the "low" reading group. *Research in the Teaching of English*, 64-109.

Nield, R. (2009). Falling off track during the transition to high school: What we know and what can be done. *The Future of Children*, 19(1), 53-76.

O'Day, J. (2009). Good instruction is good for everyone—or is it? English language learners in a balanced literacy approach. *Journal of Education for Students Placed at Risk*, 14(1), 97-119.

Olsen, L. (2008). *Made in America: Immigrant Students in Our Public Schools*. New York: The New Press.

Olsen, L. (2010). Changing course for long term English learners. *Leadership*, 40(2), 30-33.

Olsen, L. (2014). *Meeting the Unique Needs of Long Term English Language Learners: A Guide for Educators*. Washington, DC: National Education Association.

Ong, W.J. (2002). *Orality and Literacy: The Technologizing of the World*. London/New York: Routledge Press.

Orfield, G., Frankenberg, E., Ee, J., and Kuscera, J. (2014). *Brown at 60: Great Progress, a Long Retreat and an Uncertain Future*. Los Angeles: University of California.

Pettit, S.K. (2011). Teachers' beliefs about English language learners in the mainstream classroom: A review of the literature. *International Multilingual Research Journal*, 5(2), 123-147.

Protacio, M.S.O. (2013). *Investigating the Reading Engagement of English Language Learners: A Case Study of Four Middle School ELLs*. East Lansing: Michigan State University.

RAND Reading Study Group. (2002). *Reading for Understanding: Toward an RAND Program in Reading Comprehension*. Santa Monica, CA: RAND Corporation.

Ransford-Kaldon, C.R., Flynt, E.S., Ross, C.L., Franceschini, L., Zoblotsky, T., Huang, Y., and Gallagher, B. (2010). *Implementation of Effective Intervention: An Empirical Study to Evaluate the Efficacy of Fountas and Pinnell's Leveled Literacy Intervention System (LLI). 2009-2010*. Memphis, TN: Center for Research in Educational Policy.

Rogoff, B. (2003). *The Cultural Nature of Human Development*. New York: Oxford University Press.

Rueda, R., August, D., and Goldenberg, C. (2006). The sociocultural context in which children acquire literacy. In D. August and T. Shanahan (Eds.), *Developing Literacy in Second-Language Learners: Report of the National Literacy Panel on Language-Minority Children and Youth* (pp. 319-340). New York: Rutledge.

Rumberger, R., Gándara, P., and Merino, B. (2006). Where California's English learners attend school and why it matters. *UCLMRI Newsletter*, 15, 1-3.

Ryoo, K. (2009). *Learning Science, Talking Science: The Impact of a Technology-Enhanced Curriculum on Students' Science Learning in Linguistically Diverse Mainstream Classrooms*. Ph.D. Dissertation. Stanford, CA: Stanford University.

Saddler, B., and Graham, S. (2007). The relationship between writing knowledge and writing performance among more and less skilled writers. *Reading and Writing Quarterly*, 23(3), 231-247.

Sáenz, L.M., Fuchs, L.S., and Fuchs, D. (2005). Peer-assisted learning strategies for English language learners with learning disabilities. *Exceptional Children*, 71(3), 231-247.

Saunders, W.M., and Goldenberg, C. (1999). Effects of instructional conversations and literature logs on limited-and fluent-English-proficient students' story comprehension and thematic understanding. *The Elementary School Journal, 99*(4), 277-301.

Scarcella, R. (2003). *Academic English: A Conceptual Framework*. Technical Report 2003-1. Irvine: University of California, Linguistic Minority Research Institute.

Schleppegrell, M. (2001). Linguistic features of the language of schooling. *Linguistics and Education, 12*(4) 431-459.

Schleppergrell, M. (2004). *The Language of Schooling: A Functional Linguistics Perspective*. Mahwah, NJ: Lawrence Erlbaum Associates.

Shanahan, T., and Beck, I.L. (2006). Effective literacy teaching for English-language learners. In D. August and T. Shanahan (Eds.), *Developing Literacy in Second-Language Learners: Report of the National Literacy Panel on Language-Minority Children and Youth* (pp. 415-488). Mahwah, NJ: Lawrence Erlbaum Associates.

Silva, K.G., Correa-Chavez, M., and Rogoff, B. (2010). Mexican-heritage children's attention and learning from interactions directed to others. *Child Development, 81*(3), 898-912.

Silverman, R., and Hines, S. (2009). The effects of multimedia-enhanced instruction on the vocabulary of English-language learners and non-English-language learners in prekindergarten through second grade. *Journal of Educational Psychology, 101*(2), 305.

Skinner, E.A., and Pitzer, J.R. (2012). Developmental dynamics of student engagement, coping, and everyday resilience. In *Handbook of Research on Student Engagement* (pp. 21-44). New York: Springer.

Smetana, J.G., Campione-Barr, N., and Metzger, A. (2006). Adolescent development in interpersonal and societal contexts. *Annual Review of Psychology, 57*, 255-284.

Snow, C.E., Burns, M.S., and Griffin, P. (1998). *Preventing Reading Difficulties in Young Children Committee on the Prevention of Reading Difficulties in Young Children*. Washington, DC: National Academy Press.

Solari, E.J., and Gerber, M.M. (2008). Early comprehension instruction for Spanish-speaking English language learners: Teaching text-level reading skills while maintaining effects on word-level skills. *Learning Disabilities Research and Practice, 23*(4), 155-168.

Suárez-Orozco, C., Suárez-Orozco, M.M., and Todorova, I. (2008). *Learning a New Land: Immigrant Students in American Society*. Cambridge, MA: Harvard University Press.

Sullivan, A., and Brown, M. (2013). Social inequalities in cognitive scores at age 16: The role of reading. *CLS Working Papers, 2013*(13/10).

Tong, F., Irby, B.J., Lara-Alecio, R., and Koch, J. (2014). Integrating literacy and science for English language learners: From learning-to-read to reading-to-learn. *The Journal of Educational Research, 107*(5), 410-426.

U.S. Department of Education, Institute of Education Sciences, and What Works Clearinghouse. (2012). *WWC Review of the Report: A Randomized Experiment of a Cognitive Strategies Approach to Text-based Analytical Writing for Mainstreamed Latino English Language Learners in Grades 6 to 12*. Available: http://whatworks.ed.gov [November 30, 2016].

Valdés, G. (2001). *Learning and Not Learning English: Latino Students in American Schools*. New York: Teachers College Press.

Valencia, R.R. (2010). *Dismantling Contemporary Deficit Thinking: Educational Thought and Practice*. New York: Routledge.

Vaughn, S., Mathes, P., Linan-Thompson, S., Cirino, P., Carlson, C., Pollard-Durodola, S., Cardenas-Hagan, E., and Francis, D. (2006a). Effectiveness of an English intervention for first-grade English language learners at risk for reading problems. *Elementary School Journal, 107*(2), 153-180.

Vaughn, S., Cirino, P.T., Linan-Thompson, S., Mathes, P.G., Carlson, C.D., Hagan, E.C., Pollard-Durodola, S.D., Fletcher, J.M., and Francis, D.J. (2006b). Effectiveness of a Spanish intervention and an English intervention for English-language learners at risk for reading problems. *American Educational Research Journal, 43*(3), 449-487.

Vaughn, S., Martinez, L.R., Linan-Thompson, S., Reutebuch, C.K., Carlson, C.D., and Francis, D.J. (2009). Enhancing social studies vocabulary and comprehension for seventh-grade English language learners: Findings from two experimental studies. *Journal of Research on Educational Effectiveness, 2*(4), 297-324.

Volk, D., and Acosta, M. (2001). Many differing ladders, many ways to climb: Literacy events in the bilingual classroom, homes, and community of three Puerto Rican kindergarteners. *Journal of Early Childhood Literacy, 1*(2), 193-224.

Walker, A., Shafer, J., and Liams, M. (2004). "Not in my classroom": Teacher attitudes towards English language learners in the mainstream classroom. *NABE Journal of Research and Practice, 2*(1), 130-159.

Walqui, A., and van Lier, L. (2010). *Scaffolding the Academic Success of Adolescent English Language Learners: A Pedagogy of Promise.* San Francisco, CA: WestEd.

Walqui, A., Koelsch, N., Hamburger, L., Gaarder, D., Insaurralde, A., Schmida, M., and Weiss, S. (2010). *What Are We Doing to Middle School English Learners? Findings and Recommendations for Change from a Study of California EL Programs* (Research Report). San Francisco, CA: WestEd.

Wigfield, A., Gladstone, J.R., and Turci, L. (2016). Beyond cognition: Reading motivation and reading comprehension. *Child Development Perspectives, 10*(3), 190-195.

Wong Fillmore, L. (2014). English language learners at the crossroads of educational reform. *TESOL Quarterly, 48*(3), 624-632.

Wong Fillmore, L. and Fillmore, C.J. (2012). What does text complexity mean for English learners and language minority students?. In *Understanding Language: Language, Literacy, and Learning in the Content Areas* (pp. 64-74). Stanford, CA: Stanford University.

Wong Fillmore, L. and Snow, C.E. (2000). *What Teachers Need to Know about Language.* http://www.elachieve.org/images/stories/eladocs/articles/Wong_Fillmore.pdf [November 6, 2016].

Zhang, J., Anderson, R.C., and Nguyen-Jahiel, K. (2013). Language-rich discussions for English language learners. *International Journal of Educational Research, 58*, 44-60.

Zhou, M. (2000). Social capital in Chinatown: The role of community-based organizations and families in the adaptation of the younger generation. In M. Zhou and J. Gatewood (Eds.), *Contemporary Asian America: A Multidisciplinary Reader* (pp. 315-335). New York: New York University Press.

Zwiers, J. (2017). Developing oral language to foster students' academic literacy: Cultivating students' inner language of comprehending through classroom conversation. In D. Lapp and D. Fisher (Eds.), *Handbook of Research on Teaching the English Language Arts* (Ch. 8, 4th ed.). Newark, DE: International Literacy Association and the National Council of Teachers of English.

Zwiers, J., O'Hara, S. and Pritchard, R. (2014). Conversing to fortify literacy, language, and learning. *Voices from the Middle, 22*(1), 10-14. Available: http://www.ncte.org/journals/vm/issues/v22-1 [December 19, 2016].

9

Promising and Effective Practices for Specific Populations of English Learners Grades Pre-K to 12

The statement of task for this study (see Chapter 1) includes a review of programs for specific populations of English learners (ELs).[1] Accordingly, this chapter describes programs focused on ELs who are gifted and talented; living in migrant families that work in food-production industries; and living on tribal lands, specifically, American Indians and Alaska Natives. Chapter 10 provides an extensive discussion of ELs with disabilities. The committee searched for a body of evidence on promising practices for ELs who are homeless and who are unaccompanied or undocumented minors; however, such evidence generally is not specific to these populations or is lacking altogether. Thus the committee notes that systematic evaluations of practices with these specific populations are needed (see Chapter 13 for the research agenda developed by the committee).

GIFTED AND TALENTED ENGLISH LEARNERS

The underrepresentation of ELs—who are included under the umbrella term of culturally, linguistically, and ethnically diverse (CLED)—in gifted education programs has been a long-standing concern of researchers and educators (Baldwin et al., 1978; Ford et al., 2008; Lohman, 2005; Oakland and Rossen, 2005). Despite increasing recognition of the need to reform and enhance education for CLED students (Briggs et al., 2008; Harris et al., 2009), issues of overidentification for remedial classes and underiden-

---

[1] When referring to children aged 5 or older in the pre-K to 12 education system, this report uses the term "English learners" or "ELs" (see Box 1-1 in Chapter 1 for details).

tification for gifted programs remain (National Research Council, 2002). Although it has been estimated that 10 percent of those enrolled in gifted programs are CLED students (Gallagher, 2002), more recent estimates of just the EL population in school year 2011-2012 showed that only 2.7 percent of all public school students were identified as both ELs and gifted (U.S. Department of Education, 2012).

Variations in State Policies

According to the National Association for Gifted Children (2015), states vary with respect to policies aimed at the inclusion of ELs in gifted programs, as well as how they report EL status. McClain and Pfeiffer (2012) interviewed state gifted program coordinators and found that only 26 states had any policies for the inclusion of diverse populations. Moreover, whereas 20 states report race and ethnicity data on gifted programs, only 12 report information regarding EL status. Of those 12 states, 7 had identification rates of 1 percent or less; Colorado had the highest reported percentage of identified EL gifted students at 4.58 percent (National Association for Gifted Children, 2015).

Increased Identification of Gifted ELs and Their Access to Gifted Programs

Research on increasing the identification of gifted ELs and their access to gifted programs has focused on a variety of topics, including identification and selection procedures (Ford et al., 2008), test bias (Ford et al., 2008; Naglieri and Ford, 2003), professional development in teacher education programs (Ford and Trotman, 2001), and the fostering of multicultural educational reform (Bernal, 2001; Ford et al., 2008). Research to date suggests that the three factors with the greatest influence on the identification of ELs for gifted programs are (1) the assessment tools used, including measures of real-life problem solving (Reid et al., 1999; Sarouphim, 2002); (2) teacher preparation and professional development, which leads to a reduction in educator bias; and (3) district-level support (Briggs et al., 2008; Harris et al., 2009). Despite the limited evidence on the effects of programs for gifted ELs, the gifted education field is taking steps toward addressing issues of equity and access, especially for EL populations, but much more effort in this area is required (National Association for Gifted Children, 2011).

MIGRANT ENGLISH LEARNERS

Migrant students are children and youth who accompany parents and families as they relocate for seasonal or temporary employment in agriculture or fishing. These annual migrations from place to place, often across state lines, result in major disruptions in students' educational experiences. Migrant students also are deeply affected by poverty, with an average family income ranging from $17,500 to $19,999 per year, inadequate health care, crowded and poor housing, and the social and cultural isolation related to their transiency (National Center for Farmworker Health, 2016).

A recent review of the research on migrant education commissioned by the Office of Migrant Education (2011) indicates that there are approximately 470,000 school-aged migrant students (with 35 percent considered ELs and another 15 percent "out-of-school" youth ages 16-21 who have not completed but are no longer attending school). They speak primarily Spanish (81%).

School districts in states with migrant students are responsible for serving them for as long they as are in residence. These states receive funds for migrant education from the U.S. Department of Education's Migrant Education Program, which was first established under an amendment to the Elementary and Secondary Education Act (ESEA) in 1966. Funds are allocated to states under a formula based on each state's per pupil expenditure for migrant education and the numbers of eligible children in the state aged 3-21. These supplemental funds are intended to provide services in addition to those provided by the school districts and are critical supports for those schools in which migrant students are in residence for just part of the school year. Schools in the communities where migrant students register must first identify them as migrants and then assess their educational and linguistic status for placement in school and access to services.

The statute under which migrant education is mandated calls for the coordination of services across states. The Consortium for Quality and Consistency in Identification and Recruitment (ConQIR), with New York as the lead state, was established to provide inter- and intrastate coordination among the 12 states in the consortium (Colorado, Hawaii, Illinois, Louisiana, Maryland, New Hampshire, New York, North Carolina, Pennsylvania, South Carolina, Tennessee, and Vermont); four collaborating states (Florida, Kansas, Montana, and Nebraska); the Office of Migrant Education (OME); and federal migrant centers, parents, and migrant employers (Consortium for Quality and Consistency in Identification and Recruitment, 2016).

The federally funded, computerized Migrant Student Record Transfer System was created in 1969 (Lunon, 1986) to transfer student information, test scores, immunization records, and grade placement across states and districts. This low-tech but effective alternative way for transferring school records took the form of hand-carried packets, which students or parents picked up before departing one school and hand-delivered to the next one. The U.S. Department of Education was mandated by Congress as part of the No Child Left Behind Act of 2001 to provide assistance to states to develop effective methods for the transfer of student records and to determine the number of migrant children in each state (U.S. Department of Education, 2016). This system is called the Migrant Student Records Exchange Initiative (MSIX).

Services for Migrant Students

Services for migrant students vary considerably, with some states and districts having well-planned and coordinated services and others whose programs and services are less adequate. Migrant programs must address varied needs of students from pre-K through high school in a variety of programs. The adequacy of programs across this grade range depends on the availability of teachers with the training to meet the special educational and linguistic needs of migrant students. Because these students are in residence for only part of each school year in the schools they attend, they are placed in classes that have openings. In many places, schools depend on teachers who are assigned to provide supplemental language and academic services, such as instruction in English as a second language (ESL), and to fill gaps in learning that result from missed instruction time or curricular differences in the schools they have attended.

Migrant Educational Centers

State and regional migrant educational centers, many of them federally funded by the Migrant Education Program (MEP), provide valuable and necessary support to schools and directly to students in their areas. So, too, do nonprofit organizations such as the Geneseo Migrant Center in Leicester, New York, which sponsors the Migrant Library, a source for literature and other materials on migrant farmworkers that can be used by students as well as by teachers who want to learn more about the migrant experience (Geneseo Migrant Center, n.d.-a). The Geneseo organization maintains a list of migrant education centers and links to various health, legal, and parent education publications in support of the education of migrant students. Another such organization is the Interstate Migrant Education Council (IMEC), which works at the policy level to develop recommendations for improving educational programs for migrant students.

Promising Strategies for Addressing Disruptions in Schooling

The most comprehensive and recent study on promising strategies for addressing migrant students' disruptions in schooling was conducted by researchers at The George Washington University's Center for Equity and Excellence in Education (Goniprow et al., 2002) for the U.S. Department of Education's Planning and Evaluation Service. The aim of this study was to identify promising strategies for ameliorating the potential detrimental effects of disruptions in schooling on the academic performance of migrant students. The research focused on case studies of school districts in Arizona, California, Michigan, Montana, Texas, and Washington that shared students who moved back and forth between them. Districts that shared students, characterized as "trading partners," were nominated by state directors of migrant education programs as exemplary in their sharing of information, their service delivery, and their mechanisms for coordination. The researchers examined efforts to promote academic continuity and progress for students among partner districts and identified common themes in successful solutions: "shared vision of the role of migrant education, emphasis on program alignment between trading partners, use of technology, value of personal relationships, and importance of leadership" (p. ii).

Goniprow and colleagues (2002) found further that recognition of the unique challenges faced by migrant students was critical, as was the need to align the curricular content of programs for students as they moved from one locale to another. They noted the importance of personal connections among leaders in state agencies responsible for migrant education for facilitating coordination among states, as well as the key roles played by state directors in encouraging interstate activities. The use of technology was identified as important for rapid access to student information needed for placement, and for providing instruction for difficult-to-reach students (e.g., those who could not attend school because they were working or caring for younger siblings). At the time of this study (2002), the use of technology for instruction was relatively limited, but the report mentions as promising the Texas Education Agency's distance learning program for migrant students, SMART, broadcast by satellite from Texas for 8 weeks during the summer, and NovaNET, a nationwide computer-based curriculum.

The authors also found that supplemental educational strategies, such as tutorial programs and evening classes, were provided to help students catch up and complete their coursework. Technology was used to help students keep in touch via email with classmates in the schools they attended, thereby helping to alleviate disruptions in friendships as they moved from school to school.

Migrant Students in High Schools

Migrant students at the secondary level face additional challenges in completing school successfully. Their frequent moves and the loss of instructional time between moves make course completion and accrual of credits for graduation difficult. The Portable Assisted Study Sequence (PASS) program, described as a self-contained, semi-independent study course for secondary students, provides materials that out-of-school students can access online, depending on the availability of computers and the Internet (Geneseo Migrant Center, n.d.-b). For out-of-school youth, OME's Graduation and Outcomes for Success for Out-of-School Youth (GOSOSY) program develops and delivers services to help migrant students access federal or state educational resources (Graduation and Outcomes for Success for OSY, 2016).

ENGLISH LEARNERS LIVING ON TRIBAL LANDS

According to *Ethnologue*,[2] speakers remain for only 216 of the perhaps 1,000 indigenous heritage languages once spoken among American Indians and Alaska Natives in North America (Lewis, Simons, and Fennig, 2015), and all but a handful are "moribund" (Krauss, 1992). Few of these languages have more than 10,000 speakers. Navajo has an estimated 169,471 speakers;[3] Cree, 70,000;[4] Ojibwa, approximately 41,000, with 8,371 in the United States[3] and 32,460 in Canada;[5] Dakota, 18,616;[3] Apache, 13,063;[3] Keres, 12,945;[3] Cherokee, 11,610;[3] and Choctaw, 10,343.[3] Of the 19 indigenous languages of Alaska, only Yup'ik, with 10,400 speakers of Central Yup'ik[6] and 1,000 speakers of Siberian Yup'ik, can be considered relatively safe from extinction (Alaska Native Language Center, 2016).

Language revitalization is a matter of extreme urgency for members of communities whose languages are in danger of extinction (see Box 9-1). There is little disagreement on this point among these community members, but the question is who can teach these languages to children in school. Schools may not have teachers familiar with the community's indigenous

---

[2] *Ethnologue: Languages of the World* is a publication of the Summer Institute of Linguistics. It is a comprehensive reference work cataloguing all of the world's known languages. See https://www.ethnologue.com/statistics/country [January 19, 2017].

[3] See Siebens and Julian (2011).

[4] Cree has the largest speaker population of Canada's First Nations peoples. It has an estimated 70,000 speakers across southern Canada and northern Montana (see http://www.native-languages.org/cree.htm [June 27, 2017]), where they share tribal lands with the Chippewa (see http://tribalnations.mt.gov/chippewacree [June 27, 2017]).

[5] See Statistics Canada (2007).

[6] The Alaska Native Language Center offers separate counts for Central Yup'ik and Siberian Yup'ik. See https://www.uaf.edu/anlc/languages/stats [February 20, 2017].

BOX 9-1
Why Language Revitalization Is Critical

For most American Indian groups, language is a key to cultural identity, and efforts to revitalize their language by teaching it to young tribal members are important to maintaining and strengthening tribal culture. At a public information-gathering session held for this study, Tipiziwin Tolman, a Wiciyena Dakota and Hunkpapha Lakota tribal member who teaches in a Lakota Language Nest program, positioned language revitalization and maintenance in the framework of restoring health to a people who have been deeply wounded by past efforts to destroy their language, culture, and way of life:

> The maintaining of Lakota to me is my work, my personal life, my community. . . . I come from one of the most economically depressed areas in the United States. Sioux County, North Dakota, has a life expectancy of 45 years. . . . All the statistics and the social ills that you hear about my people, I live, are my reality, and are my children's reality, and there's a direct connection. We have a suicide epidemic of young people, and there is a direct connection of loss of identity through loss of language, of people [being] virtual outsiders in our own homelands, not having that connection, and not being valued or self-valued as a Lakota, because you're Lakota but you don't speak Lakota . . . you don't understand Lakota. It's a terrible reality of the children and the youth where I come from. And so I really, truly believe that we can heal ourselves, and we can heal our children, and we can heal our world through our language.

SOURCE: The information presented here is from a young adult who served on a panel on growing up multilingual at a public information-gathering session convened by the committee on May 28, 2015. She provided written permission to include her story, quotes, and name.

---

heritage language, and in communities where the remaining speakers are elderly or in fragile health, this is a problem that cannot be solved easily.[7] The problem of revitalization is more complex in Native communities that prefer keeping their languages solely as spoken when there are few remaining speakers, as in the cases of the Pueblo Peoples of New Mexico.[8] In such communities, the language can be learned only from speakers, thus making

---

[7] At a community meeting in a rural Alaskan village that was held to find ways to stem the impending loss of three Alaskan Indian languages, attendees were asked who was a speaker of one of those languages. Of perhaps 100 people at the meeting, fewer than a dozen raised their hands. Several were in wheelchairs; some had oxygen tanks beside them; all of them were elderly. They had come from villages that were as far as 150 miles from the place where the meeting was being held.

[8] Dr. Christine Sims' comments at a public information-gathering session held by the committee at the National Academies of Sciences, Engineering, and Medicine Arnold and Mabel Beckman Center in Irvine, California, on October 8, 2015.

it even more urgent to bring those who can learn the language most rapidly and easily—children—together with adults who can provide access to the language and support for learning it. In New Mexico, some of the pueblos have provided teachers for the public schools so that children can have daily pull-out classes for heritage language lessons, but this has proven to be a controversial use of school time (Sims, 2006). Many educators question whether students who are struggling academically should be spending time learning a language that appears to have no bearing on the school's curriculum.

The inclusion of culture in the curriculum for American Indian students is less controversial and more acceptable, although there are competing views as to just what that means and how native languages, an integral part of culture, should be incorporated into classroom instruction. The incorporation of culture is sometimes seen as the use of curricular materials: the history, songs, stories, and arts and crafts of a people. A broader view encompasses the relationships that exist between teachers and students, the environments in which learning is possible and occurs, the purposes for learning and education, and beliefs about what learning and knowing mean and how they happen. The term "culture-based education" describes an approach that is frequently mentioned as a means of improving instruction for Native students. Examples of such programs include The Ways, an innovative online educational program providing stories, videos, interactive maps, and educational materials for American Indian nations and schools serving communities around the central Great Lakes.[9] Another such effort is the culturally infused math curriculum program that raised math outcomes for students in rural Alaska (Kisker et al., 2012; Lipka and Ilutsik, 2014).

In a survey of programs described as culture-based education, Beaulieu (2006) found that two-thirds were not culturally related—many were after-school tutoring, homework assistance, or enrichment programs that were not culturally focused. The programs that did appear to be culturally based were ones that (1) taught culturally relevant materials on Native history and civics, such as tribal government and treaties; (2) taught culturally relevant materials through the indigenous language; (3) taught the indigenous language in immersion classes; (4) made use of culturally relevant materials, such as stories that reflected students' heritage and experiences; and (5) offered cultural enrichment through pow-wows, presentations by tribal members, and arts and crafts experiences. Such experiences are available primarily in schools with a high density of Native students; they are few and far between in schools where Native students are in the minority. Beaulieu (2006) cautions, however, that what counts is not just what is taught, but

---

[9] Produced by the Wisconsin Media Lab (http://theways.org [September 28, 2016]).

the human relationships and social and communicative interactions and activities in which instruction is embedded.

Research on the effectiveness of language revitalization programs remains limited, in part because of the lack of valid and appropriate measures for programs developed for tribal groups that are small in number. Questions remain regarding how to measure the effectiveness of such programs that not only have linguistic goals but also aim to influence students' sense of self-worth, self-efficacy, belonging to their tribal nations, and trust in others.

The paucity of evidence on the effectiveness of language revitalization programs was addressed in an executive order calling for establishment of an interagency working group.[10] This group was tasked to compile data on the academic achievement of American Indian and Alaska Native students relative to the No Child Left Behind Act, to identify and disseminate research-based practices for improving their academic achievement, and to assess the impact and role of native language and culture with respect to strategies for improving their academic achievement and school completion. As part of the research undertaken by the working group, a Program Evaluation Group was commissioned to conduct a review of promising programs and practices. This group found that, in addition to promoting indigenous self-determination, such programs and practices should enable students to achieve academic parity with other students; prepare them to participate in their tribal communities and in the larger world as well; contribute to their personal well-being; promote positive, trusting relationships between school and home; and help promote integrated school experiences that "facilitate learners' self-efficacy, critical capacities, and intrinsic motivation as thinkers, readers, writers, and ethical social agents" (McCarty and Wiley Snell, 2011, p. 4).

Language revitalization programs operate with many constraints and challenges. For example, a serious issue is the availability of teachers who know a specific native language well enough to use it to teach school subjects and are capable of designing instructional strategies that are socially and culturally compatible. Another challenge faced until recently was the constant pressure schools faced to show student progress through improved test scores on mandated achievement tests administered in English as required by the No Child Left Behind Act (Beaulieu et al., 2005; Reyhner and Hurtado, 2008).

Despite the above constraints and challenges, the Program Evaluation

---

[10] Executive Order 13336 of April 30, 2004 (*Federal Register*, Vol. 69, No. 87 [May 5, 2004] Presidential Documents). The agencies represented in this working group were from the U.S. Departments of Agriculture, Education, Health and Human Services, the Interior, and Justice, as well as other agencies designated by the working group.

BOX 9-2
Rough Rock Community School:
A Language Revitalization Program Exemplar

The Navajo school—Rough Rock Community School—in Rough Rock, Arizona, is a language revitalization program with a long history of achieving positive results. This program has been well documented and demonstrates the critical role played by community leaders and parents of students who saw language and cultural revitalization as a critical foundation for educating their children and strengthening their communities (Cantoni and Reyhner, 1998; Fishman, 1991; Reyhner, 1990).

Rough Rock Community School is a pioneer among indigenous communities in exercising local control over its educational programs. Established in1966 as the result of a grassroots effort led by Navajo tribal leaders and supportive educators, Rough Rock was a reaction to the ineffective educational programs that many of the tribal leaders had themselves experienced as children and that remained in place in the 1960s (McCarty, 2002; McCarty and Roessel, 2015). Rough Rock was envisioned as more than a school for Navajo children; the intent was for it to become "the focus for the development of the local community" (Roessel, 1977). At Rough Rock, parents and tribal leaders have been directly involved in educational decisions concerning their children and in running their own schools.

The path to establishing Rough Rock Community School was not easy for the community and its educators, posing many obstacles to self-determination and to the design and adoption of a culturally and linguistically appropriate and academically challenging education. The most serious of these obstacles was related to changes in government funding over time and the bureaucratic oversight to which programs under the U.S. Bureau of Indian Affairs were subjected. The community faced the imposition of external reviews by evaluators who had little knowledge of the community, the imposition of curricula based on the latest trends in education (e.g., basic skills-oriented learning, scripted reading instruction) and numerous delays or cuts in funding (McCarty 2002). The consequences were constant turmoil and employment instability for teachers and school administrators, resulting in frequent turnover of staff.

Nevertheless, the program survived its first several decades, and educators eventually designed a bilingual program that worked for the community. To design this bilingual education, educators had to delve into the meaning of a culturally based education for Navajos that required more than translation of English textbooks into the Navajo language; the materials had to be culturally appropriate as well. Identifying and adopting a culturally appropriate pedagogy was another major task. The key to culturally based education is that there is no one-size-fits-all instructional approach. What that meant for Rough Rock took its educators and advisors 5 years to determine. The payoff was substantial, and the team was able to create a quality bilingual language arts curriculum (Rough Rock English-Navajo Language Arts Program) that is now in its 50th year.

Group found evidence that certain language revitalization programs have a positive impact on student achievement. They found that "strong, additive, and academically rigorous Native language and culture (NLC) programs[11] have salutary effects" (McCarty and Wiley Snell, 2011, p. 14) on language maintenance and student achievement, while weak, subtractive programs do not. The group emphasized that a minimum of 4-7 years is required for students to develop the age-appropriate language skills needed for academic learning in either English or an indigenous language. It also found that time spent learning school subjects in "strong" programs did not detract from learning English, and in fact, students in such programs performed as well as or better than peers in mainstream classes (McCarty and Wiley Snell, 2011). Most important, the group found that when parents and community leaders make decisions themselves regarding content, process, and medium of instruction, Native language and culture programs "enhance student motivation, self-esteem, and ethnic pride" and provide opportunities for parents and elders to participate in student learning, thereby bringing the community and school together (McCarty and Wiley Snell, 2011, pp. 14-15). Box 9-2 describes a language revitalization program that can serve as an exemplar.

In general, a fundamental tension exists between what tribal groups regard as essential for the education of their children for full participation in their communities and what they recognize as essential for full participation in the larger society as well. Many if not most indigenous communities regard language and cultural revitalization as key to maintaining or restoring the health and vitality of communities that have undergone dramatic shifts and loss of resources over the past century and a half, but they also regard as equally important the skills and knowledge that the society expects from all children and the English skills required for academic advancement as defined by the education system.

CONCLUSIONS

Conclusion 9-1: English learners are a highly diverse group of students. There is a lack of research that explores the interactions between instructional methods and such student characteristics as language background, age, levels of proficiency and content area knowledge, and special needs.

---

[11]The Program Evaluation Group characterized "strong additive programs" as those providing instructional support in both the indigenous language and English, and identified dual language programs as examples of such programs. In contrast, the researchers characterized pull-out programs offering limited support in the indigenous language as "weaker programs" leading to subtractive bilingualism, wherein students tend to put aside the indigenous language and move toward English only.

Conclusion 9-2: The reclamation of indigenous heritage languages is an important goal for many American Indian and Alaska Native communities. Some school systems see this goal as being in conflict with the school's efforts to promote English language and literacy. However, the evidence indicates that participation in strong language revitalization programs can have a positive impact on student achievement in school.

BIBLIOGRAPHY

Alaska Native Language Center. (2016). *Alaska Native Languages: Population and Speaker Statistics*. Available: https://www.uaf.edu/anlc/languages/stats [November 30, 2016].

Baldwin, A.Y., Gear, G.H., and Lucito, L.J. (1978). *Educational Planning for the Gifted: Overcoming Cultural, Geographic, and Socioeconomic Barriers*. Reston, VA: Council for Exceptional Children.

Beaulieu, D. (2006). A survey and assessment of culturally based education programs for Native American students in the United States. *Journal of American Indian Education, 45*(2), 50-61.

Beaulieu, D.S., Sparks, L., and Alonzo, M. (2005). *Preliminary Report on No Child Left Behind in Indian Country*. Washington, DC: National Indian Education Association.

Bernal, E.M. (2001). Three ways to achieve a more equitable representation of culturally and linguistically different students in GT programs. *Roeper Review, 24*(2), 82-88.

Briggs, C.J., Reis, S.M., and Sullivan, E.E. (2008). A national view of promising programs and practices for culturally, linguistically, and ethnically diverse gifted and talented students. *Gifted Child Quarterly, 52*(2), 131-145.

Cantoni, G., and Reyhner, J. (1998). What educators can do to aid community efforts at indigenous language revitalization. In N. Ostler (Ed.), *Endangered Languages: What Role for the Specialist* (pp. 33-37). Bath, UK: Foundation for Endangered Languages.

Consortium for Quality and Consistency in Identification and Recruitment (2016). *About ConQUIR Foundations*. Available: https://www.conqir-idr.org/about.html [March 24, 2017].

Fishman, J.A. (1991). *Reversing Language Shift: Theoretical and Empirical Foundations of Assistance to Threatened Languages*. Clevedon, UK: Multilingual Matters.

Ford, D.Y., and Trotman, M.F. (2001). Teachers of gifted students: Suggested multicultural characteristics and competencies. *Roeper Review, 23*(4), 235-239.

Ford, D.Y., Grantham, T.C., and Whiting, G.W. (2008). Culturally and linguistically diverse students in gifted education: Recruitment and retention issues. *Exceptional Children, 74*(3), 289-306.

Gallagher, J.J. (2002). *Society's Role in Educating Gifted Students: The Role of Public Policy*. Storrs, CT: National Research Center on the Gifted and Talented.

Geneseo Migrant Center. (n.d.-a). *Overview of Services*. Available: https://migrant.net/migrant/overview.htm [March 24, 2017].

Geneseo Migrant Center. (n.d.-b). *The Pass Program*. Available: https://migrant.net/pass/index.htm [March 24, 2017].

Goniprow, A., Hargett, G., and Fitzgerald, N. (2002). *The Same High Standards for Migrant Students: Holding Title I Schools Accountable. Volume III: Title I Schools Serving Migrant Students. Recent Evidence from the National Longitudinal Survey of Schools. Final Report*. Washington, DC: U.S. Department of Education.

Graduation and Outcomes for Success for OSY. (2016). *Home*. Available: https://www.osy-migrant.org [March 27, 2017].

Harris, B., Plucker, J.A., Rapp, K.E., and Martinez, R.S. (2009). Identifying gifted and talented English language learners: A case study. *Journal for the Education of the Gifted, 32*(3), 368-393.

Kisker, E.E., Lipka, J., Adams, B.L., Rickard, A., Andrew-Ihrke, D., Yanez, E.E., and Millard, A. (2012). The potential of a culturally based supplemental mathematics curriculum to improve the mathematics performance of Alaska Native and other students. *Journal for Research in Mathematics Education, 43*(1), 75-113.

Krauss, M. (1992). The world's languages in crisis. *Language, 68*(1), 4-10.

Lewis, M.P., Simons, G.F., and Fennig, C.C. (Eds.). (2015). *Ethnologue: Languages of the World.* (18th ed.).Dallas, TX: SIL International.

Lipka, J., and Ilutsik, E. (2014). *Transforming the Culture of Schools: Yup¡ k Eskimo Examples.* New York: Routledge Press.

Lohman, D.F. (2005). The role of nonverbal ability tests in identifying academically gifted students: An aptitude perspective. *Gifted Child Quarterly, 49*(2), 111.

Lunon, J.K. (1986). *Migrant Student Record Transfer System: What Is It and Who Uses It?* Available: http://www.ericdigests.org/pre-926/migrant.htm [December 13, 2016].

McCarty, T.L. (2002). *A Place to be Navajo: Rough Rock and the Struggle for Self-Determination in Indigenous Schooling.* New York: Routledge Press.

McCarty, T.L., and Roessel, C.M. (2015). Tsé Ch'ízhí Diné Bi'ólta'—Rough Rock, the people's school: Reflections on a half-century of Navajo community-controlled education (US 1966). In E. Rodríguez (Ed.), *Pedagogies and Curriculums to (Re) Imagine Public Education* (pp. 49-63). New York: Springer.

McCarty, T.L., and Wiley Snell, A. (2011). *State of the Field: The Role of Native Languages and Cultures in American Indian, Alaska Native, and Native Hawaiian Student Achievement.* Policy Brief. Phoenix: Center for Indian Education, Arizona State University.

McClain, M.-C., and Pfeiffer, S. (2012). Identification of gifted students in the United States today: A look at state definitions, policies, and practices. *Journal of Applied School Psychology, 28*(1), 59-88.

Naglieri, J.A., and Ford, D.Y. (2003). Addressing underrepresentation of gifted minority children using the Naglieri Nonverbal Ability Test (NNAT). *Gifted Child Quarterly, 47*(2), 155-160.

National Association for Gifted Children. (2011). *Position Statement: Identifying and Serving Culturally and Linguistically Diverse Gifted Students.* Available: https://www.nagc.org/sites/default/files/Position%20Statement/Identifying%20and%20Serving%20Culturally%20and%20Linguistically.pdf [November 30, 2016].

National Association for Gifted Children. (2015). *2014-2015 State of the States in Gifted Education: Policy and Practice Data.* Available: http://www.nagc.org/sites/default/files/key%20reports/2014-2015%20State%20of%20the%20States%20%28final%29.pdf [November 30, 2016].

National Center for Farmworker Health. (2016). *Demographics: Farmworker Factsheet.* Available: http://www.ncfh.org/uploads/3/8/6/8/38685499/naws_ncfh_factsheet_demographics_final_revised.pdf [November 30, 2016].

National Research Council. (2002). *Minority Students in Special and Gifted Education.* M.S. Donovan, and C.T. Cross (Eds.). Division of Behavioral and Social Sciences and Education; Board on Behavioral, Cognitive, and Sensory Sciences; Committee on Minority Representation in Special Education. Washington, DC: The National Academies Press.

Oakland, T., and Rossen, E. (2005). A 21st-century model for identifying students for gifted and talented programs in light of national conditions: An emphasis on race and ethnicity. *Gifted Child Today, 28*(4), 56-63.

Office of Migrant Education. (2011). *Literature Review: Migrant Education.* Available: http://nysmigrant.org/files/Literature-Review-on-Migrant-Education.pdf [November 30, 2016].

Reid, C., Udall, A., Romanoff, B., and Algozzine, B. (1999). Comparison of traditional and problem solving assessment criteria. *Gifted Child Quarterly, 43*(4), 252-264.

Reyhner, J. (1990). A description of the Rock Point Community School Bilingual Education Program. In J. Reyhner (Ed.), *Effective Language Education Practices and Native Language Survival* (pp. 95-106). Choctaw, OK: Native American Language Issues.

Reyhner, J., and Hurtado, D.S. (2008). Reading First, literacy, and American Indian/Alaska Native students. *Journal of American Indian Education, 47*(1), 82-95.

Roessel, Jr., R.A. (1977). *Navajo Education in Action: The Rough Rock Demonstration School*. Rough Rock, AZ: Navajo Curriculum Center.

Sarouphim, K.M. (2002). DISCOVER in high school: Identifying gifted Hispanic and Native American students. *The Journal of Secondary Gifted Education, 14*(1), 30-38.

Siebens, J., and Julian, T. (2011). Native North American languages spoken at home in the United States and Puerto Rico: 2006-2010. *American Community Survey Briefs*, December. Available: https://www.census.gov/prod/2011pubs/acsbr10-10.pdf [November 4, 2016].

Sims, C.P. (2006). Language planning in American Indian Pueblo communities: Contemporary challenges and issues. *Current Issues in Language Planning, 7*(2-3), 251-268.

Statistics Canada (2007). *2006 Census Area Profiles: Profile for Canada, Provinces, Territories, Census Divisions and Census Subdivisions, 2006 Census*. Available: http://www12.statcan.ca/census-recensement/2006/dp-pd/prof/rel/index-eng.cfm [March 27, 2017].

U.S. Department of Education (2012). *Office for Civil Rights, Civil Rights Data Collection, 2011-12*. Available: http://ocrdata.ed.gov and http://ocrdata.ed.gov/StateNational Estimations/Estimations_2011_12 [March 24, 2017].

U.S. Department of Education (2016). *Migrant Student Records Exchange Initiative*. Available http://www2.ed.gov/admins/lead/account/recordstransfer.html [December 13, 2016].

10

Dual Language Learners and English Learners with Disabilities[1]

D ual language learners (DLLs) and English learners (ELs) who have been identified as having disabilities constitute a relatively small and understudied portion of the K-12 population.[2] They make up about 9 percent of the DLL/EL population and 8 percent of students with disabilities, yet these small percentages represent more than 350,000 children (Abedi, 2014). In 2013, 339,000 infants and toddlers (ages birth to 2 years), more than 745,000 children ages 3-5, and 5.8 million children and youth ages 6-21 were served under the Individuals with Disabilities Education Act (IDEA) of 2004 (U.S. Department of Education, 2015). However, DLLs/ELs with disabilities have received less attention from researchers than other children and youth with disabilities. Much of the research on DLLs/ELs with disabilities is descriptive and fairly recent, and the number of studies varies across disability categories. Given the rapid growth in the number of DLLs/ELs in schools, the large proportion of these children and youth with low academic achievement, and the prevalence of specific learn-

---

[1] This chapter includes content drawn from two papers commissioned by the committee: "Language Development of Dual Language Learner/English Learner Children with Disabilities" by Julie Esparza Brown and "English Learner Students with Disabilities: Issues of Policy and Practice" by Soyoung Park.

[2] When referring to young children ages birth to 5 in their homes, communities, or early care and education programs, this report uses the term "dual language learners" or "DLLs." When referring to children ages 5 and older in the pre-K to grade 12 education system, the term "English learners" or "ELs" is used. When referring to the broader group of children and adolescents ages birth to 21, the term "DLLs/ELs" is used. (See Box 1-1 in Chapter 1 for details.)

ing and language disabilities (about half of the population with disabilities in the United States), research on this topic is consequential and timely.

This chapter presents a critical review of the research on DLLs/ELs with disabilities through the lens of policy, practice, and research. In particular, it focuses on five of the major disability categories—specific learning disabilities (SLDs), intellectual disabilities (IDs), emotional/behavioral disorders (E/BDs), language impairments (LI, including speech/language impairments), and autism spectrum disorder (ASD). The presentation of these disability categories is intended to serve as a frame for thinking about implications for policy, practice, and research.

The chapter begins with a brief description of the different disabilities and some of the myths associated with DLLs/ELs with disabilities. This review sets the context for the remainder of the chapter, which first focuses on what policy makers and educators need to know about DLLs/ELs with disabilities. This section includes a discussion of IDEA and the Every Student Succeeds Act (ESSA), emphasizing the impact of these national policies on DLL/ELs with disabilities, including disproportionate representation, assessment and identification, instruction and services, and policies on reclassification. Next, the chapter examines what educators need to know about the existing identification and evaluation practices for DLLs/ELs with disabilities, focusing on both the multipronged approach and the response to intervention approach. This is followed by an overview of the relevant research for the different disabilities, with a focus on identification, assessment, and instruction. The chapter ends with conclusions drawn from the evidence reviewed.

OVERVIEW OF FIVE MAJOR DISABILITY CATEGORIES IN DLLS/ELS

Table 10-1 provides an overview of the defining characteristics of each of the five disability categories cited above, including identification and assessment, as well as issues associated with instruction and outcomes. The table highlights some of the broad-level outcomes that have been found for each of the specific disabilities, if possible. Box 10-1 provides an overview of the prevalence of disabilities and comorbidities in DLLs/ELs.

Despite the well-documented cognitive, educational, psychosocial, cultural, and work-related benefits associated with bilingualism (Collins et al., 2011; Kay-Raining Bird et al., 2016; Toppelberg, 2011; see Chapter 4 in this volume), parents, teachers, health professionals, and policy makers often express unsubstantiated concerns and beliefs regarding the supposed negative effects of dual language exposure in children with disabilities and their presumed difficulty or inability to become bilingual (see Kay-Raining

Bird et al., 2012; Thordardottir, 2006). Box 10-2 presents these common myths and explains how they are not supported by research evidence.

The common myths discussed in Box 10-2 unfortunately lead to misinformed and potentially damaging professional and parental practices. The practice of recommending that families of students with disabilities discontinue their exposure to the home language is, unfortunately, widespread in educational as well as in health care settings and applied to a broad range of disabilities (language, learning, emotional/behavioral, and developmental). As explained in Box 10-2, this practice is not supported for most DLLs/ELs with disabilities in most situations by the available educational, clinical, and developmental evidence; indeed, as discussed in more detail later in the chapter, evidence suggests that it may be highly detrimental. Overall, continued support for the home language through intervention or natural exposure helps develop that language while not hindering and even facilitating (through transfer of language skills) the learning of the second language (L2) (see also Chapter 4 in this volume). In "additive" environments, the two languages do not compete, but result in linguistic, cognitive, socioemotional, and cultural gains crucial for children with disabilities.

OVERVIEW OF RELEVANT POLICY ISSUES

This section provides an overview of the major federal policies that address the educational needs of DLLs/ELs with disabilities. All of the documents discussed here touch on the following areas related to educational practice for DLLs/ELs with disabilities: (1) disproportionate representation in special education, (2) assessment and identification, (3) instruction and services, and (4) reclassification as English-proficient.

Policy Related to the Disproportionate Representation of ELs in Special Education

The introduction to IDEA lists a series of findings that highlight the challenges educators face in referral, assessment, and service provision for children with limited English proficiency who are considered for or receiving special education services. It has been shown that students considered limited English proficient are disproportionately referred to and placed in special education. Disproportionate representation is defined as the extent to which membership in a given (ethnic, socioeconomic, linguistic, or gender) group affects the probability of being placed in a specific disability category (Oswald et al., 1999, p. 198). The problem is multidimensional

TABLE 10-1 Specific Disability Categories and Some Relevant Issues for DLLs/ELs

Disability	Relevant Characteristics	Identification and Assessment	Instruction and Outcomes
Specific Learning Disability (SLD)	• Affect ability to process information, causing learning difficulties • Performance below grade-level standards in eight areas (e.g., basic reading skill, reading comprehension, mathematics calculation) • Not due to cultural differences, lack of language proficiency, or inadequate instruction	• Pre-2004, discrepancy between child's ability (IQ) and academic achievement most commonly used method • Individuals with Disabilities Education Act (IDEA) allowed states to choose method: – How child responds to scientific, research-based interventions – Child's pattern of strengths/weaknesses in performance, or achievement relative to age, state-approved grade-level standards, or intellectual development • Interventions can have positive impact (Vanderwood and Nam, 2007)	• Few studies focus specifically on DLLs/ELs • Promising practices for DLLs/ELs at risk have been identified (McMaster et al., 2008) • Recurrent question is efficacy of using primary language in instruction and intervention; some research suggests positive impact (see Vaughn et al., 2005, 2006a, 2006b) • Evidence suggests interventions tailored to individual's patterns of strengths/weaknesses can have greater impact (Richards-Tutor et al., 2016)
Intellectual Disability (ID)	• Significant limitations in intellectual functioning and adaptive behavior that emerge in childhood and adolescence	• IDEA requires use of intelligence testing and adaptive behavior scoring • *Diagnostic and Statistical Manual of Mental Disorders*, 5th edition (DSM-5) in addition requires clinical assessment and relies heavily on neuropsychological profiles, rather than single scores; this is important for DLL/ELs • Use of nonverbal cognitive measures may minimize reliance on or bias due to language proficiency (see DeThorne and Shaefer, 2004) • Culture contextualization o	• Research on efficacy and impact of language of instruction remains sparse (Mueller et al., 2006) • Majority of instruction provided in English, with little attention paid to child's first language (L1) or cultural background • National survey showed that special educators assessed and instructed students in English, lacked DLL/EL-relevant training, had limited resources, and did not include parents in decision making (Mueller et al., 2006)

continued

| Emotional/Behavioral Disorders (E/BD) | • Affect educational performance over long period of time, requiring at least one of five charact2eristics (e.g., inability to build or maintain satisfactory interpersonal relationships with peers and teachers; inappropriate types of behavior or feelings under normal circumstances; general pervasive mood of unhappiness or depression)
• Distinctions in externalizing and internalizing disorders | f adaptive behaviors crucial because of variability in culture-based expectations
• Majority of individuals have externalizing disorders
• Immigrant paradox suggests that children of immigrants may have better mental health indicators than peers with nonimmigrant backgrounds (Marks et al., 2014)
• High prevalence coupled with delayed or no access to services and health care due to family's language makes DLLs/ELs a vulnerable population (Toppelberg et al., 2013)
• Delayed identification can be result of teachers' hesitation to refer because of assumptions about language acquisition (Rogers-Adkinson et al., 2012)
• Placement patterns vary across groups at regional, state, and school district levels (Artiles et al., 2005; Bal et al., 2014; Fierros and Conroy, 2002; Parrish, 2002) | • Research on instruction is scarce (Nelson et al., 2008)
• With accommodations and adaptations, effective instructional practices can be used (Rogers-Adkinson et al., 2012) |

356

TABLE 10-1 Continued

Disability	Relevant Characteristics	Identification and Assessment	Instruction and Outcomes
Language Impairment (LI)	• Persistent difficulty with acquiring and using language across modalities due to deficits in production and/or comprehension	• The American Speech-Language-Hearing Association (ASHA) and DSM-5 state that identification based exclusively on standardized language tests is problematic for DLLs/ELs; most language tests are not normed for DLLs/ELs, are culturally and/or linguistically inappropriate, and are available only for a very limited number of languages • "Assessments of speech, language and communication abilities must take into account the individual's cultural and language context, particularly for individuals growing up in bilingual environments. The standardized measure . . . must be relevant for the cultural and linguistic group." (DSM-5) • ASHA further requires a comprehensive assessment that also includes case history, documentation of home language use and exposure history, language sampling, dynamic assessment (requiring follow-up over time), systematic observation, and parent/teacher reports • Components are crucial for differentiation between language difference and LI	• Research on intervention for DLLs/ELs is limited, with most studies focusing on relative effectiveness of bilingual vs. monolingual interventions (Ebert et al., 2014; Pham et al., 2015; Restrepo et al., 2013; Thordardottir et al., 2015) • Studies show second language (L2) interventions can improve L2 outcomes • Bilingual interventions can improve both L1 and L2 outcomes • No studies have examined L1-only interventions • Questions remain about long-term effectiveness of interventions

357

	• Using language score/IQ discrepancy criterion (known as cognitive referencing) to diagnose LI is problematic (Tomblin et al., 1997) and heavily criticized as it excludes children who have LI and would benefit from services (Reilly et al., 2014); cognitive referencing may lead to underserving DLLs/ELs with LI because of other health and education disparities	
Autism Spectrum Disorder (ASD)	• Persistent deficits in social communication and social interaction across multiple contacts and restricted, repetitive patterns of behavior, interests, or activities	• Although research is incomplete, available evidence suggests linguistic status and socioeconomic status of families play major roles in detection and diagnosis • Underdiagnosed in DLL/EL families and across racial/ethnic groups • Racial/ethnic group disparities in comorbidity with ID • Parents have difficulties accessing care and referrals and advocating for their children • LI is no longer a diagnostic criterion in DSM-5; absence of LI should not operate as a barrier to diagnosis	• Although a significant body of research supports use of applied behavioral analysis, little work has been done on language of instruction and maintenance of L1

SOURCE: Data from http://www.asha.org/PRPSpecificTopic.aspx?folderid=8589935327&section=Assessment [November 1, 2017].

BOX 10-1
Prevalence of Disabilities and Comorbidities in Dual Language Learners (DLLs)/English Learners (ELs)

Researchers argue that the prevalence of language impairment (LI) in DLLs/ELs is the same as that in monolinguals (Grimm and Schulz, 2014; Kohnert, 2010). More specifically, studies of school-age Spanish-English and French-English DLLs/ELs in the United States and Canada, respectively, have shown that compared with monolingual children with LI, DLLs/ELs with LI present the same pattern and severity of difficulty (Gutiérrez-Clellen et al., 2008; Paradis et al., 2003). These findings are important for two reasons. First, they indicate that despite their LI, DLLs/ELs are not at greater risk for language learning difficulty than monolingual children with LI, attesting to the remarkable capacity of children to acquire two languages despite an underlying impairment. Second, they indicate that learning two languages under conditions of impairment does not pose unique challenges insofar as both monolinguals and DLLs/ELs with LI have the same pattern of difficulties.

Emotional/behavioral disorders (E/BD) co-occur with LI. A meta-analysis of studies that examined E/BD outcomes found that children with LI were nearly twice as likely to develop E/BD relative to typically developing children (Yew and O'Kearney, 2013). Specifically, children with LI were more likely to have internalizing problems, externalizing problems, and attention-deficit hyperactivity disorder (ADHD). Other studies have documented cross-sectional and longitudinal relationships of LI with depression and anxiety disorders, hyperactivity and impulsivity, and ADHD and oppositional behavior (Toppelberg and Shapiro, 2000). Presumably, the relationship between LI and mental disorders is present in DLLs/ELs as well, but the committee could identify only one study supporting this presumption. In a study of DLLs/ELs referred for psychiatric services, 46 percent met criteria for LI, and 41 percent met specific LI criteria (Toppelberg et al., 2002).

The prevalence of autism spectrum disorder (ASD) in children ages 8 years is being monitored by the Centers for Disease Control and Prevention (CDC) through its Autism and Developmental Disabilities Monitoring (ADDM) network. ADDM estimates are based on parents' reports of their children's diagnosis. In 2010, ADDM's estimate of the overall prevalence of ASD reached 14.7 per 1,000 (1 in 68). And international estimates of the prevalence of ASD in the Northern Hemisphere also have grown to about 1 percent in recent estimates. It is therefore crucial to monitor diagnosis trends among DLLs/ELs, as there is no reason to think that the prevalence of ASD would be lower among them; however, prevalence estimates for DLLs/ELs are not available. Moreover, the ADDM system undersamples Hispanics and Asians (the two largest DLL/EL groups), constituting, respectively, 9.9 and 2.3 percent of the ADDM sample but 17.2 and 3.3 percent of the U.S. population of 8-year-olds. Families' linguistic status negatively impacts the detection and diagnosis of ASD, and children from Hispanic and Asian families who speak a language other than English are less likely to be diagnosed and receive services when the ASD diagnosis is merited.

Socioeconomic inequality also plays a major role in the likelihood of diagnosis of ASD, as documented by another ADDM study that contrasted parent-

---

BOX 10-1 Continued

reported diagnosis and direct diagnostic assessment of ASD (Durkin et al., 2010). The authors compared ASD diagnosis and intellectual disability (ID) comorbidity across low, medium and high socioeconomic status groups based on U.S. census indicators of socioeconomic status. The study revealed that, compared with the middle socioeconomic status group, the higher socioeconomic status group was 25 percent more likely and the low socioeconomic status group 30 percent less likely to have a parent-reported diagnosis. The socioeconomic status gradients were also significant within the Hispanic, Asian, and African American groups, but importantly, prevalence rates were the same across ethnic/racial groups in the high socioeconomic status group. The socioeconomic status gradient was present but much less significant in those cases of ASD diagnosed through direct assessment, strongly suggesting that ASD prevalence was not truly lower, but that lack of access to assessment was the reason for low ASD detection in low socioeconomic status Hispanics and blacks. Hispanic and black children were more likely to have ASD with comorbid ID and less likely to have high-functioning forms of ASD. Similarly, there was no socioeconomic status gradient in children with comorbid ASD and ID, which is another indication that lower-functioning, more severe cases (i.e., ID) equalize the field and bring low socioeconomic status—largely among Hispanic and black children—to clinical attention and diagnosis.

---

and includes over- and underrepresentation.[3] Patterns of disproportionate placement of racial minorities are most salient in the high-prevalence disabilities, particularly SLD, mild ID, speech/language impairment (SLI), and E/BD (National Research Council, 2002). Box 10-3 presents a review of the placement patterns that vary at the national and state levels by disability category and year and the heterogeneity of the population.

Sections 616 and 618 of IDEA specify systems for states and the federal government to use to track such disproportionality. The secretary of

---

[3]Disproportionality is commonly measured with a relative risk ratio, which is defined as a group's "risk of identification/placement in a given category compared to [another group's] risk in the same category . . . the term relative risk [is used] because the effect of the risk factor (e.g., language status) [is] evaluated relative to some referent group [e.g., English proficient students], and [is] therefore not an absolute indicator of risk. . . . A positive risk ratio [indicates] that EL status [is] associated with an increased likelihood of special education identification or placement relative to the comparison group, whereas a negative ratio [indicates] a decreased likelihood" (Sullivan, 2011, p. 323). A ratio of 1 means that both groups have the same risk of identification. The ratio threshold for overrepresentation varies across studies, ranging from 1.2 to 2, and that for underrepresentation ranges from 0.5 to 0.9. These thresholds tend to be higher in professional practice; for example, states require relative risk ratios ranging from 2 to 5 for overrepresentation.

BOX 10-2
Common Myths

1. Children with disabilities get confused and overwhelmed by learning or being exposed to more than one language. They have significant difficulty learning one language; hence, additional languages will make language acquisition more difficult for them.

Dual language learners (DLLs)/English learners (ELs) differentiate their languages from an early age (see Chapter 4), and there is no evidence that those with disabilities get confused or overwhelmed or have additional difficulties with or negative consequences from learning two (or more) languages (Chen and Gutiérrez-Clellen, 2013; Gutiérrez-Clellen, 2000; Hambly and Fombonne, 2012; Kay-Raining Bird et al., 2016). Kohnert and Medina (2009) reviewed 64 studies covering 30 years of research and concluded that DLLs/ELs with language impairment (LI) can and do become bilingual; DLLs/ELs and monolinguals with the same impairment generally show similar levels of language ability and areas of difficulty in a given language. Moreover, in their review of all studies available on DLLs/ELs with autism spectrum disorder (ASD) (14) and Down syndrome (8) Kay-Raining Bird and colleagues (2016) found in general that the findings of this research strongly suggest that DLLs/ELs with intellectual disability (ID) or ASD, not unlike DLLs/ELs with LI, are at no greater risk for language difficulties than monolingual children with the same disorders, and that they become bilingual within the limits of their innate language ability (Hambly and Fombonne, 2012; Kay-Raining Bird et al., 2016). Thus, bilingualism does not cause LI or place children with such impairments at additional risk. All languages of a DLL/EL will be impacted by LI, although in ways specific to each language.

2. Code switching (switching between languages in a single conversation) reflects the confusion and inability of children with disabilities to keep the two languages separate. Therefore, it is a sign or a cause of LI in DLLs/ELs.

Code switching is a normal grammatical and communicatively effective behavior in all DLLs/ELs, including those with disabilities (see Chapter 4 in this volume). It is not associated with LI in DLLs/ELs and those with LI, as it is equally present in typically developing DLLs/ELs and those with LI, and therefore is not a sign or a cause of LI (Gutiérrez-Clellen et al., 2009; Thordardottir, 2006).

3. Exposure to two or more languages will worsen LI and other language learning deficits, as it causes cognitive "overload" that overwhelms an already impaired language learning capacity and reduces the affected children's chances of learning English.

Kay-Raining Bird and colleagues (2016) reviewed three studies comparing simultaneous bilinguals and monolinguals with ASD in the majority language or the language used most often in the home. They found that the two groups performed equivalently on direct measures of receptive vocabulary and general expressive and receptive language ability. One of the studies found that Chinese/English simultaneous bilinguals with ASD produced a lower number of words compared with English-speaking monolinguals with ASD if only words in English were counted. However, total vocabulary (the number of words produced in both languages combined) was significantly higher among the former children, a pattern of vocabulary abilities that has been well documented in the literature on typically developing ELs (e.g., Pearson, 2008).

Kay-Raining Bird and colleagues (2016) also reviewed recent studies of LI in ELs and concluded that balanced simultaneous bilinguals with LI do at least as well as their monolingual peers on measures of morphosyntax in both languages or only the dominant language. Sequential bilinguals with LI tend to perform more poorly on standardized tests of second language (L2) ability (but similarly on narrative structure measures). However, their performance in L2 tends to approximate or equal that of monolinguals with LI when exposure to L2 has occurred for 6 years or longer and the two languages are similar, a finding consistent with research showing that ELs in general education become proficient in English more quickly than those with disabilities.

4. The main goal should be to maximize opportunities to learn English. Parents should stop using the home language and speak to the child only in English (or other majority L2).

As noted in the *Handbook of Early Childhood Special Education* (Reichow et al., 2016), in DLLs/ELs diagnosed with ASD, growing up with two languages does not appear to have a negative impact on their language acquisition or impede their overall development (Ohashi et al., 2012). Across several studies of DLLs/ELs with ASD, researchers have emphasized the importance of considering family culture and values and identifying ways for the child to be included in the family and community (Hanson and Espinosa, 2016; Reichow et al., 2016). A qualitative interview analysis showed that mothers who did not speak the home language to their child with ASD were led to speak less and in ways that felt unnatural or uncomfortable. Kay-Raining Bird and colleagues (2016) suggest that this finding may reflect detrimental effects that can occur when parents are told they must speak to their child in the nonhome language. Therefore, research findings suggest that speaking the home language facilitates social interaction, and in turn language and social development. Children's participation in everyday interactions with their families exposes them to various social situations that build understanding of how to interact with others and how to practice communication skills (Hambly and Fombonne, 2011). In contrast, limiting the ability of children with ASD to use their home language may have negative effects on their social interactions and language development.

Given the high comorbidity of LI, specific learning disabilities (SLD), and emotional/behavioral disorders (E/BD) (Toppelberg, 2014; Toppelberg and Shapiro, 2000), research on DLLs/ELs with LI is relevant to those with these other disorders. In DLLs/ELs with E/BD, maintaining the home language has other important implications. In these children, abilities in the home language grant access to protective resources important for social, behavioral, and emotional regulation and facilitate the development of ethnic cultural identity (Marcia, 1980; Phinney, 1989; Phinney et al., 2001) and an integration strategy of acculturation, leading to biculturalism and its positive mental health and adaptational outcomes (see Sam and Berry, 2016). Together, protective processes, ethnic identity achievement, and integration lead to resilience and positive self-perception (Oppedal and Toppelberg, 2016; Toppelberg and Collins, 2016).

BOX 10-3
Variation in Placement Patterns at the National
and State Levels by Disability Category and Year
and the Heterogeneity of the Population

English learners (ELs) are underidentified at the national level (Morgan et al., 2015). However, patterns of over- and underrepresentation are observed at the state and district levels. For example, ELs were found to be both over- and underrepresented in special education in 11 California K-12 school districts, depending on grade level (Artiles et al., 2005). Specifically, in secondary grades (6-12), ELs were more than 3.5 times more likely than their non-EL counterparts to be placed in special education. In contrast, EL disability placement rates almost reached underrepresentation levels in grades K-3 (odds ratios ranging from 0.49 to 0.62), while placement odds were comparable for ELs and non-ELs in grades 4 and 5 (odds ratios of 1.13 and 1.19, respectively). Meanwhile, ELs in Arizona were placed in special education at rates comparable to those of their non-EL counterparts in grades K-12 between 1999 and 2006 (Artiles et al., 2010).

Disproportion affects ELs across disability categories. For example, the proportion of school districts in Arizona with EL overrepresentation rates in specific learning disabilities (SLDs) increased from 25 percent in 1999 to 51 percent in 2006 (Artiles et al., 2010). In contrast, the percentage of districts with EL overrepresentation rates in mild intellectual disabilities (IDs) fluctuated from 26 percent in 1999 to 17 percent in 2002 and then 26 percent in 2005. Another study from Arizona found overrepresentation of ELs with SLD and ID at the state level, but substantial underrepresentation of those with emotional/behavioral disorders (E/BDs) (De Valenzuela et al., 2006; Sullivan, 2011). These patterns led to the

---

education is responsible for using the data to monitor the presence of significant disproportionality among specific subgroups with respect to their identification as children with disabilities, placement in particular settings (e.g., regular education, separate classes, separate schools), and experience with disciplinary actions (e.g., suspensions and expulsions). One complication of this monitoring system is that under IDEA, states themselves define how they will calculate disproportionality, and recent evidence suggests that a sizable number of states have increased the cut-off score for defining disproportionality while complying with IDEA reporting and monitoring requirements (Cavendish et al., 2014). This makes it challenging for the federal government to monitor disproportionality in a consistent manner. A possible consequence is that substantially large numbers of minority learners may be placed in special education, but school districts and states may not be required to review their diagnostic practices critically as a means of ruling out inappropriate identification.

conclusion that "the identification practices among a small proportion of districts with high relative risk strongly affect statewide rates of identification" (Sullivan, 2011, p. 324).

There is emerging evidence about EL heterogeneity in disproportionate disability identification patterns based on school district data. Some districts in California differentiated between ELs with limited proficiency in their second language (L2) only and those with limited proficiency in both their first language (L1) and L2. The EL group classified as having limited L1 and L2 proficiency tended to show greater vulnerability to being placed in a disability category. In primary school, this group was about four times as likely to be placed in speech/language impairment (SLI) elementary programs and more than twice as having likely to be identified as having SLD than ELs with limited L2 proficiency (Artiles et al., 2005). ELs were also three times more likely to be identified as having SLI and about four times more likely to be identified as having SLD compared with non-ELs. In the secondary grades, this vulnerable limited L1 and L2 proficiency group was overrepresented among ELs with ID, SLI, and SLD compared with ELs with only limited L2 proficiency and non-ELs.

Another aspect of EL heterogeneity is length of residence in the United States, which may mediate disability identification rates. Evidence suggests that a small proportion (1.9%) of recent EL arrivals were placed in special education in grades 6-12 in California school districts (Artiles et al., 2005). In contrast, 18.4 percent of recent EL arrivals were placed in special education programs in grades 1-3. EL overrepresentation was greater in secondary grades than in elementary grades in this study. It is unclear whether these identification patterns were related to students' previous schooling experiences.

The U.S. Department of Education attempted to address disparities in special education through a multiyear disproportionality analysis (U.S. Department of Education, 2016). The report of that analysis does not include a statistic on underrepresentation, but includes only statistics reflecting percentage and number of districts with risk ratios above the national median (i.e., a measure of overrepresentation). This omission may be problematic in the case of ELs, as they are underrepresented at the national level: 9 percent of ELs versus 11-13 percent of the general population are identified as having a disability, and ELs constitute only 8 percent of students with disabilities but 9.5 percent of the general student population.

Policy on Assessment and Identification for DLL/ELs with Disabilities

The question of disproportionate representation of DLLs/ELs in special education (both under- and overrepresentation) may be a result of the process of assessing and identifying students for special education eligibility called "Child Find" in IDEA (Section 612(a)(3)). Child Find is a provision stating that all children with disabilities (including DLLs/ELs, although they are not specifically named) residing in a given state must be identified and evaluated to determine what special education and related services they need. A special rule for eligibility determination (often called the "Exclusionary Clause") states that a child cannot be determined eligible for special education services if the "determinant factor for such determination is a) lack of appropriate instruction in reading, b) lack of appropriate instruction in math, or c) limited English proficiency" (Section 614(b)(5)). Because educators must rule out English proficiency as a determining factor for a child's learning difficulties, the Department of Justice (DOJ) and the Office of Civil Rights (OCR) reportedly often find an impermissible delay of assessment based on DLL/EL status and/or language proficiency level. In their recent "Dear Colleague" letter, they explain that DLLs/ELs considered to have a disability should be evaluated independently of their English language proficiency (U.S. Department of Justice and U.S. Department of Education, 2015).

In addition to the Exclusionary Clause, IDEA includes a set of procedural safeguards intended to protect DLLs/ELs and their parents during the assessment and identification process. For example, local education agencies (LEAs) must ensure that the assessments and tools used to evaluate a child for disabilities and subsequent special education eligibility "are provided and administered in the language and form most likely to yield accurate information on what the child knows and can do academically, developmentally, and functionally, unless it is not feasible to so provide or administer" (Section 614(b)(3)(A)(ii)). Despite this provision, DOJ and OCR find that DLLs/ELs are often assessed only in English even though that is not their L1 (U.S. Department of Justice and U.S. Department of Education, 2015), suggesting that LEAs may be in violation of the regulations. IDEA also requires that all assessments be administered by bilingual personnel and trained interpreters, unless doing so is not possible. States are given the authority to determine the qualifications of personnel who administer assessments, and there are no specific regulations related to personnel training.

Finally, IDEA addresses the need to include parents of DLLs/ELs in the process of assessing and identifying their children for special education services. IDEA states that when an LEA proposes to initiate or rejects the initiation of evaluation, prior notices must be sent to parents and written in their L1 unless doing so is not feasible. In addition to being adequately informed of their children's referral for special education evaluation in their L1, parents have the right to participate in the team that determines a student's eligibility for special education and educational

---

BOX 10-4
Potential Influences on Proper Identification
of ELs with Disabilities

Harry and Klinger (2014) conducted a study in south Florida on racial and linguistic disproportionality and found that administrators' and teachers' beliefs about the second language (L2) and special education, knowledge of administrative processes, and staff workload mediated the rates at which schools referred ELs to special education. The researchers found that parents' roles in identifying ELs for special education were affected by the use of interpreters. In some cases, interpreters provided a strong resource, but in other cases they complicated and hindered communications. Lack of professional preparation as interpreters was the key factor in the latter cases. Language status likely mediated parents' attitudes toward the first language (L1). Spanish-speaking parents embraced and supported the use of the L1, while Creole-speaking parents tended to deny using it and favored English instruction. This study illustrates how factors both technical (use of interpreters) and contextual (professionals' beliefs, language status) mediated decisions to refer and identify ELs with disabilities, a phenomenon that can result in missed and erroneous diagnoses.

---

needs (Section 614(b)(4)(A)). Box 10-4 illustrates the complex interaction between families and trained personnel during the assessment process.

If a DLL/EL is ultimately determined to be eligible for special education services, federal policy dictates that it may be necessary to review the student's identification as a DLL/EL. This is especially the case if the student in question was identified as a DLL/EL without accommodations or alternative screeners. Such DLLs/ELs with disabilities may have been inappropriately identified as DLLs/ELs based on their disabilities. Research is needed, however, on what accommodations and alternative screeners would be most appropriate for measuring the English language proficiency of DLLs/ELs with disabilities (Shafer Willner et al., 2008, 2010).

Policy on Instruction and Services for DLLs/ELs with Disabilities

According to Section 612 of IDEA, all states are required to offer a free and appropriate public education to all students with disabilities ages 3-21, including DLLs/ELs, in the "least restrictive environment." The least restrictive environment means that, to the extent possible, children with disabilities should be educated with students who do not have disabilities, with removal from regular education classrooms limited to instances when students' disabilities prevent them from receiving adequate education in such a classroom with individualized supports. This decision is based on a student's individualized education program (IEP),[4] which outlines what special education services must be provided to the student by qualified, trained special education teachers, paraprofessionals, and related service personnel. Additionally, for children with limited English proficiency, educators should "consider the language needs of the child as such needs relate to the child's IEP" (Section 614(d)(3)(B)(ii)).

In addition to IDEA, ESSA includes regulations on academic standards. States must adopt challenging academic standards that prepare students for postsecondary education and the workforce. For the most significantly disabled students, states can create alternative academic achievement standards, but these alternative standards must be consistent with IDEA guidelines and ensure that students are prepared for postsecondary education. States also must adopt English language proficiency standards that cover four domains: speaking, listening, reading, and writing. English language proficiency standards must align with states' academic standards.

Federal policy also addresses issues pertaining to the instruction and services for DLLs/ELs with disabilities through early intervening services (for school-age children) and early intervention services (for children aged birth to 3 years). Early intervening services include academic and behavioral evaluations, services, and supports and are typically implemented before students are evaluated for special education services (often considered a general education requirement). LEAs, which can allocate some IDEA funds to early intervening services (designed for students in K-12, with particular emphasis on those in grades K-3), must report how many students receive early intervening services each year, as well as the number of students who once received such services and subsequently have received special education and related services. The act includes nothing specific about providing early intervening services for students with limited English proficiency.

DLLs with disabilities ages birth to 3 years are eligible for early intervention services, which are different from the early intervening services that target school-age children. Early intervention services are provided in natural environments, such as the child's home and community settings, to the extent possible. An individualized family service plan must be developed to outline the services and goals for the child, including the services' anticipated length, duration, and frequency (Section 636). Early intervention services target school readiness and may incorporate preliteracy, language,

---

[4]Federal guidelines governing the placement of children in special education programs require that a meeting of the student's IEP team (made up of qualified professionals and parents) be convened several times each year to evaluate the student's progress and consider decisions about the continuation and addition of services.

and numeracy skills (as well as other services related to physical and cognitive development).

Policy on the Reclassification of ELs with Disabilities as English-Proficient

In accordance with ESSA, all states must have a system for annually assessing the English language proficiency of their ELs in speaking, listening, reading, and writing. The results of these assessments must be included in state report cards that are sent to the secretary of education (Section 1111(b)(2)(H)). States can choose to exclude assessment scores of ELs who have been in the country for less than a year (in year 2, a measure of growth on assessments must be included, and by year 3, the proficiency scores must be included). These scores do not count toward the district's or state's performance, but are made publicly available. Although ELs with disabilities are not specifically cited in these regulations, white papers released by the U.S. Department of Education (2014) and the U.S. Department of Justice and the U.S. Department of Education (2015) indicate that ELs with disabilities must be included in state annual assessments of English language proficiency for students with limited English proficiency. These assessments factor into the decision to exit ELs from EL status (see Box 10-5).

BOX 10-5
The Acquisition of English and Reclassification
of ELs with Disabilities

Research suggests that learning a second language takes time and is impacted by factors such as type of bilingual instructional model, pedagogy, and learner characteristics. A recent study across seven Northwest school districts with high rates of poverty and low levels of academic achievement found that it took students in general education an average of 3.8 years to meet reclassification criteria from EL to non-EL and exit English as a second language/English language development programs. However, it took ELs in special education an average of 5.5 years to exit (Greenberg Motamedi, 2015). Nine years of longitudinal data from Los Angeles Unified School District, including 30 percent of students identified as having a disability, suggest a similar exit time frame (Thompson, 2015). Dixon (2013) found that EL reclassification took, on average, 7.4 years in general education, 5.4 years in gifted and talented programs, and 8.9 years for students with disabilities. Additionally, Dixon found that ELs with disabilities in bilingual programs took 8.8 years and those in English immersion programs 9.2 years to exit English as a second language services. Although the time frames vary, it is clear that ELs with disabilities take longer to attain English proficiency than ELs without disabilities, with some likely never attaining full proficiency.

In addition to implementing accommodations, the LEA, school personnel, and/or IEP team may have input into the decision of whether a student is proficient in English, depending on the state's definition of English language proficiency. However, the U.S. Department of Education (2014) explains that IDEA contains no provision that would authorize the IEP team to remove the EL designation before the student has attained English language proficiency based on standardized or alternative assessments. Thus, it is important that more research be conducted on valid and reliable accommodations and alternative assessments for measuring the English language proficiency of ELs with disabilities.

Taken together, evidence on policy to date reflects a complex configuration of factors mediating placement rates for ELs. Research is scarce on underrepresentation and whether placement risk varies by type of school district, student race, EL subgroup (e.g., language proficiency level), and disability. A key limitation of the research in this area is the lack of explicit theoretical grounding of studies and the formulation of theoretical propositions stemming from the available evidence (Skiba et al., 2016). Greater clarity and rigor are critically needed regarding key aspects of this research, such as what counts as over- and underrepresentation (studies use different cut-off points for disproportionality), measures of EL status (e.g., school district classification based on English proficiency versus parent reports of language use), and various methodological issues (e.g., longitudinal versus cross-sectional designs; sampling procedures; theoretical rationale for the selection of controls; definition and analysis of poverty, including its timing, magnitude, and duration) (Skiba et al., 2016).

OVERVIEW OF IDENTIFICATION AND EVALUATION PRACTICES

Professional organizations and practitioners in second language and special education fields regularly raise questions about the appropriate timing for identification of DLLs/ELs for special education services and whether reliable criteria exist for the diagnoses of specific disabilities.

In the United States, multiple factors shape the ability to differentiate developmental differences associated with acquisition of a second language (L2) from disability. First are classification issues related to the DLL/EL population and students with disabilities. Abedi (2008), for instance, found that more than 90 percent of the variance in DLL/EL classification was not related to learners' English proficiency. Rather, ethnicity, social class, and reports from parents and teachers on quality of language use played a substantial role in classification decisions. In turn, "the classification of [a DLL/EL] with disabilities remains elusive in part due to the lack of consensus in the field on who [a DLL/EL] actually is and how to refer to these students" (Minnema et al., 2005, p. 10). These classification ambiguities are related, in part, to the fact that English language proficiency is negatively associated with a disability diagnosis. For instance, Abedi (2008) reports misclassification of ELs with the lowest levels of English proficiency as learners with disabilities, while Shelton (2007) found that overrepresentation in certain disability categories in middle schools in California was more noticeable among ELs with the lowest English proficiency levels. It has also been found that ELs tend to be overlooked for early reading interventions because of limited English proficiency (Limbos and Geva, 2001).

Other factors further complicate the differentiation of L2-related differences from disabilities. These include the scarcity of research on the intersection between L2 acquisition and disability, the lack of validated assessment measures and procedures for DLLs/ELs, technical limitations (e.g., limited access to datasets that provide insight on L2/disability links, limited assessment tools), population issues (e.g., behaviors associated with L2 acquisition or with cultural/linguistic community practices that can be confused with learning disabilities), and lack of opportunity to learn (e.g., limited access to language supports and qualified teachers) (Klingner, 2014; Ortiz and Artiles, 2010). The case study in Annex 10-1 at the end of this chapter highlights the importance of these factors for proper classification and/or diagnosis. Table 10-2 lists behaviors associated with learning disabilities that are similar to behaviors exhibited by learners acquiring an L2. Some of these similarities apply to SLI as well.

Early Identification of DLLs/ELs with Disabilities[5]

DLLs/ELs are less likely than non-DLLs/ELs to be referred to early intervention and early special education, which may have serious consequences. In a nationally representative study of 48-month-olds born in 2001 (N = 7,950), Morgan and colleagues (2012) showed that speakers of a language other than English at home were 48 percent less likely than English home speakers to be referred for early intervention. Hispanics and Asians, respectively, were 56 percent and 23 percent (blacks were 36%) less likely than non-Hispanic whites to be referred for early intervention. Thus, language barriers and other factors appear to be a determinant of lack of referral for Hispanics. Lower access to health care may also be responsible for low referral rates, as pediatricians and other physicians often initiate these referrals; identification of developmental disorders by physicians occurs 1-2 years earlier than identification by preschool staff (Palfrey et al., 1987). Therefore, the role of early childhood programs, such as the Maternal, Infant, and Early Childhood Home Visiting federal program and early care

---

[5]Some passages in this section are based on and Chen and Gutiérrez-Clellan (2013) and Hanson and Espinosa (2016).

TABLE 10-2 Similarities in Behaviors Associated with Learning Disabilities and Second Language Acquisition

Behavior Associated with Learning Disability	Behavior Associated with Second Language (L2) Acquisition
Difficulty with auditory discrimination and/or phonological awareness	Students may not be accustomed to hearing sounds in the L2 that are not found in their L1. Unfamiliar sounds in the L2 may also be difficult for the student to produce.
Difficulty with sight words, words with multiple meanings, figurative language, or idioms	Students may be confused by common words, figurative language, or idioms in the L2; however, students may understand the underlying concept in their L1.
Difficulty understanding which letters make which sounds	Students may be confused by letter sounds in L2 when different from L1 or when this literacy skill has not been developed in the L1.
Difficulty with story narration and retelling	Students may have trouble with story narration and retelling when they do not have sufficient development of oral proficiency in addition to instruction in reading and writing.
Difficulty with reading fluency	Students may have difficulty reading fluently and conveying expression in their L2. Students may understand more than they are able to convey.
May seem disengaged during instruction	Students may appear disengaged during instruction in the L2 when explanations are provided without visual cues or other scaffolding techniques in place to make instruction more comprehensible.
May seem frustrated or unmotivated	Students may appear frustrated or unmotivated. This can occur if assignments are not at the appropriate level for them or when they do not understand why the assignment is meaningful or relevant.

SOURCE: Summarized from Klinger (2008).

and education (ECE) programs, which can provide referrals and connections to health care access for at-risk DLLs/ELs, cannot be overemphasized.

An important question for home visiting, ECE, health, and other professionals is whether they are accurately identifying all DLLs/ELs who have special needs and could benefit from early intervention services. As noted above, current demographics, when compared with service rates, suggest that young Hispanics with disabilities frequently are not being identified

(National Center for Education Statistics, 2007; Reichow et al., 2016; Rueda and Windmueller, 2006). Although Hispanics ages birth to 5 represent more than 15 percent of the total population, only about 2 percent of Hispanics among the birth-to-3 population receive intervention services; the percentage increases to almost 9 percent for preschoolers, which is still short of the estimated need. As discussed previously, Hispanics and ELs continue to be underrepresented in K-12 programs among children with disabilities at the national level, but in specific states (California, New York) and specific districts, they are overrepresented. These uneven and fluctuating service rates demonstrate a need for more consistent definitions and eligibility criteria for DLLs/ELs across the grades, as well as improved methods for identifying DLLs/ELs ages birth to 5 who may need special services (Reichow et al., 2016).

For DLLs/ELs with the more severe disabilities (ASD, ID) and E/BD, significant underidentification and lack of or delayed services have been documented. Rates of referral to early intervention/early childhood special education also are lower than those for non-DLLs/ELs. This differential is due, in part, to barriers to health care access (language and cultural barriers, lack of referral due to hesitation by professionals, misattribution of delays to growing up with two languages, lack of insurance, lack of parents' familiarity with the health care system). Early identification is predictive of functional outcomes for both ID and ASD. Early, high-quality intensive services can sometimes, in cases of mild to moderate ID, improve intellectual and adaptive functioning to the point that an individual no longer meets criteria for ID (according to the *Diagnostic and Statistical Manual of Mental Disorders*, 5th edition [DSM-5]). Therefore, it is particularly important to identify and provide services for early indicators of ID, ASD, LI, SLD, and E/BD.

The Office of Head Start's National Center on Cultural and Linguistic Responsiveness and Quality Teaching and Learning recently published guidelines for programs on methods for conducting developmental screening for DLLs/ELs (Office of Head Start, n.d.). These guidelines recommend two options for collecting accurate information about a child's developmental status when no valid and reliable screening instruments are appropriate for specific language groups. The first option involves gathering detailed information from the family about the child's knowledge, skills, and abilities; conducting teacher observations over the 45-day screening period; and collaborating with the family to make a referral decision. The second option entails hiring a skilled and trained interpreter. Both options require that staff consult with others who are knowledgeable about child development, speak the child's language, and are familiar with the child's culture. Staff must collect data on what the child knows and is able to do in both the home language and English, and incorporate the family's perspective on

BOX 10-6
Importance of Family Involvement in
Evaluating DLLs/ELs with Disabilities

It is important to involve parents and other family members of DLLs/ELs with disabilities both in the assessment process and at regular and possibly more frequent intervals than is the case for English-speaking populations with disabilities. Also important is obtaining the full support of parents to minimize potential fears of stigma and misinformation and to maximize access to other services that require parental advocacy and/or may be beyond what the school would routinely offer, such as applied behavior analysis, speech/language pathology services, or neuropsychological testing.

From an identification point of view, parents may be able to provide information about developmental milestones or insights about motivation or causes behind maladaptive behaviors or emotions. Parents may report a family history of specific learning disability (SLD) (dyslexia is present in 50 percent of parents of an affected child), which is a risk factor that may require closer monitoring of the child's progress. Parents also may provide a better understanding of the child's adaptive functioning at home and in other settings, clarifying questions about intellectual functioning and completing parental reports for language impairment (LI), emotional/behavioral disorders (E/BDs), and autism spectrum disorder (ASD). Section 504 of the Rehabilitation Act of 1973 requires that "enough information" be used to document that a student has a disability:

At the elementary and secondary education level, the amount of information required is determined by the multi-disciplinary committee gathered to evaluate the student. The committee should include persons knowledgeable about the student, the meaning of the evaluation data, and the placement options. The committee members must determine if they have enough information to make a knowledgeable decision as to whether or not the student has a disability. The Section 504 regulatory provision . . . requires that school districts draw from a variety of sources in the evaluation process so that the possibility of error is minimized. The information obtained from all such sources must be documented and all significant factors related to the student's learning process must be considered. These sources and factors may include aptitude and achievement tests, teacher recommendations, physical condition, social and cultural background, and adaptive behavior. In evaluating a student suspected of having a disability, it is unacceptable to rely on presumptions and stereotypes regarding persons with disabilities or classes of such persons.

Collecting "enough information" on DLLs/ELs is a crucial goal, and maintaining close communication with the family is one powerful way to achieve this goal.

the child's abilities. (Box 10-6 explains the importance of family involvement in evaluating DLLs/ELs with disabilities.) Final decisions are to be made by the appropriate staff in collaboration with families. The Head Start National Center also provides a sample form, *Gathering and Using*

Information That Families Share,[6] to assist with the data collection process. To make accurate judgments about a child's need for special services, it is critical that all home visiting and ECE professionals understand the child's level of proficiency and progress over time in both languages.

Evaluation Approaches

Research on distinguishing underlying disabilities from normal differences in language acquisition between DLLs/ELs and non-DLLs/ELs takes one of two approaches. The core premise of the first body of work is that the differentiation between learning disabilities and learning difficulties linked to L2 acquisition should rely on a systemic multipronged approach. Three components of an integrated education system that coordinates general education, special education, and bilingual education/ESL services have been identified: (1) prevention of academic failure, (2) early intervention for struggling students, and (3) special education processes adapted for DLLs/ELs (Artiles and Ortiz, 2002; Linan-Thompson and Ortiz, 2009; Wilkinson et al., 2006). This model calls for an understanding of L2 acquisition processes, attention to typical L2 acquisition behaviors that might be confused with characteristics associated with SLD, and use of consultation models that take into account multiple individual and systemic factors (e.g., DLL/EL learning histories in both languages, qualities of assessment tools/procedures used, opportunities to learn in classrooms and schools) (Artiles and Klingner, 2006; Burr et al., 2015; Klingner et al., 2010; Ortiz and Artiles, 2010; U.S. Department of Education, 2015). The second approach represents a new generation of problem-solving models that aims to predict or prevent misdiagnosis of disabilities among ELs in the context of academic interventions, such as response to intervention (RTI), which is discussed in detail below.

Multipronged Approach for Evaluating DLLs/ELs

Evaluation of DLLs/ELs for special education eligibility is a complex process that requires team decision making grounded in the expertise of special and general educators as well as L2 specialists. The evaluation process needs to provide an accurate and detailed account of what a child knows and can do developmentally, academically, and functionally in both languages (Linan-Thompson and Ortiz, 2009; Ortiz and Artiles, 2010). The assessment team needs to use evidence from both formal and informal measures and weigh the advantages and risks of using multiple languages

---

[6]See at https://eclkc.ohs.acf.hhs.gov/hslc/tta-system/cultural-linguistic/fcp/docs/dll_background_info.pdf [February 16, 2017].

during evaluation sessions. For instance, teams need to decide whether as-sessments of literacy should be conducted in L1 or L2, depending on the learning histories of learners. The assessment scores of DLLs/ELs in English may reflect risk in all areas measured. Yet measures administered in L1 may indicate that the student is in the low-risk range. Given the robust literature demonstrating the transferability of literacy skills (see Chapter 4), particu-larly across languages that share an alphabet, it is important that students' native language literacy be assessed (Durgunoglu, 2002; Durgunoglu et al., 1993) in attempting to diagnose a language or learning disability. Consider-ations for the analysis and use of evaluation results are listed in Box 10-7.

Response to Intervention (RTI) Approach

One approach to serving children with learning disabilities is the model of RTI, which can be utilized for subject learning, although the bulk of the literature on ELs focuses on reading. Box 10-8 provides an overview of the RTI model.

In an RTI model, screening assessments should be conducted each quar-ter to determine which students need additional academic support because they have not shown adequate response to intervention. At the heart of all assessment is the need for reliable and valid tools. Box 10-9 describes the curriculum-based measures (CBMs) commonly used.

Given RTI's visibility in IDEA and the fact that RTI models systemati-cally identify groups of students with varying kinds of learning needs while also offering instructional resources through evidence-based interventions, the remainder of this section is organized around the tiers of RTI. The com-ponents within each tier are specified, with particular attention to DLLs/ELs. Box 10-10 outlines general guidelines for RTI models that include DLLs/ELs.

Tier 1: Instruction and Screening

Since RTI models presume adequate and appropriate instruction in general education, RTI teams need to ensure that each EL's language profi-ciency is documented, understood by teachers, and aligned with all instruc-tion (Brown and Doolittle, 2008; Brown and Sanford, 2011). In addition, the language(s) of instruction needs to be matched to the language(s) of assessment.

Each EL must receive federally mandated ESL instruction that targets growing one language proficiency level per year. This instruction is not an intervention but rather core instruction for eligible students. Yet the instruc-tional strategies used in ESL programs need to be embedded throughout

BOX 10-7
Analyzing and Utilizing the Results of the Disability Evaluation

The following considerations are important in analyzing and utilizing the results of the disability evaluation of a dual language learner (DLL)/English learner (EL).

- Are evaluators trained to conduct the evaluation and interpret the results, including knowing how to differentiate between slow language development that is due to a lack of supporting conditions (e.g., too little exposure) and a disability?
- Does the individualized education program (IEP) or Section 504 team include participants who have knowledge of the student's language needs and training in special education and related services, as well as professionals with training in second language acquisition and DLL/EL services? Do these participants have the knowledge to recommend an education program or plan that provides the student with appropriate services and/or supports based on the student's disability and English language acquisition needs? Do these participants also understand cultural differences that may exist?
- Have the parents been invited to participate in the planning process and informed of their rights in a language they understand?
- Have trained interpreters and translated documents been made available for parents with limited English proficiency when required (e.g., parent notices under the Individuals with Disabilities Education Act [IDEA]) or when determined necessary to ensure effective communication? Is a qualified sign language interpreter available for parents who have hearing loss and need such services?
- Does the local education agency's education program address the DLL/EL's language needs and include disability-related services designed to address those needs?
- Does the IEP or Section 504 plan outline when and by whom the accommodations, modifications, and supports in the IEP or Section 504 plan will be provided?
- Will the recommended services allow DLLs/ELs with a disability to be involved and make progress in the general education curriculum and to participate in extracurricular activities?
- Is there a formal plan to monitor the progress of DLLs/ELs with disabilities with respect to language and disability-based goals?
- Have the student's general education teachers and related service providers been made aware of the IEP or Section 504 services for the DLL/EL?

SOURCE: U.S. Department of Education (2015, Ch. 6).

BOX 10-8
Overview of Response to Intervention (RTI)

RTI is a comprehensive instructional system that provides evidence-based interventions to all learners. The system is typically organized around three tiers that vary by the intensity of the interventions according to the learning needs of students (Fuchs et al., 2003). The first tier targets all students in general education, of whom 80 percent or so are expected to benefit fully. Screening tools are used to identify at-risk or struggling learners. Those learners whose screening data indicate that they are in the bottom 20 percent of the group receive additional interventions in smaller groups (tier 2 intervention). The instructional focus in tier 2 is on providing a "double dose" of instruction on the same concepts these students are learning in their classrooms. About 5 percent of students may be far below grade level and are considered to be at high risk for academic failure, and thus require the most intensive instruction in tier 3—that is, special education. In this way, "the RTI model has a systematic approach to determining whether [ELs] who are struggling and in need of special education services have difficulties well beyond those involved in learning a second language and/or opportunities-to-learn" (Lesaux and Harris, 2013, p. 74).

A key issue in the RTI literature is the determination of response and how to differentiate "responders" from "nonresponders." Torgesen (2000) estimates that 2-4 percent of the general school-age population would be considered "nonresponders" to tier 2 interventions. Linan-Thompson and colleagues (2007, p. 187) explain that "in the absence of consensus on this issue, performance level, most often measured with a benchmark score, and growth are frequently used. The benchmark is usually set by a norm group." The problem is that ELs often are not included in the norming samples. In addition, there is no consensus on the cut-off point for performance levels or growth to determine responsiveness (or lack thereof). An alternative is to use performance and growth, with peers as the reference group. The question remains, however, of "which measures yield the most accurate information regarding response to intervention" (Linan-Thompson et al., 2007, p. 187).

---

all instruction and intervention for ELs (Chamot and O'Malley, 1994; Echevarria et al., 2008; Gersten and Baker, 2000).

If RTI instruction is to be appropriate for ELs, however, RTI teams need to make some adjustments to the model. It is recommended that teams (1) separate out the screening data to examine achievement patterns of student subgroups, comparing the growth of students with similar language and cultural backgrounds; (2) ensure the provision of legally mandated English language development services to eligible students as part of general education and monitor their progress at least annually (Brown and Sanford, 2011); and (3) adjust research-based intervention programs to align with

BOX 10-9
Curriculum-Based Measures (CBMs)

Two common CBMs—that is, tools used for formative assessment—are Dynamic Indicators of Basic Early Literacy Skills Next (DIBELS Next) (Kaminski and Good, 2014) and AIMSweb (http://www.aimsweb.com) and their Spanish equivalents, Indicadores Dinámicos del Exito en la Lectura (IDEL) (Baker et al., 2006) and Medidas Incrementales de Destrezas Esenciales (MIDE), respectively (Magit and Shinn, 2002). Research suggests that CBMs are effective in predicting reading performance in both English monolinguals and English Learners (ELs) (Klingner et al., 2006; Vanderwood and Nam, 2007). Specifically, studies have consistently shown a correlation between measures of phonological awareness (Riedel, 2007), alphabetic understanding (Fien et al., 2008; Riedel, 2007; Vanderwood et al., 2008), and oral reading fluency (Crosson and Lesaux, 2010; Riedel, 2007; Vanderwood et al., 2008; Wiley and Deno, 2005) and measures of reading comprehension for ELs spanning kindergarten and 1st, 2nd, 3rd, and 5th grades. Thus, evidence indicates that CBMs are both valid and reliable predictors of reading outcomes in English among ELs (Leafstedt et al., 2004; Quirk and Beem, 2012).

Some research suggests that language proficiency impacts performance on CBMs. Quirk and Beem (2012) examined the relationship between oral reading fluency and reading comprehension among 171 ELs in grades 2, 3, and 5 and found fluency/comprehension gaps that appeared to vary by level of English language proficiency. Their results reinforce those of previous research (Crosson and Lesaux, 2010; Klein and Jimerson, 2005) that also suggested that the relationship between oral reading fluency and reading comprehension in ELs may be moderated by students' English oral language skills. For this reason, one significant concern is that CBMs often are administered only in English, even when students are receiving some instruction in their first language (L1). Although dual immersion models are expanding to languages other than Spanish, CBMs are as yet available only in English and Spanish. Brown and Sanford (2011, p. 10) offer recommendations for ensuring appropriate use of CBMs with ELs:

1. Use tools with demonstrated reliability and validity to identify and monitor students' need for instructional support in reading in both L1 and English (L2).
2. Assess students' language skills in L1 and L2 to provide an appropriate context for evaluation of current levels of performance.
3. Evaluate the potential effect of the process of L1 and L2 acquisition on current performance.
4. Plan instruction based on what is known about students' current level of performance and their literacy experiences in L1 and L2.

BOX 10-10
Considerations for Response to Intervention
(RTI) Models That Include ELs

- **Comprehensive early identification of risk for reading difficulties.** Early and ongoing screening of phonological processes as well as meaning-related skills (e.g., vocabulary, listening comprehension skills) needs to be implemented carefully with dual language learners (DLLs)/ English learners (ELs). The scope of assessments needs to be broadened over time given the uneven developmental nature of second language (L2) and reading acquisition.
- **Multiple indicators of reading development.** Decisions about reading acquisition often are based on single indicators, particularly for DLLs/ ELs. However, it is plausible that DLLs/ELs have underdeveloped skills in certain areas relative to their English-proficient peers, while they may exhibit comparable development levels in other skill domains. Thus, it is critical to document the strengths and weaknesses of DLLs/ELs before, during, and after the implementation of RTI interventions.
- **Monitoring of progress over time.** Positive learning rates may be documented at a given time on a particular skill or in a specific grade, but delays may be observable at other times or across contexts. For these reasons, it is necessary to maintain a regular assessment system that tracks responses to instruction over time.
- **A focus on the quality of classroom instruction.** The limited opportunities to learn tied to structural issues that affect DLLs/ELs (e.g., underfunded schools, lower teacher quality, school and community racial segregation, lack of access to health services) need to be addressed with a sustained focus on the quality of instruction offered to this population. Effective strategies include attending systematically to language development, building on students' background experiences, making lessons accessible (e.g., providing visual clues, posting lists of key lesson words, scaffolding), offering opportunities for practice and application, using repetition and redundant information, assessing frequently, and reteaching as needed (Echevarria and Hasbrouck, 2009). A focus on quality of instruction will allow schools to determine who benefits from instruction, improve instruction for struggling learners, compare the impact of various instructional approaches, and individualize instruction for students if needed.

SOURCE: Adapted from Lesaux and Harris (2013).

children's instructional language proficiency and cultural/experiential backgrounds (Baker et al., 2014; Rivera Mindt et al., 2008).

Tiers 2 and 3: Research-Based Interventions

Tier 2 interventions tend to follow a standardized protocol that relies on small-group instruction. A number of studies have focused on early reading skills with ELs (e.g., letter naming, phoneme segmentation, nonsense words, oral reading fluency). Successful tier 2 interventions with ELs have been reported in recent years (McIntosh et al., 2007). Research on the efficacy of tier 2 reading interventions for ELs has found significant effects on reading comprehension from interventions in text-reading but not word-reading fluency alone, suggesting that comprehension may be strongly mediated by L2 oral language and listening comprehension skills (Crosson and Lesaux, 2010). Of interest, evidence suggests that interventions tailored to an individual's patterns of strengths and weaknesses can have a greater impact than those that are standardized (Richards-Tutor et al., 2016).

Tier 3 interventions are generally more individualized relative to tier 2, although there have been studies of these interventions grounded in standardized protocols. Vaughn and colleagues (2011), for example, studied the impact of tier 3 standardized and individualized interventions and found no statistically significant differences between these two approaches. The same pattern was documented for ELs.

Nonetheless, questions have been raised about key aspects of RTI. For instance, Cirino and colleagues (2009, p. 775) conclude that "it is not clear what type of criteria should be used to establish response. . . . It is also unclear what kinds of measures are optimal for assessing responsiveness (e.g., phonology, decoding, comprehension, fluency). These issues are compounded for [ELs]." Linan-Thompson and colleagues (2007) examined nonresponders among 1st-grade ELs using three methods and found that discrepancy slope was the most accurate in identifying nonresponders. Richards-Tutor and colleagues (2012) investigated three different methods and discovered that each identified different percentages and different groups of nonresponder students. Based on this evidence, they recommended that multiple criteria be used to identify nonresponders and that caution be exercised with respect to using formulaic decision-making models—for example, by including students' educational experiences, opportunity to learn in the general education classroom in relation to their language proficiency level and cultural background, achievement in comparison with true peers, and access to literacy in the home.

Theoretical and methodological questions concerning cultural and linguistic differences have also been raised (Artiles and Kozleski, 2010; Klingner and Edwards, 2006). Some evidence suggests that interventions made no difference or had a negative impact on learners "who scored near the cut point on their fall screening test" (Balu et al., 2015, p. ES-16). It should be noted that this finding was not observed consistently across grade levels or outcomes. Furthermore, a qualitative study of the implementation of RTI with ELs in Colorado found that school personnel using the RTI model had deficit views of ELs, which were reflected in the lack of alignment between instruction and assessment, a negative school culture, lack of teacher preparation (particularly on L2 issues), and limited curricular resources (Orosco and Klingner, 2010).

RESEARCH ON IDENTIFICATION, INSTRUCTION, AND ASSESSMENT FOR DLLS/ELS WITH DISABILITIES

Identification for Specific Disabilities

The purpose of identification is to afford access to educational programs and specialized mental health interventions. However, the 2000 surgeon general's report (U.S. Public Health Service, 1999) raised concerns about ethnic minority children's access to mental health services, and Latino and other children with immigrant backgrounds have been found to be at risk for not receiving specialty mental health services (Toppelberg et al., 2013). Factors that contribute to this situation include lack of health insurance; language barriers; an unrecognized need for services; and the intersection with low socioeconomic status, childhood adversity, and neighborhood violence (Alegria et al., 2015; Toppelberg et al., 2013). These factors affect disproportionately Latinos and other immigrant groups (Flores and Vega, 1998; Organista, 2000) that have a high prevalence rate for mental health conditions such as major depression, suicidality, and posttraumatic stress disorder (Toppelberg and Collins, 2010). The high prevalence of these disorders among DLLs/ELs in general, coupled with delayed or no access to services and health care due to the family's language and other health care barriers, makes this a particularly vulnerable population (Toppelberg et al., 2013) that may require Section 504 or other accommodations.

Intellectual Disabilities

Most assessors understand that the performance of DLLs/ELs on English IQ tests is partially a function of their English proficiency. However, they erroneously believe that L1 language tests will provide more accurate and valid results. These tests are usually normed on monolingual speakers of the home language in a country other than the United States, rather than in the sociocultural and language group of individual DLLs/ELs in the United States. Brown (2008) investigated the performance of 34 3rd-

and 4th-grade ELs with medium to advanced English language proficiency on a commonly used IQ test normed on Spanish monolinguals. None of the study participants had ever been referred for interventions or special education evaluation, and all were receiving ESL services. Half of the group received Spanish instruction for literacy and math, and the other half received all-English instruction. Brown found the mean IQ score of the Spanish instruction group to be within the average range, but at 90.81, their average was lower than the normative average of 100. The English instruction group was in the below average range. Thus, multidisciplinary teams using this common Spanish language cognitive test could easily misidentify ELs in schools as having a disability, even ID. A critical view of IQ testing and borderline scores continues to be a crucial and complex topic in ID diagnosis. The case history highlighted in Annex 10-1 is a reminder of these complexities.

One option for avoiding overreliance on verbal tests is to assess cognitive abilities through the use of nonverbal cognitive tests (see DeThorne and Schaefer, 2004), some of which can be pantomimed, thus minimizing reliance on or bias due to language proficiency. Research on a community sample of 6-year-old Latino ELs using one of these tests showed IQ scores in the average range (mean 95.62; standard deviation [SD] = 11.52) and no significant IQ differences across groups of ELs who were proficient in Spanish, English, or both (means ranging from 96.24 to 101.48) (Collins et al., 2014). Of interest, a "limited proficient" group (with low skills in both languages) had IQ scores (mean 89.93; SD = 9.45) that were significantly lower than those of the English-proficient group. This type of nonverbal test may therefore be useful in assessing ELs.

DSM-5 clearly favors a complex cognitive profile resulting from neuropsychological testing over a single IQ score number. However, few neuropsychologists in the United States are bilingual or have the training or experience to evaluate DLLs/ELs (Rivera Mindt et al., 2008, 2010). Other professional workforce factors identified by Ware and colleagues (2015) include lack of properly trained interpreters, deficits in the education and training of speech/language pathologists (SLPs) and a dearth of bilingual SLPs, and lack of confidence of professionals in their own DLL/EL assessments. Misdiagnosis of DLLs/ELs with disabilities (false negatives and false positives) can have serious consequences for children who could benefit from either challenging educational opportunities (overdiagnosis) or high-quality intensive services early on (underdiagnosis) (Ware et al., 2015).

Language Impairment

Diagnosis of LI in DLLs/ELs can be complicated further by the fact that their language proficiency, with or without LI, can differ among their languages and from that of monolinguals (Kohnert, 2010; Paradis et al., 2011). Researchers and clinicians agree, however, that bilingual children with LI show impairments in both languages (Kohnert, 2010). Research has shown that, compared with typically developing DLLs/ELs, those with LI have language deficits in such areas as verb inflection, verbal fluency, phonological awareness, and phonological working memory in both languages (Aguilar-Mediavilla et al., 2014; Blom and Paradis, 2013; Girbau and Schwartz, 2008). In DLLs/ELs, slower than normal development in only one language is probably a reflection of the quality and quantity of opportunities to learn that language, whereas difficulties in both languages are more likely to reflect underlying impairment. It is for this reason that assessing DLLs/ELs in both languages is imperative.

Emotional/Behavioral Disorders

Mental disorders often have a significant effect on school performance and prosocial behavior at school. For instance, these disorders may restrict access to educational opportunities or extracurricular activities, including athletics, leading to long-term lower achievement, disengagement, withdrawal, nonparticipation in activities, and possibly absenteeism and school dropout. Schools therefore have a key role to play as a point of access for highly needed mental health services (Institute of Medicine, 1997).

Instruction and Assessment

Specific Learning Disability

A sizable body of research addresses instruction and assessment of DLLs/ELs and non-DLLs/ELs with SLD. However, relatively fewer studies focus specifically on DLLs/ELs with SLD. Ortiz (1997) and Baca and Cervantes (1989) did pioneering work on bilingual special education and produced instructional and assessment models and guidelines over the years, mainly on students with SLD. Other researchers have identified promising practices for DLLs/ELs at risk for reading disorders or with SLD at the preschool or early elementary level (Brown et al., 2013; Lovett et al., 2008; McMaster et al., 2008; Vaughn et al., 2011).

A recurrent question in this literature is the efficacy of using L1 in instruction and intervention for DLLs/ELs. Evidence supports the positive impact of interventions that use L1 instruction. In one series of studies, small-group interventions were provided in English or Spanish to 1st-grade ELs at risk for reading difficulties (Vaughn et al., 2005, 2006a). The language of intervention was matched to the language of the literacy instruction in the general education setting. Interventions included explicit instruction in oral language, listening comprehension, and reading skills and utilized strategies deemed best practices for ESL instruction. Vaughn and colleagues (2005) found significant posttest differences for the intervention groups, with an average effect size on Spanish reading measures of 0.59 (a subsequent replication study found similar results on Spanish reading measures, although with a lower effect size of 0.27). The intervention effects were maintained, and all but one student met benchmark criteria at the end of 1st grade and maintained grade-level status in 2nd grade (Linan-Thompson et al., 2006). Similarly, Cirino and colleagues (2009) conducted a 1-year follow-up intervention study in English and Spanish with ELs at risk for reading problems in 2nd grade and found significant differences benefiting the treatment group on Spanish measures of spelling decoding, fluency, and comprehension.

Richards-Tutor and colleagues (2016) conducted a systematic review of reading interventions with ELs (including ELs with SLD) published between 2000 and 2012. The findings of this work are summarized in Box 10-11.

BOX 10-11
Key Findings from Reading Intervention
Studies in English Learners

Richards-Tutor and colleagues (2016) identified 12 studies with the following key findings:

- Most studies used school designations of ELs to determine EL status (n = 7).
- Three studies included ELs with specific learning disabilities (SLD). The remaining studies included ELs at risk for SLD, though there was variability in how "risk" was defined. Four studies assessed ELs in L1 and English to determine risk.
- Intervention outcomes were not moderated by group size, length of intervention per week, or personnel delivering interventions.
- Studies showed a lack of attention to ELs' heterogeneity and the potential differential impact of interventions on EL subgroups. Two studies examined the influence of English proficiency on intervention outcomes and found no significant impact, contradicting findings from earlier studies. Reclassified ELs were not included in these studies.
- Impacts on younger ELs (K-1) were greater from interventions that targeted foundational reading skills and were tailored to student needs.
- Only 4 of 12 studies targeted vocabulary as an intervention outcome.
- Most interventions neglected the development of oral or written language skills.

Emotional/Behavioral Disorders

Research on instruction for DLL/ELs with E/BD is scarce (Nelson et al., 2008). Rogers-Adkinson and colleagues (2012) argue that with accommodations and adaptations, instructional practices found to be effective with students with E/BD can be used with DLLs/ELs with E/BD. Preciado and colleagues (2009), for example, worked with DLLs/ELs who exhibited problematic behaviors in the classroom. They used a single-subject multiple-baseline design across participants and implemented a function-based intervention with multiple components to address participants' academic and behavioral problems (participants had not been diagnosed with E/BD; one was labeled as having SLD). The intervention included direct instruction in early literacy skills, including vocabulary. In addition, a tutor supported participants in various instructional aspects, such as review of instructions for independent work and social skill learning. The researchers report a positive impact of the academic intervention on reading fluency and task completion; three of the participants showed improved behaviors.

Response to Intervention

Research on RTI with ELs is beginning to emerge; evidence to date shows that interventions can have a positive impact (Vanderwood and Nam, 2007). For instance, it has been reported that small-group interventions focused on early reading skills (i.e., phonological awareness) benefit ELs (K-1) (Leafstedt et al., 2004). Similarly, peer-based tier 1 interventions have shown a positive effect on ELs' literacy learning (Calhoon et al., 2006, 2007; McMaster et al., 2008). Other successful tier 1 and 2 interventions with ELs have been reported in the last 15 years (De la Colina et al., 2001; Denton et al., 2004; Haager and Windmueller, 2001; Linan-Thompson et al., 2003, 2006; Vaughn et al., 2005, 2006a).

A concern is that some of the research-based interventions that are commonly used in RTI have not been researched with ELs, who may respond differently from monolinguals. However, some findings on early reading with English-speaking populations have been validated in ELs (Richards-Tutor et al., 2016; Vaughn et al., 2005). A search of the U.S. Department of Education's What Works Clearinghouse revealed only eight intervention programs researched with ELs that had a positive effect on reading achievement and/or English language proficiency. In summary, Vanderwood and Nam (2007, p. 415) argue that "it is premature to conclude that RTI should be used with all low-achieving [ELs] … additional intervention research is needed to determine the most optimal intensity and length of treatment and to further address the relative effectiveness of English versus native-language instruction or intervention."

CONCLUSIONS

Conclusion 10-1: Dual language learners (DLLs)/English learners (ELs) are less likely than their non-DLL/EL peers to be referred to early intervention and early special education programs, with potentially serious consequences. Evidence indicates that early childhood education, home visiting, health, and other professionals are not identifying all DLLs/ELs with special needs—such as those with autism spectrum disorder and language impairment—who could benefit from such programs.

Conclusion 10-2: Growing up with two languages does not place dual language learners/English learners at greater risk for having a language impairment or other disability or when they have a disability, for compromising their language or cognitive development.

Conclusion 10-3: Compared with English-only interventions for language impairment, dual language interventions result in equal or even faster growth of English skills, with the additional benefit that they lead to continuing growth in the home language.

Conclusion 10-4: The disproportionate underrepresentation of dual language learners (DLLs)/English learners (ELs) with disabilities reflects policies in IDEA, which allows states to define how disproportionality will be calculated. Currently available data on rates of identification of DLLs/ELs with disabilities are insufficient, and patterns of underrepresentation and overrepresentation at the national, state, and district levels by grade and disability category are not discernible. The U.S. Department of Education's recent analyses and a resulting regulation, while a positive step, have focused only on overrepresentation, overlooking the possibility of underrepresentation for a number of disability categories and age groups.

BIBLIOGRAPHY

Abedi, J. (2008). Classification system for English language learners: Issues and recommendations. *Educational Measurement: Issues and Practices, 27*(3), 17-22.

Abedi, J. (2014). English language learners with disabilities: Classification, assessment, and accommodation issues. *Journal of Applied Testing Technology, 10*(2), 1-30.

Aguilar-Mediavilla, E., Buil-Legaz, L., Perez-Castello, J.A., Rigo-Carratala, E., and Adrover-Roig, D. (2014). Early preschool processing abilities predict subsequent reading outcomes in bilingual Spanish–Catalan children with Specific Language Impairment (SLI). *Journal of Communication Disorders, 50*, 19-35.

Alegria, M., Greif Green, J., McLaughlin, K.A., and Loder, S. (2015). *Disparities in Child and Adolescent Mental Health and Mental Health Services in the U.S.* New York: William T. Grant Foundation.

Artiles, A.J., and Klingner, J.K. (2006). Forging a knowledge base on English language learners with special needs: Theoretical, population, and technical issues. *Teachers College Record, 108*, 2187-2194.

Artiles, A.J., and Kozleski, E.B. (2010). What counts as response and intervention in RTI? A sociocultural analysis. *Psicothema, 22*(4), 949-954.

Artiles, A.J., and Ortiz, A.A. (Eds.). (2002). *English Language Learners with Special Education Needs: Identification, Assessment, and Instruction.* Washington, DC, and McHenry, IL: Center for Applied Linguistics and Delta Systems.

Artiles, A.J., Rueda, R., Salazar, J., and Higareda, I. (2005). Within-group diversity in minority disproportionate representation: English language learners in urban school districts. *Exceptional Children, 71*(3), 283-300.

Artiles, A.J., Kozleski, E., Trent, S., Osher, D., and Ortiz, A. (2010). Justifying and explaining disproportionality, 1968-2008: A critique of underlying views of culture. *Exceptional Children, 76*(3), 279-299.

Baca, L.M., and Cervantes, H.T. (Eds.). (1989). *The Bilingual Special Education Interface* (2nd ed.). Columbus, OH: Merrill.

Baker, S., Gersten, R., Haager, D., and Dingle, M. (2006). Teaching practice and the reading growth of first-grade English learners: Validation of an observation instrument. *Elementary School Journal, 107*, 199-219.

Baker, S., Lesaux, N., Jayanthi, M., Dimino, J., Proctor, C.P., Morris, J., Gersten, R., Haymond, K., Kieffer, M.J., Linan-Thompson, S., and Newman-Gonchar, R. (2014). *Teaching Academic Content and Literacy to English Learners in Elementary and Middle School.* NCEE 2014-4012. Washington, DC: National Center for Education Evaluation and Regional Assistance, Institute of Education Sciences, U.S. Department of Education.

Bal, A., Sullivan, A.L, and Harper, J. (2014). A situated analysis of special education disproportionality for systemic transformation in an urban school district. *Remedial and Special Education, 35*(1), 3-14.

Balu, R., Zhu, P., Doolittle, F., Schiller, E., Jenkins, J., and Gersten, R. (2015). *Evaluation of Response to Intervention Practices for Elementary School Reading.* NCEE 2016-4000. Washington, DC: National Center for Education Evaluation and Regional Assistance, Institute of Education Sciences, U.S. Department of Education.

Blom, E., and Paradis, J. (2013). Past tense production by English second language learners with and without language impairment. *Journal of Speech, Language, and Hearing Research, 56*(1), 281-294.

Brown, J.E. (2008). *The Use and Interpretation of the Batería III with U.S. Bilinguals.* Unpublished Ph.D. Dissertation. Portland, OR: Portland State University.

Brown, J.E., and Doolittle, J. (2008). A cultural, linguistic, and ecological framework for response to intervention with English language learners. *TEACHING Exceptional Children, 40*(5), 66-72.

Brown, J.E., and Sanford, A. (2011). *RTI for English Language Learners: Appropriately Using Screening and Progress Monitoring Tools to Improve Instructional Outcomes.* Washington, DC: National Center for Response to Intervention.

Brown, W.H., Knopf, H., Conroy, M.A., Googe, H.S., and Greer, F. (2013). Preschool inclusion and response to intervention (RTI) for children with disabilities. In V. Buysse and E. Peisner-Feinberg (Eds.), *Handbook of Response to Intervention (RTI) in Early Childhood* (pp. 339-354). Baltimore, MD: Paul H. Brookes Publishing Company.

Burr, E., Haas, E., and Ferriere, K. (2015). *Identifying and Supporting English Learner Students with Learning Disabilities: Key Issues in the Literature and State Practice.* REL 2015–086. Washington, DC: U.S. Department of Education, Institute of Education Sciences, National Center for Education Evaluation and Regional Assistance, Regional Educational Laboratory West.

Calhoon, M.B., Al Otaiba, S., Greenberg, D., King, A., and Avalos, A. (2006). Improving reading skills in predominantly Hispanic Title 1 first-grade classrooms: The promise of peer-assisted learning strategies. *Learning Disabilities Research & Practice, 21*(4), 261-272.

Calhoon, M.B., Al Otaiba, S.A., Cihak, D., King, A., and Avalos, A. (2007). Effects of a peer-mediated program on reading skill acquisition for two-way bilingual first-grade classrooms. *Learning Disability Quarterly, 30*(3), 169-184.

Cavendish, W., Artiles, A.J., and Harry, B. (2014). Tracking inequality 60 years after "Brown": Does policy legitimize the racialization of disability? *Multiple Voices for Ethnically Diverse Exceptional Learners, 14*(2), 30-40.

Chamot, A.U., and O'Malley, J.M. (1994). *The CALLA Handbook: Implementing the Cognitive Academic Language Learning Approach.* Reading, MA: Addison-Wesley.

Chen, D., and Gutiérrez-Clellen, V. (2013). Paper 6. Early intervention and young dual language learners with special needs. In Governor's State Advisory Council on Early Learning and Care (Eds.), *California's Best Practices for Young Dual Language Learners: Research Overview Papers* (pp. 209-230). Sacramento: California Department of Education.

Cirino, P.T., Vaughn, S., Linan-Thompson, S., Cardenas-Hagan, E., Fletcher, J.M., and Francis, D.J. (2009). One-year follow-up outcomes of Spanish and English intervention for English language learners at risk for reading problems. *American Education Research Journal, 46*(3), 744-781.

Collins, B.A., Toppelberg, C.O., Suárez-Orozco, C., O'Connor, E., and Nieto-Castañon, A. (2011). Cross-sectional associations of Spanish and English competence and well-being in Latino children of immigrants in kindergarten. *International Journal of the Sociology of Language, 2011*(208), 5-23.

Collins, B.A., O'Connor, E.E., Suárez-Orozco, C., Nieto-Castañón, A., and Toppelberg, C.O. (2014). Dual language profiles of Latino children of immigrants: Stability and change over the early school years. *Applied Psycholinguistics, 35*(3), 581-620.

Crosson, A.C., and Lesaux, N.K. (2010). Revisiting assumptions about the relationship of fluent reading to comprehension: Spanish-speakers' text reading fluency in English. *Reading and Writing, 23*(5), 475-494.

De la Colina, M.G., Parker, R.I., Hasbrouck, J.E., and Lara-Alecio, R. (2001). Intensive intervention in reading fluency for at-risk beginning Spanish readers. *Bilingual Research Journal, 25*(4).

De Valenzuela, J.S., Copeland, S.R., Huaqing Qi, C., and Park, M. (2006). Examining educational equity: Revisiting the disproportionate representation of minority students in special education. *Exceptional Children, 72*(4), 425-441.

Denton, C.A., Anthony, J.L., Parker, R., and Hasbrouck, J.E. (2004). Effects of two tutoring programs on the English reading development of Spanish–English bilingual students. *The Elementary School Journal, 104*(4), 289-305.

DeThorne, L.S., and Shaefer, B.A. (2004). A guide to child nonverbal IQ measures. *American Journal of Speech-Language Pathology, 13*, 275-290.

Dixon, J. (2013). *The Impact of Bilingual Education on English Language Acquisition Rates for English Language Learners, Including Exceptionalities.* Presented at the State English Learners Alliance Conference, Confederation of Oregon School Administrators, Eugene, OR, March.

Durgunoglu, A.Y. (2002). Cross-linguistic transfer in literacy development and implications for language learners. *Annals of Dyslexia, 52*(1), 189-204.

Durgunoglu, A.Y., Nagy, W.E., and Hancin-Bhatt, B.J. (1993). Cross-language transfer of phonological awareness. *Journal of Educational Psychology, 85*(3), 453-465.

Durkin, M.S., Maenner, M.J., Meaney, F.J., Levy, S.E., DiGuiseppi, C., Nicholas, J.S., Kirby, R.S., Pinto-Martin, J.A., and Schieve, L.A. (2010). Socioeconomic inequality in the prevalence of Autism Spectrum Disorder: Evidence from a U.S. cross-sectional study. *PLoS ONE, 5*(7), e11551. Available: http://journals.plos.org/plosone/article?id=10.1371/journal.pone.0011551 [December 2016].

Ebert, K., Kohnert, K., Pham, G., Disher, J.R., and Payesteh, B. (2014). Three treatments for bilingual children with primary language impairment: Examining cross-linguistic and cross-domain effects. *Journal of Speech, Language, and Hearing Research, 57*(1), 172-186.

Echevarria, J., and Hasbrouck, J. (2009). Response to intervention and English learners. *CREATEBrief*, July. Available: http://www.cal.org/create/publications/briefs/pdfs/response-to-intervention-and-english-learners.pdf [December 2016].

Echevarria, J., Vogt, M.E., and Short, D. (2008). *Making Content Comprehensible for English Language Learners: The SIOP Model* (3rd Edition). Boston, MA: Allyn & Bacon.

Fien, H., Baker, S.K., Smolkowski, K., Smith, J.L., Kame'enui, E.J., and Beck, C.T. (2008). Using nonsense word fluency to predict reading proficiency in kindergarten through second grade for English learners and native English speakers. *School Psychology Review, 37*(3), 391-408.

Fierros, E.G., and Conroy, J.W. (2002). Double jeopardy: An exploration of restrictiveness and race in special education. In D.J. Losen and G. Orfield (Eds.), *Racial Inequality in Special Education* (pp. 39-70). Cambridge, MA: Harvard Education Press.

Flores, G., and Vega, L.R. (1998). Barriers to health care access for Latino children: A review. *Family Medicine, 30*(3), 196-205.

Fuchs, D., Mock, D., Morgan, P.L., and Young, C.L. (2003). Responsiveness-to-intervention: Definitions, evidence, and implications for the learning disabilities construct. *Learning Disabilities Research & Practice, 18*(3), 157-171.

Genesee, F. (2015). Myths about early childhood bilingualism. *Canadian Psychology, 56*(1), 6-15.

Gersten, R., and Baker, S. (2000). What we know about effective instructional practices for English-language learners. *Exceptional Children, 66*(4), 454-470.

Girbau, D., and Schwartz, R.G. (2008). Phonological working memory in Spanish–English bilingual children with and without specific language impairment. *Journal of Communication Disorders, 41*(2), 124-145.

Greenberg Motamedi, J. (2015). *Time to Reclassification: How Long Does It Take English Learner Students in Washington Road Map Districts to Develop English Proficiency?* REL 2015–092. Washington, DC: U.S. Department of Education, Institute of Education Sciences, National Center for Education Evaluation and Regional Assistance, Regional Educational Laboratory Northwest. Available: http://ies.ed.gov/ncee/edlabs [November 11, 2015].

Grimm, A., and Schulz, P. (2014). Specific language impairment and early second language acquisition: The risk of over- and underdiagnosis. *Child Indicators Research, 7*(4), 821-841.

Gutiérrez-Clellen, V.F. (2000). Dynamic assessment: An approach to assessing children's language-learning potential. *Seminars in Speech and Language, 21*(3), 215-222.

Gutiérrez-Clellen, V.F., Simon-Cereijido, G., and Wagner, C. (2008). Bilingual children with language impairment: A comparison with monolinguals and second language learners. *Applied Psycholinguistics, 29*(1), 3-19.

Gutiérrez-Clellen, V.F., Cereijido, G.S., and Leone, A.E. (2009). Codeswitching in bilingual children with specific language impairment. *International Journal of Bilingualism, 13*(1), 91-109.

Haager, D., and Windmueller, M. (2001). Early literacy intervention for English language learners at-risk for learning disabilities: Student outcomes in an urban school. *Learning Disability Quarterly, 24,* 213-218.

Hambly, C., and Fombonne, E. (2012). The impact of bilingual environments on language development in children with autism spectrum disorders. *Journal of Autism and Developmental Disorders, 42*(7), 1342-1352.

Hanson, M., and Espinosa, L. (2016). Culture, ethnicity, and linguistic diversity: Implications for early childhood special education. In B. Reichow, B.A. Boyd, E.E. Barton, and S.L. Odom (Eds.), *Handbook of Early Childhood Special Education* (pp. 455-472). Switzerland: Springer International Publishing.

Harry, B., and Klingner, J. (2014). *Why Are So Many Minority Students in Special Education?: Understanding Race & Disability in Schools* (2nd Edition). New York: Teachers College Press.

Institute of Medicine. (1997). *Schools and Health: Our Nation's Investment.* Washington, DC: National Academy Press.

Kaminski, R.A., and Good, R.A. (2014). *Dynamic Indicators of Basic Literacy Skills Next (DIBELs Next).* Longmont, CO: SoprisWest.

Kay-Raining Bird, E., Lamond, E., and Holden, J.J. (2012). A survey of bilingualism in autism spectrum disorders. *International Journal of Language & Communication Disorders, 47*(1), 52-64.

Kay-Raining Bird, E., Genesee, F., and Verhoeven, L. (2016). Bilingualism in children with developmental disorders: A narrative review. *Journal of Communication Disorders, 63,* 1-14.

Klein, J.R., and Jimerson, S.R. (2005). Examining ethnic, gender, language and socioeconomic bias in oral reading fluency scores among Caucasian and Hispanic students. *School Psychology Quarterly, 20*(1), 23-50.

Klingner, J.K. (2014). *Distinguishing Language Acquisition from Learning Disabilities.* New York: Division of English Language Learners and Student Support, New York City Department of Education.

Klingner, J.K., and Edwards, P.A. (2006). Cultural considerations with response to intervention models. *Reading Research Quarterly, 41*(1), 108-117.

Klingner, J.K., Artiles, A.J., and Barletta, L.M. (2006). English language learners who struggle with reading: Language acquisition or learning disabilities? *Journal of Learning Disabilities, 39*(2), 108-128.

Klingner, J.K., Soltero-Gonzalez, L., and Lesaux, N. (2010). Response to intervention for English language learners. In M. Lipson and K. Wixson (Eds.), *Successful Approaches to Response to Intervention (RTI): Collaborative Practices for Improving K-12 Literacy* (pp. 134-162). Newark, DE: International Reading Association.

Kohnert, K. (2010). Bilingual children with primary language impairment: Issues, evidence and implications for clinical actions. *Journal of Communication Disorders, 43*(6), 456-473.

Kohnert, K., and Medina, A. (2009). Bilingual children and communication disorders: A 30-year research retrospective. *Seminars in Speech and Language, 30*(4), 219-233.

Leafstedt, J.M., Richards, C.R., and Gerber, M.M. (2004). Effectiveness of explicit phonological-awareness instruction for at-risk English learners. *Learning Disabilities Research & Practice, 19,* 252-261.

Lesaux, N.K., and Harris, J.R. (2013). Linguistically diverse students' reading difficulties: Implications for models of LD identification and effective instruction. In H.L. Swanson, K.R. Harris, and S. Graham, (Eds.), *The Handbook of Learning Disabilities* (2nd ed., pp. 69-84). New York: Guilford Press.

Limbos, M., and Geva, E. (2001). Accuracy of teacher assessments of second-language students at risk for reading disability. *Journal of Learning Disabilities, 34,* 136-151.

Linan-Thompson, S., and Ortiz, A.A. (2009). Response to intervention and English-language learners: Instructional and assessment considerations. *Seminars in Speech and Language, 30*(2), 105-120.

Linan-Thompson, S., Vaughn, S., Hickman-Davis, P., and Kouzekanani, K. (2003). Effectiveness of supplemental reading instruction for second-grade English language learners with reading difficulties. *The Elementary School Journal, 103*, 221-238.

Linan-Thompson, S., Vaughn, S., Prater, K., and Cirino, P. (2006). The response to intervention of English language learners at risk for reading problems. *Journal of Learning Disabilities, 39*, 390-398.

Linan-Thompson, S., Cirino, P.T., and Vaughn, S. (2007). Determining English language learners' response to intervention: Questions and some answers. *Learning Disability Quarterly, 30*(3), 185-195.

Lovett, M.W., Lacerenza, L., De Palma, M., Benson, N.J., Steinbach, K.A., and Frijters, J.C. (2008). Preparing teachers to remediate reading disabilities in high school: What is needed for effective professional development? *Teaching and Teacher Education: An International Journal of Research and Studies, 24*, 1083-1097.

Magit, E.R., and Shinn, M.R. (2002). *Medidas Incrementales de Destrezas Escenciales.* Eden Praire, MN: Edformation Inc.

Marcia, J.E. (1980). Identity in adolescence. In J. Adelson (Ed.), *Handbook of Adolescent Psychology* (pp. 159-187). New York: John Wiley & Sons.

Marks, A.K., Ejesi, K., and García Coll, G. (2014). Understanding the U.S. immigrant paradox in childhood and adolescence. *Child Development Perspectives, 8*(2), 59-64.

McIntosh, A., Graves, A., and Gersten, R. (2007). The effects of response to intervention on literacy development in multiple language settings. *Learning Disability Quarterly, 30*(3), 197-212.

McMaster, K.L., Kung, S.-H., Han, I., and Cao, M. (2008). Peer-assisted learning strategies: A "Tier 1" approach to promoting English learners' response to intervention. *Exceptional Children, 74*(2), 194-214.

Minnema, J., Thurlow, M., Anderson, M., and Stone, K. (2005). English *Language Learners with Disabilities and Large-Scale Assessments: What the Literature Can Tell Us.* ELLs with Disabilities Report 6. Minneapolis, MN: National Center on Educational Outcomes.

Morgan, P.L., Farkas, G., Hillemeier, M.M., and Maczuga, S. (2012). Are minority children disproportionately represented in early intervention and early childhood special education? *Educational Researcher, 41*(9), 339-351.

Morgan, P.L., Farkas, G., Hillemeier, M.M., Mattison, R., Maczuga, S., Li, H., and Cook, M. (2015). Minorities are disproportionately underrepresented in special education: Longitudinal evidence across five disability conditions. *Educational Research, 44*, 278-292.

Mueller, T.G., Singer, G.H.S., and Carranza, F.D. (2006). A national survey of the educational planning and language instruction practices for students with moderate to severe disabilities who are English language learners. *Research & Practice for Persons with Severe Disabilities, 31*(3), 242-254.

National Center for Education Statistics. (2007). *The Condition of Education 2007.* NCES 2007-064. Washington, DC: U.S. Government Printing Office.

National Research Council. (2002). *Minority Students in Special and Gifted Education.* M.S. Donovan, and C.T. Cross (Eds.). Division of Behavioral and Social Sciences and Education; Board on Behavioral, Cognitive, and Sensory Sciences; Committee on Minority Representation in Special Education. Washington, DC: National Academy Press.

Nelson, J.R., Benner, G.J., and Mooney, P. (2008). *Instructional Practices for Students with Behavioral Disorders: Strategies for Reading, Writing, and Math.* New York: Guilford Press.

Office of Head Start. (n.d.). *Screening, Assessment, Evaluation & Observation.* Available: https://eclkc.ohs.acf.hhs.gov/hslc/tta-system/ehsnrc/cde/saeo [December 2016].

Ohashi, J.K., Mirenda, P., Marinova-Todd, S., Hambly, C., Fombonne, E., Szatmari, P., Bryson, S., Roberts, W., Smith, I., Vaillancourt, T., Volden, J. Waddell, C., Zwaigenbaum, L., Georgiades, S., Duku, E., Thompson, A., and the Pathways in ASD Study Team. (2012). Comparing early language development in monolingual- and bilingual-exposed young children with autism spectrum disorders. *Research in Autism Spectrum Disorders, 6,* 890-897.

Oppedal, B., and Toppelberg, C.O. (2016). Acculturation development and the acquisition of culture competence. In D. Sam and J. Berry (Eds.), *The Cambridge Handbook of Acculturation Psychology* (2nd ed., pp. 71-92). Cambridge, UK: Cambridge University Press.

Organista, K.C. (2000). Cognitive-behavioral group psychotherapy with Latinos. In A. Freeman and J.R. White (Eds.), *Handbook of Group Cognitive Behavioral Psychotherapy*. Washington, DC: American Psychological Association.

Orosco, M.J., and Klingner, J. (2010). One school's implementation of TRI with English language Learners: "Referring into RTI." *Journal of Learning Disabilities, 43*(3), 269-288.

Ortiz, A.A. (1997). Learning disabilities occurring concomitantly with linguistic differences. *Journal of Learning Disabilities, 30,* 321-332.

Ortiz, A., and Artiles, A.J. (2010). Meeting the needs of English language learners with disabilities: A linguistically and culturally responsive model. In G. Li and P. Edwards (Eds.), *Best Practices in ELL Instruction* (pp. 247-272). New York: Guilford Press.

Oswald, D.P., Coutinho, M.J., Best, A.N., and Singh, N.N. (1999). Ethnic representation in special education: The influence of school-related economic and demographic variables. *Journal of Special Education, 32,* 194-206.

Palfrey, J.S., Singer, J.D., Walker, D.K., and Butler, J.A. (1987). Early identification of children's special needs: A study in five metropolitan communities. *Journal of Pediatrics, 111,* 651-659.

Paradis, J., Crago, M., Genesee, F., and Rice, M. (2003). French–English bilingual children with SLI: How do they compare with their monolingual peers? *Journal of Speech, Language, and Hearing Research, 46*(1), 113-127.

Paradis, J., Genesee, F., and Crago, M.B. (2011). *Dual Language Development and Disorders: A Handbook on Bilingualism and Second Language Learning* (2nd Edition). Baltimore, MD: Paul H. Brookes Publishing Company.

Parrish, T. (2002). Racial disparities in the identification, funding, and provision of special education. In D.J. Losen and G. Orfield (Eds.), *Racial Inequity in Special Education* (pp. 15-35). Cambridge, MA: Harvard Education Press.

Pearson, B.Z. (2008). *Raising a Bilingual Child.* New York: Living Language, Random House.

Pham, G., Ebert, K.D., and Kohnert, K. (2015). Bilingual children with primary language impairment: 3 months after treatment. *International Journal of Language & Communication Disorders, 50*(1), 94-105.

Phinney, J.S. (1989). Stages of ethnic identity development in minority group adolescents. *The Journal of Early Adolescence, 9*(1-2), 34-49.

Phinney, J.S., Horenczyk, G., Liebkind, K., and Vedder, P. (2001). Ethnic identity, immigration, and well-being: An interactional perspective. *Journal of Social Issues, 57*(3), 493-510.

Preciado, J.A., Horner, R.H., and Baker, S.K. (2009). Using a function-based approach to decrease problem behaviors and increase academic engagement for Latino English language learners. *The Journal of Special Education, 42*(4), 227-240.

Quirk, M., and Beem, S. (2012). Examining the relations between reading fluency and reading comprehension for English language learners. *Psychology in the School, 49*(6), 539-553.

Reichow, B., Boyd, B.A., Barton, E.E., and Odom, S.L. (2016). *Handbook of Early Childhood Special Education.* Switzerland: Springer International.

Reilly, S., Bishop, D.V.M., and Tomblin, B. (2014). Terminological debate over language impairment in children: Forward movement and sticking points. *International Journal of Language & Communicaiton Disorders, 49*(4), 452-462.

Restrepo, M. A., Morgan, G.P., and Thompson, M.S. (2013). The efficacy of a vocabulary intervention for dual-language learners with language impairment. *Journal of Speech, Language, and Hearing Research, 56*(2), 748-765.

Richards-Tutor, C., Solari, E.J., Leafstedt, J.M., Gerber, M.M., Filippini, A., and Aceves, T.C. (2012). Response to intervention for English learners: Examining models for determining response and nonresponse. *Assessment for Effective Intervention, 20*(10), 1-13.

Richards-Tutor, C., Baker, D.L., Gersten, R., Baker, S.K., and Smith, J.M. (2016). The effectiveness of readings interventions for English learners: A research synthesis. *Exceptional Children, 82*(2), 144-169.

Riedel, B.W. (2007). The relation between DIBELS, reading comprehension, and vocabulary in urban, first grade students. *Reading Research Quarterly, 42*(4), 460-466.

Rivera Mindt, M., Moughamian, A.C., Lesaux, N.K., and Francis, D.J. (2008). *Language and Reading Interventions for English Language Learners and English Language Learners with Disabilities.* Portsmouth, NH: RMC Research Corporation, Center on Instruction.

Rivera Mindt, M., Byrd, D., Saez, P., and Manly, J.J. (2010). Increasing neuropsychological services for minority patient populations: A call to action. *The Clinical Neuropsychologist, 24*(3), 429-453.

Rogers-Adkinson, D.L., Ochoa, T.A., and Weiss, S.L. (2012). Chapter 7: English language learners and emotional behavioral disorders. In J.P. Bakken, F.E. Obiakor, and A.F. Rotatori (Eds.), *Behavioral Disorders: Identification, Assessment, and Instruction of Students with EBD* (Vol. 22) (pp. 151-171). Bingley, UK: Emerald Group.

Rueda, R., and Windmueller, M.P. (2006). English language learners, LD, and overrepresentation: A multiple level analysis. *Journal of Learning Disabilities, 39*(2), 99-107.

Sam, D.L., and Berry, J.W. (2016). *The Cambridge Handbook of Acculturation Psychology* (2nd Edition). Cambridge, UK: Cambridge University Press.

Shafer Willner, L., Rivera, C., and Acosta, B. (2008). *Descriptive Study of State Assessment Policies for Accommodating English Language Learners.* Arlington, VA: The George Washington University Center for Equity and Excellence in Education.

Shafer Willner, L., Rivera, C., and Acosta, B. (2010). *Examination of Peer Review and Title I Monitoring Feedback Regarding the Inclusion and Accommodation of English Language Learners in State Content Assessments.* Arlington, VA: The George Washington University Center for Equity and Excellence in Education.

Shelton, L. (2007). *Caught in the Middle: Overrepresentation of Middle School Second Language Learners in Special Education.* Ph.D. Dissertation. Ann Arbor: University of Michigan Dissertation Express.

Skiba, R.J., Artiles, A.J., Kozleski, E.B., Losen, D.J., and Harry, E.G. (2016). Risks and consequences of oversimplifying educational inequities: A response to Morgan et al. (2015). *Educational Researcher, 45*(3), 221-225.

Sullivan, A. (2011). Disproportionality in special education identification and placement of English language learners. *Exceptional Children, 77*(3), 317-334.

Thompson, K.D. (2015). English learners' time to reclassification: An analysis. *Educational Policy* [E-pub ahead of print].

Thordardottir, E. (2006). Language intervention from a bilingual mindset. *The ASHA Leader, 11*, 6-21.

Thordardottir, E., Cloutier, G., Ménard, S., Pelland-Blais, E., and Rvachew, S. (2015). Monolingual or bilingual intervention for primary language impairment? A randomized control trial. *Journal of Speech, Language, and Hearing Research, 58*(2), 287-300.

Tomblin, J.B., Records, N.L., Buckwalter, P., Zhang, X., Smith, E., and O'Brien, M. (1997). Prevalence of specific language impairment in kindergarten children. *Journal of Speech, Language, and Hearing Research*, 40(6), 1245-1260.

Toppelberg, C.O. (2011). Promover el bilingüismo: American children should learn Spanish, and so should American child psychiatrists. *Journal of the American Academy of Child & Adolescent Psychiatry*, 50(10), 963-965.

Toppelberg, C.O. (2014). Do language disorders in childhood seal the mental health fate of grownups? *Journal of the American Academy of Child & Adolescent Psychiatry*, 53(10), 1050-1052.

Toppelberg, C.O., and Collins, B.A. (2010). Language, culture, and adaptation in immigrant children. *Child and Adolescent Psychiatric Clinics of North America*, 19(4), 697-717.

Toppelberg, C.O., and Collins B.A. (2016). Dual language children: Development, mental health, and clinical implications. In R.I. Parekh (Ed.), *Cultural Sensitivity in Child and Adolescent Mental Health* (pp. 327-350). Boston: Massachusetts General Hospital Psychiatry Academy Press.

Toppelberg, C.O., and Shapiro, T. (2000). Language disorders: A 10-year research update review. *Journal of the American Academy of Child & Adolescent Psychiatry*, 39(2), 143-152.

Toppelberg, C.O., Medrano, L., Peña Morgens, L., and Nieto-Castañon, A. (2002). Bilingual children referred for psychiatric services: Associations of language disorders, language skills, and psychopathology. *Journal of the American Academy of Child & Adolescent Psychiatry*, 41(6), 712-722.

Toppelberg, C.O., Hollinshead, M.O., Collins, B.A., and Nieto-Castañon, A. (2013). Cross-sectional study of unmet mental health need in 5- to 7-year old Latino children in the United States: Do teachers and parents make a difference in service utilization?. *School Mental Health*, 5(2), 59-69.

Torgesen, J.K. (2000). Individual differences in response to early interventions in reading: The lingering problem of treatment resisters. *Learning Disabilities Research and Practice*, 15, 55-64.

U.S. Department of Education. (2014). *Questions and Answers Regarding Inclusion of English Learners with Disabilities in English Language Proficiency Assessments and Title III Annual Measurable Achievement Objectives.* Available: http://www2.ed.gov/policy/speced/guid/idea/memosdcltrs/q-and-a-on-elp-swd.pdf [December 2016].

U.S. Department of Education. (2015). *English Learner Toolkit for SEAs and LEAs.* Washington, DC: U.S. Department of Education.

U.S. Department of Education. (2016). *Racial and Ethnic Disparities in Special Education.* Washington, DC: U.S. Department of Education.

U.S. Department of Justice and U.S. Department of Education. (2015). *Dear Colleague Letter: English Learner (EL) Students and Limited English Proficient Parents.* Available: http://www2.ed.gov/about/offices/list/ocr/letters/colleague-el-201501.pdf [December 15, 2015].

U.S. Public Health Service. (1999). *Mental Health: A Report of the Surgeon General.* Available: https://profiles.nlm.nih.gov/ps/access/NNBBHS.pdf [December 2016].

Vanderwood, M.L., and Nam, J. (2007). Response to intervention for English language learners: Current developments and future directions. In S.R. Jimmerson, M.K. Burns, and A.M. VanDerHeyden (Eds.), *The Handbook of Response to Intervention: The Science and Practice of Assessment and Intervention* (pp. 408-417). New York: Springer.

Vanderwood, M.L., and Nam, J. (2008). Best practices in using a response to intervention model with English language learners. In A. Thomas and J. Grimes (Eds.), *Best Practices in School Psychology V* (pp. 1847-1855). Bethesda, MD: National Association of School Psychologists.

Vanderwood, M.L., Linklater, D., and Healy, K. (2008). Predictive accuracy of nonsense word fluency for English language learners. *School Psychology Review, 37*(1), 5-17.

Vaughn, S., Mathes, P.G., Linan-Thompson, S., and Francis, D.J. (2005). Teaching English language learners at risk for reading disabilities to read: Putting research into practice. *Learning Disabilities Research & Practice, 20*(1), 58-67.

Vaughn, S., Cirino, P. T., Linan-Thompson, S., Mathes, P. G., Carlson, C. D., Cardenas-Hagan, E., and Francis, D. (2006a). Effectiveness of a Spanish intervention and an English intervention for English-language learners at risk for reading problems. *American Educational Research Journal, 43*(3), 449-487.

Vaughn, S., Linan-Thompson, S., Mathes, P.G., Cirino, P., Carlson, C.D., Hagan, E.C., and Francis, D. (2006b). Effectiveness of a Spanish intervention and an English intervention for first-grade English language learners at risk for reading difficulties. *Journal of Learning Disabilities, 39*(1), 56-73.

Vaughn, S., Klingner, J.K., Swanson, E.A., Boardman, A.G., Roberts, G., Mohammed, S.S., and Stillman-Spisak, S.J. (2011). Efficacy of collaborative strategic reading with middle school students. *American Educational Research Journal, 48*(4), 938-964.

Ware, J., Bethan Lye, C., and Kyffin, F. (2015). Bilingualism and students (learners) with intellectual disability: A review. *Journal of Policy and Practice in Intellectual Disabilities, 12*(3), 220-231.

Wiley, H.I., and Deno, S.L. (2005). Oral reading and maze measures as predictors of success for English learners on a state standards assessment. *Remedial and Special Education, 26*(4), 207-214.

Wilkinson, C.Y., Ortiz, A.A., Robertson, P.M., and Kushner, M.I. (2006). English language learners with reading-related LD: Linking data from multiple sources to make eligibility determinations. *Journal of Learning Disabilities, 39*(2), 129-141.

Yew, S.G., and O'Kearney, R. (2013). Emotional and behavioural outcomes later in childhood and adolescence for children with specific language impairments: Meta-analyses of controlled prospective studies. *Journal of Child Psychology and Psychiatry, 54*(5), 516-524.

ANNEX 10-1: A CASE HISTORY: AN ILLUSTRATION OF THE COMPLEXITIES OF ASSESSMENT IN ELS[7]

The following case study illustrates the complexities of assessment in DLLs/ELs. It also demonstrates how a narrow interpretation of test scores in a DLL/EL can mislead an examiner toward a diagnosis of disability.

Robby entered school in California in September 1998 and spoke only Spanish. Three months before he started school, California voters passed Proposition 227, which banned the use of languages other than English in the state's schools, despite the fact that one in four California students, like Robby, spoke little or no English. The school district serving the community where Robby lived had been quick to comply with the law and replace bilingual education with English-only classes. His parents had asked that he be placed in a bilingual class when they enrolled him in school, but were told by district administrators that he had to attend English-only classes.

---

[7]This case study was presented to the committee by Lily Wong Fillmore in January 2016.

There was nothing his immigrant parents, who spoke little English, could do.

Robby was the youngest of their four U.S.-born sons. The older boys had been in "bilingual classes" when they started school in the district, and had teachers who used Spanish and English in school even though the curriculum was taught entirely in English. This was not a true bilingual program;[8] nonetheless, the use of Spanish in school had given Robby's older brothers several years to learn English before being placed in English-only classes. Robby would have to deal with English as soon as he entered school. Nonetheless, he was eager and ready for school. His parents might have been worried about his not knowing English, but Robby was not. His brothers had learned English, and he would, too.

By watching, listening, and following the lead of his classmates who understood what the teacher was saying better than he did, Robby was able to participate in instructional activities, make some sense out of what he was supposed to be learning at school, and pick up a little English along the way. Although his parents had indicated on the language survey form, necessary for school entry, that his primary language was Spanish and that Spanish was the language used in their home, he was classified as a "fluent English speaker."[9] So Robby's language skills were never assessed formally, and as a consequence, he received no instructional support for learning English during his first 3 years in school.

Despite Robby's language barrier, his first year ended "satisfactorily." The teacher rated his performance in language arts as "satisfactory, but in need of improvement." She commented, "tries very hard, but just isn't getting the curriculum. The only letter he recognizes is 'o.'" Robby's second year in school, when he was in 1st grade (1999-2000), was by all accounts the most difficult one for him. Reading instruction in the district emphasized what was described as a phonics- and skills-based approach focused on explicit instruction. With his extremely limited grasp of English, Robby could not remember the sounds he was supposed to be matching up with letters or words with the texts he was supposed to be reading. His 1st-grade teacher was convinced that he was "language delayed and impaired."[10] She was impatient with his inability to remember things, and she apparently let him know how she felt about him.

Robby's parents reported that there had been mornings when they had to insist that he go to school whether he wanted to or not, and he was

---

[8] A true bilingual education program uses students' primary language to teach some subjects, at least initially, adding English gradually until parity in the use of the two languages is achieved.

[9] According to Robby's cumulative school record folder.

[10] Teacher's note in Robby's cumulative record.

often in tears when they picked him up after school. At some point, he decided that his 1st-grade teacher did not like him because he was a Spanish speaker. According to his parents, he stopped speaking Spanish that year. He was learning English, and although his knowledge of it was quite limited, he began using it exclusively, even at home. His parents eventually acclimated to the shift, as did his brothers. It was not difficult for the older boys because they were more proficient in English than they were in Spanish by then. But it was a difficult time for the parents. Neither could communicate easily in English. They managed the shift by speaking a mix of Spanish and English and relying on their older sons to serve as interpreters for their youngest.

By the second grade (2000-2001), Robby was no longer able to speak or understand Spanish beyond minimal levels. His English was still rudimentary, but after 2 years in school, he was an English monolingual. At home, he was not learning what he might have learned from his parents had he been able to communicate easily with them. At school, his poorly developed English skills hampered his efforts to keep up with his classmates academically. What seemed easy for his classmates was incomprehensible for him. He believed they were smart, while he was "dumb."

Robby's problems with language and learning at school followed him into the 3rd grade (school year 2001-2002), impeding his academic development to such a degree that the school sent his parents a letter in November indicating that his case was being referred to a "student study team" at a meeting to be held 3 weeks later. The letter was entirely in English, and because the parents were unable to read English, they did not understand the nature of the referral, nor did they realize that they were supposed to be present at the meeting. After this initial meeting—the only meeting that Robby's parents did not attend and the only one that the school held to discuss Robby's case—it was decided that Robby probably had severe learning disabilities and should be tested to qualify him for special education services.

Under the No Child Left Behind (NCLB) Act, which the U.S. Congress passed in 2001, schools had to demonstrate that all students were making progress toward meeting their state's standards of full academic proficiency in such subjects as English language arts, math, and science by 2014. Schools were required to show by improvements in student test scores that they were making "adequate yearly progress" (AYP) toward that goal, with serious consequences if they did not meet their AYP targets for several consecutive years.

Because of NCLB, the school district appeared eager to have students like Robby certified for special education services.[11] The assessment began

---

[11]Under NCLB, up to 1 percent of the students in a school could be tested by alternative means if they were certified as having learning disabilities.

with a review of his language status in December 2001. It was only then, 3 years after he had entered school, that the school discovered Robby's primary language was Spanish. His parents were then notified by letter (in English) that Robby's classification as a "fluent English-proficient" student was being changed to "English language learner at Beginning Level B." His parents did not understand what this change would mean and were surprised that he had been classified as "fluent English-proficient" in the first place. At that point, the school might have concluded that whatever else was preventing Robby from thriving at school, an obvious problem was that his language needs had not been recognized for the past 3 years. Instead, he was placed in a special remedial program for English reading and given speech therapy. Compounding Robby's academic problems at school was the fact that his primary language had atrophied from lack of use. He was getting imperfect English at home from his parents and was cut off from what they might have taught him in Spanish since he no longer understood it. Over time, Robby had become more and more practiced in the "learner" variety of English he and his parents spoke—he quite fluently, they but haltingly.

Each day, beginning in 3rd grade and continuing through 5th grade, during the 2-hour language arts period and part of the math period, Robby left his regular classroom and went to a "reading resource teacher." The materials and skills-focused program he received dealt nearly exclusively with phonics, which led Robby to see reading as deciphering the relationship between symbols and sounds rather than words and meaning. The longest of the "decodable" stories he worked on consisted of four sentences, so there was little chance of him discovering literary purpose in reading, either. The difference between his classmates' materials and the ones he was using was a source of substantial embarrassment to him; Robby hid his workbook and homework from his classmates.

The rest of Robby's special education program consisted of a half-hour weekly session with the speech therapist. Robby's speech therapy was premised on the language and speech assessment of an initial therapist who made no mention of Robby's need for help in learning English as a second language, or of anything that might help him deal with the difficulties he had accrued over the past 3 years as a result of the school's neglect of his language needs. Over the next 2 years, Robby fell further and further behind his classmates. His remedial program had not improved his reading ability greatly, and by the end of the 4th grade, he was referred for diagnostic testing by the school psychologist for a final disposition of his case.

Robby's psychoeducational testing was administered mainly in English, although several subtests were given in Spanish, a language Robby no longer spoke or understood. From this battery of tests the psychologist concluded: "Based on current assessment findings, Robby appears to meet eligibility criteria as a student with 'below average intellectual functioning'

(CCR [California Code of Regulations], Title V, Section 3030h)." After this report was submitted, a new code, "010," appeared on Robby's school cumulative record—the code for mental retardation.

Under the guidelines for the identification of mental retardation, the cut-off score for tests such as those Robby was given is 70. His scores were well above that cut-off in all but two subtests—the last ones given the day he was tested. Under CCR Title V, IQ test scores cannot serve as the only basis for a mental retardation determination. A child must also show "deficits in adaptive behavior" that would "adversely affect educational performance." The Vineland Adaptive Behavior Scales, a rating scale completed by Robby's teacher and one of his parents, addressed this issue. The test report summarizes as follows:

> According to both parent and teacher, Robby does not dress himself in anticipation of changes in the weather, does not make his own bed without being reminded and without assistance, and does not care for his nails without assistance and being reminded.[12] However, according to his mother, Robby is very helpful at home. Robby helps around the house with chores and running errands. In the classroom, Robby is very helpful, has good patience and self-control, and is described as a sweet and polite student.

Questions of accuracy aside, it mattered little, it appears, that the findings of this assessment had been interpreted as unsympathetically as possible. Should Robby have been tested in Spanish, for example, when he no longer understood or spoke that language (as was acknowledged in the psychologist's report)? Or should he have been tested in English, for that matter, since his English language needs had been overlooked by the school? The question of validity was not considered.

The purpose of the assessment became clear during a meeting of Robby's individualized education program (IEP) team. After discussing Robby's lack of academic progress, the IEP team declared that his "disability" was so great that his needs could no longer be met at the school he was attending. It had been decided that he would be moved to a special all-day school for non-severely handicapped children (NSH/SDC) in a different community. Robby's parents were assured that Robby's needs would be better met at the NSH/SDC school. There was no discussion of state and federal special education requirements that children be kept in the least restrictive environment possible, nor was there any discussion after Robby's parents objected

---

[12] This part of the report surprised Robby's mother when it was translated for her. She said she had not been asked about such matters, but had she been, she would have said that Robby had been dressing and caring for himself since he was 3 years of age. She said her son was not only helpful but very capable and dependable around the house.

to such a placement. The IEP team was adamant: Robby must attend the special school "for children like him" beginning in the fall.

After a visit to the NSH/SDC school to see what it was like, Robby's parents realized that their son would not have lasted long there. The classes were disorderly and noisy and the students Robby's parents met were angry, hostile, and uncooperative. They decided Robby did not need that kind of learning environment.

Friends and advocates advised Robby's parents to decline his new placement and seek a transfer to a different district if necessary. So Robby's parents kept him at home that fall rather than letting him attend the NSH/SDC school. Robby was tutored at home[13] in math, reading, and language to keep him from falling further behind. Meanwhile, Robby's parents and advocates continued to fight with the school district about Robby's placement. They pointed out that the school had not met its obligation to provide the educational services Robby needed to overcome his language barrier to the curriculum. They argued that the testing on which the placement was based was not valid and had been misinterpreted. However, the school district refused to release Robby officially. That being the case, the neighboring school districts could not enroll him because he lived outside their enrollment boundaries.

As a result of the protracted struggle over his school placement, Robby began to show signs of anxiety and depression. He began to lose confidence even in his ability to do things that he had always done easily and well. For example, he talked his parents into giving him $50 (something they could not easily afford) to try out for a youth football league. On the first day of practice, he did everything he was asked to do and excelled in his efforts. However, he refused to return to the tryouts after the first day, saying he knew he was going to fail. His parents tried to persuade him to go back; the coach called repeatedly, saying he had done very well in the tryouts and should join in the practice, but nothing worked. Robby did not want more evidence that he was inadequate.

Finally, with the help of an attorney, Robby's parents were able to schedule another IEP meeting. At this meeting, current and former teachers, psychologists, speech therapists, counselors, special education administrators, resource teachers, and specialists lined up to present arguments for the need to place Robby in an NSH/SDC school. As part of the opposition, Robby's parents prepared a statement, in Spanish, presenting their objections. Then, Robby's advocates presented his case. First, Robby knew no English when he started school, and Proposition 227 notwithstanding, under the Supreme Court's ruling in *Lau v. Nichols*, the school had an

---

[13] Robby's family friends hired a reading recovery teacher and a graduate student in linguistics to tutor him in essential subjects while his parents negotiated with the district.

obligation to help him overcome the language barrier between him and the school's curriculum. Second, despite the evidence presented of "language deficiencies and severe linguistic disorders," Robby's language development had been normal until he started school. Third, the results of the psycho-educational testing appeared to be flawed: even disregarding the questionable use of tests normed on native speakers of English with a child who was clearly an EL, it appeared that the district's school psychologist based her finding on two subtests that came at the end of the testing session—the only two parts in which Robby's performance fell below the cut-off score. When another psychologist tested Robby again, he performed above the cut-off on equivalent tests.

That was the turning point. The school psychologist who administered Robby's initial testing must have realized that the district's plan to concentrate its lowest-performing children into a few schools would not work in this case. She apologized to Robby's parents. She said the results had been misinterpreted, and she realized how greatly this had affected Robby and his family.

It has been a decade now since that meeting. The district agreed to have Robby tested by an independent testing agency to settle the question of his placement.[14] It also permitted his parents to enroll him at a different school where he might have a fresh start. With help from his friends and his teachers, Robby learned to read that year and finally was able to make some progress in school. In junior high school, Robby made the honor roll three times—a matter of considerable vindication and pride for him and his parents.

Once in high school, however, Robby had to struggle each semester against placement in remedial classes. He argued that he needed courses that would prepare him for college, not more remedial courses that led nowhere. Robby prevailed but lost anywhere from 3 weeks to a month and a half of class time each semester before being placed back in his academic classes. Nonetheless, he maintained a 3.0 grade point average in high school. On graduation day, he was despondent rather than triumphant, remembering the many barriers that had been placed in his path toward reaching that day. He realized how close he had come to not making it at all. Robby is now in his third year in college, and continues to believe school is worth the struggle.

---

[14] After 3 days of testing and observation, Robby was declared to be "normal"—a noteworthy designation only in contrast to the district's earlier finding. This was necessary to expunge the "010" designation on his file.

11

Promising and Effective Practices in Assessment of Dual Language Learners' and English Learners' Educational Progress

Assessment of the educational progress of dual language learners (DLLs) and English learners (ELs)[1] can provide concrete and actionable evidence of their learning. Sound assessment provides students with feedback on their learning, teachers with information that can be used to shape instruction and communicate with parents on the progress of their children, school leaders with information on areas of strength and weakness in instruction, and system leaders with information on the overall performance of their programs.

Well-established standards for assessing students and education systems developed through a joint effort of the American Educational Research Association (AERA), American Psychological Association (APA), and National Council on Measurement in Education (NCME) exist to guide practice (American Educational Research Association et al., 2014). According to these standards, the concept of validity is central to all assessment; it is the cornerstone for establishing the fairness of assessments, including those used with DLLs/ELs. There is a gap, however, between these professional standards, developed by consensus among relevant disciplines in the scientific community, and how assessments of DLLs/ELs at the individual student and system levels are actually conducted. Current practices vary across

---

[1] When referring to children ages birth to 5 in their homes, communities, or early care and education programs, this report uses the term "dual language learners" or "DLLs." When referring to children ages 5 and older in the pre-K to 12 education system, the term "English learners" or "ELs" is used. When referring to the broader group of children and adolescents ages birth to 21, the term "DLLs/ELs" is used.

states and districts. States will have primary responsibility for these assessments as the Every Student Succeeds Act (ESSA) of 2015 is implemented in school year 2017-2018, with its directive that school districts within a state share common assessment practices for student identification and exit from EL status.

The heterogeneity of DLLs/ELs with respect to age, first language, literacy, and access to educational services, as well as their family and community circumstances (see Chapter 3), requires careful consideration during the assessment process and the interpretation of results. Particularly for DLLs/ELs, assessment of academic learning needs to be considered in conjunction with assessment of English language development or bilingual proficiency.

This chapter summarizes what is known from research on assessment measures and practices first for DLLs and then for ELs. The discussion includes the committee's analysis of challenges in assessment design and implementation that need further investigation. The chapter ends with the committee's conclusions on promising and effective assessment practices for DLLs/ELs.

ASSESSMENT OF DUAL LANGUAGE LEARNERS

A central tenet of selecting appropriate assessment instruments is that the purpose of the assessment must guide the choice of measures, the method of data collection, and the content of the assessment (Espinosa and Gutiérrez-Clellen, 2013; Peña and Halle, 2011). This principle is clearly stated in the National Research Council (2008, p. 2) report *Early Childhood Assessment: Why, What, and How*: "Different purposes require different types of assessments, and the evidentiary base that supports the use of an assessment for one purpose may not be suitable for another." The National Education Goals Panel established four main purposes for early care and education (ECE) assessments: to promote learning and development of individual children; to identify children with special needs and health conditions for intervention purposes; to monitor trends in programs and evaluate program effectiveness; and to obtain benchmark data for accountability purposes at the local, state, and national levels (Shepard et al., 1998). Each of these purposes requires specific technical standards and assessment approaches and has inherent potential for cultural and linguistic bias. As there are unique considerations and recommendations for assessing DLLs depending on the purpose of the assessment, it is critical that ECE assessors clearly understand the purpose for assessment and match instruments and procedures to the stated purpose.

Accurate assessment of DLLs' development is critical for enhancing the quality of their care and education, as well as for understanding and improving the effectiveness of specific strategies for individual children (Espinosa and García, 2012; Espinosa and Gutiérrez-Clellen, 2013; Espinosa and López, 2007). The rapid increase in the numbers of young children who speak a language other than English in the home and attend ECE programs, combined with the expansion of state and federal funding for ECE services that carry accountability requirements, means that local and state assessment systems must be valid and appropriate for DLLs. As stated in the above-referenced National Research Council report, "Given the large and increasing size of the DLL population in the United States, the current focus on testing and accountability, and the documented deficits in current assessment practices, improvements are critical." (National Research Council, 2008, p. 258). The report goes on to summarize the recommendations from the National Association for the Education of Young Children (2005) on fair assessment of DLLs, including the use of developmental screenings, the need for linguistically and culturally appropriate assessments, a focus on improving curriculum and instruction with multiple methods and measures, the use of multidisciplinary teams that include qualified bilingual and bicultural assessors collecting data over time, the need for caution when interpreting results of standardized assessments, and inclusion of families in all aspects of the assessment process.

Virtually all experts on ECE assessment have cautioned against the use of single assessments at one point in time to identify young children's developmental status and learning needs across multiple domains of development (Daily et al., 2010; Meisels, 1999; National Research Council, 2008). Experts agree that a single assessment measure should never be used for making important educational decisions, such as those related to eligibility for services or rate of educational progress. All young children demonstrate highly variable and dynamic development depending on the context and task demands; they are also notoriously "bad" test takers with limited attention spans and frequently misunderstand the directions or task demands, which may lead to incorrect answers (Meisels, 2007; Stevens and DeBord, 2001). These challenges are compounded when children are still mastering their home or first language while also acquiring a second language during this period of rapid development.

To assess DLLs accurately, assessment professionals and ECE educators need to consider the unique aspects of linguistic and cognitive development associated with acquiring two languages during the earliest years, as well as the social and cultural contexts that influence these children's development. (See Chapter 4 for fuller discussion of the sociocultural contexts for the development of DLLs.) Important individual and contextual differences unique to the experience of growing up with more than one language will affect the development of essential skills that are often part of school readiness assessments. DLLs, for example, are much more likely than their monolingual English-speaking peers to have parents with low levels of formal education, to live in low-income families, to live in two-parent homes, and to be raised in cultural contexts that may not reflect majority culture norms (Capps et al., 2005; Espinosa, 2007; Hernandez, 2006).

Latino Spanish-speaking DLLs often have language needs that have not been identified or addressed (Espinosa and Gutiérrez-Clellen, 2013) and can lead to depressed language abilities at kindergarten entry (Fuller et al., 2015). DLLs' first and second language and literacy development also has been linked to differences in home language experiences (Hammer et al., 2011), the timing and reasons for family immigration (Portes and Rumbaut, 2014), the age and circumstances of their first exposure to English (Hammer et al., 2011), and their families' specific resiliencies and strengths (Fuligni et al., 2013).

All ECE administrators, staff, and teachers need to understand the impact of these sociocultural and language learning contexts on DLLs' development. To individualize interactions and instruction, ECE assessors need to consider the complexity and impact of these factors and then carefully select assessment instruments and procedures that match the purpose for the assessment and the characteristics of the children. Thus, the first step in ECE assessment is to collect information from the family about the DLL's early language and learning environments so these contextual factors can be carefully considered in the selection of assessment instruments, as well as in the interpretation of results and in educational decisions. Researchers have found stronger relationships between parents' reports of their children's language abilities than between teachers' reports and direct child assessments, particularly in the area of vocabulary knowledge (Vagh et al., 2009). Thus it is important that family language surveys or interviews be available in the languages families speak and include questions about which language a child first learned to speak, the language of the child's primary caregiver, the age of the child when first exposed to English, and the language spoken by other adults and peers who interact with the child regularly.

Language of Assessment

The majority of ECE assessment experts, along with the Office of Head Start (OHS) and several states, recommend that DLLs be assessed in both of their languages because assessing a DLL only in English will underestimate his or her knowledge and true abilities (California Department of Education, 2012; Espinosa and Gutiérrez-Clellen, 2013; Office of Head Start, 2015; Peña and Halle, 2011). When a DLL is assessed in only one language, concepts or vocabulary words the child knows in another language will not be represented in the results (see Chapter 4). Few states have explicit guidelines for assessing DLLs (Espinosa and Calderon, 2015); however, the federal government and several states (e.g., California and Illinois) currently require that assessments be conducted in both English and the child's home language (California Department of Education, 2012, 2015a; Illinois Department of Education, 2013; Office of Head Start, 2015). The California Department of Education, Child Development Division (CDE/ CDD), for example, has issued guidelines on the importance of a teacher or other adult being proficient in the child's home language when assessments are conducted (California Department of Education, 2012). The guidelines stress the importance of the first language as a foundation for continued development: the development of language and literacy skills in a child's first language is important for the development of skills in a second language, and therefore should be considered as the foundational step toward learning English (see also Chapter 4).

According to the new Head Start Early Learning Outcomes Framework (Office of Head Start, 2015, p. 4), moreover, "Children who are DLLs must be allowed to demonstrate the skills, behaviors, and knowledge in the Framework in the home language, English, or both languages." In addition, the National Center on Cultural and Linguistic Responsiveness has issued guidelines on how to conduct developmental screenings of DLLs in their home language and English when no appropriate standardized measures are available.[2]

These recent assessment requirements reflect a growing consensus among assessment professionals and ECE policy makers that although the field does not have adequate instrumentation with which to conduct standardized assessments in all of the languages children and families speak, there are methods for determining DLL children's competencies in multiple languages, and this information is critical in planning appropriate interventions (Gutiérrez-Clellen, 1999; Gutiérrez-Clellen et al., 2012). As noted above, many language skills and concepts learned in the child's first language have been shown to facilitate English language learning (see Chapter 4). For example, once a child knows some math concepts, such as the number 3, in the home language, the child is also likely to know the concept in the second language and needs to learn only the new vocabulary, not the concept (Sarnecka et al., 2011).

Given the large variations in preschool DLLs' amount and quality of English exposure as well as home language development (see Chapter 4), they may show uneven progress between the two languages, depending on the language tasks involved. Because of this variability and the importance of language to all academic achievement, it is impossible to obtain an accurate assessment of a DLL's developmental status and instructional needs

---

[2] Available: https://eclkc.ohs.acf.hhs.gov/hslc/tta-system/cultural-linguistic/fcp/docs/Screening-dual-language-learners.pdf [February 23, 2017].

without examining the child's skills in both languages. A child who demonstrates very little English proficiency may be in the early stages of second language acquisition but have well-developed skills in the home language, while another child that demonstrates difficulties in both English and the home language should be referred for an evaluation to determine whether special services are needed (see Chapter 8). Thus before making a referral decision, assessors need to consider each DLL's language abilities in both the home language and English: if the child is very delayed in English but shows typical skills in the home language, the child most likely has had few opportunities to learn English and needs systematic high-quality English language development (see Chapters 4 and 6). If the child has a language delay, it will show up in both languages (see Chapter 8).

It is important to note that many researchers have expressed serious validity concerns about the use of standardized measures of DLLs' English proficiency (Espinosa, 2008). Some assessment error is due to norming samples, complexity of language used, and administration procedures. To compensate for the psychometric weaknesses of current standardized tests of language proficiency within the DLL population, most researchers have recommended that assessors use multiple measures administered by bilingual, bicultural, multidisciplinary team members. These measures may include standardized tests and curriculum-embedded assessments in addition to narrative language samples and observation of children's language usage in natural settings (August and Shanahan, 2006; Gutiérrez-Clellen et al., 2006; National Association for the Education of Young Children, 2005; Neill, 2005).

Having qualified ECE assessors who are knowledgeable about the process of first and second language development during the early years is essential to understanding, interpreting, and applying the results of any assessment of DLLs. Ensuring these assessor/teacher competencies requires increased investments for ECE professionals, as discussed below.

Special Considerations for Infants and Toddlers

During the infant-toddler years (birth to 3), assessment typically includes developmental screening, observation, and ongoing assessment. The use of standardized achievement measures is not recommended for this age range. ECE providers typically observe children's behavior, language use, and progress across all domains of development in natural settings to document their growth and identify any potential learning problems. The focus of the observations is usually aligned with the major curricular goals of the program—for example, whether the child regularly shows comprehension of simple sentences by following one- or two-step directions. Although programs rarely administer standardized measures to assess individual DLLs' progress during these years, they often use standardized observation tools that track the children's learning over time (Espinosa and Gutiérrez-Clellen, 2013). One such tool, developed by the California Department of Education (2015b), is the Desired Results Developmental Profile for Infants and Toddlers (DRDP), which is required in all state-supported infant-toddler programs. Observational methods such as the DRDP that are organized around educationally significant outcomes, administered repeatedly over time, and include families' perspectives are recommended by the leading ECE professional associations (National Association for the Education of Young Children and National Association of Early Childhood Specialists in State Departments of Education, 2003; National Research Council, 2008).

These observational assessments can be thought of as formative because their results are used to plan for individualized interactions and activities to support the child's progress. All of the recommended practices for screening and assessing infants and toddlers apply to DLLs (see Greenspan and Meisels, 1996), but must be augmented by assessors who are proficient in the child's home language and knowledgeable about the child's home culture (Espinosa and Gutiérrez-Clellen, 2013; Peña and Halle, 2011).

Assessment Purposes and Procedures for Preschool DLLs

Language Proficiency

ECE assessors must first determine a DLL's proficiency in both English and the home language, as well as the distribution of knowledge across the two languages, in order to design appropriate language interventions (Ackerman and Tazi, 2015). DLLs, whether simultaneous or sequential bilinguals (see Chapter 4), typically have a dominant language, even though the differences may be subtle. Researchers have documented that most DLLs have a larger, or a specialized, vocabulary, along with greater grammatical proficiency and mastery of the linguistic structure, in one language (Paradis et al., 2011; Pearson, 2002). Typically, this is the language the child learned earliest and with which he or she has the most experience, uses more fluidly, and often prefers to use. Information provided by parents can be used as a guide in determining which language is dominant. In conducting developmental screenings or standardized assessments of language proficiency, assessment experts recommend that preschool DLLs be assessed in their dominant language first to determine the upper limits of their linguistic and cognitive abilities (Peña and Halle, 2011).

The specific measures and methods used to assess a child's language proficiency can impact the assessment results. For example, a child's English proficiency can be overestimated when a single measure is used (Brassard and Boehm, 2007; Garcia et al., 2010). Scores also can fluctuate depending on whether the measure is English-only, a sum of both languages, or based on conceptual scoring (Bandel et al., 2012). In addition, there are no national definitions of what constitutes English proficiency during the preschool years, and the number of psychometrically strong language proficiency measures for preschool DLLs is limited (Barrueco et al., 2012). Therefore, a child's designation as proficient may depend on the specific measure used and whether the assessment is based on observational data or a language assessment administered directly to the child, as well as local norms and what is expected for kindergarten entry in different communities (Ackerman and Tazi, 2015; Hauck et al., 2013; Lara et al., 2007). Therefore, the interpretation of results of standardized language tests for DLLs needs to be treated with caution and combined with other types of assessment data, such as observational records and detailed family histories.

Assessment to Improve Instruction and Individualize Practices

One of the most important purposes for ECE assessment is to guide teachers' instructional decision making and monitor each child's progress toward meeting important program goals. This is especially critical for DLLs as formative progress data collected throughout the year can be used to modify and individualize classroom strategies and identify areas of weakness that need more attention (Ackerman and Tazi, 2015; Espinosa and Gutiérrez-Clellen, 2013). When assessing DLLs' progress toward meeting program curriculum goals, it is important that progress be measured against what is typically expected of children growing up with more than one language (López, 2012). ECE assessors need to understand thoroughly the process of first and second language acquisition, the stages of second language acquisition during the preschool years, and the influences on dual language development (see Chapter 4) in order to make judgments a DLL's progress and whether it is within normal ranges. If the program is implementing a dual language approach with goals for bilingualism and biliteracy, the DLL's knowledge and progress need to be assessed continually in both languages. (See Espinosa and López [2007] and National Research Council [2008] for discussion of the potential for assessment bias when ECE teachers do not understand DLLs' language and culture.)

During the ECE years, assessments used to inform teachers and improve learning are frequently based on careful observations of children's behavior and use of language conducted repeatedly throughout the school year. The documentation of children's accomplishments can then be applied to rating scales, checklists, work samples, and portfolios completed over time (National Association for the Education of Young Children, 2005). These methods often are characterized as authentic assessments because they occur during everyday activities and allow the child to demonstrate knowledge and skills without creating an artificial context that is unfamiliar to the child and may influence performance. Observations, language samples, and interviews are considered authentic assessment methods because no specific set of correct responses is predetermined. Observations and insights from other staff members who speak the child's home language and have frequent contact with the child can also be collected through questionnaires or family interviews.

The DRDP (California Department of Education, 2015b) described above is a standardized observational instrument that is aligned with the state of California's Early Learning and Development Foundations and addresses the cultural and linguistic diversity of the state. The instrument includes eight domains of development that reflect the continuum of development from birth to early kindergarten. Most important, all ECE providers are trained in the use of the tool, its implementation, and how to interpret and apply its results to plan instruction.

As discussed by Espinosa and García (2012), many states are designing assessments administered during the first months of kindergarten that will provide data on children's "readiness" for formal schooling, as well as identify service gaps in the state's ECE system and guide linguistically and culturally appropriate instruction in the primary grades. These kindergarten entry assessments (KEAs) must be aligned with the state's early learning and development standards (ELDSs) and cover all domains of school readiness. They also must be linguistically and culturally appropriate, valid, and reliable for the population of children to be assessed, including DLLs. These KEA requirements present challenges for assessment of the school readiness of DLLs. Most states' ELDSs were designed using the typical development of monolingual English speakers as the norm against which all students are compared (Espinosa and Calderon, 2015); therefore, the language and conceptual development of DLLs is likely to be misinterpreted, underestimated, and inaccurately determined. As states continue to develop and refine their KEAs, they need to address the unique developmental trajectories of young children growing up with more than one language (Espinosa and García, 2012).

ASSESSMENT OF ENGLISH LEARNERS

Assessment of ELs once they have entered the K-12 education system is governed through a complex set of laws and policies created to protect the civil rights of ELs' national origin status (Title XI of the Civil Rights Act of 1964 and the Equal Educational Opportunities Act of 1974), as well as federal funding to enhance their academic outcomes through ESSA. In the context of these laws and policies, assessment is required for the following purposes of accountability:

- initial identification of ELs as they enter school to determine whether they are an EL and therefore qualify for targeted services, such as English language development or bilingual education;
- annual monitoring of student progress in English language proficiency (ELP) and decision making about exiting their status as an EL; and
- annual monitoring of their academic achievement in content areas in certain grades, with a primary focus on literacy and math and a secondary focus on science and other content areas.

Assessment of English Language Proficiency

The assessment of student ELP became universal after the *Lau v. Nichols* Supreme Court decision of 1974, requiring the identification of students who had limited English proficiency. Early tests, such as the Bilingual Syntax Measure (BSM) and the Language Assessment Scales (LAS), were focused primarily on English vocabulary and grammar and were used solely for purposes of identification and reclassification. ELP assessment became standards-based and administered annually through Title III of the No Child Left Behind (NCLB) Act of 2001, when states were required to administer annually ELP assessments aligned with ELP standards of the state in the domains of listening, speaking, reading, and writing. Additionally, the law mandated that the ELP standards be aligned with the state's academic standards.

The state ELP assessment was to be used for Title III accountability through annual reporting by districts of year-to-year progress across proficiency levels (AMAO1) and the percentage of ELs who attained proficient status in the assessment (AMAO2). The requirement of alignment with the academic standards was interpreted as meeting the same academic assessment targets as those required for Title I—a provision known as Adequate Yearly Progress, which history now shows was not met by most education systems.

Under ESSA, and earlier NCLB Improving America's School Act (IASA) versions of the Elementary and Secondary Education Act (ESEA), mandated ELP assessments must measure students' proficiency in the areas of speaking, listening, reading, and writing appropriate to their age and grade level. A measure of students' ability to comprehend English was also added as a requirement, with the possibility that this measure could be derived based on students' oral comprehension and reading scores. While all states are required to include the foregoing measures of ELP, under ESSA and earlier versions of the ESEA, they have been at liberty to operationalize these five measures of ELP based on definitions of underlying language skills as they judge best based on their individual state or state consortium interpretation of the research literature on English language development and professional literature on best practices in instruction of English in classrooms. Unfortunately, as noted in Chapter 6, there is no single coherent underlying theory of ELP with a strong basis in validated research at this time. While construction and validation of a comprehensive theory of ELP germane to the use of English for academic learning purposes and relevant ELP assessment is not yet at hand, important progress is being made, as discussed later in this chapter. A key step in guiding this process is the efforts of national teams of EL researchers and state and urban professional organizations that have banded together to begin to build common understandings of how to integrate EL demographic data, data from ELP and achievement assessments, and other achievement-related data systematically to provide a theoretical and empirical basis for sound and effective instruction of ELs.

Following the implementation of NCLB, two consortia of states— World Class Instructional Design and Assessment (WIDA) and English Language Development Assessment (ELDA)—were formed to develop common ELP assessments. States with larger EL populations (California, Florida, New York, Texas) developed their own assessments. The development of these assessments reflected increased concern for measuring English proficiency relevant to the learning of school subject matter associated with mastery of academic learning standards, complicating their purpose as assessment instruments. Significantly, these new-generation assessments of English for classroom learning purposes include attention to some of the key discourse-level skills outlined in Chapter 6 that need to be considered in developing a coherent theory of language proficiency applied to school learning.

Over the past two decades, there has been considerable variability across and within states in the identification, assessment, and reclassification of ELs (e.g., Abedi, 2008; Bailey and Carroll, 2015; Boals et al., 2015; Hauck et al., 2016). Linquanti and Cook (2013) provide a framework for a common definition of ELs and ELP assessment adapted from the National Research Council (2011) report *Allocating Federal Funds for State Programs for English Language Learners*, which helps frame current concerns in a coherent manner tied to establishing the validity of EL assessments. This framework includes four stages: (1) identify—determine whether a student is a potential EL; (2) classify—verify that the student is EL or non-EL; (3) establish ELP performance standards—ascertain a performance standard with which a language proficiency assessment can be compared; and (4) reclassify—monitor students' ELP until they meet the ELP performance standard, at which point students may be considered non-EL.

Language assessment for ELs in K-12 settings focuses on the assessment of English, but assessment of academic literacy in the home language is also useful. Oral language assessment of children's native language may lead to erroneous identification (MacSwan and Mahoney, 2008; MacSwan and Rolstad, 2006; MacSwan et al., 2002). For instance, while the Language Assessment Scales-Oral (LAS-O) Español and the Idea Proficiency Test I-Oral (IPT) Spanish—both assessments of children's home language proficiency—identified 74 percent and 90 percent, respectively, of Spanish-speaking ELs as limited speakers of their first language, only 2 percent of participants had unexpectedly high morphological error rates on a natural language sample (n = 145) (MacSwan and Rolstad, 2006). Doubts raised by this work led one large school district to abandon native language assessment (Thompson, 2015).

Thompson (2015) analyzed results of Los Angeles Unified School District's proficiency assessment of language and literacy in the student's native language as well as the district's proficiency expectations in English, and similarly found large numbers of children identified as "nonproficient" in their home language. However, the author notes that the native language assessments were designed specifically to measure students' proficiency in the "language used in academic settings," as well as school-based literacy. Thompson found that the assessment results were useful for predicting a window for a high probability of reclassification for ELs (see Figure 11-1). Noting concerns about the validity of oral language assessments, Thompson concludes that assessments of children's home language may play a useful role "if we frame the results not as providing information about what students lack, but as providing information about the resources students bring to the classroom," rather than serving as a measure of their language proficiency across all contexts (p. 29). In other words, variation in assessment of home language literacy is a strong predictor of subsequent academic outcomes, such as reclassification.

Therefore, it is important to obtain an accurate assessment of an EL's language development and instructional needs by examining skills in both languages. Federal law requires the assessment of ELP upon school entry. The addition of assessment of the home language, particularly those skills related to academic literacy skills, provides further valuable information about the expected developmental pathway of the student that can be used for targeted instructional services and program placement. For school-age children, it is important for home language assessment to focus specifically on the measurement of academic literacy and the language of school.

Major Changes in ESSA for English Language Proficiency

The largest change in ESSA regarding ELP assessment is its use for Title I accountability as one of the major elements that must be included in the state-developed school indicator system. Previously, ELP assessment was used to monitor districts receiving Title III funding. The ELP assessment is

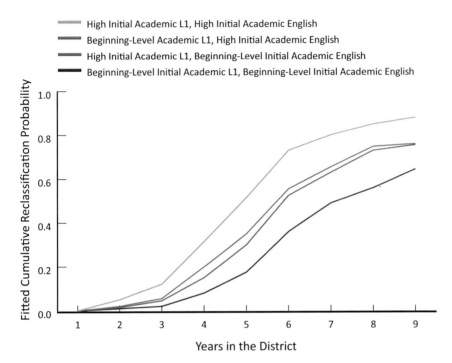

FIGURE 11-1 Fitted cumulative probability of reclassification for students entering Los Angeles Unified School District as English learners in kindergarten, by initial level of academic home language proficiency and initial academic English proficiency.
NOTE: The graph shows fitted results for students who entered the district in 2001-2002.
SOURCE: Thompson (2015).

now a required part of Title I school (not district) accountability. This shift is bringing significant system attention to the ELP assessment, since Title I addresses all students, not just ELs. While Title I regulations were being developed as this report was being written, it is clear that whatever mechanisms each state uses to ensure the quality of Title I academic assessments through its peer review process will apply in significant measure to the ELP assessment now that it is part of Title I accountability.[3]

Another change in ESSA is the requirement in Title III for standardized statewide entrance and exit procedures for identifying ELs.[4] As noted above, there is considerable variation not just across states but often across

_____

[3] A summary of EL assessment final regulations as of early 2017 under ESSA can be found at https://www2.ed.gov/policy/elsec/leg/essa/essaassessmentfactsheet1207.pdf [February 23, 2017].

[4] For relevant ESSA Title III Non-Regulatory Guidance, see https://www2.ed.gov/policy/elsec/leg/essa/essatitleiiiguidenglishlearners92016.pdf [February 23, 2017].

districts within states in the procedures and criteria used for EL identification and exiting (Cook and Linquanti, 2015; Linquanti and Cook, 2015; Linquanti et al., 2016). Under ESSA, ELs' entry into and exit from services will need to be consistent at least within states, thus allowing educators to better serve students with high rates of mobility and making the definition of an EL consistent across the state. Importantly, and as specified in ESSA, states and local education agencies (LEAs) are responsible for establishing the validity of ELP assessments consistent with technical approaches for establishing the validity and reliability of assessments and with professional standards for assessments. The latter are exemplified by the AERA/APA/NCME standards. The formulation and implementation of states' and LEAs' validity plans under ESSA will merit the careful attention of education stakeholders and will require significant planning and analysis of the resources needed to maintain consistency with the specifications of the AERA/APA/NCME standards.

The Problem of Initial Identification as a High-Stakes Process

The initial identification of ELs pursuant to ESSA and in tandem with each state's education code and requirements of the U.S. Office of Civil Rights is a central matter. Initial identification of prospective ELs, including the administration of either a screener or the full ELP assessment, must occur within 30 days of school enrollment. The committee notes that this is a high-stakes assessment because it determines services to be provided to the student. In most cases, moreover, this high-stakes decision is based on a single assessment, often administered when the student enters school in kindergarten or 1st grade and in practice even prior to the start of the school year during the registration period.

An unfortunate chain of events can affect ELs in K-12 schools when their oral home language ability is assessed without due concern for the appropriateness of the assessment instrument and systematic consideration of observational data on language use. Some research has found that such children may be identified as nonproficient in their home language because it is not assessed with valid measures and procedures (Commins and Miramontes, 1989; Escamilla, 2006; MacSwan and Mahoney, 2008; MacSwan and Rolstad, 2006; MacSwan et al., 2002). Indeed, doubts raised by this work led one large school district to abandon native language assessment (Thompson, 2015). It is well known that children identified as "non-non's" (nonproficient in both English and Spanish) have a higher likelihood of identification in special education (Artiles et al., 2005), even though the specific instruments used to identify them as non-non's are known to assess their proficiency incorrectly (MacSwan et al., 2002; MacSwan and Mahoney, 2008; MacSwan and Rolstad, 2006).

As a bottom line, the AERA/APA/NCME guidelines advise against the use of a single test for high-stakes decisions. Emerging research on the consequences of initial classification as well as reclassification decisions based on analysis of the discontinuity effects of cut scores shows long-term influences of such decisions on educational outcomes, and therefore high-stakes consequences for students (Robinson-Cimpian et al., 2016).

Reclassification of ELs

Provisions in ESSA Title I raise concerns about the reclassification of students from EL to non-EL status. This is also is a high-stakes decision for states and their LEAs with consequences for students. As described in Chapter 2, under ESSA Title I, states are required to devise and implement EL accountability models that not only identify ELs based on their performance on ELP assessments but also monitor their growth in English proficiency over time, along with their readiness to exit/transition from EL to non-EL status. Simultaneously, as part of their Title I accountability plans, states and LEAs are required to monitor ELs' academic progress and mastery of ambitious academic standards based on content achievement assessments and state-identified supplemental indicators of academic learning readiness and progress.

ESSA also requires that both states and LEAs implement validation strategies and provide empirical evidence regarding whether they are making suitable progress toward attaining accountability goals regarding transitioning of ELs at a pace and with success rates set by state plans. The AERA/APA/NCME testing standards (American Educational Research Association et al., 2014) are cited as appropriate for this purpose, although these standards were developed primarily with assessments in mind and not for validation of broad systems of indicators suitable for educational evaluation studies. Nonetheless, the standards make a scientifically sound case for consideration of additional empirical validation evidence provided by construct-relevant indicators.

The high-stakes demands on states and their LEAs described above operate at the aggregate EL level within state and LEA jurisdictions, but they also have high-stakes consequences for individual students and their classrooms and teachers by default. Beyond making sound decisions to transition ELs in the aggregate, the aspirations and intent of ESSA are clearly to support states and LEAs in implementing ELs' transition to non-EL status using decision systems with validity at the individual student and classroom levels.

One of the key findings of the Council of Chief State School Officers (CCSSO) report cited earlier (Linquanti and Cook, 2015) is that states show considerable variation in how they implement decision systems for reclassifying ELs as non-ELs. The decision to reclassify ELs carries with it the implication that they are now sufficiently proficient in English that they can learn in English and master the academic content required by a state's mandated academic standards without additional supports. The CCSSO report notes that as of 2015, all states required students to attain or exceed mandated compensatory or conjunctive performance levels on a state ELP assessment to be eligible for reclassification. However, 29 states and the District of Columbia used only an overall composite or pattern of language modality domain scores on a state ELP test as the basis for the reclassification decision. The remaining 21 states relied on an additional one to three supplemental indicators to make this decision. Additional indicators mandated by each state's education laws included performance on content achievement tests, teacher clinical input or evaluation, and other (such as parental input). Importantly, these 21 states varied in how uniformly and consistently these supplemental indicators were implemented. ESSA attempts to remedy this latter situation by mandating that states adopt and implement policies that ensure a uniform procedure for specifying and weighting such indicators across LEAs within the state. As noted in the CCSSO report, variation across states in such procedures and in the English proficiency assessments used remains an issue. Without a national standard for reclassification decisions, understanding ELs' progress across states is problematic.

The CCSSO report (Linquanti and Cook, 2015) offers nine state and LEA stakeholder recommendations for improving the validity and utility of EL reclassification decision systems (see Box 11-1). The scientific soundness of these recommendations and their contribution to establishing the validity of reclassification systems are open questions that deserve attention.

Three of the recommendations in Box 11-1 (4, 5, and 9) are worthy of further attention in this chapter because they represent innovative practices in the assessment field. These recommendations are of special importance as resources that can support the validation of classroom-based assessments of ELs' readiness to transition to non-EL status and monitoring of potential English language learning needs associated with earlier EL status that remain after students are reclassified. The bottom line is the need to know how to interpret ongoing evidence from large-scale ELP assessments, large-scale content and supplemental assessments, and local teacher-based and observation protocols to improve teachers' and LEAs' confidence that ELs are ready to function linguistically and academically with sufficient fluency to attain demanding academic standards with proper learning supports. Such information is also critical for identifying continuing English language services needed to support reclassified students' subsequent learning in English.

BOX 11-1
2015 Guidelines of the Council of Chief State School Officers for EL Reclassification

1. In strengthening reclassification policies and practices, states and districts should clearly define intended purposes and outcomes—and anticipate and address unintended negative consequences—for ELs.
2. States and districts should select reclassification criteria that directly relate to students' uses of language needed to carry out grade-level practices in academic content areas and to meet grade-level content standards.
3. States should establish the "English proficient" performance standard on the state ELP assessment using methods that take into account EL students' academic proficiency on content assessments.
4. States and districts should make EL reclassification decisions using more than an annual summative ELP assessment result; they should also examine EL students' classroom language uses as an additional reclassification criterion.
5. States and districts should ensure that local educators have training, tools, and ongoing support to effectively and consistently apply the classroom language-use criterion for reclassification decisions and are held appropriately accountable for doing so.
6. States and districts should establish common reclassification criteria and processes within states, with a goal of strengthening the reliability and validity of inferences made from local educator input and the accuracy of decisions based on multiple sources of evidence.
7. States in consortia should move toward a common English proficiency performance standard on any shared ELP assessment and acknowledge variability of other EL reclassification criteria and processes across states. They should ensure complete transparency and examine cross state comparability as new criteria and processes are implemented.
8. Consortia, states, and districts should carefully examine the application of reclassification criteria and processes for primary grade EL students, and EL students with disabilities, in order to maximize validity, reliability, and fairness.
9. Consortia, states, and districts should, as part of ensuring the consequential validity of reclassification criteria and processes, carefully examine the subsequent academic performance of reclassified ELs for as long as these students remain in the district or state.

SOURCE: Excerpted from Linquanti and Cook (2015, pp. 9-28).

Assessment of Academic Achievement

Since the 1994 reauthorization of ESEA (known as IASA), there has been statutory language about the inclusion of ELs in the academic assessments administered to all students. This language states that ELs "shall be assessed in a valid and reliable manner and provided appropriate accommodations on assessments administered to such students under this paragraph, including, to the extent practicable, assessments in the language and form most likely to yield accurate data on what such students know and can do in academic content areas, until such students have achieved English language proficiency."[5]

ESSA requires states to adopt challenging academic standards tied to assessments of proficiency in language arts/reading and mathematics administered annually in grades 3-8 and once in high school. An assessment in science at least once in elementary, middle, and high school also is still required. ESSA requires that, effective in 2017-2018, states must evaluate the progress of students on state assessments of reading/English language arts and content areas based on academic standards and models for progress determined by the states, not the federal government. As noted previously, ESSA allows states to design progress and status models that go beyond annual summative assessment results to include interim benchmark assessments measuring growth, and also to include alternative measures and indicators of students' progress and attainment of standards. This is a key difference from NCLB, which required that all states adopt annual yearly progress models based on large-scale assessments that evaluated students' progress toward 100 percent proficiency in reading/English language arts and in math and science.

Researchers and national professional groups have expressed concern about the validity and reliability of mandatory large-scale standardized tests for assessing ELs (see Abedi and Gándara, 2006; Abedi and Linquanti 2012; Durán, 2008; Kopriva, 2008; Solano-Flores, 2016; Young, 2009). Questions also have been raised as to whether and how these tests can improve classroom instruction and be based on more comprehensive assessment systems for ELs—important leading-edge research topics (e.g., Kopriva et al., 2016).

---

[5]Although this language has been in ESEA since the act's 1994 authorization in IASA, its broad parameters have resulted in its being implemented differently across reauthorizations. With computer-administered assessments, the availability of native language supports has broadened considerably.

Assessment Accommodations

Assessment accommodations have been investigated and implemented as a means of helping to address the concerns noted above. These accomodations can include linguistic modifications of test items to reduce ELP requirements, use of dictionaries or glossaries explaining construct-irrelevant terms found in assessment items, use of side-by-side English and first language presentations of assessment items, oral translations of instructions, oral reading of entire items in an EL's home language, figural and pictoral representations of item information, extended assessment time, and assessment in small groups (Burr et al., 2015; Durán, 2008; Lane and Levanthal, 2015; Solano-Flores et al., 2014).

Although accommodations are allowed, there are no widely accepted guidelines on which to use and under what circumstances, although preliminary work on such guidelines has been pursued (Rivera et al., 2008). Currently, accommodations are used inconsistently across states (Clewell et al., 2007). Also, it appears that not all accommodations are equally useful. Abedi and colleagues (2006) examined the achievement results of ELs under different conditions of accommodation. They found that ELs' performance increased by 10-20 percent on many tests when the language of test items was modified, sometimes just by simplification (Abedi and Lord, 2001), but that translating items and using a glossary without providing additional time did not lead to measureably higher achievement. The National Research Council (2011) also produced a comprehensive review of research and issues in this area, with a focus on the National Assessment of Educational Progress (NAEP) as well as other large-scale achievement assessments.

More recently, Kieffer and colleagues (2012) conducted a quantitative synthesis of research on the effectiveness and validity of test accommodations for ELs in large-scale assessments, an update of a previous synthesis published in 2006 (Francis et al., 2006; see also Burr et al., 2015; Lane and Leventhal, 2015). Based on that updated synthesis, the following recommendations constitute basic guidelines for assessment practitioners:

- Use simplified English in test design, and remove extraneous language demands.
- Provide English dictionaries/glossaries.
- Match the language of tests and accommodations to the language of instruction.
- Provide extended time, or use untimed tests.

Assessment in a Non-English Language

Assessment of content or subject matter learning in students' non-English first language is another strategy that has been actively investigated (Sireci, 2005; Sireci et al., 2016; Solano-Flores, 2012; Solano-Flores et al., 2002; Stansfield, 2003; Turkan and Oliveri, 2014). Most of this work has pursued translation of English-version test items into students' home languages. Research has found that it is highly challenging to produce translated assessment items and whole assessments that are psychometrically equivalent to their English counterparts. Nonetheless, states and counties with a need to develop and administer compatible assessments in more than one language in an academic domain have undertaken research to establish the validity of using carefully translated versions of assessments in two or more languages. The results of this research have been inconsistent. Some studies have found evidence that translated assessments do not measure target skills and knowledge as similarly and accurately as would be desired. Others have found that in isolated instances and with relaxed psychometric assumptions regarding the equivalence of assessments, academic content assessments in two languages with highly similar item content can behave comparably in terms of relative item difficulty and association with other academic measures among bilingual examinees with sufficient proficiency in the assessment's language (Sireci et al., 2016).

Assessment of content in students' non-English first language remains a prominent option under ESSA. However, as states develop and implement such assessments, they are obliged to develop reliability and validity arguments for their use that meet the Standards for Educational and Psychological Tests (American Educational Research Association et al., 2014). An important complication is that if nontranslation strategies are used and independent first language and English content assessments are developed and implemented, the two assessments need to align with the same state academic content standards and performance expectations at the same grade level if students are expected to be capable of the same kinds of learning competencies in classrooms across languages. Another important complication is that non-English first language tests make sense for ELs only if they have received or are currently receiving instruction in content areas in that language, such as in dual language instructional programs.

Assessment Validity and Test Use Responsive to Policies in Educational Practice

Assessments can be valid and reliable only for the particular purpose for which they were developed and are used; assessments that are valid and reliable for one purpose may be invalid or unreliable for other purposes

(National Research Council, 2011). As discussed below, progress toward establishing assessment validity is being made in a number of areas relevant to the characteristics of ELs, but this progress has been slow in other areas. As a result, a major retooling of assessment theory and methods may be needed to develop scientifically robust models for designing and implementing assessments and for establishing assessment validity—particularly with regard to assessments directly serving student instruction and language development.

Challenges are entailed in meeting educational goals for assessments and validating assessments for all students, regardless of background, but especially for ELs because every assessment is in part a language assessment (American Educational Research Association et al., 1999). ELs' performance on an assessment always reflects both their ability to understand the language of the assessment and their ability to generate expected responses to assessment tasks and items in the languages permitted for responses (Basterra et al., 2011; Solano-Flores, 2016).

While the use of assessment in education has traditionally been linked to policy, the nature of that linkage can vary. As mentioned elsewhere in this report, there is a growing movement to make assessment relevant to instruction and the instructional needs of students on a day-to-day and even moment-to-moment basis (Bailey and Heritage, 2008; Darling-Hammond et al., 2014; Gottlieb, 2016; Heritage et al., 2015; Jiao and Lissitz, 2015; Pryor and Crossouard, 2005). These more immediate instructional purposes for assessments are quite varied and differ from the large-scale accountability purposes related LEA and state accountability. In the latter case, the focus is on aggregate grade-, LEA-, and state-level assessment results regarding what ELs know and can do in relation to broad educational policy goals and the performance of ELs compared with other subgroups of students. Assessments can be designed and implemented in many ways to impact the everyday instruction of ELs, but three broad possibilities have emerged that point to needed validation research: (1) benchmark or interim assessments, (2) formative assessments, and (3) integrated data analytic assessment systems incorporating the first two assessment types along with other indicators of student learning status and capabilities.

Benchmark or interim assessments aligned with annual state summative assessments of achievement are being introduced by large-scale assessment developers and states. The potential value of these assessments in supporting student learning is mentioned in ESSA. These assessments can be administered periodically before administration of an annual summative assessment to gauge students' progress toward meeting state academic standards at a grade level. Their results can be used by LEAs, schools, and classroom teachers to determine the readiness of ELs and other students to master skills and knowledge that may appear on the summative annual assessments. They provide actionable information that can inform ongoing instruction or instructional interventions designed to support students' mastery of targeted skills and content knowledge where there is evidence of need at the classroom and individual student levels.

Instructionally relevant formative assessments can be constructed by local practitioners and administered as stand-alone performance assessments (Abedi, 2010) tied to current instruction, or they can be embedded in ongoing day-to-day instruction in a manner that is sensitive to instructional goals and the language and background characteristics of individual ELs and other students. Such formative assessments are sociocognitively sensitive (Mislevy and Durán, 2014); that is, they can be designed to be sensitive to students' background knowledge related to an instructional domain, prior instructional experiences, and evidence of progress in learning complex academic language skills (Bailey and Heritage, 2014; Heritage et al., 2015). Such assessments are not as easily developed as standard large-scale accountability assessments, but they are now being investigated and are encouraged under ESSA.

Finally, integrated data analytic assessment systems can guide instruction of ELs by drawing on complex data systems and an assessment approach known as evidence-centered design. A concrete example of such a system is the ONPAR assessment of science and math content instruction and mastery (Kopriva et al., 2016). This approach builds on carefully constructed models of academic content learning tasks and their performance requirements that the assessments can measure in the everyday instructional context as students develop greater skills and proficiency in a content domain. These assessments can be used to assess what ELs know and can do through computerized assessment tasks that present ELs with multimodal (e.g., textual, visual/figural) information and forms of responding tailored to their individual needs and preferences. Similar work is aimed at uncovering the deep idiosyncratic but systematic features of science tasks administered to ELs that capture fine-grained diagnostic information on how students actually interpret the meaning and performance demands of the tasks (Noble et al., 2014).

Many of these emerging developments are captured by Solano-Flores (2016) with an eye toward future research needed for a more fine-grained understanding of what ELs know and can do and importantly, as with formative assessments, what they might be able to do next toward mastery of content and domain knowledge given their language proficiency (Bailey and Heritage, 2014). They all represent key future directions for improving EL assessment and its practical value tied to both policy and instructional objectives.

The Centrality of Assessment Literacy

Understanding the purpose, design goals, implementation practices, and performance demands of assessments of ELs and the reported performance of ELs on the assessments requires assessment literacy on the part of all educational stakeholders. These diverse stakeholders include not only teachers and students themselves but also parents and community members, educational policy makers, assessment developers, teacher educators, and workforce development stakeholders. There has been as yet no systematic analysis of how to address the full range of educational needs of these different constituencies.

Important beginnings for such efforts do exist in the form of current assessment practices aligned with general policy goals for schooling (see, e.g., Koretz [2008] with regard to educational testing as a whole and Bastera et al. [2011] in the case of ELs). But more such work is needed. As assessments of ELs become more complex and ambitious with respect to what they can reveal about what students know and can do, it is important to keep in mind principles regarding the relationships among any assessment, the target actions and behaviors in the real world, and the language demands the assessment is intended to reflect. In this regard, the work of Bachman and Palmer (2010) remains seminal. It is essential for all stakeholders to appreciate that functioning competently in the face of the sociocognitive and sociocultural demands of the world is a proper focus for assessment beyond evidence of competence in the performance of assessment tasks in and of themselves.

CONCLUSIONS

Conclusion 11-1: To conduct an accurate assessment of the developmental status and instructional needs of dual language learners/English learners, it is necessary to examine their skills in both English and their home language. During the first 5 years of life, infants, toddlers, and preschoolers require developmental screening, observation, and ongoing assessment in both languages to support planning for individualized interactions and activities that will support their optimal development.

Conclusion 11-2: When used for developmental screening for dual language learners/English learners with potential disabilities, effective assessments use multiple measures and sources of information, involve consultation with a multidisciplinary team that includes bilingual experts, collect information over time, and include family members as informants.

Conclusion 11-3: Given state-established standards for progress toward college and career readiness, as well as toward meeting standards for English language development in schools, it is essential to consider the validity of English language proficiency (ELP) assessments for determining English learners' readiness for exiting services. Validity evidence is required to demonstrate that an ELP assessment appropriately measures the expected academic language demands of the classroom.

Conclusion 11-4: The appropriate use of assessment tools and practices, as well as the communication of assessment results to families and decision makers, requires that all stakeholders be capable of understanding and interpreting the results of academic assessments administered to English learners in English or their home language, as well as English language proficiency assessments. Collaboration among states, professional organizations, researchers, and other stakeholders to develop common assessment frameworks and assessments is advancing progress toward this end.

Conclusion 11-5: Exposure to subject matter instruction in English learners' first languages is critical to the validity of assessments conducted in that language. Consistent with civil rights law and Every Student Succeeds Act, research supports the use of non-English content assessments in place of English-version assessments for English learners who have been instructed in their home language. The non-English assessments are valid only if they have been carefully constructed to measure the same content and skills and to demonstrate empirically adequate psychometric consistency relative to their English-version counterparts.

BIBLIOGRAPHY

Abedi, J. (2008). Classification system for English language learners: Issues and recommendations. *Educational Measurement: Issues and Practice, 27*(3), 17-31.
Abedi, J. (2010). *Performance Assessments for English Language Learners.* Stanford, CA: Stanford University, Stanford Center for Opportunity Policy in Education.
Abedi, J., and Gándara, P. (2006). Performance of English language learners as a subgroup in large-scale assessment: Interaction of research and policy. *Educational Measurement: Issues and Practice, 25*(4), 36-46.
Abedi, J., and Linquanti, R. (2012). *Issues and Opportunities in Improving the Quality of Large Scale Assessment Systems for English Language Learners.* Paper presented at the Understanding Language Conference, Stanford, CA.
Abedi, J., and Lord, C. (2001). The language factor in mathematics tests. *Applied Measurement in Education, 14*(3), 219-234.

Abedi, J., Courtney, M., Leon, S., Kao, J., and Azzam, T. (2006). *English Language Learners and Math Achievement: A Study of Opportunity to Learn and Language Accommodation*. CSE Report 702. Los Angeles: University of California, Center for the Study of Evaluation/National Center for Research on Evaluation, Standards, and Student Testing.

Ackerman, D.J., and Tazi, Z. (2015). Enhancing young Hispanic dual language learners' achievement: Exploring strategies and addressing challenges. *ETS Research Report Series, 2015*(1), 1-39.

American Educational Research Association, American Psychological Association, and National Council on Measurement in Education. (1999). *Standards for Educational and Psychological Testing* (1999 Edition). Washington, DC: American Educational Research Association.

American Educational Research Association, American Psychological Association, and National Council on Measurement in Education. (2014). *Standards for Educational and Psychological Testing*. Washington, DC: American Educational Research Association.

Artiles, A.J., Rueda, R., Salazar, J.J., and Higareda, I. (2005). Within-group diversity in minority disproportionate representation: English language learners in urban school districts. *Exceptional Children, 71*(3), 283.

August, D., and Shanahan, T. (2006). *Developing Literacy in Second-Language Learners: Report of the National Literacy Panel on Language Minority Children and Youth*. Executive Summary. Mahwah, NJ: Lawrence Erlbaum Associates.

Bachman, L., and Palmer, A. (2010). *Language Assessment in Practice*. Oxford, UK: Oxford University Press.

Bailey, A.L., and Carroll, P.E. (2015). Assessment of English language learners in the era of new academic content standards. *Review of Research in Education, 39*(1), 253-294.

Bailey, A.L., and Heritage, M. (2008). *Formative Assessment for Literacy, Grades K-6: Building Reading and Academic Language Skills across the Curriculum*. Thousand Oaks, CA: Sage/Corwin Press.

Bailey, A.L., and Heritage, M. (2014). The role of language learning progressions in improved instruction and assessment of English language learners. *TESOL Quarterly, 48*(3), 480-506.

Bandel, E., Atkins-Burnett, S., Castro, D.C., Wulsin, C.S., and Putman, M. (2012). *Examining the Use of Language and Literacy Assessments with Young Dual Language Learners*. Chapel Hill: The University of North Carolina, Frank Porter Graham Child Development Institute, Center for Early Care and Education Research—Dual Language Learners.

Barrueco, S., Lopez, M., Ong, C., and Lozano, P. (2012). *Assessing Spanish–English Bilingual Preschoolers: A Guide to Best Approaches and Measures*. Baltimore, MD: Paul H. Brookes.

Basterra, M.D.R., Trumbull, E., and Solano-Flores, G. (2011). *Cultural Validity in Assessment: Addressing Linguistic and Cultural Diversity*. New York: Routledge.

Boals, T., Kenyon, D.M., Blair, A., Cranley, M.E., Wilmes, C., and Wright, L.J. (2015). Transformation in K–12 English language proficiency assessment: Changing contexts, changing constructs. *Review of Research in Education, 39*(1), 122-164.

Brassard, M.R., and Boehm, A.E. (2007). *Preschool Assessment Principles and Practices*. New York: Guilford Press.

Burr, E., Haas, E., and Ferriere, K. (2015). *Identifying and Supporting English Learner Students with Learning Disabilities: Key Issues in the Literature and State Practice*. REL 2015-086. Washington, DC: Regional Educational Laboratory West.

California Department of Education. (2012). *Desired Results Developmental Profile: School Readiness (DRDP-SR)*. Sacramento: California Department of Education. Available: http://www.drdpk.org [December 2016].

California Department of Education. (2015a). *A Developmental Continuum from Early Infancy to Kindergarten Entry: Infant/Toddler View*. Sacramento: California Department of Education.

California Department of Education. (2015b). *Desired Results Developmental Profile*. Sacramento: California Department of Education. Available: http://www.cde.ca.gov/sp/cd/ci/drdpforms.asp [December 2016].

Capps, R., Fix, M.E., Murray, J., Ost, J., Passel, J.S., and Herwantoro, S. (2005). *The New Demography of America's Schools: Immigration and the No Child Left Behind Act*. Washington, DC: Urban Institute.

Clewell, B.C., de Cohen, C.C., and Murray, J. (2007). *Promise or Peril?: NCLB and the Education of ELL Students*. Washington DC: Urban Institute.

Commins, N.L., and Miramontes, O.B. (1989). Perceived and actual linguistic competence: A descriptive study of four low-achieving Hispanic bilingual students. *American Educational Research Journal, 26*(4), 443-472.

Cook, H.G., and Linquanti, R. (2015). *Strengthening Policies and Practices for the Initial Classification of English Learners: Insights from a National Working Session*. Washington, DC: Council of Chief State School Officers.

Daily, S., Burkhauser, M., and Halle, T. (2010). A review of school readiness practices in the states: Early learning guidelines and assessments. *Child Trends, 1*(3), 1-12.

Darling-Hammond, L., Wilhoit, G., and Pittenger, L. (2014). Accountability for college and career readiness: Developing a new paradigm. *Education Policy Analysis Archives, 22*(86), 1-38.

Durán, R.P. (2008). Assessing English language learners' achievement In J. Green, A. Luke, and G. Kelly (Eds.), *Review of Research in Education* (vol. 32, pp. 292-327). Thousand Oaks, CA: SAGE.

Escamilla, K. (2006). Semilingualism applied to the literacy behaviors of Spanish-speaking emerging bilinguals: Bi-illiteracy or emerging biliteracy? *Teachers College Record, 108*(11), 2329-2353.

Espinosa, L.M. (2007). English-language learners as they enter school. In R. Pianta, M. Cox, and K. Snow (Eds.), *School Readiness and the Transition to Kindergarten in the Era of Accountability* (pp. 175-196). Baltimore, MD: Paul H. Brookes.

Espinosa, L.M. (2008). *Challenging Common Myths about Young English-Language Learners*. Policy Brief No. 8. New York: Foundation for Child Development.

Espinosa, L.M., and Calderon, M. (2015). *State Early Learning and Development Standards/Guidelines, Policies & Related Practices*. Boston, MA: Build Initiative.

Espinosa, L.M., and García, E. (2012). *Developmental Assessment of Young Dual Language Learners with a Focus on Kindergarten Entry Assessment: Implications for State Policies*. Working Paper No. 1: Chapel Hill: The University of North Carolina, FPG Child Development Institute, Center for Early Care and Education Research-Dual Language Learners.

Espinosa, L.M., and Gutiérrez-Clellen, V. (2013). Assessment of young dual language learners in preschool. In F. Ong and J. McLean (Eds.), *California's Best Practices for Dual Language Learners: Research Overview Papers* (pp. 172-208). Sacramento, CA: Governor's State Advisory Council on Early Learning and Care.

Espinosa, L.M., and López, M.L. (2007). *Assessment Considerations for Young English Language Learners across Different Levels of Accountability*. Washington, DC: Pew Charitable Trusts.

Francis, D.J., Rivera, M., Lesaux, N.K., Kieffer, M.J., and Rivera, H. (2006). *Practical Guidelines for the Education of English Language Learners: Research-Based Recommendations for the Use of Accommodations in Large-Scale Assessments*. Portsmouth, NH: Center on Instruction.

Fuligni, A.S., Guerra, A.W., Nelson, D., and Fuligni, A. (2013). *Early Child Care Use among Low-Income Latino Families: Amount, Type, and Stability Vary According to Bilingual Status. The Complex Picture of Child Care Use and Dual-Language Learners: Diversity of Families and Children's Experiences over Time.* Paper presented at the Biennial Meeting of the Society for Research in Child Development, Seattle, WA.

Fuller, B., Bein, E., Kim, Y., and Rabe-Hesketh, S. (2015). Differing cognitive trajectories of Mexican American toddlers: The role of class, nativity, and maternal practices. *Hispanic Journal of Behavioral Sciences*, 1-31.

García, E., Lawton, K., and Diniz de Figueiredo, E.H. (2010). *The Education of English Language Learners in Arizona: A Legacy of Persisting Achievement Gaps in a Restrictive Language Policy Climate.* Los Angeles: Civil Rights Project, University of California, Los Angeles.

Gottlieb, M. (2016). *Assessing English Language Learners: Bridges to Educational Equity: Connecting Academic Language Proficiency to Student Achievement.* Thousand Oaks, CA: Corwin Press.

Greenspan, S.I., and Meisels, S.J. (1996). Toward a new vision of developmental assessment of infants and young children. In S.J. Meisels and E. Fenichel (Eds.), *New Visions for the Developmental Assessment of Infants and Young Children* (pp. 11-26). Washington, DC: Zero To Three.

Gutiérrez-Clellen, V.F. (1999). Language choice in intervention with bilingual children. *American Journal of Speech-Language Pathology*, 8(4), 291-302.

Gutiérrez-Clellen, V.F., Restrepo, M.A., and Simon-Cereijido, G. (2006). Evaluating the discriminate accuracy of a grammatical measure with Spanish-speaking children. *Journal of Speech, Language and Hearing Research*, 49, 1209-1223.

Gutiérrez-Clellen, V.F, Simon-Cereijido, G., and Sweet, M. (2012). Predictors of second language acquisition in Latino children with specific language impairment. *American Journal of Speech-Language Pathology*, 21(1), 64-77.

Hammer, C.S., Scarpino, S., and Davison, M.D. (2011). Beginning with language: Spanish–English bilingual preschoolers' early literacy development. In D. Dickinson and S. Neuman (Eds.), *Handbook on Research in Early Literacy* (Vol. 3). New York: Guilford Publications.

Hauck, M.C., Wolf, M.K., and Mislevy, R. (2013). *Creating a Next-Generation System of K–12 English Learner (EL) Language Proficiency Assessments.* Princeton, NJ: Educational Testing Service.

Hauck, M.C., Wolf, M.K., and Mislevy, R. (2016). *Creating a Next-Generation System of K–12 English Learner Language Proficiency Assessments.* RR-16-06. Princeton, NJ: Educational Testing Service.

Heritage, M., Walqui, A., and Linquanti, R. (2015). *English Language Learners and the New Standards Developing Language, Content Knowledge, and Analytical Practices in the Classroom.* Cambridge, MA: Harvard Education Press.

Hernandez, D. (2006). *Young Hispanic Children in the U.S.: A Demographic Portrait Based on Census 2000. Report to the National Task Force on Early Childhood Education for Hispanics.* Tempe: Arizona State University.

Illinois Department of Education. (2013). *Early Language Development Standards.* Available: https://www.wida.us/standards/EarlyYears.aspx [December 2016].

Jiao, H., and Lissitz, R.W. (2015). *The Next Generation of Testing: Common Core Standards, Smarter-Balanced, PARCC, and the Nationwide Testing Movement.* Charlotte, NC: Information Age.

Kieffer, M.J., Rivera, M., and Francis, D.J. (2012). *Practical Guidelines for the Education of English Language Learners: Research-Based Recommendations for the Use of Accommodations in Large-Scale Assessments.* Portsmouth, NH: RMC Research Corporation, Center on Instruction.

Kopriva, R.J. (2008). *Improving Testing for English Language Learners.* New York: Routledge.

Kopriva, R.J., Thurlow, M.L., Perie, M., Lazarus, S.S., and Clark, A. (2016). Test takers and the validity of score interpretations. *Educational Psychologist, 51*(1), 108-128.

Koretz, D. (2008). *Measuring Up: What Educational Testing Really Tells Us.* Cambridge, MA: Harvard University Press.

Lane, S., and Leventhal, B. (2015). Psychometric challenges in assessing English language learners and students with disabilities. *Review of Research in Education, 39*(1), 165-214.

Lara, J., Ferrara, S., Calliope, M., Sewell, D., Winter, P., Kopriva, R., Bunch, M., and Joldersma, K. (2007). The English Language Development Assessment (ELDA). In J. Abedi (Ed.), *English Language Proficiency Assessment in the Nation: Current Status and Future Practice* (pp. 47-60). Davis: University of California.

Linquanti, R., and Cook, G. (2013). *Toward a "Common Definition of English Learner": Guidance for States and State Assessment Consortia in Defining and Addressing Policy and Technical Issues and Options.* Washington, DC: Council of Chief State School Officers.

Linquanti, R., and Cook, H.G. (2015). *Re-examining Reclassification: Guidance from a National Working Session on Policies and Practices for Exiting Students from English Learner Status.* Washington, DC: Council of Chief State School Officers.

Linquanti, R., Cook, H.G., Bailey, A., and MacDonald, R. (2016). *Moving Towards a More Common Definition of English Learner, Collected Guidance for States and Multi-State Assessment Consortia.* Washington, DC: Council of Chief State School Officers.

López, E. (2012). *Common Core State Standards and English Language Learners.* Portchester, NY: National Professional Resources.

MacSwan, J., and Mahoney, K. (2008). Academic bias in language testing: A construct validity critique of the IPT I Oral Grades K-6 Spanish Second Edition (IPT Spanish). *Journal of Educational Research & Policy Studies, 8*(2), 86-101.

MacSwan, J., and Rolstad, K. (2006). How language tests mislead us about children's abilities: Implications for special education placements. *Teachers College Record, 108*(11), 2304-2328.

MacSwan, J., Rolstad, K., and Glass, G.V. (2002). Do some school-age children have no language? Some problems of construct validity in the pre-LAS Español. *Bilingual Research Journal, 26*(2), 395-420.

Meisels, S.J. (1999). Assessing readiness. In R.C. Pianta and M.M. Cox (Eds.), *The Transition to Kindergarten* (pp. 39-66). Baltimore, MD: Paul H. Brookes.

Meisels, S.J. (2007). No easy answers: Accountability in early childhood. In R.C. Pianta, M.J. Cox, and K. Snow (Eds.), *School Readiness, Early Learning, and the Transition to Kindergarten* (pp. 31-48). Baltimore, MD: Paul H. Brookes.

Mislevy, R.J., and Durán, R.P. (2014). A sociocognitive perspective on assessing EL students in the age of common core and next generation science standards. *TESOL Quarterly, 48*(3), 560-585.

National Association for the Education of Young Children. (2005). *Screening and Assessment of Young English-Language Learners: Supplement to the NAEYC and NAECS/SDE Joint Position Statement on Early Childhood Curriculum, Assessment, and Program Evaluation.* Washington, DC: National Association for the Education of Young Children.

National Association for the Education of Young Children and National Association of Early Childhood Specialists in State Departments of Education. (2003). *Position Statement: Early Childhood Curriculum, Assessment, and Program Evaluation.* Washington, DC: National Association for the Education of Young Children.

National Research Council. (2008). *Early Childhood Assessment: Why, What, and How.* C.E. Snow and S.B. Van Hemel (Eds.). Division of Behavioral and Social Sciences and Education; Board on Children, Youth, and Families; Board on Testing and Assessment; Committee on Developmental Outcomes and Assessments for Young Children. Washington, DC: The National Academies Press.

National Research Council. (2011). *Allocating Federal Funds for State Programs for English Language Learners.* Division of Behavioral and Social Sciences and Education; Committee on National Statistics; Board on Testing and Assessment; Panel to Review Alternative Data Sources for the Limited-English Proficiency Allocation Formula under Title III, Part A, Elementary and Secondary Education Act. Washington, DC: The National Academies Press.

Neill, M. (2005). *Assessment of ELL Students under NCLB: Problems and Solutions.* Available: http://www.fairtest.org/sites/default/files/NCLB_assessing_bilingual_students_0.pdf [December 2016].

Noble, T., Rosebery, A., Suarez, C., Warren, B., and O'Connor, M.C. (2014). Science assessments and English language learners: Validity evidence based on response processes. *Applied Measurement in Education, 27*(4), 248-260.

Office of Head Start. (2015). *Head Start Early Learning Outcomes Framework: Birth to Five.* Washington, DC: U.S. Department of Health and Human Services, Administration for Children and Families.

Paradis, J., Genesee, F., and Crago, M.B. (2011). *Dual Language Development and Disorders: A Handbook on Bilingualism and Second Language Learning* (2nd ed.). Baltimore, MD: Paul H. Brookes.

Pearson, B.Z. (2002). Narrative competence among monolingual and bilingual school children in Miami. In D.K. Oller and R.E. Eilers (Eds.), *Language and Literacy in Bilingual Children* (pp. 135-174). Clevedon, UK: Multilingual Matters.

Peña, E.D., and Halle, T.G. (2011). Assessing preschool dual language learners: Traveling a multiforked road. *Child Development Perspectives, 5*(1), 28-32.

Portes, A., and Rumbaut, R.G. (2014). *Immigrant America: A Portrait.* Oakland, CA: University of California Press.

Pryor, J., and Crossouard, B. (2005). *A SocioCultural Theorization of Formative Assessment.* Paper presented at the Sociocultural Theory in Educational Research and Practice Conference, Brighton, UK.

Rivera, C., Acosta, B., and Shafer Willner, L. (2008). *Guide for Refining State Assessment Policies for Accommodating English Language Learners.* Washington, DC: The George Washington University Center for Equity and Excellence in Education.

Robinson-Cimpian, J.P., Thompson, K.D., and Umansky, I.M. (2016). Research and policy considerations for English learner equity. *Policy Insights from the Behavioral and Brain Sciences* [E-pub ahead of print].

Sarnecka, B.W., Wright, C.E., and Goldman, M.C. (2011). *Cross-Linguistic Associations in the Vocabularies of Bilingual Children: Number Words vs. Color Words and Common Nouns.* Paper presented at the Biennial Meeting of the Society for Research in Child Development, Montreal, Candada.

Shepard, L.A., Kagan, S.L., and Wurtz, E. (1998). *Principles and Recommendations for Early Childhood Assessments.* Washington, DC: National Education Goals Panel.

Sireci, S.G. (2005). Using bilinguals to evaluate the comparability of different language versions of a test. In R.K. Hambleton, P. Merenda, and C. Spielberger (Eds.), *Adapting Educational and Psychological Tests for Cross-Cultural Assessment* (pp. 117-138). Hillsdale, NJ: Lawrence Erlbaum Associates.

Sireci, S., Rios, J., and Powers, S. (2016). Comparing scores from tests administered in different languages. In N. Dorans and L. Cook (Eds.), *Fairness in Educational Assessment and Measurement* (pp. 181-202). New York: Routledge.

Solano-Flores, G. (2012). *Translation Accommodations Framework for Testing English Language Learners in Mathematics.* Los Angeles: University of California, Smarter Balanced Assessment Consortium (SBAC).

Solano-Flores, G. (2016). *Assessing English Language Learners: Theory and Practice.* New York: Routledge.

Solano-Flores, G., Trumbull, E., and Nelson-Barber, S. (2002). Concurrent development of dual language assessments: An alternative to translating tests for linguistic minorities. *International Journal of Testing, 2*(2), 107-129.

Solano-Flores, G., Wang, C., Kachchaf, R., Soltero-Gonzalez, L., and Nguyen-Le, K. (2014). Developing testing accommodations for English language learners: Illustrations as visual supports for item accessibility. *Educational Assessment, 19*(4), 267-283.

Stansfield, C.W. (2003). Test translation and adaptation in public education in the USA. *Language Testing, 20*(2), 189-207.

Stevens, G.G., and DeBord, K. (2001). Issues of assessment in testing children under age eight. *The Forum for Family and Consumer Issues, 6*(2).

Thompson, K.D. (2015). English learners' time to reclassification: An analysis. *Educational Policy.* Available: http://epx.sagepub.com/content/early/2015/09/23/0895904815598394.full.pdf [June 15, 2016].

Turkan, S, and Oliveri, M.E. (2014). *Considerations for Providing Test Translation Accommodations to English Language Learners on Common Core Standards-Based Assessments.* ETS Research Report No, RR-14-05 Princeton, NJ: Educational Testing Service.

Vagh, S.B., Pan, B.A., and Mancilla-Martinez, J. (2009). Measuring growth in bilingual and monolingual children's English productive vocabulary development: The utility of combining parent and teacher report. *Child Development, 80*(5), 1545-1563.

Young, J.W. (2009). A framework for test validity research on content assessments taken by English language learners. *Educational Assessment, 14*(3-4), 122-138.

12

Building the Workforce to Educate English Learners[1]

The science of child development reveals that children begin learning before birth, and their development is especially rapid during their early years (Institute of Medicine and National Research Council, 2015). As discussed in Chapter 4, the adults who interact with young children significantly influence their overall development, including their language ability. Consequently, the adults who make up the workforce that is responsible for the care and education of children bear a great responsibility for their health, development, and learning (Institute of Medicine and National Research Council, 2015). Further, the professional preparation and quality of teachers and educational administrators (principals, superintendents) is a variable that distinguishes between more and less effective schools (Lindholm-Leary, 2015). Among the many factors that affect student performance, research on all students strongly indicates that the quality of teachers has a significant impact on educational success (Ballantyne et al., 2008; Boyd et al., 2009; Loeb et al., 2014; Peske and Haycock, 2006; Samson and Collins, 2012).

This chapter addresses issues related to producing a well-prepared workforce to care for and educate children who are dual language learners (DLLs) and English learners (ELs).[2] The first section reviews the demographics of the workforce. The discussion then turns to federal policies,

---

[1] This chapter includes sections adapted from papers (Arias and Markos, 2016; Zepeda, 2015) commissioned by the committee for this report.

[2] When referring to children ages birth to 5 in their homes, communities, or early care and education programs, this report uses the term "dual language learners" or "DLLs." When referring to children ages 5 and older in the pre-K to 12 education system, the term "English

state certification requirements, competencies, preparation (including professional development), recruitment, and retention. Finally, issues related to school administrators and professional staff who provide school support services for DLL/ELs are discussed. The chapter ends with conclusions about this workforce that are linked with those in Chapters 10 and 11.

DEMOGRAPHICS

To address the needs of DLLs/ELs, policy makers, researchers, and organizations that set standards for competencies and practice need first to understand the existing composition and qualifications of the care and education professional (CEP) workforce for children from birth to 5 years of age and K-12 education professionals. This understanding is necessary to support the development of appropriate preservice programs for new educators and the design and provision of professional development for the current workforce.

To examine the CEP workforce, the committee used data from the National Survey of Early Care and Education (NSECE), a dataset collected on both center- and home-based care and education practitioners serving children birth to age 5 who are not yet in kindergarten (National Survey of Early Care and Education Project Team, 2013). Among the variables examined, the NSECE collected data regarding the age, gender, and ethnicity of and languages spoken by the current workforce. It found that 1 million and 3.8 million individuals, respectively—consisting of lead teachers, assistants, and aides—work in center-based child development centers and home-based settings.

With regard to the K-12 workforce, while the number of ELs and the associated teaching workforce both continue to grow, they are not aligned. The EL population constitutes 9.1 percent of the total K-12 student population, while English as a second language (ESL)/bilingual education (BLE) teachers[3] make up 2 percent of K-12 teachers (National Center for Education Statistics, 2013).

Educational Qualifications

A recent National Academies study examining the educational qualifications of the CEP workforce generated a recommendation that all lead educators of children from birth to age 8 have a minimum of a bachelor's

---

learners" or "ELs" is used. When referring to the broader group of children and adolescents aged birth to 21, the term "DLLs/ELs" is used.

[3] An ESL/BLE teacher is an individual who has earned a certification or license in the respective discipline.

degree, although the empirical evidence regarding the effects of this require-ment on child outcomes is inconclusive (Institute of Medicine and National Research Council, 2015). This requirement is particularly contentious as it is likely to affect the cultural and linguistic diversity of the CEP workforce. Some have argued that increasing the educational requirements for teach-ers may exclude currently employed teachers who share the ethnic and cultural diversity of the children they teach and who speak their languages (Bassok, 2013; Fuller et al., 2005). Others have found that with additional resources, these teachers can and do succeed in higher education (Sakai et al., 2014). Regardless of the debates about the value of a bachelor's degree for early educators (Zigler et al., 2011), policy makers at both the federal and state levels are requiring a minimum of a bachelor's degree with train-ing or certification in early childhood education for individuals working in the early care and education (ECE) field (Bueno et al., 2010). The 2007 reauthorization of Head Start mandated that by 2013, 50 percent of lead teachers possess a bachelor's degree in early childhood or a related field.[4]

According to the NSECE, 26 percent of center-based CEPs possessed a 4-year degree and 9 percent a graduate degree; however, data specific to members of the CEP workforce who care for and educate DLLs are not available. The distribution of college education varied by the age of children, with 45 percent of CEPs serving children ages 3-5 having a bach-elor's degree or higher, compared with 19 percent of those serving children birth to age 3 (National Survey of Early Care and Education Project Team, 2013). Home-based CEPs have a lower level of educational attainment, ranging from 16 to 19 percent with a bachelor's degree depending on whether they appear on state or national administrative lists of providers.

The Migration Policy Institute conducted an analysis of immigrants and refugees working in early childhood programs using the 2011-2013 American Community Survey from the U.S. Census Bureau. The researchers found that the educational attainment of home-based educators in the CEP workforce varied by setting and place of birth: 48 percent of immigrants and 38 percent of U.S.-born educators had less than a high school educa-tion (Park et al., 2015).

Home visitors are an expanding sector of the CEP workforce. Prior to the Maternal, Infant, and Early Childhood Home Visiting (MIECHV) Program, home visitation was provided through Early Head Start and other home visiting programs funded by federal agencies and private foundations. In 2007, Congress mandated a study of the status of DLLs participating in Head Start and Early Head Start (Administration for Children and Fami-lies, 2013). Of the 136 home visitors included in the report, 47 percent possessed a bachelor's degree or higher, 43 percent had 5 or more years

---

[4]Head Start Act of 2007, 42 U.S.C. 9843a § 648A (2)(A).

of experience, and 64.2 percent had received specialized training in early childhood.

In general, teachers and home visitors working with DLLs in Early Head Start had different educational profiles from those working with monolingual English-speaking children. The congressionally mandated report notes that "DLLs in home-based Early Head Start programs had home visitors who were less likely than home visitors for children from monolingual English homes to have received any college degree" (Administration for Children and Families, 2013, p. 69). The authors suggest that this difference may be due to Head Start's efforts to match the language and ethnicity/race of staff to the child population being served. More recently, the Mother and Infant Home Visiting Program Evaluation (MIHOPE) reviewed four MIECHV programs and produced information about the qualifications of home visitors (Michalopoulos et al., 2015). That evaluation found that 75 percent of home visitors and 98 percent of supervisors possessed a bachelor's degree or higher, which presents a different picture from that found for Early Head Start.

According to 2013 public school data from the National Center for Education Statistics (NCES), all primary public school ESL/BLE teachers have a minimum of a bachelor's degree (National Center for Education Statistics, 2013). Meanwhile, 8 percent of secondary school ESL/BLE teachers have less than a bachelor's degree—almost double the percentage of total secondary school teachers (4.4%) who lack a bachelor's degree. The percentages of ESL/BLE primary school teachers and all primary school teachers who have a master's degree or higher (53.8% and 55.4%, respectively) are comparable. A slightly higher percentage of ESL/BLE secondary school teachers have a master's degree or higher relative to all secondary school teachers (62.5% and 57.2%, respectively). With regard to experience, the majority of both primary and secondary ESL/BLE teachers have 3-9 years of teaching experience (44.7% and 41.4%, respectively). These percentages are higher than the 33.3 percent of all school teachers with the same amount of teaching experience.

Ethnic, Racial, and Linguistic Diversity

Since the ethnic, racial, and linguistic diversity of educators has been shown to affect student outcomes, it is important to consider these factors (Villegas and Irvine, 2010; Zepeda et al., 2011). The NCES data show that ELs in grades K-12 are most likely to have a general education teacher who is a white female ages 30-39. Based on a literature review, Villegas and Irvine (2010) concluded that well-qualified teachers of color can positively influence the learning experiences of students of color, as well as help alleviate the shortage of teachers in schools with high minority populations.

Although some research suggests that effective teachers in general are also effective teachers of ELs and that having foreign language skills and bilingual certification adds only a small increment to teacher effectiveness (Loeb et al., 2014), research in general shows that ELs are better able to transfer their knowledge and skills from their first language (L1) to English when the L1 is spoken in the classroom; therefore, educators who speak both their students' L1 and English may be more capable of helping them improve their social and educational outcomes (Castro et al., 2013; Chang et al., 2007; Loeb et al., 2014). In contrast to the primary school workforce, studies show that one-third to one-half of the CEP workforce comprises women of color (Whitebook, 2014), who are potentially better able to understand the cultures and languages of DLLs if appropriately matched.

According to the MPI report cited earlier, an analysis of the languages spoken by the CEP workforce found that fewer than 25 percent of these professionals spoke a language other than English. However, home-based CEPs had a higher degree of cultural and linguistic commonality with the children they taught relative to preschool teachers and program directors. The vast majority of individuals speaking languages other than English worked in home-based settings and were likely foreign-born. Spanish was the most common language spoken, followed by Mandarin and Cantonese (Park et al., 2015). Since, as pointed out by Park and colleagues, much of the CEP workforce's linguistic and cultural diversity is found in occupations with extremely low wages, the field's existing demographic characteristics present unique challenges for the educational and professional development of this segment of the CEP workforce. (For a discussion of the quality of care in informal family-based programs, which is generally lower than that in center-based programs, see Chapter 7 [Espinosa et al., 2013].)

With regard to the home visitor sector of the CEP workforce, MIHOPE found that the majority of both supervisors and home visitors described themselves as non-Hispanic white (Michalopoulos et al., 2015). In contrast, in the 2007 congressionally mandated study of Head Start and Early Head Start, 73 percent of 136 home visitors self-identified as Hispanic, with the next largest group self-identifying as non-Hispanic white (16.7%). Data on what languages these home visitors and supervisors spoke are not available for either the congressionally mandated study or MIHOPE.

In the pre-K to 12 grades, nearly 50 percent of the student population comprises students of color, while more than 80 percent of teachers are white. A recent study conducted out of the Brown Center on Education Policy at Brookings (Putman et al., 2016) investigated the potential for reducing this gap. The researchers examined four points along the teaching pipeline in which there can be "leaks": attending and completing college, interest and/or majoring in education, hiring practices, and persistence in teaching beyond a year. The results showed that achieving greater diversity in the education workforce would require changing both the college completion rates of black and Hispanic students and spurring increased interest in pursuing a teaching career (Putman et al., 2016). It should be noted that this study specifically looked at how to address gaps in racial/ethnic matching and did not take into account linguistic matching, which also needs to be addressed. Given the current shortage of teachers prepared to teach DLLs/ELs, it is important that all teachers who instruct these children be trained to work with them.

FEDERAL POLICIES

Although a number of professional organizations (Council for the Accreditation of Educator Preparation, 2013; National Association for the Education of Young Children, 2012) that oversee teacher preparation programs and the accreditation of early childhood programs pay some attention to DLLs, federal, state, and local requirements governing the licensing and certification of individuals working with infants, toddlers, and preschoolers seldom do. To varying degrees, federal funding regulates and guides the requirements for educators and home visitors in the Head Start program, the MIECHV program, Military Child Care, and the Child Care and Development Block Grant. Guidance and regulations on serving DLLs across programs such as Head Start, for example, require that every classroom in which the majority of children speak a language other than English have a staff member who can speak that language (Administration for Children and Families, 2013).

With respect to ELs, the U.S. Department of Justice and the U.S. Department of Education (2015) have stated:

> School districts have an obligation to provide the personnel and resources necessary to effectively implement their chosen EL programs. This obligation includes having highly qualified teachers to provide language assistance services, trained administrators who can evaluate these teachers, and adequate and appropriate materials for the EL programs. At a minimum, every school district is responsible for ensuring that there is an adequate number of teachers to instruct EL students and that these teachers have mastered the skills necessary to effectively teach in the district's program for EL students.

In the Every Student Succeeds Act (ESSA) of 2015, Title II explicitly mentions ELs and expectations for teacher development plans and programs. ESSA replaces the term "highly qualified" with the term "effective," defined as teachers who meet the applicable state certification and licensure requirements, including any requirements for certification obtained through alternative routes to certification or, with regard to special education teachers, the qualifications described in Section 612(a)(14)(C) of the Individuals with Disabilities Education Act (20 U.S.C. 1412(a)(14)(C)).

STATE CERTIFICATION REQUIREMENTS

Each state sets its own policies regarding employment qualifications for ECE professionals in both the public and private sectors, except for Head Start and Military Child Care, whose requirements are set by the federal government (Institute of Medicine and National Research Council, 2015). In public and private preschools, about 25 percent of teachers meet state licensing requirements. Within state-funded pre-K programs, certification, licensure, or endorsement is required.

Similarly, each state has its own requirements for K-12 teacher certification. Some states have established criteria at the preservice level, while others have specialist requirements beyond initial certification. Although all 50 states plus the District of Columbia offer a certificate in teaching ESL,[5] López and colleagues (2013) identify only 21 states that require a specialized certification to teach ELs and only 20 states that require all teachers to have knowledge specific to the education of ELs. The authors identify 7 states that have no requirements for certification or specific knowledge to teach ELs and 12 states that have preservice teacher requirements only for ESL/BLE specialists. The findings of this study demonstrate the uneven range of knowledge and skills required by each state. Additionally, according to a recent report, all 50 states plus the District of Columbia require teachers who provide instruction in English to establish that they are fluent in English, while only 39 states require that teachers who teach in a language other than English establish that they are fluent in that language (U.S. Department of Education, 2016). The issue of preparing teachers to educate ELs effectively is especially salient for states with large populations of ELs and those with increasing numbers of such students.

The following tables review state requirements for preparation of EL teachers through two lenses: states with the largest populations of ELs and those with the fastest-growing percentages of ELs. Table 12-1 identifies the 10 states most impacted by EL enrollment based on the percentages of ELs. The row for the United States provides totals for each column for all 50 states and the District of Columbia. (See Appendix B for data on all 50 states and the District of Columbia.)

Across the nation, more than 340,000 teachers are EL certified/licensed teachers working in Title III programs. Three of the 10 states with the

---

[5] 2009-2010 data from the National Comprehensive Center on Teacher Quality. Available: http://www.gtlcenter.org/sites/default/files/docs/CertificationandLicensureforTeachersofELLs.pdf [February 23, 2017].

highest percentages of ELs estimate a need for more than 15,000 certified EL teachers in the next 5 years; Nevada will require more than 16,000, an increase of 590 percent. The majority of the 10 states require teachers of ELs to have a specialist (ESL or BLE) certificate/license to work with ELs. With regard to certification and licensure, Table 12-1 shows that all 10 states offer an ESL or BLE certificate or license. It also shows that despite the large percentages of ELs in these states, only California and Florida require that all teachers complete minimal coursework in methods of teaching ELs.

In addition to ESL/BLE teachers, there is a need for ESL/BLE teacher aides, especially those who are trained to support academic learning. In 2011-2012, the average ratio of ELs to Title III teachers for the top 10 states with the fastest-growing EL populations was 66:1; the average ratio of ELs to ESL/BLE teacher aides was 36:1. Thus, in many states with the fastest-growing populations of ELs, an EL is more likely to work with an aide than a Title III teacher (see Table 12-2), and aides may not have formal qualifications to instruct children in language and content learning. (Appendix C contains student and teacher data for all 50 states and the District of Columbia.) These ratios clearly demonstrate a shortage of both Title III qualified teachers and ESL/BLE teacher aides (see Table 12-2).

From these data, the committee concludes that the variations in state policies regarding teacher qualifications to instruct ELs result in variations in the preparation and supply of teachers and aides available to work with ELs. As highlighted in the Brookings report (Putman et al., 2016), these variations indicate the need to consider policies on the preparation of high-quality teachers for this population, as well as measures to encourage novice or beginning teachers to enter this workforce.

COMPETENCIES

Some of the most influential factors in high-quality and effective practices for DLLs/ELs are the knowledge, skills, and expertise of the CEPs working with them. For children in the early grades, teacher effectiveness—defined as achieving best outcomes for children—has been identified as one of the most important variables in their achievement (García and García, 2012). There has been some development and delineation of specific educator competencies for serving DLLs/ELs (California Department of Education and First 5 California, 2011; López et al., 2012; Zepeda et al., 2011). Professional organizations and researchers have concluded that to be effective educators of these children and youth, educators need to be knowledgeable in six major content areas (Association for Childhood Education International, n.d.; Espinosa, 2013; National Association for the Education of Young Children, 2009; Zepeda et al., 2011):

TABLE 12-1 Teacher Certification: 10 States with the Highest Percentages of English Learners in 2013-2014

	2013-2014 Number of Certified/Licensed Title III Teachers[a]	Additional Certified/Licensed Title III Teachers Needed in the Next 5 Years[a]	Percent Increase in Number of Certified/Licensed Title III Teachers Needed	State Offers ESL Certificate/License[b]	State Offers BLE Certificate/License[b]	State Requires All Teachers to Complete Coursework in Methods of Teaching ELs[b]	State Requires Teachers to Obtain a Specialist (ESL/BLE) Certificate/License[c]
United States	346,715	82,380	24	51	27	5	21
California	203,395	17,104	8	Yes	Yes	Yes	Yes
Texas	24,654	13,297	54	Yes	Yes	No	Yes
Nevada	2,733	16,111	590	Yes	Yes	No	Yes
New Mexico	2,887	500	17	Yes	Yes	No	No
Colorado	7,487	1,500	20	Yes	Yes	No	Yes
Alaska	56	173	309	Yes	Yes	No	No
District of Columbia	89	345	388	Yes	Yes	No	No
Washington	1,193	2,232	187	Yes	Yes	No	Yes
Illinois	8,760	15,895	181	Yes	Yes	No	Yes
Florida	49,654	0	0	Yes	Yes	Yes	No

NOTE: BLE = bilingual education; EL = English learner; ESL = English as a second language.
[a]National Clearinghouse for English Language Acquisition (NCELA) Title III State Profiles. Available: http://www.ncela.us/t3sis/index.php.
[b]National Comprehensive Center for Teacher Quality (2009).
[c]López et al., 2013, Table A1. It should be noted that some states, such as Florida, utilize endorsements rather than certification/licensure.
SOURCE: Arias and Markos (2016.)

- understanding the structural aspects of language development (e.g., syntax, phonology) and the development of both L1 and the second language (English) (L2);
- understanding the role of culture and its linkage to language development;
- acquiring knowledge and developing skills with respect to effective instructional practices for promoting development and learning in DLLs/ELs;
- understanding the role of assessment and how to implement appropriate assessment strategies with DLLs/ELs;
- understanding the teacher's role as a professional in the education of DLLs/ELs; and
- understanding how to engage families.

TABLE 12-2 English Learners and Teachers and Teacher Aides with Formal Qualifications to Teach Them, States with the Fastest-Growing Populations of English Learners, 2011-2012

State	Number of ELs Receiving Services[a]	Number of Title III Teachers[a]	Number of ESL/BLE Teacher Aides[b]	Teacher-to-Student Ratio	Teacher Aide-to-Student Ratio
South Carolina	35,369	512	640	69	55
Mississippi	5,617	71	310	79	18
North Dakota	3,562	70	120	51	30
Kentucky	18,579	176	620	106	30
Kansas	35,082	211	1,020	166	34
Delaware	6,741	153	110	44	61
Arkansas	29,920	2,215	490	14	61
West Virginia	1,829	37	90	49	20
Maryland	55,957	1,272	NA	44	NA
Maine	4,014	105	300	38	13
Average for these 10 states				66	36

NOTE: BLE = bilingual education; EL = English learner; ESL = English as a second language.
[a]Consolidated State Performance Reports (CSPRs) for 2011-2012, available at http://www2.ed.gov/admins/lead/account/consolidated/index.html [February 23, 2017].
[b]2011-2012 School and Staffing Survey, available at https://nces.ed.gov/surveys/sass/tables/sass1112_2013312_s2s_005.asp [February, 23, 2017].
SOURCE: Arias and Markos (2016).

Additionally, a recent review of the literature on the workforce competencies important for CEPs working with DLLs (Zepeda, 2015, pp. 23-33) identifies 10 areas of knowledge and skills important for professionals who work with culturally and linguistically diverse children:

- understanding the relationship between early brain development and language development;
- understanding the different ways in which young children become bilingual and the fact that L2 acquisition takes time;
- recognizing that switching between languages is a normal part of bilingualism and not a sign of confusion;
- understanding how to support oral language development in both L1 and L2;
- conducting assessments in both L1 and L2 and ensuring that assessors understand children's L1 and are familiar with their culture;
- for particular age ranges, understanding and identifying appropriate pedagogical strategies;
- understanding how culture permeates all human activity, including parent-child interactions, and appreciating that parents may have different priorities for child growth and development than those of the wider culture;
- recognizing that children's L1 is the medium through which they learn about the values and beliefs of their culture;
- understanding that families actively respond to the individual circumstances in which they live and organize their environments in a meaningful way; and
- recognizing how personal motivation and commitment influence actions taken toward DLLs.

Likewise, consensus has emerged regarding the competencies needed by K-12 teachers to work with ELs. Three studies have identified teacher competencies over the past 15 years: Lucas et al. (2008), Markos (2011), and Menken and Antunez (2001).

Knowledge areas identified by Menken and Antunez (2001) as being critical for teachers of ELs are (1) knowledge of pedagogy, (2) knowledge of linguistics, and (3) knowledge of cultural and linguistic diversity. In a survey of postsecondary institutions offering teacher preparation programs, however, the authors found that fewer than one-sixth of them required EL-oriented content in their preparation of mainstream teachers (teachers of general education or content areas, such as mathematics, science, English, and social studies).

Lucas and colleagues (2008) conclude that for ELs, the process of learning English is interwoven with their academic content learning. They propose a set of six key knowledge points for teachers of ELs:

1. Conversational language proficiency is fundamentally different from academic language proficiency (Cummins, 1981, 2000), and it can take many more years for an EL to become fluent in the latter relative to the former (Cummins, 2008).
2. Learners of an L2 must have access to comprehensible input that is just beyond their current level of competence (Krashen, 1982, 2003), and they must have opportunities to produce output for meaningful purposes (Swain, 1995).
3. Social interaction in which ELs participate actively fosters the development of conversational and academic English (Gass, 1997; Vygotsky, 1978; Wong-Fillmore and Snow, 2005).
4. ELs with strong L1 skills are more likely than those with weak L1 skills to achieve parity with native-English-speaking peers (Cummins, 2000; Thomas and Collier, 2002).
5. A safe, welcoming classroom environment in which ELs experience minimal anxiety about performing in an L2 is essential for them to learn (Krashen, 2003; Pappamihiel, 2002; Verplaetse and Migliacci, 2008).
6. Explicit attention to linguistic form and function is essential to L2 learning (Gass, 1997; Schleppegrell, 2004; Swain, 1995).

Because ELs take longer to achieve proficiency in academic English relative to others at the same grade level who are already English-proficient, teachers must adapt instructional methods to meet their needs (Lucas et al., 2008). Therefore, Lucas and colleagues (2008, p. 366) also suggest that all teachers need "pedagogical expertise in familiarity with the students' linguistic and academic backgrounds; an understanding of the language demands inherent in the learning tasks that students are expected to carry out in class; and skills for using appropriate scaffolding so that [ELs] can participate successfully in those tasks." A classroom-based practicum experience can help develop these skills.

Combining the outcomes of the above two studies, Markos (2011) conducted a literature review synthesizing the "critical areas of knowledge" (Menken and Antunez, 2001) with the "essential understandings" (Lucas et al., 2008) and other qualities, knowledge, and skills to identify themes in the preparation of EL teachers. She identifies five themes: (1) experience with language diversity, (2) a positive attitude toward linguistic diversity, (3) knowledge related to ELs, (4) knowledge of L2 acquisition, and (5) skills for simultaneously promoting content and language learning. For a summary of the literature, see Table 12-3.

PREPARATION

Researchers have produced policy and practice recommendations regarding the preparation of educators working with DLLs/ELs (Castro et al., 2013; Samson and Collins, 2012; Samson and Lesaux, 2015). Among them are (1) leadership at the federal, state, and local levels to make the education of DLLs/ELs a priority; (2) clearer guidance from regulatory and accrediting agencies overseeing teacher certification and licensure addressing the learning needs of DLLs/ELs; (3) better coordination between the birth-5 and K-12 sectors regarding expectations for student learning; and (4) increased capacity of higher education institutions to prepare teachers to work effectively with DLLs/ELs. Three areas that are particularly salient for preparation of this educational workforce, discussed in turn below, are the capacity of higher education institutions to equip future educators to address the needs of DLLs/ELs, alternative routes to teacher preparation, and professional development approaches for those already in the classroom.

Teacher Preparation in Higher Education

Recent analyses have examined preparation programs for early childhood teachers in institutions of higher education given criticism that these programs relied on outdated content and provided inadequate experience in working with children (Bruder and Dunst, 2005). In their analysis of what constitutes critical components of preservice education, Zaslow and colleagues (2011) point out the need for a reconceptualization of teacher preparation that more directly incorporates knowledge-focused with practice-focused components. More specifically with respect to DLLs/ELs, Castro and colleagues (2013, p. 11) report that no strategic plan has been developed for preparing the early childhood workforce "to acquire competencies to foster the language and literacy development of young bilingual children."

As institutions of higher education confront the challenge of equipping the next generation of educators to instruct DLLs/ELs effectively, it will be important to consider the content of coursework offered, as well as the faculty teaching the courses and supervising classroom practice. For ELs to receive effective education in kindergarten through grade 12, teachers need to be knowledgeable in an array of curricular and instructional methods that differ from those needed to instruct English-only students (Ballantyne et al., 2008), although, as suggested by Loeb and colleagues (2014), this might only add a small increment in teacher effectiveness. In a recent analysis of California's educators of early childhood teachers, Austin and colleagues (2015) found that they reported a need for professional develop-

TABLE 12-3 Summary of the Literature Concerning the Qualities, Knowledge, and Skills All Teachers Need to Teach English Learners (ELs) Effectively

	de Jong and Harper (2005)	Gandara and Maxwell-Jolly (2006)	Lucas and Grinberg (2008)	Lucas et al. (2008)	Merino (2007)	Milk et al. (1992)	Mora (2000)	Téllez and Waxman (2005)	Walqui (2008)	Walker et al. (2004)
Experience with Language Diversity										
Study of a foreign language			X				X			
Contact with people who speak languages other than English			X							
Field experience with ELs			X	X					X	
A Positive Attitude Toward Linguistic Diversity										
Acceptance of the responsibility for educating ELs	X	X	X			X				X
An affirming view of linguistic diversity and bilingualism		X	X	X			X	X		X
Awareness of sociopolitical dimensions	X		X			X			X	
Inclination to collaborate with colleagues		X	X		X	X	X			
EL-Related Knowledge										
Connections among language, culture, and identity			X		X			X		

Knowledge of students (backgrounds, experiences, and proficiencies)		X	X	X		X	X
Understanding of families/communities of ELs		X	X			X	X
Creation of a learning environment that promotes a low affective filter	X	X	X			X	X
Knowledge of L2 Acquisition							
Differences and similarities between L1 and L2 development		X	X			X	X
Language forms, mechanics, and uses	X	X	X		X	X	X
Role of L1 literacy in developing L2	X	X	X	X	X	X	X
Skills for Simultaneously Promoting Content and Language Instruction							
Skills for designing instruction that helps ELs learn both content and language	X	X	X	X	X	X	X
Skills for understanding and implementing assessments to inform instruction and monitor progress	X	X	X	X	X	X	
Skills for collaboration with colleagues	X			X		X	X

SOURCE: Arias and Markos (2016).

ment in a number of areas, including training in working with ethnically and linguistically diverse students. Faculty at institutions of higher education awarding associate's degrees also noted a lack of institutional expertise regarding pedagogical practice centered on DLLs/ELs.

In their analysis of 226 colleges and universities offering bachelor's degrees in early childhood education (pre-K to grade 3), Ray and colleagues (2006) found that although programs indicated an interest in the needs of children with diverse ethnic, cultural, and linguistic backgrounds and DLLs/ELs, very few hours of such coursework were offered. The authors concluded that preparation programs for early childhood teachers delivered little content and practicum experiences to prospective teachers of these populations. Indeed, fewer than 15 percent of such programs—ranging from those leading to certificates, such as a child development associate, to those at the master's degree level—required coursework on teaching DLLs/ELs (Maxwell et al., 2006).

In her analysis of how institutions of higher education can increase their capacity to educate teachers in working with DLLs/ELs, Freedson (2010) notes the need to diversify these faculty with respect to their ethnic, cultural, and linguistic backgrounds. The National Prekindergarten Center's survey of early childhood teacher preparation in 2- and 4-year institutions of higher education found that approximately 80 percent of faculty were white non-Hispanic (Maxwell et al., 2006). One possible advantage of diversifying these higher education faculty is that students may be more likely to have increased cultural awareness of and tolerance for people of different races/cultures and with different beliefs (Hurtado, 2001). Further, a positive correlation has been found between the presence of nonwhite faculty in a teacher preparation program and coursework related to cultural diversity (Lim et al., 2009). However, it is unlikely that the diversification of teacher preparation faculty will occur in the short or immediate term given the challenges of building a diverse teaching workforce (Putman et al., 2016).

Important differences exist in principal and teacher demographics, training, and experience between schools with high and low numbers of ELs. In the former schools, for example, teachers were found to be more likely to have provisional, emergency, or temporary certification, and new teachers were more likely to be uncertified than teachers in schools with a less diverse population of students (de Cohen et al., 2005; New Leaders, 2013). Conversely, in schools with low numbers of ELs, specialized services for these students and relevant in-service training for mainstream teachers were less available than in schools with large numbers of ELs. In highly effective schools serving ELs, teachers had the following characteristics (Howard et al., 2007; López et al., 2013; Williams et al., 2007):

- They were certified to work with ELs, having completed required coursework in English language development (ELD) and assessment.
- In bilingual programs, they had high levels of language proficiency in students' L1 and were able to use it in their instruction.
- They demonstrated the ability to use assessment data to raise student achievement.
- They were familiar with state standards, able to align instruction with curriculum standards, had strong content knowledge, and had training in curriculum development.
- They were supportive of a collegial atmosphere for learning and improvement.
- They were familiar with the students' communities.
- They demonstrated a deep interest in and commitment to teaching.[6]

Despite policies in place to regulate the teaching of ELs, more than 70 percent of teachers had inadequate preparation to be effective with ELs (Ballantyne et al., 2008). Teachers surveyed reported that the largest gap in their training was in methods for instructing and assessing ELs (Herrera and Murry, 2006). A study in California (Gándara et al., 2005) found that most teachers who taught ELs felt they were not well prepared to meet their students' needs. Additional research likewise found that without specific training in educating ELs, teachers were not adequately prepared to teach these students (Ballantyne et al., 2008; López et al., 2013; Menken and Antunez, 2001; Zehler et al., 2003). Further, López and colleagues (2013, p. 19) found that "states requiring ESL or bilingual certification were associated with markedly higher achievement for Hispanic ELs."

Although teacher candidates may choose a specialty area such as ESL or BLE, the larger concern is preparing all teachers to work with a diverse population of students (National Research Council, 2010). As content or subject-matter experts, mainstream teachers have the responsibility to help ELs learn academic content. They also contribute to ELs' English language development by the ways in which they teach these subjects. The Common Core State Standards place responsibility for literacy development in the content areas, including science, social studies, and math, so that the language and literacy needs of students are addressed not only by ESL and English language arts teachers, but also by teachers in all other content areas. Some have proposed that all mainstream teachers be required to take a minimum of one course specifically dedicated to teaching ELs (López et al., 2013; Lucas et al., 2008). Recommended classes include instructional

---

[6]Portions of this section were adapted from a paper (Lindholm-Leary, 2015) commissioned by the committee for this report.

methods and the use of curriculum and materials specific to bilingual education programs; linguistics and language learning, including L1 literacy; academic language; formative assessment; and cultural diversity (López et al., 2013; Menken and Antunez, 2001; Samson and Collins, 2012).

Preparing teachers to instruct ELs effectively requires not only providing relevant coursework but also giving prospective teachers supervised classroom experiences with students from diverse cultures and languages and with different levels of academic learning (García et al., 2010; Hollins and Crockett, 2012; Lucas et al., 2008; Talbert-Johnson, 2006). García and colleagues (2010) call for partnerships between universities and school districts with EL communities to enable teacher candidates to apply the pedagogical knowledge acquired through coursework in the classroom with students who are culturally and linguistically diverse.

Alternative Teacher Preparation Programs

Alternative routes to teaching have increased as the result of a teacher shortage declared in the mid-1980s (Humphrey and Wechsler, 2007; Madkins, 2011). The Education Commission of the States (ECS) recently reported that overall, the nation is unlikely to be experiencing teacher shortages; however, it is still difficult to fill teaching positions in urban, rural, high-poverty, and low-achieving schools and schools with high proportions of black and Hispanic/Latino students—schools that many ELs attend (Aragon, 2016). Recent estimates suggest that approximately 20 percent of newly hired teachers were prepared in alternative certification programs (DeMonte, 2015). Alternative programs vary considerably in training approaches and content (Woods, 2016a). Three such programs are described below.

One well-known alternative program, Teach For America (TFA), is designed for individuals who have a bachelor's degree and may be working in a noneducational field. It begins with a 10-week summer institute training program for teacher candidates involving both practice and instructional components. Participants then partner with a manager of teacher leadership and development, who, along with TFA regional staff, provides coaching and mentorship once participants begin teaching. Teachers attend professional development sessions throughout the year, are committed to teaching for 2 years, and are teachers of record from the start. As such, they receive a first-year teacher's salary and benefits (Teach For America, 2016).

A second type of alternative preparation program for individuals with a bachelor's degree is the teacher residency program, which is built on the medical residency model. Individuals participate in an in-school residency for 1 year, co-teaching with a mentor while completing master's-level coursework. Residents receive feedback from their mentors, program staff, and administrators as they practice and refine their skills and knowledge in classrooms. These programs are generally offered in high-need school districts. After this first year, residents become the teacher of record at the school where they completed their residency. Upon completion of their residency, they acquire state certification and a master's degree (National Center for Teacher Residencies, n.d.; see García [2016] for an example).

Another option, Grow Your Own programs, is a collection of initiatives across the United States in which communities partner with institutions of higher education and school districts to give paraprofessionals and community members in low-income communities, including high school students ready to graduate, the opportunity to become teachers. While most alternative certificate programs require that the candidate possess a bachelor's degree before entering the program, Grow Your Own does not. The aim is to have teachers who reflect the demography of students in low-income areas and because of their backgrounds, may be more likely to teach in schools serving low-income students. Illinois began such a program by passing the Grow Your Own Teachers Act in 2004 (Grow Your Own Teachers, 2016). Another successful model of such a program is the California Teacher Pathway program (Darling-Hammond et al., 2016).

Relative to traditional teacher training programs, alternative programs such as those described above recruit and prepare a more ethnically diverse group of candidates more closely reflecting the student population who commit to teaching in high-need areas (Grow Your Own Teachers, 2016; Urban Teacher Residency United, 2014; Woods, 2016a). In the Minneapolis Teacher Residency program, for example, 40 percent of the first class of teacher residents are bilingual, and 75 percent are people of color. In the Illinois Grow Your Own program, 84 percent of the candidates are people of color (García, 2016; Grow Your Own Teachers, 2016). In Illinois, more than 40 percent of Grow Your Own teachers teach bilingual or special education. And more than 50 percent of graduates of the National Center for Teacher Residency network program teach in secondary math or science, special education, or other classrooms with ELs (Grow Your Own Teachers, 2016; Urban Teacher Residency United, 2014).

At the same time, however, the variation among alternative teacher training programs raises questions about their capacity to produce effective teachers in the numbers required by the growing population of ELs (Humphrey and Wechsler, 2007; Putman et al., 2016). Proponents of alternative pathways to teacher certification claim that these programs can help alleviate the teacher shortage in difficult-to-fill areas by decreasing the time, expense, and coursework needed to become a certified teacher. On the other hand, critics suggest that teachers prepared through alternative programs are not as qualified as those prepared through traditional, university-based programs (Clark et al., 2013).

Research on this issue has produced mixed results (Constantine et al., 2009). One study examining New York City public school teachers found that the route taken by individuals into teaching had at most small effects on their students' reading and math performance (Kane et al., 2008). Another study focused on New York City schools found that certain features of alternative programs, such as a capstone requirement, positively affected student outcomes (Boyd et al., 2009). A study that evaluated the Boston Teacher Residency (BTR) program revealed that new BTR graduates were significantly less effective than other novice Boston Public School teachers in raising students' test scores in math. By their fourth and fifth years of teaching, however, BTR graduates were significantly more effective than other Boston Public School teachers in this same category (Papay et al., 2012). The Institute of Education Sciences sponsored two large, multi-state random assignment studies evaluating the effectiveness of alternative programs compared with traditional programs based on mathematics and reading scores. The researchers found no difference in outcomes related to the preparation pathway. The exception was TFA secondary math teachers, who were shown to be more effective than teachers prepared in traditional higher education programs (Clark et al., 2013).

With regard to preparing effective teachers to address the needs of ELs, the literature points to various alternative programs across the United States that researchers believe show promise (Flores et al., 2002; Osterling and Buchanan, 2003; Skinner, 2010). However, research on the impact of these programs on student outcomes is at an early stage. More research is needed to understand fully which programs and program features produce the most effective teachers of ELs.

Professional Development

In ESSA, professional development is defined as activities that

(A) are an integral part of school and local educational agency strategies for providing educators (including teachers, administrators, other school leaders, specialized instructional support personnel, paraprofessionals, and, as applicable, early childhood educators) with the knowledge and skills necessary to enable students to succeed in a well-rounded education and to meet the challenging State academic standards; and

(B) are sustained (not stand-alone, 1-day, or short term workshops), intensive, collaborative, job-embedded, data-driven, and classroom-focused[7]

Under ESSA, grants will be awarded through the National Professional Development Project to qualified organizations, in association with state

---

[7]ESSA Public Law No. 114-95 (2015). sec. 8002, no. 42 (a) (b).

or local education agencies, to provide professional development to aid teachers and other education staff who work with ELs in meeting high professional standards, including standards for certification and licensure, and in improving classroom instruction for ELs.[8]

The education field has seen a paradigm shift away from the notion that knowledge gained in college courses transfers to pedagogical practice once the teacher is in the classroom. The new paradigm focuses on pedagogical practice through positive modeling of teacher-student interaction, with opportunities for observation, feedback, and reflection (Howes and Tsao, 2012; U.S. Department of Education, 2010). Research on professional development approaches has led to general agreement that effective professional development for working with ELs requires a sustained, intensive approach that includes modeling of effective instructional methodologies that integrate academic content with English language proficiency instruction and involves actual classroom practice, coaching and mentoring, reflective practice, and communities of learning (August and Shanahan, 2006; Calderon et al., 2011; Darling-Hammond and Richardson, 2009; DiCerbo et al., 2014; National Education Association, 2011; Neuman and Kamil, 2010; Wei et al., 2009).

Unlike the K-12 workforce, in which preparation for teaching involves first taking formal coursework at a college or university for an associate's or bachelor's degree prior to working with children, the majority of the birth-5 workforce often takes formal educational coursework concurrently with working with children (Whitebook, 2014). Thus, both preservice and in-service professional learning opportunities often occur simultaneously for the ECE workforce.

Efforts are being made to develop unique professional development approaches for CEPs serving DLLs, as well as to modify existing approaches. For example, a professional development model specifically developed for teachers who work with Spanish-speaking preschool children, the Nuestros Niños School Readiness Program, uses a combination of 3-day institutes, systematic consultations with bilingual mentors, and professional learning communities in which participating teachers exchange ideas about pedagogical practice. A randomized controlled study of the program found an improvement in participating teachers' classroom practices. Compared with children served by teachers in the control group, children served by teachers in the intervention group had better expressive word knowledge in English; better conceptual vocabulary when assessed bilingually; and positive outcomes in Spanish for vocabulary, mathematics, and letter-word identification (Castro et al., 2014).

In a modification of in-service training, the eCircle online professional

---

[8] ESSA Public Law No. 114-95 (2015). sec. 313.

development approach was modified to include add-ons to existing modules, as well as a new module on culture, language, and instruction, with short video examples on such issues as language development and family engagement. In this model, a bilingual mentor works with individual teachers on their instructional practices in both English and Spanish. A variety of other resources, such as teaching materials and progress monitoring in both English and Spanish, are used. In a randomized controlled study, teachers who experienced this professional development approach showed better oral language and literacy instruction at posttest (Landry et al., 2012).

Although research on the effects of professional development for teachers of DLLs/ELs involving coaching and mentoring shows that these approaches hold promise, close scrutiny of such programs is warranted with respect to their content in relation to desirable child outcomes and teaching practices, as well as the qualifications of those delivering this content. While there appears to be a "general consensus among researchers and policymakers around a set of child outcomes and teaching practices that should be the target of professional development programs" (Hamre and Hatfield, 2012, p. 213), the research base on DLLs/ELs and its implications for practice have not been widely incorporated into existing professional development approaches. Further, it has been suggested that research is needed on professional development programs designed to develop teacher knowledge and skills in academic English, as both EL and general education teachers are responsible for academic English language development (DiCerbo et al., 2014).

The 2011-2012 School and Staffing Survey (SASS) provided data on the percentage of K-12 teachers who reported participating in professional development for teaching ELs. Across all schools, 24 percent of teachers reported taking some professional development over the last 12 months with regard to teaching ELs (Goldring et al., 2013). In a survey of Title III districts conducted by the American Institutes of Research, the most commonly mentioned professional development topics for EL teachers were state English proficiency standards and the Sheltered Instruction Observation Protocol (Tanenbaum et al., 2012). Based on these data, it appears that more high-quality professional development programs for teachers of ELs are needed.

Calderon and colleagues (2011) have called for schools to establish causal links between teachers' professional development experiences and student outcomes based on teacher observation. To date there is little evidence to support these links. One study of three large public school districts and one charter school found little improvement in evaluations of teachers following professional development, despite the public schools having spent an average of $18,000 per teacher annually (The New Teacher Project, 2015). Further, when improvement was seen, no correlation could be identified with any specific professional development strategy. What was found in the charter management organization was a clear delineation of the roles and responsibilities of staff supporting teacher development, a mindset of high expectations and continuous growth, and feedback given to teachers on a regular basis through observation and reflection (The New Teacher Project, 2015).

RECRUITMENT

As noted previously, the demand for teachers with specialized knowledge and skills to teach DLLs/ELs is great. A major barrier to implementing bilingual education programs is the lack of qualified teachers (see Putman et al. [2016] for an analysis of the breakdown in the teaching pipeline). States are using various approaches to recruit qualified teachers, including alternative certification pathways such as those described above, partnerships with other countries to recruit teachers, job fairs specifically for teachers of DLLs/ELs, local partnerships with institutions of higher education to prepare qualified teachers, and financial incentives for teachers to add bilingual certification to their qualifications (U.S. Department of Education, 2016). Given the increase in students whose L1 is Spanish, recruiting efforts have focused on Spanish-speaking countries, in particular Spain and Puerto Rico. While these areas offer a good source of teachers, challenges associated with the recruits, such as cultural disconnects between students and teachers and difficulties for the recruits in adjusting to differences in the educational systems and life in the United States occur (Mitchell, 2016).

Schools with high populations of ELs and low-income and highly mobile populations are among those that experience the greatest challenges in recruitment and retention of qualified teachers (Simon and Johnson, 2015). As Putman and colleagues (2016) show, teacher diversity can be increased by efforts to encourage potential teachers to enter the profession. To be successful at recruiting teachers, the National Comprehensive Center for Teacher Quality suggests that a comprehensive reward package include financial incentives and strong supports, such as quality professional development, programs that provide regular coaching for new teachers, and collaborative learning communities (Hayes, 2009). Goe (2006) recommends that when hiring teachers, districts and schools match candidates' qualifications to the sociodemographic characteristics of the school. For example, recruits should possess proficiency in the L1 of many or most of the students in the schools and have completed coursework or professional development pertinent to the specific demands of teaching these students.

The alternative teacher preparation programs discussed above employ their own methods. The Grow Your Own Teachers Program reaches out to students, paraprofessionals, parents, and community members in low-

454 EDUCATIONAL SUCCESS OF CHILDREN AND YOUTH LEARNING ENGLISH

income communities to encourage them to become teachers (Grow Your Own Teachers, 2016). Teacher residency programs conduct organized and data-driven marketing campaigns to target qualified candidates in citywide neighborhoods, using such channels as Spanish language media and job fairs. They also seek referrals and work with public schools to identify candidates, such as paraprofessionals who are already working in the schools (Urban Teacher Residency United, 2014).

While many of these recruitment efforts are promising, each has its own limitations and challenges. Putman and colleagues (2016) describe four problems in building a diverse teaching workforce based on the teacher pipeline: (1) a smaller proportion of black and Hispanic than white populations now earn college degrees; (2) interest in teaching among black and Hispanic college students and graduates is lower than among white students; (3) black and Hispanic teachers are hired at lower rates than white teachers; and (4) black and Hispanic teachers are retained in their jobs at lower rates than white teachers. The authors conclude that "closing the diversity gap" between teachers and students will require a long-term strategy that increases college graduation rates among black and Hispanic students and encourages them to enter the teaching ranks.

RETENTION

Retention of teachers is another issue that affects the supply of qualified teachers for DLLs/ELs (Putman et al., 2016). Research has shown that in high-quality preservice education, providing the knowledge and skills needed for effective teaching in classrooms, along with induction support in the form of mentoring and quality professional development, helps prevent attrition (DeAngelis et al., 2013; Ingersoll and Smith, 2004; National Commission on Teaching and America's Future, 2003; Woods, 2016b). Generally, induction and mentorship of a new teacher last for the first year; however, it has been argued that to have a positive effect on student achievement, induction and mentorship should be extended for multiple years (Woods, 2016b). For example, having professional development on the appropriate pedagogical methods for teaching ELs would provide support to all teachers responsible for educating these students. Other factors that affect attrition include the characteristics of the teacher population and the student body, working conditions, and administrative support. Importantly, there is a higher rate of teacher turnover in schools with low-income and minority students, schools that, as noted earlier, generally have a higher population of ELs (Boyd et al., 2011; Guarino et al., 2006).

Two of the alternative training programs discussed in this chapter report lower rates of teacher attrition for their graduates than are commonly experienced in schools. Teachers who have become certified through the Grow Your Own Teachers Program remains in teaching for at least 5 years, reducing the 40 percent teacher turnover rate that is common in low-income schools (Grow Your Own Teachers, 2016). Once hired as full teachers, graduates of teacher residency programs also have a low rate of attrition. The National Center for Teacher Residency network reports a 3-year teacher retention rate of 87 percent and a 5-year rate of 82 percent (Urban Teacher Residency United, 2014). A review of research on teacher recruitment and retention found similar results, suggesting that graduates of alternative teacher education programs had higher retention rates than those prepared through traditional pathways (Guarino et al., 2006). These findings are consistent with the conclusion of the Brookings Institution (Putman et al., 2016) that to increase the diversity of the teaching workforce, persistence beyond 1 year is crucial. In a study of New York City teachers, however, researchers found substantially lower rates of retention beyond the second year of teaching for TFA teachers relative to those who took the traditional route to becoming a teacher or were in a Teaching Fellows pathway,[9] a time period that coincides with the end of the 2-year commitment to the TFA program (Boyd et al., 2006).

ADMINISTRATORS

School administrators include superintendents and principals; however, the available data discussed here are on principals. As the student population continues to diversify, the same cannot be said for the school administrator population. Data from 2011-2012 reveal that more than 80 percent of school principals were white. While the number of nonwhite principals has increased significantly over the past decade, they are still in the minority. Data reported in 2013, for example, showed that fewer than 7 percent of principals were Hispanic (National Center for Education Statistics, 2013).

With regard to educational attainment, the majority (61.7%) of principals have a master's degree, 26 percent have an educational specialist[10] credential, 10 percent have a doctoral degree, and 2.2 percent hold only a bachelor's degree (National Center for Education Statistics, 2013). School principals have an average of 7.2 years of experience as a principal and 12.2 years of experience as a teacher (National Center for Education Statistics, 2013). Notably, administrators in schools with high EL populations tend

[9]The New York City Teaching Fellows program is an alternative-route program that provides teachers with a teaching certificate valid for 3 years. The traditional pathway is a university-based program in which students fulfill course requirements and have a number of different field experiences, such as student teaching (Boyd et al., 2006).

[10]Education specialist degrees or certificates (of advanced graduate studies) are generally awarded for 1 year's work beyond the master's level.

to have fewer education credentials and less experience as administrators relative to schools with low EL populations, and the former schools also have teachers with similar characteristics (de Cohen et al., 2005).

Along with the fact that administrator demographics do not reflect the student population, many administrators lack the training to support a growing EL population, nor is such training currently required to become a principal (Hale and Moorman, 2003). The inadequate preparation of school leaders is highlighted by state licensure systems that fail to hold preparation programs accountable for initial licensure requirements, nor do these systems encourage professional development (Briggs et al., 2013; for additional information, see New Leaders, 2013).

National professional organizations such as the American Association of School Administrators (AASA), the National Association of Elementary School Principals (NAESP), and the National Association of Secondary School Principals (NASSP) have issued detailed policy statements on educational issues. Yet none of these organizations has a specific policy statement on the education of ELs or the competencies their members should obtain to work effectively with these students. Research points to the impact on student achievement of the instructional leadership role of school administrators and has led to the development of general standards for school administrators (see National Policy Board for Educational Administration [2015] for updated professional standards for educational leaders). Although these standards do not specifically address support for the EL population, several standards do speak to this population (Standard 3: Equity and Cultural Responsiveness; Standard 4: Curriculum, Instruction, and Assessment; and Standard 5: Community of Care and Support for Students). These standards urge administrators to account for and meet the needs of culturally diverse student bodies, including infusing the "school's learning environment with the cultures and languages of the school's community" (National Policy Board for Educational Administration, 2015).

Inadequate general preparation of administrators impedes the effectiveness of educational leaders, as well as their capacity as instructional leaders to support teachers in their schools in serving ELs. A study of middle school principals in eastern New York, for example, revealed that while 4 of 10 principals surveyed spoke a second language, only 2 of 10 had had formal training in ESL (Hagan, 2013). This lack of training can have consequences for the implementation of bilingual programs in schools. Research shows that principals who have a limited understanding of bilingualism are more likely to close their schools' bilingual programs relative to principals who believe in the benefits of bilingual education (Howard et al., 2007; Menken and Solorza, 2015). Therefore, providing professional development for school administrators to help them better understand the needs of ELs may play a crucial role in providing bilingual education.

The ECS recommends that school administrators be trained in cultural competency and instructional methods for teaching ELs so they can support and evaluate teachers of ELs, as well as develop programs in their schools and districts (Wixom, 2015). Currently, 32 states have no explicit policies requiring teachers and/or school administrators to undergo training related to the education of ELs beyond the federal requirements. Arizona, Massachusetts, New Mexico, New York, and Virginia are the only states with specific requirements for school administrators focused on research-based professional development on addressing the needs of ELs, although they differ in the emphasis placed on who should receive such training (e.g., Massachusetts requires training for only those administrators who have sheltered English instruction programs) and in when the training should occur (e.g., Virginia requires that the training be provided during the license renewal process).

PROFESSIONALS PROVIDING SUPPORT SERVICES

In addition to teachers and school administrators, ELs often have contact with other school professionals who support their education, health, and social-emotional well-being. These professionals, therefore, also require specialized training to serve ELs. It should be noted that although a variety of health professionals work with ELs, in-depth coverage of the competencies required for all of these professions was beyond the scope of this study. Since the committee's statement of task emphasized the education of ELs, the focus here is on allied health and education professionals whose roles are especially key for ELs in formal care and education settings—specifically, audiologists, speech-language pathologists, school counselors, school psychologists, and clinical psychologists.

School Counselors

Counseling is an important service for the social and emotional well-being of ELs, especially those who have experienced trauma and other adverse circumstances during migration and living in underresourced communities. The American School Counselor Association has issued a position statement calling for school counselors to "demonstrate cultural responsiveness by collaborating with stakeholders to create a school and community climate that embraces cultural diversity and helps to promote the academic, career and social/emotional success for all students" (American School Counselor Association, 2015). The association's competencies for school counselors also include knowledge of multiculturalism and its implications for school counseling programs and principles of working with various student populations based on such characteristics as ethnic and racial background, English language proficiency, special needs, religion, gender, and income. Still, some studies have found that cultural and language barriers can undermine productive relationships between Hispanic/Latino ELs and counselors (Altarriba and Bauer, 1998; Ponce and Atkinson, 1989). In contrast, another study found an increase in multicultural sensitivity among counselors-in-training who partnered with ESL students to design guidance curriculum in an ESL classroom (Burnham et al., 2009)—an example of the type of training school counselors may need to better address the needs of ELs.

Speech-Language Pathologists/Audiologists

Other school professionals, such as speech-language pathologists and audiologists, assess and work with a subset of DLLs/ELs to address developmental disabilities. The American Speech-Language-Hearing Association (ASHA)—which represents speech-language pathologists; audiologists; speech, language, and hearing scientists; and speech-language pathology and audiology support personnel—has no certification requirements for being considered a bilingual service provider. However, ASHA's definition of a bilingual service provider requires native or near-native proficiency in at least one language other than English, as well as proficiency in diagnostic and treatment services. Laws and regulations with respect to providing speech-language pathology or audiology services to bilingual clients vary among states (American Speech-Language-Hearing Association, 2016). Members are asked to self-identify as bilingual on their annual account notices. As of 2015, approximately 6 percent of members had reported being bilingual service providers in accordance with the ASHA definition.

School/Clinical Neuropsychologists

Like speech-language pathologists and audiologists, both school and clinical neuropsychologists play an important role in assessing DLLs/ELs (see Chapter 11 on the assessment of DLLs/ELs). School psychologists work with students, as well as with teachers and other school staff, to conduct psychological and academic assessments, provide culturally responsive services to students and families from diverse backgrounds, collaborate with community providers to coordinate needed services, and develop appropriate individualized education programs (IEPs) for students with disabilities (National Association of School Psychologists, 2015c). Neuropsychological evaluations often are necessary to diagnose learning disabilities and can be useful for identifying other disabilities, including autism.

Although the National Association of School Psychologists (NASP) does not provide bilingual certification or a description of competencies needed to work with DLLs/ELs, it has issued a position statement on the provision of services to bilingual students suggesting that training of school psychologists include "the developmental processes of language acquisition and acculturation, their effects on standardized test performance, and the effectiveness of instructional strategies and interventions" (National Association of School Psychologists, 2015a, p. 1). NASP lists more than 20 universities that offer graduate-level programs in multicultural and bilingual school psychology. Only two states, however—New York and Illinois—offer a bilingual credential for school psychologists (National Association of School Psychologists, 2015a). A study conducted by Aldridge and colleagues (2015) suggests that graduate programs in psychology are not adequately preparing graduates to serve DLLs/ELs.

The American Academy of Clinical Neuropsychology provides minimal guidelines for working with DLLs/ELs, suggesting that clinicians have the appropriate education and experience to work with special populations and offering alternative courses of action, such as the use of interpreters, if that education is lacking. The guidelines do not provide specific guidance on linguistic, professional, or sociocultural competencies (Mindt et al., 2008, 2010). Mindt and colleagues (2010) point to a dearth of neuropsychologists who report being adequately prepared to work with DLLs/ELs and/or possessing proficiency in languages other than English.

As a way to overcome language barriers, school psychologists, neuropsychologists, and speech-language pathologists use interpreters to assess DLLs/ELs. However, the lack of properly trained interpreters, as well as clinicians who are not trained to work with an interpreter, can increase the probability of assessment errors (Ochoa et al., 2004; Ware et al., 2015). Nearly 80 percent of school psychologists in one study used an interpreter to assess ELs, yet only 52 percent of these individuals were appropriately trained to use an interpreter (Ochoa et al., 2004). In a study of school psychologists who self-identified as bilingual, only 5 percent reported being trained to use an interpreter during their graduate studies (O'Bryon and Rogers, 2010). In a survey conducted by Kritikos (2003), more than 70 percent of monolingual and bilingual speech-language pathologists from five states reported feeling "not competent" or "only somewhat competent" when using an interpreter to assess a client who spoke a language different from their own. Considering the need for these professionals to use interpreters, an emphasis on training them in working with interpreters may be essential.

CONCLUSIONS

Conclusion 12-1: The educator workforce, including early care and education providers, educational administrators, and teachers, is inadequately prepared during preservice training to promote desired educational outcomes for dual language learners (DLLs)/English learners (ELs). The great variability across state certification requirements influences the content offered to candidates by higher education and other preparation programs to prepare them with the knowledge and competencies required by effective educators of these children and youth. The emergence of alternative teacher preparation programs is promising, but traditional institutions of higher education remain the major source of new teachers, and changes in these institutions may therefore be required to increase the pipeline of well-prepared teachers of DLLs/ELs.

Conclusion 12-2: Promising initiatives that include well-articulated professional development goals and monitoring of the application of those goals in classrooms indicate that such strategies and ongoing evaluation of their implementation can result in better outcomes for dual language learners (DLLs)/English learners (ELs). However, professional development, coaching, and continuing education for educators serving DLLs/ELs have not yet developed as a coherent set of strategies for improving the effectiveness of these providers with DLLs/ELs.

Conclusion 12-3: The preparation of educational and allied health professionals, including counselors and school psychologists, who support students' educational achievement in classrooms does not include the knowledge and competencies required to assess and support dual language learners/English learners. These professionals are involved in crucial decisions concerning the identification of learning disabilities and access to services for these children and youth and can have significant influences on their educational trajectories.

Conclusion 12-4: Matching the racial, ethnic, cultural, and linguistic diversity of the educator workforce to that of dual language learners (DLLs)/English learners (ELs) has the potential to improve student outcomes. The research base on the diversity gap between teachers and students is not definitive with respect to the best ways of reducing this gap, especially with respect to DLLs/ELs. Alternative teacher preparation initiatives represent small steps toward achieving this goal, but are not adequate to meet current needs.

BIBLIOGRAPHY

Administration for Children and Families. (2013). *Report to Congress on Dual Language Learners in Head Start and Early Head Start Programs.* Washington, DC: U.S. Department of Health and Human Services.

Aldridge, M.J., Bernstein, E., and Davies, S.C. (2013). Graduate preparation of school psychologists in serving English language learners. *eCommons*, (1). Available: http://rave. ohiolink.edu/etdc/view?acc_num=dayton1371317828 [March 22, 2016].

Altarriba, J., and Bauer, L.M. (1998). Counseling the Hispanic client: Cuban Americans, Mexican Americans, and Puerto Ricans. *Journal of Counseling & Development, 76*(4), 389-396.

American School Counselor Association. (2015). *The School Counselor and Cultural Diversity.* Available: https://www.schoolcounselor.org/asca/media/asca/PositionStatements/ PS_CulturalDiversity.pdf [April 7, 2016].

American Speech-Language-Hearing Association. (2016). *Bilingual Service Delivery.* Available: http://www.asha.org/PRPSpecificTopic.aspx?folderid=8589935225&section=Key_Issues [February 24, 2016].

Aragon, S. (2016). *Teacher Shortages: What We Know.* Denver, CO: Education Commission of the States.

Arias, M.B., and Markos, A.M. (2016). *Characteristics of the Workforce Who Are Educating and Supporting Children Who Are English Language Learners.* Unpublished manuscript commissioned by the Committee on Fostering School Success for English Learners: Toward New Directions in Policy, Practice, and Research, Washington, DC.

Association for Childhood Education International. (n.d.). *Global Guidelines for Early Childhood Education and Care in the 21st Century.* Available: http://www.acei.org/global-guidelines [March 24, 2016].

August, D., and Shanahan, T. (2006). *Developing Literacy in Second-Language Learners: Report of the National Literacy Panel on Language Minority Children and Youth.* Mahwah, NJ: Lawrence Erlbaum Associates.

Austin, L.J.E., Whitebook, M., Kipnis, F., Sakai, L., Abbasi, F., and Amanta, F. (2015). *Teaching the Teachers of Our Youngest Children: The State of Early Childhood Higher Education in California, 2015.* Berkeley: University of California, Center for the Study of Child Care Employment.

Ballantyne, K.G., Sanderman, A.R., and Levy, J. (2008). *Educating English Language Learners: Building Teacher Capacity. Roundtable Report.* Washington, DC: National Clearinghouse for English Language Acquisition.

Bassok, D. (2013). Raising teacher education levels in Head Start: Exploring programmatic changes between 1999 and 2011. *Early Childhood Research Quarterly, 28*(4), 831-842.

Boyd, D., Grossman, P., Lankford, H., Loeb, S., and Wyckoff, J. (2006). How changes in entry requirements alter the teacher workforce and affect student achievement. *Education Finance and Policy, 1*(2), 176-216.

Boyd, D.J., Grossman, P.L., Lankford, H., Loeb, S., and Wyckoff, J. (2009). Teacher preparation and student achievement. *Educational Evaluation and Policy Analysis, 31*(4), 416-440.

Boyd, D., Grossman, P., Ing, M., Lankford, H., Loeb, S., and Wyckoff, J. (2011). The influence of school administrators on teacher retention decisions. *American Educational Research Journal, 48*(2), 303-333.

Briggs, K., Cheney, G.R., Davis, J., and Moll, K. (2013). *Operating in the Dark: What Outdated State Policies and Data Gaps Mean for Effective School Leadership.* Dallas, TX: George W. Bush Institute.

Bruder, M.B., and Dunst, C.J. (2005). Personnel preparation in recommended early intervention practices: Degree of emphasis across disciplines. *Topics in Early Childhood Special Education, 25*(1), 25-33.

Bueno, M., Darling-Hammond, L., and Gonzalez, D.M. (2010). *A Matter of Degrees: Preparing Teachers for the Pre-Kindergarten Classroom.* Washington, DC: The PEW Center on the States.

Burnham, J.J., Mantero, M., and Hooper, L.A. (2009). Experiential training: Connecting school counselors-in-training, English as a second language (ESL) teachers, and ESL students. *Journal of Multicultural Counseling and Development, 37*(1), 2-14.

Calderon, M., Slavin, R., and Sanchez, M. (2011). Effective instruction for English learners. *The Future of Children, 21*(1), 103-127.

California Department of Education and First 5 California. (2011). *California Early Childhood Educator Competencies.* Sacramento, CA: California Department of Education.

Castro, D.C., Garcia, E.E., and Markos, A.M. (2013). *Dual Language Learners: Research Informing Policy.* Chapel Hill, NC: The University of North Carolina, Frank Porter Graham Child Development Institute, Center for Early Care and Education—Dual Language Learners.

Castro, D., Gillanders, C., Franco, X., Bryant, D., Zepeda, M., and Willoughby, M. (2014). *Nuestros Niños Program: Promoting School Readiness with Dual Language Learners.* Paper presented at the Head Start's 12th National Research Conference on Early Childhood—Collaboration and Coordination: Understanding Systems Supporting Young Children and Their Families, Washington, DC, July 7-9.

Chang, F., Crawford, G., Early, D., Bryant, D., Howes, C., Burchinal, M., Barbarin, O., Clifford, R., and Pianta, R. (2007). Spanish-speaking children's social and language development in pre-kindergarten classrooms. *Early Education and Development, 18*(2), 243-269.

Clark, M., McConnell, S., Constantine, J., and Chiang, H. (2013). *Addressing Teacher Shortages in Disadvantaged Schools: Lessons from Two Institute of Education Sciences Studies.* NCEE Evaluation Brief. NCEE 2013-4018. Washington, DC: National Center for Education Evaluation and Regional Assistance, Institute of Education Sciences, U.S. Department of Education.

Constantine, J., Player, D., Silva, T., Hallgren, K., Grider, M., and Deke, J. (2009). *An Evaluation of Teachers Trained through Different Routes to Certification: Final Report.* NCEE 2009-4043. Washington, DC: National Center for Education Evaluation and Regional Assistance, Institute of Education Sciences, U.S. Department of Education.

Council for the Accreditation of Educator Preparation. (2013). *CAEP Accreditation Standards and Evidence: Aspirations for Educator Preparation.* Available: https://caepnet.files.wordpress.com/2013/02/commrpt.pdf [December 1, 2015].

Cummins, J. (1981). *Bilingualism and Minority-Language Children. Language and Literacy Series.* Toronto, ON: Ontario Institute for Studies in Education.

Cummins, J. (2000). *Language, Power, and Pedagogy: Bilingual Children in the Crossfire.* Clevedon, UK: Multilingual Matters.

Cummins, J. (2008). BICS and CALP: Empirical and theoretical status of the distinction. In B. Street and N.H. Hornberger (Eds.), *Encyclopedia of Language and Education* (vol. 2, 2nd ed., pp. 71-83). New York: Springer.

Darling-Hammond, L., and Richardson, N. (2009). Teacher learning: What matters? *Educational Leadership, 66*(5), 46-53.

Darling-Hammond, L., Furger, R., Shields, P., and Sutcher, L. (2016). *Addressing Califonia's Emerging Teacher Shortage: An Analysis of Sources and Solutions.* Palo Alto, CA: Learning Policy Institute. Available: http://sedn.senate.ca.gov/sites/sedn.senate.ca.gov/files/learning_policy_institute_ca_teacher_shortage.pdf [February 23, 2017].

de Cohen, C.C., Deterding, N., and Clewell, B.C. (2005). *Who's Left Behind? Immigrant Children in High and Low LEP Schools.* Washington, DC: Urban Institute.

de Jong, E.J., and Harper, C.A. (2005). Preparing mainstream teachers for English-language learners: Is being a good teacher good enough? *Teacher Education Quarterly, 32*(2), 101-124.

DeAngelis, K.J., Wall, A.F., and Che, J. (2013). The impact of preservice preparation and early career support on novice teachers' career intentions and decisions. *Journal of Teacher Education, 64*(4), 338-355.

DeMonte, J. (2015). *A Million New Teachers Are Coming: Will They Be Ready to Teach?* Washington, DC: Education Policy Center at American Institutes for Research.

DiCerbo, P.A., Anstrom, K.A., Baker, L.L., and Rivera, C. (2014). A review of the literature on teaching academic English to English language learners. *Review of Educational Research, 84*(3), 446-482.

Espinosa, L.M. (2013). *Early Education for Dual Language Learners: Promoting School Readiness and Early School Success.* Washington, DC: Migration Policy Institute.

Espinosa, L.M., Burchinal, M., Winsler, A., Tien, H., Castro, D.C., and Peisner-Feinberg, E. (2013). *Child Care Experiences among Dual Language Learners in the U.S.: Analyses of the Early Childhood Longitudinal Survey-Birth Cohort.* Paper presented at the Dual Language Learners in Early Care and Education, American Education Research Association Annual Meeting, San Francisco, CA.

Flores, B.B., Keehn, S., and Perez, B. (2002). Critical need for bilingual education teachers: The potentiality of normalistas and paraprofessionals. *Bilingual Research Journal, 26*(3), 501-524.

Freedson, M. (2010). Educating preschool teachers to support English language learners. In E.E. García and E.C. Frede (Eds.), *Young English Language Learners: Current Research and Emerging Directions for Policy and Practice* (pp. 165-183). New York: Teachers College Press.

Fuller, B., Livas, A., and Bridges, M. (2005). *How to Expand and Improve Preschool in California: Ideals, Evidence, and Policy Options.* Berkeley: University of California, Berkeley and Davis, Stanford University, Policy Analysis for California Education.

Gándara, P.C., and Maxwell-Jolly, J. (2006). Critical issues in developing the teacher corps for English learners. In K. Téllez and H.C. Waxman (Eds.), *Preparing Quality Educators for English Language Learners: Research, Policies and Practices* (pp. 99-120). Mahwah, NJ: Lawrence Erlbaum Associates.

Gándara, P.C., Maxwell-Jolly, J., and Driscoll, A. (2005). *Listening to Teachers of English Language Learners: A Survey of California Teachers' Challenges, Experiences, and Professional Development Needs.* Santa Cruz, CA: Center for the Future of Teaching and Learning.

García, A. (2016). *Growing Their Own in Minneapolis: Building a Diverse Teacher Workforce from the Ground Up.* Available: http://www.edcentral.org/minneapolis-grow-your-own [February 22, 2016].

García, E.E., and García, E.H. (2012). *Understanding the Language Development and Early Education of Hispanic Children.* New York: Teachers College Press.

García, E.E., Arias, M.B., Harris Murri, N.J., and Serna, C. (2010). Developing responsive teachers: A challenge for a demographic reality. *Journal of Teacher Education, 61*(1-2), 132-142.

Gass, S. (1997). *Input, Interaction and the Second Language Learner.* Mahwah, NJ: Lawrence Erlbaum Associates.

Goe, L. (2006). *Planning Tool to Provide Evidence of Progress toward Equitable Teacher Distribution.* Washington, DC: National Comprehensive Center for Teacher Quality.

Goldring, R., Gray, L., and Bitterman, A. (2013). *Characteristics of Public and Private Elementary and Secondary School Teachers in the United States: Results from the 2011–12 Schools and Staffing Survey.* Washington, DC: U.S. Department of Education, National Center for Education Statistics.

Grow Your Own Teachers. (2016). *Grow Your Own Teachers: An Illinois Initiative.* Available: http://www.growyourownteachers.org/index.php?option=com_content&view=article&id=95&Itemid=27 [February 22, 2016].

Guarino, C.M., Santibanez, L., and Daley, G.A. (2006). Teacher recruitment and retention: A review of the recent empirical literature. *Review of Educational Research, 76*(2), 173-208.

Hagan, R.M. (2013). *Academic Achievement Success for ESL Students: An Approach to School Organization, Leadership, and Programs.* Unpublished Doctoral, Fordham University, New York. Available: http://pqdtopen.proquest.com/pubnum/3559465.html [December 15, 2015].

Hale, E.L., and Moorman, H.N. (2003). *Preparing School Principals: A National Perspective on Policy and Program Innovations.* Washington, DC, and Edwardsville, IL: Institute for Educational Leadership and Illinois Education Research Council.

Hamre, B.K., and Hatfield, B.E. (2012). Moving evidence-based professional development into the field: Recommendations for policy and research. In C. Howes, B.K. Hamre, and R.C. Pianta (Eds.), *Effective Early Childhood Professional Development: Improving Teacher Practice and Child Outcomes* (pp. 213-228). Baltimore, MD: Paul H. Brookes.

Hayes, K. (2009). *Key Issue: Recruiting Teachers for Urban and Rural Schools.* Washington, DC: National Comprehensive Center for Teacher Quality.

Herrera, S.G., and Murry, K.G. (2006). Accountability by assumption: Implications of reform agendas for teacher preparation. *Journal of Latinos and Education, 5*(3), 189-207.

Hollins, E.R., and Crockett, M. (2012). *Clinical Experiences in the Preparation of Candidates for Teaching Underserved Students.* Washington, DC: Council for the Accreditation of Educator Preparation.

Howard, E.R., Sugarman, J., Christian, D., Lindholm-Leary, K.J., and Rogers, D. (2007). *Guiding Principles for Dual Language Education* (2nd Edition). Washington, DC: U.S. Department of Education and National Clearinghouse for English Language Acquisition.

Howes, C., and Tsao, C. (2012). Introducing a conceptual framework of professional development in early childhood education. In C. Howes, B.K. Hamre, and R.C. Pianta (Eds.), *Effective Early Childhood Professional Development: Improving Teacher Practices and Child Outcomes.* (pp. 1-9). Baltimore, MD: Paul H. Brookes.

Humphrey, D., and Wechsler, M. (2007). Insights into alternative certification: Initial findings from a national study. *The Teachers College Record, 109*(3), 483-530.

Hurtado, S. (2001). Linking diversity and educational purpose: How diversity affects the classroom environment and student development. In G. Orfield (Ed.), *Diversity Challenged: Evidence on the Impact of Affirmative Action* (pp. 187-203). Cambridge, MA: Harvard Education.

Ingersoll, R., and Smith, T.M. (2004). Do teacher induction and mentoring matter? *NAASP Bulletin, 88*(638), 28-40.

Institute of Medicine and National Research Council. (2015). *Transforming the Workforce for Children Birth through Age 8: A Unifying Foundation.* L. Allen and B.B. Kelly (Eds.). Board on Children, Youth, and Families; Committee on the Science of Children Birth to Age 8: Deepening and Broadening the Foundation for Success. Washington, DC: The National Academies Press.

Kane, T.J., Rockoff, J.E., and Staiger, D.O. (2008). What does certification tell us about teacher effectiveness? Evidence from New York City. *Economics of Education Review, 27*(6), 615-631.

Kerchner, C.T., and Corrigan, D. (2016). California should invest in teacher residencies. *Education Week*, February 18. Available: http://blogs.edweek.org/edweek/on_california/2016/02/california_should_invest_in_teacher_residencies.html [February 22, 2016].

Krashen, S.D. (1982). *Principles and Practice in Second Language Acquisition.* Oxford, UK, and New York: Pergamon.

Krashen, S.D. (2003). *Explorations in Language Acquisition and Use: The Taipei Lectures.* Portsmouth, NH: Heinemann.

Kritikos, E.P. (2003). Speech-language pathologists' beliefs about language assessment of bilingual/bicultural individuals. *American Journal of Speech-Language Pathology, 12*(1), 73-91.

Landry, S.H., Zucker, T.A., Solari, E., Crawford, A.D., and Williams, J.M. (2012). History, scale up and improvements of a comprehensive, statewide professional development program in Texas. In C. Howes, B.K. Hamre, and R.C. Pianta (Eds.), *Effective Early Childhood Professional Development: Improving Teacher Practice and Child Outcomes* (pp. 159-189). Baltimore, MD: Paul H. Brookes.

Lim, C.-I., Maxwell, K.L., Able-Boone, H., and Zimmer, C.R. (2009). Cultural and linguistic diversity in early childhood teacher preparation: The impact of contextual characteristics on coursework and practica. *Early Childhood Research Quarterly, 24*(1), 64-76.

Lindholm-Leary, K.J. (2015). *Fostering School Success for English Learners K-12: Language and Academic Development of Dual Language Learners during the School Years.* Unpublished manuscript commissioned by the Committee on Fostering School Success for English Learners: Toward New Directions in Policy, Practice, and Research. Child and Adolescent Development, San Jose State University, CA.

Loeb, S., Soland, J., and Fox, L. (2014). Is a good teacher a good teacher for all? Comparing value-added of teachers with their English learners and non-English learners. *Educational Evaluation and Policy Analysis, 36*(4), 457-475.

López, A., Zepeda, M., and García, O. (2012). *Dual Language Learner Teacher Competencies (DLLTC) Report.* Los Angeles, CA: Alliance for Better Communities and the National Council for La Raza.

López, F., Scanlan, M., and Gundrum, B. (2013). Preparing teachers of English language learners: Empirical evidence and policy implications. *Education Policy Analysis Archives, 21*(20), 1-35.

Lucas, T., and Grinberg, J. (2008). Responding to the linguistic reality of mainstream classrooms: Preparing all teachers to teach English language learners. In M. Cochran-Smith, S. Feiman-Nemser, and D.J. McIntyre (Eds.), *Handbook of Research on Teacher Education: Enduring Questions in Changing Contexts* (3rd Edition, pp. 606-636). New York: Routledge and the Association of Teacher Educators.

Lucas, T., Villegas, A.M., and Freedson-Gonzalez, M. (2008). Linguistically responsive teacher education: Preparing classroom teachers to teach English language learners. *Journal of Teacher Education, 59*(4), 361-373.

Madkins, T.C. (2011). The Black teacher shortage: A literature review of historical and contemporary trends. *The Journal of Negro Education, 80*(3), 417-427, 437.

Markos, A.M. (2011). *Guiding Preservice Teachers to Critically Reflect: Towards a Renewed Sense about English Learners.* Ph.D. Dissertation. Tempe: Arizona State University, Available: https://repository.asu.edu/attachments/56687/content/Markos_asu_0010E_10713.pdf [December 18, 2015].

Maxwell, K., Lim, C., and Early, D. (2006). *Early Childhood Teacher Preparation Programs in the United States: National Report.* Chapel Hill: The University of North Carolina, FPG Child Development Institute.

Menken, K., and Antunez, B. (2001). *An Overview of the Preparation and Certification of Teachers Working with Limited English Proficient (LEP) Students.* Washington, DC: National Clearinghouse for Bilingual Education.

Menken, K., and Solorza, C. (2015). Principals as linchpins in bilingual education: The need for prepared school leaders. *International Journal of Bilingual Education and Bilingualism, 18*(6), 676-697.

Merino, B. (2007). Identifying cultural competencies for teachers of English learners. *UCLMRI Newsletter, 16*(4), 1-8.

Michalopoulos, C., Lee, H., Duggan, A., Lundquist, E., Tso, A., Crowne, S.S., Burrell, L., Somers, J., Filene, J.H., and Knox, V. (2015). *The Mother and Infant Home Visiting Program Evaluation: Early Findings on the Maternal, Infant, and Early Childhood Home Visiting Program. A Report to Congress.* Washington, DC: U.S. Department of Health and Human Services, Administration for Children and Families.

Milk, R., Mercado, C.I., and Sapiens, A. (1992). Re-thinking the education of teachers of language minority children developing reflective teachers for changing schools. *NCBE Focus, 6*(3).

Mindt, M.R., Arentoft, A., Germano, K.K., D'Aquila, E., Scheiner, D., Pizzirusso, M., Sandoval, T.C., and Gollan, T.H. (2008). Neuropsychological, cognitive, and theoretical considerations for evaluation of bilingual individuals. *Neuropsychology Review, 18*(3), 255-268.

Mindt, M.R., Byrd, D., Saez, P., and Manly, J. (2010). Increasing culturally competent neuropsychological services for ethnic minority populations: A call to action. *The Clinical Neuropsychologist, 24*(3), 429-453.

Mitchell, C. (2016). Need for bilingual educators moves school recruitment abroad. *Education Week, 35*(19), s5, s7.

Mora, J.K. (2000). Staying the course in times of change: Preparing teachers for language minority education. *Journal of Teacher Education, 51*(5), 345-357.

National Association for the Education of Young Children. (2009). *NAEYC Standards for Early Childhood Professional Preparation.* Available: http://www.naeyc.org/files/naeyc/files/2009%20Professional%20Prep%20stdsRevised%204_12.pdf [March 24, 2016].

National Asssociation for the Education of Young Children. (2012). *Supporting Cultural Competence: Accreditation of Programs for Young Children—Cross Cutting Theme in Program Standards.* Available: https://www.naeyc.org/academy/files/academy/file/Trend BriefsSupportingCulturalCompetence.pdf [December 1, 2015].

National Association of School Psychologists. (2015a). *Bilingual School Psychology Certification.* Available: http://www.nasponline.org/resources-and-publications/resources/diversity/cultural-competence/bilingual-school-psychology-certification [March 16, 2016].

National Association of School Psychologists. (2015b). The provision of school psychological services to bilingual students. *Communiqué, 44*(2).

National Association of School Psychologists. (2015c). *Who Are School Psychologists?* Available: https://www.nasponline.org/about-school-psychology/who-are-school-psychologists [April 1, 2016].

National Center for Education Statistics. (2013). *2013 Tables and Figures, Tables 209.1, 209.2, and 210.10.* Available: http://nces.ed.gov/programs/digest/2013menu_tables.asp [February 1, 2016].

National Center for Teacher Residencies. (n.d.). *Become a Teacher.* Available: http://nctresidencies.org/become-a-teacher [February 22, 2016].

National Commission on Teaching and America's Future. (2003). *No Dream Denied: A Pledge to America's Children, Summary Report.* Washington, DC: National Commission on Teaching and America's Future.

National Comprehensive Center for Teacher Quality. (2009). *Certification and Licensure for Teachers of English Language Learners, by State.* Available: http://www.gtlcenter.org/sites/default/files/docs/CertificationandLicensureforTeachersofELLs.pdf [December 2016].

National Education Association. (2011). *Professional Development for General Education Teachers of English Language Learners*. Washington, DC: National Education Association.

National Policy Board for Educational Administration. (2015). *Professional Standards for Educational Leaders 2015*. Reston, VA: National Policy Board for Educational Administration.

National Research Council. (2010). *Preparing Teachers: Building Evidence for Sound Policy*. Division of Behavioral and Social Sciences and Education, Center for Education, Committee on the Study of Teacher Preparation Programs in the United States. Washington, DC: The National Academies Press.

National Survey of Early Care and Education Project Team. (2013). *Number and Characteristics of Early Care and Education (ECE) Teachers and Caregivers: Initial Findings from the National Survey of Early Care and Education*. Washington, DC: Office of Planning, Research and Evaluation, Administration for Children and Families, U.S. Department of Health and Human Services.

Neuman, S.B., and Kamil, M.L. (2010). *Preparing Teachers for the Early Childhood Classroom: Proven Models and Key Principles*. Baltimore, MD: Paul H. Brookes.

New Leaders. (2013). *Change Agents: How States Can Develop Effective School Leaders Concept Paper*. New York: New Leaders.

O'Bryon, E.C., and Rogers, M.R. (2010). Bilingual school psychologists' assessment practices with English language learners. *Psychology in the Schools, 47*(10), 1018-1034.

Ochoa, S.H., Riccio, C., Jimenez, S., de Alba, R.G., and Sines, M. (2004). Psychological assessment of English language learners and/or bilingual students: An investigation of school psychologists' current practices. *Journal of Psychoeducational Assessment, 22*(3), 185-208.

Osterling, J.P., and Buchanan, K. (2003). Tapping a valuable source for prospective ESOL teachers: Northern Virginia's bilingual paraeducator career-ladder school-university partnership. *Bilingual Research Journal, 27*(3), 503-521, 539, 541.

Papay, J.P., West, M.R., Fullerton, J.B., and Kane, T.J. (2012). Does an urban teacher residency increase student achievement? Early evidence from Boston. *Educational Evaluation and Policy Analysis, 34*(4), 413-434.

Pappamihiel, N.E. (2002). English as a second language students and English language anxiety: Issues in the mainstream classroom. *Research in the Teaching of English, 36*(3), 327-355.

Park, M., McHugh, M., Batalova, J., and Zong, J. (2015). *Immigrant and Refugee Workers in the Early Childhood Field: Taking a Closer Look*. Washington, DC: Migration Policy Institute.

Peske, H.G., and Haycock, K. (2006). *Teaching Inequality: How Poor and Minority Students are Shortchanged on Teacher Quality: A Report and Recommendations by the Education Trust*. Washington, DC: Education Trust.

Ponce, F.Q., and Atkinson, D.R. (1989). Mexican-American acculturation, counselor ethnicity, counseling style, and perceived counselor credibility. *Journal of Counseling Psychology, 36*(2), 203.

Putman, H., Hansen, M., Walsh, K., and Quintero, D. (2016). *High Hopes and Harsh Realities: The Real Challenges to Building a Diverse Workforce*. Available: https://www.brookings.edu/wp-content/uploads/2016/08/browncenter_20160818_teacherdiversityreportpr_hansen.pdf [September 2016].

Ray, A., Bowman, B., and Robbins, J. (2006). *Preparing Early Childhood Teachers to Successfully Educate All Children: The Contributions of Four-Year Undergraduate Teacher Preparation Programs*. Chicago, IL: Erikson Institute.

Sakai, L., Kipnis, F., Whitebook, M., and Schaack, D. (2014). Yes they can: Supporting bachelor degree attainment for early childhood practitioners. *Early Childhood Research & Practice, 16*(1).

Samson, J.F., and Collins, B.A. (2012). *Preparing All Teachers to Meet the Needs of English Language Learners: Applying Research to Policy and Practice for Teacher Effectiveness.* Washington, DC: Center for American Progress.

Samson, J.F., and Lesaux, N. (2015). Disadvantaged language minority students and their teachers: A national picture. *Teachers College Record, 117*(2), 1-26.

Schleppegrell, M.J. (2004). *The Language of Schooling a Functional Linguistics Perspective.* Mahwah, NJ: Lawrence Erlbaum Associates.

Simon, N.S., and Johnson, S.M. (2015). Teacher turnover in high-poverty schools: What we know and can do. *Teachers College Record, 117*(3), 1-36.

Skinner, E.A. (2010). Project "Nueva Generacion" and Grow Your Own Teachers: Transforming schools and teacher education from the inside out. *Teacher Education Quarterly, 37*(3), 155-167.

Swain, M. (1995). Three functions of output in second language learning. In G. Cook and B. Seidlhofer (Eds.), *Principles and Practice in the Study of Language* (pp. 125-144). Oxford, UK: Oxford University Press.

Talbert-Johnson, C. (2006). Preparing highly qualified teacher candidates for urban schools: The importance of dispositions. *Education and Urban Society, 39*(1), 147-160.

Tanenbaum, C., Boyle, A., Soga, K., Le Floch, K.C., Golden, L., Petroccia, M., Toplitz, M., Taylor, J., and O'Day, J. (2012). *National Evaluation of Title III Implementation: Report on State and Local Implementation.* Alexandria, VA: Office of Planning, Evaluation and Policy Development, U.S. Department of Education.

Teach For America. (2016). *Your Training and Support.* Available: https://www.teachforamerica.org/teach-with-tfa/your-training-and-support [February 22, 2016].

Téllez, K., and Waxman, H. (2005). *Quality Teachers for English Language Learners.* Philadelphia, PA: Laboratory for Student Success, Temple University Center for Research in Human Development and Education.

The New Teacher Project. (2015). *The Mirage: Confronting the Hard Truth About Our Quest for Teacher Development.* Brooklyn, NY: The New Teacher Project.

Thomas, W.P., and Collier, V.P. (2002). *A National Study of School Effectiveness for Language Minority Students' Long-Term Academic Achievement.* Santa Cruz, CA, and Washington, DC: Center for Research on Education, Diversity & Excellence.

Urban Teacher Residency United. (2014). *Building Effective Teacher Residencies.* Chicago, IL: Urban Teacher Residency United.

U.S. Department of Education. (2010). *Toward the Identification of Features of Effective Professional Development for Early Childhood Educators, Literature Review.* Washington, DC: U.S. Department of Education, Office of Planning, Evaluation and Policy Development, Policy and Program Studies Service.

U.S. Department of Education. (2016). *Dual Language Education Programs: Current State Policies and Practices.* Washington, DC: U.S. Department of Education, Office of English Language Acquisition.

U.S. Department of Justice and U.S. Department of Education. (2015). *Dear Colleague Letter: English Learner (EL) Students and Limited English Proficient Parents.* Available: http://www2.ed.gov/about/offices/list/ocr/letters/colleague-el-201501.pdf [December 15, 2015].

Verplaetse, L.S., and Migliacci, N. (2008). Making mainstream content comprehensible through sheltered instruction. In L.S. Verplaetse and N. Migliacci (Eds.), *Inclusive Pedagogy for English Language Learners: A Handbook of Research-Informed Practices* (pp. 127-165). New York: Lawrence Erlbaum Associates.

Villegas, A.M., and Irvine, J.J. (2010). Diversifying the teaching force: An examination of major arguments. *The Urban Review: Issues and Ideas in Public Education*, 42(3), 175-192.

Vygotsky, L.S. (1978). *Mind in Society*. Cambridge, UK: Cambridge University Press.

Walker, A., Shafer, J., and Liams, M. (2004). "Not in my classroom": Teacher attitudes towards English language learners in the mainstream classroom. *NABE Journal of Research and Practice*, 2(1), 130-159.

Walqui, A. (2008). The development of teacher expertise to work with adolescent English learners: A model and a few priorities. In L.S. Verplaetse and N. Migliacci (Eds.), *Inclusive Pedagogy for English Language Learners: A Handbook of Research-Informed Practices* (pp. 103-125). New York: Lawrence Erlbaum Associates.

Ware, J., Lye, C.B., and Kyffin, F. (2015). Bilingualism and students (learners) with intellectual disability: A review. *Journal of Policy and Practice in Intellectual Disabilities*, 12(3), 220-231.

Wei, R.C., Darling-Hammond, L., Andree, A., Richardson, N., and Orphanos, S. (2009). *Professional Learning in the Learning Profession: A Status Report on Teacher Development in the United States and Abroad*. Dallas, TX: National Staff Development Council.

Whitebook, M. (2014). *Building a Skilled Workforce: Shared and Divergent Challenges in Early Care and Education in Grades K-12*. Seattle, WA: Bill & Melinda Gates Foundation.

Williams, T., Perry, M., Oregon, I., Brazil, N., Hakuta, K., Haertel, E., Kirst, M., and Levin, J. (2007). *Similar English Learner Students, Different Results: Why Do Some Schools Do Better? A Follow-Up Analysis, Based upon a Large-Scale Survey of California Elementary Schools Serving High Proportions of Low-Income and EL Students. Research Brief*. Mountain View, CA: EdSource.

Wixom, M.A. (2015). *State-Level English Language Learner Policies*. Denver, CO: Education Commission of the States.

Wong-Fillmore, L., and Snow, C. (2005). *What Teachers Need to Know About Language*. McHenry, IL: Delta Systems.

Woods, J.R. (2016a). *Mitigating Teacher Shortages: Alternative Teacher Certification*. Denver, CO: Education Commission of the States.

Woods, J.R. (2016b). *Mitigating Teacher Shortages: Induction and Membership*. Denver, CO: Education Commission of the States.

Zaslow, M., Tout, K., Halle, T., and Starr, R. (2011). Professional development for early educators: Reviewing and revising conceptualizations. In S.B. Neuman and D. Dickinson (Eds.), *Handbook of Early Literacy Research* (Vol. 3, pp. 425-434). New York: Guilford Press.

Zehler, A., Fleischman, H., Hopstock, P., Stephenson, T., Pendzick, M., and Sapru, S. (2003). *Policy Report: Summary of Findings Related to LEP and SPED-LEP Students*. Washington, DC: U.S. Department of Education, Office of English Language Acquisition, Language Enhancement, and Academic Achievement of Limited English Proficient Students.

Zepeda, M. (2015). *The Early Childhood Workforce for Dual Language Learners: What Do We Know and Where Do We Need to Go?* Unpublished commissioned paper. Department of Child & Family Studies, California State University, Los Angeles, CA.

Zepeda, M., Castro, D.C., and Cronin, S. (2011). Preparing early childhood teachers to work with young dual language learners. *Child Development Perspectives*, 5(1), 10-14.

Zigler, E., Gilliam, W.S., and Barnett, W.S. (2011). *The Pre-K Debates: Current Controversies & Issues*. Baltimore, MD: Paul H. Brookes.

13

Recommendations for Policy, Practice, and Research

This chapter presents the committee's recommendations for policy, practice, and research and data collection. This is followed by a research agenda that identifies gaps in current knowledge about dual language learners (DLLs)/English learners (ELs), including relevant policies, demographics, language development, effective programs and practices, DLLs/ELs with disabilities, and workforce preparation. This agenda is focused specifically on research needed to foster the educational success of DLLs/ELs.

The committee's recommendations are supported by the conclusions presented at the end of Chapters 2-12. Based on its review of the available evidence, the committee concludes that all children and youth have the capacity to become bi- or multilingual given appropriate opportunities. The ability to communicate and to learn in more than one language is universal, and is an asset that can enhance cognitive control, social and cultural competence, educational outcomes, and work skills in a global economy.

Research also reveals that many institutions responsible for early childhood and pre-K to 12 education are failing to provide DLLs/ELs with appropriate opportunities to learn. The result is persistent developmental and achievement disparities between many students classified as ELs and those who are not. The educational success and well-being of DLLs/ELs can be enhanced by aligning education and health care policies and practices with scientific evidence on effective educational programs and practices, the nature of dual language development, and the value of multilingualism and respect for cultural heritages. DLLs'/ELs' strong acquisition of their first language (L1) serves as a foundation for learning English as a language that is essential for educational success in the United States.

RECOMMENDATIONS

This section presents the committee's recommendations for practice, policy, and research and data collection.

Recommendations Pertaining to All DLLs/ELs

Recommendation 1: Federal agencies with oversight of early childhood programs serving children from birth to age 5 (such as the Child Care and Development Fund and Maternal, Infant, and Early Childhood Home Visiting Program) and state agencies with oversight of such programs should follow the lead of Head Start/Early Head Start by providing specific evidence-based program guidance, practices, and strategies for engaging and serving dual language learners and their families and monitor program effectiveness.

To ensure successful outcomes for DLLs, programs should be improved with respect to both their global overall quality and their use of specific dual language and cultural supports to meet these children's developmental needs. These improvements are needed across the range of early care and education (ECE) settings, including informal home-based and center-based programs.

Although the Head Start guidelines focus primarily on kindergarten readiness, they also include best-practice recommendations and toolkits for ensuring the cultural competency of staff, engaging families, and supporting the development of children from multilingual backgrounds. Guidelines regarding the early education of DLL children should include

- a clear statement of philosophy and goals for DLLs,
- a clear process for identifying DLLs and assessing their developmental trajectories in both their L1 and English,
- specification of qualifications for teachers of DLLs,
- direction on family engagement strategies,
- guidance on conducting community needs assessments,
- assistance in creating partnerships with community organizations and schools to increase access to high-quality education programs,
- guidance on instructional practices, and
- learning standards for infants and toddlers as well as preschoolers.

Recommendation 2: Federal, state, and local agencies and intermediary organizations with responsibilities for serving children birth to age 5 should conduct social marketing campaigns to provide information about the capacity of infants, toddlers, and preschoolers—including those with disabilities—to learn more than one language.

These campaigns should include information on the communicative, social, cognitive, emotional, and employment advantages of bilingualism and the absence of evidence of harmful effects. These government agencies and organizations, including professional associations whose members work directly with children, should also promote practices in families and programs that support the development of children's bilingualism.

Recommendation 3: Federal and state agencies and organizations that fund and regulate programs and services for dual language learners (e.g., Office of Head Start, U.S. Department of Health and Human Services, state departments of education and early learning, state child care licensing agencies) and local education agencies that serve English learners in grades pre-K to 12 should examine the adequacy and appropriateness of district- and school-wide practices for these children and adolescents. Evidence of effective practices should be defined according to the Every Student Succeeds Act.

Improvements in the care and education of DLLs/ELs will depend on a well-considered theory of change and action. Conducting self-studies through the analysis of assessment data, studying curriculum and instructional materials, observing classrooms, examining pedagogical approaches, interviewing students and parents, and working to build a culture in which learning and development are possible are all key to addressing the problems that have been identified. Changing practices is never easy and often entails professional development for all personnel involved.

Recommendation 4: Federal and state agencies and organizations that fund and regulate programs and services for dual language learners (DLLs) (e.g., Office of Head Start, U.S. Department of Health and Human Services, state departments of education and early learning, state child care licensing agencies) and English learners (ELs) in grades pre-K to 12 should give all providers of services to these children and adolescents (e.g., local Head Start and Early Head Start programs, community-based child care centers, state preschool and child development programs) and local education agencies information about the range of valid assessment methods and tools for DLLs/ELs and guidelines for their appropriate use, especially for DLLs/ELs with disabilities. The

Institute of Education Sciences and the National Institutes of Health should lead the creation of a national clearinghouse for these validated assessment methods and tools, including those used for DLLs/ELs with disabilities.

The uses of these assessment methods and tools include informing educational programming, instructional differentiation, formative assessment, continuous program improvement, and accountability. Any initial assessment of DLLs/ELs should be conducted in both the child's L1 and English and should make use of a variety of informants, including individuals who are proficient in the L1, and multiple sources of data collected over time. High-quality academic assessments should be available to ELs in grades pre-K to 12 who are in bilingual programs in their L1 to the extent practicable. Assessments of ELs' L1 should focus specifically on how the L1 is used in school and literacy settings, and test results should be interpreted to apply to each specific domain of language use.

Recommendations for Specific Populations of DLLs/ELs

Recommendation 5: The U.S. Department of Education should provide more detailed guidelines to state education agencies (SEAs) and LEAs on the implementation of requirements regarding family participation and language accommodations in the development of individualized education plans (IEPs) and Section 504 accommodation plans for dual language learners/English learners who qualify for special education. The SEAs and LEAs, in turn, should fully implement these requirements.

These guidelines should cover the following:

- identification of evidence-based resources and practices for increasing family participation that take into account parents' workplace policies and the socioeconomic, cultural, and educational circumstances of families of DLLs/ELs with disabilities;
- identification of evidence-based resources and practices that enable professionals to communicate with families of DLLs/ELs with disabilities in their L1, as well as communication strategies to use when following such guidelines is not feasible (e.g., because of a lack of bilingual school staff or of professionally certified interpreters); and
- identification of evidence-based resources and practices for conducting IEP meetings with families of DLLs/ELs with disabilities

in culturally responsive ways while discussing how to support the child's L1 and make joint decisions about the appropriate use of languages for instruction.

Recommendation 6: The U.S. Department of Health and Human Services and the U.S. Department of Education should direct programs to strengthen their referral and linkage roles in order to address the low rates of identification of developmental disorders and disabilities in dual language learners (DLLs)/English learners (ELs) and related low rates of referral to early intervention and early childhood special education services. In addition, the U.S. Department of Education should address underidentification of DLLs/ELs in its analyses, reports, and regulations in order to examine the multidimensional patterns of underrepresentation and overrepresentation at the national, state, and district levels in early childhood (birth to 5) and by grade (pre-K to 12) and for all disability categories.

The MIECHV and ECE programs overseen by the U.S. Department of Health and Human Services should also consider adapting guidelines from other federal agencies for developmental screening of DLLs and having available the appropriately trained professionals needed to conduct these screenings. Initial standardized developmental screenings that are administered to large numbers of DLLs should obtain information from multiple sources, including standardized screening instruments, observational data on the child's behavior, and parental reports, to determine whether referral for more in-depth assessment is warranted. Professionals should be aware that most standardized screening tools have not been designed or normed for DLLs; that is, they are not culturally and linguistically appropriate instruments. Teachers and assessment professionals should be trained to conduct assessments with DLLs and ELs. All procedures should be carefully documented, with final decisions being made by the team in collaboration with children's families.

To differentiate properly between language differences attributable to growing up with two languages and language delays in screening and identifying DLLs and ELs who may need special services, assessors should employ multiple measures and sources of information; consult with a multidisciplinary team that includes bilingual experts; collect information over time; and use family members as informants regarding birth, medical, developmental, and family history (Barrueco et al., 2012). These practices are consistent with expert guidelines of professional societies on assessing for language impairment, autism spectrum disorder, global developmental delay, and learning disabilities.

The recent efforts by the U.S. Department of Education to address disparities in special education through multiyear disproportionality analyses and regulations represent a positive step forward, but have focused only on overrepresentation, overlooking the critical possibility of underrepresentation (which has already been documented) for a number of disability categories.

> Recommendation 7: Local education agencies serving American Indian and Alaska Native communities that are working to revitalize their indigenous heritage languages should take steps to ensure that schools' promotion of English literacy supports and does not compete or interfere with those efforts.

Students' indigenous heritage languages are crucial to their social, cultural, and emotional well-being and to the continuation of their communities' ways of life, just as English is crucial to their participation in the economic and political life of the larger society. Both languages are necessary for American Indian and Alaska Native youth to become productive members of their communities.

Recommendations Related to the Workforce

> Recommendation 8: Research, professional, and policy associations whose members have responsibilities for improving and ensuring the high quality of educational outcomes among dual language learners (DLS)/English learners (ELs) should implement strategies designed to foster assessment literacy—the ability to understand and interpret results of academic assessments administered to these children and adolescents in English or their primary language—among personnel in federal, state, and local school agencies and DLL/EL families.

These organizations should work with institutions of higher education that prepare educators and allied professionals (school psychologists, researchers, and others) and assessment developers to ensure that assessment literacy is part of continuing education and improvement programs and that these professionals are well prepared to work with families of DLL/ELs.

> Recommendation 9: State and professional credentialing bodies should require that all educators with instructional and support roles (e.g., teachers, care and education practitioners, administrators, guidance counselors, psychologists and therapists) in serving dual language learners (DLS)/English learners (ELs) be prepared through credentialing and licensing as well as pre- and in-service training to work effectively with DLLs/ELs.

Competencies in connecting research on dual language development with best practices to guide the instruction of DLLs/ELs should be required in addition to current basic credentialing/licensing requirements. A common course of core body of content should be available for the professional development of all personnel who work with DLLs/ELs, and should include the following elements drawn from the research reviewed by the committee and consistent with its conclusions and recommendations:

- an understanding of language development and the relationship between first and second language acquisition;
- an understanding of the influences of sociocultural factors on language learning;
- knowledge of and ability to implement effective practices for promoting the successful education of DLLs/ELs, including early intervention strategies for DLLs/ELs with disabilities;
- an understanding of assessment instruments and procedures and of the interpretation and application of assessment results for DLLs/ELs;
- development of skills for establishing respectful partnerships with families of DLLs/ELs; and
- development of skills to advocate on behalf of DLLs/ELs.

The components of this common course of study should be built into preservice licensing coursework and continuing professional development requirements. Professional organizations should incorporate this common course of study into their professional offerings and advocacy efforts, and educational settings should incorporate it into their in-service education.

> **Recommendation 10: All education agencies in states, districts, regional clusters of districts, and intermediary units and agencies responsible for early learning services and pre-K to 12 should support efforts to recruit, select, prepare, and retain teachers, care and education practitioners, and education leaders qualified to serve dual language learners (DLLs)/ English learners (ELs). Consistent with requirements for pre-K to 12, program directors and lead teachers in early learning programs should attain a B.A. degree with certification to teach DLLs.**

School districts, institutions of higher education that prepare teachers and other professionals who work with DLLs/ELs, and alternative teacher preparation programs, as well as other related service providers, should increase their efforts to attract and retain personnel who are qualified to meet the needs of DLLs/ELs, including by focusing on the pool of high school graduates with seals of biliteracy and recruiting them to become teachers as part of their college education. Too few staff in the workforce know the languages and cultural customs of DLLs/ELs and their families. Programs in institutions of higher education should consider incorporating practices described in Chapter 12 into their recruitment and teacher preparation programs. Attention should be given to ensuring that teachers acquire in-depth understanding of the cultural realities of their students and the U.S. educational context through ongoing mentoring and intensive professional development.

Research and Data Collection Recommendations

Recommendation 11: The Institute of Education Sciences should promote studies focused on the impact on English learners of variations in state policies and decisions related to Every Student Success Act (ESSA) implementation. These studies should be completed in time to inform the next cycle of ESSA reauthorization in 4 years.

Specific topics addressed by these studies should include the nature of the standardized statewide entry-exit criteria, the length of time for which exited ELs are included in reports of academic progress, the minimum subgroup sample size for accountability, the models chosen for gauging progress toward English language proficiency, and the manner in which states implement the evidence-based provisions of the law for district improvement programs. The research should also document and evaluate how local district adaptations to the required state accountability systems can serve the needs of school improvement efforts.

Recommendation 12: State education agencies (SEAs) should analyze student data on the relationships among English language proficiency, academic assessments, and individual student characteristics (including students' proficiency in their L1) to determine the appropriateness of entry and exit procedures and the efficacy of targeted services. SEAs should use this information to refine entry and exit procedures and make decisions about the length of time for which exited students are included in accountability systems.

Recommendation 13: Understanding that definitions of English learners (ELs) vary from state to state, a common definition should be used by school districts, state education agencies, and federal agencies (such as the U.S. Department of Education, the Census Bureau, and the U.S. Department of Health and Human Services) in their data collection efforts and in reports related to ELs to enable comparisons and analyses across datasets.

Recommendation 14: Federal agencies that support research should develop guidelines specifying descriptors to be used to characterize dual language learners (DLLs)/English learners (ELs) and other child participants in funded research. These agencies should also develop an agreed-upon and consistent set of definitions of those descriptors, including DLL, EL, immigrant, country of origin (versus pan-ethnic or racial categories), and socioeconomic status, among others.

Reports on DLLs/ELs published by school districts and federal agencies should consistently

- include information about DLLs'/ELs' past and current language experiences and competencies;
- disaggregate panethnic and ethnic group categories, such as Latin American, Hispanic, Asian American and Pacific Islander, and African;
- disaggregate data by age group, including infants from birth to 2 years, pre-K (ages 3-5), elementary school (ages 6-12), and middle to high school (ages 13-18);
- stratify data by families' socioeconomic status;
- identify DLLs/ELs by country of origin and immigration status; and
- provide information about the participants' competence in English and their home language(s), including both oral and written language skills.

These features would increase the policy and practice relevance of the reported data by providing commonly understandable and more useful information to the public, educators, researchers, and policy makers. In addition, data collection on underserved populations, including DLLs/ELs who are from migrant/seasonal worker families, are members of transnational groups, are homeless, are unaccompanied minors, and are refugees, should be improved.

RESEARCH AGENDA

As described in Chapter 1, the committee was charged with developing a research agenda identifying gaps in knowledge about DLLs/ELs, specifically with respect to understanding the influences on their educational success. The committee found that more research is needed on the policies that govern DLLs'/ELs' education and shape their life experiences; the social, cognitive, and linguistic development and learning trajectories of ELs over the pre-K to grade 12 period; the effectiveness of alternative instructional models (including dual language models); instructional strategies that contribute to academic success; assessment methods that shape clinical and educational decisions about ELs; and the preparation of educators. Box 13-1 provides more detailed descriptions of these gaps in the knowledge base and research needed to address them.

BOX 13-1 Research Needed to Address Gaps in Knowledge About DLLs/ELs

Policy

- Investigations of states that have bilingual policies (e.g., New York and Texas) and states that have English-only policies (e.g., Arizona, Massachusetts), and the impact of implementing such policies on student achievement and educational attainment.
- Assessments of the cost-effectiveness of the array of approaches and interventions that have been implemented in the education of DLLs/ELs— and shown to be effective—to enable funding agencies, school districts, and schools to make informed decisions about the costs of implementing research-based interventions.

Demographics

- Studies of DLLs/ELs in underrepresented groups (e.g., refugees, migrant children and youth, unaccompanied minors, homeless, undocumented children and youth) to understand the effects of their DLL/EL status and other factors on their educational outcomes.
- Studies that address the lack of knowledge about groups of DLLs/ELs (e.g., those who come from different language and cultural backgrounds; have different levels of prior education; and speak alternative varieties of certain languages, such as Chinese (Mandarin versus Cantonese), and/ or belong to different cultural groups that speak the same language.
- Investigations of EL programs that include state-by-state numbers and types of language instruction educational programs and demographic information about the students enrolled in these programs.

Language Development: Birth to Age 5

- Studies of the ways in which parents from different ethnolinguistic groups in the United States use language with DLLs, and the relationship between their usage patterns and their children's later language and academic outcomes.
- Investigations of the role and importance of the quantity, quality, and structure of language exposure from parents and other child caregivers in the development of two languages in the home. Among other indices, these studies should include measures of the number of hours (as well as

BOX 13-1 Continued

proportion of time) spent in each language; and specific indices of parental language input, including number of words, different words, different
kinds of words, and grammatical variety and complexity. In addition, these
studies should indicate whether these indices are related to children's
later academic and general development and how these patterns may
differ for different L1 speakers.

- Examination of how L1 competence influences English-L2 development—
what aspects of L1 affect specific aspects of English development and
under what circumstances (similarity of the languages, level of proficiency
in each, explicit vs. no cross-linguistic instruction, etc.) and whether there
are pedagogical interventions that can enhance positive cross-linguistic
influences, especially when implemented by monolingual English-speaking teachers.

- Exploration of the developing brain architecture of DLLs/ELs during the
preschool and kindergarten years—ages when children are acquiring
language competencies needed for later language learning (2-5 years
of age). This research should aim to identify measures that differentiate
atypical developmental patterns that result from endogenous factors and
those that result from diminished exposure to a particular language or set
of languages.

- Identification of the specific language difficulties that typically developing
DLLs from different language backgrounds have with English and on effective strategies for addressing these difficulties.

- Studies of the role of technology, including whether the language development of DLLs would benefit from the use of digital learning tools (e.g.,
e-books, smartphone apps, online translators and translator devices,
media) and the conditions that enhance those benefits.

- Examination of DLLs who speak different languages (e.g., Spanish, Mandarin, Hmong) to understand effects of age at language acquisition. The
timing of exposure may intersect with type of language, such that earlier
exposure to English may be needed for some languages more than for
others.

Effective Programs and Practices: Birth to Age 5

- Research on the effectiveness of program elements and specific strategies for promoting the educational outcomes of DLLs, including the
amount and duration of L1 support necessary for DLLs with different levels of prior English exposure and teacher-child interactions that promote
improved outcomes, how much and what kind of professional development is needed for implementers of programs, and how models and strategies that have been shown to be effective with DLLs can be sustainably
implemented.

- Studies of effective accommodations and enhancements for ECE programs that promote cognitive/academic and linguistic aspects of development while building on the socioemotional/cultural strengths of DLLs.

continued

BOX 13-1 Continued

This includes effective approaches for incorporating families' knowledge of their child, culture, languages, and customs into ECE programs.

Development of English Language Proficiency: Pre-K to Grade 12

- Longitudinal investigations of the differential impact of school-entry characteristics, including high versus low levels of proficiency in English at school entry, on the learning trajectories of ELs in grades pre-K to 12. Such research should examine, in particular, what factors (e.g., socioeconomic status, interrupted schooling, L1 proficiency, quality of instruction) are associated with initial differences in English proficiency and how the English language and academic achievement of groups with different starting levels of English proficiency change across grades K-12.
- Longitudinal research on the academic outcomes of ELs from different language and cultural backgrounds and both school entry-related and in-school-related factors that influence their achievement and educational trajectories.
- Research on theories of English language proficiency that specify empirically verifiable ways in which different English language skills are related to the range of required classroom learning skills and communicative competencies that support student progress at each grade level. Specifically, research is needed on how English language proficiency theories and English language proficiency assessments reflect how ELs acquire and demonstrate their English language skills and knowledge in classrooms.

Effective Programs and Practices: Pre-K to Grade 12

- Research on the effectiveness of program elements and specific strategies for promoting academic achievement and other educational outcomes of ELs, in particular:
  - The amount and duration of L1 support necessary for ELs with different levels of prior English exposure.
  - Teacher-child interactions that promote improved outcomes.
  - For programs in which EL students are excelling, the factors that contribute to their success, including an examination of how successful EL programs equalize the status between languages to ensure the successful development of both languages, and how models and strategies that have been shown to be effective with ELs can be effectively implemented and sustained over time.
  - The features of dual language programs (e.g., student ratios of English speakers to partner language speakers in two-way programs, number of instructional hours allotted to each language, proportion of school staff and leadership that is bilingual, use of target languages within and across content areas) that influence successful acquisition

BOX 13-1 Continued

of language and content, and whether languages should be separated or mixed during classroom instruction. Specifically, more research is needed to examine whether EL and English-proficient (non-EL or former EL) students should learn together in literacy classes from the beginning, or should be separated for a portion of time to acquire a more solid foundation in their native language and more oral language development in their second language before receiving English instruction with native speakers of the partner language. This research should also investigate whether these needs vary based on student-level factors.

– Benefits of specific attributes of interventions used with English-proficient (non-EL or former EL) students for EL student outcomes, whether these attributes, if modified, would be more effective for ELs, what these modifications might be, and whether additional attributes not currently found in most interventions developed for English-proficient students are needed or would be beneficial for ELs.

- Investigation of alternative instructional strategies for ELs and their relative effectiveness with respect to English language development. In particular, research is needed to examine the differential effectiveness of explicit language instruction linked to content instruction on EL language learning and the conditions under which this approach is more or less effective than approaches that are less explicit, taking into consideration specific learner subgroups (e.g., ELs with low versus ELs with relatively high proficiency in English).
- Studies of program effectiveness that use school-based classrooms to address generalizability problems with randomized controlled designs. That is, since real classrooms are not created at random, results from randomized designs do not necessarily generalize, although they contribute to theory building.
- Case studies of school districts or schools that have overcome the obstacles to academic success for ELs to document and analyze the practices of effective schools, the development of institutional capacity for change, the engagement of all stakeholders in increasing the success of ELs, and the creation of a culture of shared responsibility for educating students of diverse backgrounds.
- Research to inform the development of effective instructional programs and strategies for addressing the needs of migrant students who are ELs frequently moving across state and district jurisdictions. The researchers should collaborate with state and regional offices of migrant education in the conduct of this research.
- Research on effective approaches to incorporating families' knowledge of their child, culture, language, and customs into instruction in grades pre-K-12.

continued

BOX 13-1 Continued

Dual Language Learners and English Learners with Disabilities

- Consideration of what accommodations and alternative screeners are most appropriate for measuring English language proficiency in DLLs/ELs with disabilities and how to interpret screening results.
- Investigation of how best to distinguish DLLs/ELs with reading, language, and related disabilities from DLLs/ELs who have not yet mastered English or have slower language development than that of typically developing children for other reasons.
- Examination of the effectiveness of different forms of intervention and support for DLLs/ELs with different types of disabilities. In particular, in the domain of language-related disabilities, there is a need for research that examines the differential effectiveness of interventions in English only, L1 only, or both English and L1. Also needed is research on the effectiveness of alternative forms of parental engagement in interventions for DLLs/ELs with disabilities.
- Creation of a dataset based on large- and small-scale studies of DLLs/ELs to permit analyses of data aggregated across studies. The availability of this dataset would maximize data use and provide more nuanced and generalizable findings and conclusions, especially regarding the complex needs and assets of DLLs/ELs with disabilities. This dataset should include detailed information about DLLs/ELs (e.g., language proficiency, generational status in the United States, developmental trajectories, socioeconomic status) as well as the communities (e.g., demographics, labor, education levels, mobility rates) and schools (e.g., indices of opportunity to learn) in which they are educated.

Preparation and Continuing Development of Educators

- Investigations to understand how preservice educator preparation programs and program features produce effective teachers of DLLs/ELs.
- In-depth examination of the philosophies and curricula of current teacher preparation and education administration programs to determine effective ways of increasing the use of current research evidence (on English language acquisition, language development, and brain development).
- Examination of appropriate ways to measure teacher and administrator effectiveness in educating DLLs/ELs.
- Examination of how short-term hiring practices (e.g., of international teachers who must depart the country after their temporary visas expire) affect program success.
- Research on the differential effectiveness of alternative in-service professional development programs and the conditions under which they are effective in producing change in teachers' use of instructional strategies that educate DLLs/ELs effectively.

REFERENCE

Barrueco, S., Lopez, M., Ong, C., and Lozano, P. (2012). *Assessing Spanish-English Bilingual Preschoolers: A Guide to Best Approaches and Measures*. Baltimore, MD: Paul H. Brookes.

Appendix A

Biosketches of Committee Members and Project Staff

COMMITTEE MEMBERS

Ruby Takanishi (*Chair*) is a senior research fellow in the Early and Elementary Education, Education Policy Division at New America. She was formerly president and CEO of the Foundation for Child Development in New York, and has a lifelong interest in how research on children's development can inform public policy and programs. Dr. Takanishi also was founding executive director of the Federation of Behavioral, Psychological, and Cognitive Sciences; director of the Office of Scientific Affairs of the American Psychological Association; executive director of the Carnegie Council on Adolescent Development; and assistant director for Behavioral and Social Sciences and Education in the President's Office of Science and Technology Policy. In 2014, she received the Distinguished Public Service Award from the American Education Research Association. Dr. Takanishi has served on several boards, including those of the Council on Foundations; Grantmakers for Children, Youth, and Families; Grantmakers for Education; the Winthrop Rockefeller Foundation; the Advisory Panel on Public Issues of the Advertising Council; the National Advisory Committee for the National Children's Study; and the National Advisory Council of the Agency for Health Care Quality and Research. She earned her B.A. and Ph.D. degrees from Stanford University.

Alfredo Artiles is Dean of Graduate Education, and the Ryan C. Harris Professor of Special Education at Arizona State University. His scholarship focuses on understanding and addressing educational inequities related to

487

the intersection of disability and sociocultural differences. He directs the Equity Alliance and co-edits *the International Multilingual Research Journal* and the book series *Disability, Culture, & Equity*. Previously, he was vice president of the American Educational Research Association (AERA). He is an AERA fellow, a Spencer Foundation/National Academy of Education postdoctoral fellow, and a resident fellow at the Center for Advanced Study in the Behavioral Sciences at Stanford University. Dr. Artiles has been principal or co-principal investigator of numerous projects. He has served as an advisor to the Civil Rights Projects at Harvard University and the University of California, Los Angeles (UCLA), the National Academy of Education, the Council for Exceptional Children, the Southern Poverty Law Center, and the Joseph P. Kennedy Jr. Foundation, among others. In 2012, he received the Palmer O. Johnson Award for best article published in an AERA journal. Dr. Artiles has held a number of visiting professorships internationally. He served as a commissioner in President Obama's Advisory Commission on Educational Excellence for Hispanics and was named 2009 Distinguished Alumnus by the University of Virginia's Curry School of Education Foundation. He holds a Ph.D. in education from the University of Virginia.

Diane L. August is currently a managing researcher at the American Institutes for Research (AIR), where she is responsible for directing the work of the Center for English Learners. Her area of expertise is research, policy analysis, and technical assistance related to the education of preschool and school-age English learners (ELs). At AIR, she serves as a senior advisor to multiple federally funded studies that involve ELs. She has also advised state-funded studies examining the trajectories of a cohort of ELs over multiple years and exploring variables that lead to their success. Dr. August has recently directed or is directing studies funded by the U.S. Department of Education focused on peer review criteria for evaluating state Title III assessment and accountability provisions, state-level dual language programming, and attributes of promising practices in the math education of ELs. Prior to her position at AIR, she was a senior research scientist at the Center for Applied Linguistics, where she directed or co-directed federally funded studies focused on language, literacy, and science development in ELs, as well as assessment of and programming for ELs. Dr. August holds a Ph.D. in education from Stanford University and has published widely in both journals and books.

Xavier Botana is currently superintendent of the Portland Public Schools, Portland, Maine. He was formerly associate superintendent of the Michigan City Area Schools. During his tenure, the district saw continued improvements in test performance and other metrics while achieving budget reductions of more than 15 percent. Mr. Botana was previously chief academic officer for Portland, Oregon, public schools, where he directed the district's teaching and learning programs, including special education and programs for ELs. His key accomplishment was articulating the "guaranteed core program" for community comprehensive high schools and establishing a districtwide training program for cultural competence with the Pacific Education Group. Mr. Botana served as chief officer for instructional design and assessment in Chicago Public Schools, overseeing the development of the district's first formative assessment program and support structure for literacy, math, and science instruction. Previously, he worked as director of English learner programs in the Illinois education department, where he spearheaded the development of the state's first assessment of English language proficiency. He was a part of the Chicago Public Schools Leadership Program, which partnered with Harvard University. He holds degrees in education from Chicago State University and has completed the coursework toward a doctorate in education and social policy at Northwestern University.

Dylan Conger is a professor at the Trachtenberg School of Public Policy and Public Administration at The George Washington University and director of the master's in public policy program. She is also a research affiliate at the institution, as well as New York University's Institute for Education and Social Policy. Her research interests include disadvantaged, immigrant, and minority youth, with a focus on education policies and urban areas. Current projects are examining the effects of public policies and programs on the educational outcomes of undocumented immigrants and English learners from early schooling through postsecondary education, estimating the effects of advanced placement and other advanced high school courses on educational outcomes, and identifying the sources of gender disparities in secondary and postsecondary educational outcomes. Dr. Conger holds a Ph.D. in public policy from New York University.

Richard P. Durán is a professor at the Gevirtz Graduate School of Education, University of California, Santa Barbara. He previously served as a research scientist at the Educational Testing Service, where he conducted studies on the validity of the SAT for use in predicting Latino students' college achievement, the validity of the GRE test, and the validity of the Test of English as a Foreign Language. He has conducted and published research on assessment validity and education policy and on educational interventions serving ELs preparing for college. He has investigated how more effective instruction could be designed to improve the academic outcomes of culturally and linguistically diverse students who do not perform well on standardized tests and who come from low-income families, and how students' self-awareness of their performance can lead to new notions of assessment. Most recently, he has been conducting research on student learning in after-school computer clubs.

Linda M. Espinosa is currently co-principal investigator for the Getting on Track for Early School Success: Effective Teaching in Preschool Classrooms project at the University of Chicago. She was formerly co-principal investigator for the Center for Early Care and Education Research—Dual Language Learners at the University of North Carolina at Chapel Hill. She was a professor of early childhood education at the University of Missouri, Columbia, and has served as co-director of the National Institute for Early Education Research at Rutgers University and vice president of education at Bright Horizons Family Solutions. She served on the Head Start National Reporting System technical advisory group and was a member of the Secretary's Advisory Committee on Head Start Research and Evaluation. Her recent work has focused on effective curriculum and assessment practices for young children from low-income dual language families. Recently, she was appointed to the New York City Universal PreK Scientific Advisory Council and completed a secondary analysis of the Early Childhood Longitudinal Study-Kindergarten (ECLS-K) cohort on the school achievement patterns of language minority children. She completed her B.A. at the University of Washington, her Ed.M. at Harvard University, and her Ph.D. in educational psychology at the University of Chicago.

Eugene E. García is professor emeritus at Arizona State University. He was dean of the Mary Lou Fulton College of Education at the Tempe campus and was professor and vice president for education partnerships at the university. He also served as professor and dean of the Graduate School of Education at the University of California, Berkeley, and as a senior officer in the U.S. Department of Education. He is conducting research in the areas of effective schooling for linguistically and culturally diverse student populations and has chaired the National Task Force on Early Education for Hispanics. He has been honored by several professional organizations for his research contributions and has received an honorary doctorate of letters from Erikson Institute, Chicago, in recognition of his contributions to the area of child development. Most recently, he was appointed to the Board on Children, Youth, and Families of the National Academies of Sciences, Engineering, and Medicine. Dr. Garcia received his B.A. in psychology from the University of Utah and his Ph.D. in human development from the University of Kansas. He has served as a postdoctoral fellow in human development at Harvard University and as a National Research Council fellow. He has received numerous academic and public honors.

Fred Genesee is professor emeritus in the Psychology Department at McGill University. He has conducted extensive research on alternative approaches to bilingual education that has systematically documented the longitudinal language development (oral and written) and academic achievement of students educated through the media of their home and another language. Currently, his work focuses on immersion students who are at risk for reading and/or language learning difficulties and how best to identify such students early in their schooling so that appropriate intervention can be provided. He is engaged in collaborative research with colleagues at McGill University that is examining the neural signatures of late second language learning in typical second language learners, simultaneous bilinguals, and internationally adopted children. Dr. Genesee has served as a consultant with parent, educational, and policy groups around the world on issues related to second language learning in school-age children, bilingual education, and dual language learning during the preschool years. He holds a Ph.D. in psychology from McGill University.

Kenji Hakuta is the Lee L. Jacks professor of education, emeritus, at Stanford University. His tenure at Stanford was interrupted briefly when he left to serve the new University of California at Merced as its founding dean of the School of Social Sciences, Humanities and Arts. He began as a developmental psycholinguist at Yale University and has authored many publications on language, bilingualism, and education. He has testified to Congress and the courts on language policy, the education of language minority students, affirmative action in higher education, and improvement of quality in educational research. Dr. Hakuta is an elected member of the National Academy of Education, a fellow of the American Educational Research Association, and fellow of the American Association for the Advancement of Science, recognized for his accomplishments in linguistics and language sciences. He has served on the boards of organizations including the Educational Testing Service, the Spencer Foundation, and the New Teacher Center. He is a well-recognized expert in the relationship between students' oral language and learning. Currently, he directs the Understanding Language Initiative at Stanford, focused on the role of language in the Common Core State Standards and Next Generation Science Standards. Dr. Hakuta received his Ph.D. in experimental psychology from Harvard University.

Arturo Hernandez is currently professor and director of the graduate program in developmental psychology at the University of Houston. He is also affiliated with the University of Houston Cognitive Science program and with the Human Neuroimaging Laboratory at the Baylor College of Medicine. Over the past 16 years, he has worked in collaboration with numerous colleagues in uncovering the factors that determine differential brain activity in bilinguals. His major research interest is in the neural underpinnings of bilingual language processing and second language acquisition in children and adults. He has used a variety of neuroimaging methods as well as behavioral techniques to investigate these phenomena, with the results of this work being published in a number of peer-reviewed journal articles. Although his work has focused on word-level processing with bilingual speakers, these efforts are aimed at investigating questions of interest to cognitive and developmental psychologists. Dr. Hernandez received his Ph.D. in cognitive science and psychology and completed postdoctoral studies at the University of California, San Diego.

Bobbi Ciriza Houtchens retired after nearly 40 years of teaching English and English language development, and now consults with and provides professional development for teachers who work with English learners and urban students across the country. She has taught in the migrant labor camps south of Miami, in the DC public schools, and in an Oaxacan middle school. She worked in the U.S. Department of Education's Office of English Language Acquisition as a teaching ambassador fellow. She also has served as a teacher trainer/mentor and as a University of California, Los Angeles, writing project consultant. She received both a B.A. and Licenciado from Elbert Covell College, an experimental college at the University of the Pacific in California, where she majored in Latin American politics, teaching English as a second language, and Spanish. She holds an M.A. in bilingual/ bicultural literacy from California State University, San Bernardino, where she served as an adjunct professor in the School of Education.

Jeff MacSwan is professor of applied linguistics and language education at the University of Maryland. His applied research program is focused on the role of language in theories of school achievement and on education policy related to bilingual learners in U.S. schools. His basic scientific research program concerns the linguistic study of bilingualism and code switching. Currently, he is editor of the *International Multilingual Research Journal*. He is also a fellow of the National Education Policy Center. He holds a Ph.D. in education from University of California, Los Angeles.

Harriett Romo is director of the Child and Adolescent Policy Research Institute (CAPRI) and a professor in the department of sociology at the University of Texas at San Antonio. She has also taught at the University of Texas at Austin and at Texas State University. She has directed grant projects at CAPRI funded by various government agencies and foundations. She has also collaborated with colleagues at the University of Washington on the language acquisition of infants in bilingual homes and has evaluated

Head Start and Early Head Start programs. Her research interests include Latino children and schooling, early childhood education, immigrant families and children, and foster care youth. She holds a bachelor's degree in education from the University of Texas at Austin, a master's in education from University of California, Los Angeles, and a Ph.D. in sociology from the University of California, San Diego, and competed postdoctoral studies in sociology at Stanford University.

Maria Sera is a professor at the Institute of Child Development, University of Minnesota. Her research focuses on the relationship between language and cognitive development. Current projects are examining the relationship between knowledge of classifiers and categories in speakers of Chinese, Hmong, and Japanese and the acquisition of second languages by preschoolers. Dr. Sera is currently conducting three studies investigating how preschoolers learn a second language. All of these studies are using experimental designs. One is comparing the role of first language vocabulary in second language learning; the second is examining the role of first language semantic and phonological organization in second language word learning; and the third is exploring the parameters of speech discrimination training that may accelerate second language learning. Dr. Sera holds a Ph.D. in developmental psychology from Indiana University.

Catherine S. Tamis-LeMonda is professor of applied psychology at New York University. Her research is focused on infant and toddler learning and development in the areas of language and communication, object play, cognition, motor skills, gender identity, emotion regulation, and social understanding and the long-term implications of early emerging skills for children's developmental trajectories. She investigates how skills in different domains reciprocally affect one another and snowball over time, and examines the role of sociocultural context in skill development and lagged associations. Her research has been funded by the National Science Foundation; National Institute of Child Health and Human Development; National Institute of Mental Health; Administration for Children, Youth, and Families; Ford Foundation; and Robin Hood Foundation. She has produced more than 150 publications in peer-reviewed journals and books and coedited *Child Psychology: A Handbook of Contemporary Issues, 1st, 2nd, and 3rd Editions.* She holds a Ph.D. in experimental psychology with a concentration in developmental psychology from New York University.

Kevin J.A. Thomas is an associate professor of sociology, demography, and African studies at the Pennsylvania State University and a research associate at the university's Population Research Institute. He previously worked as a David Bell fellow at the Harvard Center for Population and Development

Studies, and later as a research fellow at the Harvard Initiative for Global Health. He also helped produce the *World Migration* report in 2003 and has served as a consultant for several organizations, including the Migration Policy Institute in Washington, D.C., and as an expert witness on immigration issues. His research interests include migration and immigration processes among African-origin populations and racial and ethnic inequality. He has received a number of awards, including the Young Scholars Fellowship of the Foundation for Child Development. His work has been published in leading peer-reviewed outlets such as the *International Migration Review*, *Demography*, and the *Lancet*. He earned a B.A. (with honors) from Fourah Bay College, University of Sierra Leone; a master's in development administration from Western Michigan University; and master's and Ph.D. degrees in demography from The University of Pennsylvania.

Claudio O. Toppelberg is a child, adolescent, and adult psychiatrist and research scientist at Harvard Medical School and the Judge Baker Children's Center, where he directs the Child Language and Developmental Psychiatry Research Lab. He directs continuing medical education at the Child Mental Health Forum, serves on the medical staff at Children's Hospital Boston, and sits on the Harvard Medical School Department of Psychiatry research committee and the Harvard Global Mental Health Workgroup. Dr. Toppelberg is an assistant professor at Harvard Medical School and a co-investigator at the Norwegian Institute of Public Health. His research in child/adolescent development and mental health focuses on the relationships of language, neurocognitive, and emotional/behavioral development; the development of English learning/dual language children of immigrants; and reduction of socioeconomic disparities in language, neurocognitive, and emotional/behavioral development through national and state policies. His work has been published in peer-reviewed journals and received several international, national, and Harvard research awards. He is an active member of the American Academy of Child and Adolescent Psychiatry. He graduated magna cum laude from the University of Buenos Aires School of Medicine and trained in two Harvard Medical School programs in psychiatry.

Lily Wong-Fillmore is professor emeritus of education at the University of California, Berkeley. Much of her research over the past 40 years has focused on issues related to the education of language minority students in American schools. Her professional specializations are second language learning and teaching, the education of language minority students, and the socialization of children for learning across cultures. She has conducted studies of second language learners in school and community settings, including a study of the language resources of Alaska Native children in several Yupik villages along the Yukon River. She is currently engaged in studies of the academic language of complex texts as required by the Common Core State Standards, and is working with the Council of Great City Schools to develop instructional strategies for teaching such language skills to English learners and other underachieving language minority students. She also engaged over the past several decades in work focused on the revitalization of indigenous languages in the Southwest. She continues to work with leaders in several pueblos in New Mexico in support of language programs for the teaching of heritage languages to the children in those communities.

PROJECT STAFF

Suzanne Le Menestrel (*Study Director*) is a senior program officer with the Board on Children, Youth, and Families at the National Academies of Sciences, Engineering, and Medicine, where her responsibilities have included directing three consensus studies focused on children and adolescents birth to age 18. Prior to her tenure with the National Academies, she was founding national program leader for youth development research at 4-H National Headquarters. Before that, she served as research director in the Academy for Educational Development's Center for Youth Development and Policy Research and was a research associate at Child Trends. She was a founder of the *Journal of Youth Development: Bridging Research and Practice* and chaired its Publications Committee. Dr. Le Menestrel has published in numerous refereed journals and is an invited member of a research advisory group for the American Camp Association. She received the 2012 Outstanding Leadership and Service to the Extension Evaluation Profession award from the American Evaluation Association. She holds an M.S. and a Ph.D. in human development and family studies from the Pennsylvania State University, a B.S. in psychology from St. Lawrence University, and a nonprofit management executive certificate from Georgetown University.

Pamella Atayi is program coordinator for the Board on Children, Youth, and Families, supporting the board and board director, consensus studies, and a forum. She received the Sandra H. Matthews Cecil Award from the Institute of Medicine in 2013. She has more than 20 years' experience providing administrative services and has worked at various nonprofit organizations in the Washington, D.C., area, including the Evangelical Lutheran Church in the America's Public Policy Office, Catholic University of America, and World Education Services. She earned her B.A. in English from the University of Maryland University College and holds a diploma in computer information systems from Strayer University.

Rebekah Hutton is an associate program officer for the Board on Children, Youth, and Families. Previously, she was an education management and information technology consultant and worked on projects in the United States as well as Haiti, Equatorial Guinea, and Djibouti. She has also worked as a program manager and researcher at the National Center on Performance Incentives at Vanderbilt University, studying whether teacher pay for performance has measurable impact on student outcomes, and as an English language lecturer in Tourcoing, France. She received her M.Ed. degree from Vanderbilt University in international education policy and management and a B.A. degree from the University of Tennessee in French language and literature.

Amy Stephens is a program officer for the Board on Science Education of the National Academies. She is an adjunct professor for the Southern New Hampshire University Psychology Department, teaching graduate-level online courses in cognitive psychology and statistics. She has an extensive background in behavioral and functional neuroimaging techniques and has examined a variety of different populations spanning childhood through adulthood. She has worked at the Center for Talented Youth (CTY) on producing cognitive profiles of academically talented youth in an effort to develop alternative methods for identifying such students from underresourced populations. Additionally, she has explored the effects of spatial skill training on performance in mathematics and science classes as well as overall retention rates within science, technology, engineering, and mathematics-related fields for students entering the engineering program at the Johns Hopkins University. She holds a Ph.D. in cognitive neuroscience from the Johns Hopkins University and was a postdoctoral research fellow in CTY and the university's School of Education.

Appendix B

State Requirements for Teacher Certification

	2013-2014 Number of Certified/Licensed Teachers Working in Title III[+]	Additional Certified/Licensed Teachers Needed in the Next 5 Years[+]	Need to Increase the Number of Certified/Licensed Title III Teachers by ____ %[+]
National	346,715	82,380	
Alabama	2,910	224	7.70%
Alaska	56	173	308.93%
Arizona	5,422	1,317	24.29%
Arkansas	2,377	549	23.10%
California	203,395	17,104	8.41%
Colorado	7,487	1,500	20.03%
Connecticut	721	22	3.05%
Delaware	153	50	32.68%
District of Columbia	89	345	387.64%
Florida	49,654	0	0.00%
Georgia	2,195	564	25.69%
Hawaii	297	250	84.18%
Idaho	608	50	8.22%
Illinois	8,760	15,895	181.45%
Indiana	2,179	800	36.71%
Iowa	500	1,500	300.00%
Kansas	132	382	289.39%
Kentucky	174	405	232.76%
Louisiana	493	299	60.65%
Maine	109	120	110.09%
Maryland	1,023	492	48.09%
Massachusetts	1,285	500	38.91%
Michigan	532	175	32.89%
Minnesota	1,361	625	45.92%
Mississippi	91	247	271.43%
Missouri	478	921	192.68%
Montana	410	0	0.00%
Nebraska	809	80	9.89%
Nevada	2,733	16,111	589.50%
New Hampshire	143	30	20.98%
New Jersey	3,987	150	3.76%
New Mexico	2,887	500	17.32%
New York	6,211	2,025	32.60%
North Carolina	1,711	574	33.55%

State Offers ESL Certificate/License[++]	State Offers BLE Certificate/License[++]	State Requires All Teachers to Complete Coursework in Methods of Teaching ELs[++]	States Require Teachers Get a Specialist (ESL/BLE) Certificate/License[+++]
51	27	5	21
1	0	0	0
1	1	0	0
1	1	1	0
1	0	0	0
1	1	1	1
1	1	0	1
1	1	0	1
1	1	0	1
1	1	0	0
1	1	1	0
1	0	0	0
1	0	0	0
1	1	0	0
1	1	0	1
1	1	0	1
1	0	0	0
1	0	0	1
1	0	0	0
1	1	0	0
1	0	0	0
1	0	0	1
1	1	0	1
1	1	0	0
1	1	0	1
1	0	0	0
1	0	0	0
1	0	0	0
1	0	0	0
1	1	0	1
1	1	0	1
1	1	0	1
1	1	0	0
1	1	1	1
1	0	0	1

continued

	2013-2014 Number of Certified/Licensed Teachers Working in Title III[+]	Additional Certified/Licensed Teachers Needed in the Next 5 Years[+]	Need to Increase the Number of Certified/Licensed Title III Teachers by ___ %[+]
North Dakota	84	25	29.76%
Ohio	745	317	42.55%
Oklahoma	551	400	72.60%
Oregon	838	300	35.80%
Pennsylvania	1,371	331	24.14%
Rhode Island	312	50	16.03%
South Carolina	536	57	10.63%
South Dakota	24	150	625.00%
Tennessee	1,118	116	10.38%
Texas	24,654	13,297	53.93%
Utah	576	50	8.68%
Vermont	78	25	32.05%
Virginia	1,240	700	56.45%
Washington	1,193	2,232	187.09%
West Virginia	33	60	181.82%
Wisconsin	1,936	281	14.51%
Wyoming	54	10	18.52%

[+]Data in these columns are from NCELA, Title III State Profiles. Available: http://www.ncela.us/t3sis/index.php [February 23, 2017].

[++]Data in these columns are from the National Comprehensive Center for Teacher Quality (2009). Available: http://www.gtlcenter.org/sites/default/files/docs/CertificationandLicensureforTeachersofELLs.pdf [February 23, 2017].

[+++]Data in this column are from Lopez, F., Scanlan, M., and Gundrum, B. (2013). Preparing teachers of English language learners: Empirical evidence and policy implications. *Education Policy Evaluation Archives, 21*(20), 1-35.

State Offers ESL Certificate/ License[++]	State Offers BLE Certificate/ License[++]	State Requires All Teachers to Complete Coursework in Methods of Teaching ELs[++]	States Require Teachers Get a Specialist (ESL/BLE) Certificate/ License[+++]
1	0	0	0
1	1	0	1
1	0	0	0
1	0	0	0
1	0	1	0
1	1	0	0
1	0	0	0
1	0	0	0
1	0	0	0
1	1	0	1
1	0	0	1
1	1	0	0
1	0	0	1
1	1	0	1
1	0	0	0
1	1	0	1
1	1	0	0

Appendix C

Context of Educating English Learners: English Learners and Title III Teacher Population

	EL Population in 2002-2003[a]	EL Population in 2013-2014[b]	Population Change from 2002-2003 to 2013-2014
National	4,118,918	4,929,981	811,063
Alabama	10,568	20,165	9,597
Alaska	16,351	16,496	145
Arizona	140,664	90,869	−49,795
Arkansas	15,146	35,476	20,330
California	1,587,771	1,508,323	−79,448
Colorado	86,118	118,316	32,198
Connecticut	21,970	32,556	10,586
Delaware	3,445	8,356	4,911
District of Columbia	5,363	5,934	571
Florida	203,659	284,802	81,143
Georgia	70,464	98,603	28,139
Hawaii	12,853	16,553	3,700
Idaho	18,747	13,680	−5,067
Illinois	168,591	186,646	18,055
Indiana	42,560	55,986	13,426
Iowa	13,961	25,978	12,017
Kansas	17,942	51,670	33,728
Kentucky	6,343	22,517	16,174
Louisiana	11,042	17,483	6,441
Maine	2,575	5,471	2,896
Maryland	27,311	61,827	34,516
Massachusetts	50,578	73,662	23,084
Michigan	54,961	88,351	33,390
Minnesota	51,224	73,858	22,634
Mississippi	2,250	8,529	6,279
Missouri	13,121	27,793	14,672
Montana	6,642	3,443	−3,199
Nebraska	13,803	19,235	5,432
Nevada	58,753	69,969	11,216
New Hampshire	3,270	4,217	947
New Jersey	57,548	68,396	10,848
New Mexico	65,317	57,342	−7,975
New York	178,704	241,138	62,434
North Carolina	59,712	102,406	42,694

% + or – from 2002 -2003 to 2013-2014	% of Students in the State That Are ELs	Number of Certified/Licensed Title III Teachers in 2013-2014	Title III Teacher to EL Ratio
19.69%		346,715	14
90.81%	2.30%	2,910	7
0.89%	11.40%	56	295
–35.40%	6.30%	5,422	17
134.23%	7.30%	2,377	15
–5.00%	22.40%	203,395	7
37.39%	12.30%	7,487	16
48.18%	5.70%	721	45
142.55%	6.20%	153	55
10.65%	9.40%	89	67
39.84%	9.20%	49,654	6
39.93%	5.30%	2,195	45
28.79%	8.50%	297	56
–27.03%	4.50%	608	23
10.71%	9.30%	8,760	21
31.55%	5.30%	2,179	26
86.08%	4.60%	500	52
187.98%	9.20%	132	391
254.99%	2.90%	174	129
58.33%	2.10%	493	35
112.47%	2.80%	109	50
126.38%	6.50%	1,023	60
45.64%	7.40%	1,285	57
60.75%	4.70%	532	166
44.19%	7.60%	1,361	54
279.07%	1.30%	91	94
111.82%	3.00%	478	58
–48.16%	2.30%	410	8
39.35%	5.00%	809	24
19.09%	15.10%	2,733	26
28.96%	1.90%	143	29
18.85%	4.50%	3,987	17
–12.21%	15.10%	2,887	20
34.94%	2.50%	6,211	39
71.50%	6.20%	1,711	60

continued

	EL Population in 2002-2003[a]	EL Population in 2013-2014[b]	Population Change from 2002-2003 to 2013-2014
North Dakota	883	3,336	2,453
Ohio	25,610	50,414	24,804
Oklahoma	40,179	44,720	4,541
Oregon	52,331	57,376	5,045
Pennsylvania	30,731	48,446	17,715
Rhode Island	10,050	9,252	−798
South Carolina	7,467	43,080	35,613
South Dakota	4,522	5,115	593
Tennessee	26,808	35,145	8,337
Texas	625,946	809,582	183,636
Utah	43,269	38,710	−4,559
Vermont	1,057	1,614	557
Virginia	49,780	102,815	53,035
Washington	70,431	112,302	41,871
West Virginia	1,281	2,911	1,630
Wisconsin	25,764	45,771	20,007
Wyoming	3,483	3,346	−137

[a]U.S. Dept. of Education, NCES (2013). 2013 Tables and Figures. Available: http://nces. ed.gov/programs/digest/d13/tables/dt13_209.30.asp [February 23, 2017].

[b]U.S. Dept. of Education, NCES. 2014 Table and Figures. Table 204.20. Available: https:// nces.ed.gov/programs/digest/d14/tables/dt14_204.20.asp [February 23, 2017].

[c]Data in these columns are from the National Comprehensive Center for Teacher Quality (2009). Available: http://www.gtlcenter.org/sites/default/files/docs/CertificationandLicensure-forTeachersofELLs.pdf [February 23, 2017].

% + or – from 2002 -2003 to 2013-2014	% of Students in the State That Are ELs	Number of Certified/Licensed Title III Teachers in 2013-2014	Title III Teacher to EL Ratio
277.80%	2.80%	84	40
96.85%	2.50%	745	68
11.30%	7.10%	551	81
9.64%	8.40%	838	68
57.65%	2.80%	1,371	35
–7.94%	6.60%	312	30
476.94%	5.40%	536	80
13.11%	3.30%	24	213
31.10%	3.50%	1,118	31
29.34%	15.50%	24,654	33
–10.54%	5.50%	576	67
52.70%	1.50%	78	21
106.54%	7.40%	1,240	83
59.45%	9.40%	1,193	94
127.24%	0.70%	33	88
77.65%	4.90%	1,936	24
–3.93%	3.00%	54	62